COLLECTED ESSAYS

H. P. LOVECRAFT: COLLECTED ESSAYS

COLLECTED ESSAYS:
VOLUME 3: SCIENCE

H. P. Lovecraft

Edited by S. T. Joshi

Hippocampus Press

New York

Library of Congress Cataloging-in-Publication Data

Lovecraft, H. P. (Howard Phillips), 1890–1937
  [Essays]
  Collected essays / H.P. Lovecraft ; edited by S.T. Joshi. --
1st ed.
    v. cm.
  Includes bibliographical references and indexes.
  Contents: v. 1. Amateur journalism -- v. 2. Literary criticism.
  ISBN 0-9721644-1-3 (v. 1 : hardcover) -- ISBN 0-9721644-2-1
(v. 1 : pbk.) -- ISBN 0-9721644-4-8 (v. 2 : hardcover) -- ISBN
0-9721644-9-9 (v. 2 : pbk.)
  I. Joshi, S. T., 1958–   . II. Title.
PS3523.O833A6 2004b
814'.52--dc22

2004000766

Select unpublished texts have been published by permission of the Estate of
H. P. Lovecraft and John Hay Library, Brown University.

Published by Hippocampus Press
P.O. Box 641, New York, NY 10156.
http://www.hippocampuspress.com

Cover art by Virgil Finlay, used by permission of Lail Finlay.
Hippocampus Press logo by Anastasia Damianakos.
Cover design by Barbara Briggs Silbert.

First Edition
1 3 5 7 9 8 6 4 2

Cloth: ISBN 0-9748789-7-9
Paper: ISBN 0-9748789-8-7

CONTENTS

Science vied with *belles lettres* as one of Lovecraft's earliest interests, and for at least the first three decades of his life it rivalled poetry and surpassed weird fiction as his chief mode of literary expression. If we date his interest in literature to his reading of Grimm's fairy tales at the age of four, we can trace his fascination with science to the age of eight, when he stumbled upon the world of chemistry. Not long thereafter he was writing little treatises on the subject, some of which survive. But it was his discovery of astronomy in the winter of 1902–03 that gave perhaps the greatest impetus to both his literary aspirations and his philosophical outlook; for it imbued in him that sense of the "cosmic" which would ultimately find potent expression in his weird tales.

The amount of writing Lovecraft did over the next several years was prodigious. Aside from his long-running papers, *The Scientific Gazette* and *The Rhode Island Journal of Astronomy*, he produced several separate treatises; they are listed in the 20 September 1903 issue of the *Rhode Island Journal*:

Title	No. Pages
The Telescope	12
The Moon	12
On Venus	7 maps
Practical Geometry	34
ASTRONOMY	60
Solar System	27

Of these, only *The Moon* (in a revised version) survives. There was also a nine-volume "Science Library," of which three small treatises survive. All this work culminated in *A Brief Course in Astronomy—Descriptive, Practical, and Observational; for Beginners and General Readers* (1906), which Lovecraft states "got as far as the typed and hand-illustrated stage (circa one hundred fifty pages), though no copy survives" (SL 5.141). Actually, a small segment of the work does survive (see "Celestial Objects for All"), but we would very much like to have the entire monograph.

Astronomy was by no means Lovecraft's only scientific interest in youth. Meteorology claimed a surprisingly large segment of his time. His interest had evidently begun around the end of 1903; by early 1904 he had established a "Climatological Station" in his house at 454 Angell Street; it featured "6 circular windows with shutters, in case of severe storm. The instruments have not all arrived yet . . . Although the station is not, as yet, fully equipped, it *can* do much practice-work, for the storm glass is very accurate, and the wet-bulb thermometer, which was made by the observer works to perfection" (*Scientific Gazette*, 24 January 1904). A "Providence Observatory Forecast" for 5 April 1904 survives—a single sheet giving a prediction of the weather for the next day. The death of Lovecraft's grandfather, Whipple Phillips, in March 1904 and the family's subsequent move to 598 Angell Street curtailed his interest for a time, but it resumed in the fall of 1905. By early 1906 he had added a great many instruments to the meteorological observatory, including a barometer, a maximum and minimum thermometer, a dry bulb thermometer, a wet thermometer, a rain gauge, a hair hygrometer, a storm-glass, and other items. Later a wind-vane, quadrant, sundial, and magnet compass were added.

But astronomy remained Lovecraft's chief object of study, and it also led to his earliest appearances in print. His letters to the *Providence Sunday Journal* and (more remarkably) *Scientific American* in the summer of 1906 led to his becoming a regular astronomy writer for the *Pawtuxet Valley Gleaner*, a rural weekly published in Phenix, R.I. Lovecraft reports:

> During 1906, 1907, & 1908 I flooded the *Pawtuxet Valley Gleaner* with my prose articles. This rural paper was the oracle of that section of the country from which my mother's family had originally come, & was taken for old times' sake in our household. The name "Phillips" is a magic word in Western Rhode Island, & the *Gleaner* was more than willing to print & feature anything from Whipple V. Phillips' grandson. Only the failure of the *Gleaner* put an end to my activity in its columns. (SL 1.40)

No issues of the paper after the end of 1906 have come to light, but investigation suggests that the paper did indeed exist until at least the end of 1907, when it apparently merged with the *Pawtuxet Valley Daily Times*. Accordingly, we may well have lost more than 50 articles by HPL, given that his work appeared in every weekly issue after the second article.

Lovecraft simultaneously wrote monthly astronomy columns for the Providence *Tribune* (morning, evening, and Sunday editions). These articles are relatively undistinguished; they are noteworthy only because many of them included hand-drawn starcharts and other figures, thereby constituting one of the earliest instances when illustrations by Lovecraft were published.

All this work came to an abrupt end in the summer of 1908, when a nervous breakdown forced Lovecraft to withdraw from high school and retreat into hermitry for the next five or six years. He did manage, in a fleeting return to his chemical interests, to produce *A Brief Course in Inorganic Chemistry* in 1910; he describes it as a "bulky manuscript" (SL 1.75). The title is of some significance, since it was organic chemistry that had bedeviled Lovecraft in high school and also in the correspondence classes he took around 1909–10. Lovecraft also kept an astronomical notebook for the years 1909–15, but so far as can be ascertained from published descriptions of this document (it has never been made available for consultation), it was kept sporadically and in several entire years there are no entries at all. (On occasion Lovecraft carelessly states that he wrote astronomy columns for the entire period 1906–18, but he in fact wrote none between the summer of 1908 and the beginning of 1914.)

It is customarily believed that Lovecraft came out of his hermitry by means of the public feud in which he engaged in the letter columns of the *Argosy* and other Munsey magazines in 1913–14, an incident that led directly to his discovery of the world of amateur journalism (or, rather, its discovery of him). However, it is of interest to note that Lovecraft began his longest-running and most substantial astronomy column—for the Providence *Evening News* (January 1914–May 1918)—a full three months prior to his official entry into amateur journalism (April 1914). Somehow he must have gained the initiative to approach the paper and convince its editor to hire him as its astronomy columnist, perhaps as a suitably humble rival to Winslow Upton, the Brown University professor of astronomy and Lovecraft family friend who had a long-running column in the *Providence Journal*. These articles rapidly expand from a mere recital of the astronomical phenomena of the month to explications of the Graeco-Roman myths associated with the names of the planets, stars, and constellations (for which Lovecraft drew heavily upon his early reading of Bulfinch's *Age of Fable* as well as Ovid's *Metamorphoses* and other ancient texts) and glimpses of the history of astronomy. The series came to an end only because the editor of the paper required Lovecraft to simplify some of the technical language he used in the articles, something he declined to do.

Lovecraft's *Evening News* work was rudely interrupted in the fall of 1914 by the appearance of J. F. Hartmann, a local man who published an article on astrology in exactly the place in the paper where Lovecraft's column usually appeared. Not one to take such things sitting down, Lovecraft unloaded on his opponent with double barrels—first with several sober (but increasingly intemperate) attempts at rebutting Hartmann, then—when Hartmann proved surprisingly adept in fending off these attacks—with a recourse to Augustan satire. This time he drew not upon Alexander Pope (as he had done in his letter feud in the *Argosy*) but upon Jonathan Swift. Specifically, Lovecraft imitated Swift's satirical articles on the astrologer John Partridge, written under the pseudonym Isaac Bickerstaff. Lovecraft did not follow Swift exactly in this procedure: whereas Swift first made a prediction that Partridge would die on a particular day and then followed it up with a convincing account of Partridge's death (whereupon the poor fellow had considerable difficulty convincing the world that he was still alive), Lovecraft, in his "Isaac Bickerstaffe [*sic*], Jr." articles, merely parodies the vagueness of astrological predictions by extending them into the far future; while there is incidental mention of the decease of a distant descendant of Hartmann's in a notably ironic manner, this is not the focus of Lovecraft's satirical thrust. Eventually the attacks accomplished their purpose, and Hartmann vanished into silence.[1]

Lovecraft's last astronomy column, "Mysteries of the Heavens Revealed by Astronomy," written for the *Asheville* [N.C.] *Gazette-News* in 1915, is also relatively undistinguished. What he is attempting to accomplish here is a unified treatise on the fundamentals of astronomy; its emphasis on the lack of technical knowledge required to understand it underscores Lovecraft's own inability to master mathematics and other sciences—an inability that confounded his expectation of becoming a professor of astronomy. In many ways the chief interest of the *Gazette-News* articles is their very appearance; for they must have been facilitated by Lovecraft's boyhood friend Chester Pierce Munroe, who had "established himself at the Grove Park Inn, Asheville," as Lovecraft reports in "Introducing Mr. Chester Pierce Munroe" (*Conservative*, April 1915). Like the *Pawtuxet Valley Gleaner* pieces, this series also appears to be missing some instalments at the end: no copies of the paper appear to survive for a critical period of a week or so following the last surviving article, so that two or three segments appear to be lost forever.

After 1918 Lovecraft's actual writing on science declines radically, although his interest in new developments in biology, astrophysics, chemistry, anthropology, and many other sciences remained high. In 1926 the magician Harry Houdini hired Lovecraft and his friend C. M. Eddy, Jr., to write an entire book combating superstition. This work—perhaps analogous to Houdini's own previous work, *A Magician among the Spirits* (1924), a debunking of spiritualism—was to be called *The Cancer of Superstition*. Houdini had earlier asked Lovecraft to write a rush article on astrology, for which he paid $75 (see *SL* 2.79); this article apparently does not survive. A detailed synopsis prepared by Lovecraft for *The Cancer of Superstition* does survive, as do three chapters

---

1. Hartmann's articles are printed in the Appendix.

of the treatise written by Eddy; but Houdini's sudden death on 31 October 1926 derailed the plans, as his widow did not wish to pursue the project.

In reality, Lovecraft's devotion to science is exhibited more poignantly and profoundly in his weird fiction, and perhaps also in his general philosophy, than in his actual writings on science. His tales adhere rigorously to the scientific knowledge of their day, in some cases expanding upon it in a spirit of imaginative liberation; while his early grounding in science led directly to his atheism and to his hostility to superstition, mysticism, and imprecision of thought and outlook. It is perhaps just as well that Lovecraft never achieved his early goal of becoming a professor of astronomy, for such a position may well have restricted his ability to use science as an imaginative springboard in his horror fiction. But that it constituted the backbone of his thought and his literary work is evident from even the slightest of the pieces included in this volume.

—S. T. JOSHI

A NOTE ON THIS EDITION

This edition is based upon rigorous consultation of manuscripts, original publications, and relevant later appearances of Lovecraft's essays; the texts are based upon the manuscript (if extant) or first appearance unless otherwise specified. At the end of each essay, an editor's note supplies bibliographical and other information that readers might find useful for placing the item within the context of Lovecraft's life and work; footnotes elucidating specific literary, historical, and other data in the essay follow the editor's note.

For a variety of reasons it has proven impracticable to reproduce some of Lovecraft's unpublished juvenile scientific works. These include the following (all are found in the H. P. Lovecraft Papers at the John Hay Library, Brown University):

The Art of Fusion, Melting, Pudling & Casting (1899?)
Chemistry (1899?; 4 vols.)
A Good Anaesthetic (1899?)
The Railroad Review (December 1901)
The Scientific Gazette (1903–04; 32 issues)
Astronomy/The Monthly Almanack (1903–04; 9 issues)
The Planet (29 August 1903)
The Rhode Island Journal of Astronomy (1903–09; 69 issues)
Annals of the Providence Observatory (1904)
Providence Observatory Forecast (5 April 1904)
The Science Library (1904?; 3 vols.)

Publication of these works would require costly and difficult reproduction in facsimile, to capture the full flavour of the originals; in some cases, such reproduction would itself be problematical because of the faded and otherwise damaged condition of the originals. It is hoped, nonetheless, that publication of this sort might at some future date be deemed feasible.

In the notes to the astronomy columns I have chiefly sought to identify the astronomers named by Lovecraft; I have made no attempt to verify the astronomical information he presents. Lovecraft also quotes liberally from two ancient astronomical poets, the Greek writer Aratus and the Latin writer Manilius. With one exception (as indicated in the notes), Lovecraft's citations of Manilius are taken from Thomas Creech's verse translation of 1670. This book is not indicated as being in his personal library, so he must have had access to a copy at the Providence Public Library or some other source. Lovecraft's knowledge of Greek was insufficient for him to have rendered Aratus into verse, so he must have secured a verse translation of this poet as well. There were three verse translations of Aratus prior to Lovecraft's day: by John Lamb (1848),[2] E. Poste (1880),[3] and Robert Brown, Jr. (1885).[4] I have had access only to Poste's translation, which is not the one Lovecraft used; my guess is that he used the translation by Brown.

Lovecraft consistently misspelled the word *sidereal* (as *siderial*) and the constellation *Praesepe* (as *Praespe*). These misspellings are retained in this edition.

Abbreviations used in the notes are as follows:

AGN   *Asheville* [N.C.] *Gazette-News*
AHT   Arkham House transcripts
AMS   autograph manuscript
AT   *The Ancient Track: Complete Poetical Works* (Night Shade Books, 2001)
CE   *Collected Essays* (Hippocampus Press, 2004–06)
EN   [Providence] *Evening News*
ET   [Providence] *Evening Tribune*
FP   first publication
JHL   John Hay Library, Brown University, Providence, R.I.
LL   S. T. Joshi, comp., *Lovecraft's Library: A Catalogue*, rev. ed. (Hippocampus Press, 2002)
MT   [Providence] *Morning Tribune*
PVG   *Pawtuxet Valley Gleaner*
SL   *Selected Letters* (Arkham House, 1965–76; 5 vols.)
ST   [Providence] *Sunday Tribune*

I am grateful to David E. Schultz, Marc A. Michaud, Scott D. Briggs, Kenneth W. Faig, Jr., Judy Montgomery, Steve Walker, and James C. Sanford for assistance in the preparation of the text and notes. My research was chiefly done at the John Hay Library of Brown University, the Rhode Island Historical Society Library, and the University of Washington Library.

---

2. *The Phaenomena and Diosemeia of Aratus*, translated into English verse, with notes, by John Lamb (London: J. W. Parker, 1848).

3. *The Skies and Weather-Forecasts of Aratus*, translated, with notes, by E. Poste (London: Macmillan, 1880).

4. *The Phainomena; or, Heavenly Display of Aratos*, done into English verse by Robert Brown, Jr. (London: Longmans, Green, 1885).

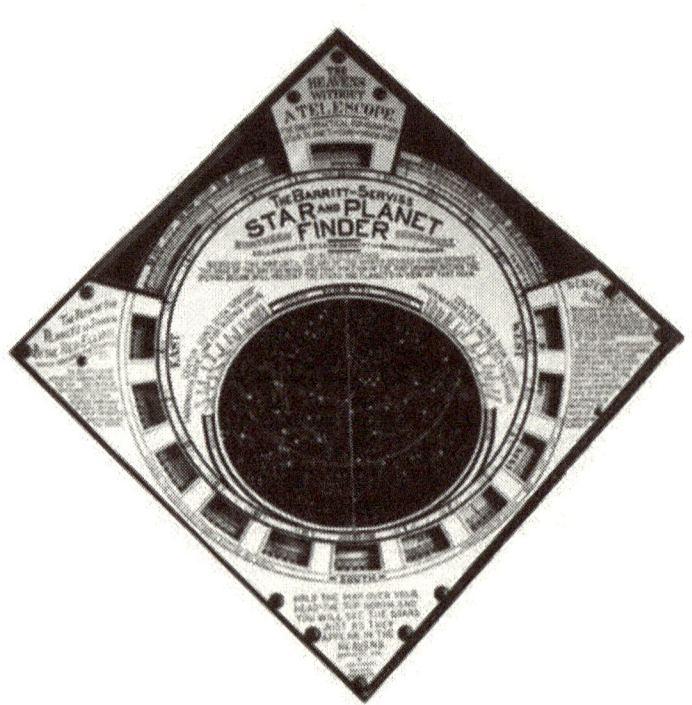

Lovecraft owned a planisphere like this one. His planisphere and telescope, given to August Derleth by Annie E. P. Gamwell on Lovecraft's death, are now owned by the August Derleth Society, Sauk City, Wisconsin.

MY OPINION AS TO THE LUNAR CANALS

I regard the lunar canals as formations analogous to the rays or streaks radiating from the principal craters. The difference is, that the "canals" are dark, while the "rays" are brighter than the rest of the moon. The explanation is, that both are matter volcanically ejected from the moon's interior in past ages, the rays, simply being composed of a more highly reflective matter than the canals. A proof of this fact is, that the rays and canals are never near each other, showing that the northern half of the moon is not as bright as the southern—I also surmise that this same holds true for mars. The only explicable phenomenon is the "oases", or round junctions of the canals, and their regularity and duplicity. (as shown in the picture)[1]

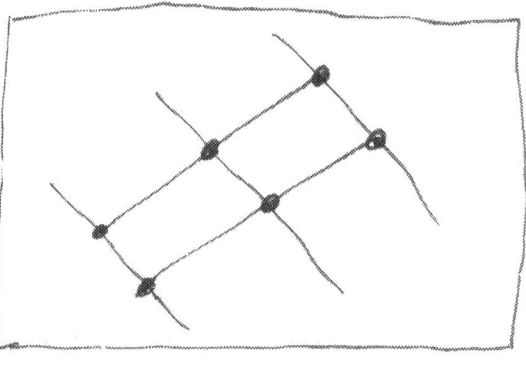

But these are probably but natural curiosities, and the canals are analogous to the rays. The lunar canals cover much less territory than the martian counterparts, this is doubtless, owing to the smallness of the moon compared with mars, and therefore it's feebler volcanic activity. As to Prof. Pickering's[2] theory—i.e.—That they are streaks of vegetation, I have but to say that any intelligent astronomer would consider it unworthy of notice, as our satellite is wanting in both water and atmosphere, the two essentials for life either animal or vegetable. Of course Lowell's[3] theory (that they are artificial) is perfectly ridiculous. But this is all the light that can be thrown on the subject until the telescope is so greatly improved as to bring the moon within a distance of a very few miles.

The End,

By

H P L

EDITOR'S NOTE Unpublished (AMS, JHL). The essay probably dates to 1903, and is apparently one of HPL's first writings since his discovery of astronomy in the winter of 1902–03.

Notes

1. The drawing is the editor's rendition of the drawing in HPL's manuscript.

2. William Henry Pickering (1858–1938), American astronomer and professor of astronomy at Harvard. His theory is found in *The Moon* (1903), which must have appeared only shortly before HPL wrote this essay.

No Transit of Mars

Providence, May 27.

To the Editor of The Sunday Journal:
   In the Journal for May 27, I notice among the letters to the editor a set of astrological predictions for 1906. Passing over the fact that astrology is but a pseudo science, not entitled to intelligent consideration, I wish to call attention to a striking inaccuracy in the aforementioned article. Its writer mentions a transit of Mars over the sun in July. Of course, as Mars is a superior planet, or one outside the earth's orbit, it cannot transit over the sun. Perhaps the astrologer refers to the conjunction of Mars July 15, but on that occasion the planet would pass behind and not across the orb of day.

H. P. Lovecraft.

EDITOR'S NOTE   FP: *Providence Sunday Journal* (3 June 1906): Sec. 2, p. 5. A letter to the editor commenting on a letter in the issue of 27 May by Thomas Hines, Jr., of Central Falls, R.I., published under the title "Hard Times Coming" (Sec. 2, p. 5). Hines had remarked: "According to the transit of Mars and Saturn, I judge that Providence and Boston will suffer from great fires this summer." The letter constitutes HPL's first published work.

Trans-Neptunian Planets

Providence, R.,I., July 15, 1906

To the Editor of the SCIENTIFIC AMERICAN:
   In these days of large telescopes and modern astronomical methods, it seems strange that no vigorous efforts are being made to discover planets beyond the orbit of Neptune, which is now considered the outermost limit of the solar system. It has been noticed that seven comets have their aphelia at a point that would correspond to the orbit of a planet revolving around the sun at a distance of about 100 astronomical units (9,300,000,000 miles).
   Now several have suggested that such a planet exists, and has captured the comets by attraction. This is probable, as Jupiter and others also mark the aphelia of many celestial wanderers. The writer has noticed that a great many comets cluster around a point 50 units out, where a large body might revolve. If the great mathematicians of the day should try to compute orbits from these aphelia, it is doubtful if they could succeed; but if all the observatories that possess celestial camera should band together and minutely photograph the ecliptic, as is done in asteroid hunting, the bodies might be revealed on their plates. Even if no discoveries were made, the accurate star photographs would almost be worth the time and trouble.

H. P. Lovecraft.

EDITOR'S NOTE   FP: *Scientific American* 95, No. 8 (25 August 1906): 135. A prescient recommendation to search for planets within the solar system beyond Neptune by the use of celestial photography. The search for such planets, gaining momentum throughout the course of the early 20th century, resulted in the discovery of Pluto in 1930—a discovery HPL immediately put to use in the story he was writing at the time, "The Whisperer in Darkness" (1930), where he identifies his imaginary planet Yuggoth (first cited in *Fungi from Yuggoth* [1929–30]) with Pluto.

THE MOON

A Brief account of all that is known concerning our satellite

7th Edition

By H. P. Lovecraft
Astronomical writer and editor

REVISED AND ENLARGED TO DATE.

Price, 50¢.

Providence, R. I., 1906.

Written November 26, 1903

Preface

The author's object in bringing this little work before the public is to acquaint all with the principal facts concerning our moon. The ignorance displayed by otherwise educated persons is appalling, but I hope that this volume will do at least *something* to remove the clouds that have hitherto shrouded moon-study.

Nov. 26, 1903—H. P. L.

————

I have just completed a thorough revision of this little work to keep it abreast of the times, and it is my earnest desire that it may be the means of turning at least a few to the as yet sparsely trodden fields of Selenography.

July 24, 1906——H. P. L.

————

REVISION JUL. 24, 1906.

The Moon, by H. P. Lovecraft

Of all the heavenly bodies there is none nearer to us than the moon, nor do we possess as intimate a relation to any other planet as we do with this little globe, only 2162 miles in diameter, that revolves around us every month. The exact period of the moon's revolution is 27d. 7h. 43m. 11s., but the motion of the earth its-self around the sun makes this appear much longer, so the apparent, or "synodic" revolution occupies 29d. 12h. 44m. 03s. As the moon travels around the earth it apparently undergoes great changes of form, called "phases", due to the different positions in which we see our satellite with respect to the sun. These phases vary in figure from a thin crescent to a full circle, and a complete set is called a "lunation". A lunation occupies one synodic revolution.

Once every month the moon is too near the sun to be seen, and sometimes, when moving exactly in the plane of the earth's orbit, it eclipses the great orb of day by passing over his face. When the moon is in line with the earth and sun, whether or not eclipsing the latter, it is said to be "new". It will then not be visible for two days. When this time has elapsed the moon can be seen in the west as a slender crescent, with horns pointing east, setting about two hours after the sun. The next night, the crescent is larger, and the time of setting is about an hour later. Thus it progresses, each night adding a little to the crescent, and about an hour to the time of setting, until, five days after its first appearance, the moon shows a half circle of light, and sets about midnight. It is then said to be in "First Quarter". From then on, the illuminated portion becomes more and more convex (or "gibbous", as it is called) until, seven days after the First Quarter, our satellite rises at sunset, in the east, a full circle of light, and after glorifying the sky throughout the night, sets just as the dawn begins to break. This is "Full Moon". The next day the side that has hitherto been a perfect semi-circle begins to diminish, and in another week the moon is again half full, the illuminated side being that which was invisible on the previous occasion. This phase is called the "Last Quarter", and the moon rises about midnight. The next few days are spent in the diminution of the edge that was straight in the crescent, this time in the east, rising two hours before daybreak, with horns pointed westward. The following day it is invisible, not to be seen again until it has passed the sun, and begun a new lunation.

Besides eclipsing the sun the moon is often eclipsed its-self. This can occur only at the full, when, if in the plane of the earth's orbit, it will of course encounter it's shadow. When the moon passes between the earth and a star or planet the phenomenon is called an "occultation". Sometimes when the moon is young not only the crescent is visible, but the entire disc, illuminated by a faint reddish light. This is then brilliantly reflected from the earth, for it must be understood that on the moon, our world shines like a brilliant orb, in fact it looks much the same as our satellite appears to us, except that it is thirteen times larger. The reason that this "earth-light" disappears as the moon waxes is, that to a lunar observer, the earth would undergo phases, being full at new moon, and vice versa.

As our satellite makes but one rotation on its axis during a revolution, it always turns the same face to the earth, letting us see but half its surface. On account of this, our world would appear immutably fixed in the lunar sky, or else not be visible at all. The apparent size of the moon as seen with the naked eye, has always been a point of dispute, some saying its diameter to be an inch, while still more compare it to a foot, yet it is a fact that a pencil held at arm's length will cover the entire disc. In angular measure, the moon's apparent diameter is 31′ 24″. Another curious thing connected with the moon as seen with the unassisted eye is the phenomenon known as the "horizontal moon". This refers to the enlarged appearance of our satellite when rising or setting. Many theories concerning this have been advanced, and it has been demonstrated that the disc should even appear smaller, indeed, a telescope at once dispels the illusion, for which as yet we know of no satisfactory reason.[1] We now come to a point where we seemingly must contradict some statements previously made, for I now assert that more than half of the moon is visible to the earth. However, the amount in excess of the half is very small, and is due to several conditions, which, taken collectively, are called "librations". To understand these, we must know that the moon describes not a circle, but an ellipse or oval around the earth, being sometimes 252,830 miles away, while on other occasions its distance is but 221,520 m. When nearest the earth it is said to be in "Perigee", and when farthest, in "Apogee". The average is about 240,000 m. There is an imaginary line in the heavens on which all the planets are supposed to travel, called the "ecliptic". However, most of them deviate more or less from it, the discrepancy being called "inclination to the ecliptic". The moon's inclination is about 5° 08' 40".

Now these two facts, ellipticity of orbit, and inclination to the ecliptic are the major causes of libration, the first enabling us to see around our satellite in easterly and westerly directions, while the latter reveals lands above the north, and below the south poles. Although, as has been said before, the moon's path does not co-incide with the ecliptic, it nevertheless intersects it at two opposite points, called "nodes". These nodes do not always occupy the same place on the ecliptic, but have a retrograde motion, occupying 18y. 213d. 21h. 22m. 46s. This period was used by the ancients for predicting eclipses, and was called the "Saros".

The moon is much smaller than the earth, its diameter being about 1/4, volume 1/49, mass 1/81, density 3/5, apparent disc 1/13, and gravity 1/7. The small gravity would cause an object weighing 7 lbs. on the earth to weigh but one, could it be transported to the moon, yet the force is sufficient to attract the waters of the earth, causing the phenomena known as tides. A striking illustration of the moon's levity as compared with the earth lies in the fact that their balancing point, or centre of gravity, lies about 1000 miles below the surface of our world.

It has been previously stated that the moon rises and sets about an hour later every night, but we must now note an exception. At the full moon nearest the autumnal equinox our satellite is observed to rise at nearly the same time for several nights. This is caused by its presence in that part of its course which makes the smallest angle with the horizon. The name "Harvest Moon" has been applied to this state of affairs. At the following full the same phenomenon takes place on a smaller scale. This is the "Hunter's Moon".

To the naked eye, the moon appears to be covered with dark spots, to which imagination gives the form of men or animals, but the telescope shows a very different sight. The entire surface is seen to be covered with mountain ranges and pitted with ring-shaped formations. These last often have small central peaks, and are thought to be extinct volcanoes, or "craters", as they are called. Any good field or spy glass will show these, but to study them in detail, an astronomical telescope is required.

In a small glass the moon looks very much like the earth, the dark spots resembling seas, etc., indeed, when such instruments were the only ones available, our satellite was thought to be inhabited, so all formations were named terrestrially, and for lack of a better nomenclature the appellations exist unchanged up to the present time. But in the 17th century scientists had concluded the moon to be devoid of life, water, or atmosphere, in other words, our satellite was set down as a dead world. Recently, however, modern progress has demonstrated that life is not yet completely absent, and that the moon possesses a thin atmosphere, low vegetation, hoar-frost, and the last stages of volcanism. This question will be more fully described in another volume. In conclusion, I will give a few directions to those desirous of studying the moon. Before commencing, learn some simple lunar map by heart, so as to be familiar with what you are about to see, then procure one of the $1.00 telescopes, which are advertised in the magazines, as they will show all the larger craters. Do not try to see the mountains at full moon, as the direct rays of the sun obscure them. The best time to observe such things is when they are on the "terminator" or the division between the light and dark sides of the lunar disc.

———

The writer confidently believes that there is no pursuit more interesting than the study of the moon, and all are urged to devote themselves to this branch of knowledge, for in the history of the world some of the most recondite facts have been brought to light by the first efforts of an amateur.

THE END

APPENDIX.
The Lunar rays.

On the moon there is a kind of formation never seen elsewhere. I refer to the bright streaks radiating outward from certain lunar craters. Prof. Pickering of Harvard holds them to be great fissures filled with hoar-frost. Your $1.00 telescope will show two "rayed" craters, i.e. Tycho and Copernicus, the former being the most interesting. The location of these craters is given in the frontispiece, which is a rough sketch made by the author May 8, 1906.[2]

Elements of the Moon:

Distance from earth (Perigee)—221,520 miles.
Distance from earth (Apogee)—252,830 miles.
Average, 240,000 m.

Siderial Revolution: 27d. 7h. 43m. 11s.
Synodical   "   : 29d. 12h. 44m. 3s.
True diameter: 2162 miles.
Ap't   " : 31′ 24″

Mass   1/81
Diameter   1/4
Volume   1/49
Density   3/5
Gravity   1/7
     EARTH – 1.

Inclination to the Ecliptic   5° 08′ 40″.

Axial Rotation same as Siderial Revolution.

EDITOR'S NOTE Unpublished (transcript, AHT). A substantial discussion of the salient facts about the moon. A list of HPL's treatises found in the 20 September 1903 issue of the *Rhode Island Journal of Astronomy* lists a 12-page work (non-extant) entitled *The Moon*; this must precede the first edition of the present treatise, dated to 26 November 1903.

Notes

1. HPL discusses this anomaly again in "The Defence Remains Open!" (1921; CE5).

2. The frontispiece is not extant.

THE EARTH NOT HOLLOW

To the Editor of the Sunday Journal:

In the Sunday Journal for Aug. 5 appeared an article concerning a book which advances the doctrine that the earth is a hollow sphere, with openings at the poles.[1] A few convincing arguments were brought up in support of the theory, but it seems to me that in most points it is contradictory to fact.

Among his arguments the author of the book, which is called *The Phantom of the Poles*, suggests that the compression at the ends of the earth is due to the apertures leading to the centre, but astronomy proves that a planet's polar compression is the result of centrifugal force, i.e. the power that causes the particles of a rotating body to retreat from the centre. All the members of the solar system are thus compressed, yet we see that they possess no polar apertures, which fact alone would almost prove by analogy that the earth is solid.

Another hypothesis introduced is that the Auroras of both hemispheres are burning volcanoes or fires, the "proof" being that they do not affect the magnetic needle. This is positively untrue, for the compass is not only disturbed but often deflected several degrees from the meridian during displays of the Northern and Southern lights. In fact, the general character of Auroral phenomena precludes the supposition that they are fires of any kind.

The rocks, gravel, wood, etc., often found in icebergs is also one of the facts with which he strengthens his theory; but they are, in all probability, the result of ocean currents.

"The open Polar seas" which are referred to as existing around both poles are likewise nearly proved to be figments of imagination, as the latest results of Arctic and Antarctic exploration seem to indicate that the North Pole is in the midst of a closely frozen ocean, while the southland is occupied by a great ice-bound continent the northern limits of which are already known to us as Graham, Victoria, and Wilkes Lands.

In regard to the surface gravity of the earth, which the new doctrine holds to be greatest at the "turning points" between the outer and inner worlds, it must simply be said that theory and experiment prove the attraction to be at its maximum on the equator, where, of course, is situated the largest amount of the earth's mass, owing to the polar compression before mentioned.

Again, the "hollow earth" theory at once becomes untenable when one reflects on the volcanic and seismic disturbances which so often convulse the crust of our planet and which, together with the fact that the heat of the ground increases with depth, tends to prove that the earth's centre is a mass of molten rock and fire.

From this we can easily see that the comparative warmth of the poles, which is emphasised most strongly, probably arises from the tenuity of the earth's crust in these localities.

In short, novel and attractive as the strange hypothesis may seem, it is certainly not possible, so we can still regard the earth as a solid body.

H. P. LOVECRAFT.

Providence, Aug. 6.

EDITOR'S NOTE FP: *Providence Sunday Journal* (12 August 1906): Sec. 2, p. 5. A refutation of an unsigned article that had appeared in the *Sunday Journal* a day before this letter was written (see n. 1). The hollow-earth theory was of venerable vintage, and had been one of the chief incitements to the Antarctic explorations of American explorer Charles Wilkes in 1838–40, the subject of HPL's non-extant juvenile treatise, *Wilkes's Explorations* (1902). John Uri Lloyd's fantasy novel *Etidorhpa* (1895), read by HPL in 1918 (see *SL* 1.54–55), also postulates a hollow earth. The conception might have partially inspired HPL's *The Dream-Quest of Unknown Kadath* (1926–27).

Notes

1. [Unsigned], "Is the World a Hollow Mockery? Mr. William Reed Thinks It Is in a Material No Less Than in a Moral Sense.—The Facts to Back Up His Ingenious Argument Set Forth," *Providence Sunday Journal* (5 August 1906): Sec. 4, p. 7. The article discussed Reed's *The Phantom of the Poles* (New York: W. S. Rockey Co., 1906).

[ASTRONOMY ARTICLES FOR THE PAWTUXET VALLEY GLEANER]

THE HEAVENS FOR AUGUST

Celestial Phenomena to Happen Next Month

Venus is, without doubt, the chief planet for August, shining each night in the West with unrivalled brilliancy. In the telescope it appears gibbous, like the moon a few days from full. Next in order of interest comes Saturn, which rises about 7.30. Its rings, which make it so attractive, are becoming less and less visible, so that in a small telescope, they appear simply as a band of light. Saturn will be nearest the earth September 4th. Mercury is invisible the greater part of the month, being lost in the sun's rays; but on the 30th he arrives at his greatest western elongation, then being visible about an hour and a half before sunrise. Mars is too near the sun to be seen, but Jupiter will be glimpsed by early risers just before the dawn.

The sun enters the sign Virgo on the 22nd. His disc is covered with spots visible in any spy-glass.

The Moon's phases occur as follows:

Full Moon ....August 4, 8 a.m.
Last Quarter ....August 11, 9.48 p.m.
New Moon...August 19, 8.29 p.m.
First Quarter...August 26, 7.42 p.m.

During the latter part of the month near the first quarter, great pleasure can be derived by studying the moon's face with optical aid. Even a field glass will shew the larger mountains.

There will be a lunar eclipse on the 4th and one of the sun on the 19th, both invisible here.

Turning to the constellations, we find the dull group called Sagittarius on the horizon, due south. Glancing above this we see Lyra, Cygnus, and Aquilo almost on the meridian. Of the spring constellations that have passed over to the west may be mentioned Boötes, Corona Borealis, and Ophiuchus. Looking north, we may discern, at equal altitudes, Cassiopeia and Ursa Minor, one on each side of the pole. The latter, in which is the famous "dipper", is in the west, pointed downward. The "little dipper" in Ursa Minor is also west of the pole. On the north horizon Auriga is rising, and in the northeast Perseus is completely risen. From this point southward, and to the west, the zodiacal constellations follow the horizon in a long procession, including Aries, Pisces, Aquarius, Capricorn, Sagittarius, Scorpio, Libra, Virgo, and Leo.

EDITOR'S NOTE: FP: *PVG* 31, No. 30 (27 July 1906): 1. The first of HPL's 17 extant articles for *PVG*, a weekly paper published in what is now Phenix, RI, a western suburb of Providence. Toward the end of each month, HPL reviews the astronomical phenomena to be seen in the following month; other articles focus on provocative or controverted issues in astronomy.

THE SKIES OF SEPTEMBER

Planetary and Stellar Motions Described

Saturn is now at his finest, coming to opposition on the 4th. He will then, of course, be nearest the earth. Venus, likewise, is best seen this month, as she arrives at greatest elongation on the 20th. At that time the telescope will reveal a "half-moon" phase, but by the end of the month the planet will be perceptibly crescentine. Mercury can be seen in the morning before sunrise until the 4th, when the proximity to the sun renders him invisible. He passes that orb in superior conjunction on the 24th, and will not be glimpsed again until November. Mars is barely visible about 4 a.m., yet not worth the seeing, as he is nearly at his greatest distance from the earth. Jupiter, however, is excellently situated for observation, rising about midnight. On the 3d of October he will be in quadrature, or at right angles to the sun. A good telescope reveals much of interest on this planet, as it has four easily visible moons, or satellites, besides many pleasing markings on its surface. Uranus and Neptune are both fairly seen with high-power glasses, but there is never anything connected with either that has much attraction.

The moon comes to its various phases in the following order:

Full Moon, 2nd .... 6.36 p.m.
Last Quarter, 10th .... 3.54 p.m.
New Moon, 18th .... 7.34 p.m.
First Quarter, 25th .... 1.12 p.m.

The sun enters Libra on the 23d, thus commencing the autumn season. His average time of rising is 5.30 a.m., and of setting, 6.00 p.m.

No eclipses or other special phenomena are booked for September.

From a stellar view-point, the present month is about the dullest of the entire year. The zodiacal group occupying the meridian is Capricornus, the Goat, principally noticeable as possessing in its head a pair of stars visible to the naked eye as a close, yet easily separable double. Above Capricornus stretches part of Aquarius, a large group that is now better seen late at night. Just below the zenith, or overhead point, we see Cygnus now past transit, and south of this may be found an aggregation of tiny groups exactly on the meridian, called Delphinus, Equuleus, and Sagitta. Turning to the north sky, Cepheus can be found between the zenith and the pole. To the west of this constellation lies Draco, and to the east Cassiopeia, while just below it is Ursa Minor, containing that most important star known as "Polaris". Of the constellations on the horizon, Ursa Major reaches down below the pole in the northwest. Auriga, which has now completely risen, claims the northeast, while the Pleiades are seen directly over the eastern horizon. From there southward, Cetus the Whale occupies the sky, and westward from that, Piscis Australis, Capricornus, and Sagittarius carry us around to the point where the Milky Way meets the earth. Ophiuchus and Serpens follow, and in the northwest Boötes has nearly disappeared. Lastly, below Ursa Major, may be seen one or two stars of Lyncus.

EDITOR'S NOTE: FP: *PVG* 31, No. 35 (31 August 1906): 1.

IS MARS AN INHABITED WORLD?

Startling Theories of Prof. Lowell on the Subject

No planet in the solar system has been the subject of more baseless speculation than Mars, the first outside the earth's orbit and the nearest to us of all. In ancient times its ruddy appearance attracted for it considerable attention, but the greatest interest came with the telescope, which revealed green and red markings, then firmly believed to be respectively seas and continents, suggesting a similarity to the earth, and indicating possible inhabitants. Late in the eighteenth century Herschel discovered on each Martian pole a white area, which waxed very large in the planet's winter, and decreased to the point of disappearance in summer.[1] This was interpreted as snow, gathering and melting, which theory holds today.

Mars was now thought without doubt to be an inhabited world. In 1877 the great Italian astronomer Schiaparelli discovered certain line-like markings on the planet, which he termed "canali", or "canals".[2] He also announced that the green spots were not seas, but areas of vegetation. The discovery of the canals was met with incredulity, but the polariscope upheld the Italian's decision concerning the green markings. This was the state of affairs until about 1890, when Mr. Percival Lowell, an American, began to carefully study the planet in the clear air of Flagstaff, Arizona, with a first-class telescope. In 1896 he gave to the world the result of his observations.[3]

The canals, he said, not only exist, but continually multiply in number. They all start from the polar caps (as the white snow areas are called), and run toward the centre of the planet in mathematically straight lines. Wherever they intersect, there is a small, perfectly round spot. Also, their breadth increases in summer, and decreases in winter. From these facts, Lowell has formed a most ingenious theory which I shall now state: Mars is supposed to be without oceans or lakes. Therefore in want of water, the only place where it exists being the poles, it is the work of intelligent beings to convey the precious fluid from the caps to the centre of the planet. The dark spots at the intersection are thought to be cities, so placed, that they may enjoy an extra water supply. The increase of the canals in summer is supposedly due to vegetation along the banks, which of course disappears with the advent of cold weather. Now these are startling conjectures which must be carefully weighed before acceptance, so we will consider each point.

The fact that Mars is nearly waterless is proven by the polariscopic observations of Prof. Wm. Pickering and others.[4] Likewise the nature of the polar caps is established, as during the melting season they are fringed with blue, which the spectroscope declares to be water. But now we come to a most serious question, "Are the canals artificial?" which of course entails a second query, "Is the planet inhabited?"

If living beings dwell on a world they must have air, water, light, and heat. Mars is known to have a least a thin atmosphere, also water, as previously stated, in the polar caps, and the sun gives considerable light and heat, although, as it is farther away, Mars would not receive as much as the earth, but of course, the Martians might be endowed with thicker skins than ours as a compensation, so we may say that the planet can be inhabited, as far as natural conditions go.

Next comes the question of the canals. They certainly have a look of artificiality, being geometrically straight, and having most exact intersections; indeed, it seems impossible that nature could produce such accurate work. But now another difficulty arises, for a thoughtful person will be apt to doubt the ability of humans to construct such great work. However, there is an answer even to this: as the Martian gravity is but a third of the earth's, therefore everything must weigh three times less than here, and the inhabitants, if they exist, must be three times as agile, and so be able to accomplish much more than our race in a mechanical way.

Thus stands Lowell's theory when analysed, not only possible, but even probable. Still, we must not be too hasty in crediting it, as ignorance is better than false knowledge.

"But if Mars is actually inhabited," ask some, "what do the people resemble?" To this no one can reply, for the lower temperature, thinner atmosphere, and other conditions would tend to produce a race quite different from ours, and as Mars is an old planet, compared to the earth, the population might be vastly more civilised and advanced than that of our globe. This, however, is mere speculation, so it is left to the fancy of the reader to form mental pictures of the population of Mars, or any more distant planet.

EDITOR'S NOTE: FP: *PVG* 31, No. 36 (7 September 1906): 1. The first of several discussions of Mars in HPL's corpus of astronomical columns. It is of interest to note that here he considers Percival Lowell's theory of the artificial construction of the Martian canals to be "not only possible, but even probable," whereas in later columns (e.g., "Mysteries of the Heavens: VII. Mars and the Asteroids" [p. 291]) he ridicules the theory as preposterous.

Notes

1. Sir William Herschel (1738–1822), German-born British astronomer. His discovery of the Martian polar caps is recorded in a paper published in 1784; rpt. in *The Scientific Papers of Sir William Herschel* (1912).

2. Giovanni Schiaparelli (1835–1910), Italian astronomer. His findings on Mars first appeared in a paper in *Astronomische Nachrichten* (1877), and were elaborated in *Osservazioni astronomiche e fisiche sull'asse di rotazione e sulla topografia del pianeta Marte durante l'opposizione del 1877* (1878).

3. Actually, Lowell's theories on the Martian canals were first enunciated in *Mars* (1895) and elaborated in *Mars and Its Canals* (1906) and *Mars as the Abode of Life* (1908).

4. Pickering's photographs of Mars date to 1888. His discovery of Martian "oases" dates to 1892.

IS THERE LIFE ON THE MOON?

Strange Revelations of Modern Science

Of late there has been no astronomical problem more disputed than that which deals with lunar life. Ever since the beginning of the nineteenth century the moon has been thought a "dead world", but now, in the twentieth, this theory is commencing to give way to more advanced ideas. The older astronomers employ a number of ways to arrive at their conclusions, and a few of them are stated below.

a. The most delicate tests have failed to reveal any signs of atmosphere around the moon.

b. Our satellite is obliged, by its long rotation, to endure great extremes of temperature.

c. The most powerful telescopes shewed nothing that indicated to their eyes life or vegetation.

d. No change was noticed on the lunar disc.

In the middle of the present century came the first ocular proof of lunar life, in the form of a changeable crater. A little mountain by the name of Linnaeus was charted in 1651 as an easily visible feature, but an eighteenth-century observer named Schroeter described it as a very small, brilliant spot.[1] However, the current explanation was that either one or the other had made a mistake. Beer and Maedler,[2] two of the earth's greatest selenographers, called its diameter 4 miles, but within a few years Schmidt mapped it at 6 to 7 miles.[3] By that time, the public was awakened to the fact that there was really truth in these observations, so the little crater was carefully watched, and the vigil was rewarded by its complete disappearance. But it soon reappeared, only ¼ mile in diameter and very bright in appearance. Since then, its size has increased to 1½ m. and later sunk to ¾.

Today this change is generally accepted as the work of active volcanism. Now no volcano can operate without atmosphere, but there could easily be a thin gaseous envelope undetected from the earth. The "lunar rays", i.e. long, brilliant streaks radiating outward from some of the craters, have always been a puzzle to astronomers. Numerous theories have been promulgated concerning their origin, some saying that they are cracks in the moon's surface while others maintain them to be streaks of lava, ejected in the remote past from the craters which they surround. But the latest and most startling theory is that they are deep furrows filled with snow. This seems incredible at first sight, considering that there are no clouds on the moon; but when we reflect that little more than hoar frost would be required to produce the glittering appearance, the theory becomes more acceptable. For this theory, the world is indebted to Prof. William H. Pickering of Harvard, the greatest living selenographer.

Another strong evidence of lunar life is the varying number of craterlets in the large ring-shaped plain known as Pluto. Every different observer has charted a different number, and in 1904 a crescentine bank, 6 × 2 miles in area, 1000 feet high that was certainly not there before, appeared on the floor of this puzzle plain. We now arrive at a point where real life is involved, for Pickering has discovered small dark streaks in some of the craters, that change from time to time, and after a careful survey has pronounced them to be low forms of vegetation.

Still another convincing proof of selenic activity is the case of the twin craters, Messier and Messier-A. They are at times exactly alike, but on other occasions very dissimilar. The explanation offered by modern science for this perplexing phenomenon is that the unequal distributing of frost causes variations of light and shade, thus distorting the familiar outlines of the two formations.

To return to volcanism, there is now before us the most startling evidence of all, for in a deep, winding chasm called "Schroeter's valley" can be seen the only active and ocular proof of seismic conditions. There an assiduous observer can detect peculiar clouds of moving whiteness, which the up-to-date selenographer interprets as nothing more or less than smoke from an active crater! These clouds are often so dense as to obscure neighbouring objects.

Now all this evidence is very convincing, and in all probability is correct, so we must consider our satellite to be a body which, although not containing any high or animal life, is yet not wholly dead.

EDITOR'S NOTE: FP: *PVG* 31, No. 37 (14 September 1906): 1. HPL draws upon his earlier works, "My Opinion as to the Lunar Canals" (p. 15) and "The Moon" (p. 17), for most of the data in this article.

Notes

1. Johann Hieronymus Schröter (1745–1816), German astronomer who observed the moon's features over many years from an observatory at Lilienthal. His findings appeared in *Selenotopographische Fragmente zur genauern Kenntniss der Mondfläche* (1791–1802).

2. Johann Heinrich Mädler (1794–1874) and Wilhelm Beer (1797–1850) collaborated on such works as *Mappa Selenographica* (1834–36; 4 vols.) and *Der Mond nach seinen kosmischen und individuellen Verhältnissen* (1837).

3. Johann Friedrich Julius Schmidt (1825–1884), German astronomer who worked mostly in Greece.

AN INTERESTING PHENOMENON

Occultation of a Star on the 25th of This Month

The moon, as everyone knows, is much nearer the earth than any other heavenly body, so it is not strange that it frequently eclipses the stars and planets that lie in its path. These eclipses are called "occultations", the term being derived from the Latin verb "occulto", to hide. The occultation of a star is a most interesting and surprising sight. Small stars are frequently hidden, larger ones more rarely, but as the moon's brightness overpowers the light of the fainter orb, few occultations are visible either to the naked eye or in a small glass. If a heavenly body is hidden by the dark edge of the moon, which is always the case before full, the sight is very striking, as the body vanishes suddenly, apparently without cause, the moon's edge being of course invisible.

Such an occultation happens on the 25th of this month, at 7.55 p.m., when the moon, a large crescent, hides the star called "X2 Sagittarii". The observer should be on hand with an opera glass about 7.45, watching the moon with care. He will then see a star a short distance away from the occulting body. At about 7.55 the star will disappear abruptly, and without previous notice.

These occultations are among the most important occurrences in astronomy, as they are the means of finding out that the moon has no dense atmosphere. (See article in last week's issue.)

Occasionally a planet is hidden by our satellite, when the phenomenon is very attractive. Such sights will always be described beforehand in the Gleaner's monthly article, so no one need be afraid of missing them.

EDITOR'S NOTE: FP: *PVG* 31, No. 38 (21 September 1906): 1.

OCTOBER HEAVENS

Celestial Scenery for the Coming Month

Jupiter can now be seen late in the evening, rising about 9.30 p.m., and coming to quadrature on the 3d. His satellites, which are visible in an opera glass, should be looked at by all possessing such instruments. Venus and Saturn are both visible during the early hours of the night, the former being at greatest brilliancy on the 25th. She can now be detected in the daytime by those who are gifted with sharp eyesight. The telescope reveals a crescent phase when pointed to this planet; indeed, but slight magnification is required to shew Venus in her true shape. Mars can be seen any clear morning before sunrise, but he is not yet in a position for interesting observations. Mercury, likewise, which may be glimpsed in the western twilight, is devoid of attraction. Uranus and Neptune, not being visible to the naked eye, will not be described here.

There are five moon-phases this month, our satellite arriving at the various points of her orbit as follows:

Full Moon, 2nd...7.48 a.m.
Last Quarter, 10th...10.39 a.m.
Full Moon, 17th ....5.43 a.m.
First Quarter, 24th ....8.50 a.m.
Full Moon, 31st .... 11.46 p.m.

On October 22nd the sun enters Scorpio, which reveals the fact that Autumn is fast advancing.

Two occultations, as described in the Gleaner for last week, will occur during October. On the 4th at 8.53 the star called "Mu Ceti" will be immersed, and at 10.42 on the 8th, "Xi-3 Orionis" will be hidden. To observe the phenomena with ease, I recommend the use of opera glasses.

Turning to the siderial heavens, we find the meridian very clearly marked for us by prominent constellations. On the horizon due south is Grus, the Crane, with Piscis Australis directly above it. Over this, in the region of the ecliptic, is Aquarius, an asterism not likely to kindle much enthusiasm in the amateur. Following the meridian still further north, we behold Pegasus, the Winged Horse. If one looks very closely at the star designated by the Greek letter "Pi", he will notice that it is double. Above Pegasus lies Cepheus, next to the pole, but it is lacking in interest.

Of the groups in the eastern sky Auriga, Taurus, Perseus, Aries, Triangula, Cassiopeia, Andromeda, and Pisces may be mentioned. Of these, Taurus is the most attractive, as he contains the Pleiades, a beautiful cluster of small stars. Although the average eye can find but six members in this aggregation, a keen-sighted English astronomer named Dawes has counted eleven, as seen on a clear night.[1] Of course, a telescope will reveal more than can be numbered.

Crossing over to the western heavens, we behold Cygnus, Lyra, Aquilo, Delphinus, Equuleus, Hercules, Draco, and Serpentarius, the same groups that were near the meridian last month. The larger part of Ursa Minor is also west of the pole.

The horizontal constellations now claim our attention. Under the pole is Ursa Major, which will rise high in the sky late at night. A little further east may be seen a few rising stars of Gemini and the Lynx. Just south of the cardinal point, part of Orion is pushing up, a precursor of brighter skies in the near future. Below this is Eridanus, a dull group, which is followed by three faint asterisms, Phoenix, Sculptor, and Grus, the latter now being in transit. On the western sky-line can be glimpsed successively the remains of Sagittarius, Serpens, Corona Borealis, and Boötes, which, bringing us back to the north, completes the circuit.

EDITOR'S NOTE: FP: *PVG* 31, No. 39 (28 September 1906): 1.

Notes

1. See William Rutter Dawes (1799–1868), *Astronomical Observations at South Villa* (1852).

ARE THERE UNDISCOVERED PLANETS?

Boundaries of Our System Still Shrouded in Obscurity

The earth which we inhabit is known to be one of many similar bodies, called "planets", that revolve around the sun in various distances. Of these, the known number is eight; consisting of four, including the earth, comparatively near the sun, all solid, and resembling each other in size and nature; besides four others, situated at immense distances, and being semi-fluid or molten in constitution. These are also much larger than the inner planets. Between the two groups of planets are about 600 very small bodies called "asteroids", which are possibly the fragments of an exploded world. The names of the inner planets are, in order of distance from the sun, Mercury, Venus, The Earth, and Mars. The outer group is composed of Jupiter, Saturn, Uranus, and Neptune. Of these, all but Mercury and Venus have one or more moons revolving around them.

The ancients knew of no planets beyond Saturn, and when Uranus was discovered in 1781, everyone supposed that the boundary of the system was reached at last, yet in 1846 Neptune was added to this list.[1] Now we must consider carefully whether there are any more of these great worlds awaiting discovery, and if so, where to find them. There are just two places in the solar system where undiscovered planets have been thought to exist, i.e. between Mercury and the sun, and beyond Neptune; for a planet in any other place would long ago have been seen.

Many people have imagined the existence of an intra-Mercurial orb, and several times the discovery of one has been announced, but in every case the assertion has been disproved. The means by which most of the pseudo-discoveries were made have been fictitious transits over the sun, and stars seen during the eclipses. Among the former, the episode of "Vulcan" will always be remembered.[2]

In 1848 the French astronomer Leverrier,[3] who discovered Neptune, thought that Mercury did not move as it should, and that the error was due to an unknown planet. He exhorted all astronomers to search carefully for this. Many years later, a poor physician named Lescarbault[4] announced the discovery of the planet in transit, and for a short time he was greatly honoured, the new orb receiving the name of "Vulcan", but after a time it was demonstrated that no such body could exist.

Another remarkable "discovery" was that made by Profs. Watson and Swift at Ann Arbor, Mich., during the eclipse of 1878, when both observers pointed out two objects, one as the hypothetical Vulcan, the other as a new intra-Mercurial. This statement, however, as well as all others like it, was quickly proved to be unfounded, as the two "planets" turned out to be well-known stars.

We must now turn to the other explorable region, i.e. that beyond Neptune. It has been observed that the order of the planets from the sun was in a regular progression, which, if so, would render planetary discovery quite easy, but this rule, which is purely accidental, fails in the case of the outer planets, so other means must be relied on. It must be understood that the enormous gravities of the large planets draw to them certain comets, making their aphelia, or points farthest from the sun, very near to their orbits. Jupiter and others have captured a great number in this way. Now it has been observed that a great many comets have their aphelia at a space of about 9,300,000,000 miles from the sun, so Prof. Forbes of the Royal Society of Edinburgh imagines a planet to exist at that distance, revolving about once in a thousand years.[5] Mr. Percival Lowell of Arizona conjectures a large body to exist about 6,550,000,000 miles out, from the same reason.[6] But it would be a very difficult task to find the elements of so distant a body, and even if some mathematician should accomplish the task of computing an orbit, it is doubtful if its theoretical place would be anywhere in the vicinity of its actual location, so it seems to the writer that the only possible way of finding such a planet is to examine photographs of every part of the sky, as is done in the discovery of asteroids.

It is not likely that the limits of our solar system are yet found, and sooner or later Mercury and Neptune must lose the distinction that they now bear.

EDITOR'S NOTE: FP: PVG 31, No. 40 (5 October 1906): 3. Another discussion of the possibility of additional planets in the solar system, both intra-Mercurial and trans-Neptunian.

Notes

1. Uranus was discovered by Sir William Herschel. HPL's non-extant treatise, "Herschel" (no. 4 of "The Science Library," c. 1903–04), probably deals with Uranus, which HPL refers to in his juvenile astronomical works as Herschel (see "August Skies" [p. 192]). For the discovery of Neptune, see further "The January Sky" (EN, 31 December 1914 [p. 133]).

2. See "Does Vulcan Exist?" (p. 331).

3. Urbain Jean Joseph Le Verrier (1811–1877), French astronomer.

4. Edmond-Modeste Lescarbault, French physician.

5. George Forbes (1849–1936), Scottish astronomer, professor of natural philosophy at Anderson's University (Glasgow), and member of the Royal Society of Edinburgh since 1887.

6. Lowell had long been concerned with the possibility of a trans-Neptunian planet, devoting the last eight years of his life to its discovery.

CAN THE MOON BE REACHED BY MAN?

Shewing That the Trip to Our Satellite, Heretofore Attempted
Only in Fiction, May Be a Scientific Possibility

Both in olden and modern times, many authors who wished to make a startling piece of fiction have recounted imaginary journeys to the moon. In 1649 a Frenchman named Jean Baudoin published a book entitled: A *Trip from the Earth to the Moon, Performed by Domingo Gonzales, a Spanish Adventurer*,[1] and from that time on, hundreds of similar works have appeared, some good, some bad; the most prominent having been written by Locke, Poe, Verne, and Wells.[2] But if any one of these authors should be asked if he thought it possible for such a voyage to be performed, a laugh would constitute a reply. Yet this is not a scientific impossibility, and some day an inhabitant of this earth may set foot on the soil of our satellite! Of course there are grave difficulties that make a lunar trip seem impossible, but if a person of the eighteenth century could have heard of the telephone, phonograph, etc., he would have been as incredulous as one who may now read these pages with a sceptical mind.

The greatest impediment to extra-terrestrial travel is lack of air, but in an air-tight compartment one could easily store enough to last the journey, carrying oxygen to re-vivify and lime to purify it. Another obstacle is the lack of gravity, which would render everything unsteady; but all essentials could be fastened to the sides of the chosen vehicle, while the passenger might support himself by convenient rests. A third difficulty is the extreme cold, but of course, artificial heat could be had. Lastly, there is always a danger of colliding with meteoric bodies, but this is so slight, that I doubt if it would deter any enthusiast.

We must now consider the greatest problem of all, i.e., the motive power. There have been a number of different methods worked out in imagination, but three of which are worthy of notice, high towers being out of the question on account of earth's rotation, also balloons, and like contrivances, which require an atmosphere to sustain them. The three investigatable plans are:

    (a)   To fire an inhabited projectile from an immense cannon.

    (b)   To interpose between the earth and the selected vehicle a screen, consisting of some material impervious to gravity.

    (c)   To send off a projectile by electrical repulsion.

We will now consider the merits and the de-merits of each.

At first sight, plan No. 1 seems quite feasible, but when we reflect that the huge projectile necessary to transport a human being must have an initial velocity of seven miles per second, which is beyond the powers of any known explosive, the proposition becomes less attractive; besides, it is not likely that anyone could stand the strain of being fired from a cannon, for the shock would be so great that no arrangement could eliminate it, to say nothing of the fall upon the moon, so we must turn to the second plan.

At the present time, however, that is quite impracticable, as nothing is yet discovered that will defy gravity, and even if it were, and the voyager had safely reached the moon, the slow rotation of the latter would render it necessary for him to circumnavigate Mars before he could reach his home again!

There now remains but one hope, electrical repulsion, and of all the three plans this seems, at present, the most rational. The existence of repulsive forces is well known. Two bodies, loaded with similar charges of electricity, repel each other, and when sufficiently light, separate. The like poles of two magnets are also mutually repelled, but at a long distance this force is perceived with difficulty. The waves of wireless telegraphy do the same. The sun repels the tails of comets, and possibly his own corona, but perhaps this force is not identical with that before described. Now while heretofore no one has created currents of sufficient intensity to repel from the earth a shell or projectile containing an astronomer, the scientific progress of a century or so may reveal some new force or apparatus that will enable this third plan to be executed.

Lastly, the reader may ask of what use the moon can be made, as it has no dense atmosphere or water, and to this I reply that an investigating party could easily manufacture air, and carry a large stock of provisions. Then the unseen side of our satellite could be explored and mapped. Prof. Pickering's discoveries of vegetation, snow, and volcanism could be verified in the most positive manner. And for those to whom avarice appeals more strongly than science, it is likely that a planet so volcanic in nature would contain beds of precious metals and stones.

However, it is not probable that, within the lifetime of anyone who now reads these pages, a journey to the moon, or any more distant orb, will be either thought of or attempted.

EDITOR'S NOTE: FP: *PVG* 31, No. 41 (12 October 1906): 2. One of the most engaging of HPL's early astronomical articles, displaying knowledge of both the science and the fiction of space travel.

Notes

1. Jean Baudoin (1590?–1650), *L'Homme dans la lune* (1648), a translation of a work by Francis Godwin, *The Man in the Moon* (1638).

2. See Richard Adams Locke (1800–1871), *Interesting Astronomical Discoveries Made in the Moon* (18350, a hoax as by "Sir John Herschel"; Edgar Allan Poe (1809–1849), "The Unparalleled Adventure of One Hans Pfaall" (1835); Jules Verne (1828–1905), *De la terre à la lune* (1865), tr. as *From the Earth to the Moon* (1869); H. G. Wells (1866–1946), *The First Men in the Moon* (1901).

THE MOON

A Brief Description of Our Satellite

Of all the heavenly bodies there is none nearer to us than the moon, nor do we possess as intimate a relation with any other planet as we do with this little globe, only 2162 miles in diameter, that revolves around us every month.

The exact period of the moon's revolution is 27d. 7h. 43m. 11s., a short time, although the motion of the earth itself around the sun makes this appear much longer, so the apparent or "synodic" revolution occupies 29d. 12h. 44m. 3s. As the moon travels around the earth it apparently undergoes great changes of form, called "phases", due to the different positions in which we see the moon with respect to the sun. These phases vary in figure from a thin crescent to a full circle, and a complete set is called a "lunation". A lunation occupies one synodic revolution.

Once every month the moon is too near the sun to be seen, and sometimes, when moving exactly in the plane of the earth's orbit, it eclipses the great orb of day by passing over his face. When the moon is in line with the earth and sun, whether or not eclipsing the latter, it is said to be "new" or in the "change". It will then not be visible for two days. When this time has elapsed, the moon can be seen in the west as a slender crescent, with horns pointing east, setting about two hours before the sun. The next night the crescent is larger, and the time of setting is about an hour later. Thus it progresses, each night adding a little to the crescent, and about an hour to the time of setting, until five days after its first appearance, the moon shews a half circle of light, and sets about midnight. It is then said to be in the "First Quarter". From then on, the illuminated portion becomes more and more convex (or "gibbous", as it is called) until, seven days after the first quarter, our satellite rises at sunset in the east, a complete circle of light. This is "Full Moon". The next day the side that has hitherto always been a perfect semi-circle begins to diminish, and in another week the moon is again half full, the illuminated side now being that which was invisible on the previous occasion. This phase is called the "Last Quarter", and the moon rises about midnight. The next few days are spent in the diminution of the edge that was straight in the last quarter, until, five days after, the moon is again a narrow crescent, this time in the east, rising two hours before daybreak, with horns pointed westward. The following day it is invisible, not to be seen again until it has passed the sun, and begun a new lunation.

Besides eclipsing the sun, the moon is often eclipsed itself. This can occur only at the full, where, if in the plane of the earth's orbit, it will of course encounter its shadow.

When the moon passes between the earth and a star or planet, that phenomenon is called an "occultation". Sometimes when the moon is young, not only the crescent is visible, but the entire disc, illuminated by a faint reddish light. This is the brilliancy reflected from the earth, for it must be understood that on the moon, our world shines like a brilliant orb, in fact, appears much the same as our satellite does to us, except that it is thirteen times larger. The reason that this "earth-light" disappears as the moon waxes is, that the earth, to a lunar observer, would undergo phases, being full at new moon, and new at full moon.

As our satellite makes but one rotation on its axis during a revolution, it invariably turns the same face to the earth, so, from the side seen by us, our world would appear immutably fixed in the heavens, while the other side might never receive its light.

The apparent size of the moon, as seen with the naked eye, has always been a point of dispute, some saying its diameter to be about an inch, while still more compare it to a foot; yet it is a fact that the entire disc may be covered with a lead pencil held at arm's length. In angular measure the moon's apparent diameter is 31 degrees and 24 minutes.

Another curious thing connected with the moon as seen with the unassisted eye is the phenomenon known as the "horizontal moon". This refers to the enlarged appearance of our satellite when rising or setting. Many theories concerning this have been advanced, and it has been demonstrated that the disc should even appear smaller; indeed, a telescope at once dispels the illusion, for which as yet no satisfactory reason has been advanced.

We now come to a point where we seemingly must contradict some statements previously made, for I now assert that more than half of the moon is visible to the earth. However, the amount in excess of the half is very small, and due to several conditions which, taken collectively, are called "librations". To understand these, we must know that the moon describes not a circle but an ellipse or oval around the earth, being sometimes 252,830 miles away, while on other occasions its distance is but 221,520m. When nearest the earth it is said to be in "Perigee", and when farthest, in "Apogee". The average is about 240,000 miles. There is an imaginary line in the heavens on which all the planets are supposed to travel, called the "ecliptic", but as a matter of fact, most them deviate considerably from it. This discrepancy is called "inclination to the ecliptic". The moon's inclination amounts to nearly 5 degrees and 9 minutes. Now these two facts, ellipticity of orbit and inclination to the ecliptic, are the major causes of libration; the first enabling us to see around our satellite in easterly and westerly directions, while the latter reveal lands above the north, and below the south pole.

Although, as has been said before, the moon's path does not coincide with the ecliptic, it nevertheless intersects that line at two points, called "nodes". These nodes do not always occupy the same places on the ecliptic, but have a retrograde motion occupying 18y. 218d. 21h. 22m. 46s. This period was used by the ancients for predicting eclipses, and was called the "Saros".

The moon is much smaller than the earth, its diameter being about 1/4, its volume 1/49, mass 1/81, density 3/5, apparent disc 1/13, and gravity 1/7. The decreased gravity would cause an object weighing 7lb. on the earth to weigh but one on the moon, yet the force is sufficient to attract the waters of the earth and cause the phenomena known as tides. A striking illustration of the moon's levity as compared with the earth lies in the fact that their balancing point, or centre of gravity, is about 1000 miles below the surface of our world. It has been previously stated that the moon rises and sets about an hour later every day, but we must now make an exception to this. At the full moon nearest the autumnal equinox our satellite is observed to rise at nearly the same time for several nights. This is caused by its presence in that part of its course which makes the smallest angle with the horizon. The name "Harvest Moon" has been applied to this state of affairs. At the following full moon the same phenomenon takes place on a smaller scale. This is the "Hunter's Moon".

To the naked eye, the moon appears to be covered with dark spots, to which imagination gives the form of men and animals, but the telescope shews a very different sight. The entire surface is seen to be covered with mountain ranges, and pitted with ring-shaped formations. These last often have small central peaks, and are thought to be extinct volcanoes, or "craters", as they are called. Any good field or spy glass will shew these, but to study them in detail a good astronomical telescope is required. In a small glass the moon looks very much like the earth, the dark spots resembling seas, etc.; indeed, when such instruments were the only available, our satellite was thought to be inhabited, so all formations were named terrestrially, and for lack of a better nomenclature the appellations exist unchanged up to the present time.

Until the latter part of the nineteenth century science has believed the moon to be dead, but the researches of Prof. Pickering tend to establish the belief that our satellite possesses a thin atmosphere, low vegetation, hoar frost, and the last stages of volcanism.

In conclusion, I will give a few directions to those desirous of studying the moon. Before commencing, learn some simple lunar map by heart, so as to be familiar with what you are about to see, then procure one of the $1.00 telescopes, which are advertised in the magazines, as they will shew all the larger craters. Do not try to see the mountains at full moon, for the direct rays of the sun obscure them. The best time to observe such things is when they are on the "terminator", or division between the light and dark sides of the lunar disc. The writer confidently believes that there is no pursuit more interesting than the study of the moon, so all are urged to devote themselves to this branch of knowledge, for in the history of the world some of the most recondite facts have been brought to light by the first efforts of an amateur.

EDITOR'S NOTE: FP: *PVG* 31, No. 42 (19 October 1906): 7. This article bears an even closer connection with "The Moon" (p. 17), whose "7th edition" had been completed only three months before. Nearly the entirety of that work has been incorporated into the present article.

[UNTITLED]

Jupiter is now well up in the evening sky. He rises at 7 p.m. on the 20th, thus coming into view quite early. Although his opposition does not occur until next month, he is, nevertheless, by far the most beautiful object to be seen in November. Venus, which has so long been ruler of the skies, makes her disappearance this month, coming to inferior conjunction on the 30th. A telescope will, however, reveal this planet as a thin crescent during the first few days. Persons desirous of seeing her should look low down in the west immediately after sunset. Saturn, with its ring still visible, shines brightly in the southeast. Great regret is occasioned by the fact that the aforementioned circle will not be seen in 1907. Mars, from a terrestrial view-point, is slowly improving. Rising at 3 a.m., he shines high in the east when overtaken by the dawn. Mercury and Uranus are invisible this month, but the former will be well situated in December. Neptune, near Jupiter, is now to be seen in a telescope.

The moon's phases will ensue in the order given below:

Last Quarter 9th, 4.45 a.m.; New Moon 16th, 3.36 p.m.;

First Quarter 22nd, 7.39 p.m.; Full Moon 30th, 6.07 p.m.

The sun enters the sign Sagittarius on the 23d, then being just 30 degrees from the winter solstice.

The fourth-magnitude star Iota Capricorni will be occulted by the five-day moon at 8.30 p.m. on the 21st. I hope all who possess glasses will observe this interesting phenomenon.

During the early morning hours of the 14th, many meteors, or "shooting stars", will be seen darting from the Gamma in the constellation Leo. These are the famous Leonids, and it would well pay anyone to remain awake the entire night of their occurrence, for the purpose of watching them. Leo will rise in the northeast shortly after twelve, and almost simultaneously the meteors will appear darting hither and thither through the sky, stopped only by the coming of the dawn.

We now arrive at the domain of the constellations, and here we find the winter groups beginning to appear. Orion has fully risen, likewise Gemini. Taurus and Auriga are high up in the sky, while the northern half of Fluvius Eridanus occupies the south-west sky. To see this asterism in full, one must travel as far south as Latitude 30 de-grees. On the meridian is Cetus, the whale. The variable Mira, in this, is now at minimum, being of the ninth magnitude. Above Cetus lies Pisces, containing the "ver-nal equinox", or point where the sun crosses the equator northward, and still higher up is Andromeda, now at its best. This constellation possesses one of the most famous nebulae in the entire sky, which may be seen with the naked eye on any clear night, in the absence of the moon. Between Andromeda and the pole, directly in the Milky Way, lies Cassiopeia, which is, on account of its conspicuous "W" shape, unmistakable. Just east of Andromeda and Pisces may be found three groups, Aries, Triangula, and Perseus. The latter contains the grandest star cluster in the heavens, which consists of a central condensation, together with numerous out-running rifts, presenting a latent beauty that defies portraiture.

In the west lie all the autumn constellations, the long list reading:

Aquarius, Aquila, Capricornus, Cepheus, Cygnus, Delphinus, Equuleus, Hercules, Lyra, Pegasus, Phoenix, Piscis Australis, and Sculptor.

Finally, in the north, Ursa Major is emerging from beneath the pole, Ursa Minor is hanging under, and Draco is descending below it. Lynx is already high in the east, and Corona has disappeared.

EDITOR'S NOTE: FP: *PVG* 31, No. 43 (26 October 1906): 8. Published without title or subti-tle, the article surveys the more notable astronomical phenomena for November.

THE SUN

Centre of the Planetary System

The sun is the centre of the solar system, and by far the largest body therein, having a diameter of 866,000 miles. A glance tells us that its constitution is not the same as that of the planets, and indeed it is not, for the bright orb is nothing less than a tre-mendous bulk of glowing gas, 1,300,000 times larger than the earth, and rotating once in 25 days. In fact it is 800 times larger than all the planets put together. Its density is but a quarter of the earth's, making it equal in consistency to a thick fluid. The force of gravity on the sun is 27 times more than on the earth, so if a person could reach the centre of the system he would be killed by his own weight.

The sun's light and heat are so great that the mind can scarcely grasp their im-mensity, for an electric arc light, the brightest known illumination, appears black in comparison to the solar rays. Should the earth be placed on the sun's surface, it would vanish and evaporate like a drop of water.

Light requires eight minutes to travel from the sun to the earth, its rate being 186,000 miles per second. The same distance is so great that if a fast train of cars had set out for the sun in 1650, it would still be far from its destination.

In a telescope, the sun is seen to be covered with irregular moving spots, sur-rounded with grey borders called "penumbrae". These are sometimes 50,000 miles in diameter, and occasionally spots over 100,000 miles wide have been observed. It is by these that the sun's rotation was discovered. The solar spots are the scenes of vast disturbances, comparable to volcanic action on the earth, yet on such a scale that even the calamities which wrecked Pompeii, Martinique, San Francisco, and Valparaiso[1] would seem as nothing beside them. The solar surface is, in fact, like a whirling ocean, the rush of gaseous fluid up and down the side of certain spots having been found to be twenty miles a second, while other eddies of molten matter have been measured at over 100 miles a second.

The exact nature of the solar spots is much disputed, some having attempted to prove from observations that they are depressions in the visible surface, or "photosphere", as it is called, while others consider them to be elevations. Prof. Newcomb holds that they are on a level with the photosphere.[2] As it is, little is known about them, save that they are cooler than the rest of the sun, which fact has been proved with delicate instruments. The substances of which the sun is composed of can be told by means of a chemical appliance known as the "spectroscope", which is also used on other objects.

When the sun is eclipsed, and his bright rays temporarily intercepted, we see that he has a vast amount of matter outside the visible disc, consisting of immense jets of fire called "prominences" and a far-reaching luminous atmosphere known as the "corona". The prominences are the result of eruptions on so great a scale that the very noise, if heard at close range, would kill a human being. The earth is small, if compared with one of these giant displays.

As the sun is all that sustains life on the planets, it will naturally be asked if its fire will ever die out. To this, it must be said that the great body's size precludes its cooling at any time within millions of years, and the discovery of an element called "Radium" in its constitution lengthens the epoch to billions, so it may be safely believed that for many generations the sun will continue to exist as a great donor of light and heat.

EDITOR'S NOTE: FP: *PVG* 31, No. 44 (2 November 1906): 5.

Notes

1. HPL refers to the eruption of Mt. Vesuvius that destroyed Pompeii (79 C.E.); the eruption of Mt. Pelée that destroyed the capital, St.-Pierre, of the Caribbean island Martinique (1902); the San Francisco earthquake and fire (1906); and the earthquake and fire in Valparaiso, Chile (1906).

2. Simon Newcomb (1835–1909), Canadian-born American astronomer. See "On the Period of the Solar Spots," *Astrophysical Journal* (January 1901). HPL owned Newcomb's *Popular Astronomy* (1880) and *Astronomy for Everybody* (1904) (*LL* 647–48).

THE LEONIDS

Directions How to Observe the Coming Shower

Of all the meteoric showers of the year, that which occurs on the 14th of this month is the most wonderful. While single "shooting-stars" are not uncommon, the sight of hundreds of brilliant streaks, all radiating from one point, is so startling that even to an old observer these "Leonids", as the members of the present shower are called, have a peculiar interest.

Meteors are small particles of matter revolving around the sun, that fall to the earth, attracted to it. Sometimes they move in companies, in which case a shower results upon their descent to the earth. A continuous belt of meteors, meeting the earth the 14th of every November, is thus called the Leonid shower. Every 33 years a thick region of the belt is encountered, giving a very brilliant display. Such will not occur again until 1932, but the ordinary phenomenon is so interesting that I will subjoin a few directions in regard to it.

Out of any star atlas trace a chart of Leo and surroundings, including about 20 degrees on each side, and mount a copy on stiff cardboard. The map is preferably white, with black stars and lettering. Take this out in the night of the shower (Nov. 13–14), being provided with a dim light by which to see it. Shortly after twelve the meteors will begin to appear, and as each one is seen, it should be plotted down on the chart together with the time of its visibility. By sunrise, which of course puts an end to the vigil, a large number of trails will be found. Now prolong the starting-point of each to the end of the chart, and the added portions will be perceived to intersect near the star marked by the Greek letter "Gamma". This is the radiant point of the meteors, or the place on the ecliptic where the belt cuts the earth's orbit.

I strongly urge all who do not mind the loss of one night's sleep to follow this plan, for by so doing, they will not only improve their own knowledge, but aid the science of astronomy, should they care to publish their results.

EDITOR'S NOTE: FP: *PVG* 31, No. 45 (9 November 1906): 5.

COMETS

The Wanderers of Our System

Comets, those strange astronomical nonentities, are members of the solar system that revolve in very elongated and uneven orbits. As usually seen, they consist of a nucleus, or condensation, followed by tails, or streamers of light, which, curiously enough, are always repelled from the sun, causing them to precede the nuclei when moving away from the great luminary. Comets are extremely light in density, but otherwise from that, little concerning their physical condition is known, the most prevalent theory being that they are composed of minute particles, enclosed in atmospheres. These bodies are so light that they are deviated from their course by the attraction of planets, especially the large ones, such as Jupiter, so one can never tell when a comet's path will change in direction. From this, it is considered possible for such a body to strike the earth, although the chances are all against such a collision. Even should it occur the levity of the attacking body would prevent any serious damage.

Besides comets belonging to the solar system, there are many which roam aimlessly through space, and are attracted to our sun by chance proximity. A comet of this kind never returns unless a large planet happens to keep it by its gravitation.

While most comets are visible only in a telescope, a few are very bright. These have usually received names, or are known by the date of their appearance. Those of 1680 and 1843 were among the most beautiful. The latter will return in 2219. Halley's comet, with a revolution of 76 years, is another bright body. It will next appear in

1910. The great comet of 1811 is likewise worth mention. Among the long-period comets, Donati's may be noted. It appeared in 1858, but will not again be seen until 3858, its period of revolution being about two thousand years.

Comets often have two or more tails. That of 1744, which was quite brilliant, had six, while the faint comet of Dorelly, in 1903, had two, as observed by the writer.

These celestial wanderers were formerly regarded as precursors of calamity, but modern progress has destroyed such gross superstition, and comets are now welcomed rather than dreaded.

EDITOR'S NOTE: FP: *PVG* 31, No. 46 (16 November 1906): 1.

DECEMBER SKIES

Celestial Events for the Christmas Month

Jupiter arrives at his best this month, coming in opposition on the 28th. Even an opera glass will then shew four of his attendant satellites, and possibly outline his disc. Saturn, in quadrature on the 1st, illumines the southwest. He is ever attractive to telescopists. Mercury, in greatest elongation on the 18th, is also of interest. This planet may be found in the east before sunrise any morning near the middle of the month. Venus and Uranus are invisible, both being near solar conjunction. Neptune may be located near Jupiter any night with the aid of a spy glass, but he hardly repays the trouble.

The moon's phases are as follows:

Last Quarter, 8th.. 8.45 p.m.
New Moon, 15th .... 1.54 p.m.
First Quarter, 22nd.. 10.04 p.m.
Full Moon, 30th .... 1.44 p.m.

The sun enters Capricornus on the 22nd, at 1 p.m., thus inaugurating the winter season.

Those who are addicted to very late hours may witness the occultation of 56 Geminorum on the 4th at 2.36 a.m., although its interest is inconsiderable, the star being only of the fifth magnitude. Besides this no special phenomenon is predicted for December.

Among the stars a multitude of very beautiful groups is in sight. Orion is high in the southeast, and no one can mistake it, as its great size and bright stars both serve to make it a most conspicuous object. Attention is called to the row of three brilliant stars in its centre, variously called the "belt", "yard", "kings", etc.; also the line of faint dots below it, which contains the famous Orion nebula. Above Orion, Taurus, with its Pleiades and Hyades, is nearly on the meridian, which is held by Aries. The latter constellation, supposed to represent a ram, has little of interest. Over these, Perseus is in transit, Algol, the famous variable, being almost exactly on the line. This constellation reaches nearly from the zenith to the Pleiades. Following the Milky Way from Cassiopeia along Perseus, we come to Auriga, the Wagoner, which holds the brilliant Capella. Continuing to trace the stream we pass Gemini, now at a respectable altitude. Jupiter and Neptune are now both in this asterism.

Far in the southeast, beyond Orion, lie the two dogs, Canis Major and Canis Minor. Sirius, the chief star of the former, and the brightest in the whole sky, is now visible in full splendour. In the southwest we must not fail to note Pisces, Pegasus, and Andromeda, which done, we may turn to the north. Here Ursa Minor hangs straight down below the pole on the meridian in lower transit. Further to the east the fore part of Leo's sickle has come up, and south of that, the head of Hydra is seen. The Milky Way to the south Lepus and Canis Major lead us on to Fluvius Eridanus, the river. Cetus and Aquarius occupy the horizon until the west point is reached, where are found Delphinus and Equuleus. In the northwest Cygnus is sinking, and to the east Ursa Major now makes a right angle with the horizon, while Draco is in lower transit.

EDITOR'S NOTE: FP: *PVG* 31, No. 48 (30 November 1906): 5.

THE FIXED STARS

An Account of the Siderial Heavens

When we go out at night and gaze up at the cloudless sky, we see, except for the moon, planets, and an occasional comet, naught save stars, a countless host of glittering lights. Their beauty prompts nearly everyone to inquire what they are, and how far away they are situated, yet the true answer never fails, at first, to produce a feeling of incredulity, for every member of that silent multitude is a sun, perhaps larger than ours, seeming so small only because it is located at a distance so great as almost to approach infinity.

Such are the fixed stars. I say fixed, but this apparent rest is false, for they are moving, every one of them, at an inconceivable rate of speed. Yet they do not revolve around any central orb, but roam hither and thither at random. As an example, I may remark that our own sun, which is of course a star, is now flying towards a mammoth body known to us as "Vega". A beginner may imagine that the two will someday collide, but he can rest assured that the laws of the universe are too rigid to allow anything of the kind to happen.

To render easy the description of the stars in reference to their brilliancy, all have been classed in orders called "magnitudes". This word is misleading, for in truth it has no relation to a star's real size, but only to its apparent brightness. The 21 brightest stars have been called "stars of the first magnitude", the next in brilliancy "of the second", and so on down to the sixth, where naked-eye visibility ends.

Groups of stars presenting some characteristic figures are called "constellations", and are known by the Latin name of the objects they represent. The likeness is, however, in most cases badly "stretched".

Fifteen first-magnitude stars are visible in our latitude, their names being appended below, in order of their brilliancy: 1, Sirius; 2, Vega; 3, Arcturus; 4, Capella; 5, Rigel; 6, Procyon; 7, Betelgeux; 8, Aldebaran; 9, Altair; 10, Antares; 11, Spica; 12, Regulus; 13, Fomalhaut; 14, Deneb; 15, Pollux. There are 60 stars of the second magnitude, and 130 of the third. The names of these should be learned from any reliable star atlas, such as Upton's or Burritt's.[1] The number of stars of the lesser magnitudes is too great to estimate.

There are but 25 stars in the heavens whose distances from our sun have been measured, but these suffice to illustrate the immensity of the universe. The average space between our sun and any other is about two hundred thousand billion miles, a number beyond comparison or adequate comprehension. A bright star called Alpha Centauri is the nearest known to the solar system, yet the distance is twenty-five thousand billion miles.

Such enormous distances are not usually expressed in miles, but in "light years". These are the spaces traversed over by light, at a rate of 186,000 miles a second, in a year. Now some stars are 100,000 light years apart. This means that light requires 100,000 years to pass from one to the other. Thus, if a star is 200,000 light years from earth, we do not see it as it is now, but as it was 200,000 years ago. Indeed, we have no right to say that a star actually is in a certain place, for since the light we see started from its source, the body itself may have perished.

Some stars are "variable", that is, changeable in brightness, in regular intervals, varying from a few minutes to many years. Of these, Algol, in Perseus, and Mira, in Cetus, are the most famous. The former has a short period, and the latter a very long one. Several explanations have been offered for this variability, the most likely being that they rotate, having one side brighter than the other.

As was said before, all the stars are travelling through space, yet it takes over 300,000 years to perceive even a slight change in the constellation figures. Some of the stars approaching us are: Arcturus, at 50 miles a second; Vega at 45, Polaris at 45, and Pollux at 40. Those receding are: Gamma at 50 miles, Castor at 30, Capella at 30, Regulus at 20, and Sirius, also at 20.

When one has observed the heavens for some time he will notice that certain stars have decided colours—Betelgeux, Aldebaran, and Antares being red; Arcturus, Capella, and Pollux orange; Sirius, Vega, and Spica white, while others of all shades exist. Chemistry shews us that these colours are most significant; in fact, a star tells us its age by its colour, a young sun being white, turning successively yellow and orange in middle life, and shedding ruby rays when dying. Our own star, or sun, is thought to be of the orange class.

Totally dead stars are known to exist, but, of course, they are invisible. Sometimes a new star will flame up for a time and then die out. This is perhaps a celestial conflagration, on a scale too great to be conceived of. The most famous new stars are those which happened in 1572 and 1901.[2] If any of these suns possessed inhabited planets, the entire race must have been exterminated by the great calamities. Besides these temporary stars, there are instances recorded of stars which have disappeared. There is nothing strange in this, since suns are constantly dying and new ones being formed.

We have hitherto dealt with single or isolated stars, but I will now call attention to another class, known as doubles and multiples. These consist of two or more stars revolving around each other. There are over 600 such systems known at the present time, 50 of which have over two members. The revolution periods of most of these have been ascertained, the shortest being that of Kappa Pegasi, 11 years, and the longest that of Zeta Aquarii, 1625 years. Likely many more exist whose periods exceed 5000 years, but they have not yet moved enough for astronomers to calculate their orbits with precision.

There are some systems in which one or more members have cooled or died out, making them known only by their attraction on the others. Procyon has such a dark companion.

Some famous star systems are: Sirius, with a period of 53 years; Castor, 1000 years; and Zeta Cancri, a triple in which the second star revolves around the first in 60 years, and the third around both in 600 years. The space between the components of such systems exceeds the distance of the farthest solar planet from our sun.

Thus are the dimensions of the visible universe, yet when it is known that even this may be but one of many, man and his tiny globe sink into insignificance before such infinity.

EDITOR'S NOTE: FP: *PVG* 31, No. 49 (7 December 1906): 4.

Notes

1. Elijah Hinsdale Burritt (1794–1838), *Atlas Designed to Illustrate Burritt's Geography of the Heavens* (1850); Winslow Upton (1853–1914), *Star Atlas* (1896). HPL owned both volumes (see *LL* 138 and 900), Burritt in a rev. ed. of 1856.
2. HPL refers to the "new" star that flamed up near Algol; he refers to it at the conclusion of "Beyond the Wall of Sleep" (1919).

CLUSTERS—NEBULAE

Strange Bodies of Interstellar Space

If an attentive observer make a careful survey of the heavens, even with the unassisted eyesight, he will at once perceive the existence of a class of bodies differing from their neighbours. These are misty little patches of diffused light, resembling, on a small scale, the Milky Way. If he now apply opera or field glass to some of these strange bodies, he will become acquainted with a new fact, that they are not all alike, for a few are instantly seen to be composed of innumerable little stars, while the rest retain their hazy aspect. And if a still higher magnification be used, more will be resolved into components until at last a limit is reached, clearly indicating that the peculiar objects are to be divided into separate classes, the first those resolvable into stars, and the second, those apparently gaseous and continuous. In the language of astronomy, the members of the resolvable class are called "clusters", while the others retain the name of "nebulae" (singular, nebula).

Clusters of every degree of aggregation may be found. At one extreme may be placed the Pleiades in Taurus, plainly resolvable to the naked eye, while, for instance, that near the star called 47 Teucani is to be separated in only the most powerful of telescopes. The contemplative mind, on viewing a cluster, will be sure to inquire if the components are actually in proximity, or apparently so, the result of distance. The answer to this is, that both kinds exist. The grand group in Hercules is without doubt a true cluster, being, in fact, a veritable swarm of suns, while the Praespe, in Cancer, is, in all probability, the result of chance. The Milky Way is to be included in the former division.

Nebulae are enormous masses of glowing gas under high pressure, and extremely hot in temperature. Their principal point of interest is that they are nothing less than solar systems in the making. To understand this one must first learn the nebular hypothesis of creation, as given by Laplace.[1] This runs as follows: Before the existence of the stars and solar system, nothing save nebulae occupied space. These, rotating, cast off rings, that later hardened into planets, which continue to revolve and rotate, forming the present systems. Now the nebulae of today are considered remains of this early condition, for instances may be cited of all states of creation, for example, that in Canes Venatici is a mass of light with a sun condensing in the centre, while those in Andromeda, Aquarius, and Pegasus reveal rings that will some day be planets. Most nebulae are so large that our solar system is an atom in comparison, but they will contract as they cool.

EDITOR'S NOTE: FP: PVG 31, No. 51 (21 December 1906): 5.

Notes

1. Pierre Simon, marquis de Laplace (1749–1827), French astronomer and physicist and author of the landmark treatise *Exposition du Système du monde* (1796), propounding the nebular hypothesis.

JANUARY HEAVENS

The dawn of the year 1907 reveals three planets in the evening sky: Jupiter, still at his best, having been in opposition on Dec. 28; Saturn, past his prime, yet visible in the early evening; and Neptune, in opposition on the 2nd. Of these, Jupiter is by far the most interesting, since he is now nearest the earth, subtending a disc of 50 seconds, or nearly a minute of arc. In the morning, two planets grace the heavens: Venus, in greatest brilliancy on the 4th; and Mars, now very well seen in a telescope. The latter rises at 2.10 a.m. in the 15th. Among the visible orbs, Mercury and Uranus must be placed.

The moon's phases will be as follows:

Last Quarter, 7th..9.48 a.m.
New Moon, 14th ....10.57 a.m.
First Quarter, 21st ....3.42 a.m.
Full Moon, 29th ....8.45 a.m.

The second day of January marks the earth's perihelion, or nearest approach to the sun, which luminary enters the sign of Aquarius on the 23d.

Two eclipses occur this month, one of the sun on the 14th, and one of the moon on the 29th. The first of these is total, so will, although invisible here, attract much attention from astronomers. The second barely escapes observation in the Pawtuxet Valley, since the day breaks but five minutes previous to its beginning.

There will be an occultation of the star Delta Cancri at 10.22 p.m. on the 1st.

The evenings of January shew the most brilliant stellar display that the heavens can afford, as the very richest part of the sky is upon the southern meridian. Orion is culminating, Rigel, its brightest star, being almost in transit. Capella, in Auriga, passes not half a minute before it, exactly on the zenith. Taurus, so replete with celestial treasures, has been in the west but thirty minutes. Gemini is rapidly approaching the meridian. In this group lie the famous "twin" stars, Castor and Pollux. The Milky Way stretches from the northwest to the southeast, bearing Cygnus, Cassiopeia, Perseus, and Auriga, ending between the two dogs, Canis Major and Canis Minor. Turning north, the principal constellation at all times of the year is Ursa Major, the circumpolar, whose "dipper" is familiar to all. This is now high above the horizon. Polaris is, of course, in its accustomed place, the bulk of Ursa Minor being to the east. Noting the horizontal groups from north eastward, we see successively Boötes, Leo, Hydra, Argo Navis, Lepus, Columba, Eridanus, Pisces, and Pegasus, until Cygnus brings us around to the north once more.

EDITOR'S NOTE: FP: PVG 31, No. 52 (28 December 1906): 5.

[ASTRONOMY ARTICLES FOR THE PROVIDENCE *TRIBUNE*]

IN THE AUGUST SKY

Saturn, which will be in opposition next month, has now arrived in the evening sky, rising on the 1st at 8:45 p.m. and on the 31st at 7. His rings are barely visible in the telescope, and in another year they will be temporarily obscured. Venus, however, is the chief of the planets, illuminating the western sky each night after sunset. On Sept. 20 it will reach its greatest apparent distance from the sun, so at present it shews a slightly gibbous phase, making it less attractive than it will be in a few months, for although now dazzlingly brilliant it has not yet reached the time of greatest brightness, which will occur on the 25th of October.

Jupiter is just emerging from the sun's rays, being visible a short time before sunrise. The amateur telescopist will always find something of interest connected with this planet, for its ever-moving satellites and beautifully shaded belts make it one of the most pleasing objects in the heavens. Mars, however, is still too close to conjunction for ordinary vision.

Mercury's inferior conjunction happens on the 12th, but by the 30th he will have reached his greatest western elongation, being visible to early risers just above the sunrise point. At that time a good telescope will reveal a "half moon" phase. In this country there will be no difficulty in locating the elusive little planet, but to observers in higher latitudes a sight of Mercury is rare indeed, and it is even said that Copernicus, the great founder of modern astronomy, passed his life without as much as a glimpse of it.

The Moon's phases will be as follows: Full moon, 4th; last quarter, 11th; new moon, 19th; and first quarter, 26th, giving bright evenings for both the beginning and ending of the month. Those who possess field or spy glasses will derive pleasure from viewing the half moon on or around the 26th of the month, for the craters on the inner edge can be easily perceived with but a slight magnifying power.

A lunar and a solar eclipse will occur this August, neither, however, being visible in Providence. Among the constellations may be noticed some especially bright groups on or near the meridian; Altair in the south, Lyra and Cygnus almost overhead.

The groups of spring have passed to the west, among them being Boötes, Corona, and Serpentarius. In the north, Ursa Major is heading for the horizon to the west of the Pole, while at an equal altitude Cassiopeia is ascending in the east. On the horizon is Auriga, with the bright gem Capella, just rising, and a little further eastward is Perseus, famous for its variable star, Algol.

The rest of the horizon is occupied by the zodiac; Aries rising due east; Pisces, Aquarius, and Capricornus being at good altitudes, while Sagittarius is transiting. To the west Scorpio is still in its splendour, the fiery Antares shining brightly. This star is of a profound red tint, and, as its name implies, is often compared to Mars. Scorpio as a whole rather resembles a boy's kite, and forms one of the most striking of all the summer groups. Libra, Virgo, and Leo are past their prime; indeed, the last named has almost set.

It must not be imagined that these zodiacal constellations coincide with the signs of the same name, for a slow changing process called "precession" has caused each sign to occupy the constellation preceding that which bears its name. The sun enters the sign Virgo on the 22d, and already the shortening of the days is perceptible.

Sunrise occurs at 4:36 a.m., and sunset at 7:05 p.m. on the first of the month, but on the 31st the two periods are respectively 5:08 a.m. and 6:21 p.m.

EDITOR'S NOTE FP: *MT* 1, No. 25 (1 August 1906): 6; *ET* 1, No. 121 (1 August 1906): 6. The first of 20 monthly articles written for the Providence *Tribune* (morning, evening, and/or Sunday editions). The star-charts that accompanied many of the articles represent the first (and nearly the last) instances when illustrations by HPL were published.

THE SEPTEMBER HEAVENS

Celestial Motions for the Coming Month

Venus is now near her best, coming to greatest elongation on the 20th. At that time exactly one-half of her disc may be seen. Of late, great importance has been attached to this planet on account of its surface markings, which are among the most difficult objects in astronomy. If any permanent spots were detected, the period of rotation might be ascertained, but in spite of the efforts of many observers nothing has been discovered on the bright orb save dark indefinite shadings that are too transitory to indicate the axial motion.

Turning to the eastern quarter of the sky, we find Saturn also in full glory. His opposition occurs on the 4th, when he will, of course, be nearest the earth. Notwithstanding the unfavourable view which is had of his rings this year, the giant orb is very attractive, for a small telescope will reveal three satellites out of the ten that attend him. Besides, the great polar compression, which cannot well be seen except in the absence of the rings, is always of interest.

In the morning two planets illuminate the sky; Mercury, which can be seen low in the east during the first few days of the month, but which passes the sun in superior conjunction on the 24th, and Jupiter, now a most conspicuous object, coming to quadrature on October 3. The latter is in a position to be observed by everyone, and nothing can be found in the entire sky that presents a finer aspect through a moderate-sized telescope. On the 15th Jupiter rises about 11 p.m.

Mars might be added to the morning list, as he is barely visible at 4 a.m., but in all glasses except the largest he is practically worthless.

Uranus and Neptune are seen fairly well with high optical assistance, both being near quadrature, but the amateur observer will find nothing connected with either of these planets that has much interest.

The Sun enters Libra on the 23d, thus commencing the autumn season. He rises on the 1st at 5:10 a.m., setting at 6:20 p.m., but on the 30th the days are shorter by an hour and a half.

The Moon is, of course, as attractive as usual, being full on the 2nd, in Last Quarter on the 10th, New the 18th, and arriving at First Quarter just after midnight on the 25th. The owners of large telescopes would do well to study the moon carefully near the full, with a view to detecting surface changes. Our satellite has long been considered a "dead world", but modern research reveals a slight variability in the figure of several lunar formations, which seems to indicate that life is not wholly extinct. The craters called Eratosthenes and Plato are the seats of most of the changes, therefore demanding the maximum amount of attention.

No eclipses or other special phenomena are predicted for September.

From a stellar viewpoint the present month is the least interesting of the entire year. Capricornus, the "Sea-Goat", is on the southern meridian, but is remarkable only for a pair of stars visible to the naked eye as a close double.

Above Capricornus is the western half of Aquarius, a large group that is now best seen after midnight.

Just below the zenith we behold Cygnus, now past transit, and south of this may be found an aggregation of tiny groups exactly on the meridian, called Delphinus, Equuleus, and Sagitta.

In the northern sky, Cepheus is between the zenith and the pole. To the west of this constellation lies Draco, to the east Cassiopeia, while just below it is Ursa Minor, containing that most important star called "Polaris".

This bright orb, because it is situated almost at the pole of the heavens, does not behave like the ordinary stars, but appears stationary, about forty-two degrees above the horizon of Providence, while all the others seem to revolve around it. Consequently those which are nearer to it than its altitude never set, but describe circles in the heavens, the radii of which are proportional to their distance from the pole. Constellations so situated are called "circumpolar", and as the altitude of the pole is equal to the latitude of the observer it will at once be seen that at the ends of the earth all stars are circumpolar, the pole being at the zenith, while at the equator everything will rise and set.

Of the constellations that line the horizon, Ursa Major reaches down below the pole in the northwest. Auriga, which has now completely risen, claims the northeast, while the Pleiades are seen directly over the eastern horizon.

This group contains six stars plainly glimpsed by the naked eye, and ancient legends assert that a seventh was once visible. A telescope shews hundreds, besides an extensive nebulous background, which might, by higher optical powers than the present-day astronomer can command, be resolved into myriads of tiny stars. The appearance of this famous and beautiful cluster in the evening sky is always indicative of autumn.

From the Pleiades southward, Cetus occupies the heavens. This mammoth group contains one of the most wonderful variable stars in the sky, called Mira, which is sometimes a bright gem of the second magnitude, while on other occasions it sinks down to the ninth, when, of course, it is invisible to the unassisted eyesight.

Further westward is Piscis Australis, or the Southern Fish, which holds the brilliant star Fomalhaut. As this group is so far south it is not well seen in our latitude, but to an observer in Florida or Texas it is indeed a beautiful sight.

On the meridian, as was before mentioned, is the zodiacal group Capricornus, and Sagittarius, also in the zodiac, carries us around to the point where the Milky Way meets the earth.

Ophiuchus and Serpens follow, while in the northwest Boötes has nearly disappeared.

Lastly, below Ursa Major, may be seen one or two stars of the Lynx.

EDITOR'S NOTE   FP: MT 1, No. 52 (1 September 1906): 6; ET 1, No. 148 (1 September 1906): 6.

ASTRONOMY IN OCTOBER

Autumn Views of the Celestial Bodies During the Present Month

Jupiter can now be seen late in the evening, rising about 9:30 p.m., and coming to quadrature on the third. He cannot fail to attract general notice, for his appearance low in the northwest is very striking; indeed, the planet is so bright that he often casts a perceptible shadow, which no other star-like object except Venus can do.

Fig. 1—Jupiter.

Four of Jupiter's satellites are visible with low optical powers, and they are among the most interesting celestial objects to be seen this month. In their motion around the primary body, they often transit over, cross behind, and are eclipsed by it, giving, in fact, a miniature representation of the solar system. Fig. 1 shews Jupiter as seen in a small telescope.

Venus and Saturn are both visible during the early hours of the night, the former being at greatest brilliancy on the 25th. She is a beautiful crescent, the phase being visible even in a spy glass, and it is likely that sharp eyes can now detect her in the day-time. The markings on this planet, which were mentioned last month, should be sought after by all who possess telescopes. If really existing, they would resemble the dark shadings depicted in Fig. 2.

Fig. 2—Venus.

Mars can be seen any clear morning before sunrise, as he ascends above the horizon over two and a half hours before the break of day. A three or four-inch telescope will now shew indistinct markings on this orb, which, however, cannot be clearly studied until 1907.

During the last days of October, persons with penetrating sight may possibly catch a glance at Mercury, low down in the evening twilight, but to the majority of observers, he is effectually hidden.

Uranus, barely visible to the naked eye, is in the constellation Sagittarius, therefore being out of sight except in the earliest moments after sunset, while Neptune, which is just beyond the power of the unassisted vision, does not rise until nearly midnight.

The moon's phases are as follows:

    Full Moon, 2nd .... 7:48 a.m.
    Last Quarter, 10th .... 10:39 a.m.
    New Moon, 17th... 6:43 p.m.
    First Quarter, 24th.. 8:50 a.m.
    Full Moon, 31st... 11:46 p.m.

Thus two full moons adorn the sky this month, a rather unusual occurrence.

On Oct. 23d the sun enters Scorpio. Although a telescope will still shew spots on his disc, the solar activity is nothing as compared with that in 1905.

Among the special phenomena may be noted two occultations, that of M Ceti on the 4th at 3:53; and one of A3 Orionis at 10:42 on the 8th. Both stars, however, are so faint as to require the aid of a telescope in observing their disappearances.

Fig. 4—The Evening Sky for October.

Turning to the siderial heavens, which are shewn by the map forming Fig. 4, we find the meridian very clearly marked out for us by prominent constellations. On the southern horizon is Grus, the Crane, with Piscis Australis directly above it. Over this, in the region of the ecliptic, is Aquarius, famous principally for a large nebula, similar in appearance to Saturn and his ring. Nebulae of this form are supposed to consist of the matter from which stars and planets are evolved, so this mass of diffused light may be considered as a solar system in the making.

Following the meridian still further north, we behold Pegasus, the Winged Horse. If one looks very closely at the star designated by the Greek letter "Pi," he will notice that it is double. A binocular greatly enhances the beauty of this. In fact, every student of the heavens should own at least an opera glass, as I shall, in the course of these articles, point out from time to time objects particularly adapted to such instruments.

Far above Pegasus lies Cepheus, next to the pole, but it is totally devoid of interest.

Of the groups in the eastern sky, Auriga, Taurus, Perseus, Aries, Triangula, Cassiopeia, Andromeda, and Pisces may be mentioned. Taurus is by far the most interesting, for besides the Pleiades, he possesses still another mass of stars, a "V"-shaped cluster called the "Hyades". This contains the bright red orb Aldebaran. Fig. 3 shews the Hyades as seen in an opera glass.

Fig 3—The Hyades Cluster.

Crossing over to the western heavens, we find Cygnus, Lyra, Aquila, Delphinus, Equuleus, Hercules, Draco, and Serpentarius, the same groups that were near the meridian last month. The larger part of Ursa Minor is also west of the pole. This portion is known to everyone as the "little dipper", or "lesser plough".

The horizontal constellations now claim our attention. Under the pole in lower transit is Ursa Major, which will rise high in the sky later at night. A little further east may be seen a few rising stars of Gemini and the Lynx. Just south of the cardinal point, part of Orion is pushing upwards, a precursor of brighter skies when the year is further advanced. Below this is Eridanus, a dull group, which is followed by three faint asterisms, Phoenix, Sculptor, and Grus, the latter now being in transit.

On the western sky-line can be glimpsed successively the remains of Sagittarius, Serpens, Corona Borealis, and Boötes, which bringing us back to the north, completes the circuit.

EDITOR'S NOTE FP: *MT* 1, No. 77 (1 October 1906): 10; *ET* 1, No. 172 (1 October 1906): 9.

THE SKIES OF NOVEMBER

Planets, Stars and Meteors Conspicuous This Month

Venus, which has so long been ruler of the evening sky, makes its disappearance this month, coming to inferior conjunction on the 30th. The planet may, however, be seen low down in the west during the first few days, when a telescope will reveal a most attenuated crescent. The present stage of Venus's revolution has a point of great popular interest attached to it, because it is claimed by some that this thin semicircle of light may be seen in its true form with the naked eye.

Jupiter is now well up in the evening sky. He rises at 7 p.m. on the 20th, thus coming into view quite early. Although his opposition does not occur until next month, he is, nevertheless, by far the most beautiful object to be seen in November.

The ring is still visible about Saturn as seen in a moderate-sized telescope, and great regret is occasioned by the fact that 1907 will not reveal it.

Mars is steadily improving from a terrestrial point of view. Rising at 3 a.m., he shines high in the east when overtaken by the dawn.

Neptune, near Jupiter, is now to be seen in a telescope.

The moon arrives at her various phases in the following order:

Last Quarter, 9th	4:45 a.m.
New Moon, 16th	3:36 a.m.
First Quarter, 22d	7:39 p.m.
Full Moon, 30th	6:07 p.m.

It is a mistake to suppose that a telescope is required to learn the configuration of the dark spots on the face of our satellite, for the writer has, with the naked eye alone, traced and recognised the 12 leading formations.

A beginner who desires to become acquainted with lunar topography must first try to forget the familiar outlines of the "man in the moon", the "lady", etc. He then should carefully study the face of the silent orb (when full or nearly so) and make a sketch of all that he sees.

The sun enters Sagittarius on the 23d, which thing, however, is of little interest or value.

One moderately attractive occultation occurs this month, i.e., that of Iota Capricorni on the 21st at 8:30 p.m. As the star is of the fourth magnitude, and as the moon will be only five days old, the phenomenon will be especially pretty in an opera glass.

November possesses, in the way of meteors, one of the most wonderful displays of the whole year. I refer to the Leonids, or the "shooting stars" that appear to radiate from the star Gamma in the constellation Leo. This shower occurs every year, and is unusually bright every 33 years. The display of 1906 will not be one of these special showers, although many meteors are expected. The observer, if he would see them, must rise at midnight, on the 13th, and prolong his vigil until sunrise. Leo will rise into view shortly after 12, and almost simultaneously the meteors will appear, darting hither and thither through the sky, all, however, being traceable to the star Gamma Leonis, the point where the orbit of the earth intersects the belt of meteors.

Figure 1 is a map of Leo, shewing the radiant point. This can be easily found by remembering its position in the famous "sickle". The apparent place of Leo above the eastern horizon at 2 a.m. is shewn by the left-hand boundary of the map.

We now arrive at the domain of the constellations, shown by Figure 2. Here we find the winter groups beginning to appear.

Orion has fully risen, likewise Gemini. Taurus and Auriga are high up in the sky, while the northern half of Eridanus Fluvius occupies the southwest sky-line. One must travel as far south as latitude 30 degrees to see the whole of this asterism, including its principal orb, Achernar, which ranks high among stars of the first magnitude.

On the meridian is Cetus, the whale, whose variable star Mira was described last September. The latter is now at minimum, being of the ninth magnitude.

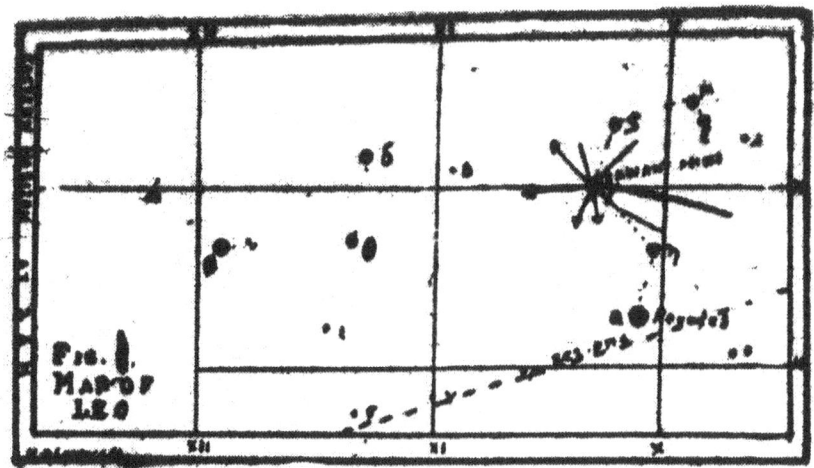

Fig. 1—Map of Leo.

Fig. 2—The Evening Sky for November.

Above Cetus lies Pisces, containing the "vernal Equinox", or point where the sun crosses the equator to the north, and still higher up is Andromeda, now at its best.

Between Andromeda and the pole, directly in the Milky Way, lies Cassiopeia, which is, on account of its conspicuous "W" shape, unmistakable.

Just east of Andromeda and Pisces may be found three groups, Aries, Triangula, and Perseus. The latter contains one of the most famous star clusters in the northern sky. This attractive swarm of suns appears, in the telescope, to be composed of a central condensation, together with numerous outrunning rifts, presenting a latent beauty that defies portraiture.

In the west lie all the autumn constellations, the long list reading: Aquarius, Aquila, Capricornus, Cepheus, Cygnus, Delphinus, Equuleus, Grus, Hercules, Lyra, Pegasus, Phoenix, Piscis Australis, and Sculptor.

Finally, in the north, Ursa Major is emerging from beneath the pole. Ursa Minor is hanging under and Draco is descending below it.

Lynx is already high in the east and Corona has disappeared.

EDITOR'S NOTE FP: MT 1, No. 104 (1 November 1906): 5; ET 1, No. 199 (1 November 1906): 4.

THE HEAVENS FOR DECEMBER

Unusually Brilliant Skies During the Closing Month of 1906

Jupiter, coming to opposition at 10 a.m. on the 28th, leads the host of planets. Even an opera glass will now reveal his four brighter satellites, and possibly outline his disc. This giant orb rises at 6:15 p.m. on the 1st, and at 4:20 on the 31st.

Saturn, which arrives at quadrature on the 1st, is next in interest, although not nearly as well seen as in September. He sets about 9:45 p.m.

Mercury reaches greatest western elongation on the 18th, and may be found in the east before sunrise any morning near the middle of the month. A telescope magnifying about a hundred diameters will clearly shew the varying phases of this planet.

Mars, rising at 2:30 a.m., is another morning orb, now being quite well seen.

Venus and Uranus are both near solar conjunction, therefore invisible.

Neptune may be located near Jupiter any night by the aid of a spy glass, but he hardly repays the trouble. Nevertheless, his place, as well as those of the other planets, is given on the accompanying map.

The phases of the moon will ensue as given below:

Last Quarter, 8th.. 8:45 p.m.
New Moon, 15th .... 1:54 p.m.
First Quarter, 23d..10:04 a.m.
Full Moon, 30th .... 1:44 p.m.

The Sun enters Capricornus on the 23d at 1 p.m., thus turning northward, and inaugurating the winter season. By the end of the month 10 minutes will have been added to the length of the days.

The Evening Sky for December.

An occultation of 56 Geminorum occurs at 3:26 a.m. on the 4th, but its interest is inconsiderable.

Besides that, no special phenomena are predicted for December.

The constellations now visible, as shewn by map, are among the brightest of the entire year.

Orion is high in the southeast, and no one can mistake it, as its great size and bright stars attract the attention of all. This constellation contains the famous row of three stars, variously known as the "belt", "yard", "kings", etc., also the great nebula, which may be located in the group of faint stars below this "belt".

Above Orion, Taurus, with its beautiful clusters, is nearly on the meridian, which is held by Aries, the Ram.

Over these, Perseus is in transit, Algol, the famous variable, being almost exactly on the line. This group extends nearly from the zenith to the Pleiades.

Northwest of Perseus lies Cassiopeia, and east of it is Auriga, the Wagoner, which holds the brilliant Capella.

Continuing in the same direction we arrive at Gemini, now at a respectable altitude. The planets Jupiter and Neptune are now both in this asterism.

Near Gemini is the inconspicuous group known as Cancer, which once marked the sun's highest northern declination. Its principal feature is a faint cluster called "Praespe", or the "Manger", visible as a nebula to the naked eye, but resolvable in an opera glass.

Far in the east, beyond Orion, lie the two dogs, Canis Major and Canis Minor. Sirius, the chief star of the former, and the brightest in the whole sky, is now to be seen in full splendour.

In the southwest we must not fail to note Andromeda, Pegasus, and Pisces, relics of the autumn sky, which done, the north claims our view.

Here Ursa Major hangs straight down below the pole, on the meridian in lower transit. Further on the east Leo Minor, Leo, and Hydra have partially risen.

Ursa Major now makes a right angle with the horizon, while Draco barely clears it. Westward, Cygnus, Lyra, and Hercules are sinking, and high above the pole are three dull groups, Cepheus, Camelopardalis, and Lynx.

In the extreme south, Columba, Lepus, Horologium, Fluvius Eridanus, Cetus, Phoenix, Officina Sculptoria, and Aquarius carry us around the horizon to the west point, north of which Delphinus and Equuleus are setting.

EDITOR'S NOTE FP: *MT* 1, No. 130 (1 December 1906): 10; *ET* 1, No. 224 (1 December 1906): 11 (unsigned).

THE HEAVENS IN JANUARY

Astronomical Events of the Opening Months in 1907

The dawn of the year 1907 reveals three planets in the evening sky: Jupiter, still at his best, having been in opposition Dec. 28; Saturn, yet visible in the early evening, and Neptune, in opposition on the 2nd.

Of these, Jupiter is by far the most interesting, since he is now nearest to the earth, subtending a disc of 50 seconds, or nearly a minute of arc.

In the morning two planets grace the heavens: Venus, in greatest brilliancy on the 4th, and Mars, now very well seen in a telescope. The latter rises at 2:10 a.m. on the 15th.

Among the invisible orbs, Mercury and Uranus must be placed.

The moon will be in last quarter on the 7th; new on the 14th; in first quarter on the 21st, and full on the 29th.

The second day of January marks the earth's perihelion, or nearest approach to the sun. It appears strange at first sight that this should occur during the cold weather, yet it is a fact, for our planet is so far from the sun that the small variations in distance from it cannot affect the temperature, which is governed solely by orbital inclination.

Two eclipses occur this month, one of the sun on the 14th and one of the moon on the 29th. The first of these is total, so will, although invisible here, attract much attention from astronomers. The second barely escapes visibility in Providence, since the day breaks but five minutes prior to its beginning.

The sun enters the zodiacal sign Aquarius on the 23d.

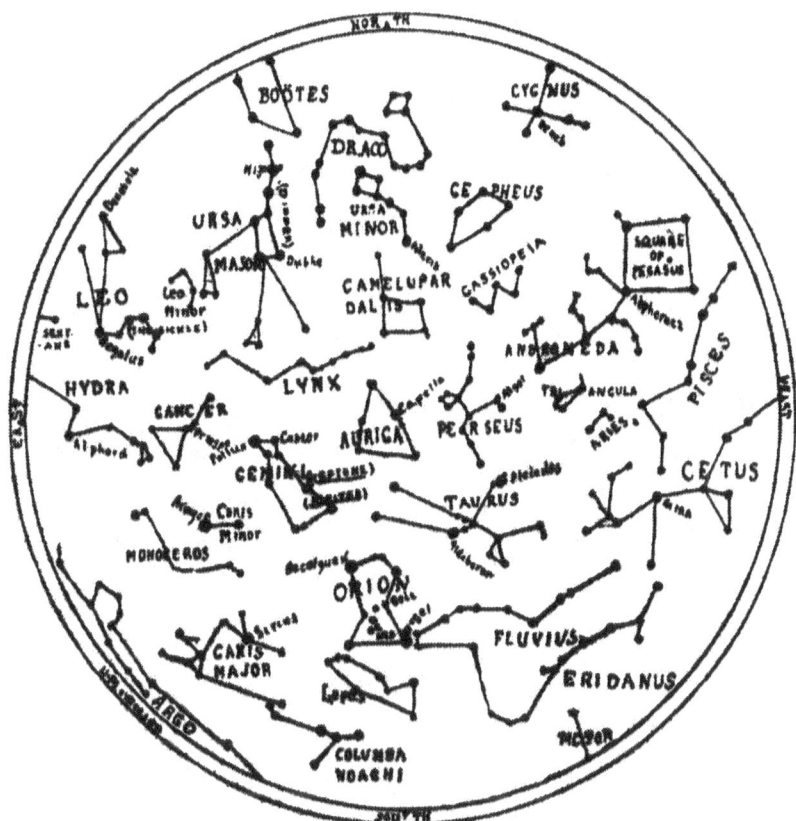

The Evening Sky for January.

The evenings of January shew the most brilliant stellar display that the heavens can afford, as the very richest part of the sky is upon the Southern meridian.

Orion is culminating, Rigel, its brightest star, being almost in transit. Capella, in Auria, passes not half a minute before it, exactly on the zenith. Taurus, so replete with celestial treasures, has been in the West but 30 minutes.

Gemini is rapidly approaching the meridian. In this group, besides its stars Castor and Pollux, are now the planets Jupiter and Neptune.

The Milky Way, which, for the sake of simplicity, has been omitted from the accompanying map, flows from the Northern horizon to the Southeast, and bearing successively Cygnus, Cassiopeia, Perseus, and Auriga, ends between the two dogs, Canis Major and Canis Minor.

Below Sirius the other stars of Canis Major may be seen forming a very attractive asterism.

Turning north the principal constellation at all times of the year is the circumpolar called Ursa Major, the "dipper" in which is familiar to all. This is still at right angles with the horizon, although much higher up than in December.

Polaris is, of course, in its accustomed place, the rest of Ursa Minor being to the east.

The groups around the horizon, starting from the north to east, are now to be considered. A few stars of Boötes which never set lie a trifle east of the cardinal point. Coming around a few degrees Leo has completely risen, while farther to the south are seen the head and neck of Hydra.

In the southeast one may find all that is visible of Argo Navis in this State. From latitude 30 degrees southward the whole of this constellation is to be seen, including its brightest star Canopus, which is second only to Sirius in lustre.

Due north lie Lepus and Columba Noachi.

West of the meridian is Fluvius Eridanus, and still further on Pisces, Pegasus, and Cygnus are about to set.

EDITOR'S NOTE FP: MT 1, No. 156 (1 January 1907): 8; ET 1, No. 224 (1 January 1907): 9.

THE HEAVENS IN FEBRUARY

Celestial Phenomena During the Shortest Month in the Year

Jupiter and Venus, the two finest planets in the whole sky, are both seen to advantage in February. The former, now subtending a disc of nearly 45 seconds in the evening sky, lies in the constellation Gemini, and is daily receding from the earth. It has not, however, gone beyond the range of good seeing, for its opposition occurred the 28th of last December.

Venus shines brightly each morning before the dawn, rising at about 4 a.m. as an average. This planet reaches its greatest western elongation on the 9th, when it is, of course, at its best. At the time mentioned a "half-moon" phase will be presented. During the first part of the month Venus will shew a large crescent.

Mars, who shares the morning sky with Venus, is now most conspicuous. Few who are watching can fail to recognise this ruddy orb, as it ascends above the horizon at 1:45 a.m., coming into plain visibility about 2:30.

A telescope of medium power will at present reveal many of the Martian spots and canals, if favourably situated.

Saturn, for all practical purposes, has gone. At its next approach to the earth the ring surrounding this planet will be almost invisible, from the fact that it will be tipped or inclined nearly "edgewise" to the plane of the ecliptic.

Uranus has not yet advanced enough for visibility, but Neptune, near Jupiter, is well seen in any telescope.

Mercury is in the west after sunset during the last days of the month, coming to greatest elongation on the 1st of March.

The sun enters Pisces, the last sign of the zodiac, on the 21st.

No eclipse or other unusual phenomena are predicted for February.

The moon's phases will be as follows:

Last Quarter, 1st... 7:53 p.m.
New Moon, 12th .... 10:42 p.m.
First Quarter, 19th .... 11:35 p.m.
Full Moon, 28th ....1:23 a.m.

Chart of the Evening Sky during February.

Our satellite, in its monthly revolution, will make its nearest approach to the earth on the 10th and will be farthest away on the 21st.

Turning to the constellations of the evening sky at 9 p.m., as shewn by the map, we find the brilliant groups of January still in sight, although somewhat changed in location.

Sirius, the brightest star in the sky, has now passed the meridian by 30 minutes and will set at 1:30 a.m. Stars as far south as this stay above the horizon but a short time in our latitude, a contrast to the northern circumpolars.

Gemini, with Castor and Pollux, is on the meridian, practically in the zenith. This constellation is at present the most northward member of the zodiac.

Canis Minor is within half an hour of transit. Procyon, in this, is a very attractive star. The name "Procyon" is derived from the two Greek words meaning "before the dog", owing to the fact that it rises before Sirius, although it culminates and sets later.

West of the meridian, just free of the Milky Way, is Orion, the most interesting constellation in the sky. Possessing two first-magnitude stars, besides the famous "belt", this asterism always attracts attention.

Auriga, of which Capella is the dominant star, can be easily recognised in the northwest, still high in the sky.

Turning to the circumpolar region, Ursa Major is seen steering for the zenith from the east. The object of greatest interest in this group is the star Mizar, at the handle of the "dipper". This appears as double, even to the naked eye.

Ursa Minor is almost entirely southeast of the pole, which approximately marks its northern extremity.

The groups around the horizon at this time are as follows:

In the north a few stars of Hercules and Corona Borealis (not shewn on the map) have risen, and almost the whole of Boötes, with the bright orange star Arcturus, is in view. Due east Virgo is rising, and in the south Hydra is uplifting itself. Crater, sometimes included with the preceding, is completely in sight.

The Milky Way, bearing part of Argo Navis, is just east of the meridian, and Canis Major is immediately to the west. Lepus, Fluvius Eridanus, Cetus, and Pisces line the horizon from south to west, the last two groups being partially set. Pegasus has entirely disappeared. Andromeda is following fast, and the Milky Way, with a few stars of Cygnus, lies almost directly below the pole.

Taurus is still high up, and Leo, with its beautiful stars Regulus and Denebola, has attained a good altitude, while Perseus still graces the northwest.

EDITOR'S NOTE FP: MT 2, No. 28 (1 February 1907): 9.

THE HEAVENS IN MARCH

Astronomy for the Opening Month of Spring

Mercury, the most difficult to see of all the planets, comes to greatest eastern elongation on the first, therefore shining in the West after sunset near that date. There is little of interest to be perceived on this body except its varying phase, which will, during the present period of visibility, change from a semi-circle of light to a beautiful crescent.

Jupiter is another evening planet, and is still in a fairly good location, as on the 23d of the month it arrives at quadrature, or that place in its apparent annual course, which is 90 degrees from the sun.

One point of attraction connected with the present stage of its revolution is that this giant planet reveals a sensible phase. The phase in question is, however, only a slight shading off at one edge of the disc, for Jupiter is outside the earth's orbit, so can never shew a crescent. This shading off causes an appearance similar to that of the moon about a day from full.

In the morning sky we find Venus again approaching the sun. This bright orb, which was in greatest elongation on Feb. 9, now presents a gibbous aspect. It still rises about 4 a.m., but is less brilliant than formerly.

Mars, also a morning planet, is steadily improving. It rises about 1 a.m. at the middle of the month. No one could possibly confuse any other heavenly body with Mars, as it shines with an intense reddish light which is unmistakable. On the 8th this planet comes to quadrature, therefore shewing a strongly marked gibbous phase.

Saturn is invisible throughout the month, as it comes to solar conjunction on the 9th. When next seen it will occupy the morning sky.

Uranus is just emerging from the sun's rays, yet he hardly repays observation.

Neptune, in quadrature on the 31st, is still visible.

The sun passes the vernal equinox at 1 p.m. on the 21st, thus entering the sign Aries and commencing the spring season. At this time the axis of the earth is at a right angle with the imaginary line joining our planet to the sun, giving equal day and night in both hemispheres.

The solar spots have lately been unusually prominent.

The moon's phases will occur in the following order:

Last quarter, 7th ....3:04 a.m.

New moon, 14th ....1:05 a.m.

First quarter, 21st .... 8:10 p.m.

Full moon, 29th .... 2:44 p.m.

Perigee falls on the 8th; Apogee on the 20th.

Three visible occultations of stars occur during March. Although none are so prominent but what they require the use of an opera glass, I will give their dates: Omicron Sagitarii, March 9th, 1:38 a.m.; Zeta Geminorum, 23d, 12:10 p.m.; Delta Cancri, 24th, 10:53 p.m.

The following showers of meteors are scheduled for the month: Beta Leonids, 13th; Chi Cepheids, 18th; Beta Ursids, 24th; Eta Coronids, 27th; Zeta Draconids, 28th. Of these, the fall of the Beta Ursids on the 24th will probably be the most attractive, although several fine displays of the Beta Leonids have recently occurred.

These showers are named from the stars that mark their radiant points, for example the "Eta Coronids" radiate from the star Eta in Corona Borealis.

The evening constellations for March (at 9 p.m.) are shewn by the accompanying map.

The zodiacal group now on the meridian is the small and inconspicuous asterism known as Cancer, which is remarkable only for its cluster, ordinarily visible to the naked eye as a diffused spot of light, but separable into stars by even the feeblest optical assistance. This object, called "Prasepe", or "The Manger", is situated midway between the two stars Gamma and Delta Cancri.

Below Cancer, the head and neck of Hydra, the longest constellation in the sky, have now reached the meridian.

The grand assembage of stars noted in January and February, Orion, Taurus, Auriga, Perseus, Gemini, Canis Major, and Canis Minor, are still in view, but have passed over to the west. The zenith is now occupied by a portion of Lynx, a faint group, part of which is circumpolar.

Looking north, between Ursa Major and the Pole, is the tail of Draco, the Dragon, which nearly encompasses Ursa Minor in its folds. The head of this group is now turned toward the east, apparently viewing Hercules, a mammoth group, which has just risen.

Below the handle of the "dipper" lies the constellation known as Canes Venatici, or the Hunting Dogs, principally notable for a rather bright star called "Cor Caroli", which is situated in an otherwise barren region.

In the northwest, Cepheus and Cassiopeia are visible, the latter making nearly a right angle with the horizon.

Looking south, Leo has nearly reached the transit point, and Virgo, now completely risen, follows closely.

The groups around the horizon will next take our attention.

The Heavens for March.

Due north, a few stars of Cygnus are seen, marking the Milky Way. Further east, all of Hercules has risen. Southward from this, Corona Borealis, now entirely seen, is followed by the head of Serpens, a constellation which will prove to rival even Hydra in length when fully above the horizon.

Boötes, with Arcturus, has gained somewhat of an altitude, and Virgo is now quite high.

Passing the east point we see Crater and Corvus, beyond which the enormous bulk of Argo Navis carries us over to the west, where all the bright groups of winter are nearing the sky-line, together with Columba, Lepus, and Eridanus.

Travelling around to the north again, we meet successively Taurus, Aries, and Triangula, until the last half of the great Andromeda, still in plain sight, completes the circum-horizontal belt of constellations.

EDITOR'S NOTE FP: MT 2, No. 53 (2 March 1907): 12; ET 2, No. 53 (2 March 1907): 3.

APRIL SKIES

The Heavens for the Coming Month

Jupiter is still visible in the evening sky, although declining in brilliancy. As it sets about midnight those who desire to view this planet at a high altitude should look as soon as it is sufficiently dark, about half-way between the zenith and the western horizon, where its brilliancy causes it to be a most conspicuous object. For the benefit of those who possess telescopes I will give the dates of a few of the most prominent phenomena of Jupiter's satellites.

On the first of the month there will be an eclipse of the fourth satellite, the disappearance taking place at 6:16 a.m. and the reappearance at 9:18. Five days later, on the 6th, the first satellite will transit across the disc of its primary, entering at 8:30 and leaving at 10:55. The 14th marks the date of an occultation, also of the first satellite, which disappears at 7:53, reappearing at 11:23.

Toward the end of April two more well-seen phenomena take place, namely, an eclipse of the third satellite on the 28th from 8:02 to 11:12 p.m. and another occultation of the first from 6:11 to 9:43. Some of these commence so early that only the end will be visible.

Near Jupiter lies Neptune, the only other planet visible evenings, but as this faint body is to be seen only in a telescope few will notice it.

Turning to the morning sky we find a more attractive array of planets. Mars, now past quadrature, is climbing higher and higher into the heavens, rising about half an hour after midnight, while Saturn, almost fully emerged from the sun's rays, follows it above the horizon at nearly 2:30 a.m. Venus continues to approach the sun, shewing a disc rapidly increasing to fulness, yet decreasing in apparent diameter. This planet rises about 3:30 a.m., or nearly the same time as Saturn. Uranus is near Venus, yet scarcely worth the notice of amateurs. Mercury comes to western elongation on the 14th, thus being visible in the east about an hour before sunrise near that date. Its phase will vary from a large crescent to a gibbous shape.

The moon's configurations will ensue as given below:

Last quarter, 5th ....10:20 a.m.
New moon, 12th.. 2:06 p.m.
First quarter, 20th .... 3:38 p.m.
Full moon, 28th ....1:05 a.m.

Our satellite is twice in Perigee this month, namely, on the 2d and 30th. Apogee falls on the 18th.

The sun enters Taurus on the 20th. It rises at 5 a.m. and sets at 6:30 p.m. as an average. The large spot which was so prominent in February and March has now greatly decreased in size.

As three stellar occultations are especially prominent this month I will mention the times of their occurrence: Theta Librae, April 2 at 4:20 a.m.; Chi Orionis, the 17th, at 11:20 p.m., and Chi Ophiuchi at 1:05 a.m. on the 30th.

Among the meteoric displays for April may be mentioned the following: Eta Cra-

The Evening Sky for April.

terids, on the 17th; Nu Boötids and Beta Serpentids, 18th; Mu Serpentids, 19th; Lyrids, 20th, and 102 Herculids, 25th.

The Lyrid Shower on the 20th is by far the finest of these phenomena, although it cannot be well observed until after midnight.

The constellations at 9 p.m., as shewn by the accompanying map, will next take our attention. The southern sky is now occupied by the striking zodiacal constellation called Leo, which really consists of two distinct groups. The larger of these is the famous "sickle" containing the bright star Regulus, and the other, situated east of the sickle, is shaped like a right triangle, holding the second magnitude star Denebola. Below Leo is the single visible star of the constellation Sextans and above it is Leo Minor.

West of the meridian parts of the splendid constellations Orion, Taurus, Canis Major, Canis Minor, Gemini, Auriga, etc., are still in view.

In the east Boötes is now high in the sky, Arcturus, its brightest star, being almost directly over the cardinal point.

Immediately westward of Boötes lies the well-known Ursa Major with its famous "dipper", or "plough", as it is often called. Under the handle of the dipper may be seen Canes Venatici, a rather inconspicuous group. East of Ursa Major is a long but faint constellation known as "Lynx". In the northwest Hercules is gaining altitude, and above this is a most attractive circle of stars known as Corona Borealis or the Northern Crown.

The enormous length of Hydra is now fully seen. The head under the zodiacal constellation Cancer shines in the southwest, while the tail, situated below Virgo, is in the southeast, plainly shewing over how great a space the long asterism extends.

Just above Hydra, on the meridian, is Crater, a rather uninteresting group, and eastward of this is Corvus, a small but pleasing trapezium of moderately bright stars.

In the north, below the pole and immersed in the Milky Way, is Cassiopeia, always recognisable on account of its "W" shape. Bisecting the polar angle made by Ursa Major and Cassiopeia we find in the east a tiny but beautiful constellation which has just risen. This is Lyra, famous for its principal star Vega, a bright, bluish-coloured orb of the first magnitude.

Ursa Minor is east of and above the pole. Below this group is Cepheus and west of it are Camelopardalis and Perseus.

In the northeast Cygnus is rising; further south the greater part of Serpens is visible and still more southerly Libra has entirely appeared. The star Alpha in Libra is a very pleasing double, its character being visible even in a small opera glass.

East of Libra is Virgo, now at a good altitude. The principal feature of this constellation is the white star Spica, which is of considerable brilliancy. Above Virgo is Coma Berenices, a pretty cluster of small stars resembling the Pleiades.

The southeast horizon is occupied by the northern half of Centaurus, a constellation that is only partly visible in this section of the country. The brightest star in this group, which is seen from the latitude of New Orleans, is considered to be the nearest neighbour of the solar system, being only 25,000,000,000,000 miles away, a distance that is very small in interstellar space, notwithstanding its immensity in terrestrial units.

Argo Navis holds the southwest, bringing us around to Monoceros, or the Unicorn, a spreading group which occupies the space between Canis Major and Canis Minor. This group completes the list of evening constellations for April.

EDITOR'S NOTE FP: *ET* 2, No. 78 (1 April 1907): 15.

THE HEAVENS IN MAY

Celestial Motions for the Coming Month

The morning sky will be unusually brilliant during May, for it holds nearly all of the prominent planets.

Saturn, which rises about 1:30 a.m., is the chief feature. An unique interest is at present attached to this orb, because its encircling ring system is almost totally invisible. Such a state of affairs happens in intervals of about 15 years, or half of Saturn's revolution, when the plane of the rings lies edgewise to the earth.

A moderately large telescope will now reveal, as a dark band, those parts which cross the disc of the planet, while a very powerful instrument might shew the entire edge, as a most attenuated bar of light.

Not until 1909 will the system again assume its normal aspect.

Venus is another body which adds to the attractiveness of the morning sky. Rising about 3:20 a.m., this planet shines brightly for nearly an hour before sunrise. In a telescope it shews a phase of marked convexity.

Mars, which is now past its quadrature, surmounts the horizon even before midnight, but is not yet sufficiently advanced in its orbit to be visible to evening observers. At the middle of the month it rises at 11 p.m., shewing a round red disc to all who are possessed of telescopes magnifying over 25 times. No one need hope, however, to see the canals and satellites of this planet without an immensely powerful glass.

Somewhat near Mars, in the constellation Sagittarius, is the telescopic orb known as Uranus.

Turning to the less attractive evening sky, we find two planets, Jupiter and Neptune, both near together, and rapidly receding from favourable vision. The satellites of the former planet will make the following especially prominent configurations:

May 1, 7:42 p.m., occultation of satellite 2; 4th, 8:20 p.m., occultation of satellite 4; 5th, 7:35 p.m., occultation of satellite 3; 7th, 8:10 p.m., occultation of No. 1; 8th, transit of No. 1, ending at 7:40; 15th, transit of No. 1, ending at 9:40; 16th, eclipse of No. 1, ending at 7:52; 17th, transit of No. 2, beginning at 8:20; 22d, transit of No. 2, beginning at 9:20, and 30th, occultation of No. 1, at 8:42.

Mercury is practically invisible throughout the month, coming to superior conjunction on the 24th.

The moon's phases will ensue in the order given below:

Last Quarter, 4th.. 4:45 p.m.

New Moon, 12th .... 3:59 p.m.

First Quarter, 20th ....8:28 a.m.

Full Moon, 27th ....9:18 a.m.

Perigee is on the 28th, Apogee on the 16th.

The sun enters Gemini on the 22nd. Sunrise occurs at 4:40 a.m. and sunset at 6:42 p.m. on the first of the month, but by the 31st the two periods are respectively 4:11 a.m. and 7:13 p.m., shewing an increase of an hour in the length of the day.

There is to be an occultation of Theta Librae at 9:24 p.m. on the 26th, which will, however, lack interest, inasmuch as the star is only of the fourth magnitude.

The following meteoric showers are the most prominent among those predicted for May: May 1, Upsilon Herculids; 5, Theta Ophiuchids; 6, Eta Aquariids; 11, Alpha Coronids; 14, Gamma Delphinids; 29, Draconids; 30, Iota Pegasids. Of these, the Eta Aquariid display on the 6th will probably prove the most attractive.

The constellations at 9 p.m., as shewn by the accompanying map, will next be considered.

The zodiacal constellation now on the meridian is Virgo, which contains the brilliant white star Spica. This group is now seen to the best advantage. Its principal stars, seven in number, form a sprawling "Y", Spica, before mentioned, being at the foot of the letter.

Below Virgo is the tail of Hydra, and the attractive little constellation known as Corvus, which is just past transit.

Leo has now entirely passed the south point, which is held by Coma Berenices.

The western sky contains those groups which were in or near their prime last month, such as Crater, Sextans, Leo Minor, Lynx, Cancer, etc.

Looking north, Cassiopeia is in its lowest position below the pole, and the Milky Way lies close to the horizon almost directly east and west. In the northeast the greater part of Cygnus is now in view, above which is Lyra with its brilliant gem Vega. Between Vega and Arcturus, in Boötes, which is now very high, lies the great constellation Hercules, together with Corona Borealis.

Chart of the Skies for May.

Tracing the horizon as usual from the northeastward, we first encounter one or two stars of Andromeda, which are just within the circumpolar belt. Next comes Cygnus, already mentioned, with parts of Sagitta, and Vulpecula (not shewn on the map) closely following. A little further south, we find Ophiuchus and Serpens completely risen. In the southeast, the forepart of Scorpio is visible, with Libra above it.

From southeast to due south, we see the group called Lupus, and the upper part of Centaurus, west of which a stray star or two of Argo Navis brings us to that part of the horizon where Monoceros, Gemini, and Canis Minor are setting.

In the northwest, Auriga and Perseus, both partially obscured, bring us around to the north once more.

In the region of the pole, Ursa Minor is seen pointing directly upward, reaching past Draco to Ursa Major, which is but little northwest of the zenith. South of this is Canes Venatici.

Below the pole, Cepheus and Camelopardalis complete the list of constellations visible on May evenings.

EDITOR'S NOTE FP: *MT* 2, No. 104 (1 May 1907): 5; *ET* 2, No. 104 (1 May 1907): 6.

THE HEAVENS IN JUNE

Planetary and Stellar Configurations for the Opening Month of Summer

Mars, in some respects the most interesting of all the planets, has now arrived in the evening sky. Although its opposition will not occur until the 6th of July, it is, nevertheless, sufficiently advanced to be plainly visible at 10 p.m. At that time it will be very conspicuous, shining low in the southeast with a bright, ruddy light that renders it unmistakable. On the 10th of the month it rises about 9:30 p.m.

Jupiter and Neptune, which are still nominally evening planets, have become practically invisible on account of their ever-increasing proximity to the sun. Soon they will both be in conjunction.

Mercury will come to greatest eastern elongation on the 27th, thus being visible in the west after sunset, and shewing a half-disc if viewed with a telescope.

Venus and Saturn are morning planets this month. The former is quite rapidly approaching the sun, becoming less and less attractive as the days pass, while the latter is steadily increasing in apparent size and brightness. The absence of the rings makes the present year a very good time to observe the satellites of the Saturnian system.

Uranus is nearing its best, as its opposition comes early next month. The moon's phases will be as follows:

Last Quarter, 3d .... 10:20 p.m.
New Moon, 10th .... 6:50 p.m.
First Quarter, 18th .... 9:55 p.m.
Full Moon, 25th .... 4:27 p.m.

Perigee occurs on the 25th, Apogee on the 11th.

The sun enters Cancer on the 22nd at 9 a.m., thus commencing the summer season. This evening, of course, marks the longest day of the year, which possesses 15 hours 14 minutes of continuous sunlight. After this the days steadily shorten, shewing a decrease of two minutes by the end of the month.

There is at present a great degree of activity on the sun's disc. Early last month a group of spots was discovered whose configuration exactly resembled an interrogation point.

None of the occultations which occur this month will be sufficiently prominent to merit our attention.

Among the coming displays of meteors may be mentioned the following: June 7, Beta Herculids; 13th, Eta Cepheids; 15th, Kappa and Beta Cygnids; 20th, Delta Cepheids; 28th, Delta Cygnids. It may be seen from the foregoing data that meteoric activity is at present confined to a region extending between 16 and 23 hours of right ascension, and from zero to 70 degrees of north declination. No eclipses or similar phenomena are indicated for June.

As shewn by the accompanying map,[1] the quiet summer groups occupy the main portion of the evening sky. The meridian line is now very clearly marked out by the great constellation Boötes, which stretches southward from the very zenith toward the horizon. Immediately east of Boötes is Corona Borealis, a group of most attractive appearance, and to the west lies Coma Berenices.

The zodiacal constellation now on the meridian is Libra, which is neither conspicuous nor beautiful, being notable only for a naked-eye double star.

Virgo, with its star Spica, is only just past transit, and is yet seen to good advantage, although Leo is quite low in the sky.

Turning to the east we find those constellations which lined the horizon last month now high in the heavens. Cygnus, with its bright star Deneb, and Lyra, with its ever-attractive Vega, are both well in view, while Hercules and Ophiuchus are approaching the zenith.

In the north, Ursa Major is now swinging over to the west, the head of the outlined animal being almost on the same level as the pole. Ursa Minor is stretching upward along the meridian, as if balancing on the north star, which is supposed to mark the lesser bear's tail. Above Ursa Minor is Draco, very nearly in upper transit.

Below the pole are the other northern groups. Auriga is almost set, Capella being on the horizon's very edge. Lynx is but little above it. Almost in lower transit is Camelopardalis, an asterism, which is conspicuous more for its long name than for any special characteristic. To the east, Cepheus and Cassiopeia have begun to ascend.

Turning to the constellations around the horizon, we first encounter part of Andromeda, low in the northwest. Southward of this is a collection of tiny groups, known as Delphinus, Equuleus, and Sagitta. The first of these is a very attractive rhombus in shape.

Almost due east is Aquila, with its brilliant star Altair. This is one of the finest summer groups. In the southeast is part of Sagittarius, the ninth constellation of the zodiac, which is quite interesting when fully risen. Scorpio holds the south, although not yet in transit. This group is unmistakable, since its shape perfectly resembles that of a kite. Scorpio contains the brilliant red star Antares, one of the most striking features in the sky. Exactly on the meridian is Lupus, the wolf.

To the west are the remains of several constellations that were more or less prominent during the recent past, among which may be mentioned Centaurus, Hydra, Corvus, and Crater. In the northwest, portions of Cancer, Gemini, and Auriga bring us around again to the north point.

EDITOR'S NOTE FP: MT 2, No. 131 (1 June 1907): 8.

Notes

1. No star chart was published with this article.

ASTRONOMY IN AUGUST

The Heavens for This Month.—Mars the Ruling Planet

Mars is still the ruling planet of the evening sky, being, to all appearances, as bright as it was last month. The favourable opposition of July 6 was watched by hundreds of observers, and many valuable photographs of the planet were secured. The south polar cap, which is now most prominent, is rapidly melting from exposure to the sun, and a bluish fringe, caused by the melted snow, is forming around it. Soon this cap will be invisible in small telescopes, while the northern pole is becoming more and more brilliant from swiftly accumulating snow. Mars now sets at about 1 a.m.

Saturn, still seemingly ringless, is visible late in the evening. Toward the end of the month it rises at 7:30 p.m.

Jupiter is again coming into view, this time as a morning planet, rising about 2:45 a.m. By the 25th this planet will be so well seen that I give the dates of the most prominent phenomena of its satellites as follows:

Aug. 25, 4:16 a.m., transit of Satellite III. (beginning).

Aug. 29, 3:41 a.m., eclipse of Satellite I. (beginning).

Aug. 29, 4:03 a.m., transit of Satellite II. (ending).

Aug. 30, 3:56 a.m., transit of Satellite I. (ending).

The belts of Jupiter are now generally visible in ordinary telescopes.

Uranus is still near its prime, and Neptune is just appearing in the morning sky.

Mercury will come to greatest western elongation on the 12th, then being visible a short time before daylight, just above the sunrise point, and shewing a half-disc.

Venus is also a morning planet, but is now too near the sun to be well seen since it does not rise until nearly daybreak.

The moon's phases will be as follows:

New moon, 9th............1:36 a.m.
First quarter, 16th ....4:06 p.m.
Full moon, 23d ....7:15 a.m.
Last quarter, 30th.......10:28 p.m.

The Sun enters Virgo on the 23d. Sunrise occurs at 4:36 a.m. and sunset at 7:05 p.m. on the 1st, but by the 31st, the days are one hour and 15 minutes shorter. No eclipses or noteworthy occultations will happen during August.

The most prominent meteoric showers are as follows: Aug. 4, Beta Triangulids; 10th, Eta Perseids; 16th, Mu Perseids; 17th, Kappa Cygnids; 21st, Alpha Aurigids; 23d, Omicron Draconids; 25th, Gamma Pegasids; 29th, Delta Dra-

The Skies for August.

conids. Of these, the Eta Perseid display on the 10th is the finest, since it almost rivals the November Leonid shower.

The accompanying map shews the constellations on the meridian Aug. 20, at 9 p.m., for, beginning with this article, I shall, instead of giving a general account of all the visible constellations, describe in detail only those which are in transit, therefore best seen, mentioning such objects in them as may be easily observed with an opera glass.

Following the meridian from north to south, the first constellation of any importance, excepting Ursa Minor, is Draco, the Dragon, which lies immediately above the pole. The pole of the celestial sphere formerly lay near Thuban, the brightest of the 80 stars in this group. In Draco, the star marked by the Greek letter "Nu" is double, and easily resolvable by an opera glass. Another pleasing feature is the orange-coloured star Gamma.

Above Draco, and almost directly in the zenith, is Lyra, the Harp, a small constellation of but 21 stars. To the naked eye the chief attraction of this group is Vega, a bright bluish gem of the first magnitude, but opera glass observers find a greater interest in the star Epsilon, which appears double. A good telescope will resolve each component of this pair into another double, making a really quadruple object.

Between the zenith and the south nothing but the Milky Way, as shewn by the shaded area on the map, occupies the meridian, until we come to Sagittarius, the Archer, a group of 70 stars, which is just above the horizon. This constellation is replete with interesting opera glass objects. The upper half is often resolved into a subgroup in the form of an inverted saucepan, usually called the "Milk Dipper". Sagittarius is pre-eminently a field of clusters and nebulae. Below and to the right of Mu, in the milk dipper, lies a beautiful object, designated by the catalogue number of "8M", or "Messier 8". This has the appearance of a telescopic comet, but is really a combination of a star cluster and a nebula. While its appearance in an opera glass is excellent, a telescope is required to shew in detail the nebulous masses and rifts of which it is composed. Above the milk dipper is a cluster called 24M, which may, by the use of a powerful opera glass, be resolved into its component stars. A good plan to follow when observing these difficult objects is to look with the side rather than the front of the eye. 25M is the most beautiful of all the Sagittarian clusters. It is visible in an opera glass and consists of several definite layers of stars, one above the other. On the old maps Sagittarius was depicted as a Centaur, with bow and arrows.

Where the meridian meets the southern horizon may be seen the inconsequential group called Corona Australis, or the Southern Crown, but as none of its six principal stars is above the fifth magnitude, or in any way worthy of notice, we will pass it over and conclude our observations for August.

EDITOR'S NOTE FP: MT 2, No. 183 (1 August 1907): 8; ET 2, No. 181 (1 August 1907): 12.

THE HEAVENS FOR SEPTEMBER

Astronomy During the First Month of Autumn

Saturn now occupies the point of greatest interest, since it will arrive at its opposition the 17th of the month. The ring has again become visible, but may be seen only as a faint line of light.

Second only to Saturn is Mars, which is now about 50,000,000 miles away from the earth. A small telescope will now reveal both the northern and southern polar caps of this planet as well as the principal dark markings. Mars sets at about 11:30 p.m. this month.

Jupiter is the ruler of the morning sky, rising at 1:17 a.m. The belts and occasional spots on this giant orb may now be observed by any medium-sized telescope. Some of the most prominent configurations of Jupiter's satellites for September will be as follows:

> Sept. 5, 3:53 a.m., transit of Satellite II (beginning).
> Sept. 6, 3:36 a.m., transit I (beginning).
> Sept. 15, 2:25 a.m., transit of I (ending).
> Sept. 19, 3:32 a.m., eclipse of III (beginning).
> Sept. 21, 3:53 a.m., eclipse of I (beginning).
> Sept. 22, 4:24 a.m., transit of I (ending).
> Sept. 28, 4:35 a.m., eclipse of II (beginning).
> Sept. 29, 4:04 a.m., transit of I (beginning).
> Sept. 30, 4:20 a.m., transit of II (ending).

The roman numerals in the preceding table indicate the number of the satellite in order of distance from Jupiter. I record the phenomena of only the four brightest satellites.

Venus will be invisible this month, being in superior conjunction on the 14th. Mercury is likewise hidden from view, its conjunction occurring on the 6th. Uranus and Neptune are both fairly well seen.

The sun enters Libra on the 23d, thus marking the advent of autumn. Sunrise and sunset occur at respectively 5:09 a.m. and 6:20 p.m. on the 1st, but at 5:40 a.m. and 5:29 p.m. on the 31st.

The moon's phases will occur in the following order:

> New Moon, 7th .... 4:04 p.m.
> First Quarter, 14th .... 10:40 p.m.
> Full Moon, 21st .... 4:34 p.m.
> Last Quarter, 29th..6:37 a.m.

Perigee occurs on the 18th, Apogee on the 2nd. No eclipses are scheduled for September.

There will be an occultation of XI Ophiuchi on the 14th at 8:20 p.m. The star is of the fourth magnitude.

The following are the most noteworthy meteoric displays to be seen next month: Sept. 3, Nu Andromedes; 7, Epsilon Perseids; 15, 16 Camelopardalids; 21, Alpha Arietids; 22, Gamma Pegasids, Delta Cepheids, and Kappa Taurids; 27, 15 Orionids. None of these showers are of great brilliancy or importance.

Daniell's Comet, which was discovered on June 10, and which has since become visible to the naked eye, may be seen dimly before sunrise near the cluster 44M in Cancer, rising at about 3:35 a.m. It now has the appearance of a nebula, and is almost as far from the earth as the earth itself is from the sun. By the end of the month it will be invisible.

The accompanying map represents the constellations on and near the meridian for Sept. 20 at 9 p.m.

The zenith is now occupied by Cygnus, the Swan, a large, spreading constellation of about 80 principal stars. This group contains several objects which may be seen to advantage with opera glasses. The star Albireo, at the extreme end of the constellation, is double, the components being yellow and blue in colour. Omicron, near the bright Deneb, is a multiple star. Any glass will shew it double, while a moderately powerful instrument will reveal the existence of a third component to the system. Near Deneb and the star Gamma will be found multitudes of small stars visible with slight optical assistance, and very attractively arranged.

Passing southward we go by the diamond-shaped group Delphinus and the tiny constellation Equuleus, until the western half of Aquarius, the Water-Bearer, is arrived at. In this group, directly on the meridian, is a finely arranged aggregation of small stars near Mu and Epsilon. Aquarius also contains other objects, which will be described next month.

Low in the south is Capricornus, the Sea Goat. Two interesting doubles are the chief attractions of this constellation. The star Giedi, which is the uppermost of the two principal orbs of Capricornus, is a very wide double, being separable even by the naked eye under favourable conditions. Dabih, just below Giedi, is not so easily resolved, but is much more attractive in an opera glass, since the components are blue and yellow in colour, reminding one somewhat of Albireo in Cygnus. Capricornus being the most southerly group now in the meridian, the list of celestial objects for September must close.

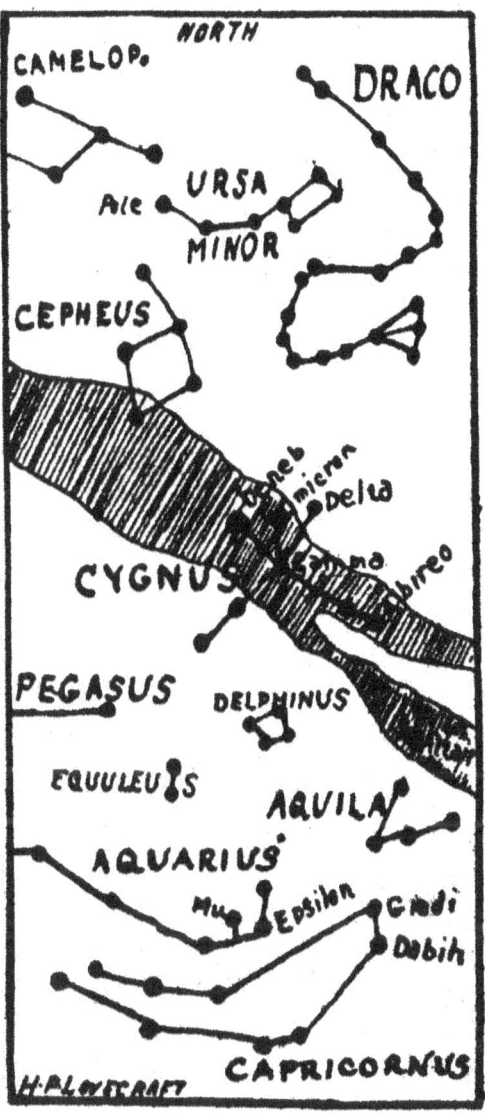

Skies for September.

EDITOR'S NOTE FP: ST 2, No. 35 (1 September 1907): 8.

THE SKIES OF OCTOBER

Celestial Events for the Coming Month

Saturn is still the leading planet of the evening sky, having been in opposition on Sept. 17. The ring may be seen at all times as a thin line of light, visible each side of the planet's centre. Saturn sets at about 3 a.m. this month.

Mars is fast losing brilliancy and attractiveness, since it is three months past its opposition. Toward the end of October it will be noticed that this planet is slightly gibbous in shape, a phase that will be more marked in the near future.

Jupiter is now the principal planet of the morning sky, rising at approximately 11:45 p.m. The belts, polar compression, and other features of this orb make it one of the best objects in the heavens for small telescopes. The principal phenomena of Jupiter's satellites for October will be as follows:

Oct. 7—2:07 a.m., Eclipse of Satellite I., Beginning.
Oct. 7—4:05 a.m., Transit of II., Beginning.
Oct. 8—2:45 a.m., Transit of I., Ending.
Oct. 14—4 a.m., Eclipse of I., Beginning.
Oct. 15—2:26 a.m., Transit of I., Beginning.
Oct. 23—1:40 a.m., Eclipse of II., Beginning.
Oct. 24—1:11 a.m., Transit of I., Ending.
Oct. 25—1:36 a.m., Transit of II., Ending.
Oct. 25—2:48 a.m., Eclipse of III., Ending.
Oct. 30—2:15 a.m., Eclipse of I., Beginning.
Oct. 30—4:16 a.m., Eclipse of II., Beginning.
Oct. 31—12:40 a.m., Transit of I., Beginning.
Oct. 31—3:06 a.m., Transit of I., Ending.

Venus is invisible, being close to the sun, just past superior conjunction. It sets about 20 minutes after the close of day, hence will be an evening planet when next seen.

Mercury is at its best for evening observation on the 23d, when it comes to greatest eastern elongation.

Uranus and Neptune are still in rather good positions.

The sun enters Scorpio on the 23d. Sunrise and sunset are at 5:41 a.m. and 5:28 p.m. on the 1st, at 6:15 a.m. and 4:40 p.m. on the 31st.

The moon's phases will be as follows:

New Moon, 7th ....5:21 a.m.
First Quarter, 14th ....5:02 a.m.
Full Moon, 21st ....4:16 a.m.
Last Quarter, 29th..2:52 a.m.

Perigee occurs on the 14th, Apogee on the 28th.

No eclipses or favourable occultations are predicted for this month. Among the principal meteoric displays may be mentioned the following: Oct. 2, Chi Cepheids; 3, Beta Taurids; 11, Epsilon Piscids; 14, Epsilon Arietids; 14, Sigma Ursa Majorids; 18, XI

Orionids; 20, Alpha Cetids; 20, Beta Canis Majorids; 29, Delta Geminids. Of these the XI Orionid shower on the 18th is by far the best.

Daniell's Comet has now entirely passed from view. The constellations on the meridian this month, as shewn by the accompanying map, are rather dull. The first group in any way worthy of notice is Pegasus, the Winged Horse, which is but little south of the zenith. This constellation is composed of two distinct parts. First a line of small stars stretching far westward, and second, the Great Square, a large subgroup which also contains part of Andromeda.

Pegasus possesses few objects for the opera glass, the only conspicuous one being the star Pi, which is a wide and easy double.

Below Pegasus is Aquarius, the Water Bearer, the 11th constellation of the zodiac. This group is so large that it occupies the meridian for two consecutive months. It is the eastern half which is now best seen. The chief objects of this part of Aquarius are Tau, a beautiful white and orange double, and 104, a wide but rather faint pair of stars.

Low in the sky is Piscis Australis, the Southern Fish. This is noticeable only for Fomalhaut, its brightest star, which is a reddish-tinted object of the first magnitude.

Grus, the Crane, which is just below Piscis Australis, is so near the horizon that it cannot be well seen in the latitude of Providence, hence the list of October objects must end.

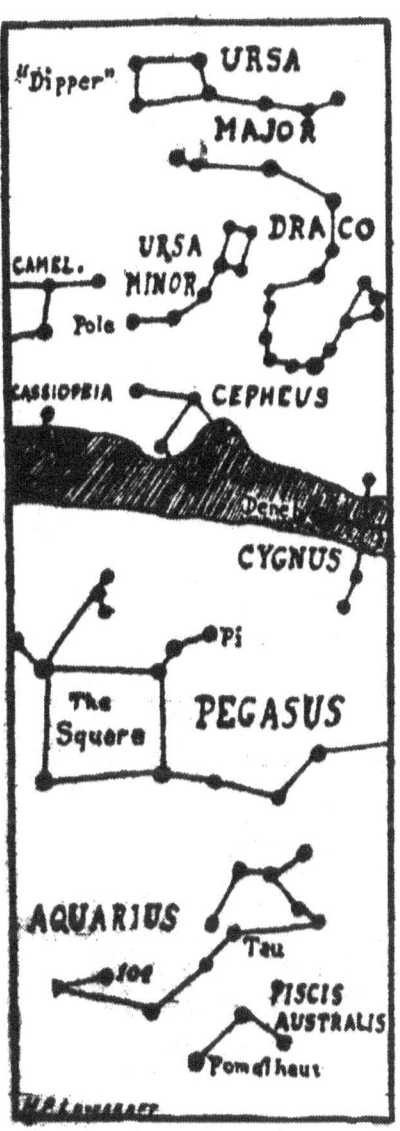

October Skies.

EDITOR'S NOTE FP: *MT* 2, No. 235 (1 October 1907): 2; *ET* 2, No. 232 (1 October 1907): 13.

THE HEAVENS IN NOVEMBER

Transit of Mercury Forms Chief Event of the Coming Month

The principal astronomical phenomenon which is to transpire during the month of November is the transit of Mercury over the sun's disc on the morning of the 14th. The occurrence is one of great rarity, never happening at intervals of less than seven years, and often in even greater periods; indeed, 14 years have elapsed since the last transit.

The phenomenon itself is simply a passage of the planet Mercury between the earth and the sun, which renders it visible to us, projected as a black spot on the solar disc, but its astronomical importance is very great, since it affords the best method for computing the size and motions of Mercury, as well as ascertaining the uniformity of the sun's axial rotation. Transits of Mercury occur, of course, at the planet's inferior conjunction, but only at times when this aspect coincides with a part of Mercury's orbit which is near the ecliptic, or earth's annual path. The transit of Nov. 14, 1907, is not entirely visible in the latitude of Providence, since the beginning occurs before daybreak. At 6:33 a.m. the sun will rise as usual, and the unassisted eye can detect nothing strange upon its disc. If, however, an opera glass, properly shaded, be turned toward the sun, a tiny black dot will be seen, in the northeast of the visible surface. This will slowly move westward, until by 8:48 it will have reached the edge of the disc. At this stage, the owners of telescopes should look for the phenomenon called the "black drop", which is an optical deception that causes Mercury to appear elongated when near the sun's edge. At 8:51 the transit will be over. Fig. 1 illustrates the occurrence.

Figure 1
*Path of Mercury over the
Sun's Disc.*

Turning to the regular phenomena, we find Jupiter rapidly approaching the evening sky. Its quadrature occurs on the 5th, and its rising time is about 9:45 p.m. In the telescope, this planet shews a slight shading off on the edge turned away from the sun, its nearest approach to a phase. The November phenomena of Jupiter's satellites will be as follows:

Nov. 5, 2:13 a.m., Transit of Satellite II., ending. Nov. 6, 4:08 a.m., Eclipse of I., beginning. Nov. 7, 2:39 to 5 a.m., Transit of I. Nov. 8, 3:40 a.m., Transit of II., beginning. Nov. 8, 11:32 p.m., Transit of I., ending. Nov. 12, 2:25 p.m., Transit of III., beginning. Nov. 14, 4:32 a.m., Transit of I., beginning. Nov. 14, 2:30 a.m., Eclipse of I., beginning. Nov. 16, 1:20 a.m., Transit of I., ending. Nov. 22, 2:23 p.m., Eclipse of I., beginning. Nov. 23, 12:52 to 3:12 a.m., Transit of I. Nov. 24, 1:22 a.m., Eclipse of II., beginning. Nov. 26, 1:06 a.m., Transit of II., ending. Nov. 29, 4:16 a.m., Eclipse of I., beginning. Nov. 29, 10:40 p.m., Eclipse of III., ending. Nov. 30, 2:42 to 5:02 a.m., Transit of I. Nov. 30, 10:44 p.m., Eclipse of I., beginning.

Saturn is still well seen, although it is now less brilliant than it has been during the past few months. The ring has not yet opened sufficiently to be seen as such. Saturn sets about 1 a.m.

Mars arrives at quadrature on the 11th. It will then shew a perceptible gibbous phase in any instrument powerful enough to shew it as a disc. For all surface observations, however, this planet is now very unfavourably situated.

Venus now sets about 40 minutes after the sun, hence is not advanced enough for favourable seeing. Uranus is receding from view, while Neptune is approaching its best.

The sun enters Sagittarius on the 22nd. Sunrise and sunset occur at 6:17 a.m. and 4:39 p.m. on the first; at 6:52 a.m. and 4:13 p.m. on the 30th. No eclipses are predicted for November.

Two excellent occultations will occur this month, that of Zeta Tauri at 10:05 p.m. on the 21st, and that of Delta Geminorum at 9:04 p.m. on the 23d. The Great Leonid meteor shower will probably be noted about the 14th of the month, in the early morning hours. Last year very few meteors were seen, but so uncertain is the phenomenon that it is quite likely to be of considerable magnitude this month. Other meteoric displays are as follows: Nov. 1, Epsilon Arietids; 2, E. Taurids; 16, Nu Ursids; 17, Gamma Camelopardalids; 20, Kappa Laurids; 27, Gamma Andromedes; 30, Mu Pegasids and Epsilon Ursids. The Gamma Andromedes, which fall on the 27th, are especially worthy of notice.

The month of November marks the arrival of the first winter star groups, the meridian, as shewn by Fig. 2, being occupied by Andromeda. This constellation, although large, contains but one opera glass object, the great nebula 31M. This is the largest and brightest object of its kind in the entire sky,

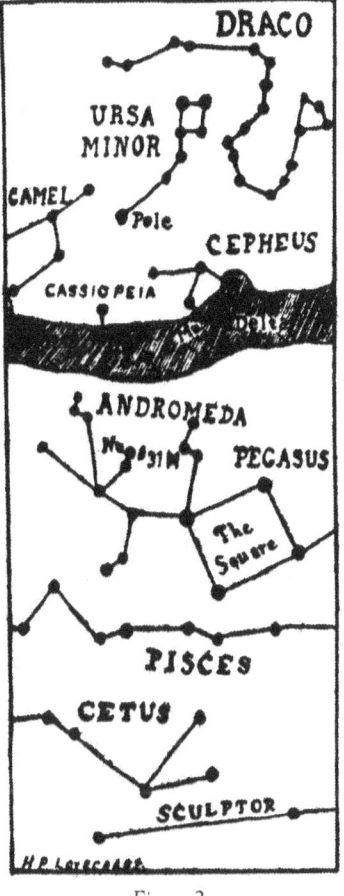

Figure 2
Evening Sky for November

and is thought to be made up of rapidly rotating spirals of gaseous matter, but the observer with low powers must content himself by seeing it as an elongated ellipse of misty light, with the barest suggestion of a central condensation. 31M is just visible to the naked eye, and is situated very near to the star Nu, by whose aid it may be easily found.

Above Andromeda are two groups, Cepheus and Cassiopeia. The former contains two fine objects. The star Delta is double, the components being blue and orange in colour. Mu, a little to the left of Delta, is a very red star, beautiful on that account. Cassiopeia is unmistakable on account of its "W" shape, but possesses no opera glass objects save a rich region of the Milky Way. This group ends the list of November objects, since the Southern constellations, Pisces, Cetus, and Sculptor, are not worthy of notice here.

EDITOR'S NOTE FP: MT 2, No. 262 (1 November 1907): 5 (unsigned); ET 2, No. 259 (1 November 1907): 17 (unsigned).

HEAVENS FOR DECEMBER

Planetary and Stellar Motions for the Closing Month of 1907

Jupiter is now the leading feature of the evening sky, rising at about 7:45 p.m. Although its opposition will not occur until Jan. 29 this planet is already in a very favourable position for observation.

Saturn arrives at quadrature on the 13th. Its rings are nearly edgewise to the earth, making them invisible in small telescopes, although large instruments now reveal certain bright protuberances on them which are not seen except at rare intervals. Mars is past quadrature, thus possessing very little of interest.

Mercury, whose transit last month attracted general attention, comes to its greatest western elongation on the 1st, thus being visible in the east before sunrise. Venus is now visible every night, low in the west immediately after the close of day. It sets over an hour after the sun, thus shining brightly in the evening twilight. In a telescope it shews a small, nearly full disc. Uranus is invisible, being close to conjunction, while Neptune is at its best.

The moon's phases will be as follows:

New Moon, 5th .... 5:22 a.m.
First Quarter, 11th .... 9:16 p.m.
Full Moon, 19th........... 12:55 p.m.
Last Quarter, 27th......... 6:10 p.m.

Perigee occurs on the 6th, Apogee on the 22nd.

The sun enters Capricornus on the 22nd, thus marking the advent of winter. The days are shortest from the 20th to the 24th, their average length being 9 hours and 4 minutes. An unusually large number of spots are now visible, even to the naked eye on the solar disc.

There will be an occultation of Delta-3 Tauri on the 17th at 7:05 p.m. The follow-

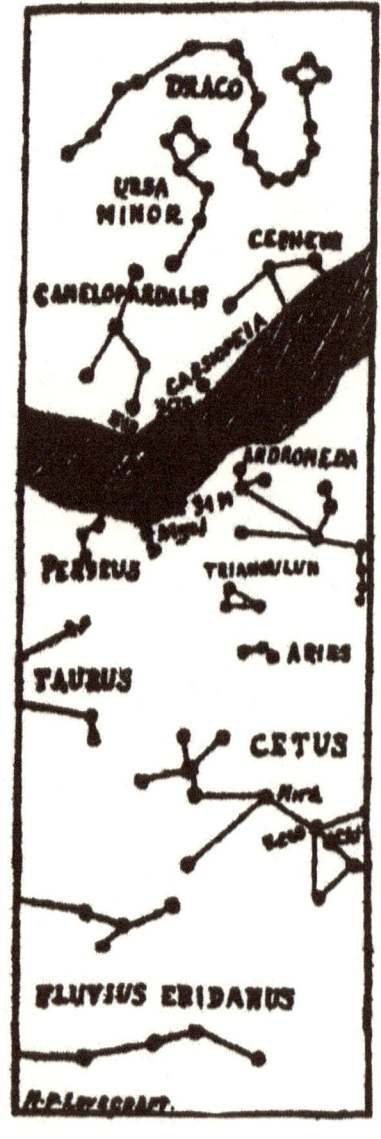

ing meteoric showers are expected to occur during December: Dec. 1, Eta Perseids; 4, Beta Ursids and Delta Geminids; 6, XI Taurids; 8, Pi Leonids and Alpha Draconids; 10, Alpha and Beta Geminids; 22, Chi Draconids; 24, Gamma Boötids; 25, Theta Geminids. Of these the Alpha Geminid shower on the 10th is usually the most attractive.

Turning to the constellations we find two noteworthy groups on the meridian, namely, Perseus and Cetus. Perseus, the first of the strictly winter groups to reach transit, is especially prominent in two respects, since it contains the greatest star cluster in the entire sky, as well as the noted variable star Algol or Beta Persei. The great cluster may be viewed to advantage in any good opera or field glass, appearing in the former instrument as a luminous cloud and in the latter as a resplendent area of small stars. Surrounding Alpha Persei is a beautiful arrangement of tiny orbs which forms a widespread cluster. Another cluster is 34M, the observation of which, however, requires the use of a good field glass.

The quintuple star Eta, also in Perseus, reminds one of Jupiter and its four largest satellites, as seen in a small telescope, all the components being in a straight line with the largest next the end.

Near the southern horizon is the constellation known as Cetus, the Whale. The principle object in this group is Mora, or Omicron Ceti, a variable whose brilliancy fluctuates between the second and ninth magnitudes. Other features of Cetus are the double stars Chi and Zeta, the latter being separable even to the naked eye.

EDITOR'S NOTE FP: *ST* 2, No. 47 (1 December 1907): 15.

THE HEAVENS IN JANUARY

Astronomical Phenomena for the Coming Month

The principal celestial event due to happen next month is the opposition of Jupiter on the 29th. This planet is, with the exception of Venus, the brightest in the entire sky, hence will form a most conspicuous object during the winter evenings. It is now in the constellation Cancer, rising about sunset and setting about sunrise.

Venus will be visible low in the west each evening. It should be looked for in the twilight as it sets, but little over two hours after the sun. Its phase is not sensibly less than that of last month.

Saturn, now past quadrature, is losing interest, although it will linger in the evening sky until March. Mars is likewise in a rather unfavourable position. Mercury arrives at superior conjunction on the 14th, hence will not be seen during January.

Uranus is invisible, being in conjunction on the 4th, but Neptune comes to opposition on the same date, thus presenting a favourable opportunity for observation.

The moon's phases will be as follows:

New moon, 3d .... 4:43 p.m.
First quarter, 10th .... 8:53 a.m.
Full moon, 18th .... 8:37 a.m.
Last quarter, 26th .... 10:01 a.m.
Perigee occurs on the 4th, Apogee on the 18th.

The sun enters Aquarius on the 22nd. On the 1st it rises at 7:14 a.m., setting at 4:22 p.m., but by the 31st the days are 48 minutes longer. The earth is nearest the sun, or in perihelion, on the 2d. There will be a total eclipse of the sun on the 3d, which, however, cannot be seen here.

The most prominent meteoric displays for January are as follows: Jan. 2, Quadrantids; 5, Theta Ursids; 11, XI. Boötids; 17, Chi Cygnids; 19, Zeta Draconids; 22, Chi Librids; 25, Iota Candrids. Of these the Quadrantid Shower on the 2d, whose radiant point is near the star 44 Boötis, will probably be the most interesting.

The meridian at 9 p.m., as shewn by the map, now contains some of the finest constellations in the heavens. Due south is Orion, the hunter, a group which, on account of its great size and brilliant stars, can never fail to attract wide attention. The principal features of Orion as seen with the naked eye are Betelgeux, a brilliant red star in the upper portion; The Belt, a line of three fairly bright stars in the central part; and Rigel, a bluish orb of the first magnitude, situated in the extreme southern section of the group. In an opera glass, also, Orion is a splendid sight. The region just below the belt, called the "Sword", contains 42M, one of the finest nebulae in the northern sky. In an opera glass this appears to entirely surround the star Theta. Pi-5, in the western portion, is an attractive white and orange double. Near Bellatrix and Phi are multitudes of small stars, forming a miniature milky way. The same conditions are also observable near the belt.

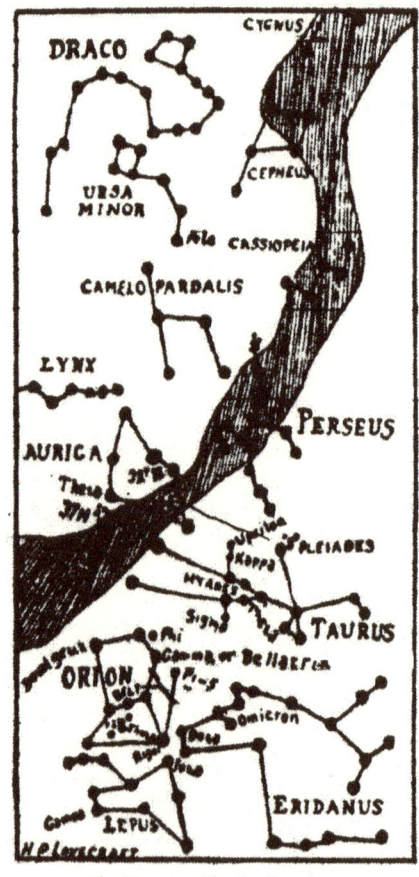

Above Orion is Taurus, the grandest of the Zodiacal groups. This constellation is especially replete in interesting opera glass doubles, the stars Theta, Kappa, Sigma, and Nu being easily separable with low powers. Taurus also contains two of the finest clusters in the northern sky, the Pleiades and the Hyades. The former possesses six stars easily visible to the naked eye, one more seen with difficulty, several hundred observable in an opera or field glass, and an infinite number discernible in a good telescope, besides a nebulous background, which might, by very high powers, be resolved into countless more. The Hyades form a "V"-shaped group, which contains Aldebaran, the brightest star in the constellation.

Auriga, just above Taurus, is preeminently a field of fine clusters, no less than five being within its confines; 33-7, 37M, and 38M are observable with field glasses, while the aggregation of stars near Theta is visible in any opera glass.

Turning to the southern groups, Eridanus is first encountered. This contains Omicron, a fine white and orange double, as well as an attractive cluster near Beta.

The Evening Sky for January.

Lepus, below Orion, also contains two excellent opera glass objects. Gamma is a fine double, while a small star near Iota is notable for its deep red colour.

EDITOR'S NOTE FP: *ET* 3, No. 1 (1 January 1908): 4; *MT* 3, No. 2 (2 January 1908): 10.

FEBRUARY SKIES

Celestial Evenings for the Coming Month

Venus is now high up in the evening sky, not setting until three hours after the sun. It still presents a gibbous aspect in a telescope, but this phase is constantly decreasing.

Owing to the position of the orbit of Venus with respect to the sun and earth, its apparent disc, as seen by us, increases as its phase decreases, hence it appears smallest when almost full, and largest when a thin crescent, nearly between the sun and the earth. It is, of course, invisible when exactly full, or in inferior conjunction.

Mercury, whose orbit is situated similarly to that of Venus, is at its best on the 13th, when it arrives at greatest eastern elongation. It may be seen at that time about an hour after sunset, low in the west, presenting a half phase if viewed with a sufficiently powerful telescope.

Mars and Saturn are still in the evening sky, but are too far advanced in their courses to be of great interest.

Jupiter is still near its best, being but little past opposition. It is visible in the eastern sky, shining with a brightness which rivals that of Venus. Uranus is still invisible, while Neptune is very favourably situated.

The moon's phases will be as follows:

New Moon, 2nd.................. 3:36 a.m.
First Quarter, 8th .... 11:28 p.m.
Full Moon, 17th .... 4:05 a.m.
Last Quarter, 24th............... 1:24 p.m.

Perigee occurs on the 1st, Apogee on the 14th.

The sun enters Pisces on the 17th at 11 a.m. It rises and sets at 6:59 a.m. and 4:27

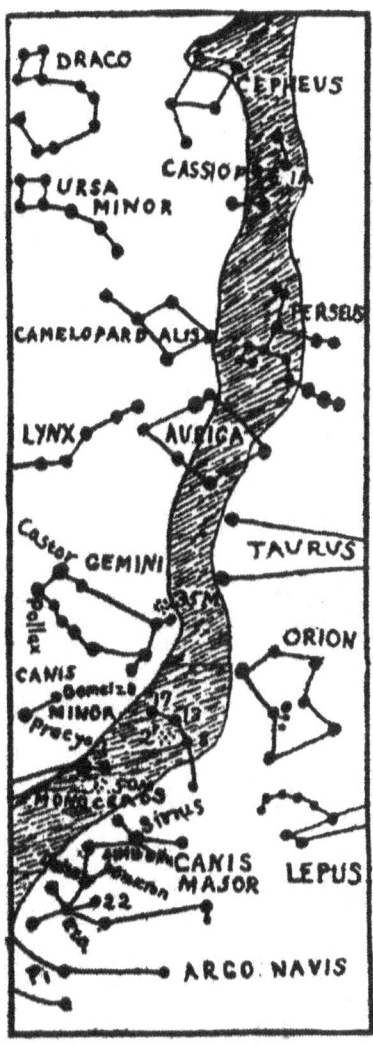

The Evening Sky in February.

p.m., respectively, on the 1st. On the last day of the month, which is the 29th, since 1908 is a leap year, the times are 6:21 and 5:33, shewing an increase of 1h. 14m. in the length of the days.

No eclipses will occur this month.

The following meteoric showers are predicted for February.

Feb. 1, Alpha Draconids; 7, Alpha Aurigids; 15, Alpha Serpentids and Beta Ophiuchids; 16, Tau Leonids; 20, Rho Herculids.

The meridian at 9 p.m., as shewn by the accompanying map, is unusually attractive this month. High up in the south, just below the zenith, is the constellation known as Gemini, or the Twins. This group contains the famous stars Castor and Pollux. Both of these are fine doubles, but much beyond the reach of an opera glass. They are, however, centres of beautiful star fields which form an attractive sight even with the lowest powers. Gemini also contains the great cluster 35M, which is within the reach of any good opera or field glass.

Immediately below Gemini are two constellations, Canis Minor and Monoceros. The former contains Procyon, a first magnitude star, and Gomelza, an interesting triple star, the components of which form a right triangle. Monoceros, or the Unicorn, is noticeable principally for the thick fields of small stars surrounding the large stars, 8, 13, and 17, and for the clusters 2-7 and 50M.

We now arrive at Canis Major, the Greater Dog, one of the most interesting constellations in the heavens. The first object to be noted in connexion with this group is Sirius, or the Dog-Star, the brightest stellar orb in the entire sky. Sirius shines with a brilliant greenish white light, although it is said to have been red in the past. Nu, also in Canis Major, is a triple star, easily seen as such. The star 22 is noticeable on account of its deep red colour.

Among the clusters in this group, 41M is the most prominent. The fine fields of small stars between Delta and Omicron complete its opera glass subjects.

Between Canis Major and the southern horizon is the western extremity of Argo Navis, a constellation which will be more fully treated of next month. Pi, in this group, is an interesting orange star.

EDITOR'S NOTE FP: *ET* 3, No. 28 (1 February 1908): 5.

THE HEAVENS IN MONTH OF MARCH

Jupiter and Venus Principal Celestial Objects

Neptune is the Least Prominent of All the Planets
in the Evening Sky, Being Invisible to the Naked Eye.—
The Moon's Phases.

Venus is now without doubt the most conspicuous object in the early evening sky, shining high in the southwest. It is moving eastward at a rate surpassing that of the sun, hence is visible longer and longer after sunset as the days pass. Its brilliancy is also rapidly increasing, so that few can fail to notice it. This planet is now situated in the extreme eastern part of the constellation Pisces. In a telescope it shews a gibbous phase, like that of the moon between first quarter and full. This phase decreases as the planet's brilliancy increases. Venus will be the leading planet of the evening sky until late in June, as its inferior conjunction occurs on July 5.

Jupiter is already high up in the southeast. It is located in the constellation Cancer, near the star Delta. As Cancer has no conspicuous stars, the planet appears especially brilliant against such a background. It retrogrades, or moves westward, until the 30th, when it is stationary, preparatory to the resumption of its direct or eastward journey among the stars. Jupiter is still in a fine position for observation by those who possess telescopes powerful enough to reveal the motions of its satellites or to study the belts.

Mars, situated in the constellation Aries, is descending lower and lower in the southwest after sunset. It is now near Venus and may be seen as a red star setting about four hours after the sun. It is quite noticeable, as no other bright stars are in the vicinity, although contrast with Venus, which is very close to it, tends to lessen the effect. Mars will linger in the evening sky until August.

Neptune is the least noticeable of all the planets in the evening sky, not being visible except in a telescope. At present it is in Gemini, near the centre of the constellation. It may be identified by those who possess suitable instruments from its proximity to the star Delta.

Saturn has now entirely vanished from the evening sky, passing behind the sun in conjunction on the 20th. In a month or two it will be visible in the east before sunrise as a morning star.

The morning sky is now singularly devoid of bright planets. Uranus is the first planet to rise after midnight. It is in the constellation Sagittarius, situated just above the bowl of the "Milk Dipper". Mercury, the other morning planet for March, will not be seen during the first half of the month, but comes to visibility toward the end, arriving at greatest western elongation on the 27th. If an observer desires to locate Mercury at that time he should closely examine that portion of the sky just above the sunrise point. The planet will be identified by its slightly reddish colour and scintillating appearance. In a telescope it reveals a semi-circular phase.

The moon's phases will be as follows:

New Moon, 2nd.. 1:57 p.m.

First Quarter, 9th .... 4:42 p.m.

Full Moon, 17th .... 9:28 p.m.

Last Quarter, 25th..7:32 a.m.

Perigee occurs on the 1st and 29th, Apogee on the 13th. Our satellite is in conjunction with the following planets on the dates mentioned: March 5, Venus; 6, Mars; 11, Neptune; 13, Jupiter; 26, Uranus; 30, Mercury.

The sun enters Aries at 7:16 a.m. on the 21st, thus crossing the equator northward and commencing spring. Sunrise and sunset occur at 6:20 a.m. and 5:31 p.m. respectively on the 1st and at 5:29 and 6:09 on the 31st, shewing an increase of 1 hour 26 minutes in the length of the day during the month. No eclipses are due to occur in March.

Among the meteoric showers of the month those of the Beta Leonids on the 13th and of the Beta Ursae Majorids on the 24th are the most attractive. Cancer is the fourth sign of the zodiac, but, owing to the motion of the earth's pole around that of the ecliptic and the consequent motion of the equator around the ecliptic itself, a phenomenon called precession, it has come to be the fifth constellation east of the vernal equinox, where the zodiac begins. Cancer, which is now almost in the zenith, is a rather dull group, but contains one object of universal interest. This is the famous cluster 44M, called the "Praespe", situated between the stars Gamma and Delta. The Praespe appears like a faint nebula when viewed with the naked eye, but the slightest optical assistance reveals it as a dense aggregation of tiny stars.

Low down, near the southern horizon, is the great group known as Argo Navis or the Ship Argo. This constellation takes up a large space in the southern celestial hemisphere, although but a small part of it can be seen in the latitude of Providence. South of latitude 30 degrees the entire asterism may be observed, especially the bright star Alpha or Canopus, which has not a superior in all the heavens, Sirius alone excepted. The principal opera glass objects of Argo Navis are the double stars Kappa, Mu, and XI and the clusters 38-8, 45M, and 93M. Argo has recently been divided into four smaller groups, descriptive of different parts of the celestial ship; these are Malus, the mast; Vela, the sails; Puppis, the stern, and Carina, the keel.

EDITOR'S NOTE FP: MT 3, No. 53 (2 March 1908): 4; *ET* 3, No. 54 (3 March 1908): 6 (illustration only; as "The Evening Sky in March").

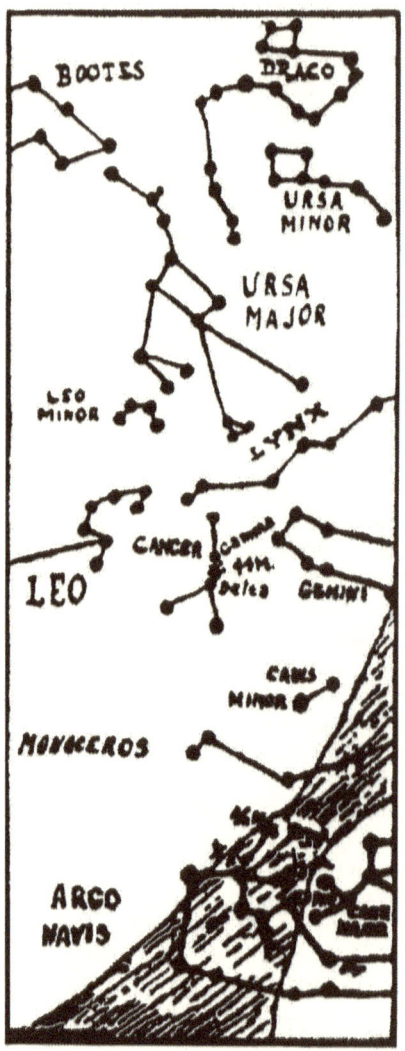

The Evening Sky in March.

SOLAR ECLIPSE FEATURE OF JUNE HEAVENS

Supposed Discovery of an Eighth Satellite Attending Jupiter is Attracting Much Attention to That Planet.— The Evening Sky Offers Field for Study.

Venus, now a slender crescent, is sinking lower and lower into the western sky. At the same time its apparent diameter is increasing, so that its phase will be almost invisible to the naked eye. The planet is observed with difficulty toward the last of the month, owing to its ever-decreasing apparent distance from the sun. On July 6 it will pass the sun in inferior conjunction, becoming visible in August as a morning planet, with greatest brilliancy on the 11th of that month. Venus now sets about 10 p.m.

Jupiter is still high in the west, although less favourable for observation than during last month. This planet is now of particular interest owing to the supposed discovery of an eighth satellite attending it. The discovery was made by an observer at the Greenwich Observatory, who found its image on a plate which had been used to photograph Jupiter. It is either a satellite or an asteroid, and subsequent photographs seem to indicate that it is the former. Its faintness renders it invisible to the human eye, even through the most powerful telescopes. The sensitive photographic plate is alone able to record its existence. Mercury comes to greatest eastern elongation on the 6th. It will then be in a favourable position for observation in the western sky after sunset. It is at that date very near Mars, which will serve as a valuble guide in locating it. In a telescope Mercury will shew a semicircular phase. Toward the end of the month this planet will disappear, arriving at inferior conjunction on July 5. Saturn is now well up in the morning sky, rising about midnight. The ring system is gradually increasing in visibility, and will soon be perceptible as more than the line of light which is at present seen.

Mars is near Mercury, very low in the western evening sky. It is practically worthless for observational purposes, and will be gone in August. Its principal value this month is in locating Mercury. It will be near Venus on the 22nd. Mars sets at about 9 p.m.

Uranus is now in the "Milk Dipper" of Sagittarius, faintly visible to the naked eye. Its position is becoming more and more favourable. On the other hand Neptune is invisible, being close to conjunction with the sun.

The moon's phases for the month are as follows:

First Quarter, 6th .... 11:56 p.m.
Full Moon, 14th ....8:55 a.m.
Last Quarter, 21st..12:36 a.m.
New Moon, 28th ....11:32 a.m.

Perigee occurs on the 16th, Apogee on the 4th. The moon comes to conjunction with the following planets on the following dates: Mars, June 1; Venus, 2; Jupiter, 3; Uranus, 15.

The sun enters the zodiacal sign Cancer on the 21st at 3 p.m., thus marking the beginning of summer. The 21st is of course the longest day, being 15 hours and 17 minutes from sunrise to sunset. On the 1st the sun rises and sets at 4:10 a.m. and 7:14 p.m., respectively; on the 21st at 4:07 and 7:24, and on the 30th at 4:10 and 7:25. An annular eclipse of the sun will occur on the 28th. This is an eclipse in which the moon passes centrally over the sun's disc, yet fails to wholly obscure it, leaving a ring of light visible.

The name "annular" as applied to this kind of eclipse is derived from the Latin "annulus", a ring, referring to the ring of sunlight visible around the moon's disc. Annular eclipses occur at times when the sun is near the earth and when the moon is far away, making the former appear so much the larger that the latter fails to cover it completely. As seen at Providence the annual effect is missing, the phenomenon being visible only as a partial eclipse. The first contact of sun and moon occurs at 9:51 a.m., and the eclipse lasts until 12:59 in the afternoon. Observers should view it only through very dark glasses, as the sun's light, even at maximum obscuration, is sufficient to injure the eyes.

The principal meteor showers for June are as follows: June 7, Beta Herculids; 13th, Eta Cepheids; 15th, Beta and Kappa Cygnids; 20th, Delta Cepheids; 28th, Delta Cygnids.

The evening sky is now filled with the characteristic constellations of summer, which are in general less striking in appearance than the winter groups. The principal constellation on the meridian at 9 p.m. is Boötes, which extends southward from the zenith. Below Boötes is Libra, whose interesting objects were described last month. Eastward is Corona Borealis, and Coma Berenices lies to the west. High in the western sky is Virgo, still seen to advantage. Below it is Leo, now past its prime. In the east are Cygnus, Lyra, Hercules, and Serpentarius, the last two being near the zenith. Northward we find Ursa Major past the pole and entering the western sky. Ursa Minor now lies along the meridian above the pole. Above it is Draco, just north of the zenith. Below and a little to the east of the pole is Cepheus, just commencing its upward journey.

The list of horizon constellations begins with Camelopardalis, which is in the north, directly under the pole. Proceeding eastward we arrive at part of Andromeda and the whole of Cassiopeia, the last-named group being entirely in the circumpolar belt. Beyond Cassiopeia the horizon is barren as far as the east, where may be found Delphinus, Equuleus, Sagitta, and Aquila. The last named is one of the most attractive of the summer groups, containing the bright reddish star Altair. Farther southward we see Sagittarius just rising, preceded by Scorpio, whose interesting objects will be described next month. At the southern intersection of meridian and horizon is Lupus, the Wolf, which is too far south to be well seen in these latitudes. Looking westward, Centaurus is first seen, followed by Hydra, with its two dependent groups Corvus and Crater. In the northeast part of Cancer, together with the planet Jupiter, is setting, north of which portions of Gemini and Auriga complete the circuit of horizontal groups.

EDITOR'S NOTE FP: *MT* 3, No. 131 (1 June 1908): 4; *ET* 3, No. 130 (1 June 1908): Sec. 2, p. 2. HPL's monthly columns come to an abrupt end here, presumably as a result of the nervous breakdown he suffered at this time, which caused his withdrawal from high school at the end of his third year (he had skipped nearly the whole of the 1905–06 term) without a diploma.

THIRD ANNUAL REPORT OF THE PROV. METEOROLOGICAL STATION

1906

by H. P. Lovecraft, Director of the Station

(Jan. 16, 1907)

I. DESCRIPTIVE.

The Providence Meteorological Station, at the beginning of 1907, consists of a shelter, with a northern exposure, attached to the side of a small building, or office; a rain gauge, above it, a spectroscope, a full meteorological library, etc. The entire outfit has one edifice to its self. The following conditions are noted:

1. Pressure
2. Temperature
3. Wind
4. Rainfall
5. Weather.

The equipment of the station is as follows:

Mercurial Barometer by Spooner
Sixe's Thermometer by Taylor
Rain Gauge by Queen and Co.
Wind Vane by Gage and Co.
Storm Glass by Large
Stan. Thermometer by Wilder
Diffraction Spectroscope by Ives.

Our observations are made in the subsequent order:

Max. and Min.
Temperature
Sky and Clouds
Spectroscopic Rain-Bands
Rainfall
Pressure.

Forecasts are issued daily. A few sub-stations are maintained. Since Dec. 24, 1906, observations are taken at 8.30 a. m. The main station is directed by H. P. Lovecraft, 598 Angell St., Providence, R. I. The main sub-station, No. 2, is directed by H. B. Munroe, 66 Paterson St. No. 2 is mainly for comparison.[1]

II. PROGRESS.

During the year 1906 many important events connected with the station took place. On Jan. 1, an entirely new shelter was supplied, and later in the month a complete set of new instruments by Queen was purchased. A vane by Gage and Co., was added in April. During September, the observations from the shelter were discontinued for a time, although the general weather conditions were steadily noted. On Dec. 24, the location of the station was changed for the first time since 1904. Whereas it formerly occupied the roof of the R. I. JOURNAL building, it now has an edifice of its own, the rain gauge surmounting, and the shelter having a northern exposure, as formerly. At this time hygrometry was superseded by spectroscopy, and a new Sixe's thermometer added. The station again filled out U. S. Gov't form No. 1009.

III. NOTABLE WEATHER EVENTS.

The following are some occurrences that were specially noted here.

JAN.	3	Hailstorm, (Night)
	4	Heavy Fog (Morn)
	10	Cold Day, Zero.
	21–22	V. Warm Spell, (64)
	24	High Pressure, (30.76)
	28–30	Clear Days.
FEB.	2–3	V. Cold Weather.
	6–7	do.
	11	V. High Pressure (30.961)
	14	Sleet and Hail
	18	Thick Mist (Night)
	22	Hy. N. W. Winds
MAR.	3	Hy. Rain
	10	First Cumuli Processions.
	15	Large Snow
	22	Hy. N. W. Winds
	24	High Pressure (30.901)
APR.	30	Thunderstorm 2h 30m
MAY	5	Thunderstorm
	13	Warm Day (90)
	16	do. (88)
	18	do. (96)
	18	Meteor (Evening)
	18	Electrical Storm (Night)
	19	Thunderstorm, (Night)
	24.	do.
	27–9	Long Rain (3.25 inches)
JUNE	5	Thunderstorm (Night)
	6	do.
	9	Severe Thunderstorm
	16–19	Long Rain
	23	Thundershowers
JUL.	1	Thunderstorm (Early Morning)
	2	do.
	3	Hy. Rain (1.25 inches)
	4	Thunderstorm 6 p.m.
	10	Thunderstorm 5 p.m.
	24	Thunderstorm 4 a.m.
AUG.	1–4	Bad Weather
	4	Thunderstorm 7 p.m.
	6	Thunderstorm 5 p.m.
	7	Hy. Rain, 3 to 11 a.m.

	15–16	Many Meteors
	23	Thunderstorm (Night)
	27	Hy. S. W. Winds (Morn)
SEP.	1–3	Cold Spell
	7–11	Good Weather
OCT.	7	Great Meteor, 10:10 p.m.
NOV.	11	Thunderstorm, last of season.
	15	First Large snow
	30	Hailstorm (Night)
DEC.	27–Jan. 1, 1907	Warm Spell.
	30	High Pressure (30.675)

IV. CLOUD PHOTOGRAPHY.

This work was performed by a new 6.5 × 8.5 camera. The following types were taken:

Cumulus
Cirrus
Stratus
Cirro-Stratus
Cirro-Cumulus
Cumulo-Stratus
Cumulo-Nimbus, or Thunder-Cloud.

Celestial views were also taken. The camera lens is by Darlot, body by Edwards, and back by Blair Optical Co.

V. SPECTROSCOPIC WORK.

On Dec. 24, 1906, when so many changes were made, the Prov. Meteo. Station procured a diffraction spectroscope by Ives. The object of this was to observe the condition of the atmosphere with respect to aqueous vapour. It is well known that atmospheric moisture causes a dark shaded band, called the "Rain Band", in the solar spectrum near the "D" line. This band, with respect to intensity, is observed daily, and is, as an index to coming rain, far superior to the hygrometer, as will be at once seen by the scientific reader. As a frontispiece to this volume, I give a few charts of atmospheric spectra.

VI. RECORDS.

The records of the Prov. Meteo. Station are preserved in full by the "Science Year Book", an English publication, which we have always used. This is open to free public inspection at any time. We have arranged with the U. S. Gov't for their form No. 1009 (Monthly) and these will be sent, duly filled out by us, to anyone, for $1.00 per year. Any single month's form will be given for ten cents. Forecasts are sent daily for $3.50 per year. The monthly gov't forms contain data on Temperature, Rainfall, Wind, and Weather, with monthly summaries.

VII. FORECASTS.

Every morning, at 9.00, a forecast is issued for the following day, from observations taken at 8.30 a.m. These are the result of the most careful study, observation, calculation, and comparison, and as a test of their accuracy, all are referred to the past. Since the addition of the spectroscope they are even surer than before, as it is practically impossible for precipitations to occur without giving previously a rain band in the spectrum.

VIII. CO-OPERATION.

A lesser station is in co-operation with us. This, No. 2, is conducted by Mr. H. B. Munroe of 66 Paterson St. The director of No. 2 notes only temperature and general weather, observing at 8 a.m., at which hour all of the stations formerly observed. No forecasts are issued by Mr. Munroe.

———

The Providence Meteorological Station was founded Jan. 24, 1904, and has since made no halt in progress or improvement. We hope that our work during 1907 may keep up to this standard, and we are certain that it will.

IX. GENERAL DATA.

BY THE MAIN STATION NO. I.

Highest Temp.	96	On May 18 and Jun. 28
Lowest Temp.	00	On Jan. 10.
Mean Temp.	48.	
Greatest Rainfall,	3.25 inches, on May 27–9	
Highest Barometer,	30.961, on Feb. 11, 1906.	

FINIS

EDITOR'S NOTE Unpublished (transcript, AHT). One of the few surviving documents testifying to HPL's interest in meteorology and to his diligence in recording notable meteorological phenomena for the entire year 1906.

Notes

1. The reference is to Harold Bateman Munroe, one of HPL's boyhood friends. Munroe also imitated HPL by issuing his own hectographed newspapers, in the manner of HPL's *Rhode Island Journal of Astronomy*.

CELESTIAL OBJECTS FOR ALL

An Easy Guide to Astronomical Observation with
Opera, and Field Glasses.

By H. P. Lovecraft.
Author of "A Brief Course in Astronomy"[1]

Educational Series, No. 6.

ILLUSTRATED
And with a series of 11 special maps.

FIRST EDITION

PROVIDENCE
The R. I. Journal
1907

FIRST EDITION
PUBLISHED JULY 28, 1907
H. P. Lovecraft

Preface

The following little treatise is designed to furnish the amateur astronomer with a list of objects for observation which may be studied with such simple instruments as are possessed by all. The greater part of this work is also printed in "A Brief Course in Astronomy" by the same author.

No attempt has been made to give practical exercises requiring angular measurement, since the treatise is purely popular.

H. P. LOVECRAFT

Providence, July, 1907.

Good Supplementary Reading

Burritt, The Geography of the Heavens
Maunder, Astronomy Without a Telescope
Serviss, Astronomy With an Opera Glass[2]

Contents

FRONTISPIECE: LUNAR MAP.[3]

LIST OF ILLUSTRATIONS AND STAR MAPS

Note

The greater part of this book has been incorporated into the author's larger work, A BRIEF COURSE IN ASTRONOMY.

Chapter I   Introduction

Of all the erroneous ideas that have become rooted in the human mind, none is so baseless as the belief that large telescopes are required for the popular study of the heavens. It is true that for close observation of the surfaces of the planets, the figures of the nebulae, etc., quite good sized instruments are needed, but it is truer still that even an opera or field glass is quite enough for the observations which an amateur would be likely to make.

THE INSTRUMENT

The selection of a suitable instrument is a task of more or less difficulty, for although a field glass will give more power than an opera glass, yet the latter is far more pleasant and comfortable to use, since the image is brighter, the field of view is larger, and there is less apparent tremor when supported by the hands alone.

Hence I would advise those who wish to observe merely as a past-time to procure an opera glass, and those who intend to pursue the study further, perhaps with a telescope, eventually, to procure a good field glass, which, although not quite so convenient to use, will amply repay its purchaser. The really best plan is to own a glass of both kinds, using the opera glass on stars, and the other on the observation of sun, moon, and planets. All of the objects described in these pages are visible with an opera glass, unless the contrary is distinctly stated.

Opera glasses are usually made to magnify about 3 diameters, field glasses, 6. The reader should be very careful to procure a glass in which the fields of view of both tubes blend exactly into one circle. If this precaution is neglected, it will cost the observer much time and patience in attempting to view celestial objects.

OBSERVATION

It is assumed that the reader has some elementary knowledge of astronomy, and some degree of familiarity with the constellations, so I will at once proceed to the subject of observation.

The chief point to be mentioned in connection with the subject is the caution to serve objects only when they are on or near the meridian. Otherwise they are seen through many layers of atmosphere, hence are not as clear as when high in the sky. Always wait until it is very dark before attempting to observe delicate stellar objects, and never attempt to study them in bright moonlight. On the other hand, the moon and planets are best seen in twilight, indeed, the author has secured most beautiful views of Venus' crescent at this time of the day.

In attempting to glimpse faint clusters, nebulae, etc., it is advisable to observe from the side, rather than the front of the eye, since the former is more sensitive to small quantities of light. Lastly, do not be discouraged if you fail to see every object as described, for the first time, for celestial observation is more a matter of skill and eye-training than would ordinarily be supposed.

Chapter II   The Solar System

The various orbs that compose the great system of which our own earth is a part are the first objects to be considered. The natural order in which the solar system is taken up begins with the sun, and goes outward, hence we will consider each object in an isolated manner.

THE SUN

If the observer's glass be properly covered with dark glass, a few spots may be seen on the sun, and a powerful field glass might show the penumbrae of some of them. The glass for eye protection is preferably of a bluish color, and must nearly approach opacity. It is best that it should be fastened to the large end of the glass. If sufficiently large, one piece will serve both barrels.

MERCURY

There is nothing of interest on the surface of Mercury for opera glass observers, yet the little planet forms a pleasing sight when near its elongation. It should be sought for when the sun is about an hour below the horizon, low down, directly over the sunrise or sunset point.

VENUS

When near inferior conjunction, the crescent phase of this planet is plainly visible with the smallest of glasses, indeed, many have claimed to have seen it with the naked eye. It would be well for the amateur to try this, as a test of keen eyesight.

THE EARTH

Next in the solar system comes our own earth, but as that is so obviously ought of the domain of opera-glass astronomy, we will only consider its satellite, the moon.

THE MOON

We now come to the most interesting of celestial objects, whatever be the means employed for observation. The frontispiece is a map of the moon as seen in an opera glass. All the features depicted may be clearly discerned. In observing the moon, all objects to be seen, except dark plains or rays, must be near the terminator, or line separating illumined from unillumined parts, because otherwise they cast no shadows, therefore being practically invisible.

In lunar geography, or "Selenography" as it is called, Latin names are used, hence Mare means Sea; Sinus, Gulf; Oceanus, Ocean, and so on. These names were applied at a time when the dark spots were thought to be large bodies of water. Mountains and volcanic craters are named after great scientists.

I will now proceed to describe a few of the most striking formations. (The numbers refer to the frontispiece)

The Mare Crisium (A) is the first object visible on the young moon, being a small plain surrounded by high mountains. A cap, called Promontorium Agarum, projects into the Mare, and is visible in an opera glass. The Mare Serenetatis (B) is first seen about four days after new moon. It is in many respects similar to the Mare Crisium. The eastern (left hand) edge of this plain is bounded by the Apennine range of hills (1) which is plainly defined even in a very tiny glass. South of the Mare Serenetatis lies the Mare Tranquilitatis (C) which is devoid of interest. Maria (plural of Mare) Nectaris (D) and Foecunditatis (E), which are still farther south, are attractive in outline. Among the Western crater-mountains are Cleomedes (2) north of the Mare Crisium, and Langrenus (3) of the Mare Foecunditatis. Between the Maria Crisium and Serenetatis lies Proclus (4) a small, but very brilliant mountain. East of the Mare Tranquilitatis is situated a group of three fine craters, Theophilus (5), Cyrillus (6), and Catharina (7). A short distance east of these is another fine group of three, Ptolemy (8), Alphonsus (9), and Arzachel (10). South of this set is the crater Tycho, the centre of an immense system of lunar rays, or the long bright streaks that radiate from some formations. Strange to say, the lunar rays are not visible except at full moon, when nearly all other features are almost invisible. Below Tycho are two craters, Clavius (20) and Maginus (19) which are very imposing in appearance when on the terminator, but which disappear almost entirely at full moon. Returning to the plains, we note the Mare Imbrium (G) east of the Mare Serenitatis, and the Oceanus Procellarum (H) still further east. Connecting the Mare Serenitatis with the Oceanus is the Mare Vaporum (F). On the southern border of the Oceanus lie the Maria Humorum (I), and Nubium (J). These, with the Mare Frigoris (K) in the extreme north, finish our list of dark markings. The crater Copernicus (12), the centre of a fine ray system, is situated in the Oceanus Procellarum. A telescope greatly improves the appearance of this crater, yet in anything it is a beautiful object. North of Copernicus, at the end of the Apennines, is Eratosthenes (13) famous as one of the possible locations of lunar life. Above the Mare Imbrium lies Plato (14), a large but shallow crater, to the east of which is the Sinus Iridum (15) a beautiful "bay" surrounded by fine mountains. Some distance to the southeast lie two craters, Aristarchus (16) and Herodotus (17). These are very small, yet are by far the most brilliant spots on the moon. Further south, and east of the Oceanus Procellarum, Grimaldi (18), a dark crater, completes our list of opera glass craters. Besides those mentioned, many other small craters will be seen, giving a most pleasing and ragged aspect to lunar scenery, in fact, the study of the moon has few equals, no matter what instrument be used. A most instructive pastime is to map the dark spots on the full moon, and compare the result with the frontispiece.

MARS

The most powerful field glass will probably fail to show the planet Mars as a disc. The reddish color, however, is very pronounced.

THE ASTEROIDS

These are totally beyond the powers of opera and field glasses.

JUPITER

The four satellites of Jupiter may be seen with any field glass, and an opera glass will probably reveal two or three.

SATURN

Under favourable conditions, the ring of Saturn may be seen as a slight elongation.

URANUS AND NEPTUNE

Both of these planets are visible as faint stars in opera glasses, yet their study seldom repays the observer.

COMETS

With the aid of opera glasses, highly interesting drawings of these objects have been obtained. In this work it is well to use the most powerful glass available.

METEORS

Although the observation of these interesting objects is a matter too sudden to admit of the use of an opera glass, yet all should watch vigilantly for meteors during the night. For each one, the following data must be noted: (1) Time of visibility. (2) Estimated brightness, in comparison to well known stars. (3) Duration of visibility. (4) Path in the sky, told by familiar constellations. Such a record, faithfully kept, will later prove of great value.

Such is the Solar System as it may be seen by all. We will next turn our glasses to the sidereal heavens, or domain of other suns.

Chapter III   The Siderial Heavens

Of all the work which may be done with opera and field glasses, none save the study of the moon is as attractive as the study of the siderial heavens.

Here may be found objects in plenty which are amply within the powers of any opera or field glass. In the following catalogue of celestial objects, the author has selected those objects such as may be easily and conveniently seen from the Latitude of the Central United States.

The number following the name of each constellation refers to the map on which that group may be found. The accompanying series of 11 star maps has been prepared expressly for this work, and shows the region of sky near the meridian for the 20th of the given month at 9 p. m. They are good for any year. Only such objects as are described in the catalogue have been entered on the charts.

A SELECT CATALOGUE OF 90 CELESTIAL OBJECTS VISIBLE IN OPERA AND FIELD GLASSES. ARRANGED ALPHABETICALLY BY CONSTELLATIONS.

Compiled by H. P. Lovecraft.

ANDROMEDA (X)

31M, near y, Great Nebula, appears as an ellipse of misty light. Brightest at centre.

AQUARIUS (VIII and IX)

τ, Double star, colors, white and orange.
104, Naked eye double. Many fine star fields near μ and ε.

ARGO NAVIS (II)

κ, μ, ζ, Double stars.
π, Orange star.
38, Cluster.
46M, Cluster.
93M, Good Cluster.

AURIGA (I)

33⁷, 37M, 38M, Field Glass Clusters. Near β, fine star cluster.

BOOTES (V)

α, called Arcturus, Bright reddish orange star, surrounded by a cluster.

CANCER (II)

44M, Fine cluster, called "Praespe".

CANIS MAJOR (II)

α, Sirius, or the dog star. Brightest star in the entire sky.
ν, Triple Star.
22, Red Star.
41M, Cluster.
Fine star fields between δ and o.

CANIS MINOR (II)

β, called Gomeisa, Triple star.

CAPRICORNUS (VIII)

α, called Giedi, Double star, very easy.
β, called Dabih, Double star, blue and yellow.

CASSIOPEIA (X)

Fine region of the milky way.

CEPHEUS (X)

δ, Double star, blue and orange.
μ, Red star.

CETUS (XI)

o, called Mira, famous variable, mags. 2–9.
χ, ζ, Double stars.

COMA BERENICES (IV)

Beautiful and close aggregation of stars.

CORONA BOREALIS (V)

Fine semicircle of stars.

CORVUS (VIII)

ζ, Double Star.

CYGNUS (VIII)

β, called Albireo, fine field glass double, colors, blue and yellow.
o, Multiple star. Double to naked eye, triple in opera glass, quadruple in field glass.
Fine star fields near α and γ. Milky Way is very rich in Cygnus.

DRACO (VII)

γ, Orange Star.
ν, Double.

ERIDANUS (I)

o, Double Star, white and orange. Star group near β.

GEMINI (II)

35M, star cluster, one of the most beautiful in the heavens. Fine star fields near α and β.

HERCULES (VI)

13M, Fine cluster, but rather beyond the powers of an opera or field glass.

LEO (III)

β, called Denebola, Double star, triple in field glasses.
γ, Double star, yellow and white.
ε, Triple star.
ζ, Quadruple star.

LEPUS (I)

γ, Double star. Near ι, very red star.

LIBRA (V)

α, Double star.
β, Green star.

LYRA (VII)

ε, Double star. A telescope reveals each component to be double.
ζ, Double star, quite difficult.

MONOCEROS (II)

2^7 and 50M, clusters.
Fine star fields around 8, 13, and 17.

ORION (I)

π^5, Double star, white and orange.
42M, Great nebula, surrounding the star ϑ. Great many small stars near γ and φ, and near belt.

PEGASUS (IX)

π, Double star, Easy Test for even naked eye.

PERSEUS (I)

β, called Algol, famous variable. Great cluster, finest in heavens.
34M, cluster.
Multitudes of stars near α.
ζ, Quintuple star, components in a st. line.

SAGITTARIUS (VII)

8M, Combination of a star cluster and nebula.
24M, Beautiful cluster.
25M, Another fine cluster.
Milky way is very rich in Sagittarius.

SCORPIO (VI)

α, called Antares, very red star of 1st magnitude.
δ, Small, fine pair of stars.
ζ, Double, blue and red, near it are other stars and a cluster.
μ, ν, and 22, Doubles.
4M, 6M, and 7M are good clusters.

SERPENTARIUS (VI)

Also called Ophiuchus et Serpens.
ϑ, Field glass double, surrounded by swarm of stars.
ρ, Triple star.

TAURUS (I)

θ, κ, σ, ν, Double stars.
The Hyades: "V" shaped cluster containing Aldebaran, a bright reddish star.
The Pleiades: A cluster of 6 stars visible to the naked eye, incalculable number in a good field glass.

URSA MAJOR (IV)

α, called Dubhe, difficult double.
ζ, called Mizar. Has a naked eye companion called "Alcor". Field glass shows still another companion.

URSA MINOR (V)

α, The pole star, Double in opera glass, multiple in field glass.

VIRGO (IV)

Star groups near o and π.

Perhaps these pages do not contain descriptions of all the objects visible in opera or field glasses, yet the author thinks that enough has been given to arouse at least in a few readers, a new interest in astronomy, as interpreted by simple instruments, which will perhaps cause them to pursue the study further, and with more powerful apparatus.

FINIS

THE GREEK ALPHABET

The small letters are most frequently used in Astronomy. The character σ is used in the middle and at the beginning of a word. The letter ς is used at the ending only.

A α	Alpha	N ν	Nu
B β	Beta	Ξ ξ	Xi
Γ γ	Gamma	O o	Omicron
Δ δ	Delta	Π π	Pi
E ε	Epsilon	P ρ	Rho
Z ζ	Zeta	Σ σ ς	Sigma
H η	Eta	T τ	Tau
Θ θ	Theta	Υ υ	Upsilon
I ι	Iota	Φ φ	Phi
K κ	Kappa	X χ	Chi
Λ λ	Lambda	Ψ ψ	Psi
M μ	Mu	Ω ω	Omega

EDITOR'S NOTE Unpublished (transcript, AHT). An excerpt from HPL's major (but, aside from the present item, non-extant) scientific work of his teenage years, *A Brief Course in*

Astronomy (see n. 1), giving basic information on the selection of a telescope and guidelines for the observation of the planets and constellations.

Notes

1. Of this work, dating to 1906, HPL notes that "it got as far as the typed and hand-illustrated stage (circa one hundred fifty pages), though no copy survives" (*SL* 5.141).

2. The works referred to (the first and the third owned by HPL) are: Elijah Hinsdale Burritt, *The Geography of the Heavens,* and *Classbook of Astronomy* (rev. ed. 1853; *LL* 139); Edward Walter Maunder (1851–1928), *Astronomy without a Telescope* (1903); and Garrett P. Serviss (1851–1929), *Astronomy with an Opera-Glass* (8th ed. 1906; *LL* 779). Of the first, given to HPL by his maternal grandmother, Robie Alzada Place, HPL noted that it "is today the most prized volume in my library" (*SL* 1.7).

3. The frontispiece, figures, and maps are non-extant.

VENUS AND THE PUBLIC EYE

To the Editor of the Sunday Journal:
    The general ignorance of the public as regards the science of astronomy has often been noted and deplored. Garrett P. Serviss, in his well-known work entitled "Astronomy With an Opera Glass,"[1] tells of an instance in which the planet Venus was mistaken for an electrically lighted balloon by the greater part of the population of New York city. This occurred in 1887, yet the following incident tends to illustrate the lamentable fact that the public knowledge of celestial science has advanced little, if any, since then.

    While in the business section of this city on Christmas Eve, at about 6 p. m., the writer noticed excited groups of people on the street corners, and mystified individuals everywhere pointing to the western sky. Following the direction of the many upraised fingers he beheld the planet Venus, which was shining with great brilliancy, and appeared to be the centre of attraction. This great apparent concern in astronomy seemed encouraging, to say the least, and the writer began to believe that the general apathy which the public usually exhibits was being thrown off, and that an awakening of scientific interest was taking place within the breasts of the population, when this belief was shattered by remarks overheard from a knot of cultivated and apparently well-educated men.

    It seems that the general idea existed that the planet was nothing more or less than the searchlight from some airship, either that which was recently purchased by a local merchant, or that supposed to be owned by Wallace E. Tillinghast of Worcester, Mass. Upon further listening the writer heard many remarks as to the "perfect control to which the aëroplane must be subject, in order that the light shine so steadily," and many estimates of its "distance above the earth," varying from half a mile to two miles. When apprised of their error, the gentlemen of the aforementioned group exhibited only mild surprise.

    Such a revelation of general ignorance is depressing in effect. In all probability the reports of strange lights lately seen in the sky have caused the multitude to turn their gaze heavenward, and to seize upon Venus, which is by far the brightest of all star-like objects, as the searchlight of the supposed "airship," for which they really look in vain.

Yet, actually, the appearance of Venus should not cause people of intelligence to indulge in such suppositions, as its brilliant presence in the heavens is by no means uncommon. Even now it is not as bright as it will be next month.

The moral of the preceding is that if the general public will not avail itself of the astronomical information afforded by the publication of Prof. Upton's excellent articles in the Journal on the first of each month,[2] suitable free lectures should be provided to impart such knowledge to it.

H. P. LOVECRAFT.

Providence, Dec. 24.

EDITOR'S NOTE   FP: *Providence Sunday Journal* (26 December 1909): Sec. 2, p. 5. One of the few surviving works from HPL's period of hermitry (1908–14) following his withdrawal from high school—a period during which HPL "could hardly bear to see or speak to anyone, & liked to shut out the world by pulling down dark shades & using artificial light" (HPL to R. H. Barlow, 10 April 1934; ms., JHL). If nothing else, the present letter testifies that HPL did venture out of doors on rare occasions. For his continuing interest in astronomy, see his "Astronomical Notebook" (Appendix, p. 332).

Notes

1. See "Celestial Objects for All," n. 2.

2. Winslow Upton, professor of astronomy at Brown University and a friend of the Lovecraft family (see *SL* 1.21, 38), wrote a long-running monthly astronomy column in the *Providence Journal*. For this reason, HPL's own astronomy columns had to be written for other local papers.

[ASTRONOMY ARTICLES FOR THE PROVIDENCE *EVENING NEWS*]

THE JANUARY SKY

At the beginning of the year 1914, the evening sky presents a spectacle of more than ordinary splendour, for besides the usual brilliant constellations of the season, there are visible two of the brightest and most interesting of the planets; Mars and Saturn.

The chief astronomical event of the month of January will be the opposition of Mars on the 5th, at which time both the planet and the earth will be on the same side of the sun; Mars therefore approaching nearer to us and shining more brilliantly, than in any other part of its revolution. It is visible each evening, high up in the eastern sky, rising about sunset, and being situated in the constellation Gemini. There are two very bright fixed stars in this group, but the planet so far surpasses either of them in lustre, and is of such a pronounced reddish colour, that it cannot be mistaken. The present opposition of Mars will offer no such favourable opportunity for the study of the planet's surface as was afforded by the opposition of 1909, since the latter occurred under exceptional conditions which are found only once in about 15 or 17 years. It may be well here to remark, that the date of the arrival of Mars at its exact astronomical point of opposition often differs by several days from the moment of closest proximity to the earth.

Saturn is now very well situated for observation, having been in opposition on Dec. 7. It may be seen quite near Mars, being in the constellation Taurus. The planet is most easily found by noticing the prominent group of stars in Taurus called "The Hyades", which have the shape of the letter "V", with a bright ruddy star at the top of the left-hand branch. If we imagine this branch to be prolonged, we shall at a short distance encounter Saturn, which is almost directly in line with it. While the object is pleasing even to the unassisted vision, it is far more interesting when seen through a telescope, for then only can its marvellous system of encircling rings be seen. The angle at which we behold these rings varies greatly during the long revolutions of Saturn around the sun. In 1907 they were turned edgewise toward the earth, therefore being invisible, but at present they are shewn under almost the best possible conditions. They will not disappear again until 1931.

Jupiter has now withdrawn from view, being in conjunction on the 20th, and consequently lost in the sun's rays throughout the month.

Venus has likewise retired to the vicinity of the sun. Though it might during the first few days of January be espied in the morning twilight just before sunrise, low down near the eastern horizon, it will soon have vanished completely.

Mercury will make no appearance in the coming month, since its superior conjunction falls on the 24th. Uranus, in conjunction on the 28th, is also invisible.

The telescopic planet Neptune arrives at its opposition on the 17th. But the event is without interest to the amateur.

The moon's phases will occur as follows:

First Quarter, 4th ....8:09 a.m.
Full Moon, 12th ....12:09 a.m.
Last Quarter, 18th.. 7:30 p.m.
New Moon, 26th .... 1:34 p.m.

Our satellite comes to Perigee on the 18th and to Apogee on the 3d and 31st. On the 9th it will be in conjunction with Saturn and on the 11th with Mars.

On Jan. 3 the earth reaches its perihelion, or point of nearest approach to the sun. The days are now lengthening perceptibly, the 31st being over three-quarters of an hour longer than the 1st.

There is now under observation a new comet, visible in small telescopes and daily growing brighter. It cannot yet be told whether or not it will become visible to the naked eye, but if its brilliancy continues to increase at the present rate it will probably do so.

Turning from the phenomena of the solar system to those of the sidereal heavens, we find in the January evening sky the brightest stars and most striking constellations of the entire celestial sphere. It will be my custom in these articles to describe the stars each month as they appear at about 9 p.m. on the 15th, which description will roughly answer for all the evenings of the month.

Of supreme interest, lying almost directly south in the sky, is the immense and magnificently brilliant constellation Orion. This group is of all stellar arrangements the most impressive and unmistakable; once seen, it is never forgotten. In its northeast corner is the bright reddish star Betelgeux, a gem of prime magnitude, and in the southwestern extremity shines the no less radiant Rigel, whose light is bluish-white in hue. In the centre of the constellation is that famous diagonal row of three stars of the second magnitude which is variously called "The Belt", "The Ell and Yard", or "The Three Kings". Below the belt hangs that somewhat curving, but roughly vertical line of smaller stars which is known as "The Sword", and which contains the Great Nebula of Orion, an object of much renown in astronomy, but which to be well seen requires the use of a telescope.

Above Orion is the Zodiacal group Taurus, the Bull, a constellation second in splendour only to Orion itself. In Taurus are those two famous asterians called "The Pleiades", or "The Seven Stars", and the "V"-shaped "Hyades", which latter contains at the top of its left-hand branch the bright star Aldebaran.

Westward of Taurus is Aries, the Ram, another Zodiacal group, and eastward along the Zodiac lies Gemini, or the Twins, wherein the two heavenly brothers, Castor and Pollux, are each represented by a brilliant star. Still farther eastward is Cancer, the Crab, which contains the celebrated cluster of stars called "Praespe", or "The Manger".

The Via Lactea, or Milky Way, flows across the sky from the northwestern to the southeastern horizon, bearing within it successively Cepheus, a rather uninteresting group; Cassiopeia, a bright constellation shaped like a flattened "W"; Perseus, a lustrous assemblage of stars which contains a great cluster, and the famous variable star Algol; Auriga, the Wagoner, whose principal star is the brilliant Capella; Canis Minor, the Lesser Dog, with its bright star Procyon; and grandest of all, Canis Major, or the Greater Dog, in which shines that most luminous of all fixed stars, the piercingly radiant Sirius.

Reverting to the northwest, we observe Andromeda, which extends just south of Cassiopeia. Andromeda contains a brilliant and famous nebula, which is barely visible to the naked eye, but which most persons not familiar with the heavens fail to glimpse.

Northward we see Ursa Major, the Greater Bear, with its familiar "Plough", or "Dipper", now ascending from the horizon. Following the direction pointed out by the two stars forming the front of the Dipper's bowl, we come to Polaris, the practically stationary guardian of the north celestial pole, or place in the sky whither points the upper end of the earth's axis. Polaris marks the end of the tail of Ursa Minor, the Lesser Bear, or, to use a less classical nomenclature, the end of the handle of the "Lesser Dipper", which now seems to hang down toward the horizon.

The constellations around the horizon, enumerated from the north point eastward, are Draco, the Dragon, a long sinuous group lying beneath Ursa Minor; Leo, the Lion, a splendid constellation not yet risen high enough for profitable observation; parts of Hydra and Argo Navis; Columba, the Dove, above which lies Lepus, the Hare; Eridanus, a group whose brightest star, Achernar, is never seen in the latitude of Providence; Cetus, the Whale, which contains the curious variable star Mira; Pisces, the Fishes, a Zodiacal group; Pegasus, the Winged Horse; and finally, the brilliant Cygnus, or the Swan, whose beauty is hidden by its low place in the sky, but which will be a notable object by next summer.

EDITOR'S NOTE FP: *EN* 44, No. 38 (1 January 1914): 6. The first of 53 monthly columns for the Providence *Evening News*, the most expansive and interesting of HPL's astronomy columns.

THE FEBRUARY SKY

Mercury, the least seen of all the principal planets, will assume its most favourable aspect in the evening sky of the coming month. Being always near the sun, this small body discloses itself only by twilight, either low in the west just after sunset, as in the present instance, or close to the eastern horizon just before the break of day. The difficulty of observing Mercury is very great; indeed, it is related that the celebrated Copernicus, under the skies of Prussia, could never in his entire life catch sight of it, and that the late Mr. Hind, an English astronomer, saw it but once without the aid of a telescope.[1] In our more southern latitude, however, it is by no means infrequently beheld. The planet attains its best position, that of greatest apparent distance from the sun, on the 22nd, and will be visible for a few days before and after that time, twinkling like a bright reddish spark in the west about three-quarters of an hour after sunset. On the 26th, Mercury will be near the thin crescent of the infant moon, which latter may assist in its identification. Both will be extremely close to the horizon, and must be sought for as soon after sunset as the increasing darkness permits; even then the observer who dwells amidst the structures and smoke of the city is not likely to find them. Since Mercury is an inferior planet, or one which lies within the orbit of the earth, it shews in the telescope a complete set of phases like those of the moon. During the present period of visibility, the planet's phase will change from a gibbous figure to a crescent, being a half-circle on the 22nd.

Mars, though past its opposition, continues to shine refulgently in the southern evening sky. It is now moving westward amongst the stars, but will resume its direct eastward motion on the 12th of the month. This planet has lately been made the subject of so much careless and speculative writing, that the public is in danger of acquiring very false notions concerning its nature and the evidences of intelligent life upon its surface. The much-advertised "Martian canals", whose apparent rectilinear form and regular arrangement have led a few visionary observers to believe them artificial, are by no means the definite, prominent objects that they seem in modern drawings; and while they do present a certain semblance of straightness and regularity, there is nevertheless nothing in their aspect which could cause a conservative astronomer to think them other than natural features. They are but seldom seen, and are never distinctly defined, even in the largest of telescopes; in fact, the normal telescopic appearance of Mars is best shewn by drawings made before their discovery, when observers sought less to depict lines and shadings which lie at the extreme limit of visibility. As to animal life on Mars, we may say only that there is as yet no good proof either of its existence or of its absence.

Saturn, which lies westward of Mars in the heavens, is second to it in lustre. It is now approaching its quadrature, setting at about half past two in the morning during the middle part of the month. The rings are inclined 26 degrees of arc toward the earth, being within one degree of their greatest possible inclination. It is universally known at the present time that these remarkable objects are in reality nothing more than dense aggregations of tiny revolving masses, which, on account of their great numbers and peculiar arrangements, give the appearance of solid, flat, concentric rings. Science has indeed progressed since 1837, when Thomas Dick, in his volume on "Celestial Scenery", declared them to be solid, probably inhabited, and capable of sustaining a population of 8,078,102,266,080.[2]

The superior conjunction of Venus will occur on February 11th, wherefore that planet cannot be seen during the month. Jupiter and Uranus are also lost to view. Neptune, invisible to the naked eye, lies on the border between the constellations Gemini and Cancer, and can there be found with a properly mounted telescope on any clear evening.

The phases of the moon will occur as follows:

First Quarter, 3rd ....5:33 a.m.
Full Moon, 10th .... 12:35 p.m.
Last Quarter, 17th...4:38 a.m.
New Moon, 24th .... 7:03 p.m.

The moon will adorn the evening sky from the 1st to the 13th, and again during the last two or three days of the month. Perigee is on the 13th; Apogee on the 28th. Our satellite will be in conjunction with the following planets on the following dates: Saturn, 5th; Mars, 7th; Mercury, 26th. Between the times of first quarter and full moon, it will run high in the heavens, running low about the time of last quarter.

At the time of new moon on the 24th, an annular eclipse of the sun will take place, which will not, however, be visible in this part of the world. As seen in the South Pacific Ocean, the moon passes centrally over the face of the sun, yet fails to cover the latter completely, leaving visible a thin ring or "annulus" of light. Annular eclipses occur when the moon is near its Apogee, or point of greatest distance from the earth, at which times it shews a smaller apparent disc than the sun's.

In the month of February, the standard clock and the sun-dial come to their closest agreement, thus placing noon exactly midway between sunrise and sunset. The length of days increases 1 hour and 11 minutes during the month.

In the evening sky of February we find most of the brilliant constellations which we noticed last month still in sight, though somewhat changed in location. Cygnus and Pegasus have disappeared in the west, while Leo, Hydra, and the ship Argo are becoming prominent in the east. Gemini, the highest of all the Zodiacal constellations, now occupies the meridian, its bright star Castor performing its transit but about 10 degrees south of the zenith. We are accustomed to associate the name Cancer with the highest point of the Zodiac, but we must not forget that the slow processional motion of the celestial equator around the ecliptic has carried each Zodiacal constellation out of the sign or place which it formerly occupied, so that the famous thirteen signs of the Zodiac, which represent thirteen different parts of the ecliptic, have, although they retain their original names, been left behind by the thirteen respective constellations of like title, and are each occupied by the constellation next preceding. The sign of Cancer, at the northern limit of the ecliptic, was formerly marked by the constellation Cancer, but the latter has been carried beyond, and Gemini, the constellation next preceding, has taken its place.

Looking northward this month, we find Ursa Major east of the pole star, and preparing to ascend above it, while Cassiopeia is declining in the west. Ursa Minor is below and to the right of the pole, and Draco lies beyond it in the same direction. Polaris itself, sometimes called by its Greek name Cynosura, is ever of interest. Its lack of apparent motion sets it apart from the other stars of the sky, and it has for centuries been the guiding beacon of the mariner. However, the same slow processional motion which carries the equator around the ecliptic, shifting the Zodiacal constellations ahead of the signs, acts as well in the polar regions, carrying the poles of the heavens around those of the ecliptic, so that Cynosura has not always occupied, and will not always occupy, its present important position. In early Egyptian times the star Thuban, in Draco, was at the north celestial pole, and in the course of thousands of years to come, the bright Deneb, in Cygnus, and the resplendent Vega, in Lyra, will successively reign in place of Cynosura.

The constellations around the horizon, reckoned eastward from the north point, are Boötes, the Herdsman, as yet but partially risen; the most western portion of the Zodiacal group Virgo, the Virgin; the central regions of Hydra, the Water-Snake, with Crater, the Cup, which stands upon his back; the northern half of Argo Navis, or the ship Argo, now seen at its best; the insignificant Columbia Noachi, or Noah's Dove; fragments of the extensive constellations Eridanus, Cetus, and Pisces; and finally Andromeda, still seen to advantage, but soon to sink from view.

The chill discomforts of winter are now mitigated by celestial prophecies of returning spring. In February the sun enters the sign of Pisces, or the Fishes, which typifies, according to the ancient inventors of the Zodiac, that season when the streams are freed from their icy bondage and afford a plentiful supply in the line and net of the early fishermen.

EDITOR'S NOTE FP: *EN* 44, No. 63 (31 January 1914): 6.

Notes

1. John Russell Hind (1823–1895), British astronomer who discovered 10 asteroids, 2 comets, and several variable stars. See his book, *The Solar System* (1852).
2. Thomas Dick (1774–1857), *Celestial Scenery* (1837). The volume is included in Dick's *Works* (1849; 10 vols. in 5), owned by HPL (*LL* 240).

THE MARCH SKY

Jupiter, the brightest of all the planets save Venus alone, is now visible for the first time this year, appearing low in the southeastern sky just before sunrise. Its time of rising precedes that of the sun by 1 hour and 16 minutes on the 1st of the month; by 3 hours and 8 minutes on the 31st. Jupiter is absolutely unmistakable, being at present situated in the constellation Capricornus, which contains no bright stars. The nearest star of any considerable lustre is Altair, in the Eagle, but this object is much less brilliant and far higher up in the heavens than is the planet, so that the latter ought under no circumstances to be confounded with it.

Mars and Saturn continue to be the principal planets of the evening sky. Both are decreasing in brilliancy, but Mars the more rapidly, for while last month Mars outshone Saturn, we find that in March the latter is the brighter of the two. On the 1st of the month, Saturn sets at 1:18 a.m.; Mars at 3:37 a.m. On the 31st, Saturn sets at 11:23 p.m. and Mars at 3:07 a.m. Saturn is in the constellation Taurus, Mars in Gemini; wherefore both lie in the western heavens during the evening hours. In the telescope Mars now begins to shew a decidedly gibbous aspect, which will be most marked at its time of quadrature next month. Since this planet is situated beyond the orbit of the earth, it can never exhibit a complete set of phases, but merely becomes slightly shaded off at the edge turned opposite the sun, about the time when in its apparent course it reaches a point 90 degrees from that luminary. Saturn is in quadrature, or 90 degrees from the sun, on the 2nd of this month, but on account of its remoteness it shews no departure from its normal figure. A good telescope three inches in aperture will exhibit the black line of division between the two outer rings, the faint belts on the planet's surface, and two or three of the satellites.

Mercury and Venus are at present too near the sun for observation, but will both appear next month; Mercury in the morning and Venus in the evening sky. The faint Uranus is gradually withdrawing from the solar glares, but it presents no features of interest to the casual observer. It now lies in the constellation Capricornus, quite near to Jupiter, with which it will be in conjunction on the 4th. Neptune may be found with a telescope in right ascension 7 h. 50 min. north declination 20 deg. 37 minutes. This is almost on the dividing line between Cancer and Gemini.

The moon's phases will be as follows:

First Quarter, 5th ....12:03 a.m.
Full Moon, 11th .... 11:19 p.m.
Last Quarter, 18th.. 2:39 p.m.
New Moon, 26th .... 1:09 p.m.

Perigee is on the 12th, Apogee on the 27th. The moon runs high above the 5th and low above the 18th. On the 4th it will be in conjunction with Saturn; on the 6th with Mars; and on the 22nd with Jupiter.

On the night of the 11–12th, there will be a partial eclipse, in which the earth's shadow will cover nine-tenths of the moon's diameter. The entire phenomenon will be visible in Providence, the various circumstances taking place at the following times:

Moon enters penumbra ....March 11, 8:41 p.m.
Moon enters shadow ....March 11, 9:42 p.m.
Middle of eclipse...March 11, 11:13 p.m.
Moon leaves shadow ....March 12, 12:44 a.m.
Moon leaves penumbra ....March 12, 1:45 a.m.

The penumbra is the semi-shadow made by the partial interception of the sunlight from the moon by the earth. The passage of the moon through the penumbra appears to us as if the lunar disc were being traversed by light clouds.

Transferring our attention to the constellations, we behold all the splendid groups of winter now advanced to the western sky, while the east is occupied by the less striking stars of spring. The Zodiacal constellation now in the meridian is the small and inconspicuous Cancer, remarkable only for the well-known cluster of stars called "Praespe" or "The Manger", which is visible to the naked eye as a faint, diffuse patch of light, situated midway between the two stars Gamma and Delta Cancri. The true stellar nature of Praespe was one of the first telescopic discoveries of Galileo, and may be perceived even in a good opera glass. South of Cancer, the head and neck of Hydra, the longest constellation in all the heavens, have now reached the meridian. Hydra bears upon his back two smaller groups; Crater, the Cup, and east of it, Corvus, the Crow, both visible in the southeastern sky on March evenings.

In the north, Ursa Major is soaring aloft, though not yet passing over the pole. Below it lies Draco, whose head is now turned toward the east, as if to view Hercules, an extensive group at present but partly risen. Low in the heavens to the west of the pole, Cepheus and Cassiopeia are visible, the latter making nearly a right angle with the horizon. Polaris is at any place fixed as far above the horizon, as the place is north of the earth's equator. Since our latitude is about 42 degrees, it follows that we always see Polaris about 42 degrees above the northern horizon, whilst all the other stars and constellations appear to revolve around it. Of course, those which lie less than 42 degrees from the pole never set, but remain ever visible, describing complete circles in the heavens, and being called "circumpolar". The principal groups which are circumpolar in this latitude are Ursa Major, Ursa Minor, Cassiopeia, Cepheus, and Draco.

High in the southeast are now seen Coma Berenices and the stately Zodiacal constellation Leo. On the horizon, considered in order eastward from the north point, are Hercules, not yet fully risen; Corona Borealis, or the Northern Crown; Boötes, with the bright ruddy star, Arcturus, shining conspicuously; the Zodiacal constellation Virgo, with the lustrous Spica; the tail of Hydra, with Corvus perched upon it; the long extent of Argo Navis; the unimportant Columba Noachi; some remnants of the departing Eridanus; the Zodiacal group Aries; several stars of Andromeda; and lastly, just beneath the north pole, those few faint stars of Cygnus which fall within the limits of the circumpolar region.

On March 21, at 6 a.m., the sun reaches the vernal equinox and enters the Zodiacal sign Aries, crossing the celestial equator on its annual northward journey and opening the welcome season of spring. Until 1752, the phenomenon roughly marked the beginning of the common year, which commenced on March 25, but when the Gregorian calendar was adopted the date of New Year's was set back to Jan. 1. The days gain 1 hour and 24 minutes in length this month, being nearly equal to the nights just before the time of the sun's entrance into Aries.

A recent astronomical discovery of considerable interest is that of a very large asteroid, or minor planet, announced in February by the Rev. Joel H. Metcalf, a well-known amateur observer of Winchester, Mass.[1] The new-found object is at present thought to have a diameter of about 500 miles, which, if correct, would make it one of the largest, if not actually the largest, of all the asteroids. Later investigators may prove that this hastily estimated diameter is much too great, but we can in any event be certain that the body is one of no mean dimensions. Dr. Metcalf also strongly suspects that he has found three new asteroids besides the one of whose existence he is sure.

The asteroids are a numerous group of tiny planets which lie between the orbits of Mars and Jupiter, and whose discovery was prompted by the belief that, according to the law of proportion of planetary distances, some body ought to exist in that region. Giuseppe Piazzi, a celebrated astronomer of Palermo, Sicily, commenced the long series of discoveries on the night of Jan. 1, 1801, by finding that object which he later named Ceres, after the tutelary divinity of his native island.[2] Within seven years three more asteroids were discovered—Pallas in 1802 by Olbers, Juno in 1804 by Harding, and Vesta in 1807 by Olbers. In 1845 a fifth, called Astraea, was added to the list by Hencke.[3] Three were found in 1847, and since that time no year has passed without the discovery of from one to over 100. Almost 1000 minor planets are now known to exist, the rate of discovery being so rapid that great difficulty is had in keeping account of those already found. The most recent receive no names, but are identified by numerals. Photography is now the principal means used in searching for new asteroids, cameras being mounted and turned by clockwork so that they may follow the apparent diurnal motion of the heavens during exposures of several hours, the plates then shewing the fixed stars as dots, but revealing as streaks any moving objects such as asteroids which may have been in the field of view. This method was first used by Dr. Max Wolf of Heidelberg, who has discovered more asteroids than any other person up to the present time.[4] Rev. Dr. Metcalf, who has discovered 40 asteroids and many comets, employs a slightly different photographic method of his own invention.

The great success of this talented clergyman as an amateur astronomer and discoverer recalls many other instances of divines, both Protestant and Catholic, who have united with their religious acquirements a profound knowledge of celestial science.

EDITOR'S NOTE FP: *EN* 44, No. 88 (2 March 1914): 8.

Notes

1. Joel H[astings] Metcalf (1866–1925), a Unitarian minister at various New England congregations with an interest in astronomy. He discovered 41 asteroids, 6 comets, and several variable stars.

2. Giuseppe Piazzi (1746–1826), Sicilian astronomer. His discovery of Ceres is related in *Risultati delle osservazioni della nuova stella scoperta il dì gennaio 1891 nell'Observatorio di Palermo* (1801).

3. HPL refers to the German astronomers Heinrich Wilhelm Matthäus Olbers (1758–1840), Carl Ludwig Harding (1765–1834), and Karl Ludwig Hencke (1793–1866).

4. Maximilian Franz Joseph Cornelius Wolf (1863–1932), German astronomer who discovered hundreds of asteroids at the Baden Observatory constructed for him by the grand duke of Baden.

THE APRIL SKY

In the month of April all the major planets will be visible; three in the morning, and four in the evening sky.

Venus, the brightest star-like object in the heavens, has now returned to view, and may be seen in the evening twilight near the western horizon. The planet sets about an hour after sunset on the 1st, and about an hour and three-quarters after sunset on the 30th. It moves during April from Pisces through Aries into Taurus, being near the Pleiades at the end of the month. Through the telescope, Venus shews a decreasing gibbous phase, as yet but little different from a full disc. Later in the year it will become an exceedingly conspicuous object.

Jupiter is the most brilliant planet of the morning sky, shining higher and higher up in the east. Its lustre is increasing quite rapidly, so that while in March it was almost exactly as bright as Sirius, it now outshines any of the fixed stars. Jupiter is ever of interest to the owner of a small telescope, since its beautiful and easily visible markings, as well as its retinue of constantly moving satellites, make it a particularly pleasing object for observation with limited magnifying powers. The planet is oval in figure, being greatly flattened at the poles, and is traversed by light and dark belts of indefinite outlines parallel to the equator, and becoming indistinct toward the edge of the disc. The four brighter satellites are visible even in a good pocket spy-glass.

Mercury reaches its greatest western elongation on the 7th of the month, being then visible with difficulty low in the east before sunrise. In these latitudes, western elongations of Mercury which occur in spring are never as favourable as those which occur in autumn, wherefore the present phenomenon will not be especially interesting to observers here.

Mars arrives at quadrature on April 10th, then setting at about 1:15 a.m. So rapidly is its brilliancy increasing, that by the end of the month it will be no brighter than Pollux, which shines near it. The planet moves a considerable distance amongst the stars during April, travelling about half a degree each day, and passing out of Gemini into Cancer.

Saturn, though past its quadrature, nevertheless remains an attractive ornament of the evening sky. It still retains great lustre, being about as bright as Rigel, in Orion. Saturn sets at 11:31 p.m. on the 1st and at 9:39 p.m. on the 30th.

The moon's phases will occur as follows:

First Quarter, 3d... 3:41 p.m.
Full Moon, 10th ....8:28 a.m.
Last Quarter, 17th..3:52 a.m.
New Moon, 25th ....6:22 a.m.

The moon runs high on the 3d and 20th; low on the 14th. It will be near Saturn on the 1st, Mars on the 3d, Neptune on the 4th, Jupiter and Uranus on the 18th, Venus on the 27th, and Saturn again on the 28th. Perigee falls on the 10th, Apogee on the 23d.

The sun enters the sign Taurus on the 20th. During the month the days gain 1 hour and 17 minutes in length.

On April evenings the southern meridian is occupied by the beautiful Zodiacal constellation Leo, or the Lion. This extensive group is composed of two distinct divisions, the larger and western part resembling a sickle and containing the brilliant Regulus; the other having the shape of a right triangle, and containing Denebola, a star of the second magnitude. The six prominent stars of the "sickle" represent the head and breast of the celestial lion, Regulus marking the heart and thereby earning its Latin name of Cor Leonis. The western end of the right triangle corresponds to the lion's haunch, while Denebola, as its name signifies in Arabic, lies at the tip of the tail. West of the meridian, most of the magnificent winter constellations still linger above the horizon, though now bereft of that peculiar splendour which they possessed a few months ago. In the east, Boötes, the Herdsman, has ascended to a good altitude, its principal star, the reddish or orange Arcturus, far outshining all the other stars in the vicinity. Arcturus is considered by most observers to be the brightest star visible in our latitude, Sirius alone excepted. Of the northern stars, only Capella and Vega are comparable to it in lustre. West of Boötes is the small constellation Canes Venatici, or the Hunting Dogs. The only star of any importance in this group is an orb of the third magnitude known as Cor Caroli, or the Heart of Charles. Accounts differ as to whether this name was given in memory of the murdered Charles I or in honour of the return of Charles II. South of Canes Venatici lies a faint patch of light somewhat like Praespe, in Cancer. This is the small group called Coma Berenices, or Berenice's Hair, which when seen through a field glass shews itself to be composed of many faint stars. In the northeast, and rapidly gaining altitude, is Hercules, above which shines the beautiful circle of stars forming the Northern Crown. The vast length of Hydra is now displayed to best advantage, extending form the southwest, where the head lies just beneath Cancer, to the southeast, where the tail reaches almost to the region under Libra. The two small groups on Hydra's back, Crater and Corvus, are closely approaching the meridian, Crater, the more western, being about to cross that imaginary line. Above Hydra, and still entirely in the eastern heavens, is the Zodiacal constellation Virgo.

In the northern sky, we see the Plough about to culminate above the pole, the two stars called the "Pointers" being roughly on the meridian. Below this group are Draco and Ursa Minor, both east of the pole and increasing in altitude. Cassiopeia has descended low in the northwest, while Cepheus is due north, near the horizon, performing its lower transit. Proceeding eastward around the horizon, we find that Lyra, the Lyre, is appearing, the brilliant Vega being just visible through the dense vapours which obscure all bodies at low altitudes. As seen from the latitude of Providence, Vega lies but little outside the limit of the circumpolar region, hence is never long hidden from our view. Next to Lyra is Hercules, now almost entirely in sight. South of it, the compound constellations Serpentarius, or Ophiuchus et Serpens, is partially above the horizon. The Zodiacal group Libra, or the Balances, is rising in the southeast, and farther south, portions of Centaurus, the Centaur, are to be seen. The southern and more brilliant half of Centaurus is never visible here. Indeed, the constellation cannot be completely observed at any place above the 30th parallel of north latitude. In the section perpetually hidden from our northern eyes is Alpha Centauri, a star extremely interesting not only on account of its great brightness, but because it is the nearest to us of all the stellar bodies. The prodigious immensity of the space between our solar system and the rest of the universe is well illustrated by the fact that this nearest of the stars lies 25,000,000,000,000 miles away. It is about 9000 times farther off than is Neptune, the farthest of the planets, from the sun. The distance of Alpha Centauri, though almost beyond human comprehension, is but slight when compared with other stellar distances, most of which are far too great for expression in terms of any terrestrial unit, and which are therefore measured by a special unit called the "light year". A light year contains 5,509,588,236,000 miles, and is the distance travelled over in one year by the waves of light, at their incredibly rapid rate of 186,000 miles per second. All distances on the earth are relatively so small, that the time consumed by light in going from one locality to another is practically negligible; we see all terrestrial objects as they are at the present moment, and can scarcely imagine a case where an interval must elapse between the emission of light by a body, and our perception of it. In such a case, of course, we should see the body not as it is, but as it was when it emitted the light which makes it visible to us, just as we hear the report of a distant cannon some seconds later than the actual firing, owing to the slow motion of sound.

Alpha Centauri is four and one-third light years away. Since its light has taken four and one-third years to travel hither, it follows that the inhabitants of the earth must this month behold it not as it is now, but as it was in December, 1909, four and one-third years ago. This being so, what are we to think of those remote stars which astronomers have estimated to be 100,000 light years away? The mind can form no conception of gulfs so vast as these.

We observe such stars as they were 100,000 years before our day; in the stupendous intervals since they sent forth the light which we now see, they may themselves have faded forever. Adding in the grandeur of this idea is the fact that nearly all of the visible stars are separated from each other by spaces as great as that which separates any of them from our own solar system.

Next to Centaurus, and extending from the south point to the southwest, is Argo Navis, which, like its neighbour, is never wholly seen in these northern latitudes. In the invisible part of this group lies Canopus, the second brightest star in all the heavens. The horizon just west of Argo is occupied by Canis Major, beyond which we find successively Orion, Taurus, Perseus, and a few stars of Andromeda, which brings us again to the north, and completes the circle of horizontal constellations.

EDITOR'S NOTE FP: *EN* 44, No. 113 (31 March 1914): 8.

MAY SKY

Saturn, which has been a conspicuous object in the evening sky since late autumn, this month withdraws to the vicinity of the sun and passes out of view. During the first half of May it can be seen low in the west just after sunset, lying in the constellation Taurus. On the 1st it sets almost three hours later than the sun; by the 10th this space is lessened to about two hours and a quarter; on the 20th the planet sets only an hour and a half after sunset, and thereafter it will be too near the sun for observation. Its conjunction occurs next month. While Saturn is sinking from sight in the western twilight, it meets and passes Venus, which is destined to supersede it in the evening sky. The two planets will be near each other on the 16th at 9 a.m., when Venus will be 3 deg. 10 min. north of Saturn.

Venus is moving steadily eastward, slowly gaining on the sun, and crossing from Taurus to Gemini. At the end of the month, it sets 2 hours and 12 minutes after sunset. Venus is not yet an attractive object for study with the telescope, since it is still quite distant, and nearly circular in outline. As it draws near the earth and shews its phases during the coming summer and autumn, it will be much more interesting to the amateur observer.

Mars remains an important feature of the evening sky, setting on the 1st at 12:53 a.m., and on the 31st at 11:34 p.m. It spends the entire month in Cancer, though traversing almost the whole breadth of that constellation. About the middle of May it will be near Praespe, and will form with the bright star Regulus, in Leo, and Procyon, in Canis Minor, an immense isosceles triangle whose base is much greater than its altitude. Mars will not disappear until late autumn.

Jupiter will be invisible throughout the month, passing beyond the sun in superior conjunction on the 17th at 5 a.m. On the 28th it will be in conjunction with the also invisible Saturn.

Uranus, which lies in the morning sky, will be in quadrature on the 2nd of the month, and stationary on the 17th.

Neptune may be found with a telescope in the early evening sky, lying in the eastern part of the constellation Gemini. Its position on the 15th will be Right Ascension 7 h. 10 min., North Declinatiom 30 deg. 35 min. It will next month pass into Cancer.

The moon's phases for May will be as follows:

First Quarter, 3d..1:29 a.m.
Full Moon, 9th... 4:31 p.m.
Last Quarter, 16th.. 5:12 p.m.
New Moon, 24th .... 9:35 p.m.

Perigee falls on the 8th, Apogee on the 30th. The moon runs low on the 11th, high on the 26th. It will be near the following planets on the following dates: Neptune, 1st; Mars, 2nd; Uranus, 15th; Jupiter, 16th; Venus, 27th; Neptune, 29th; Mars, 30th.

For observation with a small telescope, there is no more interesting object in all the heavens than the moon. Its light and dark shadings are visible to the naked eye, while the inequalities in its surface may be clearly perceived even with the feeblest of magnifying powers. The lunar mountains are not well seen at full moon, for the direct illumination then prevents them from casting the shadows needed to make them appear plainly in relief. They are best studied when on or near the "terminator" or line separating the light and dark portions of the disc, for there the shadows are longest. Perhaps the most attractive view of the moon to be had with a weak glass, is that obtained at or near the time of first quarter, when the terminator is occupied throughout its length by prominent markings. Toward the northern end are then seen the crater Archimedes and the range of mountains called the Apennines, whilst along the southern half are clustered innumerable craters of various sizes and depths. These craters are generally much larger than those upon the earth, and are undoubtedly the result of tremendous volcanic forces which once existed in the moon.

The sun enters the Zodiacal sign Gemini on May 31st. It moves seven degrees northward this month, causing the days to gain 58 minutes. On the 31st, the sun will be above the horizon for 15 hours.

The new comet which was mentioned in *The Evening News* astronomical article for January is still approaching the earth, and may possibly be seen without a telescope in the autumn. This object was discovered last December by Prof. Paul T. Delavan of the National Observatory at La Plata, Argentine Republic.[1] It was for some time confused with Westphar's periodic comet, but its separate identity now seems fairly well established.

Turning to the constellations, we find the southern meridian occupied by the Zodiacal group Virgo, whose most brilliant star, the pure white Spica, will soon perform its transit. The seven leading stars of Virgo form a large, very rough letter "Y", with Spica at the base. This constellation represents Astraea, the goddess of Justice, who is supposed to hold Libra, the Balances, in her hand. South and southwest of Virgo are the eastern portions of Hydra, and the dependent groups Crater and Corvus. The latter, which is a very easily recognisable trapezium of rather bright stars, has but lately crossed the meridian. Leo has now passed into the western sky, while Coma Berenices is in transit just above Virgo. East of Virgo, Libra has ascended to a considerable altitude. The stars of winter have largely disappeared in the West, though Procyon, Castor, Pollux, and Capella still linger above the horizon. Cancer remains in a favourable situation. In the east we find two stars of surpassing lustre; Vega, in Lyra, and Arcturus, in Boötes. Arcturus is far higher in the sky than is its rival. Between Vega and Arcturus lie the constellations Hercules and Corona Borealis.

The circumpolar groups next claim our attention. Ursa Major is now directly above the pole, in its characteristic vernal position, while Cassiopeia, its opposite, is directly beneath the pole, in lower transit. Cepheus has begun to ascend in the east, and Draco, far above it, will soon follow Ursa Major in the meridian. Ursa Minor, also, lacks but little of being in upper transit.

On May evenings the Milky Way lines the horizon, extending from the southwest, where parts of it are disappearing with the winter groups, round through the north to the southeast, where other parts are coming into view with the stars of summer. At no other time is so great a length of it exposed at once, yet at no other time is it less easy to see, for as every observer knows, such a faint object is practically obliterated by vapours when low in the sky.

Tracing the constellations around the horizon as usual, from the north point eastward, we first behold Cygnus, with the bright Deneb, rising in the northeast. This group is almost circumpolar at Providence; indeed, a few of its stars fall within the circle of perpetual visibility, so that the whole can never be long absent from our evening skies. It will be better seen when it has attained a greater altitude. East of Cygnus, a star or two of Aquila, the Eagle, is above the horizon, and still farther east, the rather indefinite Ophiuchus et Serpens is almost completely in view. In the southeast, part of the Zodiacal constellation Scorpio, the Scorpion, has risen, those stars representing its head and claws being in sight. Its principal star, the flaming Antares, is very low in the sky, but will be seen as a brilliant red orb as the evening advances. Next to Scorpio lies Centaurus, which carries us as far as the south point. On the southwestern horizon we see few or no stars, that region being occupied by barren portions of Argo Navis. Due west, the bright Procyon, in Canis Minor, is visible, whilst north of it can be seen Gemini, with Castor and Pollux, and Auriga, with the brilliant Capella. North of Auriga, Perseus is sinking from sight, and Cassiopeia, directly beneath the pole, brings us round again to Cygnus, thus concluding the list.

EDITOR'S NOTE FP: *EN* 44, No. 141 (1 May 1914): 8.

Notes

1. I.e., Pablo T. Delavan, Argentine astronomer and head of the observatory at the University of La Plata. See the satirical use to which HPL puts this comet in "Delavan's Comet and Astrology" (p. 264).

THE JUNE SKY

Venus, slowly increasing in brilliancy, is now the most interesting feature of the evening sky. It shines each night low in the west, setting about two hours after the sun, and shewing in the telescope a gibbous phase comprising over eight-tenths of the entire surface. The planet is now moving east and south, passing out of Gemini into Cancer.

Mercury arrives at its greatest eastern elongation on the 19th of the month, then being visible in the evening twilight, just above the sunset point. The present elongation is by no means as favourable to observers as that of last February, yet a careful watcher should have little difficulty in locating the elusive planet. On the 19th it will be about six degrees south of Pollux, in Gemini, and on the 25th it will be near the thin crescent of the new moon.

Mercury and Venus both present peculiar problems to the telescopic observer, in that their surfaces seem practically destitute of well-defined markings, therefore affording no satisfactory means whereby we may discover their periods of rotation. Different observers, fancying themselves to have found real topographical features on these two bodies, have attempted to determine the lengths of their days, but so conflicting are the results thus obtained that we cannot but consider them as open to dispute. The cases of the two planets are remarkably similar. Certain authorities assert that they both rotate like the earth, once in about 24 hours, whilst others maintain with equal positiveness that each turns on its axis in the same time that it revolves around the sun, thus behaving as does the moon toward the earth, and keeping one half perpetually turned to the central body, the other half perpetually turned away. The elder astronomers universally accepted the shorter periods as true; the opposite opinion was first held by the late Schiaparelli of Milan and has been enthusiastically confirmed by Prof. Percival Lowell of Flagstaff, Arizona.

The time of rotation of Mercury was first investigated in the late eighteenth and early nineteenth centuries by the celebrated German astronomer, Johann Schroeter, who believed that when the planet has a crescentic phase, the south horn becomes blunted once in 24 hours 5 minutes. Schroeter, assuming the phenomenon to be due to the shadow cast by a mountain of great altitude, inferred that the intervals between successive truncations represent rotations of Mercury on its axis. On the other hand, the greatest of all telescopic observers, Sir William Herschel, could never distinguish any features whatsoever upon Mercury. In 1882, the English astronomer, Danning,[1] thought that he saw the blunting of the southern horn, which Schroeter had previously remarked, and in addition announced the discovery of vague spots on the disc, from whose motion he deduced a rotation of about 25 hours. However, in 1889, Prof. Schiaparelli, after observing Mercury in strong twilight to avoid the glare usually surrounding the planet, declared he saw some brown stripes and streaks of an entirely different character from the markings before noticed, whose behaviour would indicate that Mercury turns on its axis but once in its solar revolution of 88 days. If the results of Schiaparelli be correct, and they are now much favoured by astronomers, then Mercury must have on one side eternal day, and on the other, eternal night,

In the case of Venus, present evidence seems to point rather toward the short period as correct. In the "Annus Mirabilis", 1666, the Italian observer Giovanni Domenico Cassini announced the discovery of bright and dark spots on the surface of the planet, from whose motion he deduced a rotation of about 28 h. 21 min.[2] His son Jacques, observing in France, later confirmed this result.[3] Herschel denied the existence of markings on Venus, but Schroeter, in 1789, stated that the crescent of this planet, like that of Mercury, is blunted periodically, by the shadow of lofty peaks. In this manner the German confirmed the earlier conclusions of the two Cassini. This period has since been independently determined by De Vico in 1840, by Niesten in a series of observations extending from 1881 to 1890, and by Flammarion in 1894.[4]

In 1890 Prof. Schiaparelli asserted that the conduct of certain white spots on Venus indicate a long period of rotation, probably identical with the planet's revolution about the sun, that is, 225 days. Prof. Lowell states most positively that the rotation and devolution are equal, basing his belief on the conduct of certain supposed streaks, most of which he says radiate like spokes from the centre of the planet's disc. The majority of observers are unable to see the markings described by Schiaparelli and Lowell, although many possess vastly superior telescopes. In 1892 Trouvelot[5] announced a period of about 24 hours, and in 1900 Belopolsky,[6] using a spectroscope, inferred from the motion of the lines in the spectrum of the planet, that the rotation is quite rapid. Prof. T. J. J. See, U.S.N., of California,[7] has recently shewn mathematically that according to certain mechanical laws, Venus probably rotates in the short period of 23 h. 31 min. Thus the latest and most authoritative astronomers confirm the early results of Giovanni Domenico Cassini, and exhibit Venus as a veritable counterpart of the earth, not only in size, but in the length of its day as well.

Mars is now the only prominent superior planet visible in the early evening sky. It sets at 11:33 p.m. on the 1st, and 10:17 p.m. on the 30th. During June the planet moves from the extreme eastern part of Cancer to the vicinity of Regulus, in Leo, passing less than a degree north of that star on the 23d. The appearance of Mars and Regulus in close proximity will afford a good opportunity to compare the ruddy hue of the planet with the pure white of the star. Mars will be the fainter of the two. On the 27th, when Mars will be about two and a half degrees east of Regulus, the crescent moon will pass only 36 minutes of arc south of the planet, forming with it and the star a pleasing triad.

Jupiter shines with great brilliancy in the morning and late evening sky, appearing shortly before midnight. On the 1st of the month it rises at 11:37 p.m., and on the 30th at 10:23, thus coming above the horizon at nearly the same time that Mars descends below it. Jupiter is in Capricornus, moving eastward until the 11th of the month, and westward after that date.

Saturn arrives at conjunction on the 13th, being therefore invisible throughout the month. Uranus is in Capricornus, west of Jupiter, and now retrograding amongst the stars. Neptune, on the border between Gemini and Cancer, is drawing toward the sun and out of view. It will be in conjunction with Venus on the 16th, and in conjunction successively with the young moon and then Mercury on the 25th.

The moon will have five phases this month, as follows:

First Quarter, 1st ....9:03 a.m.
Full Moon, 8th..12:18 a.m.
Last Quarter, 15th...9:20 a.m.
New Moon, 23d...10:33 a.m.
First Quarter, 30th .... 3:25 p.m.

Perigee falls on the 5th, Apogee on the 17th. The moon runs low on the 8th, high on the 23d. It will be near the following planets on the following dates: Uranus, 10th; Jupiter, 12th; Mercury, 27th; Venus and Mars, 27th.

The sun this month attains the highest point in its apparent annual course, entering the sign Cancer and thus opening the summer on the 22nd at 2 a.m. The days are then at their maximum, being 15 h. 14 min. in length. By the end of the month their length will have decreased by three minutes.

The quiet constellations of summer now occupy the greater part of the evening sky. The Zodiacal group now on the meridian is Libra, which, though neither conspicuous nor beautiful, is notable for a double star whose components can be separated with the naked eye. Above Libra, the meridian line is marked out by Boötes, which is flanked on the east by Corona Borealis, and on the west by Coma Berenices. Virgo is just past transit, whilst Leo is declining in the west. In the east we find at good altitudes those constellations which last month lined the horizon. Cygnus, with its bright star Deneb, is now well in view, whilst Lyra, Hercules, and Ophiuchus are mounting high in the heavens.

In the north, Ursa Major is swinging down westward of the pole, and Cassiopeia is beginning to arise from beneath the latter. Ursa Minor extends along the meridian above the pole as though balanced on the tip of its tail, and higher still is Draco, now in upper transit.

Due north, a few stars of Perseus which fall within the circumpolar region commence the list of constellations around the horizon. Eastward of these a few stars of Andromeda and Pegasus are beginning to appear. A little north of the east point the tiny rhombus forming Delphinus, the Dolphin, is in sight. Almost due east, Aquila, the Eagle, with its brilliant star Altair, is now well seen. Low in the southeast the Zodiacal group Sagittarius, the Archer, has partly risen, while Scorpio is entirely visible. Lupus and Centaurus hold the southern horizon, and westward of these we find the long coils of Hydra, with the attendant constellations Corvus and Crater. Just north of the west point, Cancer is about to set, and still farther north a portion of Gemini, with Castor and Pollux, remains in view. Capella, about to set in the northwest, completes the catalogue.

On June evenings the Milky Way is in the eastern sky, flowing from the north, where it bears within it the constellation Cassiopeia, to the southeast, where it mixes with the stars of Scorpio and Sagittarius.

EDITOR'S NOTE FP: *EN* 45, No. 11 (29 May 1914): 12, 5.

Notes

1. Unidentified.

2. Giovanni Domenico Cassini (1625–1812), Italian astronomer chiefly known for determining the rotation periods of Jupiter, Mars, and Venus.

3. Jacques Cassini (1677–1756), Italo-French astronomer, son of Giovanni Domenico Cassini, also known for work in geodesy.

4. HPL refers to the astronomers Francesco de Vico (1805–1848; Italian), Jean Louis Nicolas Niesten (1844–1920; Belgian), and Camille Flammarion (1842–1925; French). Flammarion also exhibited an interest in occultism; HPL owned his *Haunted Houses* (1924; *LL* 319).

5. Etienne Léopold Trouvelot (1827–1895), French astronomer and naturalist who specialised in the observation of solar prominences at the observatory at Meudon.

6. Aristarkh Apollonovich Belopolsky (1894–1934, Russian astrophysicist who worked chiefly at the Pulkovo Observatory.

7. Thomas Jefferson Jackson See (1866–1962), American astronomer, U.S. Navy professor of mathematics, and director of the observatory at Mare Island, California.

THE JULY SKY

Saturn is now rapidly emerging from the sun's rays, and becoming visible low in the northwest just before dawn. On the 1st it rises only 36 minutes before the sun, but by the 31st it will have gained over two hours, rising at about 1:30 a.m. The planet is moving eastward from Taurus toward the boundary of Gemini, traversing during this journey a fragment of the constellation Orion which reaches up into the Zodiac. Saturn may be found by prolonging for a considerable distance the line formed by the left-hand branch of the Hyades. The planet will be seen not far from the star Zeta, which lies at the tip of the Bull's southern horn.

Venus continues to be the chief planet of the evening sky, glowing with unrivalled brilliancy in the west after sunset. On the 1st it sets about two hours after the sun, and on the 31st about an hour and three-quarters after the sun. The gibbous phase of Venus is now becoming quite noticeable in a telescope, the illuminated surface diminishing during the month from eight-tenths to seven-tenths of the entire disc. At the same time the planet is steadily growing brighter, since in its approach to the earth the increasing apparent size of the disc more than compensates for the decreasing phase.

Before Venus will have attained to its greatest brilliancy, the phase will have shrunk to a crescent, yet that crescent will be of vastly larger proportions than is the gibbous figure which the planet now shews. Venus moves during July from the eastern part of Cancer to the eastern part of Leo, passing about a degree north of Regulus on the 13th.

Mars is still east of Venus, but is rapidly being overtaken by the latter. The red planet is visible in the western evening sky, setting on the 1st at 10:16 p.m. and on the 31st at 8:56. It moves this month from the middle part of Leo to the boundary of Virgo. Mars is now no brighter than a star of the second magnitude.

Jupiter, shining with great splendour, has now entered the earlier evening sky, and will next month come to opposition. It rises on July 1st at about 9:40 p.m. and on the 31st at about 7:30. It is still retrograding in Capricornus, and, being near no bright stars, is absolutely unmistakable as it appears in the southeastern heavens.

Mercury, in inferior conjunction on the 16th, is practically invisible throughout July, though by the end of the month it will be drawing toward its western elongation.

Uranus is in the constellation Capricornus, not far from Jupiter, so that it is now visible quite early at night. Its opposition will occur on the 3d of August. Neptune arrives at conjunction on the 21st, wherefore it will not appear this month.

The moon's phases will be as follows:

Full Moon, 7th..9:00 a.m.
Last Quarter, 15th...2:32 a.m.
New Moon, 22nd.. 9:38 p.m.
First Quarter, 29th .... 6:51 p.m.

Perigee comes on the 3d and 28th, Apogee on the 15th. The moon runs low on the 5th, high on the 19th. On the 9th it will be in conjunction with Uranus, on the 10th with Jupiter, on the 20th with Saturn, and on the 26th with Venus and Mars.

The sun this month moves southward about 4¾ degrees, entering the Zodiacal sign Leo on the 23d. The days lose 43 minutes during July. On the 2nd of the month the earth will be in aphelion, or greatest distance from the sun, which fact somewhat tempers the fervour of summer in these latitudes.

The comet of Delavan will this month withdraw from the vicinity of the sun, and come into view in the northeastern sky just before sunrise. It is not visible to the naked eye, but will probably become so in the course of the next two or three months. During July, Delavan's passes through Taurus and Auriga, becoming circumpolar in August. It will be noticed that comets, unlike planets, are not confined to the Zodiacal circle, but may rove about in all parts of the sky. This is because their orbits have no tendency to lie in that plane to which all of the planetary orbits roughly conform.

In turning to our monthly survey of the constellations, we are led to wonder at the origin of these ancient yet mostly arbitrary arrangements. Whilst we know them by Latin names, and associate them with the legends of Graeco-Roman mythology, it is not to be imagined that their history is thus traced back to its source. As the classical authors did most toward perpetuating the names and fanciful derivations of the various groups of stars, so are the classical myths concerning them most widely regarded; yet the antiquity of almost all the constellations is far greater than is indicated by the Grecian tales. Fragments of early attempts at celestial nomenclature, re-descended to us through the ages from diverse and widely separated nations, shew a surprising degree of identity, and render it almost certain that a large number of the figures we know were invented in prehistoric times, when mankind was in an agricultural or pastoral state, and before the various modern divisions of humanity extended. Very obscure are the reasons for selecting most of the objects which are imagined to be depicted amongst the stars. Some groups, it is true, were perhaps suggested by remote resemblances in the arrangements of the stars themselves, such as in the Northern Cross, in Cygnus, or in the Plough or Dipper in Ursa Major; yet the majority cannot plead this excuse, and many of the real resemblances which we find, are to objects other than those of which the groups are named.

Scorpio, the Zodiacal constellation on the meridian this month, is one of the few groups that justifies its appellation, for although its outline most strongly suggests a boy's kite, it is not wholly unlike a scorpion. At the heart of the venomous creature shines the fiery red Antares, a star of the first magnitude, whose name, derived from the Greek, means "Rival of Mars". Above Scorpio is the dull compound group comprising Ophiuchus and the Serpent, while over this, and reaching beyond the zenith, is the vague form of Hercules. Just west of Hercules, and barely past transit, is Corona Borealis, reputed to be the diadem given by Bacchus to Ariadne. In the west are those constellations which were last month on or near the meridian, including Boötes, with the peerless Arcturus, Canes Venatici, Coma Berenices, Libra, and Virgo, with the shining Spica. High in the east are Cygnus, with the brilliant Deneb, Lyra, with the lustrous Vega, Delphinus, with its rhombic outline, and Aquila, with the bright Altair.

In the north, Draco is above the pole, while Ursa Major is west of it, standing perpendicularly to the horizon. Just beneath Draco lies Ursa Minor, now beginning to shew an inclination westward. East of the pole we find Cassiopeia at a good altitude, with Cepheus directly above it.

The constellations around the horizon will next be noticed. The few circumpolar stars of Perseus have moved east of the north point, and farther east a considerable part of Andromeda is in view. About three-quarters of the expanse of Pegasus has risen, though the Great Square is not yet wholly above the horizon. In the southeast, parts of the Zodiacal constellations Aquarius and Capricornus are appearing, while Sagittarius is completely visible. Scorpio lies due south, and west of it are successively Lupus and Centaurus. The tail of Hydra and the familiar trapezium of Corvus are setting in the southwest, beyond which the horizon is for some distance quite void of stars. In the northwest, Regulus, the brightest star in Leo, is about to set, while farther on we see only the Lynx, a faint, partly circumpolar constellation which brings us once more to the north.

In order to obtain a perfectly satisfactory view of the starry heavens, it is necessary to observe them from some place in the rural or suburban districts, as opposed to the urban] districts, where the eye may be blinded and fatigued by artificial lights. The appearance of the night sky in the country is beautiful beyond the comprehension of those accustomed to make their observations in the city. The Milky Way, but a vague band of dim, cloudy luminosity to the town student, is to the rustic astronomer a clear resplendent arch, traceable in all its details and ramifications, while hundreds of the smaller stars, never seen above the glare of brilliantly illuminated streets, stand out with distinctness in the black rural sky. The powerful arch lamps lately introduced in Providence are a serious hindrance to astronomical study, hence in the city the celestial vault should be viewed mostly from streets where the less dazzling incandescent lamps are employed.

EDITOR'S NOTE FP: *EN* 45, No. 37 (30 June 1914): 6.

THE AUGUST SKY

The most [. . .] astronomical event of the month of August is the total solar eclipse which occurs on the 21st. The belt of totality, or path of the moon's shadow over the earth, extends from the Arctic Islands north of Canada across Northern Greenland, central Norway and Sweden, Western Russia, Turkey and Persia to Western India. As a partial eclipse, it may be viewed from a much wider territory comprising the Northeastern part of North America, the entire area of Europe, the Western half of Asia, and the Northeastern part of Africa. In Rhode Island, where only a small fraction of the solar surface will be darkened, the phenomenon will not be of the highest interest, but within the region of totality, the conditions are such that they claim the closest attention of astronomers, and attract observers from all other parts of the world. The obscured sun is there seen to be encircled by a wide and gorgeous "corona" or crown of light, with occasional long rays or streamers darting far out into space. Forming a narrow, irregular fringe about the edge of the disc are fiery "prominences", whose red colour contrasts strongly with the pure white radiance of the surrounding corona. The prominences and corona are solar atmospheres which cannot be beheld save during total eclipses, since the intense refulgence of the luminous surface otherwise hides them. Their appearance is variable, some eclipses shewing them in more impressive manner than others. Whenever opportunity is offered, they are studied with the greatest of care by means of the telescope, the camera, and the spectroscope. Prof. David Todd of Amherst college,[1] a particular student of this subject, will observe the coming eclipse in Russia, either near Riga or at a village near Kiev, both of which places lie along the zone of totality. Since at a given spot the total phase will last but little over two minutes, he will make his observations from an aëroplane flying in the same direction as the moon's shadow at the rate of 120 miles an hour, chasing the eclipse, as it were, and considerably prolonging for himself the period of totality. As seen at Providence, the eclipse of August 21 will occur in the early morning, beginning at 5:50 and lasting about thirty minutes. The edge of the moon will encroach but slightly upon the sun's northern edge; yet the spectacle deserves notice, and should be quite widely observed here. A dark or smoked glass must of course be used by all observers to protect the eye from the dangerous intensity of the solar rays.

The array of planets in the August sky, both morning and evening, is extremely attractive. Mercury comes to greatest western elongation on the 5th, being then visible in the east before sunrise, and lying in the constellation Gemini, a considerable distance south of Pollux. It soon, however, recedes from our sight, approaching the sun, and passing beyond that luminary in superior conjunction on the 30th.

Saturn is the other morning planet, rising on the 1st at 1:26 a.m. and on the 31st at 11:34 p.m. It shines with about the same brilliancy as that of the fixed star Rigel, and is situate east of the Pleiades, northeast of the Hyades. Its motion this month is not great, but takes it just across the boundary line into Gemini. The system of rings, very favourably inclined toward the earth, offers a most pleasing object for observation with the telescope.

Jupiter is now at its best for the year, being in opposition and therefore nearest the earth on the 10th of the month. It rises on the 1st at 7:28 p.m., on the 10th at sunset, and, having passed into the evening sky, sets at 3:14 a.m. on the 31st. Appearing each evening in the southeastern heavens, Jupiter seems a worthy rival of Venus, which shines in the west. Though Venus is really much the brightest, the other planet is no mean counterpart. Jupiter continues its slow retrograde motion in Capricornus. It is too far south to be at its best for observation in these northern latitudes, but the amateur telescopist will enjoy none the less the contemplation of its beautiful belts and shifting satellites.

Venus reigns supreme in the western evening sky, travelling this month from the eastern part of Leo to the immediate vicinity of the star Spica. Venus overtakes and passes Mars on the 5th. The phase of Venus is gradually approaching the semicircular form; at the close of the month it will have decreased to less than six-tenths of a circle. The planet sets on the 1st at 8:52 p.m., and on the 31st at 7:55.

Mars, now quite dull and worthless as a telescopic object, still lingers in the early evening heavens, setting on the 1st at 8:55, and on the 31st at 7:36. It is moving from the eastern boundary of Leo into Virgo, passing through the western part of the latter constellation during August. On the 5th it is overtaken by the swifter Venus, which passes only ten angular minutes to the south of it. The two planets in such very close proximity will form an interesting pair, the faint ruddy Mars appearing as though it were but a satellite of the resplendent yellowish-white Venus.

Uranus arrives at its opposition on the 2nd of the month, thereby becoming an "evening star". It is scarcely visible to the naked eye, and has little about it to interest the amateur. It now lies near Jupiter in Capricornus. Neptune was in conjunction last month, and although by the end of August it may be beginning to withdraw from the solar glare to the morning sky, it needs no further notice here.

The phases of the moon for August will be as follows:

Full Moon, 5th.. 7:41 p.m.
Last Quarter, 13th.. 7:56 p.m.
New Moon, 21st ....7:27 a.m.
First Quarter, 27th .... 11:53 p.m.

Apogee comes on the 12th, Perigee on the 24th. The moon runs low on the 1st and 28th, high on the 16th. It will be near Uranus on the 5th, Jupiter on the 6th, Saturn on the 16th, Mars and Venus on the 24th.

The sun enters the sign Virgo on the 23d, and with its southward motion causes the days to decrease by nearly an hour and a quarter.

Before the month is over, Delavan's comet will possibly have been seen with the naked eye. This comet is now becoming circumpolar, the position on the 31st being in the faint modern constellation Lynx, at Right Ascension 8 h. 15 min. 43 sec., Declination 48 deg. 35 min. 9 sec.

The Zodiacal constellation on the meridian in August is Sagittarius, the Archer, represented on the charts as a centaur bearing a bow. This group is now the most southern member of the Zodiac, the precessional motion of the earth's axis having carried the winter solstice within its confines, just as it has carried the summer solstice into Gemini. Though having no star of the first magnitude and but one of the second, Sagittarius possesses in richness what it wants in show. Its western extremity is immersed in the Milky Way, the inverted ladle-like figure formed by the stars Zeta, Tau, Sigma, Phi, Lambda, and Mu being called the "Milk-Dipper". Mu marks the end of the Milk-Dipper's handle; above it, and visible to the naked eye in the absence of the mean and artificial lights, lie two beautiful clusters of stars known as 24m and 25m. 24m has a breadth almost three times that of the moon when full, and appears like a protuberance on the outline of the

Milky Way. 25m is situate a little distance to the east. An opera or field glass will exhibit many other interesting clusters in this vicinity, particularly m, [sic] which is a sort of cluster and nebula combined, and which has an appearance rather like that of a telescopic comet. This lies below the star Mu. Above Sagittarius are Aquila and Ophiuchus; still higher up, and almost in the zenith, are Cygnus, Lyra, and Coma Berenices. In the east the rising constellations foretell the advent of autumn. Pegasus and Andromeda are gaining altitude, whilst the tiny asterisms Delphinus, Equuleus, and Sagitta, the Arrow, are already high in the heavens, the latter, which lies above Altair, being almost on the meridian. In the north, Ursa Major is descending at the left of the pole, while Cassiopeia, already very high, is ascending at the right. Above Cassiopeia, Cepheus is approaching upper transit. Ursa Minor lies above and to the left of Polaris, and Draco coils itself just beyond. Lynx is on the horizon beneath the pole, while east of it a solitary star of Auriga has arisen. In the northeast most of Perseus and all of Triangulum are in sight. The rest of the horizon is almost entirely occupied by a long procession of Zodiacal constellations; Pisces rising due east, Aquarius and Capricornus completely visible in the southeast, Sagittarius on the meridian and Scorpio just west of it, Libra in the southwest, and Virgo setting due west. From the west to the north point are found only fragments of Leo Minor, together with those parts of Ursa Major which precede the Plough in their circuit of the sky.

We are now in the midst of that season of about 40 days known since ancient times as the "Dog Days", or "Dies Caniculares". The beginning of this term was designed to coincide with the "heliacal" rising of Sirius, the Dog-Star; that is, with the first appearance of that body on the southeastern horizon just before sunrise, after its long absence from the nocturnal heavens. The phenomenon of procession and the different aspect of the sky as beheld from different latitudes causes the conventional date on July 25, given usually as the commencement of the Dog-Days, to differ widely from any actual time of the heliacal rising of Sirius. The Dog-Days are considered to end of the 5th of September. The traditions surrounding the Dies Caniculares are very interesting and very ancient. In Egyptian times the appearances of Sirius in the morning twilight, preceding the rising of the Nile, counselled the farmers to sow their grain. From this important function, the star acquired a religious significance, and was the object of much worship. Seven ruined temples have been discovered which were so built that the beams of Sirius, heliacally rising, should strike the great altars. Even the name "Sirius" is thought by some students to the derived from "Osiris", the name of the greatest of the Egyptian gods. In Asia, the heliacal rising of Sirius was regarded as the source of the extreme heat of late summer, a belief to which Virgil more than once alludes;[2] whilst among the Romans a dog was each year sacrified to the star at this season.

EDITOR'S NOTE FP: *EN* 45, No. 64 (1 August 1914): 8.

Notes

1. David Todd (1855–1939), professor of astronomy and director of the observatory at Amherst College (1881–1920).
2. See, e.g., Virgil, *Georgics* 4.425f.

THE SEPTEMBER SKY

The closest attention of astronomers is at present directed toward Delavan's Comet, which is faintly visible to the naked eye, and which may soon become quite conspicuous. This body now lies in the constellation Lynx, but before September is over will have crossed into Ursa Major, being directly beneath the Plough at the end of the month. Although after the 15th the comet will appear low in the southwest during the early evening hours, it cannot be well seen save in the northeast before dawn. On the 3d of October it will be nearest the earth. In a good telescope Delavan's Comet now exhibits a tail about a degree in length.

Turning to the planets, we find Venus and Jupiter still sharing the supremacy of the evening sky. Venus glows with ever increasing lustre in the west after sunset, coming to greatest elongation on the 18th. It will then shew an exactly semicircular phase, which will afterward change to a crescent. The marvellous brilliancy of Venus toward the close of the month will probably cause many persons ignorant of astronomy to mistake it for an artificial light; indeed, one evening about five years ago Westminster street was lined with curious and excited watchers who pointed out the planet as the searchlight of an aëroplane.[1] Venus moves this month from an immediate neighbourhood of Spica, in Virgo, to the boundary line between Jupiter and Scorpio.

Jupiter shines brilliantly in the southern sky, setting at 3:14 a.m. on the 1st, and 1:04 a.m. on the 30th. It is still retrograding in Capricornus, and though somewhat past its opposition, has not yet sensibly diminished in splendour.

Saturn, in quadrature on the 25th, is preparing to enter the evening sky. It is now situated in Gemini, rising on the 1st at 11:33 p.m., and on the 30th at 9:42. Though not near its maximum brilliancy, it is none the less a very conspicuous object, being now about as bright as the star Capella in Auriga.

Mars, while still nominally an evening planet, has now approached the sun too closely to permit of observation. Mercury will likewise be invisible this month.

Uranus is well seen with the telescope in the evening sky, whilst Neptune is emerging from the sun's rays in the morning heavens.

The moon's phases for September will be as follows:

Full Moon, 4th...9:01 a.m.
Last Quarter 12th... 12:48 p.m.
New Moon, 19th .... 4:38 p.m.
First Quarter, 26th ....7:08 a.m.

Apogee is on the 5th, Perigee on the 21st. The moon runs high on the 12th, low on the 25th. It passes near the following planets on the following dates: Jupiter, 2nd; Saturn, 13th; Venus, 23d; Jupiter, 29th. There will be a partial lunar eclipse on the 4th, invisible at Providence.

The sun enters the Zodiacal sign Libra on the 23d at 5 p.m., thus commencing the Autumn season. The days decrease about 1 hour and 20 minutes during September.

Activity upon the solar surface, very inconsiderable during the past two years, has now begun to increase. Last month there appeared on the sun a spot of great size, surrounded by a penumbra, and attended by several smaller spots and faculae.

The solar eclipse of August 31, while not seen here on account of clouds, was observed with great success along the path of totality both in Sweden and in belligerent Russia. The fiercest battles between mortals are of small consequence in the vast system of infinity, and the celestial bodies perform their accustomed motions without regard to the state of war or peace upon this one tiny sphere. That men of science are not to be deterred from their objects by even the gravest of international hostilities is shewn as well today as in 1870, when Prof. Janssen escaped from besieged Paris in a balloon, in order to observe a total solar eclipse in Algeria.[2]

The array of constellations in the September sky is singularly devoid of beauty and interest; the groups of summer departing, whilst the resplendent pageant of the winter stars has not yet appeared above the eastern horizon. The Zodiacal constellation on the meridian is Capricornus, the Sea-Goat, remarkable only for a pair of stars just separable with the naked eye. Above and east of Capricornus is Aquarius, the Water-Bearer. Still higher up, Aquila has crossed the meridian and entered the western sky, while Cygnus lies exactly in the zenith. Of the three tiny groups south of Cygnus, we find Delphinus on the meridian, Equuleus just east, and Sagitta just west of that imaginary line. In the western sky are Lyra, Hercules, Corona Borealis, and Ophiuchus et Serpens. In the east are Triangulum, Aries, Andromeda, Pegasus, and Pisces.

Looking northward we see Ursa Major descending beneath the Pole-Star, and Ursa Minor, with Draco beyond it, lying west of that orb. Cepheus, with Cassiopeia closely following, is approaching upper transit, whilst Perseus, east of the pole, is mounting along in full splendour.

On the horizon below the pole is Lynx, to the east of which Capella is beginning to appear through the mist. Farther east, the Pleiades are about to rise into view. Southward, the bulk of Cetus is in sight, and low in the southeast shines Fomalhaut, the brightest star in the Southern Fish. Due south there are no stars on the horizon, but west of the meridian Sagittarius still remains completely visible, beyond which Scorpio has partly disappeared. Due west Libra has wholly vanished, so that we next encounter Boötes, whose bright star Arcturus grows dim as it sets. Between Boötes and the north point, Canes Venatici and Ursa Major complete the circle of constellations.

Of particular interest to Rhode Islanders is the opening of Mr. F. E. Seagrave's new private observatory in North Scituate, about two miles north of the village.[3] The building stands on an eminence 342 feet above sea-level, free from the smoke and lights of the city, and commanding a magnificent view of the celestial vault. The principal telescope, over eight inches in aperture, is contained in a brick tower with a revolving dome, whilst a number of other astronomical and meteorological instruments occupy two rooms east of the tower. Mr. Seagrave, who is connected with the astronomical department of Harvard University, and who is one of the foremost astronomers of the present time, formerly had an observatory on Benefit Street in this city.[4]

Rhode Island, now possessing two observatories of the most approved type, is indeed well represented in the astronomical world.

EDITOR'S NOTE FP: *EN* 45, No. 89 (1 September 1914): 8.

Notes

1. See "Venus and the Public Eye" (p. 99).
2. Pierre Jules César Janssen (1824–1907), French scientist who worked in astronomy, spectroscopy, and photography.

3. Frank Evans Seagrave (1860–1934), Rhode Island astronomer who went on three solar eclipse expeditions (1878–1901), did important work on Halley's comet in 1909–10, and established an observatory in North Scituate, R.I., in 1914.

4. The George R. Drowne House (1862) at 119 Benefit Street.

THE OCTOBER SKY

Venus, shewing a crescentic phase in the telescope, will arrive at its greatest brilliancy on the 23d of the coming month, being then almost ten times brighter than the resplendent star Sirius. The planet shines just above the western horizon each evening like a dazzling lamp, attracting much attention as the twilight deepens. Toward the end of the month its crescent will have become so very large and thin, that the phase may be perceptible through a good opera or field glass. Venus will be in Scorpio during October, lying about a degree south of the bright red star Antares at the time of greatest brilliancy. On the 21st of the month, the slender crescent of the young moon will pass only 24 angular minutes north of Venus, the two bodies in such close proximity forming an extremely pleasing spectacle. The planet sets at 7 p.m. on the 1st, and at 5:30 on the 31st, thus being visible but a short time each evening.

Venus when brightest is readily visible by day, though not usually seen at such a time unless its exact place in the heavens be known. When Napoleon arrived in Paris after his Italian wars, he was given a fete by the Directory at the Luxembourg. On this occasion he observed the populace assembled round the palace gazing at the sunny sky above, and as he looked upward himself, he beheld Venus, brightly gleaming in the full light of mid-day. The crowd, misled by the persistent delusions of judicial astrology, were acclaiming the planet as the guiding star of the great Conqueror of Italy, and it is related that Bonaparte himself was not above taking satisfaction in what he deemed so propitious an omen. Though we should now know better than to associate such a phenomenon with human events, or to connect it with the fortunes of any modern conqueror, Kaiser, or nation, we may derive much pleasure from the daytime observation of Venus. This is by no means difficult if we but know when and where to look for it. For the amateur observer without an equatorially mounted telescope, the best way to find Venus during the day is to construct a sight or pointer which shall indicate the place in the heavens to be occupied by the planet at a certain hour; preferably, that place on the southern meridian where the planet will transit. To do this, cut from stiff cardboard a right triangle having a base of nine inches and an altitude of three and a half inches, or any dimensions in the same proportion, so that the angle between the base and hypothenuse shall be about 20 degrees. Select a spot commanding a good view of the southern horizon, and there mount the triangle on a stick or post so that it shall lie exactly north and south by the compass or pole star, with the base perfectly horizontal and the altitude or upright side south. The hypothenuse or slanting side will then point to the approximate place in the sky where Venus will cross the meridian on or about the day of greatest brilliancy. On Oct. 23 the planet transits but little after 2 p.m., hence those who desire to find it may simply look along the hypothenuse of the triangle at that time. Venus can thus be found with ease though it will be too near the horizon to appear to best advantage. This method should be followed by the possessors of small telescopes, for the daylight gives a fine opportunity to study Venus without the dazzling glare which surrounds the planet at night.

Jupiter, which lingers in the southern sky long after the setting of Venus, continues to shine with great splendour. It still remains in Capricornus, retrograding until the 9th of the month, and afterward moving eastward. On the 1st it sets at 1:04 a.m., and on the 31st at 11:04 p.m.

Saturn is visible in the later evening sky, rising at 9:42 on the 1st, and 7:40 p.m. on the 31st. It is in the western part of Gemini, moving directly until the 15th of the month, and afterward retrograding. The rings are inclined very favourably for observation with the telescope, and the planet is now one of the most attractive features of the heavens.

Mercury arrives at its greatest eastern elongation on the 15th, it being visible low in the west just after sunset around that date. This planet will on the 7th of next month perform a transit across the sun's disc, a rare phenomenon which we shall consider more particularly in the November article.

Mars is close to the sun, and will not be well seen for many months to come. Uranus and Neptune are both in quadrature this month; the former, in the evening sky, on the 31st, and the latter, in the morning sky, on the 24th. Neither can be seen without a telescope.

The moon's phases will occur as follows:

Full Moon, 4th..12:59 a.m.
Last Quarter, 12th...4:38 a.m.
New Moon, 19th ....1:34 a.m.
First Quarter, 25th .... 5:44 p.m.

Apogee is on the 6th, Perigee on the 18th. The moon runs high on the 9th, low on the 22nd. It will approach the various planets as follows: Saturn, 10th; Venus, 21st; and Jupiter, 26th. On Oct. 15th, at 3:43 a.m., the bright outer edge of the waning crescent moon will occult the star Regulus, in Leo. About an hour later, at 4:45, Regulus will reappear from behind the dark or invisible edge, a rather striking phenomenon, since there will be no apparent cause for the sudden return of the star.

The sun enters the Zodiacal sign Scorpio on the 2nd. The shortening of the days is now very perceptible, and heralds the advent of winter. During October the mornings lose 34 minutes, and the afternoons 46.

Delavan's comet continues to be very plainly visible to the naked eye. On the 2nd of the month it will be nearest the earth, its distance from us being somewhat over one and a half times that from the earth to the sun. On the 26th it will be nearest the sun, or in perihelion. During the first half of October the comet may be seen either low in the northwest just after sunset, or in the northeast before sunrise, but it is moving so rapidly amongst the stars that it will soon desert the morning in favour of the evening sky. Its course in the heavens this month extends from a point under the handle of the Plough to one in Boötes. It will lie about seven degrees north of Arcturus on the 26th. During September the writer observed this interesting object with and without instruments on a number of occasions from 4 a.m. until dawn. It had about the brightness of a star of the fourth magnitude, appearing to the naked eye as a blurred, elongated patch of light; rather faint, yet easily visible. In an ordinary pair of opera-glasses this blur resolved itself into a star-like nucleus, a bright coma, and a short, broad tail. In a pair of prism binoculars magnifying eight diameters these details were better seen, whilst in a three-inch astronomical telescope with powers of 50 and 100, the comet was indeed a beauteous sight. On Sept. 16 a small telescopic star could be discerned shining through the feeble luminosity of the tail. Delavan's is the first bright comet which has graced our skies since the appearance of Halley's over four years ago, and no lover of astronomy should neglect to observe it while it remains in view. It is believed to be moving in a very elongated orbit, so that it will not return for over 60,000 years.

Whilst the comet of Delavan is thus claiming attention in the north, another cometary body of considerable brilliancy has arrived in the southern heavens. This latest celestial visitor was discovered on Sept. 18 at the Cape Observatory in South Africa, and though not ascending above the horizon in these northern latitudes, can be seen with the naked eye by observers in the southern hemispheres. Its location is at present in the constellation Eridanus, not far from the bright star Achernar. Reports as yet fail to indicate whether or not it may move northward and become visible in New England.

Turning to the siderial sky, we find the dull groups of Autumn predominating, though the first of the brilliant stars of Winter are beginning to appear. The Zodiacal constellation now on the meridian is Aquarius, a group with no bright stars and of very little interest. Above it, the meridian line is marked out with considerable precision by the two more western stars of the Great Square of Pegasus. This square, though generally assigned to Pegasus, really encroaches upon the constellation Andromeda, which lies to the east, for one of its stars forms part of the latter group. West of Pegasus, Cygnus has just crossed the meridian. Aquila, southwest of Cygnus, is still well seen. Just west of Cygnus is Lyra, whose brilliant star Vega outshines all the other stars in that region. Hercules, below Lyra, is fast approaching the horizon. In the east are Cetus, Pisces, Aries, and Perseus. Cetus, the Whale, is a group of considerable extent, its general outline being that of an inverted letter "Y". At the fork of the "Y" is the famous variable star Mira, whose name, meaning "The Wonderful", is amply justified by its fluctuations in brilliancy between the second and ninth magnitudes. Mira undergoes its variations in a period of about 11 months, during half of which time it is visible to the naked eye. When brightest, its lustre is 400 times greater than when fainter. This is the first star ever discovered to be variable, its nature having been noticed in 1596 by David Fabricius.[1]

In the northern sky we now find Ursa Major exactly below the pole, Cepheus and Cassiopeia high above that point, and Ursa Minor and Draco descending at the left of it. Looking eastward around the horizon, we see just beyond Ursa Major the rising form of Lynx. Farther east Auriga has gained a good altitude, its brilliant star Capella shining very conspicuously. Slightly north of the east point Taurus has completely risen, its bright red star Aldebaran and its two beautiful clusters of stars, the Pleiades and the Hyades, appearing in full splendour. Southward a few stars of Eridanus are coming into view, beyond which Cetus and the unimportant groups Phoenix and Sculptor are seen. Almost on the meridian is Piscis Australis, or the Southern Fish, whose bright star Fomalhaut shines quite prominently despite its low altitude. Fomalhaut is the only star of great brilliancy in that part of the sky, hence cannot be mistaken.

Capricornus extends eastward from Piscis Australis to Sagittarius, which has partly set in the southwest. Due west, Ophiuchus et Serpens is setting, north of which Corona Borealis is about to sink from visibility. Beyond Corona, a part of Boötes brings us round to Ursa Major and the north once more.

The Milky Way is now a beautiful sight, extending from the northeast, where it flows between Capella and the horns of the Bull, through Perseus, Cassiopeia, Cepheus, and Cygnus, to the western sky, where it divides into two branches; one reaching the horizon through Ophiuchus et Serpens, the other through Aquila and Sagittarius.

EDITOR'S NOTE FP: *EN* 45, No. 113 (30 September 1914): 6.

Notes

1. David Fabricius (1564–1617), German astronomer.

THE NOVEMBER SKY

Foremost among the celestial events of the coming month is the transit of Mercury over the sun's disc on the morning of the 7th. Although an inferior planet passes between the earth and the sun at every inferior conjunction, it ordinarily performs this passage either above or below the exact line connecting the two, being at such times invisible on account of the sun's overpowering refulgence. At rare intervals, however, the planet comes exactly in line between the solar and terrestrial spheres, thus appearing to us as a small black spot outlined against the fiery disc of the sun. A phenomenon of this sort is called a "transit". Transits of Mercury are far more frequent than those of Venus, for while the latter orb has not transited the sun since 1882 and will not again till 2004, the former crosses the solar disc at irregular intervals of from three to 13 years, or about 12 times in a century. So small is the apparent size of Mercury as seen from the earth that a telescope is required to observe its transit. On the morning of Nov. 7 the sun will rise at 6:26, with Mercury already on the disc. The planet will move northward and westward along a chord near the southern edge, leaving the disc at 9:10 a.m. These phenomena afford the observer a very satisfactory means of measuring the size and shape of Mercury, as well as the exact figure of its orbit. Transits of Mercury always occur either in May or in November. The last previous transit, which was visible at Providence and observed by the writer, occurred in November, 1907; the next, which cannot be seen here, will take place in May, 1924. Not until Nov. 14, 1953, can the inhabitants of this state have the privilege of beholding another.

Mercury, having emerged from its transit, will arrive at greatest elongation west on the 23d of the month, then being visible as a twinkling orb in the east just before sunrise.

Venus may be seen early in November as a very bright body close to the southwestern horizon after sunset. It will, however, soon be lost in the sun's rays, arriving at inferior conjunction on the 27th. Toward the end of next month it will appear low in the eastern sky before dawn.

Jupiter and Saturn share the honours in the evening sky. The former is moving directly in Capricornus, and will be in quadrature on the 6th. It sets at 11:03 p.m. on the 1st, and at 9:24 on the 30th. Saturn is retrograding in Gemini, and now entering the earlier evening sky. On the 1st it rises at 7:39 p.m., and on the 30th at 5:35.

Mars will be invisible throughout the month, whilst Uranus and Neptune may both be seen with optical aid; the one in the evening and the other in the morning sky.

The moon's phases will be as follows:

Full Moon, 2nd	6:43 p.m.
Last Quarter, 10th	6:37 p.m.
New Moon, 17th	11:02 a.m.
First Quarter, 24th	8:39 a.m.

Apogee falls on the 2nd and 29th, Perigee on the 16th. The moon runs high on the 6th, and low on the 19th. It will be near Saturn on the 7th and near Jupiter on the 23d.

The sun enters the Zodiacal sign Sagittarius on the 22nd. During November the days lose about one hour.

Delavan's comet, now receding from the earth, has proved a beautiful and interesting object, though not so generally observed as its appearance warranted, on account of its having been best seen in the morning sky. Prof. E. E. Barnard of the Yerkes Observatory[1] made several successful photographs of the comet, shewing the bright head and two diverging tails. When seen under the most favourable conditions the tails could be traced almost eight degrees from the head with the naked eye, though they were never bright except for about two degrees. Mr. Seagrave of this state has studied Delavan's comet to great advantage in the pure air and absolute darkness of his newly completed observatory at North Scituate.

Meteors or "shooting stars" will be rather abundant during November, especially in the early morning hours of the 14th, 15th, and 16th, when the annual Leonid shower occurs, and in the early evenings of the 23d, 24th, and 25th, when displays of the Andromedes may be expected. These streams of meteors are supposed to be the fragments of disintegrated comets. Of the two November groups, the Leonid shower is generally the most notable. The number of meteors seen varies from year to year, being sometimes very small, and on other occasions very great. In 1833, 240,000 Leonids are estimated to have fallen, the phenomenon causing much fear among the ignorant, and driving into frenzies the superstitious blacks of the Southern states. The records of the Ladd Observatory in this city shew far smaller figures for recent years, the two principal displays, in 1898 and 1901, yielding only 318 and 312 meteors, respectively. The ordinary number may be roughly set at from 25 to 50.

As the earth becomes more and more cheerless from the approach of winter, we find compensation in the increasing splendour of the starry sky above. The high eastern heavens now glisten brightly with the gems of Perseus, Taurus, and Auriga, whilst the rising forms of Orion and Gemini are beginning to lend their lustre to the gorgeous ensemble which will gild the nocturnal arch for many months to come. The Zodiacal constellation on the meridian in November is the dull and inconspicuous Pisces, or the Fishes, whose chief interest lies in the "vernal equinox" or point where the sun crosses the celestial equator on its northward journey. Below Pisces is the great bulk of Cetus, the Whale, whose second brightest star, Deneb Kaites, is almost in transit. Above Pisces are the contiguous constellations Pegasus and Andromeda, the latter and more easterly group extending up to the zenith itself. Just east of Pisces are Aries and Triangulum, both soon to attain the meridian. In the west lie the few remaining constellations of summer, together with some of the autumn groups, including Cygnus, Lyra, Aquila, Delphinus, Equuleus, Sagitta, Aquarius, and Capricornus.

Low in the north we find the Plough already tilted upward as if to begin its annual ascent east of the pole. High up on the opposite side of Polaris are Cassiopeia and Cepheus, the former in upper transit and the latter just past it. Ursa Minor and Draco are west of the pole, and about to descend beneath it.

On the horizon just east of Ursa Major is the modern constellation Lynx, almost completely risen, beyond which shines Gemini, with the heavenly twins Castor and Pollux. Due east the stately form of Orion is appearing; a magnificent sight indeed with its two lustrous stars Betelgeux and Rigel, and its sparkling "belt" and "sword". As the brilliancy of Orion gives it beauty, so does its great extent give it a dignity befitting that beauty. Manilius has well said of this giant among constellations: "His arms extended stretch o'er half the skies."[2] South of Orion the starry streams of Eridanus are in view, though the brightest parts of that group are never visible in our northern latitude. Due south are Sculptor and Phoenix, west of which Fomalhaut still brightens the horizon. In the southwest Capricornus has not yet begun to set, and Aquila, due west, also remains entire. In the northwest the setting stars of Hercules carry us round again to Ursa Major.

Most important of all recent advances in astronomy is the photographic discovery of a ninth satellite to Jupiter, made by Mr. Seth B. Nicholson[3] on July 21st of this year with the Crossley reflector at the Lick Observatory. On the night of the discovery Mr. Nicholson was making photographs of the giant eighth satellite, and noticed a strange image on his plates. Subsequent photographs revealed its motion and proved its nature. The new-found body is of the 19th magnitude, and invisible to direct vision, even in the most powerful telescopes. It lies beyond the orbits of the four bright moons, and is believed to revolve around Jupiter in a period of approximately three years, having a retrograde or backward motion like that of the eighth satellite.

The discovery of satellites round the various planets commenced as soon as the telescope was applied to the heavens. On Jan. 7, 1610, Galileo first observed three of the moons of Jupiter, finding a fourth on the 13th of the same month. Huyghens,[4] in 1655, discovered a similar attendant to Saturn. In 1671 Cassini found another satellite of Saturn, repeating this discovery in December 1672, and finding yet two more in March 1684. Sir William Herschel discovered two satellites of Uranus in January 1787, and two more of Saturn in August 1789. In October 1846 Lassell found the single known satellite of Neptune, whilst in September 1848 Prof. Bond of Harvard found Saturn's eighth moon.[5] Lassell in 1851 enriched science by discovering two more satellites of Uranus. In August the late Prof. Asaph Hall of the United States Naval Observatory discovered the two tiny attendants of Mars.[6] In 1892 Prof. E. E. Barnard, now of the Yerkes but then of the Lick Observatory, discovered the fifth satellite of Jupiter, and in 1898 Prof. W. H. Pickering of Harvard added a ninth to Saturn's known retinue. In January 1905 Mr. Perrine of the Lick Observatory discovered photographically the sixth and seventh satellites of Jupiter,[7] and Prof. Pickering in July of the same year discovered by the same method the tenth satellite of Saturn. In January 1908 an eighth moon of Jupiter was found, also photographically, by Mr. Melotte of the Royal Observatory at Greenwich.[8] Mr. Nicholson's achievement this year brings the number of known satellites in the solar system up to 27, including our own moon.

That the recent discovery of Jupiter's ninth satellite will be followed by many similar discoveries in the near future is very likely. The celestial camera has opened for science the door to regions inaccessible to the actual vision of the human eye, and will inevitably bring to light a large number of the tiny and hitherto unknown bodies which must be revolving round the larger and more distant planets.

It is with regret that the writer notes at the present time a rather virulent epidemic of astrological quackery in this city.[9] Belief in the fortune-telling power of the stars and planets is of course superstition of the grossest sort, and a most incongruous feature of this enlightened age; yet astrology is a plague which has proved most difficult to eradicate, and only too many persons of indifferent education are still the dupes of its absurd pretensions.

Since it is practically impossible under our existing laws to prosecute and punish astrologers who do not use the mails in plying their nefarious trade, we must attack the evil at another point, and seek to undermine astrology by diffusing astronomical truth, and thus lifting the public above the range of the charlatans who now flourish because of the general condition of ignorance.

EDITOR'S NOTE FP: *EN* 45, No. 139 (31 October 1914): 10.

Notes

1. Edward Emerson Barnard (1857–1923), astronomer at the Lick Observatory (1887–95) and the Yerkes Observatory (1895–1923).

2. Marcus Manilius (1st century C.E.), Latin poet and author of the *Astronomica* (c. 25 C.E.), a didactic poem on astrology. The line is found at 1.388 (tr. Thomas Creech, 1670).

3. Seth Barnes Nicholson (1891–1963), instructor of astronomy at the University of California (1913–15) and astronomer at the Mt. Wilson Observatory (1915–57). He discovered the 9th, 10th, 11th, and 12th satellites of Jupiter.

4. Christiaan Huygens (or Huyghens) (1629–1695), Dutch physicist and astronomer and one of the leading scientists of the Renaissance.

5. HPL refers to the British astronomer William Lassell (1799–1880) and the American astronomer William Cranch Bond (1789–1859), astronomical observer at Harvard University (1839–59).

6. Asaph Hall (1829–1907), astronomer at the U.S. Naval Observatory (1862–91).

7. Charles Dillon Perrine (1867–1951), American astronomer who worked at the Lick Observatory (1893–1909) and the Argentine National Observatory at Cordoba (1909–36).

8. Philibert J. Melotte, British astronomer.

9. The reference is to J. F. Hartmann's astrology articles (pp. 334–48), to which HPL wrote several rebuttals; see "[Science vs. Charlatanry]" (pp. 260–72).

THE DECEMBER SKY

Saturn, the most interesting of all the planets for observation in ordinary telescopes, will arrive at its opposition on the 21st of the coming month, then appearing at its best. The ring system is still displayed to us at an angle practically as favourable as that which we beheld at the preceding opposition, and affords users of small instruments an excellent opportunity to detect the line of division between the two principal rings. According to Proctor,[1] the division may be seen with a two-inch glass, but this can only be when atmospheric conditions are unusually good; the writer has found difficulty in perceiving it through a telescope three inches in aperture. It is most plainly marked at the "ansae" or parts of the ring system which, on account of perspective, appear broader than the rest, and resemble two handles, one on each side of the planet. The discovery of the true nature of Saturn's rings is one of the most interesting chapters in astronomical history. When Galileo, in 1610, gave Saturn its first telescopic observation, he beheld the disc apparently flanked on each side by a lesser planet, and announced to his friend Kepler, that he had observed the planet to be triple. Soon, however, he noticed that the attendant bodies were disappearing, and when, in December, 1612, they totally vanished, he was utterly confounded, doubting the reality of his own observations, and thereafter ceasing altogether to study Saturn. The varying phases of the rings caused succeeding astronomers to advance every conceivable theory regarding their shape. Scheiner in 1614 believed that the two visible extremities of the ring were bodies attached to the planet.[2] Hevelius, who observed Saturn from 1643 to 1650, thought that it was attended by two detached crescentic bodies.[3] His contemporary Riccioli held a slightly different opinion, considering the two crescents attached to the planet. At another time Riccioli advanced the theory that the planet is attended by two globes joined to it by solid bands.[4] Perhaps the most peculiar belief was that of the eminent philosopher Gassendi,[5] who pictured Saturn as an immense ellipsoid, with a vast circular opening near each extremity. In 1656, the Dutch astronomer Huyghens demonstrated beyond the possibility of doubt the annular nature of Saturn's system, thus solving the problem which had troubled the scientific world for 46 years. Saturn this month hovers around the boundary between Taurus and Gemini, appearing brighter than any visible fixed star save Sirius alone. It rises at 5:34 p.m. on December 1, and on the 31st at 6:39 a.m.

The other prominent evening planet is Jupiter, now past its quadrature and sinking in the western sky. It sets on the 1st at 9:23 p.m., and on the 31st at 7:52. The planet is still a very brilliant object, though by no means at its best.

Venus is rapidly withdrawing from the sun's rays, and by the end of the month will shine with intense brilliance in the eastern sky before sunrise. The striking splendour of this planet in the east at the Christmas season may, as sometimes in the past, cause the ignorant to hail it as the Star of Bethlehem returned. Greatest brilliancy will occur on the 2nd of January. The phase of Venus is now a slender but gradually augmenting crescent, which should be discernible with very slight magnifying power. On the 1st of December Venus rises only 26 minutes before the sun, but on the 31st it rises at 4 a.m.

Mercury will not be visible this month, since it is approaching superior conjunction. Mars is likewise hidden from view, its conjunction occurring on the 24th of the month. Uranus is in the constellation Capricornus, soon to leave the evening sky, whilst Neptune, in Cancer, is drawing toward its opposition.

The moon's phases for December will be as follows:

Full Moon, 2nd.. 1:21 p.m.
Last Quarter, 10th..6:32 a.m.
New Moon, 16th .... 9:35 p.m.
First Quarter, 24th ....3:25 r.m. [sic]

Perigee is on the 15th, Apogee on the 27th. The moon runs high on the 3d and 31st, low on the 16th. It will be near Saturn on the 4th, Jupiter on the 20th, and Saturn again on the 31st.

The entrance of the Sun into the Zodiacal sign Capricornus on December 22nd proclaims the advent of our winter, yet by a curious paradox is also the beginning of the great luminary's annual return northward. The latter and more cheerful significance of the winter solstice has made that phenomenon a cause of feasting and rejoicing amongst various races since the earliest prehistoric times, and has indirectly fixed the date for the observance of Christmas. The true season of Christ's nativity is not definitely known, that event having once been celebrated on the 6th of January in connexion with the feast of the Epiphany. The selection of December 25th as Christmas day occurred in the fourth century, and was undoubtedly a result of a desire to make the celebration coincide with the ancient Roman Saturnalia, which was a development of the primitive winter festival called Brumalia.[6] Many of our present Yuletide customs are derived from the winter festivals of the Druids and of our Saxon ancestors. Though we must for months to come endure the rigours of inclement weather, we may find a consoling proof of the sun's return in the increasing length of the days. Between the first of the month and the winter solstice the days lose 16 minutes, but from the 22nd to the 31st, a gain of five minutes is to be noted.

The eastern evening sky is now bestrown with the myriads of sparkling diamonds that form the constellations of winter. High in the celestial vault shine Orion, Taurus, Auriga, and Gemini, with their resplendent stars Betelgeux, Rigel, Aldebaran, Capella, Castor, and Pollux; whilst nearer the horizon are the two Dogs, with the brilliant Procyon and the peerless Sirius.

Aries, the Ram, is the Zodiacal constellation nearest the meridian, it being just past transit at 9 p.m. on Dec. 15th. Although the name of this group is forever associated with the vernal equinox, we must remember that the motion of the earth's axis in space has shifted the equinox to Pisces, so that Aries is now the second instead of the first constellation of the ecliptic circle. This group is of small extent, and has but two prominent stars, Hamal and Sheratan, both of the second magnitude.

Burritt, in his "Geography of the Heavens", calls attention to the fact that Hamal and Sheratan form a characteristic example of many pairs of bright stars in various parts of the heavens, whose brightest member lies east of the other. Other pairs of this class are Castor and Pollux in Gemini, and Procyon and Gomelza in Canis Minor. Mesarthim, or Gamma Arietis, an object of the fourth magnitude, is the first star ever known to be double. In 1664 the astronomer Hooke, whilst observing a comet in his telescope, came upon Mesarthim by accident, and discovered to his surprise that it is in reality composed of two stars of equal magnitude.[7] Just east of Aries, and rapidly approaching the meridian, is Taurus, the Bull, with its two famous and beautiful clusters. Above Taurus and Aries, and close to transit, is Perseus, a group which, though having no star of the first magnitude, is none the less of surpassing splendour. The Milky Way is here beheld at its richest, while the famous cluster about the star Chi is a magnificent sight in any telescope. The larger stars of Perseus form a graceful curved line that becomes easily impressed upon the memory. Algenib, the brightest star, is of the second magnitude, whilst Algol, the other prominent object, is a variable star whose fame rivals that of Mira in Cetus. Algol, whose name is the Arabic for "Daemon",[8] is as truly representative of the variables of short period as is Mira of the variables of long period. It is ordinarily of the second magnitude, but once in every two and a half days it suffers a temporary obscuration, which lasts over eight hours, and which when greatest reduces it to about the fourth magnitude. This variation is probably caused by the fact that Algol is actually double, the bright visible star having a dark companion which partially eclipses it at regular intervals. The French astronomer, Joseph Lalande, who died in 1807, used in his later years to spend entire nights on the Pont Neuf in Paris, shewing the phenomena of Algol to such passersby as might be interested.[9] West of Perseus is Andromeda, still at its best for observation. South of this group we meet successively Pisces and Cetus, the easternmost parts of the latter being not yet past transit. West of Andromeda Pegasus is declining toward the horizon. In the north Ursa Major is gradually turning to form a right angle with the horizon, whilst Draco is succeeding it beneath the pole. Ursa Minor is hanging downward as though suspended from the tip of his tail. About the pole Cassiopeia has crossed to the west, and Cepheus, immediately below it, is now sinking perceptibly. In the northwest Cygnus has descended too low to exhibit its full splendour, whilst Lyra, with the bright Vega, is about to set. East of the ascending Plough the horizon is occupied by the faint modern constellation Leo Minor, or the Lesser Lion. Farther east we behold the Zodiacal constellation Cancer, the Crab, completely risen. Due east the dull Monoceros, or the Unicorn, is quite outlustred by the neighbouring winter groups. In the southeast the refulgent beams of Sirius announce the appearance of the Greater Dog, next to which Columba, the Dove, is seen. Below Orion is Lepus, the Hare, while the immense extent of Fluvius Eridanus flows from this point to the southern meridian. Achernar, the principal star of Eridanus, is one of the brightest in the heavens, but unfortunately is never visible as far north as Rhode Island. Beyond the meridian the unimportant groups Sculptor and Phoenix carry us round to the southwest, where the brilliant Fomalhaut is setting. Near by is Aquarius, already half withdrawn from view. North of the east point, the small constellations Delphinus, Equuleus, and Sagitta bring us again to the point where Vega is disappearing.

While in the summer and early autumn we are most concerned with that part of the Milky Way which meets the southern horizon in the neighbourhood of Scorpio and Sagittarius, our attention is now being directed toward that opposite region which flows downward through the two Dogs, and which will next month be unfolded to us in even greater splendour.

EDITOR'S NOTE FP: *EN* 46, No. 10 (30 November 1914): 8.

Notes

1. Richard Anthony Proctor (1837–1888), British astronomer. HPL owned his *Half-Hours with the Telescope* (13th ed. 1902; *LL* 708).

2. Christoph Scheiner (1573–1650, German astronomer who chiefly studied sunspots).

3. Johannes Hevelius (1611–1687), astronomer and instrument maker born in what is now Gdansk, Poland. See his *Dissertatio de nativa Saturni facie* (1656).

4. Giambattista Riccioli (1598–1671), Italian astronomer and geographer.

5. Pierre Gassendi (1592–1655), French philosopher and astronomer best known for resurrecting the atomic theory of Democritus.

6. See "Brumalia" (p. 319).

7. Robert Hooke (1635–1703), British scientist who worked in optics, astronomy, and physics.

8. See HPL's fictional use of Algol in "Beyond the Wall of Sleep" (1919).

9. Joseph-Jérôme Lefrançais de Lalande (1732–1807), French astronomer best known for his astronomical tables.

THE JANUARY SKY

Venus, fairest of all the planets, greets the opening year with her brightest beams. Maximum brilliancy occurs on the 2nd of January, at which time the planet will form a spectacle of exceeding beauty in the southeastern heavens just before dawn. Venus is still receding from the sun, and will next month arrive at greatest western elongation. During January Venus traverses the constellations Scorpio and Ophiuchus, being in the general vicinity of the bright red star Antares. On the 1st of the month it rises at 4 p.m., and on the 31st at 3:50. The phase of Venus as seen in the telescope varies from a crescent of moderate thickness to an almost semicircular figure as the planet approaches its elongation.

Saturn, which was in opposition the 21st of last month, continues to shine with full splendour in the evening sky. It is now retrograding near the boundary between Taurus and Gemini, adding its lustre to a region already resplendent with the beams of brilliant fixed stars and the shimmering ribbon of the Galaxy. On the 1st of the month Saturn sets at 6:29 a.m.; on the 31st at 4:13.

Jupiter, though still conspicuous, is descending lower and lower in the southwestern sky. It gleams brightly during the early evening, setting on the 1st at 7:51 p.m., and on the 31st at 6:26. By the end of the month it can be seen only through the twilight.

Mercury will be in superior conjunction on the 5th, and by the end of the month may possibly be glimpsed by sharp eyes near the western horizon just after sunset. Its elongation, however, will not occur until February.

Mars remains invisible, having been in conjunction on the 24th of December. Uranus is likewise hidden from view, coming to conjunction on the 1st of next month.

Neptune will be in opposition on January 30th, then appearing under the best possible conditions. This remote planet is never visible to the naked eye, but with the aid of a telescope may be found in the constellation Cancer, Right Ascension 8 h., 4 min., North Declination 20 degrees. The apparent disc of Neptune is so small, that considerable magnifying power is required to distinguish it from a fixed star.

The discovery of Neptune was one of the most remarkable achievements of astronomical science, being no mere accident, but the result of long and extremely precise calculation. In the first half of the nineteenth century the motions of Uranus, as computed by the most accurate mathematicians, shewed the effects of gravitation exerted by some large unknown planet outside its orbit. With only this attraction on Uranus as a guide, two able young astronomers, Mr. John Couch Adams of England,[1] and M. Leverrier of France, commenced separately and independently to calculate the position and elements of the undiscovered world; a task of unparalleled difficulty, offering an opportunity for the exercise of the highest faculties with which mankind is blessed. Adams was the first to announce his result, which he communicated in 1845 to Mr. Airy, then astronomer royal, expecting the latter to use the data in making a telescopic search for the new planet.[2] Airy, however, neglected to act promptly on the computations of Adams, and put them aside until the following year, when the confirmation calculations of Leverrier aroused him. Then, at Airy's request, Prof. Challis of the Cambridge, Eng.,[3] observatory instituted a careful search of the region wherein the planet was thought to lie; but though he actually saw it many times, the want of accurate charts prevented him from distinguishing it from the many small stars in its vicinity. Meanwhile, Leverrier had sent his computations to Encke, head of the observatory at Berlin, where some very accurate celestial maps were being prepared.[4] The supposed place of the unknown planet had by chance already been covered by the new charts, so that two assistant astronomers, the late Dr. Galle and M. D'Arrest,[5] at once proceeded to use the maps in making a telescopic search according to Leverrier's directions. Galle observed each known fixed star through the instrument, calling its name to D'Arrest, who marked it off upon the map. At length Galle perceived a tiny point of light which had no place on the chart, and which was evidently the suspected planet. By the next evening the new object had sensibly moved, proving beyond a doubt that on September 23, 1846, another great planet had been found. For some time afterward the French displayed a rather unscientific desire to surpass Mr. Adams' share in the finding of Neptune, allotting all the credit to M. Leverrier. Now, however, the fame of the English mathematician is everywhere more properly recognised. That the discovery was not made from his calculations seems entirely the fault of the astronomer royal who neglected them so long.

The Moon will this month have five phases, as follows:

Full Moon, 1st ....7:21 a.m.
Last Quarter, 8th... 4:13 p.m.
New Moon, 15th ....9:43 a.m.
First Quarter, 23d...12:33 a.m.
Full Moon, 30th .... 11:41 p.m.

Perigee falls on the 12th, Apogee on the 24th. The Moon runs low on the 13th, high on the 27th. It will pass near Venus on the 12th, Jupiter on the 17th, and Saturn on the 27th.

The Sun enters the Zodiacal sign Aquarius on the 20th. During January the days gain 46 minutes.

On the 2nd of the month the earth will be in perihelion, or at its nearest point to the sun. It seems strange to us in the Northern Hemisphere, that we should be closest to the sun during the season of coldest weather, yet we must realise that it is not our solar distance but our inclination toward or away from the sun, that determines our seasons. The only effect of our winter proximity to the sun is a tempering of the fiercest cold. To the inhabitants of the Southern Hemisphere, of course, this effect is wanting, since winter occurs during our summer, when the earth is farthest away from the sun. Their seasons therefore present far more disagreeable extremities of temperature than ours.

Turning to the constellations, we find that the revolving seasons have brought to our view the same resplendent array which we beheld just a year ago. Indeed, the face of the siderial sky is in every season the same as at the corresponding time of any other year, the planets alone presenting aspects of infinite diversity. But it is with renewed interest and more affectionate regard, that we hail each successive advent of the various familiar and friendly groups. To the lover of the sky, each star and constellation becomes associated with its respective season, and no phenomena of earth are more typical of the cold January than the lighting up of the nocturnal vault by the meridian beams of Orion, Taurus, Auriga, and The Dogs.

Orion is the most splendid of constellations, and has achieved a place in the traditions of every race and nation. In classical mythology, whence we derive it, Orion was a giant hunter, and the hero of many conflicting legends. According to one account he was the son of Neptune and Euryale, killed by a scorpion for his boast that he could conquer every animal on earth. The Greek and Roman poets preserve the old belief that the rising of Orion causes destructive storms and tempests; hence Virgil speaks of a time "when sudden, dire Orion rous'd the sea."[6] These fancied connexions between earth and sky survive to this day amongst the unlearned, and form a fertile field for the baseless speculations of astrologers and other wild eccentrics.

Taurus, the Bull, which now lies just above Orion on the meridian, is the most refulgent of all the constellations of the Zodiac, and brings to mind a wealth of mythological associations. In prehistoric times it was very appropriately the first group of the ecliptic circle, since it then marked the sun's place at the opening of spring. A suggestion of this ancient condition is found in Virgil, who tells us to perform certain agricultural tasks "Candidus auratis aperit cum cornibus annum Taurus."[7] (When shining Taurus opens the year with golden horns.) The Hyades, a beautiful V-shaped cluster containing the bright red star Aldebaran, form one of the principal features of Taurus. This cluster, rising at the time of the autumnal rains, was connected by the superstitious ancients with stormy weather, and its stars are often called in poetry "The rainy Hyades".

The most famous cluster in Taurus, however, is that of the Pleiades, or Seven Stars, whose name is derived from the Greek verb "plein", to sail, referring to their use by the mariner as a guide over the desolate wintry seas. But six of the Pleiades are now readily visible to the naked eye, though tradition insists that a seventh once shone with equal brilliancy. Alcyone, the brightest Pleiad, was thought during the last century to be the central sun about which all the rest of creation revolves, but this theory has since been completely exploded. Taurus represents the bull into which Jupiter turned himself when he bore off Europa from Asia. The Pleiades and Hyades have an independent mythology, representing the daughters of Atlas, set in the heavens an account of their virtue and piety. Vague legends of nearly all primitive nations connect the Pleiades with some terrible past disaster to the entire human race.

Some of the constellations now appearing above the eastern horizon cheer us as harbingers of the coming spring. The Sickle of Leo, with the bright Regulus, is now completely in view, whilst the head of Hydra follows close upon the Lesser Dog. The Plough in Ursa Major is at right angles to the horizon, and preparing for its ascent above the Pole. To the west the dull groups of Autumn are vanishing, and Deneb, in Cygnus, has well nigh sunk from view. The Galaxy flows from the northern horizon to the southeast, where Argo Navis, newly risen, floats in the golden stream.

EDITOR'S NOTE FP: *EN* 46, No. 35 (31 December 1914): 8.

Notes

1. John Couch Adams (1819–1892), British astronomer. See his *Scientific Papers* (1896–1900; 2 vols.).

2. George Biddell Airy (1801–1892), British astronomer and astronomer royal at Greenwich (1835–81).

3. James Challis (1803–1882), British astronomer and director of the Cambridge Observatory (1836–61).

4. Johann Franz Encke (1791–1865), German astronomer best known for his work on comets.

5. HPL refers to the German astronomers Johann Gottfried Galle (1812–1910) and Heinrich Louis d'Arrest (1822–1875).

6. Virgil, *Aeneid* 1.535–36 (HPL's translation, apparently).

7. Virgil, *Georgics* 1.217–18.

THE FEBRUARY SKY

The elusive Mercury, so seldom identified by beginners in astronomy, will attain its greatest eastern elongation on the 6th of February, then twinkling rather brightly near the western horizon just after sunset. This is the most favourable opportunity of the present year to see Mercury in the evening sky, and the small planet should be diligently sought for near the time given. On the first evening of the month, Mercury will lie very close by the brilliant Jupiter, so that it ought then to be quite easily found. At 2 a.m. of the same night it will pass only about half a degree north of the giant planet, though both will be far below the horizon at that hour. During the present period of visibility, Mercury will be in the constellation Aquarius. Two days after its greatest elongation, Mercury will arrive at perihelion, or nearest point to the sun, and on the 11th it will change its motion from direct to retrograde. On the 21st, the planet will pass the sun in inferior conjunction, preparing to appear next month as a "morning star". Before Feb. 6th, Mercury will shew in the telescope a gibbous phase, decreasing to a semicircle by the date mentioned. After that, until it becomes lost in the solar rays, the planet's figure will be a steadily shrinking crescent.

Refulgent Venus, now a "morning star", likewise attains greatest elongation and a semicircular phase on the 6th of the month, then shining high above the eastern horizon before dawn. Before that time its phase will be crescentic, and afterwards, gibbous. On February 1st Venus rises at 3:52 a.m., and on the 28th at 4:06. During the present month Venus will pass from Ophiuchus into Sagittarius, moving almost completely across the latter constellation.

An interesting feature connected with Venus is the frequency with which the supposed discovery of a satellite has been announced. It has now been pretty completely proven that there is no such attendant body, yet during the seventeenth and eighteenth centuries some of the most eminent astronomers believed themselves to have found evidence of its existence. In the morning twilight of Jan. 25, 1672, the famous Italian observer Cassini beheld southwest of the crescent of Venus an object of like phase, about a fourth the size of the planet, and distant from it by about as great a space as the planet's diameter. At 4:15 a.m. on August 18, 1686, when Venus was gibbous on the western edge, Cassini saw the phenomenon again; the lesser body being of the same phase as Venus, a quarter of its size, and lying eastward at a distance equal to three-fifths of the planet's diameter. Cassini, mindful of the elusiveness of the problematical object, declined to speak dogmatically concerning it, but cautiously remarked, 'that he was in doubt whether it were not a satellite of Venus'. The telescope employed by Cassini in the making of these observations was of the old-fashioned "aerial" type, with a simple double-convex objective of 34 feet focal length, and without a tube. On October 28, 1740, at sunrise, Mr. Short[1] beheld through a 16½-inch reflecting telescope magnifying 60 diameters a small star-like object about 10 seconds of arc from Venus. With powers of 140 and 240, the lesser body shewed a phase like that of the planet, being of about a third the size of the latter. During the month of May, 1760, Mr. Montaigne[2] made some very detailed observations of the hypothetical body. On the 3d he saw a crescent 20 angular minutes from the similar crescent of Venus, and a fourth of the latter in size. The next day the "satellite" appeared to have moved through 30 degrees of a circle around Venus. Observations on the 7th and 14th convinced Montaigne that the body was a true revolving satellite. He was of the opinion that its surface is very dark, thus causing it to be discerned only with the greatest difficulty. The most probable explanation of these pseudo-discoveries is that the smaller object seen was an optical illusion caused by the nature of the telescopes used; a mere reduced image of Venus. The astronomer Wargentin[3] possessed a refracting telescope of good quality, which always shewed such a false satellite of Venus, but which revealed the spurious nature of the phenomenon when turned on its axis.

Saturn is now the leading planet of the evening sky, shining brilliantly near the star Zeta Tauri, which marks the tip of the Bull's southern horn. The planet retrogrades until the 26th of the month, when it commences a direct or eastward motion. On the 21st it comes to perihelion. Saturn sets on the 1st at 4:18 a.m., and on the 28th at 2:25. It is needless to say that the ringed world will this month be the focus to which all amateurs' telescopes will converge.

Jupiter has sunk low in the western evening sky, and may be glimpsed only during the very early part of the month, flickering brightly through the unsteady twilight air. On the 1st it will be close to the fainter Mercury, setting at 6:36 p.m. The giant planet is now in the constellation Aquarius, steadily moving eastward. Jupiter passes beyond the sun in conjunction on the 24th, and will next appear low in the early morning heavens.

Mars is still lost in the sun's rays, and will not come into view until spring. Uranus is also invisible, being in conjunction on Feb. 1st. Neptune is favourably situated in the evening sky, though perceptible only through the telescope.

The moon will this month have but three phases, a rather infrequent state of affairs peculiar to February. Last month there were five phases, and in March there will also be five. Not since February, 1902, has there been another month with less than four. The present abbreviated set of phases is as follows:

Last Quarter, 7th...12:11 a.m.
New Moon, 13th .... 11:31 p.m.
First Quarter, 21st .... 9:58 p.m.

Perigee comes on the 7th, Apogee on the 21st. The moon runs low on the 9th, high on the 23d. It will pass near Venus on the 10th, and near Saturn on the 23d.

The Sun enters the Zodiacal sign Pisces on the 19th. During February the days gain one hour and 11 minutes. The clock and sun-dial now coincide most completely, noon falling half way between sunrise and sunset. On the 13th there will be an annular eclipse of the sun, invisible at Providence, but seen at its best in northern and western Australia, and in Papua, or New Guinea. As a partial eclipse it may be observed from several other places in or bordering on the Pacific and Indian oceans; Japan, the Malay Peninsula, and the African coast being included within the extreme limits of the phenomenon.

The resplendent winter constellations still reign in fullest glory though all are situate farther west than when we last noticed them. Orion, Taurus, and Auriga have passed the meridian, on which now shines the magnificent Sirius, or the Dog-Star, with Procyon and the heavenly twins, Castor and Pollux, lying successively above it. Sirius, the brightest of all the stars in our firmament, has received the most admiring attention from poets both ancient and modern. Manilius wrote of it:

"All others he excels; no fairer light
Ascends the skies, nor sets so clear and bright."[4]

Canis Major, or the Greater Dog, in whose jaws Sirius is supposed to be set, is considered to be the principal hound of Orion, though some ancient writers, including Homer, take Sirius by itself as the giant hunter's dog. Procyon, in Canis Minor, which now shines above and to the left of Sirius, is a very bright star whose charms are somewhat unappreciated on account of the vaster beauties of its more famous neighbour. The name "Procyon" is derived from two Greek words, "pro", before, and "kyon", dog, alluding to the fact that this star rises just before the Dog-Star, as though heralding the advent of the latter. Above the Lesser Dog is the splendid Zodiacal constellation Gemini or the Twins, whose bright stars Castor and Pollux represent the celestial brothers from whom the whole group is named. Castor and Pollux were once of equal magnitude, but a marked difference in brilliancy now exists, Castor being the fainter. The two have always conveyed the idea of relationship, and it is almost impossible for us to think of them separately. Though neither attains the standard first magnitude, the pair are among the most admired objects in the sky. The Heavenly Twins, or Dioscouri, were the sons of Jupiter and Leda, and play a very conspicuous part in Graeco-Roman mythology. Castor was a skilled horseman, whilst Pollux excelled in feats of arms. As Martial said:

> "Castor alert to tame the foaming steed,
> And Pollux strong to deal the manly deed."[5]

The brothers participated in the famous Argonautic expedition, and later cleared the sea of pirates, the latter deed making them the patron deities of the mariner. Castor was at first mortal, but Pollux was immortal. When the former was killed at a feast the pleas of his brother caused Jupiter to grant immortality to him as well; it being provided, however, that only one of the two should be on earth at the same time. Later Jupiter set them both in the heavens as a reward for their pure and noble fraternal affection. The Romans deeply revered the Gemini, and believed that during the battle of Lake Regillus,[6] in answer to the prayers of the Dictator Aulus Postumius, they appeared on their white horses to aid the forces of the young republic against the league of thirty Latin cities which were attempting to restore Tarquinius Superbus to the throne on the Palatine. The peasantry were long afterward accustomed to point out a mark upon a volcanic rock near the scene of this victory as the hoof-print of one of the Twins' horses. The importance of the Gemini in Latin thought is well illustrated by the favourite Roman oath "Ecastor!" or "By Castor!" and "Aedepol!" or "By Pollux!"

Encouraging signs of spring are now beginning to appear in the east. The whole of the Lion is well in sight, whilst Crater, set on the coils of Hydra, is just emerging from the mists of the horizon. The western part of Virgo is slowly unfurling itself, and Coma Berenices is clearly in view. Northward, the Plough is climbing high, while Cassiopeia is descending correspondingly. Perseus is still at its best in the northwest. Some of the western groups soon to disappear below the horizon are Eridanus, Cetus, and Andromeda. Aries will remain visible for a long time.

The inspiring effect of astronomical study on the cultured lay mind is very impressively shewn in a recent essay concerning "The Spiritual Significance of the Stars", by Mr. Leo Fritter,[7] a talented young attorney of Columbus, Ohio, and a leader in amateur journalistic circles. In the infinite celestial universe, with its unbending laws and resistless forces, this author discerns the pattern for all human laws and institutions; the only example of that perfection for which mortals vainly strive, and the only adequate guide for them in their child-like gropings after truth. In man's ability [to understand the] complex system of flying suns and whirling planets that fill the boundless space around him, Mr. Fritter sees, something of a divine nature; something that shews man to be "akin to the central intelligence who presides over this huge dynamo of cosmic energy".

Such lofty sentiments, the natural result of the rational and reverent contemplation of the heavens by an intellect of high quality, form a refreshing contrast to the vulgar superstitions of the sordid astrologer, who beholds in infinity only a cheap little fortune-telling contrivance, designed for the exclusive benefit of one tiny, insignificant world.

EDITOR'S NOTE FP: *EN* 46, No. 61 (30 January 1915): 8.

Notes

1. James Short (1710–1768), British scientist who worked chiefly in optics, although he also made astronomical observations.

2. Unidentified.

3. Pehr Wilhelm Wargentin (1717–1783), Swedish astronomer who supervised the construction of an observatory in Stockholm and concentrated his studies on the moons of Jupiter.

4. Manilius, *Astronomica* 1.410–11 (tr. Thomas Creech; "Yet" for all in the first line and "none" for "nor" in the second line in Creech).

5. Martial (M. Valerius Martialis, 40?–104? C.E.), *Epigrams* 7.57. HPL's is a very loose translation, which in Martial is full of obscene puns.

6. The battle of Lake Regillus (a lake in Latium, in central Italy) was, by Roman tradition, said to have taken place in 498 B.C.E. See the account in Livy 2.19–21.

7. Leo Fritter was a longtime amateur journalist and colleague of HPL. The article appeared in the *Woodbee* (January 1915) and is discussed by Lovecraft in some untitled notes on amateur journalism in the *Conservative* (April 1915; CE 1.36).

THE MARCH SKY

Mercury, visible in February as an evening star, this month appears in the morning sky, arriving at its greatest western elongation on the 20th. It will then be visible low in the east before sunrise. This is not an especially favourable elongation, since morning appearances of Mercury are always best in the autumn rather than in spring.

Venus continues to shine brilliantly in the early morning heavens, rising at 4:06 a.m. on the 1st and at 3:59 on the 31st. It is now approaching the sun and shews in the telescope a gibbous phase. During March Venus moves out of Sagittarius, completely across Capricornus, and into Aquarius.

Saturn, shining in the west, and attaining its quadrature on the 17th, is the only bright planet of the evening sky. It is still lingering east of the Hyades, on the boundary between Taurus and Gemini, moving slowly along the Zodiac. On the 1st it sets at 2:25 a.m., and on the 31st at 12:29. In its present position amid so many bright stars, Saturn is perhaps a little more difficult than usual to identify. We may find it, however, by prolonging eastward the line formed by the lower or left-hand branch of the Hyades, at whose tip lies the brilliant red star Aldebaran.

Jupiter, in conjunction last month, may become visible in the morning twilight, just above the eastern horizon, by the end of March. On the 31st it will rise not quite an hour before the sun. The planet is now moving eastward through Aquarius.

Mars is not yet sufficiently withdrawn from the solar glare to be visible, but will soon make its appearance in the morning sky. On the 31st it rises but three-quarters of an hour before the sun.

Uranus is preparing to appear in the morning, while Neptune is still well seen with the telescope in the evening.

The moon will this month have five phases, as follows:

Full Moon, 1st	1:33 p.m.
Last Quarter, 8th..	7:28 a.m.
New Moon, 15th	2:42 p.m.
First Quarter, 23d...	5:48 p.m.
Full Moon, 31st	12:38 a.m.

Perigee is on the 4th, Apogee on the 20th. The moon runs low on the 8th, high on the 23d. It passes near Venus on the 11th, and near Saturn on the 23d.

The Sun enters the Zodiacal sign Aries on the 21st, at noon, thus opening the long awaited and eagerly welcomed season of spring. This happy annual event gave rise to a multitude of joyful religious ceremonies amongst primitive peoples; which ceremonies, transferred to the Jewish and Christian faiths, appear respectively in the observance of the Passover and of Easter.

On Feb. 10 a new comet was discovered in the constellation Ophiuchus, by J. E. Mellish of Cottage Grove, Wisconsin.[1] Though invisible to the naked eye, it may be seen in a small telescope, and is under observation at the Ladd Observatory here.

The brilliant constellations of winter have passed over to the western sky, while the plainer groups of spring are now well up in the east. The Zodiacal constellation on the meridian is Cancer, the Crab, which in ancient times marked the position of the sun at the beginning of summer. The chief object of interest in Cancer is the faint cluster of stars called "Praespe", or the "Manger", which appears to the naked eye as a dull, nebulous blur of light. On each side of the "Manger" are the two inconspicuous stars Gamma and Delta Cancri, usually known as the "Aselli", or "Little Asses", which are supposed to be feeding from the manger. The credulous ancients believed that the weather could be predicted by noticing the various ways in which the Manger and the Aselli are veiled by light clouds. The celebrated Greek astronomical poet Aratus, in his "Diosemia" or "Prognostica", relates how the obscuration of Praespe alone denotes tempests, the dimming of the Northern Ass a south wind, and the dimming of the Southern Ass a cold north wind.[2] It is, of course, needless to say that these supposed indications have no real foundation, but are as false as the ridiculous prophecies of the astrologers. The mythological history of Cancer may be traced back to a very early period. In the Egyptian zodiac this group represented the scarabaeus, or sacred beetle; while among the Chaldaeans and Hindoos it was, as in classical and modern times, a crab. The Greeks regarded Cancer as the crab sent by vindictive Juno to attack the heel of Hercules when that hero was engaged in his mortal combat with the Lernaean Hydra. As matters turned out, Hercules was able to conquer both Hydra and Cancer, all three subsequently achieving a place in the heavens.

Immediately below Cancer on the southern meridian is the head of Hydra, the coiled body extending eastward for a vast distance, and being not wholly risen even now. In the Grecian myths, Hydra was a nine-headed monster who infested the marshes near Lake Lerna, in the Peloponnesus. When one of his heads was cut off, two would grow in its place. To slay this creature was one of the labours of Hercules, who burned off the heads with a heated iron. According to the Egyptians, this constellation represents the river Nile.

The eastern heavens now tell us of the arrival of spring. High up shines Leo, the Lion, with its Sickle and Right Triangle, the former containing the bright star Regulus, or the Little King. Virgo is almost completely risen, Spica shining brilliantly just above the horizon. Perched on the back of Hydra is Corvus, the Crow, whose irregular but compact figure is very clearly distinguishable in the southeast. In the northeast Boötes is ascending the vault, bearing with him that ruddy vernal gem:

"The bright Arcturus, fairest of the stars."[3]

Corona Borealis, as the night progresses, mounts above the mist and reveals its beautiful circular outline.

In the north the Plough is beginning to assume its characteristic spring position, soaring above the pole in inverted fashion. The Milky Way flows from the northern to the southern horizon in a splendid bend which passes through the gorgeous western sky.

One of the rarest treats yet afforded local lovers of astronomy was the able and beautifully illustrated lecture on the heavens given by Prof. Brooks,[4] the eminent astronomer and discoverer of comets, at the Y.M.C.A. on Broad street last month. Prof. Brooks is professor of astronomy in Hobart college, and director of the Smith Observatory at Geneva, N.Y.

Besides giving a wealth of information concerning the science to which he has devoted his life, the venerable lecturer outlined an original theory regarding the nature of the fifth satellite of Jupiter, which has seldom been mentioned in textbooks or the press. This satellite, as the writer remarked in *The Evening News'* astronomical article for November, was discovered in 1902 at the Lick Observatory by Prof. E. E. Barnard. It is of very small size, lies very close to its primary, and performs its revolution in an incredibly short period. Now, three years before Barnard discovered this peculiar object, Prof. Brooks had found a periodic comet consisting of four fragments, whose orbit was, as is the case with many comets, influenced by the enormous gravitation of Jupiter, and which consequently passed very close to that giant planet in the course of its revolution. It was learned by calculation that in 1886 this comet had approached to within 200,000 miles of Jupiter's surface, thus coming inside the orbit of the nearest large satellite. Wherefore Prof. Brooks, realising the immense attraction exerted by Jupiter, believes that a part of his comet was at that time detached from the rest, and held by the great planet, forever to revolve around it as a moon; and, that it is this comet-born moon which Barnard later discovered as the fifth satellite. The theory of Prof. Brooks is indeed startling. It is hard for us to think that the fifth satellite is really new, and not merely newly found; that it was no satellite at all until the year 1886. Besides, our knowledge of comets does not lead us to believe that they contain any matter sufficiently solid to form a planetary satellite, even so small a one as this. However, Prof. Brooks still places faith in his hypothesis, and is inclined to regard the fifth moon of Jupiter with a sort of proprietary interest, as though it were his own celestial real estate, as he humorously expressed it. Such a skilled, earnest, and faithful astronomical worker is certainly entitled to a greater share of the sky than are most men.

EDITOR'S NOTE FP: *EN* 46, No 85 (27 February 1915): 10.

Notes

1. John E. Mellish, American astronomer who worked at the Yerkes Observatory in Lake Geneva, Wis.

2. Aratus of Soli (315?–240? B.C.E.) was a Greek poet on astronomy, agriculture, and other subjects. *Diosemiai* is the name given to the final section (ll. 733–1154) of Aratus' sole extant work, the *Phaenomena*. The passage to which HPL alludes occurs at ll. 892–908.

3. Manilius, *Astronomica* 5.357–58 (tr. Thomas Creech).

4. William Robert Brooks (1844–1921), British-born American astronomer who resided chiefly in western New York state, where he built his own observatory, the Red House Observatory, in his garden. He taught at Hobart College from 1900 until his death.

APRIL SKIES

Saturn, now past its quadrature, continues to be the only prominent planet in the evening sky. Each night it shines brightly in the western heavens, setting on the 1st at 12:38 a.m., and on the 30th at 10:40 p.m. The brilliancy of Saturn has been rapidly diminishing since its opposition last December, for while it then surpasses all visible fixed stars save Sirius, it is at present no brighter than Rigel. The planet changes but little in apparent place amongst the stars, still remaining on the border of Taurus and Gemini. Turning to the morning sky we find Jupiter now emerging from the solar rays and shining with great lustre in the east. On the 1st it rises at 4:34 a.m., less than an hour ahead of the sun, but at the end of the month it will rise at 3:50 a.m., nearly two hours before the great luminary. The brightness of the planet is steadily increasing, being now almost the same as that of Sirius. Jupiter is moving directly in the eastern part of Aquarius, approaching the boundary of Pisces. As Jupiter slowly withdraws from the vicinity of the sun it encounters Venus, another "morning star", which is bound in the opposite direction. On the morning of the 15th these two brilliant planets will be very close together, presenting a highly interesting sight, and offering an excellent opportunity for comparison. Venus, it is needless to say, will appear by far the brighter. The exact time of conjunction is 11 a.m., in daylight, of course, at which hour Venus will pass only nine minutes of arc south of Jupiter.

Venus rises on April 1st at 3:58 a.m., and on the 30th at 3:28 a.m. Its motion amongst the stars takes it through Aquarius into Pisces, so that near the end of the month it lies close to the vernal equinox, or prime meridian of the sky. As seen through a telescope the planet is gibbous. A third "morning star" is the red planet Mars, which is now sufficiently removed from the sun to be faintly discernible near the eastern horizon just before dawn. On the 1st it rises at 4:45 a.m., and on the 30th at 3:39. Mars moves from the eastern part of Aquarius into Pisces, passing the vernal equinox on the 16th.

Mercury, in greatest elongation west on the 20th of March, lingers in the early morning twilight during the first few days of April, forming with Jupiter, Venus, and Mars a rather remarkable array of morning planets. However, it will vanish before the middle of the month, arriving at superior conjunction on May 1st.

Uranus is well up in the morning sky, while Neptune, in quadrature on the 18th, is visible with a telescope in the evening.

The moon, after having five phases in January, only three in February, and five again in March, returns this month to the more ordinary number, as follows:

Last Quarter, 6th...3:12 a.m.
New Moon, 14th ....6:36 a.m.
First Quarter, 22nd...10:39 a.m.
Full Moon, 29th ....9:19 a.m.

Perigee comes on the 1st and 30th, Apogee on the 17th. The moon runs low on the 4th, high on the 19th. It will pass near Venus on the 10th, Jupiter on the 11th, Mars on the 12th, and Saturn on the 19th.

The sun enters the Zodiacal sign Taurus on the 20th. During April the days gain an hour and 17 minutes.

The new comet of Mellish, whose discovery was mentioned in last month's article, is increasing in brilliancy, and may be seen in very small telescopes. Whether or not it will become visible to the unassisted sight cannot yet be told. Calculations made at the Students' Observatory, Berkeley, California, indicate that the comet will come to perihelion, or nearest point to the sun, on July 20th.

The starry skies of April are distinctly the skies of spring, the gorgeous groups of winter having sunk almost from view in the misty west. The Zodiacal constellation on the meridian is Leo, the Lion, whose right-hand portion is a perfect Sickle, with the bright star Regulus, the Little King, at the end of the handle; and whose left-hand division is a geometrically correct right-angled triangle, with Denebola, a star of the second magnitude, at the intersection of base and hypothenuse. Leo presents magnificent outlines, and is the most splendid of all the spring groups. In classical mythology, Leo represents the terrible Nemaean lion slain by Hercules and set in the heavens by Jupiter as a reminder of the furious fray. But long before Hellenic times this constellation was figured as a lion. The Egyptians, in their most ancient zodiacal schemes, gave to its stars a leonine form, perhaps on account of its being occupied by the sun in that torrid season when the lions, oppressed by the drought of their native deserts, appeared in the inhabited regions and sought relief in the waters of the swollen Nile. The name of the star Regulus is supposed by Burritt to arise from that of the consul Marcus Regulus, one of the most famous of Roman heroes.[1] Such, however, is probably not the case. The star was very early known as Rex, or the King, and was supposed by the ancients to rule all the heavens. "Regulus", or "The Little King", is merely a diminutive title applied to it by the astronomer Copernicus.

Below the Lion, Hydra spreads his monstrous length, bearing on his back the two small "parasite" constellations Corvus, the Crow, and Crater, the Cup. The neat geometrical outline of Corvus is at all times unmistakable, and renders its annual appearance one of the most characteristic of the various signs of spring. In the southeast shines Virgo, with its bright gem Spica, while due east we behold Arcturus in all its splendour, and Canes Venatici, with its sole conspicuous star Cor Caroli, or the Heart of Charles. The four stars Denebola, Spica, Arcturus, and Cor Caroli form a perfect rhombus which is known as the "Diamond of Virgo". In the north we see Ursa Major above the pole, and Cassiopeia below it. Low down in the northeast the bluish-white rays of the lustrous Vega are beginning to penetrate the vapours of the horizon. Farther east, Hercules has almost completely risen. Above Hercules is Corona Borealis, whose sparkling starry circlet is one of the most delicately beautiful of all the quiet figures of the spring and summer skies. Still higher up, beyond Arcturus, is that faintly glimmering mass of tangled beams which we know as Coma Berenices. The winter portion of the Milky Way is now fading in the west, while the summer portion is not yet above the eastern horizon. The section about to appear is perhaps the more generally observed of the two, since the radiance of the other is almost forgotten in the presence of the refulgent stars that lie along its course.

It is with a feeling of sentimental regret that we learn of the final disposition of the great Rosse telescope, which has for 70 years been admired as the largest specimen of its kind in the world. The gigantic and venerable glass has not been able to keep pace with the advancing arts, and having become obsolete as an instrument of astronomical research, has taken its place as an historical curiosity in the Science Museum at South Kensington, London. This immense reflecting telescope, whose massive mirror measures six feet in diameter, was constructed personally by the indefatigable scientist who owned and employed it, William Parsons, third Earl of Rosse, of Birr Castle, Ireland.[2] Plans for the telescope were announced in 1840, and on April 13, 1840, the mirror was cast in a foundry built especially for that purpose. This mirror was not of silvered glass, as is the case with the reflectors of today, but of a speculum metal consisting of copper and tin alloyed in the proper proportions. When cast, the mirror weighed three tons. The reflecting surface was ground and polished by steam-powered machinery, and the mirror set in a wooden, iron-hooped tube 56 feet long and seven feet in diameter. The telescope was too cumbrous for the equatorial mountings of that time, so was mounted instead on a large universal hinge affixed to a firm foundation, and supported by chains and pulleys attached to enclosing walls of masonry. This mounting was completed in 1845 and the telescope then declared ready for use. Its scope was somewhat restricted since its arrangement prevented its being directed to all parts of the sky. The Rosse instrument so much exceeded all others in size, that upon its completion it was expected to accomplish wonders in astronomical discovery. It did not, however, fulfil the highest anticipations of its owner or of the scientific world in general, though many valuable observations were performed by its aid. Now that the famous giant has fallen, the five-foot reflectors of the Harvard Observatory at Cambridge and the Mount Wilson Observatory in California are the largest telescopes in the world. Yet at no far distant date the Rosse record will not only be equalled but surpassed, for there is now under construction at the Mount Wilson Observatory a mirror 100 inches, or eight and one-third feet in diameter. This marvellous object, ground and polished according to the most recent scientific methods, may be expected to excel the old leviathan as much in quality as in quantity, and we have reason to look forward to great advances in celestial knowledge when it is finally put in use.

EDITOR'S NOTE FP: *EN* 46, No. 113 (1 April 1915): 7.

Notes

1. Marcus Regulus was consul of Rome in 256 B.C.E. and, during the Punic wars, sacked the Carthaginian city of Tunis in 256 but was later captured by the Carthaginians and spent the rest of his life in captivity.

2. William Parsons, third earl of Rosse (1800–1867), Anglo-Irish astronomer who in 1845 completed the construction of a telescope with a 72-inch disk near his family seat at Birr Castle, County Offaly, Ireland.

THE MAY SKY

Mercury, in superior conjunction on the first of the month, arrives at its greatest eastern elongation on the 31st. On and around the latter date it will shine twinklingly in the western sky just before the setting of the sun, lying quite near the brighter planet Saturn, which will aid in its identification. Saturn itself is sinking lower and lower in the western evening sky. On the first it sets at 10:36 p.m., and on the 31st at 8:52. It will next month draw near the sun and vanish from our sight.

Jupiter, on the other hand, is fast gaining in height and brilliancy. It shines refulgently each morning, rising on the 1st at 2:50 a.m., and on the 31st at 1:02. The planet is still in direct motion, this month crossing from Aquarius into Pisces.

Venus remains conspicuous as a "morning star", though gradually drawing near the sun. On the 1st it rises at 3:27 a.m., and on the 31st at 2:55. Its motion this month takes it from Pisces into Aries.

Mars is slowly mounting higher in the morning sky, rising on the 1st at 3:38 a.m., and on the 31st at 2:30. It keeps close to Venus throughout the month, passing from Pisces into Aries. On the 14th of May the two planets will be in conjunction, Mars lying less than a degree north of Venus. The contrast between the white, lustrous Venus and the red, now inconspicuous Mars will be very marked.

On the 7th of the month Uranus comes to quadrature in the morning sky. Its slight motion in Capricornus is direct or eastward until the 21st, then retrograde or westward. Neptune, though past quadrature, is still favourably seen in the evening, lying now in the constellation Cancer.

The moon's phases for May will be as follows:

Last Quarter, 6th..12:23 a.m.
New Moon, 13th .... 10:31 p.m.
First Quarter, 21st .... 11:50 p.m.
Full Moon, 28th .... 4:33 p.m.

Apogee comes on the 24th, Perigee on the 28th. The moon runs low on the 2nd and 29th, high on the 16th. It will be near Jupiter on the 9th, and on the 11th will be successively near Venus and Mars. On the 17th it will approach Saturn.

The sun enters the Zodiacal sign Gemini on the 21st of the month. During May it moves northward about seven degrees, bringing the fullest joys of spring, and increasing the length of the days by 58 minutes. By the close of the month, there will be 15 hours of sunshine each day.

Mellish's comet continues to grow brighter, and may be visible to the naked eye this month. It will be nearest the earth about the middle of June, it then being only 40,000,000 miles away, and 165 times brighter than when discovered last February. Though it may prove a conspicuous object, it will not be visible in New England after this month, since its motion is taking it rapidly southward. During the first part of May it can be found in the little modern constellation Scutum Sobieskii, just north of Sagittarius, which is well up in the southeastern sky by midnight.

The Zodiacal constellation of the meridian this month is Virgo, the Virgin, a rather extensive group whose principal stars form a crude figure resembling the letter "Y". At the base of this celestial letter beams the lustrous Spica, a beautful, pure white star of the first magnitude. In classical mythology Virgo is held to be Astraea, the goddess of Justice, last of the ancient deities to leave the earth. In the fabulous golden age, when all men were just and happy, the various gods dwelt much amongst mortals, cheering our ancestors in their labours and aiding them in their endeavours. But when mankind grew vicious, sinking from the golden to the silver, from the silver to the brazen, and from the brazen to the iron age, the sons of heaven departed one by one until only Astraea was left. Finally, disgusted at the depravity of the mortal race, even Astraea took flight, ascending to the skies where she now shines as the constellation Virgo. As Ovid relates it:

> "Faith flees, and piety in exile mourns;
> And Justice, here oppress'd, to Heav'n returns."[1]

In the character of Astraea, Virgo is represented as holding in her hand the Balances of justice, the constellation Libra. Another legend holds Virgo to be the Grecian maiden Erigone, daughter to Icarius the Athenian. Her father being slain by some peasants whom he had inflamed with wine, Erigone hung herself out of filial piety on the spot where he had perished. On the charts Virgo / of filial piety on the spot where he / Spica as an ear of corn which she holds.[2] This association with the harvest season is very interesting, recalling prehistoric times when Virgo's place in the Zodiac justified such a connexion. The Egyptians deemed Virgo to be a representation of the great goddess Isis, whilst the peoples of the Tigris-Euphrates civilisation called it after their own deity Ishtar, Ashtoreth, or Astarte.

Just north of Virgo, and exactly on the zenith at Providence, may now be seen that elusive, glittering, shimmering cluster of small stars which form the constellation Coma Berenices, or Berenice's Hair. The legend of this group is quite interesting, though not prehistorically mythological. Berenice was the wife of Ptolemaeus Soter, king of Egypt, and when her royal husband departed for the war in Assyria, she vowed to sacrifice her luxuriant golden tresses to Venus in the event of victory. The king having won, Berenice cut off the locks and deposited them in the temple of Venus, but they were one day missed from the shrine where she had placed them. Finally Conon, the court astrologer, a sage no doubt almost as wise as our star-gazing contemporary Mr. Hartmann, pointed them out in the heavens, whither Jupiter had transferred them.

> "There Berenice's locks first rose so bright,
> The heav'ns bespangling with dishevell'd light."[3]

Just south of Virgo on the meridian is the neat little trapezium of stars forming the constellation Corvus, the Crow. This group, though by no means dazzling in its brilliancy, is yet of great attractiveness to the discriminating eye, being one of the most pleasingly characteristic of all the features of the vernal heavens. The effulgent winter constellations are now almost entirely gone. Procyon, in Canis Minor, still lingers in the West, but the Greater Dog has set. The Twins yet remain in sight, but Taurus has disappeared. Capella continues to light up the northwest, but is fast approaching the horizon. The only bright constellation in the higher western heavens is Leo, still in full glory. The presence of Crater, Hydra, Cancer, and Lynx adds but little beauty to this part of the sky. In the north we perceive that the Plough is now tilted slightly downward toward its summer position west of the pole, while Draco, behind it, is approaching upper transit. Cassiopeia is directly under the pole, and Cepheus has just begun its ascent. Cygnus, with the bright Deneb, is almost wholly in view, whilst Lyra, with the matchless Vega, is conspicuous in the northeast. Other eastern groups are Hercules, Ophiuchus, Libra, Corona Borealis, and Boötes, the latter, with its bright Arcturus, being close to the zenith. Low in the southeast Scorpio is rising, the fiery Antares just shewing its ruby beams through the horizontal vapours. On the southern horizon is part of Centaurus, the Centaur, that extensive and resplendent constellation whose brightest beams are never beheld in so northern a latitude as this. Alpha, the chief star in this group, is the nearest of all stellar bodies to our own solar system. The Centaurs, in mythology, were a race of monsters whose lower parts were like those of horses, but whose upper portions were human. They lived in Thessaly and Arcadia, and were reputed to have been the inventors of pastoral poetry. One of their number, Chiron by name, had been instructed by Apollo and Diana, and was so learned that he became a great teacher, under whose care many Greek heroes, including Aesculapius, Hercules, Jason, Achilles, and Aeneas were reared. Chiron was said even to have invented the constellations. Upon his death, this semi-equine sage was set in the heavens by Jupiter. The fabulous history of Centaurus is much confused with that of the Zodiacal group Sagittarius, which also represents a centaur, and opinion is about equally divided as to which of the two is Chiron. Historical mythologists endeavour to account for the origin of the legends concerning centaurs by supposing them to refer to a race of hardy Thessalians who spent much of their time on horseback.

The high position of Providence in the astronomical world has lately been strengthened in no mean fashion by the addition of a costly and delicate new Italian instrument to the already fine equipment of the Ladd Observatory on Doyle Avenue. This instrument, the gift of Mr. Samuel H. Tingley of this city, is a device for the study of the solar prominences, those gigantic jets of red flame which are seen playing about the darkened disc during total eclipses of the sun. The prominences, parts of the chromosphere, or sun's inner atmosphere, are not generally visible except during total eclipses, but may be studied at other times by means of the spectroscope and allied special instruments. The newly donated piece of apparatus was manufactured especially for Mr. Tingley with utmost skill and well-nigh incredible precision at the best scientific workshops in Italy, so that our local observatory has now an opportunity to compete with the largest and best astronomical institutions of the country in the prosecution of solar research.

EDITOR'S NOTE FP: *EN* 46, No. 138 (30 April 1915): 8.

Notes

1. Ovid, *Metamorphoses* 1.149–50 (tr. John Dryden [1693]; "flies" for "flees" in Dryden).
2. There appears to be a textual problem in this passage; the text is printed here exactly as given in the original appearance.
3. Pope, *The Rape of the Lock* (1714), Canto 5, ll. 129–30 ("Not" for "There" in Pope).

THE JUNE SKIES

At the beginning of the coming month the evening sky will be graced by the presence of two bright planets, Mercury and Saturn; both of which, however, will sink from sight within the space of two or three weeks.

Mercury was in greatest elongation east on May 31, and will therefore be visible just above the western horizon in the evening twilight, not reaching inferior conjunction till June 27th; while Saturn, coming to conjunction on the 28th, will lie not far from it, setting on the 1st at 8:51 p.m., and on the 10th at 8:22.

The morning sky is more fortunate in its adornment, containing the ever brilliant Venus and Jupiter, as well as ruddy Mars, whose lustre is steadily increasing. Venus, fairest of all the planets, rises on the 1st at 2:54 a.m., and on the 30th at 2:51. It is slowly approaching the sun, passing this month from Aries into Taurus, and lying on the 17th almost exactly midway betwixt the famous Pleiades and Hyades clusters. As Venus draws near the solar orb, Jupiter correspondingly recedes from it, arriving at quadrature on the 19th. The giant planet rises on the 1st at 1:01 a.m., and on the 30th at 11:07 p.m. It will soon enter the evening sky, supplying the deficiency made by the withdrawal of Mercury and Saturn. Jupiter's motion, still direct, bears it a little farther into the constellation Pisces, the vernal equinox being quite closely approached at the end of June. The planet will, however, turn backward next month without having actually reached this important celestial circle.

Mars has now become a reasonably conspicuous object, attaining by the close of the month a brilliancy but little below that of the stars Regulus, Deneb, and Fomalhaut. It moves during June from Aries into Taurus, rising on the 1st at 2:20 a.m., and on the 30th at 1:33 a.m.

Uranus is now well past quadrature, and drawing rapidly toward to the evening sky, though its dulness will cause it to be little observed. Neptune, still less attractive in its lustre, is sinking out of the evening sky, and will next month come to conjunction.

The moon's phases for June will be as follows:

Last Quarter, 4th...11:32 a.m.

New Moon, 12th .... 1:57 p.m.

First Quarter, 20th ....9:24 a.m.

Full Moon, 26th .... 11:27 p.m.

Apogee falls on the 10th; Perigee on the 25th. The moon runs high on the 12th and low on the 25th. It will approach the following planets on the following dates: Jupiter, 5th; Mars, 9th; Venus, 10th.

On June 22nd, at 7 a.m., the sun reaches the Tropic of Cancer, the highest point in its apparent annual course, thus proclaiming the advent of summer and giving us the longest day of the year. The solar disc will on that occasion be above the horizon for 15 hours and 14 minutes. By the end of the month, three minutes will have been lost by the days. Solar activity, for the past few years at a low ebb, is gradually becoming more evident, as is attested by the recent appearance of a large group of spots on the shining surface. The frequency of solar spots, as determined by the German astronomer Schwabe,[1] varies in periods of 11 years, five from a minimum to a maximum, and six from a maximum to a minimum. The last previous minimum was in 1911, hence we may expect to see the greatest possible number next year. These fluctuations appear to be connected, in some manner not yet perfectly comprehended, with certain phenomena of terrestrial magnetism. The solar spots are by most observers held to be depressions in the visible surface of the great central luminary, created by gaseous eruptions of a degree almost beyond our conception. Some of them vary from 50,000 to 100,000 miles in diameter, dwarfing to insignificance the earth on which we dwell. They are generally surrounded by grey fringes called "penumbrae", whose diameter occasionally reaches 150,000 miles. When we consider that the sun is a mass of incandescent vapour whose temperature is about 7000 degrees Centigrade, we may imagine feebly the strange nature of the spots. They are probably cyclonic in form, since under high magnification their penumbrae seem to be composed of attenuated filaments, all converging toward the centre of the spots, and having something of a spiral contour. The darkness of the spots is only relative, due to contrast with the incredibly effulgent surface on which they appear. The spots recently seen were more than 20 in number, two of which were each over 15 times the size of the earth.

Mellish's comet has not fulfilled the highest expectations which it aroused in the early spring. Its brilliancy has not been at all considerable, and Profs. Lampland and Slipher[2] of the Lowell Observatory at Flagstaff, Arizona, now report that the original mass has undergone a disruption like that which destroyed the famous comet of Biela in 1852. Whether the breaking up of Mellish's comet will give rise to a swarm of meteors as did Biela's cannot yet be told. It is at present a prevailing theory amongst astronomers, that all meteors have arisen from the disintegration of comets; and if this be true, we are now witnessing one of the actual processes of creation.

It was recently announced that Prof. Paul T. Delavan, the discoverer of last year's conspicuous comet, had succeeded in finding another, but latest advices from Prof. Stroemgren[3] of Copenhagen indicate that this body is Temple's well-known periodic comet, now drawing near its perihelion. However, it will be remembered that Delavan's comet of 1913–14 was for some time held to be Westphal's comet, so that we must not yet positively reject this astronomer's second announcement.

Turning to the constellations, we behold the characteristic groups of summer ascending in the east, while those of spring are for the most part past the meridian. The Zodiacal constellation just now lying due south is Libra, the Balances, a group containing 51 stars, of which two are of the second magnitude and two more of the third. The individual names of these stars are derived from the Arabic tongue, testifying to the immense debt which we owe the painstaking astronomers of the mediaeval Saracencaliphate. Their length and difficult pronunciation, however, as exemplified by "Zubeneschamali" and "Zebenelgubi", rather incline us to favour the more modern Greek letter system of Bayer. Libra did not exist as a separate constellation in the older classical Zodiac, but was introduced by the famous Marcus Terentius Varro, "most learned of all the Romans".[4] It was previously considered either as the balance of Virgo, or the claws of Scorpio. However, its separate position in prehistoric Egyptian and Chaldaean Zodiacs has been asserted. Just west of Libra, and but lately past the meridian, is Virgo, with the brilliant Spica, whilst high above them both shines Boötes, holding the matchless Arcturus. Amongst the earlier Greeks Boötes represented Lycaon, King of Arcadia, who was turned by Jupiter to a wolf on account of his practice of offering human sacrifices to Pan. This same mythology, however, is also claimed for Lupus, a fainter group now on the southern horizon, and barely appearing through the mists. Another legend connects Boötes with Icarius, who was slain by some shepherds whom he had aroused with liquor. According to a third tale, this constellation typifies Erichthonius, who first taught the use of the four-horse chariot. But most frequently was Boötes called by the name "Arctophylax", or "Guardian of the Bear", and in this capacity figured as driving Ursa Major in its circuit round the pole. Aratus, the most famous astronomical poet of antiquity, thus writes:

> "Behind, and seeming to urge on the Bear,
> Arctophylax, on earth Boötes named,
> Sheds o'er the Arctic car his silver light."[5]

Just east of Boötes glows the exquisite circle known as Corona Borealis, which represents the crown given by Bacchus to his mortal wife, Ariadne, and set by him in the sky at her death. Below Corona lies the massive constellation formed by Ophiuchus and the Serpent which he bears and sometimes designated by the collective name Serpentarius. Ophiuchus is the celestial form of Aesculapius, the great healer, son of Apollo and the nymph Coronis, and pupil of Chiron the centaur. When this marvellous physician was born, his future achievements were foretold by Ocyrrhoe, daughter to Chiron, for which rash prophecy the seeress was metamorphosed into a mare. So great was the skill of Aesculapius, that he at last became able to raise the dead;

whereat Pluto, sovereign of the nether world, made complaint before Jove concerning the unnatural restoration to life of his rightful subjects. The father of Gods and men, perceiving the justice of Pluto's plea, removed Aesculapius from the earth; but in acknowledgment of his merits, gave him eternity amidst the stars. The serpent was a shape assumed by Aesculapius when he journeyed to Rome to cure the plague, and under which he was there worshipped; hence in the heavens both human and serpent forms are figured.

In the northern sky we now observe Ursa Minor above the pole, as though balanced on the top of his tail, whilst Ursa Major is headed downward. Cassiopeia, preceded by Cepheus, is commencing its ascent, and Draco is almost in upper transit. In the northwest Cygnus is well in view, whilst the piercing bluish-white beams of Vega come from a high station in the nocturnal vault. Aquila, with the bright Altair, shines pleasantly above the eastern horizon, south of which Sagittarius is beginning to appear. The Scorpion claws stealthily along the southern horizon, reaching almost to the meridian where Libra, Lupus, and Centaurus are seen. In the west are the constellations of Spring: Hydra, Corvus, Crater, Virgo, Leo, Coma Berenices, and Canes Venatici. Close to the horizon and soon to set are Cancer, Gemini, and Auriga. The Milky Way, traceable from the north to the southeast, flows through Cassiopeia, Cepheus, Cygnus, Aquila, Ophiuchus, Sagittarius, and Scorpio; its chief richness, better to be displayed in the later summer, being in the two latter groups.

EDITOR'S NOTE FP: *EN* 47, No. 1 (1 June 1915): 8.

Notes

1. Samuel Heinrich Schwabe (1789–1875), German astronomer who in 1843 made the first definite statement on the periodicity of sunspots.

2. Carl O. Lampland (1873–1951), American astronomer who was assistant director of the Lowell Observatory from 1903 until his death. Earl C. Slipher (1883–1964), American astronomer who joined the staff of the Lowell Observatory in 1905 and remained there until his death. He was a pioneer in planetary photography.

3. Svante Elis Strömgren (1870–1947), Danish astronomer who was professor of astronomy at Copenhagen University (1907–40) and director of its observatory.

4. M. Terentius Varro (116–27 B.C.E.), best known for *De Lingua Latina* (On the Latin Language); most of his works do not survive. He was referred to as "the most learned of the Romans" (*vir Romanorum eruditissimus*) by Quintilian (*Instutio Oratoria* 10.1.95).

5. Aratus, *Phaenomena* 91–93.

THE JULY SKIES

During July the early evening heavens will be entirely destitute of bright planets, while all of these bodies may be distinguished more or less favourably in the morning. Mercury, which last month passed out of the evening sky, will this month appear in the morning, arriving at its greatest western elongation on the 18th, and being visible about that date as a twinkling reddish spark outlined at dawn against the pale eastern heavens, close to the horizon. On the 10th Mercury will be near both the thin crescent of the waning moon, and the bright planet Venus. On the 22nd it will be near Saturn, which will have emerged from the sun's glare into the morning sky.

Venus is gradually withdrawing toward the sun, and will soon be lost amid the latter's refulgence. On the 1st it rises an hour and twenty minutes before the solar orb, while by the 31st this interval is reduced to an hour. Venus will be very near Saturn on the 17th, passing but little more than half a degree north of the ringed planet. The course of Venus amongst the stars during July takes it from the eastern part of Taurus entirely through Gemini, to the western confines of Cancer.

Mars is now well up in the morning sky, rising on the 1st at 1:32 a.m., and on the 31st at 12:43. The planet's path this month lies wholly in Taurus, extending from the western to the eastern portion of that constellation, and passing between the Pleiades and the Hyades.

Jupiter is now the most advantageously situated of all the planets, being a very conspicuous object in the southeastern sky after midnight. On the 1st of the month it rises at 11:06 p.m., and on the 31st at 9:06. The planet is in Pisces, near the vernal equinox, moving directly until the 19th, and retrograding after that date.

Saturn, before the end of the month, will emerge from obscurity and shine near the eastern horizon at dawn. On the 31st it will rise two hours and five minutes before the sun.

Uranus is near opposition, and therefore visible under quite favourable conditions, but it is at all times too faint for profitable observation by amateur astronomers. Neptune arrives at conjunction on the 23d, and is accordingly hidden from sight in the solar rays.

The moon's phases will occur as follows:

    Last Quarter, 6th .... 12:54 p.m.
    New Moon, 12th .... 4:31 a.m.
    First Quarter, 19th .... 4:09 p.m.
    Full Moon, 26th .... 7:11 a.m.

Apogee comes on the 8th, Perigee on the 24th. The moon runs high on the 9th, low on the 23d. It will be near Jupiter on the 3rd, Mars on the 8th, Venus and Mercury on the 10th, and Jupiter again on the 30th.

The sun enters the Zodiacal sign Leo, the Lion, on the 23d, moving southward about four and three-quarters degrees during the month. The days lose 43 minutes between the 1st and the 31st.

On July 5th the earth will be in aphelion, or farthest point from the sun. It is fortunate for us that we dwell in the northern hemisphere, where summer occurs when the earth is at its greatest distance from the sun, and winter when the earth is nearest that body, for this varying distance is thus able to mitigate the severity of our seasons. In the southern hemisphere, which includes Australia, South Africa, Argentina, and Chile, the seasons are opposite; perihelion occurs in summer, that is our winter, and aphelion at the present season, the southern winter and our summer. Thus the southern seasons are rendered the more unpleasantly extreme by the same causes which soften the otherwise violent contrasts in our own.

The comet lately found by Delavan has now been conclusively identified with Temple's periodic comet, hence is after all no new discovery.

The Zodiacal constellation on the meridian in July is Scorpio, the Scorpion, whose long, kite-like figure is unmistakable as it makes its short sojourn in the visible sky, hanging low over the southern horizon. Marking the heart of the fabled Scorpion glows the deep red star Antares, which is, as its Greek name reveals, frequently compared to the planet Mars, an almost equally ruddy object. But the causes of redness in the star and in the planet are extremely dissimilar. Mars, a non-luminous globe reflecting the light of the sun, displays its characteristic hue merely because the soil of its surface chances to be red; whilst the colour of Antares, an incandescent gaseous object sending forth its own waves of light, arises from the conditions under which the light is generated, and affords some index to the quality and constitution of the star. Astronomers and astrophysicists, in investigating the colours of the various sidereal bodies, have generally agreed that the relative age of a star may be estimated by the predominating tint in its rays. Thus a comparatively new star, or one but lately evolved from the nebulous condition, is usually bluish-white in hue. Those further advanced in development are pure white, turning eventually to deepening shades of orange; whilst an old star, or one whose lustre is about to die out, is red, the shade growing deeper as extinction approaches. According to this rule, then, Antares is a star of great age, and will in the course of a few million years have ceased to shine. Antares is flanked on each side by a star of the third magnitude, its prominence being thus much enhanced. The tail of the scorpion extends in a curved line east of Antares, and causes the starry figure to bear an unusual resemblance to the object which it is supposed to represent.

The mythological history of Scorpio is connected with that of Orion, as described in these columns last January. Orion having been killed for his presumption by the Scorpion, both were set in the heavens, it being provided that neither one should appear above the horizon in the presence of the other. Wherefore Orion blazes refulgently in winter, but drifts away into the western twilight each spring, that Scorpio may shine in his turn. In the autumn Scorpio leaves the sky, and Orion mounts above the eastern hills. This subject affords an amusing instance of ignorance or neglect on the part of a great author. In a passage in Victor Hugo's "The Man Who Laughs", two sailors in a boat are examining the misty winter sky. The captain declares he cannot see the belt of Orion, whilst the other replied in naive dejection, that he cannot see Antares![1] The constellation Scorpio is in reality vastly older than the Grecian myths, its legendary lore extending to early Egyptian and Chaldaean times. It was generally thought to have a sinister significance, and to possess an occult connexion with that equally evil object, the planet Mars; indeed, the few astrological quacks and dupes who have survived to the present day still prate stupidly about the "malignant sign of Scorpio, birthplace of malefic Mars and his house".

Directly over Scorpio is the rambling compound constellation Ophiuchus et Serpens, while still higher up, and just east of Corona Borealis, is the vague, dull form of Hercules. In the west are all the groups of spring; Leo, Virgo, Corvus, Libra, and Boötes. Northward we behold Draco, the Dragon, in upper transit, Ursa Major pointed down toward the horizon, and Ursa Minor leaning to the west above the pole. Cepheus and Cassiopeia are ascending in the eastern circumpolar region, whilst Andromeda has partially risen in the northeast. Pegasus, also half in sight, lies southward from Andromeda, while due east Aquarius is appearing. In the southeast Capricornus has unfolded its westernmost extremity, while Sagittarius is in full view. Higher up in the eastern heavens are Aquila, the Eagle, with the bright Altair; Lyra and Cygnus, bearing respectively the lustrous stars Vega and Deneb; and the three tiny asterisms Delphinus, Equuleus, and Sagitta, the first named of which presents a neat little rhombic figure commonly called "Job's Coffin".

Delphinus represents the dolphin that saved the bard Arion from drowning, and forms part of a very beautiful and interesting legend. Arion was a musician and courtier to Periander, Tyrant of Corinth. Having journeyed to Sicily to enter a musical contest, he left victorious for home. But the golden prize he had won excited the covetous passions of the sailors on his ship, who cast him overboard after allowing him to sing one last melody to the strains of his lyre. However, the song had drawn a school of dolphins about the vessel, and one of them offered to bear him in safety to the land. As a poet has written:

> "But (past belief) a dolphin's arched back
> Preserv'd Arion from his destin'd wrack;
> Secure he sits, and with harmonious strains
> Requites his bearer for his friendly pains."[2]

Delphinus landed the lyrist on the promontory of Taenarus, in Sparta, whence Arion made haste to Corinth, arriving ahead of the murderous ship's crew, and causing the friendly monarch Periander to have the robbers crucified.

The list of the world's great telescopes will soon receive a notable addition in the form of another reflector which will share with the common telescope at Harvard and the Mount Wilson telescope in California the distinction of being unsurpassed in size. This new instrument, five feet in clear aperture, is being constructed for the Observatorio Nacional at Cordoba, Argentina, which is at present under the direction of Prof. C. D. Perrine, formerly of the Lick Observatory. The glass for the mirror was cast in France, weighs one ton, and is eight inches in thickness. Construction is by Warner and Swasey, and the instrument when completed will be contained in a tube 6 feet in diameter and 27 feet in length. The weight of the finished telescope will be 14 tons. While the five-foot record for size will soon be surpassed by the 100-inch glass now being built at Mount Wilson, the new Cordoba instrument will yet remain the largest telescope in the southern hemisphere.

EDITOR'S NOTE FP: *EN* 47, No. 27 (30 June 1915): 6.

Notes

1. See Victor Hugo (1802–1885), *L'Homme qui rit* (1869; Eng. tr. as *The Man Who Laughs*), Part 1, Book 2, ch. 3.
2. The poet is HPL himself.

THE AUGUST SKIES

Venus is now withdrawing from visibility, preparatory to its superior conjunction of September 13th. At the very beginning of August, it may be seen as a brilliant orb, poised just above the sunrise point in the early morning twilight, but before the month closes it will have approached the sun too closely to be observed.

Saturn, as Venus departs, replaces the latter as a conspicuous morning planet. On the 1st it rises at 2:20 a.m., two hours and five minutes before the sun, and on the 31st at 12:35, over four and a half hours before the sun. The ringed planet is in direct motion, being now about half way across the constellation Gemini. Though at present rather dull in appearance, Saturn will soon commence to gain lustre, and will wax very brilliant during the ensuing months.

Mars, which is being overtaken quite swiftly by Saturn, rises on the 1st at 12:42 a.m., and on the 31st at 12:06. Its increasing brightness is as yet hardly perceptible, though it gains about a tenth of one stellar magnitude during the month. The planet's motion amongst the stars carries it out of Taurus well into Gemini.

Jupiter though not yet in opposition has entered the evening sky, rising on the 1st at 9:04 p.m., and on the 31st at 6:57. Its brilliancy increases nearly two tenths of a magnitude during August. The planet is now retrograding through the extreme western portion of Pisces.

Mercury will be invisible throughout the month, arriving at superior conjunction on the 14th.

Uranus comes to opposition on the 7th, then appearing under the best possible conditions. At this point in its apparent course it is usually visible to the naked eye, but since it never exceeds the sixth magnitude, it is seldom noticed or identified by the amateur. Uranus is now retrograding in Capricornus. Neptune, in conjunction last month, is a negligible quantity.

The Moon's phases for August will be as follows:

Last Quarter, 2nd .... 4:27 p.m.
New Moon, 10th .... 5:52 p.m.
First Quarter, 17th .... 9:17 p.m.
Full Moon, 24th .... 4:41 p.m.

Apogee is on the 4th, Perigee on the 20th. The moon runs high on the 5th, low on the 19th. On the 6th it will pass near Mars, on the 7th near Saturn, on the 23d near Uranus, and on the 26th near Jupiter.

The sun enters the Zodiacal sign Virgo on the 23d, thus sadly announcing the waning of summer. During August the days decrease by almost an hour and a quarter.

On the 10th occurs an annular eclipse of the sun, invisible except on the Pacific Ocean and the contiguous parts of Asia. Its annular nature can be observed only from a very restricted path, which touches no important land areas. The year 1915 contains the least possible number of eclipses; two of the sun. Seven is the greatest possible number; five of the sun and two of the moon, or four of the sun and three of the moon. All these, however, are extremes; four being the most common number of eclipses to occur within a single year.

Turning to the constellations, we find that Sagittarius, the Archer, is the Zodiacal group on the meridian at 9 p.m. this month. Sagittarius contains no star of the first magnitude, but is interesting on account of its partial immersion in the Milky Way, and its possession of many clusters and nebulae conspicuous in an opera or field glass. In our latitude this constellation lies close to the southern horizon, while in England it is even less favourably seen. The mythological history of Sagittarius is, as has been remarked before in these columns, often confused with that of Centaurus, since each is represented on the maps and globes as a Centaur. However, Centaurus is generally taken as Chiron, the wise teacher, while Sagittarius is recognised as Nessus, the famous opponent of the peerless hero Hercules. One day, as Hercules was travelling with his bride Dejanira, he came to the swift-running river Evenus, across which he knew not how to convey his spouse. The centaur Nessus, standing close by, offered to assist the fair by carrying her to the opposite shore on his back whilst Hercules should swim. This he did, but no sooner had he reached the land, than he commenced to gallop off with his precious burden, treacherously leaving the son of Jove to battle with the foaming torrent. But Hercules, perceiving the abduction of Dejanira, slew Nessus with an arrow poisoned from the venom of the Lernean Hydra. As Ovid says:

> The Centaur's back admits the feather'd wood,
> And through his breast the barbed weapon stood,
> Which when, in anguish, through the flesh he tore,
> From both the wounds gush'd forth the spumy gore.[1]

Nessus, expiring, soaked his robe in his own blood, which had received the Hydra's poison, and gave the envenomed garment to Dejanira, falsely telling her that if her affection of Hercules should cool, the wearing of this robe by him would restore its ardour. Years later, occasion having arisen, Dejanira innocently sent the poisoned robe to her husband to wear at a sacrifice. Scarce had the hero donned the fatal cloth, when he commenced to burn as with fire. In vain he sought to remove it, for its horrible folds clung to him like his very skin. Thus did Sagittarius, or Nessus, accomplish his revenge. Raging in agony, Hercules repaired to the summit of Mount Oeta, there built his own funeral pyre, and after bequeathing his mighty bow and deadly arrows to his comrade Philoctetes, resigned himself to the flames of death. But Jove, admiring and pitying his valiant son, let the fire consume only the mortal part of him, raising the purified, immortalised Hercules to the heights of Olympus, there evermore to dwell amongst the Gods.

Above Sagittarius lies Aquila, the Eagle, containing the brilliant star Altair. This constellation was anciently thought to portend tempests when it rises before the sun, a belief embodied in the works of the celebrated Greek astronomical poet Aratus. Of the classical legends surrounding Aquila, three are of equal importance. According to one account, this bird is the form into which was metamorphosed Merops, king of Cos. Others hold the Eagle to represent the shape assumed by Jupiter when he bore off the lad Ganymede from his playmates on Mount Ida, taking him up to Olympus to succeed Hebe as cupbearer to the Gods. The third story calls Aquila the bird that supplied Jupiter with the thunderbolts that he used during the wars between the Gods and the Giants. As Manilius says:

> He's worthy Jove, since he, a bird, supplies
> The Heav'n with sacred bolts, and arms the skies.[2]

In general the Eagle was considered king of the feathered tribe, and in particular the sacred bird of Jupiter. The lower part of Aquila is by some classified as a separate constellation. Tycho Brahe, the famous old Scandinavian astronomer, named it Antinous, in memory of that beautiful Bithynian youth who became the favourite of Hadrianus, the Roman emperor. Antinuous, having been told by an oracle that his death would save the imperial master from peril, drowned himself in the Nile. Hadrianus, touched by the supreme sacrifice of his young courtier, built him a temple on the river bank where he had perished, and filled the empire with portraits and statues of him. The worship of Antinuous as a god was later introduced by the emperor.

Looking almost directly overhead we may now behold Lyra, the Lyre, whose refulgent star Vega is one of the wonders of the north celestial hemisphere. This is one of the few groups which partially justify their names, and it is not difficult to trace the outlines of the ancient musical instrument among the various stars that compose the constellation. According to the Greeks, Lyra was the celestial lyre given by Apollo to the matchless musician Orpheus. So entrancing were its strains that wild animals, tamed for the moment, flocked round the player; swift-running rivers stilled their flowing to hear the notes; and even the trees and rocks, the very hills and mountains, moved closer that they might drink in the heavenly chords. The nymphs of the woods, the naiads of the brooks and fountains, are the hamadryades of the groves, all gathered about the inspired one, rapt in ecstasy at the music of his lyre. The nymph Eurydice became the bride of the player, but soon after their nuptials, was killed by the sting of a serpent. Orpheus, in despair, descended to the lower regions with his lyre, charming all who heard, and even causing those who had been condemned to eternal torment to forget their unhappy lot whilst they listened. Pluto, King of the Nether World, was so moved by the sweet sounds that he consented to restore Eurydice to earth, provided Orpheus would not look backward during the journey to the land of the living. This provision, at first eagerly accepted by the musician, was soon broken, and he was forced to depart alone with his lyre, as he had come. In grief, he sought solitude, thereby so enraging the women of Thrace, that they tore him to pieces. The lyre is a small stringed instrument, like a miniature harp. It was a favourite amongst the ancients, who composed verses to be sung to its accompaniment, thus originating the term "lyric" poetry. It was the chosen instrument of Apollo and the Muses.

West of the meridian now lie Hercules, Ophiuchus et Serpens, Scorpio, Libra, Corona Borealis, and Boötes. The western half of Virgo has already set. In the north we observe both Draco and Ursa Minor west of the pole, with Ursa Major beneath them, headed for that upright position which it assumes on autumnal evenings. We may next month behold the well-known Plough or Dipper without inversion. Cassiopeia, with Cepheus above it, has mounted high in the east. In the northeast Perseus is beginning to appear, whilst the whole of Andromeda is now in sight. Pegasus is gaining height in the heavens, and portions of Pisces are coming into view due east. In the southeast Aquarius is almost completely visible, and Piscis Australis will soon rise. Capricornus is well in the southeastern sky; below and to the west of Aquarius, and just east of Sagittarius. Soon to come to transit are Cygnus, Sagitta, Delphinus, and Equuleus.

The Milky Way this month spans the celestial vault as a glowing ribbon extending from a place on the horizon just east of the north point, to one just west of the south point. Its richness in the constellations Scorpio and Sagittarius is great, and the spectacle thus afforded by the southern evening heavens is one which will amply repay the observer with or without optical assistance.

EDITOR'S NOTE FP: *EN* 47, No. 53 (31 July 1915): 8.

Notes

1. Ovid, *Metamorphoses* 9.128–30 (tr. John Gay; from "Garth's Ovid" [1717]; *LL* 664).
2. Manilius, *Astronomica* 1.344–45 (tr. Thomas Creech).

SEPTEMBER SKIES

Jupiter, blazing to full splendour in the southeastern evening sky, arrives at its opposition on the 17th of the month. For the amateur observer with an ordinary telescope the planet is ever a source of delight, being perhaps the best seen of all celestial bodies save the sun and moon. Seen now under the best possible circumstances, it is the cen-

tre of attraction for all glasses large and small. The naked eye perceives only a dazzlingly bright star-like object, but when optical assistance is secured we behold a large,
variegated disc, slightly oval in outline, with four attendant satellites by its side. The
oval figure is due to Jupiter's polar compression, and the conspicuous belts on the surface are perhaps of cloud-like nature, since their appearance and mutability alike indicate an atmospherical rather than a solid condition. Jupiter is indeed supposed to
contain little or no solid matter, being a sort of plastic semi-sun like the other large
outer planets. The belts run parallel to the equator, in whose plane the satellites also
revolve. While all four larger satellites are often seen beside Jupiter, they are occasionally occulted by their primary, eclipsed by its shadow, or seen in transit across its disc.
Owing to the angle at which we observe the transits of Jupiter's satellites, we may often
see both the satellite and its darker shadow in transit. The dates and conditions of
these occultations, eclipses, and transits, are carefully predicted in the Nautical Almanack, which may well be consulted by the owners of telescopes. The five fainter satellites are, of course, utterly beyond our powers.

The ringed Saturn is to the morning sky what Jupiter is to the evening sky. Rising
at 12:34 a.m. on the 1st and at 10:44 p.m. on the 30th, it is rapidly increasing in brilliancy, coming to quadrature next month. The expansion of the ring system has decreased but little, and the planet will be an object of great beauty during the coming
autumn and winter.

Mars also adorns the morning heavens, rising on the 1st at 12:05 a.m., and on the
30th at 11:33 p.m. The ruddy orb is not yet of striking brilliancy, though it may be recognised with ease. During September it moves from the western part of Gemini
through that constellation to the very border of Cancer. Mars and Saturn will be in
conjunction with each other on the 10th at 6 p.m., Mars passing only one degree and
eight minutes north of the larger planet. The opportunity for comparison or contrast
afforded during the ensuing night will be favourable indeed.

Mercury will be in greatest elongation east on the 28th, then appearing as a faint
ruddy spark in the western evening twilight, low hanging above the sunset point. The
present elongation is not a conspicuously favourable one, since evening appearances of
Mercury are best made during spring.

Venus, in superior conjunction on the 12th, will be practically invisible throughout the month, though it is interesting to note how some observers have tried by daylight observations to follow the planet almost to the exact moment of this aspect, and
to observe its very earliest appearance afterward. Superior conjunction, of course,
technically marks a change from "morning star" to "evening star". In 1813 Dr. Thomas
Dick commenced a series of observations on Venus at points very near superior conjunction, succeeding thirteen years later in glimpsing the planet only a few hours before the exact aspect. He was of opinion that Venus might be seen through proper
glasses even at the precise moment of superior conjunction, as a perfect circle, save
when it should chance to pass unusually close to, or behind, the sun. Dr. Dick likewise
investigated the conditions surrounding inferior conjunction, finally obtaining a good
view of the thin crescent only 36 hours after the conjunction. From all his studies in
this direction, he finally laid down the law that Venus, though often invisible for
months to the naked eye during the course of a single apparent or synodic revolution,
can never in that period be hidden from the painstaking telescopic observer more than
sixteen and a half days; indeed, that in certain more favourable revolutions, Venus
may be seen uninterruptedly on every clear day, the only break being the few moments
of absolute non-illumination which attend inferior conjunction when the waning cres-

cent has at last disappeared, and the slender waxing crescent is as yet unborn.

Uranus is still near its best in the evening sky, whilst users of telescopes may now perceive Neptune in the early morning.

The Moon's phases for September will be as follows:

Last Quarter, 1st..9:57 a.m.

New Moon, 9th ....5:53 a.m.

First Quarter, 16th ....3:21 a.m.

Full Moon, 23d ....4:35 a.m.

Apogee falls on the 1st and 29th, Perigee on the 14th. The Moon runs high on the 2nd and 29th, low on the 15th. On the [ ]th it will be near Mars and Saturn, on the 9th near Uranus, and on the 22nd near Jupiter.

The Sun enters the Zodiacal sign Libra on the 23d at 10 a.m., thus ushering in the dismal autumnal season and giving us equal days and nights. This balance of light and darkness is doubtless the reason why the sign came in ancient times to be known as the scales of Astraea, the Goddess of Justice. As Virgil tells us in his Georgics:

> "But when Astraea's balance hung on high,
> Betwixt the nights and days divides the sky,
> Then yoke your oxen, sow your winter grain,
> Till cold December comes with driving rain."[1]

In the sidereal heavens we this month find but a dull ensemble of constellations; indeed, September may be said to mark the interval betwixt the waning of the mildly beautiful summer groups and the advent of the dazzlingly refulgent stars of winter. The Zodiacal contellation on the meridian is Capricornus, the Sea-Goat, whose attractions are limited to one apparent double star in its western extremity. In mythology Capricornus represents the form into which the demigod Bacchus changed himself when overtaken by the monster Typhon. All the gods were one day feasting on the banks of the Nile, when the monster appeared without warning. Each deity assumed an animal shape and escaped in the speediest possible manner. Bacchus became a goat, but since he essayed to cross the river, his submerged parts assumed a fish-like form, whilst his head and fore parts remained goat-like. Capricornus is therefore delineated on the globes as a creature half goat and half fish. Just above Capricornus are the western portions of Aquarius, which will soon succeed it on the meridian. To the west lie the remaining constellations of summer: Sagittarius and parts of Scorpio on the horizon, with Aquila, Ophiuchus et Serpens, Hercules, Corona Borealis, and Lyra higher up. Boötes and Canes Venatici are low in the northwest. Returning to the meridian, we find the small groups Delphinus, Equuleus, and Sagitta high in the sky, whilst Cygnus glows resplendent at the very zenith. Cygnus, the Swan, is notable for its cruciform outline, and is frequently known as the "Northern Cross". At the head shines the bright Deneb, a gem of prime magnitude, whilst at the foot we may behold Albireo, a star of less lustre, but more beauty in the telescope, since it constitutes a striking blue and yellow double. Cygnus is that friend and kinsman of the unfortunate Phaethon, who, after the latter had perished in the river Eridanus, pined in fraternal grief beside its banks. He beheld the three weeping sisters of Phaethon turn into poplar trees through their sorrow, and finally, having angered the gods by his continual haunting of the stream, he was himself turned into a swan, evermore to float about in sadness upon the placid waters.

In the northern heavens the signs of autumn are quite apparent. The Plough, right side up, is sliding beneath the pole, while Cepheus and Cassiopeia are correspondingly mounting above that pivot. Ursa Minor and Draco are west of the pole, whilst Perseus, in all his splendour, is in full view eastward. In the northeast Auriga is rising, with Capella just in sight. A little farther south a shimmering spot of hazy luminosity near Pleiades, and the near approach of the first resplendent winter groups. Higher up are Aries, Andromeda, and Pegasus. Due east we behold Pisces completely risen, and Cetus about half in sight. The southeastern sky contains Aquarius, the Water-Bearer, beneath which shines the solitary bright star Fomalhaut, part of the constellation Piscis Australis, or the Southern Fish. Piscis Australis is supposed to be drinking or swimming in the stream of water which issues from the urn of Aquarius. As Aratus remarks:

> "The Southern Fish beneath Aquarius glides
> And upwards turns to Cetus' scaly sides;
> Rolls from Aquarius' vase a limpid stream,
> Where num'rous stars like sparkling bubbles gleam."[2]

That the cultured reading public is in general assuming an increasing interest in the science of the heavens is well attested by the fact that this year's honours as chief essayist in the United Amateur Press Association, perhaps the most representative of all country-wide societies of young literary workers, have been bestowed upon Mr. Leo Fritter for his admirable astronomical sketch, "The Spiritual Significance of the Stars", which was reviewed in these columns last February. The diffusion of elementary astronomical information, disencumbered of its dull mathematical complexities, cannot but introduce to the entire thinking world a subject rich in beauty and lofty in inspiration, which can, as no other study can concretely do, raise the mind far above the petty ills and annoyances of common life.

EDITOR'S NOTE FP: *EN* 47, No. 79 (1 September 1915): 8.

Notes

1. Virgil, *Georgics* 1.208–11 (tr. John Dryden [1697]). Virgil's text does not mention Astraea by name.

2. Aratus, *Phaenomena* 389–94.

OCTOBER SKIES

Saturn, steadily gaining in lustre, arrives at its quadrature on the 10th of this month, then appearing conspicuously in the eastern midnight sky. On the 1st it rises at 10:43 p.m., and on the 31st at 8:45. It is still in direct motion through the constellation Gemini, thus embellishing a group already resplendent with its own constituent orbs.

Jupiter still reigns as monarch of the evening sky, shining each night in the southeast with dazzling effulgence. Its beauty is the more prominent by reason of its solitude, since the planet is now retrograding near the western boundary of Aquarius, a region wholly devoid of bright stars. Jupiter sets on the 1st at 4:28 a.m., and on the 31st at 2:43 a.m. One of the reasons for Jupiter's great attractiveness to the amateur observer is the large disc which it exhibits in common telescopes. With a power of only 50 diameters its size appears equal to that of the full moon as seen with the naked eye, whilst with the more usual power of 100 it is of course twice as large. Yet such is the force of optical illusion, that the novice invariably underestimates the size of the disc as he views it through the tube. When the power of 50 is used, Jupiter's disc at first strikes the eye as vastly smaller than the moon, and only when the two orbs are in close juxtaposition can the comparison be graphically made. If in such a case the observer will look through the telescope at Jupiter with one eye, meanwhile keeping the other eye open and directed at the full moon, he can by moving the telescope make the magnified image of Jupiter coincide with the unmagnified moon, whereupon the two discs will be found of identical size, neither one overlapping the other. This underestimation of the size of a telescopic image is not confined to Jupiter alone, but occurs in connexion with all the planets. Mars, in particular, disappoints the beginner. The brilliancy of Jupiter to the naked eye this autumn has had the usual perplexing effect upon those not familiar with astronomy, and has given rise to all manner of conjectures concerning its supposed artificial nature. This has been particularly the case on European battlefields, where it is reported that the planet has actually almost been fixed upon in the belief that it is a German dirigible. The citizenry of Paris have likewise eyed the giant orb in fear, imagining it to be the searchlight of a hostile aëroplane. But as press reports shew, all are not equally stupid regarding the splendid object which gilds the southeastern sky. Intelligent soldiers, spending their nights in the open, have besieged well-known French astronomers with questions about it, such questions leading in many cases to a genuine interest in and study of the heavens. Thus the great conflict is not wholly without its redeeming features. Many inhabitants of the towns, transplanted to the open fields of France, and bivouacked under the crystal skies of that country, have gained much real inspiration and love of Nature from their experiences.

Mars, now near its quadrature, is well seen at or after midnight. On the 1st it rises at 11:32 p.m., and on the 31st at 10:53. Its ruddy brilliancy is perceptibly increasing, and by the end of the month it will outshine the standard first magnitude. During October Mars will move from the western boundary of Cancer almost entirely across that constellation. Early next year, when Mars comes to opposition, its appearance will be very striking, and it will probably become the subject of just such speculation as Jupiter is now receiving. The writer recollects that at the opposition of 1907 a number of persons inquired whether it was a signal or artificial light of some sort sent up from a point southeast of Providence.

Mercury may possibly be glimpsed at sunset above the western horizon during the first two or three days of this month, since its greatest eastern elongation occurred on September 28. It will, however, soon disappear, arriving at inferior conjunction on the 22nd. It will next month be seen in the morning sky.

Venus continues invisible for all practical purposes, though it is now nominally an "evening star", and will soon shine resplendently just above the western horizon in the early evening. Upon its first appearance next month its disc will be little less than a full circle, which will wane successively to a half-circle and a crescent during the ensuing months of visibility.

Uranus, so hard to find with a common altazimuth telescope, may be detected this month by reason of its occultation on the 16th at 9:40 p.m. The moon, being nearer to us than is any other heavenly body, frequently intervenes betwixt the earth and some star or planet, shutting off the latter object from our sight. This phenomenon, which is called an "occultation", is very striking when the object occulted happens to disappear behind the moon's dark or invisible edge, for in such a case the cause of disappearance is unseen, and the object seems to vanish startlingly out of a clear sky. The occultation of a star is absolutely instantaneous, since such bodies are no more than mere points of light even in the largest of telescopes; but a planet, when occulted, seems to fade more gradually, since a perceptible interval is required for the moon's edge to creep over its disc. In the average small telescope Uranus does not shew a disc, but the observer who carefully watches the slightly gibbous moon on the evening of the 16th cannot fail to note the tiny object which it approaches at about half-past nine, and which about 9:40 is seen gradually to sink out of sight as the moon's dark edge covers it. This object is the distant planet Uranus, thus pointed out for the benefit of those who might not otherwise be able to find it. Neptune is in quadrature on the 26th, but is without interest for the amateur astronomer. It will be in conjunction with Mars on the 11th.

The moon's phases for October are five in number, and will occur as follows:

Last Quarter, 1st...4:44 a.m.
New Moon, 8th .... 4:42 p.m.
First Quarter, 15th ....8:51 a.m.
Full Moon, 22nd.. 7:16 p.m.
Last Quarter, 30th.. 11:40 p.m.

Perigee falls on the 11th, Apogee on the 27th. The moon runs low on the 13th, high on the 27th. It will be near the following planets on the following dates: Saturn, 1st; Mars, 2nd; Uranus (occultation), 16th; Jupiter, 19th; Saturn, 29th; and Mars, 31st. The present month is indeed rich in lunar conjunctions.

The sun enters the Zodiacal sign Scorpio on the 23d, thus proclaiming the advancement of the autumn. The days lose an hour and 22 minutes during the month.

The starry skies of October contain the heralds of winter's resplendent pageant. Taurus is now wholly above the eastern horizon, whilst Auriga and Perseus, mounting high, are other samples of the splendour soon to arrive. The Zodiacal constellation on the meridian this month is Aquarius, the Water Bearer, one of the least interesting of all the celestial circle. Though generally depicted on the globes as a bearded man holding an urn of water, this group is considered to represent the beautiful Phrygian boy Ganymede, son of the Trojan king, whom Jupiter, in the guise of an eagle (Aquila), snatched up from amongst his playmates on Mount Ida to become cupbearer to the gods in place of Hebe, who had abandoned that position to wed the hero Hercules. Other classical tales identify Aquarius with Deucalion, who with his wife Pyrrha formed the only surviving pair after the deluge sent by Jupiter to punish the wickedness of mankind. This virtuous couple, who had escaped from the flood by ascending the uncovered summit of Mount Parnassus, desired at once to re-create the entire human race. Inquiring of an oracle how to accomplish this purpose, they were told to cast behind them the bones of their mother. Since Earth is the common mother of us all, and since the rocks may be said to constitute her skeleton, Deucalion and Pyrrha gathered a quantity of stones, which they scattered widely about them. These stones, as soon as they reached the ground, were instantly metamorphosed to human creatures, from whom we are all descended. A third legend connects Aquarius with Cecrops, the first king of Athens, who came from Egypt to found the celebrated Grecian city, and who implanted the seeds of that culture and learning for which Athens was afterward so distinguished. Pre-classical myths all coincide in giving to Aquarius a watery character, a circumstance perhaps due to the fact that the sun traverses this group during the rainy season. The Egyptians believe that when the Nile rises, Aquarius is sinking his great urn into the waters to replenish its contents.

Just above Aquarius, and just south of the zenith, now shines Pegasus, the Winged

Horse. Pegasus was a being born of the blood of the gorgon Medusa, which dripped from her severed head as the hero Perseus bore it away in triumph after slaying her. The young horse was captured and tamed by the goddess Minerva, who gave him as a present to the Muses. When he arrived at the abode of the Nine, on the summit of Mount Helicon, he gave the yielding earth a blow with his hoof, creating the beautiful fountain Hippocrene. In classical mythology Pegasus plays no inconsiderable part, having been used as a steed by Bellerophon, who slew the Chimaera, and according to some accounts having served Perseus himself in his rescue of the Aethiopian princess Andromeda. On account of his connexion with the Muses, Pegasus is ever associated with the art of poesy and considered the mount of those who succeed in numbers, as shewn by the following lines in praise of a young poet, wherein the bard is favourably compared to the astronomer:

> The winged steed above th' horizon flies,
> And lends his lustre to the vaulted skies;
> But whilst we view him in the distant space,
> Kleiner leaps on, and guides his flight with grace![1]

In the west are the groups of summer and of early autumn. Sagittarius and Ophiuchus et Serpens are setting, whilst Capricornus, Aquila, Cygnus, Delphinus, Equuleus, Sagitta, Lyra, Hercules, and Corona Borealis are still in full view. In the north we find the Plough below the pole, now right side up, and soon to attain lower transit. Ursa Minor and Draco are west of the pole, and Cepheus, with Cassiopeia close following, is above it. The lustrous stars Capella and Aldebaran, in Auriga and Taurus respectively, illumine the northeast, while farther south on the horizon Eridanus is beginning to appear. In the southeast are the faintly seen groups Sculptor and Phoenix, and due south, almost too near the horizon to be visible, is Grus, the Crane. Above Grus, and directly beneath Aquarius, shines the Southern Fish, whose one bright star Fomalhaut lends beauty to a region otherwise rather desolate.

EDITOR'S NOTE FP: *EN* 47, No. 104 (1 October 1915): 8.

Notes

1. The lines are by HPL and refer to his amateur colleague, the poet Rheinhart Kleiner (1892–1949).

NOVEMBER SKIES

Venus, after a year's absence, this month returns to the evening sky; being visible toward the end of November as a very brilliant orb close to the southwestern horizon just after sunset, and disappearing each night as the twilight grows deeper. On the 30th Venus sets at 5:26 p.m., a little less than an hour and a quarter after the sun. Through a telescope the planet exhibits a small disc but little departing from a full circle, and possessing no well-defined spots or other configurations. On account of this absence of plain markings, the surface of Venus has ever been a to subject of much conjecture amongst astronomers. The older observers were unanimous in attributing to the disc a variety of indefinite shadings, visible only in powerful telescopes and under particularly favourable conditions, which seemed to rotate once in about a day of nearly the same length as ours. But more recently this conclusion has been disputed, several astronomers having maintained that the faint markings on the planet are streak-like in nature, and that Venus, as shewn by them, rotates only once during its revolution of 225 days about the sun, thus keeping one hemisphere always facing the solar rays, with the other always turned away in darkness. It cannot as yet be said that either faction of opinion has well proved its case, but the whole controversy is a graphic illustration not only of the elusive nature of the topographical features of Venus, but of the general delicacy of the data from which our present knowledge of many astronomical facts is deduced. Venus this month moves from Libra through northern Scorpio and southern Ophiuchus into Sagittarius.

Mercury arrives at greatest western elongation on the 7th, being then visible through the early morning twilight near the southeastern horizon just above the sunrise point. The disc will appear through the telescope as a half-circle, being crescentic before, and gibbous after, the exact time of elongation. Like Venus, Mercury has no plainly defined configurations on its surface, and its period of rotation is disputed in exactly the same manner as is that of the larger inferior planet. Comparing the two cases, however, there is this difference to be noticed; that the evidence regarding Venus seems to incline toward the older theories, and the short, earth-like period of rotation, whilst Mercury probably acts as the more modern observers believe, rotating but once during its solar revolution of 88 days, and turning but one face toward the sun.

Mars has now become a brilliant and conspicuous object in the morning and later evening sky, rising on the 1st at 10:52 p.m., and on the 30th at 9:56. On the 9th the planet arrives at quadrature. The disc of Mars, unlike those of Mercury and Venus, is replete with markings and variegations. Near the poles are dazzling white tracts, probably of snow or hoar-frost, which melt and freeze again in the summer and winter of the planet, respectively. The other parts of the surface are either greenish or reddish, the latter hue predominating, and lending to the planet that appearance of ruddiness which is so pronounced to the naked eye. The famous "canals", dark, narrow streaks extending across the disc with almost mathematical precision, and believed by extreme thinkers to be the artificial works of intelligent inhabitants of Mars, are not visible in ordinary telescopes. Being a superior planet, Mars does not undergo the manifold changes of phase seen in Mercury and Venus, but appears for the most part as a perfect circle. About the time of quadrature, however, a slightly gibbous aspect is assumed, which may be noticed throughout the present month. During November Mars moves out of Cancer into Leo, being quite close to the bright star Regulus as the month ends.

Jupiter continues to be the principal evening planet, since its superior, Venus, is seen for so short a time in the twilight. The giant orb sets on the 1st at 2:12 a.m., and on the 30th at 12:15. Jupiter is now near the eastern boundary of Aquarius, retrograding until the 15th of the month, and afterward moving directly.

Saturn, now past its quadrature, is entering the evening sky. On the 1st it rises at 3:44 p.m., and on the 30th at 6:43. It is now retrograding in the central part of the constellation Gemini. The advent of Saturn, Mars, and Venus, before the departure of Jupiter, will lend to the evening skies of the coming winter a lustre all the more glorious because of the resplendent fixed stars of the season.

Uranus, in the evening sky, arrives at quadrature on the 5th, whilst Neptune, in the morning sky, is past quadrature.

The moon's phases for November will be as follows:

New Moon, 7th ....2:53 a.m.
First Quarter, 13th .... 6:06 p.m.
Full Moon, 21st .... 12:36 p.m.
Last Quarter, 28th.. 5:11 p.m.

Perigee occurs on the 8th, Apogee on the 23d. The moon runs low on the 9th, high on the 23d. It will approach Uranus on the 13th, Jupiter on the 16th, Saturn on the 25th, and Mars on the 28th.

The sun enters the Zodiacal sign Sagittarius on the 22nd. During November the days lose approximately one hour in length.

The evening sky now grows refulgent with the rising of the winter constellations. Out of the east come Gemini and Orion, the latter the most splendid of all the starry host, while high in the heavens shine Taurus, Auriga, and Perseus. By midnight the two Dogs will have come to view.

The Zodiacal constellation on the meridian at 9 p.m. of the 15th is Pisces, a dull, uninteresting, and loosely arranged group whose only claim to renown is its present possession of the "vernal equinox", or point where the sun's upward path intersects the equator of the heavens. This intersection was anciently in the constellation to Aries, and the equinox is therefore still mathematically called the "first point of Aries", but the phenomenon of precession has caused a gradual movement of the celestial equator along the ecliptic, or sun's path; wherefore the technical "signs" of the Zodiac no longer correspond with the constellations for which they are named. In future ages the vernal equinox will move from Pisces to Aquarius and so on in a westward or retro-grade direction around the ecliptic.

Above Pisces, and practically at the zenith, is Andromeda, famous for the posses-sion of one of the greatest nebulae in all the sky. This nebula is faintly visible without a telescope, appearing as a tiny, elongated bit of misty light. Andromeda, together with Cassiopeia and Cepheus, which adjoin it on the north; Perseus, which bounds it on the east; Pegasus, which bounds it on the west; and Cetus, which lies far south of it, across Pisces; forms the nucleus of one of the most interesting of mythological tales, trans-planted in its entirety to the sky, where all its participants shine as distinct constella-tions. Andromeda was a princess of Aethiopia, daughter of King Cepheus and Queen Cassiopeia. Having declared herself more beautiful than the Nereides of the waves, Neptune, the ocean-god, sent Cetus, a vast sea monster, to harass the coast of Ce-pheus' kingdom as a rebuke to the vain presumption of the queen. When Cepheus consulted the oracle of Jupiter Ammon for means of relief, he was told that the curse would be withdrawn only on condition that the Princess Andromeda be bound to a rock on the shore and left for Cetus to devour. This having been done, the chained Andromeda in terror awaited the coming of the destroying monster. But meanwhile the Jove-born Perseus, fresh from his victory over the gorgon Medusa, and mounted on the winged horse Pegasus, was flying across the stricken domain. Observing Andro-meda and her plight, he descended and slew the dire sea-creature that even then had approached to devour the royal victim. As Ovid says, in Eusden's translation:

> "Thus the wing'd hero now descends, now soars,
> And at his pleasure the vast monster gores.
> Full in his back, swift stooping from above,
> The crooked sabre to its hilt he drove."[1]

The Princess thus rescued, Perseus led her in triumph to her parents and there wedded her, after turning all his rivals to stone by shewing to them the fatal head of Medusa. Jupiter, looking upon his son Perseus with favouring eye, caused the whole event to be immortalised in the heavens. The first-born son of Perseus and Andromeda was named Perses, from whom the ancient sovereigns of the Persian Empire claimed their origin.

The western sky is filled with the departing groups of autumn and late summer. Piscis Australis, Capricornus, and Aquarius are fully visible, as is also Aquila, whose bright star Altair shines conspicuously over the horizon due west. Vega, farther north, more than rivals Altair with its intense bluish-white brilliancy. Cygnus, Delphinus, Equuleus, and Sagitta are still well seen. In the north Ursa Major is below the pole in lower transit, the Plough being already tilted as if in preparation for its winter ascent of the northeastern heavens. Ursa Minor hangs downward from the pole, while Draco is gradually following Ursa Major toward lower transit. Eastward the winter groups are appearing in full splendour, and toward the south the watery windings of Fluvius Eridanus are seen. Due south Sculptor and Phoenix are on the horizon, though neither is worthy of particular attention. The Milky Way now extends in an arc from the northeastern to northwestern horizon, nowhere touching the southern sky, but flowing through Auriga, Perseus, Cassiopeia, Cepheus, and Aquila. During the coming winter months its splendid southern branch, wherein floats the starry ship Argo, will delight the eye.

The eagerly awaited 100-inch reflecting telescope of the Mount Wilson Observatory in California is now approaching completion, and will probably be in active use within a year. This instrument, as before mentioned in these columns, will be the largest telescope in the world, surpassing by far even the famous old leviathan of Lord Rosse.[2] Dr. George Ellery Hale[3] of the observatory entertains high hopes concerning the gigantic instrument, and believes that its advent will usher in a new era of astronomical progress. According to recent estimates, a full hundred million hitherto unknown stars will reveal themselves to its expansive mirror and powerful eye-pieces or photographic plates. Through our present anticipation of such strides in observational astronomy, we are able to appreciate the expectant sensations which animated the scientific world in the days of 1845, just before the long-heralded Rosse telescope became a perfected reality.

EDITOR'S NOTE FP: *EN* 47, No. 129 (1 November 1915): 8.

Notes

1. Ovid, *Metamorphoses* 4.717–19 (tr. Laurence Eusden; from "Garth's Ovid").

2. For Rosse, see "April Skies" (p. 145), n. 2. HPL uses the term leviathan deliberately, as the telescope was referred to as the "Leviathan of Parsontown" (the old name for the town of Birr).

3. George Ellery Hale (1868–1938), American astrophysicist who was director of the Mt. Wilson Observatory (1904–23) and later helped to raise funds for the Mt. Palomar Observatory.

DECEMBER SKIES

Jupiter, still the leading planet of the evening sky, comes to quadrature on the 12th of the month, being visible in the south and southwest. On the 1st it sets at 12:14 a.m., and on the 31st at 10:23. The planet is moving directly near the boundary between Aquarius and Pisces, crossing during December from the former to the latter constellation. Jupiter this month undergoes its nearest approach to an actual change of phase. The giant orb never attains the markedly gibbous appearance noticed in Mars at quadrature, but any large telescope can clearly exhibit the slightest shading off of the edge turned away from the sun when Jupiter is at or very near this aspect. The well-known amateur observer Webb, author of "Celestial Objects for Common Telescopes", detected Jupiter's phase in 1838 with a comparatively small instrument, and stated that it may be best seen in twilight.[1] The phenomenon has also been illustrated in occultations of stars or satellites by the disc of Jupiter. When the shaded edge approaches the object to be covered, it obscures that object before the latter seems to touch completely the illuminated area, just as the dark edge of the gibbous moon occults a star or planet whilst the bright surface is some little space removed.

As Jupiter sinks lower and lower in the western heavens, Venus, now easily to be seen, gains altitude as if to meet it. This queen of planets sets on the 1st at 5:27 p.m., or one hour and thirteen minutes after the sun, but by the 31st will have progressed upward so far as to linger above the horizon till 6:31, or two hours and nine minutes after the close of day. The course of Venus amongst the stars this month extends throughout the length of Sagittarius and well into Capricornus. Venus is still gibbous in phase, nearer the circular than the semicircular form. Not until spring will it be seen at its best.

Mars now adorns with great prominence the later evening sky, rising on the 1st at 9:54 p.m., and on the 31st at 8:17. The brilliancy of the red planet is rapidly increasing, for although it is not now so bright as Rigel, it will by the end of the month surpass any visible fixed star save Sirius alone. During December, Mars moves through the western part of Leo, passing only two and a half degrees north of the bright star Regulus on the 13th. The planet is of course by far the brighter of the two, yet its proximity to the star will create a spectacle by no means uninteresting.

Saturn, in full ringed splendour, will adorn the evening sky, being now not far from opposition. On the 1st it rises at 6:42, and on the 31st at 4:29. The ring system is still inclined at a very favourable angle toward the earth, and shews a broad illuminated expanse. From now onward, however, the visible area will decrease, until, in 1921, the rings will be seen edgewise from the earth, appearing only in the best telescopes, and being wholly invisible through the majority of instruments. This virtual vanishment is scarce to be marvelled at, when we consider that the thickness of the system probably does not exceed 100 miles. As December begins, Saturn will vastly outshine Mars, but by the close, Mars will have amply caught up, though Saturn's brilliancy is also increasing at its own slow rate.

Mercury will remain invisible throughout the coming month, being in superior conjunction on the 15th. Uranus, now past quadrature, is faintly seen in the early evening sky, whilst Neptune, drawing toward opposition, is visible through the telescope later in the evening.

The moon's phases for December will occur as follows:

New Moon, 6th .... 1:04 p.m.
First Quarter, 13th ....6:38 a.m.
Full Moon, 21st ....7:58 a.m.
Last Quarter, 29th..7:59 a.m.

Our satellite is in Perigee and runs low on the 6th, being in Apogee and running high on the 20th. On the 8th the thin new crescent, low in the western sky after sunset, will lie not far from the brilliant planet Venus. The distance is less on the preceding night, but the moon will then be too recently emerged from its change to be seen. On the 13th, the moon's quadrature or first quarter occurs but little after the quadrature of Jupiter, wherefore the two orbs will approach each other, forming a combination highly pleasing to the artistic eye. On the 22nd, Saturn will lie but two and three-quarters degrees south of the practically full moon, whilst four days later, on the 26th, the gibbous waning moon will pass five and three-quarters degrees south of Mars.

On December 22nd at 5 p.m. the sun will enter the Zodiacal sign Capricornus, thus commencing its annual ascent of the ecliptic circle, and ushering in the dreary season of winter. But in the upward turning lies the promise of vernal warmth to come, hence the winter solstice has ever been a season of rejoicing rather than of repining. Amongst all primitive peoples the sun's entrance into Capricornus has been the source of seasonal celebration, and the prehistoric Italian ceremonies for this occasion in later ages fixed successively the dates of Roman Saturnalia and the world-wide Christian feast of the Lord's Nativity. During December the days suffer a net loss of eleven minutes, losing sixteen between the 1st and the 22nd, and gaining five between the 23rd and 31st.

The gorgeous east is now ablaze with the dazzling pomp of winter's celestial train. The regal Sirius glows with peerless refulgence, whilst Procyon brightly heralds its superior. The Zodiacal constellation now on the meridian is Aries, the Ram, which though not of overpowering brilliancy is yet of great interest and attractiveness. Aries represents the golden-fleeced ram of mythology, around which are grouped such an infinite variety of exciting legends. He was originally given by Mercury to Nephele, Queen of Thessaly, to carry her two children Phryxus and Helle through the air to a place of safety in Colchis after Athamas, the King, had put her away and taken a second bride, who wished the babies slain. The little prince and princess were strapped to the back of Aries, who straightway leaped aloft on his flight toward Asia. But at the narrows which separate Europe from the east, the Princess Helle fell to her death in the sea below, thus giving to those waters the name "Hellespont". Under the modern title of "Dardanelles" the Hellespont is now once again the scene of historic death, and may the royal babe of ancient legend rise in spirit from the waves to bless the valiant legions of England![2] Phryxus was more fortunate than his sister, for he escaped uninjured, and was safely borne to Colchis, where King Aeetes gave him protecting welcome. The youthful prince sacrificed his bearer to Jupiter, and permitted Aeetes to hang the ram's golden fleece in a sacred grove, where it was guarded by a never-sleeping dragon. But the Thessalians took it amiss that the fleece of Aries should thus repose on foreign shores, and Jason, son of Aeson, set out with his famous Argonautic expedition to bring it back. King Aeetes proved unwilling to surrender the golden fleece to Jason, and agreed to part with it only on condition that the young Thessalian yoke two fire-breathing, brazen-footed oxen to a plough, and sow in a neighbouring field the magic dragon teeth of Cadmus, from which would spring armed and hostile warriors. Alone, the task could never have been accomplished, but Jason was assisted by the sorceries of Medea, daughter of Aeetes, who endowed him with power to tame the fiery oxen and to turn the earth-grown solders against each other instead of against him. Medea likewise lulled to sleep the wakeful dragon that guarded the golden fleece, and, as Valerius Flaccus tells us:

> "Exulting Jason grasp'd the shining hide,
> His last of labours, and his envy'd pride."[3]

Jason, with Medea as his bride, returned Aries' golden fleece to Thessaly, where it was finally received with acclamations and rejoicing.

Direct below Aries in the southeastern sky is Cetus, the sea monster sent by Neptune to devour Andromeda as punishment for the emolus [enormous?] vanity of her mother Cassiopeia. The aquatic nature of this constellation has been persistently assumed by all the races of antiquity, and long before the famous Grecian myth the Chaldaeans deemed it a leviathan of the deep. Above Aries is the old group called Triangulum, east of which, and just about to transit, is the sparkling Perseus with his starry streams. Perseus was the son of Jupiter and Danae, daughter of Acrisius the Argive king. Acrisius had been told by an oracle that his death would come from his daughter's son, wherefore he enclosed Danae in a brazen tower, resolving that she should never wed. But Jove, admiring the maid from Olympian heights, descended as a shower of gold and married her in secret. When her son Perseus was born, Acrisius placed both Danae and the infant in a chest and set them adrift on the tide. Tossed by the winds, they floated eventually to the isle of Seriphus, where reigned King Polydectes. As the years elapsed, the king made suit to Danae, who, not desiring to wed him, appealed to Perseus, now near manhood, for protection. Polydectes, evil of mind and anxious to rid himself of this obstacle, sent Perseus to the far confines of creation to slay the hideous Gorgon Medusa, hoping that the hero might thus himself be destroyed. Medusa was a monster whose head was covered with writhing snakes instead of hair, and whose face, if seen by any mortal, would at once turn him to stone with its frightfulness. But the Jove-born Perseus was aided by the gods in his attempt. Mercury lent him his winged sandals, Pluto his helmet which makes the wearer invisible, and Minerva her shield or Aegis, whose burnished surface might enable him to view the Gorgon by reflection, avoiding the direct sight which would petrify him. Thus armed and aided, Perseus slew Medusa, cut off her head, and flew away from the scene of his victory; as some say, mounted the back of the winged horse Pegasus, who sprang from the Gorgon's gore. When he reached the North African realm of King Atlas, father of the Pleiades and the Hyades, and most gigantic of men, Perseus was refused hospitality, whereupon he produced Medusa's head, the sight of which turned Atlas to stone. As the metamorphosis came over the king, his bulk increased till he grew to be a mountain, and by the will of the gods he was sentenced forever to bear all the heavens upon his shoulders. From the domain of Atlas Perseus winged his way to Aethiopia, the kingdom of Cepheus, where he saved and wedded the Princess Andromeda. Then he returned to Seriphus with his bride, joining his mother and turning the perfidious King Polydectes to stone with the Gorgon's head. As successor he enthroned Dictys, who had first saved his mother and himself from the sea. Meanwhile news arrived that Acrisius, grandfather of the hero, had been driven from power and imprisoned by his brother Praetus. Perseus, with Danae his mother and Andromeda his wife, hastened to Argos, turned the usurping Praetus to stone, and replaced Acrisius upon the throne. The old king, regretful of his action casting his daughter and grandson into the sea, welcomed his liberator with contrition, and accorded him the honour due a prince of his line. But the prophecy of the ancient oracle was after all to be realised. One day whilst Perseus was playing at quoits, his discus by accident struck the aged sovereign, causing his death as at first predicted. Perseus thereupon became king, and after him reigned Perses his son, the line reaching down to the throne of Persia, whose rulers, through their descent, claimed kinship with Jove himself. We now behold the hero set in the sky, his uplifted sword glistened with myriads of starry gems, and in his left hand the head of the Gorgon, which he clutches by its snaky locks.

In the western sky now shine the groups of earlier autumn; Cygnus, Andromeda, Pegasus, Pisces, Aquarius, and Piscis Australis, whose bright star Fomalhaut is just about to set. Close to the western horizon are Equuleus and Delphinus, whilst Lyra is soon to disappear in the northwest. The Plough has now begun its winter ascent of the eastern circumpolar region, and Cassiopeia, high above the pole on the opposite side, has commenced to decline correspondingly. Cepheus is west of the pole, and Draco beneath it. The Lesser Bear hangs face downward from Polaris. In the northeast the Zodiacal constellation Cancer has appeared, south of which Monoceros, the Unicorn, is coming to view. Still farther south the resplendent Dogs gleam through the silvery ripples of the Milky Way, whilst the high eastern and southern heavens are bespangled with twinkling stellar gems as a fair field is dotted with bright flowers. The beauty of Gemini, enhanced by the temporary presence of the planet Saturn, is matched by that of Auriga, whose flaming jewel Capella is slowly nearing the zenith. Taurus, with Aldebaran, the Pleiades, and the Hyades, is not far from the high southern meridian, whilst the unrivalled Orion, monarch of all the skies, glows superbly in the southeast. Fluvius Eridanus, rising beneath Orion, streams proudly down toward the horizon till its phosphorescent waves are lost to view in the midst.

Observing with awe and rapture this annual display of celestial glory, the lover of the sky must needs marvel at the callousness of those whose nocturnal gaze never mounts above the garish glare of the sordid city. How trivial seem the rays of the lamp to him who is wont to look upon assembled suns and worlds!

EDITOR'S NOTE FP: *EN* 47, No. 153 (30 November 1915): 8.

Notes

1. Thomas William Webb (1807–1885), *Celestial Objects for Common Telescopes* (rev. ed. 1904–07, 2 vols.; *LL* 927 [HPL had only Vol. 1]).

2. HPL refers to the Gallipoli peninsula that forms the western shore of the Dardanelles. The Allies twice attempted—in April-May and in August 1915—to force their way through the Dardanelles, but were repulsed by the Turks both times, with immense casualties. Between December 1915 and January 1916 the Allies completely evacuated the area.

3. Valerius Flaccus (1st century C.E.), *Argonautica* 8.117–18. The translation is by HPL, as Valerius Flaccus was not translated into English verse until 1999. The first prose translation (by H. G. Bloomfield) was published in 1916.

JANUARY SKIES

D uring the opening month of 1916 all the major planets, faint and bright alike, will be visible in the evening sky. Mercury, unseen throughout December, makes a favourable evening appearance in January. On the 20th it will arrive at greatest eastern elongation, being visible at or about that time as a pinkish spark, outlined against the western twilight just after sunset. Its phase as seen through a telescope will be semicircular, though the disc will exhibit no markings. The next appearance of Mercury will be in the morning, at the close of next month.

Venus has now so much advanced, that it forms a conspicuous figure in the evening sky. Setting on the 1st at 6:31 p.m. and on the 31st at 7:48, it is now comparatively high in the heavens, lingering much over two hours after sunset, and thus having the opportunity to exhibit its intense glow to great advantage against the inky curtain of full darkness. By the last of the month it sets a full 2 hours and 52 minutes after the sun. In phase Venus is still strongly gibbous, not coming to semicircular form till April. Paradoxically enough, the actual illuminated surface as seen by us increases in spite of the decreasing phase. This is because the planet swiftly approaches the earth as it wanes. The rather thin crescent of Venus at greatest brilliancy possesses a far larger absolute surface than the almost complete circle which we behold near superior conjunction.

Mars is now an object of great beauty and splendour, being close to its opposition and advantageously placed in the evening sky. On the 1st it rises at 8:46 p.m., and on the 31st at 5:38. The planet is retrograding in the constellation Leo, changing on the 1st from direct motion. Mars will be an "evening star" during the entire year, though its brilliancy will steadily decrease after its opposition next month. By December it will have lost most of its present attractiveness.

Jupiter, though past its quadrature, continues to blaze with great effulgence, progressing westward to meet its rival Venus. Next month the two will be close together, presenting an unique spectacle, and affording a chance for comparison in which Jupiter will suffer. The giant planet this month sets at 10:24 p.m. on the 1st, and at 8:52 p.m. on the 31st. It is now in Pisces, moving directly, and lending lustre to an otherwise barren region in the southwestern sky.

Saturn is now in fullest splendour, coming to opposition on January 4th. To the telescopic observer, this immense ringed world is ever a delight, presenting as it does a spectacle absolutely unparalleled in all the sky. The expansion of the ring system is now slightly diminished, but is still great enough to exhibit all the beauties of the rings. Common instruments will reveal the dark line of division betwixt the two outer rings, a feature particularly plain at the "ansae", or two opposite parts of the system shown to us most broadly by perspective. Saturn is still in Gemini, rising on the 1st at 4:28 p.m., and setting on the 31st at 5:24 a.m.

Uranus is still in the evening sky, though soon to quit it. Early next month it will come to conjunction and disappear amidst the solar refulgence.

The faint Neptune, on the other hand, is this month at its best, arriving at opposition on the 22nd. Though invisible to the unassisted vision, this planet may be detected with very little optical aid if one but know where to search for it. Its appearance, however, scarce repays the finder, since its supposed belts and variations of superficial brilliancy are doubtful even in the most powerful of instruments.

The moon's phases for January will be as follows:

New Moon, 4th .... 11:45 p.m.
First Quarter, 11th .... 10:38 p.m.
Full Moon, 20th ....3:29 a.m.
Last Quarter, 27th.. 7:35 p.m.

Perigee falls on the 4th, Apogee on the 17th. The moon runs low on the 3d and 30th, high on the 17th. It approaches the following planets on the following dates: Venus, 7th; Jupiter, 10th; Saturn, 18th; Mars, 22nd. At the time of full moon on the 20th, there will be a partial lunar eclipse visible at Providence as follows:

Moon enters Penumbra..1:06 a.m.

Moon enters Shadow..2:55 a.m.

Middle of Eclipse ....3:40 a.m.

Moon leaves Shadow...4:24 a.m.

Moon leaves Penumbra..6:14 a.m.

The eclipsed area is comparatively slight, comprising but 0.137 of the moon's diameter at maximum. The penumbra is the half-shadow or tract from which the intervening earth excludes only a part of the sun's light. The actual shadow, or "umbra", as it is astronomically designated, is that area from which all sunlight is cut off. To a person situated on the moon in the completely shadowed parts, the phenomenon would be a total eclipse of the sun by the earth. On the 3d of next month there will be a total eclipse, visible in Rhode Island as partial, which will doubtless prove of even greater interest than the more imminent eclipse of the moon.

The sun enters the Zodiacal sign Aquarius on January 20th, thereby announcing the dreariest period of the year. It has been suggested that the figure of this sign, an old man pouring from an urn a stream of icy water, originated through its association with the coldest and bitterest of seasons. During the month the days gain 46 minutes in length, verifying the rough old New England couplet:

"When the days begin to lengthen,
The cold begins to strengthen."

But a condition slightly counteracting the frigidity of our Northern winter is the fact that the earth is at this season nearest the sun. Actual perihelion occurs on the 2nd of this month. Of course, this benign tempering of climate is confined solely to super-equatorial regions. In the southern hemisphere, Argentina, Chile, South Africa, and Australia, it is now summer, with the heat of that torrid period only accentuated by the proximity of our globe to the sun. July, the southern midwinter, will find the earth in aphelion, its remoteness from the sun cruelly accentuating the bitterness of the cold. We of the United States and Great Britain should congratulate ourselves on our position with respect to the equator.

The starry skies of January are without doubt the most brilliant of all the year, as if endeavouring by their refulgence to compensate for the suffering of the cold earth. The Zodiacal constellation on the meridian is Taurus, the Bull, famous alike for its two glorious star cluster, the famous Pleiades and the V-shaped Hyades; and for the bright red star Aldebaran, which reposes at the top of the left-hand branch of the latter cluster. In mythology, Taurus is the milk-white bull into which Jupiter turned himself when he bore off Europa, daughter of Agenor, from Asia. As Mr. Addison very beautifully translates from Ovid:

"The ruler of the skies, the thund'ring god,
Who shakes the world's foundations with a nod,
Among the herd of lowing heifers ran,
Frisked in a bull, and bellow'd o'er the plain.
His skin was whiter than the snow that lies

Unsully'd by the breath of Southern skies;
Small shining horns on his curl'd forehead stand,
As turn'd and polish'd by the workman's hand.
His eye-balls roll'd, not formidably bright,
But gaz'd and languish'd with a gentle light."[1]

Below Taurus and almost on the meridian is the Giant Hunter Orion, king of all the starry host. With its two resplendent stars, Betelgeux and Rigel, its glittering belt, its sparkling sword, and its shimmering nebula, this group well deserves its classification as foremost of the constellations. Below Orion is Lepus, the Hare, a furtive little object in whose pursuit the great huntsman ever takes delight. West of Lepus, on and past the meridian, flow the northern branches of the River Eridanus, whose brighter parts, including the lustrous star Achernar, never ascend above the horizon of Providence. Eridanus is an old name for the River Po, in Northern Italy or Gallia Cisalpina. Its mythological interest lies in its having served as the grave of the ill-fated Phaeton, son of Phoebus the Sun-God, who one day rashly undertook the difficult task of driving his father's blazing chariot across the sky. Phoebus had instructed the youth how to avoid the terrible dangers of the heavens, but Phaeton, becoming affrighted at the bewildering array of signs, constellations, and planets, lost control of the celestial steeds and drove so near the earth that he scorched and withered all beneath him. The frightful heat baked all the Aethiopians to their present blackness, and seared the Libyan and Saharan regions till they became eternal deserts. Jupiter, perceiving the disaster wrought by the reckless boy, finally struck him down with a thunderbolt,

"Till in the Po his blasted corpse was hurl'd,
Far from his country, in the western world."[2]

The sisters of Phaeton, weeping beside Eridanus' banks, were turned into poplar trees, whilst Cygnus, his friend, was changed to that Swan who now shines in the sky. It has been conjectured that the myth of Phaeton refers to some past period of terrible heat or drouth.

Above Taurus, and almost precisely in the zenith, glows Capella, brightest star of the constellation Auriga, the Waggoner. This group represents Erichtenius, fourth King of Athens and son to Vulcan, who invented the chariot, and was the first to drive a four-horse team. West of Auriga, and but little past transit, shines the effulgent Perseus with his carving sword. Near him are Andromeda and Triangulum, whilst below these groups lie Aries and Pisces. Cetus is declining in the southwest, while Pegasus is already descending below the northwestern horizon. North of Pegasus, Cygnus is just going out of view.

In the north we find the Plough at right angles to the horizon, commencing its annual winter ascent. Close following, but still beneath the pole, is Draco, the Dragon. Ursa Minor is swinging eastward, while Cepheus, with Cassiopeia above it, lies west of the pole. Cor Caroli, the brightest star of Canes Venatici, has barely appeared in the northeast. Farther south the Sickle of Leo is wholly visible, with Cancer and Leo the head and fore parts of Hydra now in sight. Next to Cancer, and now containing the planet Saturn, is Gemini, with its famous pair of bright stars, Castor and Pollux.

In the southeast blaze out the brilliant beacons of winter. The two Dogs, the Milky Way, and the upper part of Argo Navis, all help Orion in gilding the nocturnal dome. West of Argo and Canis Major is Columba, the Dove, scarcely a fitting object in these martial days.

Through each succeeding year the same starry sights unfold themselves to our gaze, yet never do we tire of beholding them. As cherished friends they return at expected intervals, cheering us with their refulgent presence and guiding our thoughts today, even as they guided the primitive acts of our semi-barbaric ancestors thousands of years ago.

EDITOR'S NOTE FP: *EN* 48, No. 25 (31 December 1915): 8.

Notes

1. Ovid, *Metamorphoses* 2.848–58 (tr. Joseph Addison [1704] as "Europa's Rape"; two lines omitted by HPL).
2. Ovid, *Metamorphoses* 2.323–24 (tr. Joseph Addison [1704] as "The Story of Phaeton"; "on" for "in" in the first line in Addison).

FEBRUARY SKIES

The month of February will, from an astronomical point of view, be chiefly distinguished by the total solar eclipse which falls on the 3d, and which will be visible in Providence as a partial eclipse. The path of the moon's obscuring shadow, which constitutes the zone from which the phenomenon may be observed as total, extends mostly over the Atlantic and Pacific oceans, leaving the South American countries of Colombia and Venezuela and the island of Guadaloupe as the only land areas from which the complete totality can be watched. As a partial eclipse, the occurrence may be seen throughout the United States, Mexico, and Central America; in the greater part of Canada, and in the northern half of South America, Iceland, the British Isles, France, Spain, and northwestern Africa will likewise be favoured.

In Rhode Island the eclipse will be of but moderate magnitude, less than half the solar disc being darkened. At about 10:25 a.m. the moon's edge will commence to encroach upon that of the sun. At about 11:30 the eclipse will be at its greatest, approximately four-tenths of the solar disc being hidden. The phenomenon will end at 12:35 p.m. So conspicuous a spectacle deserves observation by all local lovers of the heavens. Whether watched with the unaided eye or with optical assistance, a dark or smoked glass must be used; since the direct solar glare is unendurable to the sight.

Of the various planets visible this month, Venus shines unsurpassed. It is now comparatively high in the western sky during the early evening, setting 2 hours and 52 minutes after the sun on the 1st, and 3 hours and 24 minutes after the sun on the 29th. The phase of Venus is still gibbous though now gradually approaching the semicircular form. The planet's brilliancy increases steadily, and before many weeks will give rise to the customary tales of a "strange light in the west" amongst the ignorant. Venus this month moves from the eastern part of Aquarius to the eastern part of Pisces, crossing the vernal equinox about the 13th.

Jupiter, still of intense lustre, is now near Venus, meeting the latter almost exactly at the vernal equinox. On the evening of the 13th the two resplendent orbs will be in very close proximity, offering a sight well worthy of admiring observation. The relative brilliancy of these planets may then be advantageously compared. Actual conjunction occurs on the 4th at 2 a.m., when Venus will lie but 37 minutes of arc north of Jupiter, but they will by that time have sunk below the horizon. Jupiter sets on the 1st at 8:51 p.m., and on the 29th at 7:30.

Mercury, in inferior conjunction on the 5th, attains visibility at the end of the month, glowing like a spark in the low eastern heavens before dawn. Greatest elongation will occur on the 1st of March.

Mars, now of superlative ruddy refulgence, arrives at opposition on the 9th; being then nearest the earth, and appearing most advantageously as it ascends the eastern heavens just after the close of day. It is retrograding amongst the stars, passing during February from the vicinity of Regulus in Leo, to a point well within the confines of Cancer. Of all the planets, Mars has probably received the greatest amount of popular attention, since its peculiar and variable telescopic appearance invests it with an air of mystery in no way lessened by the vague conjectures made concerning the existence of human, or at least intelligent, life upon its surface. It is scarce needful to remark, that the red planet is now under the closest observation by astronomers in every part of the world. On January 24th it was announced at the Lowell Observatory, Flagstaff, Arizona, that five canal-like markings or rifts had appeared in the "north polar cap", or white tract supposedly of snow, which surrounds the north pole of Mars during the northern winter of that planet. According to the radical theories of Lowell, the new rifts are the visible result of vegetation springing through the melting snow. The conservative scientist, however, withholds comment on phenomena such as these, preferring to accumulate accurate information without the prejudice of premature theorising, until a time shall arrive when he may possess evidence of more conclusive and enlightening character.

Uranus is this month wholly invisible, being in conjunction on the 5th; but Neptune faintly shines in the evening sky, having been in opposition in January.

The moon's phases for February will be as follows:

New Moon, 3d...11:06 a.m.
First Quarter, 10th .... 5:28 p.m.
Full Moon, 18th .... 9:29 p.m.
Last Quarter, 25th..4:24 a.m.

Perigee falls on the 1st and 29th, Apogee on the 13th. The moon runs high on the 12th, and low on the 27th. It approaches the various planets as follows: Venus and Jupiter on the 6th, Saturn on the 14th, and Mars on the 18th.

The Sun enters the Zodiacal sign Pisces on the 19th. During February the days gain one hour and eleven minutes. Apparent or sundial time is this month almost exactly the same as the mean, or clock time; noon occurring precisely midway betwixt sunrise and sunset.

The present month is notable for the possession of the intercalary or "Leap Year" day, whose periodical recurrence maintains the regularity of our calendar. The selection of February to consign this day is due to the older arrangement of the months whereby February concluded the civil year.

Turning to the constellations we discover the resplendent groups of winter still reigning with undiminished lustre. Orion is now past the meridian, which post of prominence is occupied by Sirius, the brightest star of all the sky. So incomparably brilliant is this luminary gem, that we are sometimes forgetful of the richness and attractiveness of the rest of the constellation, Canis Major, in which it belongs; yet that group would rank high even if without its peerless Dog-Star.

Much above, and slightly east of Canis Major lies Canis Minor, whose bright star Procyon not only precedes the Dog-Star when rising, but lingers after him as he sets. The Zodiacal constellation on the meridian is Gemini, most northerly of all the twelve, and lying but little below the zenith. Besides its own sparkling fixed stars Castor and Pollux, it now contains the planet Saturn, whose effulgence imparts an added splendour. Just east and but slightly south of Gemini is Cancer, faint in itself, but notable as the former location of the summer solstice. Toward the end of the month the planet Mars will lend to this group a transient glory. In the west are the bright constellations whose appearance in the east last autumn heralded the present array of stellar brilliants. Taurus is still at its best, whilst Auriga and Perseus beam without diminution of lustre. Lower in the sky are Eridanus, Aries, and Andromeda, while Cetus and Pisces have partially set. In the north we find Draco beginning to ascend, with Ursa Major considerably above it. Ursa Minor is likewise rising, being at present below and to the right of the Pole-Star. Cepheus is sinking toward lower transit, with Cassiopeia close behind it. The region immediately above the pole is quite devoid of bright stars. In the northeast Boötes has not yet risen, though the misty beams of Coma Berenices are beginning to penetrate the thick air of the horizon. Virgo is half in sight due east. Whilst Leo is rapidly mounting the vault, southeast Hydra is uncoiling, the small parasitic group Crater, the Cup, being just visible. Low in the south floats Argo Navis, though the brighter parts of this group are never seen in the latitude of Rhode Island. Its splendid star Canopus, second only to Sirius in lustre, is visible in the extreme southern part of the United States.

February, though a winter month, has in it something of cheer and promise which the others lack. The ascending sun now shews its approach in the slightly increasing temperature, whilst the Zodiacal sign Pisces, the Fishes, into which it now moves, typifies the season of melting rivers and the resumption of labour by the fisherman. On the 2nd of February falls the old Popish festival of Candlemas, with which is connected the curious but baseless meteorological tradition, that if the weather then be fair, a resumption of winter's worst rigours may be expected to ensue.

Spots on the sun, for the past few years quite rare, may henceforth be looked for in greater numbers; since a period of frequency is now close at hand. The last previous maximum was in 1908, and according to the conditions of the cycle as best calculated, the next will occur in 1917 or 1918.

EDITOR'S NOTE FP: *EN* 48, No. 52 (1 February 1916): 8.

MARCH SKIES

Venus, now of intense lustre, is the dominant feature of the March sky; blazing forth each evening high above the western horizon. On the 1st, it sets at about 9 o'clock, nearly three hours and a half after the sun, and on the 31st, at 10:06, nearly four hours after sunset. As the month advances the planet's phase approaches closer to the semicircular configuration which will exist at the time of greatest eastern elongation in April. The course of Venus amongst the stars during March extends from the eastern part of the constellation Pisces, entirely across Aries, and just into Taurus, ending not far from the celebrated Pleiades cluster.

Jupiter, though visible low in the west during the first few evenings of the month, soon withdraws from sight, and will be in conjunction on the 1st of April. Its brilliancy has faded to a magnitude no greater than that of the region of the sky which lies just east of the vernal equinox. Jupiter sets on the 1st at 7:30, about two hours after the sun; and on the 14th at 7:05, only an hour after sunset.

Mars, in opposition last month, still graces the southern and southeastern heavens with but slightly diminished splendour. On the 1st it sets at 5:40 a.m., and on the 31st at 3:28. It spends the entire month in the constellation Cancer, retrograding until the 22nd, and afterward moving directly. In general, it forms the apex of a rather flat celestial triangle, the ends of whose bases are marked by the bright stars Regulus, in Leo, and Procyon, in Canis Minor.

Mercury arrives at greatest western elongation on the 1st, being at that time visible near the eastern horizon just before sunrise. The present period of visibility is not, however, exceptionally favourable since Mercury's best morning appearances are made in the autumn. At the time of elongation, the planet will lie in the dull constellation Capricornus.

Saturn arrives at quadrature on the 30th. It is still a leading object in the evening sky, shining refulgently in the south and southwest, and lingering amongst the stars in the central part of the constellation Gemini. As the month commences, the planet is in westward or retrograde motion, but after the 11th it moves eastward, or directly. Saturn sets on the 1st at 3:25 a.m., and on the 31st at 1:24.

Uranus is now emerging from the solar glare, being faintly visible in the morning sky, whilst Neptune, approaching its quadrature, shines even more faintly during the evening hours.

The moon's phases for March will be as follows:

New Moon, 3d.. 10:58 p.m.
First Quarter, 11th .... 1:33 p.m.
Full Moon, 19th .... 12:27 p.m.
Last Quarter, 28th..11:22 a.m.

Apogee falls on the 12th, Perigee on the 26th. The moon runs high on the 11th, low on the 24th. It approaches the following planets an the following dates: Mercury, 1st; Jupiter, 5th; Venus, 7th; Saturn, 13th; and Mars, 25th.

On the 20th of March, at 5:47 p.m., occurs the happiest astronomical event of the year; the sun's entrance into the Zodiacal sign Aries, with its consequent northward crossing of the equator and opening of the beneficent season of spring. This annual occurrence, typifying the reawakening of Nature and the renewal of life, has in all ages and amongst all northern races been hailed with delight and religious celebration; so that no nation today is without some sort of spring festival based upon the ancestral traditions surrounding the return of the sun. Many of our Easter customs are directly descended from the vernal rites of our prehistoric forefathers. During March the days gain one hour and 24 minutes, and are of about the same length as the nights. The sun, in this period, moves northward 11 degrees and 21 minutes.

The solar eclipse which occurred on the 3d of last month was observed with success in many localities. Dr. William R. Brooks, director of the Smith Observatory and Professor of Astronomy at Hobart College, Geneva, N.Y., who will be remembered in Providence for the interesting lecture he delivered here a year ago, made valuable observations during the course which he discerned not only the mountainous roughness of the moon's edge as it was darkly outlined against the solar surface, but two prominent spots near the centre of the solar disc as well.

The sidereal sky, though still radiant with the glory of the departing winter groups, begins now to assume a characteristically vernal aspect. The Zodiacal constellation on the meridian at 9 p.m. is Cancer, the Crab, a faint asterism whose chief permanent interest lies in the dimly glittering cluster of little stars known as "Praespe" or "The Manger". Just at present, however, the resplendent and ruddy Mars adorns the scene.

Just below Cancer is the head of Hydra, a group of such length that the tip of the tail is hardly yet above the southeastern horizon. Still lower in the south is Argo Navis, the Ship Argo, but a small part of which is ever visible in a latitude so far north as that of Rhode Island. As we view it, it floats proudly in the Milky Way at the place where that golden stream meets the southern horizon. Argo Navis represents the first ship ever constructed by man, the celebrated vessel built by Argus for the Thessalian prince Jason, when the latter started out on his famous quest of the Golden Fleece. Jason was the son of Aeson, King of Thessaly, but his father falling ill, the throne was occupied by Pelias, his uncle, brother to Aeson. Now Pelias, covetous of permanent power, resolved to put Jason out of the way, but fearing downright murder, decided to send him abroad in search of the golden fleece of the ram Aries, who had conveyed the children Phryxus and Helle out of Europe, and whose pelt now hung in a sacred dragon-guarded grove in Colchis, under the care of Aeetes the King, who had received the boy Phryxus years before. The ram having come originally from Thessaly, Jason was directed to return it thither. Being chosen for so perilous a mission, Jason at once assembled about him a more illustrious convocation of demigods and heroes than ever before or since were met together. There might be found nearly every celebrated youth of godlike and heroic fame: Hercules, mighty son of Jove; Castor and Pollux, heavenly twins of universal renown; Orpheus, magic lyrist whose dulcet strains might move even the hills and mountains; Nestor, famed hero; Theseus, he who was to slay the Minotaur; and Zetes and Calais, brawny sons of Boreas, the North Wind. As Mr. Pope has written in his "Ode for St. Cecelia's Day":

> So when the first bold vessel dar'd the seas,
> High on the stern the Thracian rais'd his strain,
>   While Argo saw the kindred trees
>   Descend from Pelion to the main.
>   Transported demigods stood round,
>   And men grew heroes at the sound.[1]

The daring Argonauts, having set sail, touched first at Lemnos, then at Mysia, where the beautiful youth sent ashore for fresh water was made prisoner by the enamoured nymphs of the fount he there discovered. Hercules, missing the lad, went in search of him, but neither soon returning, the Argo quit the Mysian shore without the two. Arriving in Thracia, the Argonauts found and consulted the sage Phineus, who directed them how to get safely by the Symplegades or Clashing Isles, which moved about in the entrance to the Euxine Sea and crushed betwixt them all vessels that dared attempt to pass by. Instructed by Phineus, the voyagers let loose a dove when they reached the Isles, thus causing them to clash together. The dove being fleet of wing, escaped with the loss of its tail feathers, and in the moment of rebound after the clash, the Argo passed safely betwixt the perilous obstructions. The advice of Phineus was given in gratitude for the benefaction of the Argonauts in relieving him of a terrible torment. Jupiter, in punishment for acts of cruelty, had deprived Phineus of his sight, and caused him ever to be harassed by certain birds called Harpies, creatures with the heads of women, the claws of vultures, and pale, hungry faces. Whenever a meal was placed before Phineus, the Harpies would straightway seize upon it and bear it off. These pestilential birds were driven off by the Argonauts after some labour, and Phineus was thus freed of his torture.

When Jason and his companions reached Colchis, they discovered many obstacles in the way of attaining the sought-for fleece. Fire-breathing oxen were to be yoked to a plough, dragon's teeth were to be sown, and the crop of armed men arising from these teeth were to be vanquished. Then the sleepless dragon guarding the sacred grove of the fleece was to be overcome. Aided by the sorceries of the King's daughter, Medea, Jason finally triumphed, sailing away with the fleece and with Medea as his bride. After his return to Thessaly, Jason found his spouse of great aid in restoring his aged father, Aeson, to health and youth, and in disposing of the wicked Pelias. The Argo was taken from the sea and set up in a sanctuary on the Isthmus of Corinth, in a grove sacred to Neptune. One day as Jason was standing by admiring his faithful vessel, the ancient wooden stern collapsed, crushing the daring Argonaut to death beneath it. The Argo, reposing in state, was so often patched up, that finally no piece of the original wood remained, though the outline still existed. Learned sages of Greece then fell into great dispute, whether or not the object remaining might justly be deemed the true and original Argo. What was their result, I know not, but the ship itself may be seen each clear winter night, low on the southern horizon, and lying east of the Dog-Star.

The western sky now bears all the stellar brilliants of winter; Orion, the two Dogs, Gemini, Auriga, Taurus, and Perseus being in full view. Columba, Eridanus, and Aries are setting. In the north Ursa Major is well prepared for his passage above the Pole, whilst Ursa Minor is lifted at the right of the pole, parallel with the horizon. Cepheus, followed by Cassiopeia, is sinking beneath Polaris. In the northeast the glittering semicircle is above the mists, while Boötes, with that most splendid of all heralds of spring, the bright Arcturus, is well in view. Arcturus, with its orange-reddish refulgence, is one of the most characteristic and captivating of all the signs of the vernal season. Due east the Zodiacals group Virgo is rising, the sparkling Spica being now well seen. In the southeast, the neat little trapezium of Corvus, the Crow, is displayed. High in the south is Leo with its stately Sickle and trim triangle. Regulus marks the base of the Sickle's handle and serves to illume a region otherwise rather desolate.

The skies of March, taken as a whole, are among the most pleasing panoramas unfolded to the admiring observer. In them the effulgent charm of winter yet remains, whilst the groups scaling the eastern sky are happily prophetic of the milder times soon to ensue.

EDITOR'S NOTE FP: *EN* 48, No. 76 (1 March 1916): 6.

Notes

1. Alexander Pope, "Ode for Musick, on St. Cecilia's Day" (1713), ll. 38–43.

APRIL SKIES

Venus this month appears under the best possible conditions for the telescopic observer, arriving at greatest eastern elongation on the 24th, and being therefore at its greatest apparent distance from the sun. It shines each evening with unparalleled radiance, high in the western sky as the darkness gathers, setting on the 1st at 10:05 p.m., and on the 30th at 10:45. Though the planet is most impressive to the casual spectator after the coming of full darkness, when its superlative lustre is emphasised by the absence of solar illumination, the telescopist finds in this brilliant impressiveness a serious obstacle to his study; since the dazzling glare of the highly reflective surface fatally obscures the distinctness of its outlines. Therefore the average astronomer makes his observations by twilight, when the bright orb first twinkles out in the slowly darkening heavens, and the disc may be seen as a sharply defined image, even when subjected to considerable magnification. Indeed, the advanced student of the sky, possessing for his telescope an equatorial mounting whose graduated circles may enable him to direct the tube to any desired mathematical point on the celestial vault, generally watches Venus in the daytime, finding the planet by means of its right ascension and inclination as recorded in the Nautical Almanack. When thus viewed with the greatest care and the best optical aid which science can devise, the surface of Venus undoubtedly reveals certain actual topographical configurations. Various authorities differ concerning the exact aspect and nature of these markings, but their faint presence is indisputable, and they may at some future time furnish us with more knowledge of that luminous world which is so much akin to our own. The presence of a very dense, cloudy, and reflective atmosphere about Venus is probably the reason alike for the planet's extreme brilliancy, and for the vagueness and impermanence of its features. If the surface be inhabited the dwellers thereon must but seldom behold the clear heavens outside their atmospheric veil. Venus of all heavenly bodies most nearly resembles the earth, and is most likely to sustain an analogous race of men. Its size is but little less than that of the terrestrial globe, whilst its day or period of rotation is, despite some contrary opinion, probably similar. The year is shorter, having but 225 days, and the climate is warmer, Venus being much nearer the sun; but the shorter year is scarcely a material factor, and the higher temperature might well be endured by organisms not unlike mankind; since the dense air, laden with gaseous vapour, must serve to mitigate the tropical ardour of the solar rays. The inclination of the planet's axis to the plane of its orbit, which determines the character of the seasons, is yet to be exactly defined; but several competent astronomers have made estimates which justify the supposition that the seasons of Venus do not widely differ, save in length, from those which we experience upon the earth. Speculation concerning the inhabitants of other worlds is always fruitless, but in view of the popular and extended discussions about possible intelligent life on Mars, it seems excusable to indulge in similar discussion regarding Venus, whose conditions are certainly better adapted to the maintenance of life than are those of the small and frigid Mars. The apparent form of Venus' disc during April will approximate the half-circle, this phase being exact at the time of greatest elongation. The planet this month moves directly across the constellation Taurus, beginning near the far-famed Pleiades.

Mars, though relegated to comparative insignificance by the superior refulgence of Venus, still adorns the evening sky with great splendour, shining to advantage long after the Queen of Planets has set. Being outside the earth's orbit, Mars is not restricted like Venus and Mercury to the immediate vicinity of the sun, but may be beheld far into the night. On the 1st of April it sets at 3:27 a.m., and on the 30th at 1:14. Though the present period of visibility is not an especially favourable one, Mars is receiving much attention from those astronomical students who specialise in planetary research. The planet is this month in direct motion, travelling a short distance in the eastern part of the constellation Cancer.

Saturn, while now past quadrature, nevertheless forms a pleasing and conspicuous ornament of the western evening sky. It lies in the constellation Gemini, setting on the 1st at 1:24 a.m., and on the 30th at 11:30 p.m. The ringed world is drawing closer and closer to Venus, and will next month be in conjunction with the latter. This conjunction will be of particular interest, since Venus will then be very near greatest brilliancy, offering an unusually striking contrast to the vastly duller Saturn.

Jupiter will be in conjunction with the sun on April 1st, being therefore invisible save at the very last of the month. On the 30th the giant planet will rise a little more than three quarters of an hour before the sun, and may possibly be seen as a "morning star", very low in the east as the twilight of dawn turns to day. Jupiter is in slow direct motion, still lingering in the dull constellation Pisces, just east of the vernal equinox.

Mercury, in superior conjunction on the 14th, will be invisible throughout the month. The faint Uranus is gaining height in the morning sky, whilst the still fainter Neptune, in the evening sky, reaches quadrature on the 20th.

The moon's phases will occur as follows:

New Moon, 2nd...11:21 a.m.
First Quarter, 10th ....9:36 a.m.
Full Moon, 18th ....12:08 a.m.
Last Quarter, 24th... 5:38 p.m.

Apogee falls on the 9th, Perigee on the 21st. The moon runs high on the 7th, low on the 21st. It will be near Venus on the 6th, Saturn on the 9th, Mars on the 12th, and Jupiter on the 30th.

The Sun enters the Zodiacal sign Taurus on the 20th, moving northward in such a manner that the days will gain over an hour and a quarter during the month. The activity of the solar surface is increasing as the time of maximum spottedness draws near, and large clusters of spots may be expected at any time by the telescopic observer. Various pseudo-scientific speculators use the solar spot cycle as a basis for ridiculous long-range predictions of the weather, founding their fallacious doctrines on the vague relation which seems to exist between the sun and terrestrial magnetism. It is hardly necessary to remark to the intelligent, that no scheme of this sort is worthy of attention; but for the benefit of the unenlightened, the United States Weather Bureau has recently been forced to publish an official and authoritative denial of the validity of all long-range meteorological forecasts. The extent to which unscrupulous charlatans employ astronomy in deluding and defrauding the public is indeed distressing, for despite the efforts of scientists and the dicta of Government observers, there is today issued in the city of St. Louis a weekly magazine, read avidly by the rural population of the entire nation at the cost of one dollar per year, wherein appears an absurd system of predicting weather by the motion and aspects of the planets. The outrageous ludicrousness of this system is shewn on the very surface, by the inclusion of "the planet Vulcan", a body which is now conclusively known not to exist at all, but which was thought for a little while during the last century to have been discovered close to the sun, within the orbit of Mercury. Fraud such as this should be vigorously suppressed as a menace alike to truth, and to the prosperity of the less educated public.

Turning to the contemplation of the fixed stars, we this month discover the majestic Leo, or the Lion, as the Zodiacal constellation on the meridian during the evening. This massive and impressive group, with its sickle and right triangle, scarcely needs description, and is a worthy and luminous herald of the milder days of spring. Below Leo, and extending eastward almost to the horizon, is the sinuous Hydra, which bears on its back the two little groups Crater and Corvus. Of these two, Corvus is by far the more attractive, conspicuous, and well defined; its trapezium-like figure being one of the most characteristic sights of the vernal season as it traverses the low southeastern sky. West of Leo is Cancer, with its faint cluster of stars known as "Praespe". Still farther west is the radiant Gemini, and below them both are the remnants of the winter groups: Canis Minor still high enough for favourable vision, and Canis Major, Orion, and Taurus about to set. These once splendid winter brilliants seem to have lost their magic scintillance with the crisp frosty air of their appointed season; for as they now linger in the softer air of spring they seem scarce brighter or more animated than the fresher, if duller, constellations which are unfolding themselves in the east.

In the north, the Great Bear is soaring above the pole, the Plough being nearly in upper transit. Ursa Minor is tilted upward to the right of the pole, whilst Cepheus and Cassiopeia are on the horizon below it. Draco coils eastward and above the pole. Slightly westward, Perseus is about to set, with Auriga close following. But as Auriga carries the effulgent Capella from view, Boötes, in the east, well compensates for its loss with the bright Arcturus. A little below Boötes is the graceful, though not particularly brilliant, circlet known as the Northern Crown. Low on the northeastern horizon a radiant beam of bluish white pierces the dense vapours. This is the matchless Vega, now about to return for the coming spring and summer. A little south of this, Hercules is rising to view, while due east the twisting serpent announces the coming of Ophiuchus. In the southeast Libra has completely risen, above which Virgo shines in quiet dignity, with the brilliant Spica gleaming whitely. On the southern horizon the upper parts of Centaurus, the Centaur, are dimly seen, though but little of this group is ever visible as far north as Providence.

After midnight a new and glowing pageant will unfold itself to the watcher. Scorpio with the fiery Antares; Aquila with the bright Altair; and the rich summer reaches of the Milky Way will reward his vigil. But for those who keep more ordinary hours, such sights belong rather to the summer than to the spring.

EDITOR'S NOTE FP: *EN* 48, No. 103 (1 April 1916): 8.

MAY SKIES

V enus, now past greatest elongation and rapidly approaching the sun, arrives at greatest brilliancy on the 27th of the coming month, then gleaming with high lustre in the western heavens during the twilight and early evening hours. It may indeed be seen in full daylight as well, by those who know its position on the celestial sphere;

and many sharp eyes will doubtless glimpse it as it crosses the meridian, high in the southern heavens, at about 2:45 each afternoon near the time of maximum brightness. The planet this month moves from the northeastern part of the constellation Taurus to the central part of Gemini, setting on the 1st at 10:45 p.m., and on the 31st at 10:05. Venus, viewed through the telescope, now shews a crescentic phase, shrinking from moderate thickness to considerable tenuity as the month progresses. To the naked eye, the aspect of Venus is now both startling and beautiful. The ignorant at such seasons of brilliancy frequently mistake the planet for an artificial light, and it is not improbable that lively rumours of hostile aëroplanes and Zeppelins will circulate freely during the ensuing weeks.

Close to Venus in the early evening sky is Saturn, now much past quadrature, and insignificant indeed as compared with its brighter neighbour. On the 24th the two orbs will be in conjunction, offering a spectacle of more than ordinary beauty and interest. Saturn sets on the 1st at 11:30 p.m., and on the 31st at 9:40.

Mars comes to quadrature on the 14th, shining with no mean effulgence in the high southern and southwestern evening sky; setting on the 1st at 1:44 a.m., and on the 31st at 12:13. The planet this month moves from the eastern boundary of the constellation Cancer, well into Leo, passing very close to the bright star Regulus on the 24th. The brilliancy of Mars has decreased very materially since the time of opposition, having fallen more than two standard magnitudes. The planet is now exactly as bright as the fixed star Aldebaran, in Taurus, and somewhat brighter than its present stellar neighbour Regulus.

Mercury arrives at greatest eastern elongation on the 12th, then appearing as a sparkling bit of pinkish light near the western horizon during the evening twilight hour.

Jupiter, now emerging from the solar glare, is the only bright planet in the morning sky. On the 1st it rises at 3:53 a.m., being barely discernible above the eastern horizon at dawn; but on the 31st it appears at 2:06, fully two hours before the sun.

Uranus, in the morning sky, will come to quadrature on the 10th, whilst Neptune, in the evening sky, is past quadrature.

The moon will have five phases during May, as follows:

New Moon, 2nd...12:29 a.m.
First Quarter, 10th ....3:47 a.m.
Full Moon, 17th ....9:11 a.m.
Last Quarter, 24th...12:16 a.m.
New Moon, 31st .... 2:37 p.m.

Apogee falls on the 7th, Perigee on the 19th. The moon runs high on the 5th, low on the 19th. It will approach the following planets on the following dates: Venus, 6th; Saturn, 7th; Mars, 10th; and Jupiter, 28th.

On May 21st the sun enters the Zodiacal sign of Gemini, moving northward about seven degrees during the month. The days increase by nearly an hour between the 1st and the 31st, the sun being above the horizon for fifteen hours on the latter date.

The sidereal skies of May shew in the west the last retreating remnants of winter's gorgeous host, and in the east the rising van of summer's stately array. The major part of the vault is given over to the quiet stars of spring. The Zodiacal constellation now on the meridian is Virgo, the Virgin, whose principal star, Spica, beams with a pure white lustre of prime magnitude. Below Virgo is Corvus, the Crow, perched upon the tail of Hydra, and easily recognisable by its plainly defined and compact trapeziform contour. Corvus represents, according to some accounts, the favoured raven of Apollo, whose hue was once white as the fleecy clouds of his native Grecian skies.

Chancing one day to learn of the perfidy of the nymph Coronis, whom Apollo loved, Corvus bore the tale to his master, who thereupon slew Coronis with an arrow. But the deed having been done, Apollo regretted his hasty act, and mourned for the nymph; blaming the tale-bearer as the cause of his woe, and turning the raven to that inky blackness which now marks the species. Another tale holds Corvus to be the metamorphosed form of the daughter of Coronaeus, king of Phocis, who, having been pursued by Neptune, was saved and turned to a bird by Minerva. The new-created raven was for some time the favourite bird of the goddess, but was later dismissed for telling tales and supplanted by Nyctimene, the Owl. Ovid, in his Metamorphoses, brings both of these legendary ravens into conversation, relating how the daughter of Coronaeus vainly warned the bird of Apollo not to bear tales to his master.[1] All the races of antiquity, save the Arcadians or primitive Chaldaeans, coincide in giving Corvus a bird-like character; the Arcadians interpreted the constellation as a horse.

West of Corvus is Crater, the Cup, called by the Greeks the goblet of Apollo, and by the Romans, that of Bacchus. Its form is vague as compared with that of the Crow. Stretching beneath Corvus and Crater, and apparently supporting the two small groups, is the immense length of Hydra, the Water-Serpent, whose head has now traversed far into the western sky.

Above Virgo, and practically in the zenith, is the faint, nebulous bit of light which indicates the constellation Coma Berenices, east of which Boötes is rapidly bringing the bright Arcturus toward transit. West of Virgo, Leo still shines with undiminished beams, while still farther westward along the Zodiac path, Cancer and Gemini are successively seen.

In the north we discover Cassiopeia directly beneath the pole, and but little above the horizon, in lower transit. At this position, the characteristic figure of the letter "W" is best seen. Cepheus has passed lower transit and is preparing to ascend the celestial dome. Ursa Major and Ursa Minor are both above the pole, whilst Draco is quite near upper transit. The mythological history of Draco is beclouded by many conflicting accounts. One legend avers that it represents the dragon who dwelt in the cave in the ancient grove near the plain of Panope, where Cadmus, the Tyrian prince, was directed by an oracle whilst searching for his sister Europa, who had been carried off from Asia by Jupiter in the disguise of a milk-white bull. At the mouth of the cave was a crystal fount, and when the companions of Cadmus essayed to fill their pitchers in the clear waters, the dragon burst forth upon them, raising his head higher than the tallest trees, and slaying all the Tyrians by means of his sinuous and cruel folds, or his poisonous breath. Cadmus, missing his men, went in search of them, and having discovered their fate, proceeded to give battle to the dragon. After much labour he conquered and killed the beast with his javelin, and in response to an oracle, extracted the teeth and sowed them in the fertile plain around. From these teeth sprang up a crop of armed warriors, who after some strife amongst themselves, offered themselves to the service of Cadmus, and under his guidance founded and peopled the city of Thebes on the very spot where they had sprung out of the earth. But Draco had been sacred to Mars, and Cadmus was cursed with the slaying of him. One day Cadmus impiously remarked that if a serpent were so precious to the Gods, he would fain be one himself, whereupon he was changed into one. Some of the dragon's teeth must have been preserved till later times, for we again meet with them in the legend of Jason and the Golden Fleece. A different tale identifies Draco with the dragon who guarded the Golden Apple of the

Hesperides and who was slain by Hercules. Another story, which has an astronomical foundation, associates Draco with the dragon flung by Minerva into the skies during the Gigantomachia, or War of the Gods and Giants. With such force did the goddess throw the twisting monster, that its coils became entangled with the axis of the heavens, wherefore it is fixed evermore to be whirled around the pole in the northern skies. The axis of the earth at one time pointed to the star Thuban, or Gamma, in Draco, wherefore that orb may be considered as the predecessor of our present Polaris. The astronomers and astrologers of ancient Egypt built temples oriented to this star, which they worshipped on account of its peculiar position. When the precession of the equinoxes began to carry the star away from the celestial pole, they changed the construction of their temples to follow it; not realising that it was merely the direction of the earth's axis which gave rise to the phenomena they admired. Of course, after the star had been left behind by the earth's axis, it ceased to have the properties of a pole-star, but began to describe the apparent revolutions common to all circumpolar stars; indeed, both Deneb, in Cygnus, and Vega, in Lyra, will successively serve as pole-stars thousands of years hence. Other groups in the north on May evening are Auriga and Perseus, setting toward the west, and Cygnus and Lyra, rising eastward. Hercules and Corona Borealis are already high in the vault. Further south, Ophiuchus et Serpens may be seen in part. In the southeastern Scorpio is rising, the fiery red rays of Antares now shining through the mists of the horizon. Antares is one of the characteristic features of the summer sky, and will lend a striking adornment to the celestial sphere during the month to come. Libra, the Balances, hang high in the southeast contiguous to Virgo. Sprawling along the southern horizon just east of the meridian in the northern edge of Centaurus, the Centaur, a group never completely seen as far north as Rhode Island. Two of its stars, Iota and Theta, are fairly well marked, but as a whole this constellation is distinctly a southern feature. In Australia, South Africa, and South America, Centaurus is one of the most prominent objects of the sky, exhibiting its two intensely brilliant stars Alpha and Beta, the former of which is the nearest of all the sidereal bodies to our solar system.

EDITOR'S NOTE FP: *EN* 48, No. 130 (3 May 1916): 8.

Notes

1. See Ovid, *Metamorphoses* 2.542–611.

JUNE SKIES

The coming month will witness the departure of both Venus and Saturn from the evening sky. Venus, having been at greatest brilliancy on May 27, is now drawing toward inferior conjunction, and decreasing rapidly in phase. On the 1st it sets two hours and 51 minutes after sunset; but will by the 20th or 25th have approached the sun too closely to remain visible save through the telescope in full daylight. On the 20th it will set about an hour and ten minutes after the sun. Since the waning of Venus is accompanied by a corresponding approach to the earth, it follows that the visible crescent increases in apparent semidiameter as it decreases in thickness, thus presenting a very striking outline shortly before it finally disappears. So large is the planet's disc at this period, that any ordinary opera glasses will suffice to reveal the phase which was before discernible only through the telescope. Indeed, many persons of unusually acute vision have detected the crescentic shape without any optical aid whatsoever. When Venus is close to inferior conjunction, the telescopist may not infrequently behold a great prolongation of the crescent, a prolongation at times so considerable that the cusps seem to meet, forming a complete circle. This phenomenon is due to the refraction and reflection of light by the dense and abundant atmosphere of the planet, and is analogous to the luminous fringe about the disc which some observers have noticed when Venus is just approaching upon the solar surface in transit. A phenomenon less easily explained is the dim glow seen on the supposedly invisible parts of the planet, forming a spectacle like that commonly called "the old moon in the new moon's arms"; when, though the moon be only a crescent in phase, we perceive all the rest of its surface faintly illuminated by radiance reflected from our own earth. Venus has no such source of reflected light; and its atmosphere, however thick, cannot possibly account for the strange illumination. Some observers have suggested that the planet's surface is phosphorescent, whilst others attribute the faint light to electromagnetic causes, comparing it roughly with the more fitful phenomena of the terrestrial Auroras.

Saturn, languishing low in the western sky during the early evening, has about it little of interest this month. On the 1st it sets at 9:40 p.m., and on the 20th at 8:35, an hour and ten minutes after the sun. On the 22nd it will be in rather close conjunction with the also disappearing Venus, after which time it will gradually slip away into the mists of the twilight.

Mars, though not now of great lustre or attractiveness, still adorns the evening sky, setting on the 1st at 12:13 a.m., and on the 30th at 10:45 p.m. It is in direct motion, passing this month from the central to the eastern part of the constellation Leo.

Jupiter is the most prominent planet of the morning sky, rising on the 1st at 2:07 a.m., and on the 30th at 12:23. It moves directly during June, crossing from the constellation Pisces into Aries.

Mercury is in inferior conjunction on the 5th, but becomes visible later in the month. arriving at greatest western elongation on the 30th. It will then shine low in the east at dawn, being not far from the attenuated crescent of the waning moon on the morning of the 2th. [sic]

Uranus, in the morning sky, is now past quadrature; whilst Neptune, in the evening sky, is drawing toward conjunction.

The moon's phases for June will be as follows:

First Quarter, 8th	6:59 p.m.
Full Moon, 15th	4:42 p.m.
Last Quarter, 22nd	8:16 a.m.
New Moon, 30th	5:43 a.m.

Apogee falls on the 3d and 30th, Perigee on the 16th. The moon runs high on the 1st and 8th, low on the 15th, crossing the equator on the 9th and 21st. It will approach Saturn and Venus on the 3d, Mars on the 7th, Jupiter on the 24th, and Mercury on the 2th. [sic]

On June 21st, at 1:24 p.m., the sun enters the Zodiacal sign Cancer, thereby opening the genial season of summer. This, the longest of days, contains 15 hours and 14 minutes. Between the 21st and the end of the month the days lose three minutes.

The Zodiacal constellation on the meridian during June evenings is Libra, the Balances, whose legendary character was doubtless determined by the fact that when the group was named, the sun entered its confines just at the autumnal season of balanced days and nights. This condition, brought about by the precession of the equinoxes, did not exist in those prehistoric ages when the other signs of the Zodiac were delineated, hence we may assume that Libra is the youngest of the twelve, and was created in its present form during historical times. To the eye, this constellation is wanting in lustre and general interest, though its principal star shews double in an opera glass, and its second star, visible just above the chief one, is of a peculiar greenish hue.

High over Libra, and reaching southward along the meridian from the zenith itself, is the impressive extent of Boötes, the Herdsman, whose resplendent star Arcturus is now somewhat past transit. Just east of Boötes, and soon to attain the meridian, is Corona Borealis, or the Northern Crown, a starry diadem whose glittering beauty imparts to it a merited prominence in the skies of summer. Its brightest star is of the second magnitude, and is variously known as Gemma or Alphecca. In the year 1866 one of the obscurer stars in Corona Borealis, usually invisible to the naked eye, blazed out in unexpected brilliancy, rivalling Gemma itself for a time, but soon fading back to its accustomed insignificance. Corona Borealis represents the golden crown given to Ariadne, daughter of Minos, King of Crete, by her divine husband Bacchus on the occasion of their marriage. Minos was at one time an overlord of Athens, and each year demanded a tribute of seven youths and seven maidens from the Athenians, to be devoured by the Minotaur, a monster having the body of a bull and the head of a man, who dwelt in a vast Cretan labyrinth skilfully constructed by Daedalus. So perfect was the labyrinth, that no one entering could ever find his way to safety again, but would sooner or later be discovered and slain by the Minotaur. At last the celebrated hero Theseus, godlike son of King Aegeus of Athens, resolved to break the cruel supremacy of Minos, or to perish in the attempt. Accordingly he sailed to Crete as one of seven youths demanded by Minos, but with the resolution to slay, and not be slain by, the monster of the labyrinth. Having arrived at the court of King Minos, Theseus attracted the attention, and won the affection, of Ariadne, the King's daughter, who provided him with a sword for slaying the Minotaur, and a silken thread which he might take with him into the labyrinth to use as a guide in finding his way out. The destruction of the Minotaur and the liberation of the Athenians having been successfully accomplished, Theseus wed Ariadne, and departed with her for Athens; but upon the advice of Minerva, given in a vision, he abandoned his bride on the isle of Naxos, where she mourned his desertion with bitter lamentations. Venus took pity on the weeping princess, and promised to her an immortal husband in place of the mortal whom she had lost, whereupon Bacchus appeared and married her, placing upon her brows a crown of gold as token of the wedding. When, after a long and happy life, Ariadne died, her immortal husband flung the jewelled coronet toward the skies. As it mounted it grew more brilliant, each gem blazing with a more than earthly lustre from its golden setting, till at length it found a place of perpetual splendour in high heaven, between the kneeling Hercules and the Herdsman who drives the Bears around the pole.

In the eastern sky we may now behold that array of constellations which some have called "The Region of the Birds". A tendency to group certain types of constellation figures seems to have existed at the time the old asterisms were formed, since we may here, as in other places, discern a similarity in the mythological representations. Cygnus, the Swan, and Aquila, the Eagle, are obviously birds, whilst Lyra, the Lyre, is generally depicted on the ancient charts as being carried by an eagle. Cygnus and

Aquila are both in the Milky Way, whose summer branch is just beginning to gain notice in the east. Above these groups may be found another pair of ancient and extensive constellations, Hercules and Ophiuchus et Serpens. Neither contains any brilliant stars, or possesses any sharp outlines, yet both combine take up a vast amount of space in the summer sky. In the west are the groups of spring; Virgo, with its bright Spica; Hydra; Corvus; Crater; Leo, with its characteristic Sickle and Right Triangle and its two attractive stars Regulus and Denebola; Coma Berenices with its faint, misty glittering; Cancer, just about to set; and last of all Gemini, sole remnant of winter's starry glory, and visible only by the feeble departing beams of Castor and Pollux.

In the north we behold Ursa Minor directly above the Pole, with Ursa Major sloping down toward the west. Draco, above Ursa Minor, is in upper transit, Cepheus is well up in the east, and Cassiopeia has commenced to ascend the vault after lower transit. Virtually on the horizon, slightly westward of the north point, is the blazing Capella, sadly dimmed by its unfavourable position, and preparing to disappear for its brief season of obscurity. In late summer and early autumn we shall enjoy its orient rays.

East of the north point the first stars of Pegasus and Andromeda are appearing, whilst farther south the well-defined little constellation of Delphinus, or the Dolphin, is entirely in sight. In the southeast Sagittarius is commencing to appear, while Scorpio, laved by the Milky Way and splendent with its red Antares, has crawled wholly to view. Directly south on the horizon are Lupus, the Wolf, and Centaurus, the Centaur, neither of which may be seen to advantage in a latitude as far north as ours.

EDITOR'S NOTE FP: *EN* 49, No.1 (1 June 1916): 6.

JULY SKIES

The evening sky is now practically devoid of bright planets; Venus and Saturn having disappeared, and Mars having lost most of its former lustre.

Venus arrives at inferior conjunction on the 3d, then theoretically crossing into the morning sky, where it will actually appear later in the month. On the 20th it will rise about an hour and a half before the sun, shining as an effulgent object low in the east as the twilight of dawn grows stronger. On the morning of the 27th it will pass quite near the thin, waning crescent of the old moon, offering a rather pleasing spectacle. On the 31st the planet will rise two hours and 20 minutes before the sun, being by that time the prominent object in the morning sky. Venus now exhibits to the telescopist a crescent of great tenuity; which thickens, however, at a very rapid rate. Greatest brilliancy will occur next month, and greatest western elongation in September.

Saturn follows Venus in conjunction on the 12th, being therefore invisible throughout the month. In August it will appear low in the eastern morning sky, suffering a highly interesting occultation by the moon.

Jupiter shines high and resplendently in the morning sky, arriving at quadrature on the 27th. It rises on the 1st at 12:22 a.m., and on the 31st at 10:28 p.m. During July it will move a short distance through the western part of the constellation Aries.

Mercury, in greatest western elongation on June 30, will be visible as a twinkling reddish spark near the eastern horizon at dawn during the first three or four days of July. Soon disappearing, it will reach superior conjunction on the 28th.

Mars still lingers in the evening sky, though now bereft of beauty and conspicuousness. On the 1st it sets at 10:44 p.m., and on the 31st at 9:22. During July it passes
from the east-[. . .]tion on June 30, will be visible well into Virgo.

Uranus, approaching its opposition, is drifting into the evening sky, whilst Neptune, in conjunction on the 25th, is invisible.

The moon's phases for July will be as follows:

First Quarter, 8th ....6:55 a.m.
Full Moon, 14th .... 11:40 p.m.
Last Quarter, 21st.. 6:33 p.m.
New Moon, 29th .... 9:15 p.m.

Perigee falls on the 14th, Apogee on the 28th. The moon crosses the equator on
the 6th, runs low on the 12th, crosses the equator again on the 18th, and runs high on
the 25th. On the 6th it will be near Mars, on the 22nd near Jupiter, and on the 27th
near Venus. A partial lunar eclipse, visible at Providence, will occur on the night of the
14–15th, as follows:

Moon enters Penumbra... 9:18 p.m.
Moon enters Shadow.. 10:19 p.m.
Middle of Eclipse .... 11:46 p.m.
Moon leaves Shadow...1:12 a.m.
Moon leaves Penumbra ....2:14 a.m.

The eclipse will be of considerable magnitude, eight-tenths of the moon's diameter
being immersed in shadow at the time of maximum obscuration.

The Sun moves southward four and three-quarters degrees this month, entering
the Zodiacal sign Leo on the 23d. The days lose 41 minutes. On the 3d, the Earth will
be in aphelion, or at the point of greatest distance from the Sun. The annual occurrence of this condition during the most fervid period of the Northern summer is a
source of mitigating relief to the inhabitants of our hemisphere. On the 29th of the
month there will be an annual eclipse of the sun; invisible here, but visible in the East
Indies and Australasia. The annual effect may be perceived along a path extending
through southern Australia and the island of Tasmania, whilst in other places the phenomenon will appear as an ordinary partial eclipse.

The Zodiacal constellation on the meridian this month is Scorpio, the Scorpion,
perhaps the most distinctively gorgeous stellar object in the summer sky. Whilst its
outline bears more than the usual resemblance to the creature for which it is named, it
resembles still more a kite, with streaming tail extending down close to the southern
horizon. In our latitude, most of the splendour of Scorpio is lost on account of its slight
altitude, but those of our neighbours who are hastening to the troubled Rio Grande
will behold it in full regal pomp, richly clad in the shimmering robes of the Milky Way.
Antares, the chief star of the group, is of the first magnitude, and possesses a fiery red
colour to be seen in no other star of equal brilliancy. Above Scorpio lies the extensive
and inextricably tangled double group, Ophiuchus et Serpens, which commemorates
the famous physician of classical antiquity, Aesculapius, son of Apollo and Coronis. It
was in this constellation that the famous temporary star observed by Kepler burst forth
late in September, 1604. Brighter even than the planet Jupiter, it scintillated in a most
remarkable manner, and was assiduously watched by the astronomers of the time.
When it had left the evening sky, and, after the usual period of invisibility, appeared in
the early morning in December, its lustre had much faded. During 1605 it sunk from
the first to the third magnitude, and disappeared during the long period of combined

invisibility and cloudy weather extending between October, 1605, and February, 1606. The origin of such temporary stars is still rather uncertain, though it is generally believed that they result from collisions betwixt dark celestial objects, which suddenly liberate vast amounts of light and heat from the concussions.

Progressing upward still farther, we encounter the large but rather vague and uninteresting constellation Hercules, which reaches past the zenith into the northern sky. Hercules contains a famous and immense cluster of stars, invisible to the naked eye, but perceptible through an opera-glass as a faint blur of light. According to Sir William Herschel, this cluster contains about 14,000 stars. Its shape is approximately spherical, and the late J. Ellard Gore[1] estimated that each member has a diameter of 45,000 miles, being separated by a distance of nine trillion miles from its next neighbour. Garrett P. Serviss has indulged in some very interesting calculations of the appearance of the heavens as viewed from the surface of any possible planets which might attend the stars of this cluster. In the [. . .]ed as 13M.

Looking westward from Hercules, we behold successively the beautiful circlet of Corona Borealis, and the stately outline of Boötes, with the matchless Arcturus. Still farther to the west is the nebulous glitter of Coma Berenices, yet seen to advantage. Looking downward again, we see Libra just west of Scorpio, and Centaurus on the southern horizon. Far to the west the neat trapezium of Corvus is just disappearing, the extremity of the Hydra's tail close following. Virgo is still completely in view, but Leo is sinking through the vapours to invisibility.

In the north we find the Plough at right angles to the horizon, toward which it is steered. Draco and Ursa Minor are above the pole, while Cepheus and Cassiopeia are mounting the heavens at its right.

The groups of later summer and autumn are now commencing to creep above the eastern horizon. Considerable portions of Pegasus and Andromeda are already unfolded to our view, whilst Aquarius and Capricornus adjoin them. Lyra and Cygnus are soaring aloft, the former being not far from transit. Bathed in the Milky Way is Aquila, the Eagle, whose bright star Altair shines nobly through the silvery mist. Between Aquila and Pegasus are those interesting little asterisms Sagitta, the Arrow, Delphinus, the Dolphin, and Equuleus, the Little Horse. Of these, Delphinus is by far the best known and most easily identified, having a well-defined geometrical outline that readily captures the casual glance.

Low in the southeast, directly east of Scorpio, lies the attractive expanse of Sagittarius, the Archer, which, though containing no star of prime magnitude, is yet one of the chief beauties of the summer heavens. The upper stars of this constellation form the figure of an inverted ladle or dipper with a short handle, called the "Milk Dipper", from its suggested use in ladling the shimmering flood of the Milky Way, which flows thick about it. Sagittarius, together with Scorpio, exhibits the Milky Way at its best, further enriching the scene by a profusion of clusters and nebulae, most of which may be well discerned either with the naked eye, or with an ordinary opera glass.

On July 25 begin the traditional "Dies Caniculares", or Dog Days, whose name refers to the star Sirius, a body that once rose heliacally at this season. Though precession has altered the astronomical conditions, the memory remains, and we still understand Virgil when he says:

> "'Twas noon, the sultry Dog-Star from the sky
> Parch'd Indian swains; the rivell'd grass was dry."[2]

The fancy of the imaginative ancients found ample grounds for connecting the dazzling rays of the star with the scorching heat of the season.

EDITOR'S NOTE FP: *EN* 49, No. 27 (1 July 1916): 8.

Notes

1. J[ohn] Ellard Gore (1845–1910), Irish astronomical writer and member of the Royal Irish Academy.
2. Virgil, *Georgics* 4.425–27 (tr. John Dryden).

AUGUST SKIES

Venus, now in the morning sky, attains its greatest brilliancy on the 9th of the month, then glowing with peerless lustre in the western part of the constellation Gemini. The planet is steadily withdrawing from the solar rays, and will next month arrive at greatest elongation.

Jupiter also adorns the morning sky, though it is gradually drifting into the evening heavens. On the 1st it rises at 10:27 p.m., and on the 31st at 8:28. Its motion amongst the stars is slow, and has not yet carried it out of the western section of Aries.

Mars sheds its faint ruddy beams in the west each evening, setting on the 1st at 9:21 p.m., and on the 31st at 8:04. Its motion during August carries it from the western part of Virgo to a point in that constellation very close to the bright star Spica.

Mercury, having been in superior conjunction late in July, will be invisible throughout August.

Saturn this month emerges from the glare of the sun, appearing low in the eastern sky before dawn. On the 1st it rises only an hour and twenty minutes before the sun, but on the 31st it will rise at 1:32 a.m., over three hours and a half before the great luminary. Saturn is now in the extreme eastern part of the constellation Gemini, soon to cross over into Cancer. On the morning of the 25th, Saturn will be occulted by the thin crescent of the waning moon. Occultations of the bright planets are rather interesting and uncommon phenomena which well repay observation. At 3:16 a.m. the bright convex edge of the moon will gradually commence to cover the well-known figure of Saturn and its rings, soon hiding the planet completely. At 4:20 a.m., in the strong twilight, Saturn will begin to reappear from behind the dark invisible edge of the lunar disc, thus seemingly unfolding itself from the empty heavens. This emersion will be particularly entertaining to watch. The occurrence, of course, is best seen through a telescope powerful enough to exhibit Saturn as a disc of considerable magnitude; yet even the naked eye may derive much pleasure from the spectacle. At the time of the occultation the moon will be but three days from its change.

Uranus arrives at its opposition on the 10th, then being at its best for observation. At this point in its course, the planet is dimly visible to the naked eye, if its place in the heavens be exactly known. This faint though immense sphere was the first planet discovered since the dawn of civilisation, its brighter fellows having been known and recorded in the earliest ages. Uranus was first noticed by the illustrious Dr. Herschel on March 13, 1781. At first mistaken for a comet, its steady light and well-defined disc soon proved its planetary nature; and it was named by its discoverer "Georgium Sidus", or the Georgian Star, in honour of the King, who had acted as a beneficent patron toward the astronomer. Continental astronomers called the new planet "Herschel", after the eminent scientist who first made known its existence. Later the German astronomer, Dr. Bode, proposed the name Uranus, which better conforms to the ancient mythological system of celestial nomenclature, and which has become the present appellation of the planet. After the discovery of Uranus, it was found that the faint orb had been previously observed many times without identification as a planet. On December 13, 1690, the Astronomer Royal, Mr. Flamsteed, had recorded it as a star, whilst the French astronomers Le Monnier and Arago had each seen it many times. Bradley had observed it once, and Mayer had included it in a catalogue of fixed stars, under the number 964.[1] Uranus is one of the larger bodies of our solar system, being about 31,000 miles in diameter; yet its remoteness from the sun, a distance of 1,780,000,000 miles, causes it to shine but feebly. Its superficial configurations are not well defined, consisting apparently of vague belts like those of Jupiter and Saturn. This planet revolves around the sun in a period of about 84 years, and has a probable rotation of about 11 hours. It is attended by four satellites, whose names Ariel, Umbriel, Titania, and Oberon, are derived from Semitic and Teutonic mythology instead of from the more familiar Graeco-Roman legends.

Neptune is still lost in the sun's rays, having lately been in conjunction.

The moon's phases for August will be as follows:

First Quarter 6th .... 4:06 p.m.
Full Moon, 13th ....7:00 a.m.
Last Quarter, 20th..7:53 a.m.
New Moon, 28th .... 12:25 p.m.

Perigee falls on the 12th, Apogee on the 24th. The moon runs low on the 9th, high on the 22nd, crossing the equator on the 2nd, 16th, and 29th. It will be near Mars on the 4th, Jupiter on the 18th, Venus on the 24th, and Saturn (in occultation) on the 25th.

The sun's southward motion, which carries it into the Zodiacal sign Virgo on the 23d, gives a melancholy prophecy of the coming autumn, and shortens the days by an hour and a quarter.

The Zodiacal constellation on the meridian in August is Sagittarius, the Archer, whose richness in clusters and nebulae well to compensates for its want of bright stars. The Milky Way flows through the western part of the group, imparting a quiet splendour appropriate to the season. Higher in the southern sky, the hulk of Ophiuchus et Serpens is giving place to Aquila, the Eagle, on the meridian. Aquila contains the bright star Altair, which, as compared with most of the fixed stars, lies rather near our solar system. Yet comparatively near as Altair may be, it nevertheless requires 17 years for light to travel to us from its part of space. Not far from the exact zenith is Lyra, the Lyre, with the incomparable Vega. Unlike Altair, Vega is situate at an immense distance from us, wherefore its intrinsic brilliancy must be enormous. It is undoubtedly vastly brighter than our own sun. The star Beta in Lyra is variable in lustre, changing from the third to the fourth magnitude in periods slightly less than 13 days. It is believed that Beta Lyrae is really a double star, with one component brighter than its mate; and that its fluctuations in brilliancy are due to alternate eclipses of the faint star by the bright, and the bright by the faint.

Epsilon Lyrae is another interesting star. To the keen eyesight, and more easily with an opera glass, it appears double; whilst a good telescope shews each of the components to be double as well, making a quadruple system. Delta Lyrae marks that point in space whither our own sun and its system are travelling at the speed of about 11 miles per second.

Hercules, with its wealth of mythological associations, is barely past the meridian; whilst Cygnus, hardly less reminiscent of classical lore, will shortly attain that celestial circle. Cygnus was a friend of the unfortunate Phaethon, who was hurled to death in the River Eridanus, or Po, after his rash attempt to drive the flaming car of his father, the Sun-God. Cygnus mourned unceasingly by the river banks, and frequently sought to recover the body of his former companion from the watery waste, till at last Jupiter turned him to a swan and set his image in the skies.

> With pensive grace the melancholy Swan
> Mourns o'er the tomb of luckless Phaethon.
> On grassy banks the weeping poplars wave,
> And guard with tender care the wat'ry grave.
> Would that I might, should I too proudly claim
> An heav'nly parent, or a god-like fame,
> When flown too high, and dash'd to depths below,
> Receive such tribute as a Cygnus' woe;
> The faithful bird, that dumbly floats along,
> Sighs all the deeper for his want of song![2]

In the western sky Corona Borealis, Scorpio, and Libra remain well in view, while farther west Boötes and Coma Berenices are still prominent. Virgo has partially set, and Leo has entirely disappeared. In the north Ursa Major is preparing to descend beneath the Pole, whilst Ursa Minor now extends westward from that point. Cassiopeia is at the right of the pole, with Cepheus immediately above it. In the northeast the resplendent Perseus is rising, whilst Andromeda is already in full. Pegasus soars aloft, heralded by the small groups Delphinus, Equuleus, and Sagitta. Due east some of the dim stars of Pisces are rising, south of which Aquarius and Capricornus are wholly visible. Piscus Australis will soon rise, bringing into view the bright Fomalhaut, whose lustre attracts so much attention in the autumn and early winter.

Numerous meteors, or "shooting stars", may be expected on August evenings, since the orbit of the earth intersects a rather thick belt of these bodies at this point. Meteors are the smallest of celestial objects, varying from large rocks to minute grains of dust in size. When the earth encounters them, they strike the atmosphere and become ignited through friction, then shining as we see them. Some are entirely consumed in mid-air, whilst others leave solid masses which descend to the earth's surface as aerolites, or meteoric stones. These are the only celestial bodies which may be actually touched by human hands.

Very interesting to the astronomical public is the recent revival of the old theory that our universe has a "central sun" or body about which all the other stars revolve. In 1845 the German astronomer Maedler attempted to prove that Alcyone, in the Pleiades, is such a central sun, but his theory was exploded soon after its inception. Later it was held that the proper motions of the stars are all rectilinear, and within the last twenty years the Dutch astronomer Kapteyn[3] has made extensive researches concerning "star-drifts", or groups of seemingly unrelated stars whose motion has a common direction. Now, however, Mr. O. R. Walkley[4] has put forward an hypothesis which exalts the gorgeous southern star Canopus, in Argo Navis, to the position of central sun. Canopus is a body of prodigious size and brilliancy, outshining our sun 47,000 times, and appearing in our skies second only to Sirius in lustre. It is not well to accept the new theory without more exact demonstration; but its tenets, as thus far shewn, are at least worthy of careful examination. Analogy would naturally suggest the idea of a central sun, since all lesser celestial motions take the form of revolutions of certain bodies about centres. Satellites revolve around the planets; the planets revolve about the suns hence we may well imagine that the stars, or suns of space, revolve around some still superior body. But theory and analogy are of little value in science unless sustained by observation; wherefore it is upon actual celestial measurements, and not from the constructive imagination, that we must base our acceptance or rejection of this fascinating idea of Mr. Walkley's.

EDITOR'S NOTE FP: *EN* 49, No. 52 (1 August 1916): 6.

Notes

1. HPL refers to the astronomers Johann Elert Bode (1747–1826; German), John Flamsteed (1646–1719; British), Pierre-Charles Le Monnier (1715–1799; French), Dominique François Jean Arago (1786–1853; French), James Bradley (1693–1762; British), and Christian Mayer (1719–1783; German). HPL appears to be in error in citing Arago, whose work occurred many years after the discovery of Uranus.

2. The poem ("On Receiving a Picture of Swans") is by HPL, written in September 1915 (see *SL* 1.12).

3. Jacobus Cornelius Kapteyn (1851–1922), Dutch astronomer whose major contributions were in the field of stellar astronomy.

4. Unidentified.

SEPTEMBER SKIES

In the skies of September all the major planets will be visible, though not all glowing with fullest lustre.

Jupiter, now well within the confines of the evening sky, rises on the 1st at 8:27 p.m., and on the 30th at 6:25. It is retrograding amongst the stars of Aries, to which constellation it lends no little splendour.

Venus attains its greatest western elongation on the 12th, then beaming with much effulgence in the constellation Cancer, not far from the celebrated cluster Praespe, or The Manger, and shewing through the telescope a phase like that of the half-moon. By the end of the month it will have assumed a decidedly gibbous appearance. The planet is now at the highest point in the morning sky, rising on the 1st at 1:29 a.m., and on the 30th at 1:52. At the time of greatest elongation it will rise about 3 hours and 50 minutes before the sun, affording an ample opportunity for extended observation.

Saturn, this month entering the constellation Cancer, rises on the 1st at 1:31 a.m., and on the 30th at 11:44 p.m., thus being a prominent feature of the morning heavens. On the morning of the 6th the ringed planet will be in conjunction with Venus, passing only three degrees north of the latter. Saturn and Venus have followed unusually similar courses of late, the present conjunction being the third since May.

Mars, though now past all profitable observation, lingers on in the early evening sky; setting on the 1st at 8:03 p.m., and on the 30th at 6:55. Mercury will reach greatest eastern elongation on the 9th, then being visible in the twilight near the western horizon just after sunset. Uranus is quite favourably situated in the evening sky, being near the moon on the 9th. Neptune has now become visible through the telescope in the morning, lying not far from Venus on the 13th, and coming to conjunction with the moon on the 22nd.

The moon's phases for September will be as follows:

First Quarter, 4th .... 9:26 p.m.
Full Moon, 11th .... 3:31 p.m.
Last Quarter, 19th..12:35 a.m.
New Moon, 27th ....2:34 a.m.

Perigee falls on the 9th, Apogee on the 21st. The moon runs low on the 5th, crosses the equator on the 11th, runs high on the 19th, and crosses the equator again on the 26th. It will be near Mars on the 1st, Jupiter on the 15th, Saturn on the 21st, Venus again on the 23d, and Mars again on the 30th. The full and waning moon of September is generally known as the "Harvest Moon", on account of its uncommonly long sojourn in the evening heavens. At most seasons of the year the moon, after being full, rises as usual about an hour later every night, thus soon withdrawing its light from the early nocturnal sky. This month, however, as though to guide the harvester and permit him to continue his labours after the sun has set, our satellite lingers in the evening sky for some time into its wane, rising but a few moments later each successive night. This fact is caused by the full moon's presence in the Zodiacal sign Aries, which makes so small an angle with the eastern horizon, that the moon when passing through it is less repressed in relation to the horizon at consecutive risings than when in any other part of its course, though its rate of motion be in each case the same. While the phenomenon is known as "Harvest Moon", the following full moon, which partakes in a lesser degree of the same qualities, is called the "Hunter's Moon". Of course, the moon occupies the sign Aries at other times than these, but in such instances it is not near full, hence the small difference in the time of its successive risings is not generally remarked.

On the 23d of this month the sun enters the sign Libra, thus proclaiming to a melancholy world the advent of dismal Autumn, and affording an equality betwixt the days and nights. During September the days lose an hour and twenty minutes.

Turning to the constellations, we find in the sky the dullest array of the entire year. The Zodiacal group on the meridian is Capricornus, the Sea-Goat, which has no star brighter than the third magnitude. The principal stars, Giedi or Alpha, and Dabih or Beta, lie in a vertical line directly below Altair, in the Eagle, and are both double as seen with an opera glass. Giedi, indeed, shews its two-fold nature without optical aid. Above Capricornus lie the three small but ancient asterisms Delphinus, the Dolphin, Equuleus, the Little Horse, and Sagitta, the Arrow. The principal stars of Delphinus form a tiny but easily recognised figure of diamond shape, commonly known by the rather inexplicable name of "Job's Coffin". Equuleus represents Celeris, brother to Pegasus, and chosen steed of Castor; or according to other accounts, it typifies the first of all the equine tribe, the horse created by Neptune. Neptune and Minerva held a contest for the position of tutelary divinity of infant Athens, declaring that which of them should invent that article most useful to mankind, should preside over the new-built city. Neptune smote the earth with his trident, whereupon there sprang forth a horse, the like of which had never before been seen; but Minerva offered as her invention the olive tree, and was awarded the supremacy. Sagitta represents the arrow shot by Hercules at the Stymphalian Birds. Above these little groups lies the resplendent expanse of Cygnus, just west of which is Lyra, with the fulgent Vega. Most of the other summer constellations are in the western sky, including Sagittarius, Aquila, Ophiuchus et Serpens, Hercules, Corona Borealis, and Boötes. Scorpio has almost completely set. In the North we find Ursa Major assuming its upright position as it prepares to glide beneath the pole. Ursa Minor stretches out westward of Polaris. The mythological history of these two Bears is one of the best known tales in Ovid's Metamorphoses, and has been very prettily translated therefrom by Mr. Addison.[1] Ursa Major was once Callisto, nymph of Diana's train. Having received the favour of Jove, she was turned to a bear by the jealous act of Juno. Long afterward her son Arcas, beholding her as a bear whilst hunting, was about to transfix her with an arrow, little dreaming he would thereby be slaying his own mother. But Jupiter beheld the scene, and averted the catastrophe, by turning Arcas also to a bear, and setting both mother and son in the sky. Juno, however, was not to be foiled in her jealous purposes. Beholding the heavenly honour accorded to her former rival, she besought Oceanus and Tethys, deities of the deep, to deny the bears a resting place at night in the waves. The gods consented, and accordingly Ursa Major and Ursa Minor are circumpolar constellations, describing circles around the pole of the heavens, but never setting in the soothing surges of the northern seas. Of course, this legend and its astronomical result are applicable only to those middle northern latitudes in which lived the classic races who shaped the Graeco-Roman tales, and in which we also live. Near the equator they appear to rise and set, and far in the southern hemisphere they are not visible at all.

East of the north point a few evidences of the starry splendour of the approaching winter are in view. Perseus, resplendent with his gleaming sword, is fully risen, whilst just above the horizon the peerless beams of Capella, in Auriga, are piercing the vapours. A little farther south a delightful spot of shimmering light is commencing to resolve itself into the beautiful Pleiades cluster, thus heralding the approach of the mighty Taurus. Aries and Pisces are both completely in sight, while the foremost portions of Cetus are also appearing. High in the eastern sky are Pegasus and Andromeda, four of whose stars combine to form the "Great Square of Pegasus". In the south, Aquarius is about to succeed Capricornus on the meridian, while below all other groups Piscis Australis displays its solitary bright star, Fomalhaut, a gem of prime magnitude. The Milky Way flows diagonally across the sky from northeast to southwest, passing through Auriga, Perseus, Cassiopeia, Cepheus, Cygnus, Aquila, Ophiuchus et Serpens, Sagittarius, and what remains of Scorpio.

Those observers who still remain on their summer sojourns in the rural and mountainous regions may derive much greater pleasure from the delicately faint constellations of the season than those who view the sky from the more clouded and vitiated air of the city. The groups which here impress the eye as devoid of beauty or interest, there seem very near to the fortunate spectator, presenting intimate revelations of stellar arrangements which we but ill perceive through our curtain of smoke and lamplight. In the following lines, addressed to an observer in the highlands of northwestern Massachusetts, we are shewn how great is the advantage of altitude and rustic surroundings.

> Whilst town astronomers, with straining eyes,
> Search out the wonders of the distant skies;

With optic tube in feeble fashion trace
The cloud-film'd features of ethereal space;
While scribbling pedants paint with prosy line
The various orbs, and when and how they shine;
(Those orbs so faintly and so little known—
Realities in books and globes alone—)
On Zoar's proud height, of heav'n itself a part,
Gamwell sees all, without the need of art![2]

EDITOR'S NOTE FP: *EN* 49, No. 79 (1 September 1916): 6.

Notes

1. See Ovid, *Metamorphoses* 2.401–541 (tr. Joseph Addison [1704] as "The Story of Calisto" [*sic*]).
2. The poem is by HPL, referring to his cousin Phillips Gamwell (1898–1916).

OCTOBER SKIES

On the 23d of the month, Jupiter will arrive at its opposition; being then nearest the earth, shining at its brightest, and rising about sunset. All through the night it will glow resplendently without a rival; till close to dawn, when it has reached the low western sky, its lustre will be matched and surpassed by that of Venus in the east.

Jupiter, called by Proctor the "Giant of the Solar System", is the largest of the planets. Its distance from the sun is 482,000,000 miles; its year is equal to about twelve of ours, whilst its day contains only ten of our hours. It is 88,000 miles in diameter, being in volume 1300 times greater than the earth. Jupiter's distance from us varies from about 390,000,000 miles at opposition, to about 580,000,000 miles at conjunction. The planet stands nearly upright in its orbit, its axis being inclined but three degrees from a perpendicular. The result of this fact is the absence of well-defined seasons, perpetual spring reigning everywhere on its surface. However, other conditions offset any benefits caused by this seemingly happy state. Gravity on the surface of Jupiter is nine times greater than that upon the earth; so that a man would find difficulty in moving about on the colossal globe. Jupiter, at least the visible portion, appears to be in a somewhat plastic state; in fact, may be regarded as almost liquid or gaseous. Like the sun, it does not rotate uniformly; the average axial period is 9 hours and 56 minutes. This rapid rotation, together with the pliant structure of the planet, have caused the equatorial regions to bulge out, thus producing a very great polar compression, which at once strikes the eye of the telescopic observer. Even through very small instruments, the surface of Jupiter is seen to be covered with broad, alternate light and dark belts, parallel to the equator. The disc is brightest and most clearly defined at the centre, the belts becoming indistinct toward the edge. Jupiter is the first of the group of outer planets, which are all immense in size and plastic in constitution, as contrasted with orbs like the earth, which are smaller and solid.

The atmosphere of Jupiter is very dense, as shewn by the conduct of the belts, which are palpably atmospherical phenomena of some sort. These belts frequently change shape, move, join another, or break up; like the stratus clouds of our own sunset skies. Since the planet receives but a 27th of the amount of solar light and heat that is given to the earth, it is evident that in order to account for the rapid formation and motions of its clouds, phenomena requiring a high temperature, the body beneath these clouds must itself possess and radiate great heat. In fact, we may well assume that Jupiter is in a half-molten state; it is a kind of semi-sun, as it were, though it gives forth no light. Its density is nearly the same as that of the sun. Occasionally spots more permanent than the belts are noted upon the surface of the planet. These are probably connected with the great mass beneath the stratum of clouds, thus indicating that though very hot and plastic, this mass is at least in some degree coherent. The famous red spot which appeared in 1877 is even now visible at times, though infinitely fainter than when it was first observed. It is unnecessary to state that no inhabitants could possibly dwell upon Jupiter, or upon any of the four outer planets. Jupiter is attended by nine satellites, four of which are very large, and easily seen in small telescopes. These four were discovered in 1610 by Galileo. They present a most interesting sight in any telescope, being often eclipsed by the shadow of their primary, occulted by that body itself, or projected upon its disc in transit, preceded or followed by their shadows, as their position with respect to the sun determines. Their names, in order of distance outward from Jupiter, are Io, Europa, Ganymede, and Callisto. In powerful telescopes they shew sensible discs, and upon their surfaces spots may be discerned. Prof. W. H. Pickering has discovered that Callisto always faces Jupiter as the moon faces the earth, and Mr. Douglass,[1] an assistant of Prof. Percival Lowell, believes that Ganymede behaves likewise, a fact suspected by the celebrated Dr. Herschel over a century ago. Conclusions respecting the habitability of these orbs would be baseless. If they do possess inhabitants, a thing by no means impossible, their astronomers must indeed be fortunate, for words cannot describe the grandeur with which Jupiter shines in their nocturnal skies. The other five satellites of Jupiter are very faint indeed. One of them was discovered by Barnard in 1892, two more by Perrine in 1905, another by Melotte in 1908, and the ninth and latest by Nicholson in 1914. The last four are so difficult to observe, that they have never been directly glimpsed by human eye. They were discovered by photography, for the camera is much more sensitive to faint beams of light than is the sight of man, and exposure can be protracted to a great extent. The satellite which was discovered in 1892 lies within, and the four more recently found lie outside, the orbits of the four larger satellites. The satellites discovered by Melotte and Nicholson, respectively, behave in a most extraordinary manner; revolving round Jupiter backwards, thus appearing to break a fundamental law of the solar system. Adequate explanations, however, have been lately offered.

Venus, having been in greatest western elongation last month, is now slowly retreating toward the visibility of the sun; though still shining with unrivalled effulgence, high in the eastern morning sky. On the 1st it rises at 1:52 a.m, about 3 hours and 50 minutes before the sun; and on the 31st at 1:52 a.m. [sic], about 3 hours and 5 minutes before the sun. The swift motion of Venus amongst the stars carries it this month from the western part of Leo, entirely across that constellation and well into Virgo. On the 6th it will pass close to the bright star Regulus, lying only a few minutes of arc to the south.

Mercury, in inferior conjunction on the 5th, becomes visible about the middle of the month; arriving at greatest western elongation on the 20th. It will then be visible in the morning sky, just above the eastern horizon as dawn approaches. Morning elongations of Mercury are most favourably seen in the autumn, hence the present appearance will be well worthy of observation.

Mars, setting at 6:54 p.m. on the 1st, and at 6:00 on the 31st, is nominally an evening planet, but is practically past observation. During October it moves from the constellation Libra into Scorpio, bringing it at the end of the month in the general vicinity of its ruddy stellar analogue, Antares.

Saturn, in full ringed splendour, will be in quadrature on the 23d, and is now gradually drawing toward the evening sky. On the 1st it rises at 11:43 p.m., and on the 31st at 9:50. Its motion this month is direct, extending a brief space through the western half of the constellation Cancer.

Uranus is still well seen through the telescope in the evening sky, whilst Neptune, in the morning sky, comes to quadrature on the 28th.

The moon's phases for October will be as follows:

First Quarter, 4th ....6:00 a.m.
Full Moon, 11th ....2:01 a.m.
Last Quarter, 13th.. 8:00 p.m.
New Moon, 26th .... 3:37 p.m.

Perigee falls on the 6th and 31st, Apogee on the 19th. The moon runs low on the 2nd and 30th, high on the 15th; crossing the equator on the 9th and 23d. It will approach Jupiter on the 12th, Saturn on the 19th, Venus on the 23d, and Mars on the 28th. The full moon this month is known as the "Hunter's Moon", on account of the manner in which it lingers in the evening sky after the full. This condition, as stated last month, arises from the same causes as those of the Harvest Moon.

The sun enters the Zodiacal sign Scorpio on the 23d, thus astronomically announcing the ruthless encroachments of autumnal chill. As a recent bard has written of this time of year:

> See now the teeming field and fruitful vine
> Their bounteous care for graceful man resign,
> While o'er the radiant summer's less'ning breath
> Spread azure mists, the robes of coming death.
> The morning groves in alter'd aspect weep,
> And wait in splendour for the wintry sleep.
> Where once was verdure, leaves of brazen hue
> Succeed the gold and red that come to view;
> The dying flow'rs excite a pitying tear,
> And man laments the swift-revolving year.
> Earth gains the rest that frosty breezes bring,
> And still'd in slumber, waits the sun of spring.[2]

In the sidereal sky of October we observe the dulness of early autumn giving place to the first heralds of the bright winter pageant. The Zodiacal constellation on the meridian is Aquarius, a group but little renowned for beauty or interest. Above Aquarius is Pegasus, the Winged Horse; while still higher up Cygnus has just passed the meridian. Capricornus is west of the meridian, as are also the minor groups Delphinus, Equuleus, and Sagitta, together with Aquila, the Eagle, with its bright star Altair. Still farther west Lyra shines, with Vega blazing in undisputed eminence. On the western horizon we may behold Sagittarius and Ophiuchus partly set, and Hercules soon to commence its descent from visibility. Corona Borealis is flinging to us its parting beams, whilst Arcturus, though visible just after sunset, is not in sight at 9 p.m., our stated hour of observation. In the north we find Ursa Major below the pole, with the so-called "Dipper" right side up for the only time in its annual round. Cassiopeia and Cepheus are above the pole, whilst Ursa Minor and Draco are west of that point. In the northeast Auriga is completely above the horizon, its bright Capella giving forth a radiance which compensates for the lately departed beams of Arcturus. Capella is in our latitude very nearly circumpolar, and is never invisible throughout an entire night. In June, when it departs from the evening sky, it rises early enough to be visible in the morning sky. It might incidentally be remarked, that Vega is also never out of sight at some hour or another on every night of the year. South of Auriga, the resplendent Zodiacal constellation Taurus has just completed its ascent above the horizon. Aldebaran and the Hyades gleam merrily through the vapours, whilst the Pleiades, at a greater altitude, twinkle with silvery lustre. The high eastern sky now glitters with the rays of Perseus and Andromeda. Farther south, Aries, Pisces, and Cetus shine with less conspicuous radiance. Low hanging above the horizon is the bright Fomalhaut, in Piscis Australis, soon to attain the meridian. This star is much used by navigators in calculating the position of their ships, and is in this connexion called one of the four "Royal Stars", the others being Regulus, Aldebaran, and Antares. These stars are all about six hours of right ascension apart, hence form important markings or graduations on the clock-face of the sidereal sky. Garrett P. Serviss, referring to the absence of other bright stars in the vicinity of Fomalhaut, compares that strangely fascinating orb to "a distant watch-fire gleaming in the midst of a lonely prairie".

The Dominion Observatory near Victoria, B.C., has now put into operation, or will soon do so, a gigantic reflecting telescope which will, until the completion of the Mt. Wilson telescope, be the largest in the world. This immense instrument is equipped with a mirror six feet in diameter, thus equalling in size the famous old Rosse telescope, lately dismantled, and surpassing by a foot the reflectors at Harvard and Cordoba, and the present Mt. Wilson reflector. The modern supremacy of the reflecting telescope is due principally to the rise of astronomical photography, a work to which reflectors are vastly better suited than refractors. In the later days of the eighteenth century and the first half of the nineteenth, reflectors were acknowledged as the superior type; but within the last sixty years the refractor has been a prime favourite with astronomers, especially in America, so that many had come to consider the reflector as practically obsolete. Photography, however, has brought the latter type into its own once more, and the greatest instruments of today are of the same sort as that with which Dr. Herschel scoured the sky in the reign of George III.

EDITOR'S NOTE FP: *EN* 49, No. 104 (2 October 1916): 6.

Notes

1. L. Andrew Ellicott Douglass (1867–1962), American astronomer who in 1894 went with Percival Lowell to the new Lowell Observatory in Flagstaff, Arizona. In 1906 he moved to the University of Arizona as professor of astronomy and physics.

2. The poem is by HPL and is original to this article.

NOVEMBER SKIES

Jupiter still adorns the evening sky with supreme lustre, shining high in the west during the most convenient hours for observation. It is now retrograding in the extreme western part of the constellation Aries, crossing back into Pisces later in the month. The planet sets on the 1st at 5:32 a.m., and on the 30th at 3:20.

Saturn is visible later in the evening, rising at 9:49 p.m. on the 1st, and at 7:50 on the 30th. Its splendour, while not comparable to that of Jupiter, is nevertheless considerable; and it forms a striking object as it shines amidst the dull stars of the constellation Cancer. The planet's motion is direct until the 12th, and thereafter retrograde.

Venus is still a dazzling and conspicuous ornament of the morning sky, rising on the 1st at 3:47 a.m., about three hours and a half before the sun, and on the 30th at 3:53 a.m., just three hours before the sun. It shines rather high in the east before dawn, moving this month through the constellation Virgo. On the 20th it will pass but little more than four degrees north of the bright star Spica.

Mars no longer merits our consideration as an object of interest. It is still in the evening sky, but glows very feebly indeed. On the 1st it sets at 6 p.m., and on the 30th at 5:30, only an hour and a quarter after the sun.

Mercury will be invisible throughout November, arriving at superior conjunction on the 23d.

Uranus, in quadrature on the 8th, is visible with a telescope in the evening sky, whilst Neptune, now past quadrature, lies in the morning heavens.

The moon's phases for November will be as follows:

First Quarter, 2nd... 12:51 p.m.
Full Moon, 9th... 3:18 p.m.
Last Quarter, 17th... 5:00 p.m.
New Moon, 25th .... 3:50 p.m.

Apogee occurs on the 15th, Perigee on the 27th. The moon runs high on the 13th, low on the 20th, crossing the equator on the 5th and 19th. It will be near Jupiter on the 8th, Saturn on the 15th, and Venus on the 22nd.

The Sun enters the Zodiacal sign Sagittarius on the 22nd. The grey and dismal days lose an hour in length during the month.

Meteors in fairly large quantities will probably be visible in the morning sky on the 14th, 15th, and 16th, when the earth crosses the Leonid belt; and in the evening sky on the 23d, 24th, and 25th, when the treame [sic] of Andromedes is encountered. Meteors, or "shooting stars", are rather deceptive both in appearance and in popular nomenclature, for whilst the true stars are, with the possible exception of certain nebulae, the largest and most distant of all things we can behold, these "shooting stars" or meteors are the smallest and nearest of the celestial orbs; being scarce larger than rocks, pebbles, or grains of dust, and coming into actual contact with our atmosphere, some indeed reaching the surface of the earth itself. Meteors are members of the solar system, revolving around the sun in the same manner as do comets; in fact, it is thought probable that meteors have taken their origin from the disintegration of comets. Their brilliancy is due to their combustion in our air, which latter ignites them with the intense heat caused by its friction upon them as they strike it at extremely high rates of speed.

So small are most meteors, that they are entirely consumed before reaching the ground, depositing only an ash or dust which has been recognised amongst the Arctic and Antarctic snows, and upon the beds of the oceans. Meteors are the only heavenly bodies which forcibly encounter the earth during their passage through space, for while the general laws of motion do not permit of collisions betwixt members of the system, these tiny "shooting stars" are so widely diffused that it would be strange indeed if one did not occasionally strike our planet, either because the latter may happen to lie in its path, or because terrestrial gravity may deflect it toward us. It is thought that meteors become incandescent about 75 miles above the earth's surface. At regular periodic intervals the earth encounters large clusters of meteors, causing great numbers to be seen during the course of a single night. Such a phenomenon is called a "meteoric shower". Each year at stated dates occur many meteoric showers, some of which are much more conspicuous than others. The meteors in such a shower all seem to come from a single point in the sky, which lies, of course, in the direction from which the cluster strikes the earth. This point is called the "radiant point" of the shower, and all showers are named from the constellations in which their respective radiant points are situate; for instance, the meteors whose radiant point is in Leo are called "Leonids". Two annual meteoric displays are of especial prominence; the Perseid shower of August, and the Leonid shower of the present month. Of these, the Leonid shower is by far the richer in "shooting stars". While most meteors are so small that they are wholly burnt up before striking the earth, there are a few of greater magnitude that pass through the atmosphere without completely losing their solidity, descending to us as meteoric stones, extremely hot from friction and combustion. Such bodies are known as "meteorites" or "aerolites", and are the only kind of celestial objects that may be touched by earthly hands. Specimens of these objects are carefully preserved in museums, and subjected to chemical analysis, whereby they are found to consist either of rocky matter or of nearly pure metals such as Iron and Nickel. Within their pores are frequently included great volumes of the inert gas Helium. In size they vary from immense masses to fragments scarcely larger than pebbles.

At times many aerolites, probably all of the same original mass, fall at once, as in the showers of stones over the Middle Western States in 1876, and over Spain in 1896. Besides those stones which are seen to descend from the sky, many great masses bearing indisputable evidence of celestial origin have been found in various parts of the earth. One found in Greenland by Admiral Peary[1] weighs almost 100 tons, whilst others weighing 27, 17, and 15 tons are known. We need not enumerate in this catalogue the "meteor" which three years ago fell into the Sakonnet river near the stone bridge [at] Tiverton, and which was exhibited at 10 cents a glance in a vacant shop in Fall River. This object, a piece of ordinary slag, was merely the nucleus of one of those numerous hoaxes with which the annals of science abound.

Turning to the constellations as they appear at 9 p.m., about the middle of the month, we behold the effulgent heralds of the gorgeous winter stars. In the east blaze Taurus and Gemini, with Capella a little to the north, but above them all in glory is Orion, whose magnificent bulk is not completely visible. As Manilius wrote:

> "First next the Twins see great Orion rise;
> His arms, extended, stretch o'er half the skies.
> His stride is large, and with a steady pace
> He marches on, and measures a vast space.
> On each broad shoulder a bright star display'd,

And three obliquely grace his hanging blade.
In his vast head, immers'd in boundless spheres,
Three stars less bright, but yet as great, he bears;
But farther off remov'd, their splendour's lost:
Thus grac'd and arm'd, he leads the starry host."[2]

The Zodiacal constellation on the meridian is Pisces, the Fishes, whose dulness is almost totally unrelieved by bright or interesting stars. Below it is the western part of Cetus, the Whale, with Deneb Kaitos, a star of the second magnitude, soon to transit. This Deneb must not be confused with the star of similar name in Cygnus. The word "deneb" is the Arabic word for "tail", and is applied to stars in the tails of more than one imaginary constellation figure. That in the tail of Cygnus, however, is most frequently called Deneb, and unless some qualifying adjective be present, the term may be considered to apply exclusively to it. Deneb Kaitos is also known as Diphda. Below Cetus lie two faint groups which are but ill seen in the northern hemisphere, and which were given no names in classical times. The uppermost is called Sculptor, or Apparatus Sculptoris, representing the tools and materials of a sculptor, whilst the constellation beneath it is Phoenix, named after a legendary bird. Sculptor was named by Lacaille, the illustrious French astronomer, while Phoenix was created by Bayer, the inventor of our present system of stellar nomenclature, in 1603.[3] Phoenix has one star of the second magnitude, which may be seen as a fleck of isolated brightness, barely above the southern horizon, by those who enjoy an unobstructed view of that part of the heavens. The Phoenix was first described by Herodotus, and later by Ovid and Tacitus. Not until the time of Sir Thomas Browne was it known to be merely a mythical creature. It was said to live five hundred years, at the end of which time a young bird would arise from the remains of the one which had perished. This circumstance gives rise to the hackneyed metaphor about a new institution which springs from an old one, or a town rebuilt after destruction; such things being said to rise "Phoenix-like".

Directly overhead shines Andromeda, with the adjacent part of Pegasus, the two easterly stars of the "Great Square" serving to mark the meridian. West of the meridian are the groups of earlier autumn, including Piscis Australis, Aquarius, Capricornus, Delphinus, Equuleus, Sagitta, Aquila, Cygnus, and Lyra. Hercules has nearly disappeared below the northwestern horizon, while Corona is wholly out of sight. In the north we behold Cassiopeia above the pole, and Ursa Major below it; the Plough having assumed an upward tilt preparatory to its winter ascent of the northeastern heavens. Cepheus has now begun its descent from above the pole, and Ursa Minor and Draco are preparing to glide beneath that point. Lynx, one of the modern constellations devised by Hevelius, is now almost wholly in sight eastward of the Great Bear. All the east is ablaze with the first of the winter stars. Orion, Gemini, Taurus, Auriga, and Perseus are visible in the early evening, and by midnight the two Dogs will have joined the pageant. Along the southeastern horizon flows Eridanus, in whose waves the whale Cetus ponderously disports. Above Cetus is Aries, a small constellation just now made splendid by the presence of the planet Jupiter.

The Milky Way spans the northern sky like an Auroral arch, culminating where Cassiopeia marks one of its richest portions. From east to west its shining stream involves the constellations Gemini, Auriga, Perseus, Cassiopeia, Cepheus, Cygnus, Lyra, and Aquila.

There is now on exhibition at the museum of Roger Williams Park a remarkable collection of astronomical photographs, taken by the celebrated Prof. Percival Lowell of Flagstaff, Arizona, whose theories concerning the planet Mars are so widely known. The pictures are in the form of glass transparencies, exhibited in a darkened room, and illuminated from behind, so that they stand out with vivid clearness, as though the celestial objects represented were in truth beheld through the lens of a great telescope.

The collection portrays the buildings and instruments of the Lowell Observatory, as well as the heavenly bodies there photographed. Mars, the particular subject of Prof. Lowell's researches, is shewn in many aspects; the peculiar canaliform markings, which he has conjectured to be artificial, appearing with distinction in the pictures. Other planetary, cometary, and sidereal bodies are likewise displayed with pleasing accuracy. Those who were fortunate enough to attend Prof. Lowell's illustrated lecture at Sayles Hall in 1907,[4] will take especial interest in these photographs. That the Lowell theory concerning the presence of intelligent life on Mars is found untenable by the majority of conservative astronomers, need deter no one from an admiring inspection of a collection which is perhaps the best of its kind in existence. No difference of opinion can rob Prof. Lowell of his place as possibly the foremost living observational astronomer.

EDITOR'S NOTE FP: *EN* 49, No. 129 (31 October 1916): 2.

Notes

1. Robert E. Peary (1856–1920), American arctic explorer. Peary discovered the meteorite on an expedition to Greenland in 1894. He removed it in 1896–97 and sold it to the American Museum of Natural History in New York.

2. Manilius, *Astronomica* 1.387–93 (tr. Thomas Creech; "stately" for "steady" in the third line in Creech).

3. HPL refers to the French astronomer Nicolas Louis de Lacaille (1713–1762) and the German astronomer Johann Bayer (1572–1625). Bayer radically revised Ptolemy's star catalogue and introduced the modern system of star citation, whereby each star in a constellation is assigned a Greek letter. See his *Uranometria* (1603).

4. HPL was one of them; see his discussion in *SL* 1.21–22.

DECEMBER SKIES

Jupiter and Saturn, the former past opposition and the latter soon to arrive at that aspect, divide attention in the evening sky. Jupiter is the brighter of the two, and beams at a good altitude in the south; Saturn, itself of no mean lustre, gilds the east. Jupiter is this month is the eastern part of the constellation Pisces, retrograding until the 21st, and thereafter moving directly. It sets on the 1st at 3:19 a.m., and on the 31st at 1:16. Saturn is still retrograding in Cancer, being rather near the western edge by the end of the month. It rises on the 1st at 7:49 p.m., and on the 31st at 5:39.

In the morning sky, Venus reigns unrivalled. It is still seen to considerable vantage in the southeast, rising on the 1st at 3:53 a.m., and on the 31st at 5:05. It forms a veritable "Star of Bethlehem" for the Christmas season. During December the planet moves from the eastern part of Virgo entirely across Libra and into Scorpio, encroaching upon the southern extremity of the non-zodiacal constellation Ophiuchus. On the

28th it will pass six degrees north of the flaming red star Antares, offering a highly interesting spectacle.

Mars, though invisible, is still nominally an "evening star", setting on the 1st at 5:29 p.m., and on the 31st at 5:21. It will be in conjunction with Mercury on the 22nd.

Uranus is drawing toward conjunction, and is therefore but ill seen in the evening sky. Neptune, approaching opposition, is visible with a telescope late in the evening.

The moon has five phases this month, as follows:

First Quarter, 1st .... 8:56 p.m.

Full Moon, 9th... 7:44 a.m.

Last Quarter, 17th.. 1:06 p.m.

New Moon, 24th .... 3:31 p.m.

First Quarter, 31st .... 7:07 a.m.

Apogee falls on the 13th, Perigee on the 25th. The moon runs high on the 9th, low on the 23d, crossing the equator on the 2nd, 13th, and 29th. It will be near Jupiter on the 5th, Saturn on the 12th, and Venus on the 22nd.

The sun enters the Zodiacal sign Capricornus on the 21st, thus inaugurating the unwelcome season of winter. But in the very act of attaining the winter solstice, the bright orb gives forth a cheering prophecy of spring; since it is at this point in his course that he turns once more to the north. The significance of this good omen was not lost upon even the most primitive of mankind, hence we discover winter festivals of rejoicing amongst all early tribes and nations. These prehistoric feasts were generally attended by symbolic ceremonies, such as the display of evergreens to typify the perpetual survival of Nature, and the turning of the Yule-log to represent the coming solar light and heat. The winter celebrations of the early Italians were called "Brumalia", from the word "bruma", meaning winter.[1] After the rise of Rome, the old holiday observance was given a new significance, being called "Saturnalia", and dedicated to the god Saturn, whose reign in Italy was said to have marked the Golden Age of that land. Some time after the Roman Empire had adopted Christianity as its state religion, it was decided to preserve the tradition of the Saturnalia by celebrating the birth of Our Saviour at the old season of merriment; and thus, through an indirect succession, we may trace our Christmas cheer and customs to an astronomical source.

On Nov. 21st a new comet was discovered by the well-known amateur astronomer, Rev. Joel H. Metcalf of Winchester, Mass. The object is exceedingly faint, and was found only by the evidence of the sensitive photographic plate.

In the sidereal heavens we behold the rising of the most refulgent orbs of the year, the eastern sky blazing with that splendid array of which Aratus thus writes:

"First rise athwart the Bull—majestic sight—
Orion's giant limbs and shoulders bright;
Who but admires him, stalking through the sky
With diamond-studded belt and glitt'ring thigh?
Nor with less ardour, pressing on his back
The mottled Hound pursues his fiery track;
Dark are his lower parts as wintry night,
His head, with burning star, intensely bright;
Men call him Sirius, for his blasting breath
Dries mortals up in pestilence and death."[2]

The Zodiacal constellation on the meridian is Aries, the Ram, which once stood at the head of the ecliptic band, marking the sun's place at the beginning of spring. Below Aries is Cetus, the Whale, which contains the interesting variable star Mira. This body, whose very name signifies "wonderful", is one of the most remarkable objects in the sky, fluctuating in brilliancy betwixt the second and ninth magnitudes in periods of about 331 days. The variation is not regular, since the star often fails to attain the second magnitude at its times of maximum brilliancy, whilst the period occasionally departs from the average length by almost a month. Phenomena of this type are very difficult to interpret, and the exact conditions attending to the variations of Mira are still enveloped in mystery.

Nearly in the zenith is Perseus, whose glittering radiance well crowns the celestial dome. Here we find another famous variable star, albeit one of vastly different type. This is Algol, whose name is the Arabic word for "demon". Algol is ordinarily of the second magnitude, but sinks every two and a half days to the fourth, its light being reduced for about eight hours at each obscuration. West of Perseus is Andromeda, with Pegasus still farther west. Below these groups lies the dull Pisces, whose few beauties are made brighter by the lines of Aratus:

> "Where the equator cuts the Zodiac's line
> On the blue vault, the glitt'ring Fishes shine.
> Though far apart, a diamond-studded chain,
> Clasping their silver tails, unites the twain."[3]

Pisces, through precession, has come to take the place of Aries as leader of the Zodiac, though in reckoning the motions of sun, moon, and planets, we are accustomed to ignore the change, and to assume that the old "signs" are in their ancient situations. This creates a sharp distinction between the actual Zodiacal constellations, and the now purely arbitrary "Signs of the Zodiac". In the southwest Aquarius is setting, whilst the bright star Fomalhaut barely lingers about the horizon. However, at this season of early dusk, we may transfer our hour of observation to 5:30 p.m., then beholding Fomalhaut in full splendour near the meridian. It is well to remember that we may, by choosing various hours of observation, obtain glimpses of many objects not visible in the usual evening panorama. If we view the sky two hours earlier or later than usual, we see the constellations as they would appear, respectively, a month earlier or later at our usual hour. Thus if we call 9 p.m. our regular time of observation, we can this month see the October sky at 5 p.m., the November sky at 7 p.m., the January sky at 11 p.m., the February sky at 1 a.m., the March sky at 3 a.m., and the April sky at 5 a.m. By dawn we may view the same groups which we behold in the evening during May. It is sometimes interesting to study the constellations at an unusual hour, and to discover what we are accustomed to call the "spring stars" in a wintry setting. Conversely, the present December sky was visible as early as September, just before sunrise, so far as the constellations are concerned. Lyra, with the brilliant Vega, shines very low in the northwest. Cygnus is somewhat higher up, but is steadily sinking. Looking north, we find Draco and Ursa Minor beneath the pole, with Ursa Major sharply tilted upward toward the east. Cassiopeia and Cepheus are past upper transit, the latter being well started on its descent of the sky. In the east Cancer has just appeared with Gemini and Canis Minor above it. Low in the southeast is Canis Major with the peerless Sirius in full glory. High in the eastern heavens are Orion, Taurus, and Auriga; each containing stellar beacons of gorgeous lustre. South and west of Orion, the river Eridanus flows down to the horizon, which it now intersects exactly at the meridian. The brightest parts of this group are never visible in our latitude. The Milky Way reaches across the sky from northwest to southeast, including within its confines the constellations Lyra, Cygnus, Cassiopeia, Perseus, Auriga, Gemini, Canis Minor, and Monoceros; the last named being a minor modern group now rising. Later in the evening we may view the more splendid parts of the Galaxy, which involve the eastern half of Canis Major and the visible region of Argo Navis.

The astronomical world now mourns the loss of one of its foremost celebrities; Prof. Percival Lowell, whose collection of celestial photographs is now on exhibition in this city, having died on November 12th. Dr. Lowell was perhaps the greatest observational astronomer of our time; certainly the greatest authority on matters pertaining to the planets. His investigations concerning the surfaces and topography of Mercury, Venus, Mars, Jupiter, and Saturn are the most valuable of their kind, whilst his detailed study of Mars alone is a work unparalleled in the history of science. His observatory, designed primarily for researches on Mars, was established in 1894, in a locality selected especially for its clearness of atmosphere; being situate at Flagstaff, Arizona, at an altitude of 7000 feet above sea level. The original large telescope of the Lowell Observatory is a 24-inch refractor for visual work, made by the celebrated Alvan Clark[4] of Cambridge, and pronounced by that skilful artificer his best production. This exceptional instrument, together with the very favourable locality of Flagstaff, gave Prof. Lowell a marked advantage over the majority of observers. An immense 40-inch reflecting telescope for photographical work was added to the equipment in 1909, making the observatory without a peer for its particular purpose. Prof. Lowell began to attain his widest celebrity in 1896, when he published his first book on the planet whose study had become his life work. His theory concerning the artificiality of the Martian "canals" brought him ridicule as well as praise, but the value of his observations is undoubted. He mapped the surface of Mars as no cartographer had ever mapped it before; and brought to light a host of new facts bearing upon its seasonal changes. He demonstrated the presence of oxygen and aqueous vapour in the atmosphere of Mars. In refutation of those who charged that some of his discoveries were mere optical illusions, he succeeded in photographing many of the topographical features whose existence had been doubted. Dr. Lowell was a recognised authority on cosmical physics and in 1909 delivered a memorial series of lectures on that subject in Huntington Hall, Boston, during which he rather startled the press and public by mentioning the possibility of the annihilation of the solar system through collision with a dark star. Before his adoption of astronomy as a constant profession, Dr. Lowell was a student of Oriental affairs, residing for a time in Japan and Corea, and acting as advisor to the Corean Special Commission which visited this country. His books reflect both these and the astronomical phases of his useful and varied career. The academic honours conferred upon Prof. Lowell by various societies and institutions in Europe and America were manifold. He never occupied an active professorship, but bore his title through honorary connexion with the Massachusetts Institute of Technology. He was a graduate of Harvard, of which university his brother is now president.[5]

In assigning to Percival Lowell his place amongst the eminent men of science, it will not be necessary for posterity to endorse or reject his theories regarding life on Mars. His solid achievements, consisting of actual contributions to astronomical knowledge, are sufficient to enshrine his memory side by side with that of Galileo and of Sir William Herschel.

EDITOR'S NOTE FP: *EN* 50, No. 3 (1 December 1916): 8.

Notes

1. See "Brumalia" (p. 319), probably written about this time.
2. Aratus, *Phaenomena* 322–32.
3. Aratus, *Phaenomena* 239–43.
4. Alvan Clark (1804–1887), American instrument maker who, with his sons Alvan Graham Clark (1832–1897) and George Bassett Clark (1827–1891), operated the firm of Alvan Clark & Sons in Cambridgeport, Mass.
5. A. Lawrence Lowell (1856–1943), president of Harvard from 1909 to 1933.

JANUARY SKIES

Saturn, to the telescopic observer the most unique and impressive of the planets, is now visible under the best possible conditions, arriving at its opposition on Jany. 17. It is at present retrograding near the boundary line betwixt the constellations Cancer and Gemini, crossing from the former into the latter during the course of the coming month. On the 1st, it rises at 5:38 p.m. On the 31st, having passed opposition, it sets at 6:19 a.m. During the convenient evening hours it may be observed high in the eastern sky, somewhat south of the bright stars Castor and Pollux. Saturn, though attractive in all circumstances, is preëminently a telescopic object. The naked eye, dwelling upon its bright yet strangely leaden-hued rays, is wholly unprepared for the sight revealed by a telescope of moderate power; for through the latter is beheld a golden ball, much like that of Jupiter in appearance, yet entirely surrounded by three immense flat rings of light, which nowhere touch the planet itself. This arrangement is absolutely unparalleled. In all the expanse of heaven no counterpart exists. Saturn itself is inferior only to Jupiter in size amongst the planets, and is believed to have the same constitution; that is, an extremely high temperature and a plastic or molten nature. Upon its surface may be discerned belts which, though not so readily seen in small telescopes, are nevertheless like those of Jupiter; and which are believed to arise from the same causes. That Saturn is hotter and even less solid than Jupiter may be inferred from its very low specific gravity; for the planet is lighter than water. It is, in fact, the least dense of all the planets. Gravity upon the surface of Saturn is variable. At the equator, it is less than on the earth, but at the poles it is greater. Because of its plastic condition, Saturn, like Jupiter, has an irregular rotation and greater polar compression. The polar compression, indeed, is the greatest possessed by any planet in our system. Saturn's distance from the sun is 886,000,000 miles; its distance from the earth varying from 774,000,000 to 1,028,000,000 miles. It was once the most remote of the known planets, of which distinction it was deprived by the discovery of Uranus in 1781. It revolves around the sun in a period of 29½ years, turning on its axis in a mean period of 10 hours and 14 minutes. Its diameter is 73,000 miles, and its axis is inclined 27 degrees from a perpendicular to the plane of its orbit. Its synodic period, or interval between successive oppositions as seen by us, is 378 days. When viewed with a telescope, Saturn's disc, like that of Jupiter, appears brightest at the centre. The belts, owing to the planet's greater axial inclination, are sometimes seen as curved lines, whilst Jupiter's are always horizontal. The brightest belt, that at the equator, is of a faint pink colour.

The poles are surrounded by dull areas. The rings of Saturn were discovered by Galileo; who did not, however, understand their real nature. Huyghens, in 1656, first knew them for what they are. With low magnifying powers, they appear as one and such they were first thought to be. Cassini, twenty years after their discovery, found that there are at least two, with a clear black line of demarcation between; and in 1850 Bond discovered the third ring, which is nearer the planet than the others, and so dark and transparent that it has been called the "gauze" or "crepe" ring. The opinion has been recently advanced by some, that the crepe ring is not separate, but a continuation of the inner bright ring. The plane in which the rings of Saturn lie is that of the planet's equator, which departs 28 degrees from that of the earth's orbit. The result of this condition is that we see them tilted at various angles, sometimes edgewise; when, on account of their extreme tenuity, they all but disappear; but we never behold them as circular bands with the ball or body of Saturn in the centre. The set of phases resulting from the angles at which the rings are beheld from the earth, occupies a complete revolution of Saturn around the sun; that is, nearly thirty years. Twice during this time, once in fifteen years, the rings nearly disappear, being turned edgewise toward our planet. The last such disappearance took place in 1907; the next will occur in 1922. We now behold them fairly well expanded. The rings of Saturn are not solid bodies, as they seem, but are merely swarms of tiny separate particles like miniature satellites; all revolving together in the same plane, and thus giving an appearance of solidity whilst actually pursuing independent paths. This fact was first suspected as early as 1715, but not proved until after 1850. The stability of the system of rings has often been discussed. It has even been intimated that the rings have contracted, thus approaching the planet, since the beginning of their telescopic observation. The rings of Saturn do not exceed 100 miles in thickness. The outermost ring is about 170,000 miles in diameter, and 11,000 miles in width. The division discovered by Cassini is 2000 miles wide. The inner bright ring is 10,000 miles wide and about 9000 miles from the surface of Saturn. Saturn has ten satellites, more than attend any other planet; five of which are visible in ordinary telescopes. Titan, the largest, was discovered in 1655 by Huyghens. The tenth, a body of incredibly slight magnitude for such an object, was discovered by W. H. Pickering in 1905. It is called Themis. The names of the satellites in order of distance from Saturn are: Iapetus, Hyperion, Themis, Titan, Rhea, Dione, Tethys, Enceladus, Mimas, and Phoebe. The prodigious spectacle presented to their possible inhabitants by the ball and rings of Saturn, defies our conception.

Jupiter, in quadrature on the 17th, lends to the evening sky a lustre even greater than that of Saturn. It is moving eastward through the dull constellation Pisces, approaching very closely the confines of Aries at the end of the month. It sets on the 1st at 1:15 a.m., and on the 31st at 11:25 p.m. During the most opportune hours of the evening, it may be found high in the western sky.

Mercury is also to be reckoned amongst the evening planets of the month, coming to greatest eastern elongation on the 2nd. It is then visible as a bright pinkish spark against the background of the western twilight just after sunset. This visibility, however, is of short duration, the planet attaining its inferior conjunction on the 19th. At the very end of January, Mercury will reappear low in the eastern morning sky; though being visible only to very careful observers. On the 30th it will be close to Venus, which will, of course, outshine it vastly.

Venus is rapidly approaching the sun and preparing to withdraw from the morning sky. On the 1st it rises 2 hours and 8 minutes before the sun, but on the 31st it precedes that luminary above the horizon by little more than one hour. It moves this month from the constellation Ophiuchus well into Sagittarius.

Mars is now lost in the solar rays, though technically still an "evening star". On the 1st it sets almost an hour after the sun, but on the 31st it follows that orb to the nether hemisphere within 27 minutes. Next month it will be in conjunction, appearing later in the year as a "morning star".

Uranus, very close to Mars in the heavens, is likewise visible; whilst Neptune, in opposition on the 26th, is at its best in the evening sky.

The Moon's phases for January will be as follows:

Full Moon, 8th	2:42 a.m.
Last Quarter, 16th	6:42 a.m.
New Moon, 23d	2:40 a.m.
First Quarter, 29th	8:02 p.m.

Apogee falls on the 10th, Perigee on the 23d. The moon runs high on the 5th, low on the 20th; crossing the equator on the 13th and 26th. It will be near Jupiter on the 1st, Saturn on the 9th, Venus on the 21st, and Jupiter again on the 29th. At the time of full moon on January 7–8 there will be a total lunar eclipse; visible at Providence under the following circumstances:

Moon enters Penumbra	11:36 p.m.
Moon enters Shadow	12:50 a.m.
Totality begins	2:00 a.m.
Middle of Eclipse	2:45 a.m.
Totality ends	3:29 a.m.
Moon leaves Shadow	4:39 a.m.
Moon leaves Penumbra	5:53 a.m.

The long period of totality, comprising nearly an hour and a half, will afford an interesting spectacle; since the lunar disc is scarcely ever wholly obscured by the earth's eclipsing shadow, being nearly always visible as a dull, smoky, reddish object. In the eclipse of 1884 the moon totally disappeared from the sight of the naked eye; a phenomenon of great rarity. The light reaching the lunar surface under these circumstances is that which the earth's atmosphere refracts, and is consequently somewhat dependent upon the state of the weather in those parts of the earth which are near the edge of the terrestrial disc as beheld from the moon. A lunar eclipse is, of course, an eclipse of the sun by the earth as seen by an observer on the moon.

The sun enters the zodiacal sign Aquarius on the 21st of the month, bringing us the dreariest and most inclement conditions of the year. The days gain 46 minutes between the 1st and the 31st. On January 23d there will be a partial solar eclipse, invisible in Rhode Island, but visible in central and western Europe, western Asia, and northeastern Africa. The year 1917 contains seven eclipses, the greatest possible number; four of the sun and three of the moon. This annual array will end, as it began, with a total lunar eclipse visible in this city, which will occur on the 28th of next December. None of the intervening eclipses will be visible here.

On the 2nd of this month the earth arrives at perihelion, or nearest point to the sun; a circumstance which is not without effect in tempering the rigours of our northern winter.

A comet known as Wolf's is now visible in the telescope, and may attain considerable lustre next summer when it draws toward its perihelion.

The constellations of the season are the most gloriously refulgent of all the year. Taurus, with the red Aldebaran and the twinkling Pleiades and Hyades, is on the southern meridian; whilst Orion, just below it, is soon to reach that line, bringing to culmination the lustrous Betelgeux and Rigel, and the famous "belt" and "sword". In the very zenith glows Auriga, with its dazzling star Capella, west of which is the richly adorned Perseus. In the southeast Canis Major presents a picture of unrivalled splendour, with Sirius, brightest of all the stars, blazing with accustomed fire. Higher in the east are Procyon, in Canis Minor, and Castor and Pollux, in Gemini. Low in the east the gigantic Sickle of Leo is rising, the bright Regulus being well in view. Cancer, above it, exhibits a less striking but no less captivating beauty with its faint cluster called "Praespe". In the west are the groups of autumn, including Cetus, Eridanus, Aries, Pisces, Andromeda, Pegasus, and Cygnus; the last two about to sink from sight. In the north we find the Plough tilted at right angles to the horizon and rapidly ascending the vault. Draco is beneath the Pole, as is also Ursa Minor. Cassiopeia and Cepheus are west of that celestial pivot, both appearing to advantage.

The death of Rev. Ira [sic] R. Hicks[1] of St. Louis on the 12th of last October brings to mind the enormous and regrettable power of false science amongst a great number of intelligent though not wholly educated persons. This individual, an earnest but hardly discriminating student of the skies, devoted the entire latter part of his life to the formation and operation of an elaborate system of weather prediction, based on the motions of the various planets; and succeeded in obtaining thousands of credulous admirers through his monthly and annual publications. Hicks was probably sincere in his peculiar beliefs, yet unconsciously accomplished no little harm to astronomy by virtue of his persistent maintenance of fallacious theories. Among the more patently absurd errors of his speculation was his continued faith in the existence of the supposed intra-Mercurial planet Vulcan, whose unreality was demonstrated years ago. Misguided propagandists and thinkers like "Prof." Hicks constitute one of the most powerful of all arguments for the increased diffusion of true scientific knowledge. The public, if rightly instructed in the rudiments of astronomy, could not for an instant have been duped by the flagrantly impossible idea that planetary motion and terrestrial weather can be connected. Yet it is to the credit of the late theorist that he never swerved from the propagation of what he deemed truth; and never missed an opportunity to improve, according to his ideas, the intellectual condition of the proletariat. His public notoriety was considerable, and his esteem amongst his readers immense. That this esteem was deserved, is well proven by his always good intentions. He exemplifies the seemingly inevitable truth that no man unselfishly dedicated to the cause of science, however much he may err in its practice, can wholly escape that touch of dignity and nobility which the pursuit of knowledge imparts to its followers.

EDITOR'S NOTE FP: *EN* 50, No. 26 (2 January 1917): 8.

Notes

1. Iri R. Hicks (1845?–1916), astronomer and weather forecaster in St. Louis.

FEBRUARY SKIES

Saturn is still the leading planet of the evening sky, shining high in the east during the early hours, and crossing to the west toward midnight. It sets at 6:18 a.m. on the 1st, and at 4:23 on the 28th, thus being visible practically all night. It is now retrograding in the extreme eastern part of the constellation Gemini, near the boundary of Cancer. Its rings, belts, and satellites well repay telescopic observation.

Jupiter, intrinsically brighter than Saturn, is less favourably situated, being now past quadrature and declining in the western sky. It is in direct motion in the western part of the constellation Aries, setting on the 1st at 11:25 p.m., and on the 28th at 10:00.

Mars, in conjunction on the 28th, is invisible throughout the month. When next seen, it will be a morning planet, remaining as such during the rest of the year.

Venus is now approaching the sun, and will soon be lost amid the overpowering refulgence of that orb. On the 1st it rises 1 hour and 4 minutes before the sun, thus being seen with ease through the twilight of dawn; but by the 28th its time of rising will precede that of the sun by only 26 minutes, rendering its observation a matter of much difficulty. Its phase now closely approximates a perfect circle, 0.97 of the disc being illuminated at the end of the month. During February Venus moves from the eastern part of the constellation Sagittarius completely through Capricornus and just into Aquarius.

Mercury, in greatest western elongation on the 12th, will be visible low in the eastern sky just before dawn for several days before and after that date. On the 19th it will be rather near the very thin crescent of the aged moon. During the present period of visibility, Mercury will cross from the constellation Sagittarius into Capricornus. This planet, the smallest in our system save the asteroids, has a diameter of only 3000 miles. It is the nearest of all the planets to the sun, having a mean solar distance of 36,000,000 miles, and performing its orbital revolution in 88 days. This proximity to the sun renders Mercury the most difficult of the major planets to observe; since it never recedes more than 28 degrees from the central luminary, and can therefore never be seen with the naked eye except at or near the times of its greatest elongations; low in the west soon after sunset, or in the east before the break of day, as it is this month. The most favourable evening appearances are those which take place in the spring; as a morning star, it is best seen in the autumn. Its present aspect is thus not particularly favourable. As seen in the morning sky, this planet was thought by the ancients to be a different body from that seen in the evening, hence was known to them by two names: "Apollo" as a morning star, and "Mercury" as an evening star. The difficulty of glimpsing Mercury is well illustrated by the fact that Copernicus, the great father of modern astronomy, was never in his life able to see it; and that Mr. Hind, a British astronomer, is said to have observed it but once without the aid of a telescope. The planet is brightest when in a gibbous phase; that is, when between superior conjunction and one of its elongations. It will therefore be more brilliant after than before the 12th of this month. Mercury's synodical period, or time of apparent revolution around the earth from one inferior conjunction to another, is 116 days. The surface of Mercury reflects light but feebly, and has but few definite markings as seen in the telescope. The older observers believed that they could distinguish high mountains on the planet, but later astronomers have failed to substantiate their conclusions. The time of rotation of Mercury is a matter of much dispute; since while some declare that it is much like the earth's, others affirm quite as strongly that the planet turns on its axis only once during its revolution around the sun; thus acting as does our own moon toward the earth, and keeping one half always turned to the central body, the other half always turned away. If this be true, then Mercury must possess in one hemisphere perpetual sunlight, and in the other, perpetual darkness. The existence of an atmosphere around Mercury is likewise disputed. Of all the members of the solar system, Mercury has the greatest density; being, curiously enough, about equal to the metal mercury in specific gravity. The planet has no satellite. The excessive amount of solar light and heat received by Mercury on account of its proximity to the sun precludes the possibility of the existence upon its surface of inhabitants in any way similar to those of the earth. Mercury passes in transit betwixt the earth and sun at intervals of from three to thirteen years; then being visible in the telescope as a black spot crossing the solar surface. Such phenomena always take place either in May or in November. Gassendi, in 1631, was the first person to observe a transit of Mercury. Mercury last performed a transit on Nov. 7, 1914, whilst future transits will occur in 1924, 1927, 1937, and 1940. Not, however, until Nov. 14, 1953, can the inhabitants of Providence enjoy the privilege of beholding one.

Uranus is invisible this month, being in conjunction on the 8th. Neptune is seen to advantage in the evening sky.

The moon's phases for February will be as follows:

Full Moon, 6th.. 10:28 p.m.
Last Quarter, 14th.. 8:53 p.m.
New Moon, 21st .... 1:09 p.m.
First Quarter, 28th ....11:44 a.m.

Apogee falls on the 6th, Perigee on the 20th. The moon runs high on the 2nd, low on the 16th; crossing the equator on the 9th and 22nd. It will be near Saturn on the 5th, Mercury on the 19th, and Jupiter on the 25th.

The sun enters the Zodiacal sign Pisces on the 19th, thereby marking that final and half yielding stage of winter which is not wholly without prophecies of the coming spring. During February the days increase their length by an hour and eleven minutes. Apparent solar time at this season comes into temporary agreement with ordinary mean time, so that the clock and sundial now coincide. Noon falls exactly half way between sunrise and sunset.

Turning to the constellations, we find the brilliant pageant of winter yet undimmed; though all the lustrous and familiar groups have moved toward the west. Precisely on the meridian is the peerless Dog-Star, while the other brilliants of Canis Major cluster resplendently beneath it. It is interesting to note that despite the extreme brilliancy of Sirius as we behold it, it is not a particularly large star, as such things are reckoned. It is rather larger than our sun, but the source of its lustre lies more in its proximity than in its size. Yet near as it is, eight years are required for the force of light, at its inconceivably rapid rate of 186,000 miles per second, to travel between it and our solar system. Above and to the east of Canis Major lies Canis Minor; and above and to the west is the great Orion. Sirius, together with Procyon in Canis Minor and Betelgeux in Orion, forms a large and impressive equilateral triangle of bright stars. An old jingle thus describes it:

> "Let Procyon join to Betelgeux
>   And pass a line afar,
> To reach the point where Sirius glows,
>   The most conspicuous star;
>
> Then will the eye delighted view
>   A figure fine and vast,
> Its span is equilateral,
>   Triangular its cast."

Sirius now lies on the western edge of the Milky Way, but its type of motion reveals the fact that it was once on the eastern edge. Its radiance is now pure white, though ancient allusions lead us to believe that it was a red star in classical times. This type of change is highly unusual, since the order of chromatic change in the stars is generally the direct opposite; white stars tending to turn orange and eventually red. Sirius is known to be a "young" star; that is, a star not far advanced on the path of stellar evolution and decadence. Its spectrum is of a characteristic type, and other orbs of similar spectra are known as "Sirian Stars". The outstanding feature of this spectrum is the indication of Hydrogen in immense quantities.

Orion, Taurus, and Auriga gild the vault in the west; whilst Eridanus, Cetus, Aries, Perseus, Andromeda, and portions of Pisces are visible farther west. In the north we find the Plough high in the sky, though not yet above the pole. Ursa Minor is below and to the right of the pole, as is Draco. Cassiopeia is west of the pole, with Cepheus beneath it, preparing to glide under the pole. Eastward the heavens proclaim the coming spring. Cancer and Leo soar aloft, and the head and foremost coils of Hydra are high in the sky. Crater has just appared in the southeast, and portions of Virgo are in sight. Later in the evening the bright Arcturus will emerge from behind the curtain of the northeastern hills. Coma Berenices has now attained a perceptible altitude, and shimmers with accustomed grace and elusiveness in the northeast; Canes Venatici, with its one bright star Cor Caroli, shining beside it. The Milky Way stretches from the north to the southeast, flowing through Cepheus, Cassiopeia, Perseus, Auriga, Taurus, Gemini, Canis Minor, Canis Major, and Argo Navis in its course. The crisp brilliance with which it glistens on these wintry evenings contrasts sharply with the delightfully languid sheen it presents as it glows amid the stars of Scorpio and Sagittarius on summer nights.

EDITOR'S NOTE FP: *EN* 50, No. 52 (1 February 1917): 6.

MARCH SKIES

To many readers of these monthly chronicles of the heavens, certain technical terms used in describing the apparent motions of the planets have doubtless seemed obscure and meaningless. It is accordingly the writer's design to attempt an explanation of those which most frequently occur in articles of this sort. First of all, we must clearly understand the circumstances under which the inhabitants of the earth view the other bodies of the solar system. Our planet is the third in order of distance from the sun;

Mercury and Venus lying within its orbit and being called "inferior" planets; and Mars, Jupiter, Saturn, Uranus, and Neptune outside, and being termed "superior" planets. In defining the rather complex apparent motions of these bodies it is necessary to remember that such are the result of their real motions as seen from an object itself moving—our own earth. Naturally the inferior planets will have a very different type of apparent motion from that of the superior planets, since their position in relation to us is so radically different. The various typical or important points in the apparent course of a planet are called "aspects". The principal aspects of the inferior planets are four in number, viz.: Inferior and Superior Conjunctions, and Greatest Elongations East and West.

In order successfully to comprehend the meaning of these terms, let us follow an inferior planet throughout one of its apparent revolutions. We will begin at a time when it is invisible to our eyes, lying on a line between us and the sun, and therefore rising and setting with the latter. It is then nearest to us, and is said to be "Inferior Conjunction". "Conjunction" is a word used to express the relation of two celestial bodies which are in a line north and south; in this case the two bodies are the planet and the sun, but when the sun is one of the bodies concerned its name is not generally mentioned; the expression "in conjunction", when applied to one body without the mention of another, meaning, by general custom, that the body is in conjunction with the sun. Usually when an inferior planet is in inferior conjunction, it passes just a little north or south of the sun; but at rare intervals it passes directly across the disc of the great luminary, becoming visible as a black speck on the shining surface. Such a phenomenon is called a "transit", and is far more common with Mercury than with Venus. Some time after inferior conjunction, the planet emerges from the solar glare, shining low in the eastern sky just before sunrise, and shewing in the telescope a very thin crescentic phase.

As time passes, the phase increases, and the planet withdraws more and more from the sun, being visible higher and higher in the early morning sky until at length it shews a phase, like that of the half-moon, and is at its greatest apparent distance west of the sun. It is then said to be in "Greatest Elongation West". This is the best time to observe an inferior planet in the morning. After this, the planet turns and approaches the sun, its phase meanwhile increasing and becoming gibbous. Finally, having attained an approximately full phase, it is again lost in the solar rays, coming once more in line with the sun and earth, but this time lying beyond the sun, instead of between us and that body. It is now farthest from the earth, and is said to be in "Superior Conjunction". Were it not rendered invisible by the blinding refulgence of the sun, it would shew a perfectly round disc, like that of the full moon. Having passed beyond the sun, the planet next becomes visible low in the western sky just after sunset, still shewing in the telescope a practically full phase.

As it recedes from the sun, mounting higher and higher in the early evening sky, its phase decreases; after a while becoming a semicircle. The planet is then at its greatest apparent distance east of the sun, and is said to be in "Greatest Elongation East". This is the best time to observe it in the evening sky. Now the planet appears again to approach the sun, and the crescentic phase is a second time assumed. At last it becomes lost in the sun's radiance, and once more arrives at inferior conjunction. The foregoing description applies equally to Mercury and to Venus; though Venus, of course, recedes at its elongations nearly twice as far from the sun as does Mercury.

In considering the case of the superior planets, we are confronted by an entirely different set of aspects and conditions of visibility; for these bodies are not confined to the eastern morning sky, or the western evening sky, but partake to a great degree of the general annual drift of the constellations from east to west. The principal aspects of the superior planets are four in number, viz.: Opposition, Conjunction, and two quadratures. In tracing the apparent course of a superior planet we had best begin when it is nearest the earth, and opposite the sun as seen by us.

It is then said to be in "Opposition", rising at sunset, culminating, or reaching its highest point in the heavens, at midnight, and setting at sunrise. Shewing in the telescope a full, round disc, it is at its best for observation; a condition quite in contrast with that of the inferior planets, which are invisible when nearest the earth. Thus we are enabled to study the superior bodies with a far higher degree of facility and success. After opposition, a superior planet rises earlier and earlier each day, thus appearing higher and higher in the eastern sky each night; until, having advanced a quarter of a circle, or 90 degrees of angular measure, it culminates at about six in the evening, being then in "Quadrature". When at this point Mars shews a perceptible phase, or departure from the circular form; whilst Jupiter exhibits a slight shading off on the edge turned away from the sun. The other superior planets, however, are too far distant to be affected in this manner.

After quadrature, the planet drifts farther and farther westward, until at length it approaches the sun and is lost in the glare of that body, passing beyond it in "Conjunction". It is then farthest from the earth. Soon the planet reappears in the morning sky on the other side of the sun, emerging from invisibility as does an inferior planet after its inferior conjunction. As time passes, it rises earlier and earlier, until after a while it comes above the horizon about midnight and is in "quadrature" again. This is on the other side of the orbit, or 180 degrees from the other quadrature. Mars and Jupiter here repeat their exhibitions of phase. Continuing to rise earlier each night, the planet now enters the evening sky, finally rising at sunset and reaching another opposition.

Of the various brights, only Jupiter and Saturn are visible this month, both in the evening sky. Jupiter, setting on the 1st at 9:58 p.m., and on the 31st at 8:30, is sinking lower and lower in the west. It is moving directly through the constellation Aries, brightly adorning a region not remarkable for lustrous stars.

Saturn is visible under rather more favourable conditions; gleaming high in the south each evening, and slowly retrograding in the extreme eastern part of the constellation Gemini. It lingers in the sky long after the departure of Jupiter, setting on the 1st at 4:22 a.m., and on the 31st at 2:30 a.m. It shines just south of the bright stars Castor and Pollux.

Mercury reaches superior conjunction on the 29th, being invisible throughout the month. Venus, in superior conjunction next month, has practically deserted the morning sky. Mars has not yet emerged from the sun's rays, and Uranus is almost equally involved in solar radiance. Neptune is telescopically visible in the evening sky, being not yet in quadrature.

The moon's phases for March will be as follows:

Full Moon, 8th.. 4:58 p.m.

Last Quarter, 16th..7:38 a.m.

New Moon, 22nd... 11:05 p.m.

First Quarter, 30th ....5:36 a.m.

Apogee falls on the 5th, Perigee on the 21st. The moon runs high on the 1st and 28th, low on the 15th; crossing the equator on the 8th and 22nd. It will be near Saturn on the 5th, Jupiter on the 25th, and Saturn again on the 31st.

The sun enters the Zodiacal sign Aries on the 20th at 11:38 p.m., thus bringing to our hemisphere the benignant and long awaited season of spring. During March the days increase by an hour and 24 minutes.

In the eastern sky we now behold the characteristic constellations of the vernal season. The familiar trapezium of Corvus has appeared above the horizon, while Spica, in Virgo, shines brilliantly a little to the north of it. Arcturus has gained a considerable, [*sic*] and Corona Borealis is entirely in sight. Higher in the sky, Coma Berenices, Leo, and the head of Hydra are to be seen, while Cancer is the Zodiacal constellation on the meridian. In the western heavens all the bright groups of winter yet remain; Orion, Canis Major, Canis Minor, Gemini, Taurus, Auriga, and Perseus shining with great lustre; albeit lacking that peculiar crispness which attend their midwinter appearance. In the north we behold the Plough climbing above the pole, and Ursa Minor stretched out to the right of that point. Draco, balanced on its head, lies beyond Ursa Minor. Cepheus is beneath the pole with Cassiopeia closely following.

The Milky Way is entirely in the western sky, but after midnight the shimmering summer streams will rise bearing in them the bright stars of Scorpio.

EDITOR'S NOTE FP: *EN* 50, No. 73 (28 February 1917): 6.

APRIL SKIES

Saturn, in quadrature on the 14th, is the leading planet of the April skies; being visible high in the west on each clear evening. On the 1st it sets at 2:19 a.m., and on the 30th at 12:26 a.m. It lies in the eastern part of the constellation Gemini, in direct motion, and having approximately the same bearings that it possessed last month while it was retrograding. Its brilliancy is steadily decreasing, though the diminution does not become very noticeable during this month.

Jupiter is drawing near the sun and settling out of sight in the western twilight at early evening. On the 1st it sets two hours and 20 minutes after the sun, therefore being fairly well visible near the horizon; but by the 30th it will set only 25 minutes after the sun, being then too near the solar orb for good observation. While visible, it is easily the brightest star-like object in the sky.

Mercury comes to greatest eastern elongation on the 24th, being then seen at its best. Spring elongations east of the sun are especially favourable times to observe the planet in the evening twilight, hence all are urged to take advantage of this opportunity, looking for the planet just above the sunset point before the darkness becomes intense. It will appear as a ruddy or pinkish speck of rather bright light, lying close to Jupiter on the 16th. At the time of greatest elongation, Mercury will be but little south of the famous Pleiades cluster in the constellation Taurus.

Venus, in superior conjunction on April 26th, and Mars, in conjunction on the 28th of last February, are both invisible. Later on they will appear in the evening and the morning sky, respectively.

Uranus, having emerged from the sun's rays, is visible through a good telescope in the morning sky; whilst Neptune, in quadrature on the 22nd, is fairly well seen in the evening, also with optical aid. Neither of these two large though faint planets has any particular attraction for the amateur observer.

The Moon's phases for April will be as follows:

Full Moon, 7th...8:49 a.m.
Last Quarter, 14th.. 3:12 p.m.
New Moon, 21st ....9:01 a.m.
First Quarter, 29th ....12:22 a.m.

Apogee falls on the 2nd and 29th, Perigee on the 17th. The moon runs low on the 12th, high on the 24th; crossing the equator on the 5th and 18th. It will be near Saturn on the 27th.

On the 20th the sun enters the Zodiacal sign Taurus, the days increasing an hour and 17 minutes during the month of April. Spots have recently been very numerous on the solar disc, mainly near the equator.

In taking up our monthly survey of the constellations, we are impelled to inquire into the place of this fascinating pursuit in the larger science of astronomy. In a strictly technical sense, the tracing of the various apparent groups of stars is not a part of astronomy at all; yet an accurate knowledge of them and their mythological figures is of course as essential to the astronomer as a knowledge of geography is to the terrestrial explorer. While some of the constellations are of modern making, most of them have existed since prehistoric times. They were well known in their present form to the ancients, and are the subject of frequent allusions in classical writings. Ptolemy,[1] in the second century A.D., recorded 48 constellations [. . .] to the objects for which they are named is in most cases very remote, so that we are often inclined to wonder how the ancient nomenclature came to be established. In learning the features of the sky a good star atlas or planisphere, particularly the latter, is much to be desired. Hammett's Planisphere,[2] which may be obtained at any bookstall for a dollar, was used by the writer in his early studies, and seems quite unequalled for its purpose. In learning the constellations we should at first seek to become familiar with those groups which are always visible in our latitude. Of these the well known "Plough" or "Big Dipper" in Ursa Major is the most readily recognised, and should serve as a starting point from which we may proceed to other parts of the sky. The "Dipper", which contains seven stars, may always be found with ease. In spring it is in the north above the pole in an inverted position; in summer it is in the northwest with the bowl downward; in autumn it is on the northern horizon beneath the pole, right side up; whilst in winter it is in the northeast with the bowl uppermost. These statements refer to its position at the most convenient hour of evening observation. The two stars in the front of the bowl are called "The Pointers", since the line which they form points directly to the star Polaris, at the north celestial pole.

In our latitude, Polaris lies a little less than half way up from the northern horizon to the zenith, having no perceptible motion, since the axis of the earth points to it. It is the principal star of the constellation Ursa Minor, which swings round it in a very restricted circle, and possesses the general appearance of a small dipper. Almost exactly opposite Ursa Major, on the other side of the pole, is Cassiopeia, which has the shape of a flattened letter "W". It may be found beneath the pole in spring, east of it in summer, above it in autumn, and west of it in winter. Cepheus is a faint group that precedes Cassiopeia in its circuit of the skies. Draco, a dull, expansive constellation, lies beyond Ursa Minor from the pole. The foregoing groups never leave our sky and may well guide us to those more southerly asterisms which the successive seasons bring us.

The elegant amusement afforded by the study of the constellations is immensely enhanced by a knowledge of their mythological history, which has been touched upon from time to time in these columns. The constellations this month are typical of the spring sky. The Zodiacal group on the meridian is Leo, the Lion, an extensive array of stars containing two divisions. The western and larger part is known as the Sickle, from its shape, and contains the bright star Regulus; while the other part has the form of a right triangle and contains Denebola, a star of the second magnitude. Regulus has in astronomical lore an importance which its brilliancy does not fully warrant; an importance due to the fact that when the constellation was formed, this star marked the place of the sun in the sky at the summer solstice. Beneath Leo wind the coils of Hydra, whose head is now past the meridian. Its two dependent groups, Crater and Corvus, are still in the east. The southeast is illuminated by the expanse of Virgo, the bright star Spica lending lustre to an area almost destitute of other brilliant bodies. Farther north is Boötes, with the resplendent Arcturus, west of which shimmers the elusive radiance of Coma Berenices. Above Coma Berenices is Canes Venatici, whose brightest star Cor Caroli forms with Denebola, Spica, and Arcturus a perfect rhombus called the "Diamond of Virgo". In the west are most of those effulgent winter groups which shone so conspicuously a few months ago. Now, as they linger in the milder air of the early spring evenings, they seem scarcely the same constellations, so tempered and softened is their radiance. Taurus, Orion, Perseus, Gemini, Auriga, and the two Dogs are still in view, though most of them will soon set. Cancer is still high in the sky, but little west of the meridian. In the north the various circumpolar groups are all in the characteristic spring positions described earlier in this article. In the northwest Lyra is rising, the bluish-white beams of Vega piercing the vapours of the horizon with surprising intensity. Farther south Hercules is rearing his formless bulk, above which glitters the attractive diadem of Corona Borealis. Due east Ophiuchus et Serpens is rising, some of the convolutions of the celestial Snake being already at a considerable altitude. In the southeast Libra is entirely in view, while nearer the south the upper parts of Centaurus are projecting themselves into the visible hemisphere. The whole of this great constellation we can never see in the latitude of Rhode Island. The Milky Way has passed far to the west, and will soon substitute its summer branch for the wintry stream we now behold. That branch, by virtue of its location amidst stars of milder glow, generally attracts more notice than the stream which laves the distractingly brilliant shores of Canis Major, Canis Minor, Gemini, Taurus, Auriga, and Perseus.

On March 19 a new comet was discovered by J. E. Mellish, which though invisible to the naked eye, is observable in a small telescope. It is of approximately circular outline, with a well-defined nucleus, but possesses no tail. At present it is visible in the evening after sunset, lying near the boundary betwixt Aries and Pisces. By the 8th of the month it will be rather bright, though its proximity to the sun will probably prevent successful observation without optical aid. It will attain perihelion, or nearest point to the sun, on the 12th. In ancient times, no portent was regarded as more dreadful than the advent of a comet, but intellectual enlightenment has brought about a change in our attitude toward these as well as other things; and comets are now welcomed with scientific interest, rather than feared with superstitious terror.

EDITOR'S NOTE FP: *EN* 50, No. 102 (2 April 1917): 6.

Notes

1. Ptolemy (Claudius Ptolemaeus, *fl.* 146–170 C.E.), Alexandrian writer on astronomy, mathematics, and other subjects. He is the author of *Mathematike Syntaxis* (more commonly known by its Arabic name, *Almagest*), a complete treatise on astronomy in 13 books.

2. *Hammett's Planisphere: Showing the Principal Stars Visible for Every Hour in the Year from Lat. 40 Degrees N.* (Boston: J. L. Hammett Co., 1900).

MAY SKIES

The principal planetary event of the coming month is the appearance of Venus in the evening sky after an absence of nearly a year. On the 1st, it sets practically with the sun, being therefore lost amidst the dazzling rays of that luminary; but by the 31st it will have moved so far as to linger above the horizon for three-quarters of an hour after sunset, thus disclosing itself to the keen observer whose view of the western heavens is unobstructed by natural or artificial barriers. It should be sought as early as possible, whilst the twilight is yet strong, and will be found in the constellation Taurus. The phase of Venus as beheld through the telescope is now a virtually complete circle of slight diameter. As the ensuing months pass, the disc will wane in phase and increase in magnitude; attaining a half-moon figure by the end of November, when greatest eastern elongation will occur. Its brilliancy, even under the present unfavourable conditions, exceeds that of any other star-like object in the sky. An interesting addition to the mass of conflicting data regarding the rotation of Venus is afforded by the recent conclusions of Mr. D. H. Wilson,[1] who has not only made observations of his own, but given careful study to the charts and sketches of previous observers. Whilst roughly endorsing the theory of a long rotation, Mr. Wilson believes that the period does not quite equal the planet's sidereal revolution of 225 days, but that it comprises an interval of somewhat less than 224 days. This condition, if true, would cause rather strange circumstances of night and day upon the surface of Venus. It is at present safer to withhold judgment on these observations and inferences, awaiting authoritative corroboration or disproof.

Mercury, visible for the first two or three days of May in the west after sunset, will arrive at inferior conjunction on the 16th, being therefore invisible during the major portion of the month. Its next appearance will be in the morning sky of June.

Mars, by the end of the month, will rise an hour before the sun, thus being visible to the assiduous observer as a morning planet. It now lies in the constellation Aries, but is rapidly drawing toward the confines of Taurus. Its brilliancy is at present inconsiderable, though later in the year it will shine more conspicuously. Mars will not attain quadrature till December.

Jupiter, in conjunction on the 9th, will be practically invisible throughout the month, reappearing in June as a morning planet.

Saturn, but lately past quadrature, is the leading planet in the evening sky; setting on the 1st at 12:35 a.m., and on the 31st at 10:30 p.m. It is in direct motion in the extreme eastern part of the constellation Gemini, arriving at the boundary of Cancer by the end of the month. As beheld during the most convenient hours of observation, immediately after nightfall, it hangs low in the northwestern heavens. Mr. F. E. Seagrave, the celebrated astronomer whose activities have enhanced so materially the scientific renown of Rhode Island, has lately published the result of a series of micrometrical investigations of Saturn's rings, made two years ago at his laboratory in North Scituate. These results appear to contradict the prevalent theory that the rings are gradually approaching the ball of the planet, and convey the impression that the

Saturnian system is relatively stable. The question is one of no mean importance in astronomy and astrophysics, and deserves research of the greatest amplitude and fullest detail. That a Rhode Islander should contribute so largely to our knowledge of it, is a circumstance which cannot but be gratifying to local pride.

Uranus, in quadrature on the 14th, is visible in the morning sky. Neptune, somewhat past quadrature, still remains in the evening heavens.

The moon's phases for May will be as follows:

Full Moon, 6th.. 9:43 p.m.
Last Quarter, 13th... 8:48 p.m.
New Moon, 20th .... 7:47 p.m.
First Quarter, 28th .... 6:34 p.m.

Perigee falls on the 13th, Apogee on the 27th. The moon runs low on the 8th, high on the 22nd; crossing the equator on the 2nd, 15th, and 29th. It will be near Saturn on the 25th.

The Sun enters the Zodiacal sign Gemini on the 21st, moving northward this month to the extent of seven degrees. The days increase about an hour during May, being fifteen hours in length at the end of the month.

Turning to the constellations, we discover upon the southern meridian the Zodiacal group Virgo, its refulgent star Spica soon to transit. Below Virgo is the conspicuous trapezium of stars forming Corvus, the Crow, one of the most characteristic groups of the vernal season. Corvus is perched upon the coils of Hydra, most of which has already passed the meridian. West of Corvus is Crater, the Cup, a group of similar size but less definite outline. Above Crater, and just west of Virgo, the stately and majestic bulk of Leo still shines with undiminished splendour, while farther west the shimmering cluster of Praespe serves to distinguish the faint constellation Cancer. Beyond Cancer, and soon to sink below the horizon, is Gemini; which with Canis Minor to the south and Auriga to the north, forms the last of the bright groups of vanished winter.

Returning to the meridian, we find above Virgo the glittering field of faint stars known as Coma Berenices; while still higher up, and practically in the zenith, is Canes Venatici with its single conspicuous star Cor Caroli. In the north, Ursa Major is above the pole, whilst Ursa Minor is soon to assume a similar position. Cassiopeia is close to the horizon in lower transit; and Cepheus, just ahead, is beginning its annual ascent of the vault. Draco curves sinuously from a point due east of the pole to one directly above it. Of the non-circumpolar northern groups, Perseus is just sinking from sight west of Cassiopeia, while Cygnus is rising east of Cepheus. Lyra, with the resplendent Vega, has now attained a good altitude, and forms the most striking feature of the eastern sky. Above it is the vague but extensive constellation Hercules, south of which is the equally vague and equally extensive Ophiuchus et Serpens. Higher in the sky is the sparkling Northern Crown, and the effulgent star Arcturus in Boötes. In the southeast, next to Virgo, is Libra. Above the southeastern horizon in fierce gorgeousness crawls the Scorpion with its brilliant fire-red star Antares; a fitting portent of the flaming scenes of fury which await our warriors on the Hun-infested plains of France. Scorpio is the most spectacular and characteristic of the summer groups, and will blaze radiantly in the months to come. West of Scorpio, and reaching completely to the meridian, the uppermost parts of Centaurus line the horizon. The entire group, including its brightest stars, is never visible in this latitude. Alpha Centauri, the brightest star of the constellation, is the nearest of our stellar neighbours, lying at a distance of 25,000,000,000,000 miles from the solar system. That so vast an interval in terrestrial

terms should be reckoned as infinitesimally small in terms of sidereal space, is an elo-
quent testimonial to the unbounded magnitude of the visible universe, to say nothing
of the stupendous conception of absolute infinity. The consideration of boundless time
and space is indeed the most thought-provoking feature of astronomical science. Humanity with its pompous pretensions sinks to complete nothingness when viewed in
relation to the unfathomed abysses of infinity and eternity which yawn about it. The
entire period of existence of mankind, or of all organic life, or of the earth, or of the
sun and solar system, or of the visible universe itself, is but an inconsequential instant
in the history of the whirling spheres and ether-currents that compose all creation; a
history which has neither beginning nor ending. Man, so far from being the central and
supreme object of Nature, is clearly demonstrated to be a mere incident, perhaps an
accident, of a natural scheme whose boundless reach relegates him to total insignificance. His presence or absence, his life or death, are obviously matters of utter indiffer-
ence to the plan of Nature as a whole. Even the vast universe we behold is but an atom
in the absolutely unlimited expanse which stretches away on all sides. It is small wonder that the Marchioness, in M. Fontenelle's old volume "Entretiens sur le Pluralit, des
Mondes", grew dizzy at the thought of infinity, and exclaimed that "surely we ourselves
are almost lost among so many millions of worlds!"[2] A recent writer has attempted a
portrayal of astronomical infinity in blank verse, describing a dream or vision in this
fashion:

> "Alone in space, I view'd a feeble fleck
> Of silvern light, marking the narrow ken
> Which mortals call the boundless universe.
> On ev'ry side, each as a tiny star,
> Shone more creations, vaster than our own.
> As on a moonless night the Milky Way
> In solid sheen displays its countless orbs
> To weak terrestrial eyes, each orb a sun;
> So beam'd the prospect on my wond'ring soul;
> A spangled curtain, rich with twinkling gems.
> Yet each a mighty universe of suns—
> And all the universes in my view
> But a poor atom in infinity."[3]

The discoveries of celestial science have indeed altered our perspective in radical
manner, and made evident the triviality of many things commonly deemed vital and
important.

The great 72-inch reflecting telescope of the Dominion Observatory at Victoria,
B.C., mentioned in these columns last October, has at last been mounted and placed
in use. Until the completion of the immense Mt. Wilson reflector, it will enjoy the distinction of being the world's largest telescope, equalling in size the famous but now
dismantled instrument of Lord Rosse. The new telescope, however, possesses many ad-
vantages over the Rosse "leviathan", having a mounting of the most approved equatorial pattern, instead of being propped up clumsily by means of chains and pivots
between walls of masonry. After a long period of supremacy of the refracting telescope,
celestial photography with its special demands has brought about a new reign of the
reflector.

EDITOR'S NOTE FP: *EN* 50, No. 127 (1 May 1917): 5.

Notes

1. Unidentified.
2. Bernard Le Bovier de Fontenelle (1657–1757), *Entretiens sur la pluralité des mondes* (1686), usually translated as *Conversations on the Plurality of Worlds*. The comment appears in the conversation titled "The Fifth Evening."
3. These are lines 152–56, 160–65, and 169–70 of the central section (titled "Aletheia Phrikodes") of "The Poe-et's Nightmare" (1916; *AT* 22); in that poem the last two lines read: "That all the universes in my view / Form'd but an atom in infinity."

JUNE SKIES

The principal planets of the June evening sky are Venus and Saturn, both shining low in the west during the early hours of darkness. Venus, remaining above the horizon after the sun for three-quarters of an hour on the 1st, and for an hour and ten minutes on the 30th, glows with intense lustre, though by no means so brilliantly as it will blaze in the months to come. Its motion amongst the stars during June carries it from the eastern part of the constellation Taurus almost entirely across Gemini.

Whilst Venus is thus emerging from the solar glare, Saturn is being rapidly overtaken by the sun; sinking lower and lower in the heavens each night, and arriving at conjunction in July. On the 1st it sets at 10:30 p.m., and on the 30th at 8:40, but an hour and a quarter after sunset. The planet now lies in the western part of the constellation Cancer, moving slowly and directly.

Mercury, Mars, and Jupiter all lie rather close to one another in the morning sky, being visible near the eastern horizon just before sunrise. On the morning of the 6th Mercury and Mars will be immediate neighbours, having been in conjunction at the preceding midnight. Two mornings later, on the 8th, Mars and Jupiter will be extremely close together, coming to a conjunction of only 41 minutes of arc at the following noon. On the next morning, the 9th, Mercury and Jupiter will approach each other, being in conjunction at 2 a.m. On the morning of the 12th Mercury and Mars will again form a pair, having been in conjunction at 11 p.m. of the preceding day. Mercury attains greatest western elongation on the 11th at midnight. The region of the sky wherein this sociable assemblage of celestial wanderers takes place, is that roughly marked by the boundary betwixt Aries and Taurus. Mars rises on the 1st at 3:10 a.m., and on the 30th at 2:20. It is not well seen by the telescopic observer, nor is it particularly attractive to the unassisted vision. Recent progress in Martian research has brought out two interesting facts connected with the planet. The late Prof. Lowell last year announced the existence of certain minute dots on the surface, each lying within one of the polygons formed by the intersections of the "canals".

From each dot fine lines extend out web-like to the corners and sides of the surrounding polygon; these lines being vastly more delicate than the actual "canals" themselves. The other discovery, made by the celebrated observer Antoniadi, is that of a definite relationship between the melting of the Martian polar caps and the sun's period of spot activity. M. Antoniadi,[1] from examination of data and drawings extending back to 1856, has found that the caps shrink by far the more swiftly when the spots on the sun are most numerous; a circumstance confirming the theories of those who declare that the sun's radiation is most intense at spot maxima.

Jupiter rises at 3:20 a.m. on the 1st, and at 1:45 on the 30th, outshining both of the other planets in its vicinity.

Uranus, now past quadrature, is approaching the evening sky. Neptune, in conjunction next month, lies near Venus and Saturn in the early evening heavens.

The Moon's phases for June will be as follows:

Full Moon, 5th..8:07 a.m.

Last Quarter, 13th...1:38 a.m.

New Moon, 19th ....8:02 a.m.

First Quarter, 27th ....11:03 a.m.

Perigee falls on the 8th, Apogee on the 24th. The Moon runs low on the 6th, high on the 18th; crossing the equator on the 11th and 26th. It will be near Jupiter, Mars, and Mercury on the 17th, Venus on the 20th, and Saturn on the 21st.

The Sun enters the Zodiacal sign Cancer on the 21st at 7:14 p.m., thus opening the genial season of summer. The days are then at their longest, giving us about 15 hours a quarter of sunlight. Between the 21st and the end of the month they will decrease by three minutes. On June 19th there will be a partial eclipse of the sun; invisible at Providence, but well seen in the Arctic region. About three-quarters of the solar disc will be obscured at maximum.

Wolf's comet, discovered on April 27, 1916, comes to perihelion on the 16th of this month. It will be visible in a small telescope until September, glowing faintly in the northern sky. This object was found at greater distances from the earth and sun than those of any former comet at the time of discovery; it having been 380,000,000 miles from the earth and 460,000,000 miles from the sun when first seen. On June 16th it will pass within 80,000,000 miles of the earth, and about 156,000,000 miles from the sun. It is a periodic comet; having a parabolic orbit, and a sidereal revolution of about 50 years. After its appearance this summer, it will vanish in the neighbourhood of the sun; reappearing briefly and faintly in the fall of 1918, before it finally vanishes for its half-century sojourn in impenetrable space.

Viewing the sidereal sky, we discover upon the southern meridian the faint Zodiacal constellation of Libra, the Balances, whose only feature of interest is a double star easily discernible as such by the naked eye. Immediately west of Libra, and scarcely past transit, is Virgo, whose bright star Spica shines in rather solitary splendour. About Libra and Virgo, and approximately on the meridian, is Boötes; bearing the refulgent orange-red star Arcturus. This orb is of great size, even as stars are reckoned, being about 100 times larger than our own sun. It is also distinguished for its rapid "proper motion", it having traversed a distance in the sky equal to twice the apparent diameter of the moon since the days of classical antiquity. This fact reminds us that, although we are accustomed to call the stars "fixed", they are actually rushing through space at incredibly rapid rates; only their enormous distance giving them that comparatively unchanging aspect which we know. Delicate instruments are able to record the changes in a star's position during many years; and the spectroscope, whose prismatic image or "spectrum" of an object moves in one direction when the object is receding and in the other direction when it is approaching, enables us to learn that many stars apparently at rest are in reality moving in the line of sight; that is, moving exactly toward or away from us. The rates at which the stars are travelling differ greatly. All are very high, yet the distances involved are such that a period of over 3000 years is necessary for us to perceive any distinct alterations in the figures of the constellations. Certain nebulae, as distinguished from stars proper, are thought to move 621 miles per second. The rates of the visible stars are considerably less. 1830 Groombridge, the most swiftly moving of all the stars, flies on at the velocity of 200 miles per second; whilst 61 Cygni, the next in speed, advances about 100 miles per second. About 25 to 50 miles per second is the speed most frequently observed. Our own star or sun is of course in motion like the rest, carrying the whole solar system at the rate of 16 miles per second toward a point in the sky marked out by the constellation Hercules. This direction has been called the "apex of the sun's way".

East of Boötes lies the Northern Crown, while west of it may be perceived the misty tract of light composing Berenice's Hair. Closely analysed, the latter group may be found to contain three stars of the fourth magnitude and 17 of the fifth, together with a multitude of fainter orbs which impart to it its nebulous appearance. None of these has any individual name, though the asterism is an ancient and historic one. Beyond Virgo and Coma Berenices, Leo is declining in the west; while still farther along the Zodiac Cancer is still seen in full, and Gemini is sinking from sight. In the southwest Hydra is visible in its vast entirety, together with the dependent constellations Crater and Corvus.

In the north Draco may be seen in the full splendour of upper transit. Just beneath it is Ursa Minor, likewise above the pole, and appearing as though balanced on the tip of its tail. The Greater Bear is now inclined downward, at the west of the pole, whilst Cassiopeia, its opposite in the circumpolar sky, is beginning its eastward ascent. Cepheus, which precedes Cassiopeia in the journey around the pole, has attained a fair latitude in the east. Beyond Cepheus is Cygnus, the Swan, well seen for the first time since its disappearance in the west last winter. Deneb, its brightest star, is generally classed as of the first magnitude, though it is not a particularly brilliant specimen of its type. Lower and farther south, the keen observer may detect the neat but tiny rhombus marking Delphinus, the Dolphin; and but little above it may be seen the effulgent rays of Altair, the prime jewel in the constellation Aquila, the Eagle. A great part of the eastern sky is at present occupied by the two large but vague constellations Hercules and Ophiuchus et Serpens, the former of which contains a notable cluster of stars, visible in a good opera glass and catalogued as 13M. This little cluster, so insignificant as viewed by us, is said to contain within its modest compass more than twice as many stars as are visible to the naked eye in the entire sky. In the southwest Scorpio blazes in full view, revealing its kite-like outline and its deep red star Antares. Immediately behind it Sagittarius is rising, the boundary betwixt the two groups being phenomenally replete with nebulae and star clusters visible in opera or field glasses. This pair of Zodiacal constellations is also remarkable for the richness of the Milky Way in its vicinity. Low down, where the southern meridian meets the horizon, stalks the sinister outline of Lupus, the Wolf, a southern group not well seen in the latitude of Rhode Island.

A recent discovery of immense importance to our knowledge of the structure of the universe is that of the incredibly rapid rotation of certain large spiral nebulae. It has been found that many of these vast objects, whose distance is virtually inconceivable, revolve on their axes at rates as high as 200 miles per second; a condition which necessitates the revision of many long-accepted theories regarding their nature. Each fresh advance of celestial science demonstrates with new force how little and how rudimentary is our present information regarding the larger outlines of the visible creation wherein we dwell.

EDITOR'S NOTE FP: *EN* 50, No. 153 (1 June 1917): 3.

Notes

1. Eugène M. Antoniadi (1870–1944), astronomer of Greek ancestry who focused on the study of Mars. He was appointed director of the section on Mars of the British Astronomical Association.

JULY SKIES

Saturn and Venus, the one approaching and the other receding from the sun, are this month quite close together; passing each other in conjunction on the 4th. They are to be found low in the western sky just after sunset, disappearing below the horizon as the evening advances. Venus by far outshines its neighbour, despite the enormous superiority in actual bulk which Saturn possesses. Soon after this conjunction, Saturn will disappear, arriving at its solar conjunction on the 27th. Venus steadily mounts higher in the sky; setting an hour and a quarter after the sun on the 31st, and glowing with an increasingly conspicuous lustre. During July this brilliant planet moves entirely across Cancer into Leo, passing about a degree north of the bright star Regulus on the 27th. In the telescope Venus still exhibits a gibbous phase, through its contour in becoming closer and closer to the half-circle.

Mars has now well emerged from the vicinity of the sun, rising almost three hours before that luminary by the end of the month. It is a noticeable though not predominant feature of the morning sky, moving during July from the constellation Taurus, between the Pleiades and the Hyades, in direct motion.

Mercury, in superior conjunction on the 12th, is practically invisible throughout the month. Neptune, in conjunction on the 28th, soon follows it into invisibility. Uranus, in opposition next month, is well seen in the evening sky by those who possess telescopes.

The moon's phases for July will be as follows:

Full Moon, 4th.. 4:40 p.m.
Last Quarter, 11th..7:12 a.m.
New Moon, 18th .... 10:00 p.m.
First Quarter, 27th ....1:40 a.m.

Perigee falls on the 6th, Apogee on the 22nd. The moon runs low on the 3d and 30th, high on the 15th; crossing the equator on the 9th and 23d. It will be near Jupiter on the 14th, Mars on the 16th, and Venus on the 21st. On the 4th there will be a total eclipse of the moon, invisible here.

The sun enters the Zodiacal sign Leo on the 23d, moving southward four and three-quarters degrees this month. Between the 1st and the 31st the days lose 43 minutes. On the 3d the earth will reach aphelion, or greatest distance from the sun, which has a slight effect in tempering the heat of the season in our Northern hemisphere. On the 18th there will be a partial eclipse of the sun, invisible at Providence, but visible from the Indian Ocean and the Antarctic regions.

The Zodiacal constellation on the meridian this month is Scorpio, the Scorpion, whose well-marked outline and bright stars have given it a deserved celebrity. Chief amongst its brilliants shines Antares, a flaming red orb of much lustre, whose name indicates its similarity to the planet Mars. Antares lies at the heart of the imaginary Scorpion, hence has often been designated as Cor Scorpii. The Chinese, noting the resemblance betwixt Antares and a flame, called the star "The Great Fire." This ruddy gem is on each side flanked by a star of the third magnitude, a condition which emphasizes its splendour and renders it the more conspicuous to the casual beholder. The whole constellation of Scorpio bears a pronounced resemblance to a kite, the effect being most manifest to southern observers on account of the location of the group. Scorpio contains one star of the first magnitude, two of the second, seven of the third, eight of the fourth, and ten of the fifth. The tail of the fabled beast lies in a singularly rich portion of the Milky Way, adjacent to Sagittarius. The mythological significance of Scorpio is peculiarly appropriate to the times, since it is traditionally associated with warfare and violence. As the Roman poet Manilius tells us:

> Bright Scorpio, arm'd with pois'nous tail, prepares
> Men's martial minds for violence and wars;
> His venom heats and boils their blood to rage,
> And rapine spreads o'er the unlucky age.[1]

Above Scorpio lies the vast expanse of Ophiuchus et Serpens, a group having little but size to recommend it to the student's attention. Still higher up is Hercules, equally uninteresting and almost as vast, whose magnificent cluster is visible to the unassisted vision as merely a luminous blur. This group contains 113 stars; of which one, called Ras Aigethi, is of the second magnitude; nine of the third, and 19 of the fourth. The remote ancients regarded this constellation with a curious sense of mystery, acknowledging its prehistoric antiquity and assigning to it no name save "The Man Upon His Knees". In Chaldaea it is said to have typified Ishdubar, who slew a monstrous dragon; and in Phoenicia it represented the God Melkarth. Classical lore identified it with Ixion, Prometheus, and Theseus at various times, finally settling down to the notion of Hercules, most celebrated of the Grecian heroes and demigods. Hercules was the son of Jupiter and Alcmena, and early incurred the hatred of the ever-jealous Juno, who sent two serpents to kill him whilst he was yet an infant. But young as he was, he succeeded in strangling both of the monsters as he lay cradled with his half-brother Iphicles in the shield of Amphitryon, his stepfather. The youth was educated by the famous centaur Chiron, and at the age of 18 slew a great lion that was ravaging the country. He also accompanied the Argonauts on their famous quest of the Golden Fleece. When a young man, having accidentally killed a friend, he gave himself by the advice of the Delphian Oracle into the service of Eurystheus the king, for a term of 12 years, during which time he performed the 12 great labours which have rendered his name the most apt of all personifications of incredible strength. The 12 labours of Hercules are usually given as follows: (1) The killing of the Nemean Lion, whose skin he wore ever after. (2) The destruction of the nine-headed Lernean Hydra. (3) The capture, alive, of the golden-horned and bronze-footed stag. (4) The capture of the Erymanthian Boar. (5) The cleansing of the Augean Stables at Elis, in which 300 oxen had been confined for 30 years. He accomplished this labour by digging a ditch and leading the waters of the rivers Alpheus and Peneus through the filthy stalls. (6) The killing of the huge man-eating Stymphalian Birds of Arcadia. (7) The capture, alive, of the wild bull of Crete. (8) The capture of the horses of Diomedes, that fed on human flesh. (9) The seizure of the girdle of Hippolyta, queen of the warlike Amazons. (10) The killing of the monstrous King Geryon of Gades (Cadiz, Spain) and the driving of his man-eating oxen back to Greece. (11) The obtaining of the three Golden Apples of the Hesperides by the aid of Atlas, during which adventure he held the entire sky on his shoulders for five days. (12) The bringing up to earth of the three-headed dog Cerberus, who guarded the gate of the infernal regions. After the completion of these labours, Hercules again killed a friend; for which he was forced to serve Omphale, Queen of Lydia, for a year. He then married Dejanira, and returned to the Peloponessus. Once, as he and his wife were endeavouring to cross a stream, the centaur Nessus offered to allow Dejanira to ride upon his back; but as soon as she had mounted, attempted to run off with her. Hercules, observing this, at once bent his bow and slew the monster; who, in his dying breath, directed the hero's wife to collect the blood which flowed from his gaping wound, and soak in it one of her husband's robes; which, if ever he became neglectful of her, would restore his affection if worn by him. Now this was but a vindictive scheme of the expiring centaur; for in reality the wearing of the blood-soaked robe would cause the most acute torment of body, ending in death. Some time after, suspecting that Hercules was becoming alienated from her, Dejanira sent him the robe which she had prepared according to the centaur's direction for use at a sacrifice; and no sooner had the hero donned it than he commenced to suffer the most horrible pain and burning. He tried to tear off this fatal vestment, but its venomous folds adhered to his flesh. Unable to obtain relief, Hercules gave his arms to his friend Philoctetes and caused himself to be burned alive on a great pyre on Mount Oeta. But only the mortal part of him was consumed; his immortal portion being carried up to Olympus, where he received as his wife Hebe, the cup-bearer of the Gods.

West of Hercules is the attractive circle of the Northern Crown and the familiar outline of Boötes, the latter containing the resplendent star Arcturus. In the western sky are all the groups of spring; Leo, close to setting, Virgo, still seen to advantage, Corvus, about to disappear, Libra just past transit, and Centaurus, barely seen above the vapours of the southern horizon. In the north we see Draco in upper transit, while Ursa Minor leans westward. Ursa Major is west of the pole, whilst Cepheus and Cassiopeia are ascending eastward of that point. In the northeast portions of Pegasus and Andromeda are appearing, while farther south parts of Aquarius and Capricornus are in sight. Sagittarius, immersed in a particularly rich portion of the Milky Way, graces the southeast, and higher in the eastern sky are Aquila, Delphinus, Equuleus, Sagitta, Lyra, and Cygnus.

These groups of summer, while by no means so resplendent as those of the winter months, are nevertheless possessed of a quiet beauty all their own, which well accords with the genial languor of the season.

EDITOR'S NOTE FP: *EN* 51, No. 25 (2 July 1917): 4.

Notes

1. Manilius, *Astronomica* 4.217–22 (tr. Thomas Creech; a very loose translation).

AUGUST SKIES

Mercury, in greatest eastern elongation on the 22nd, is visible in the early evening sky for several days before and after that date. It should be sought low in the west as soon after sunset as the increasing dusk permits it to be glimpsed. In appearance it is sparkling and ruddy, though not at all conspicuous. The phase of Mercury is easily perceptible in a small telescope of good quality, though the planet possesses no particular features of interest for the amateur observer.

Venus is the principal planet of the evening sky, setting at 8:30 p.m. on the 1st, and at 7:35 on the 31st. Its lustre is now very great, and each day carries it to a more favourable position for study. Next winter it will blaze with immense refulgence. Venus this month moves from the constellation Leo into Virgo.

Jupiter, second to Venus in lustre, is gradually entering the evening sky; rising on the 1st at midnight, and on the 31st at 10:10 p.m. It now lies in the central part of the constellation Taurus, enriching a region already brilliant with fixed stars. The giant planet will next month be in quadrature.

Saturn, in conjunction last month, is reappearing in the morning sky, rising two and a half hours before the sun by the end of August. It is situate in the faint constellation Cancer, near the cluster called Praespe. Saturn is bright, but not comparable in this respect to Jupiter, which shines far to the west of it.

Mars will be visible in the morning sky, rising on the 1st at 1:40 a.m., and on the 31st at 1:13. It moves this month from the western to the eastern part of the constellation Gemini, glowing with slowly increasing lustre.

The faint Uranus is now at its best, coming to opposition on the 14th. Neptune, in conjunction on the 28th of last month, is practically invisible.

The moon's phases for August will be as follows:

Full Moon, 3d		12:11 a.m.
Last Quarter, 9th		2:56 p.m.
New Moon, 17th		1:21 p.m.
First Quarter, 25th		2:08 p.m.

Perigee falls on the 3d, Apogee on the 18th. The moon runs high on the 12th, low on the 26th, crossing the equator on the 5th and 19th. It will be near Jupiter on the 11th, Mars on the 13th, Saturn on the 16th, and Mercury and Venus on the 20th.

The sun enters the Zodiacal sign of Virgo on the 23d. Between the 1st and the 31st the days decrease by nearly an hour and a quarter.

Turning to the constellations, we find upon the southern meridian the Zodiacal group Sagittarius, the Archer, whose glittering expanse is fascinating to the naked eye, and doubly so through an opera glass. Its western portions are involved in the luminous currents of the Milky Way, which also lave the shore of Scorpio. The stars Zeta, Tau, Sigma, Phi, Lambda, and Mu in Sagittarius form an interesting sub-group shaped like an inverted ladle, and called the "Milk Dipper", since it is figuratively of use in ladling the golden stream which flows by it. Above the star Mu at the end of the handle are visible two attractive star clusters, catalogued as 24M and 25M. This region, indeed, is well sprinkled with clusters and nebulae which any good field glass will disclose.

Clusters, nebulae, and the Milky Way are far more important objects in the science of astronomy than they seem to the casual observer; since from their appearance and phenomena are based nearly all our speculations regarding the structure and dimensions of the universe. Though these three types of misty light [reveal?] a similar aspect to the unaided gaze, telescopic examination proves their fundamental differences. A cluster may generally be resolved into stars, like the Milky Way, with the use of powerful magnification; but a true nebula, being a continuous mass of growing gas, defies all attempts of this sort. A few clusters, like the noted Pleiades and Hyades in Taurus, exhibit their true nature without a telescope. Clusters are never the chance results of perspective; there being in all cases a real proximity and relation between the various component stars, as frequently proved by a common motion in the same direction. The Milky Way is one of the most beautiful objects of the night sky. This faint stream of silvery light, spanning the heavens as it sometimes does in a great arch reaching from horizon to horizon, has in all ages inspired the fancy of poet and philosopher alike. That this apparently continuous glowing ribbon is in reality an aggregation of innumerable stars, is now understood by all; and though not actually proven till the time of Galileo and his telescope, was suspected by many even in ancient times. It is not probable that the Milky Way is merely a fortuitous collection of stars; certain facts render it likely that this shining band affords to us a veritable index of our position in space and possesses a fundamental relation to the structure of the visible universe. It is remarkable that all temporary stars, most of the brighter ordinary stars, and a large proportion of the fainter stars are grouped in or near the Milky Way. The Milky Way is not a perfectly regular band of light, its contour being diversified by numerous rifts, divisions, and ramifications. The places along its course are especially destitute of stars, standing out in black contrast to the surrounding fields of light, and receiving the apt name of "Coal Sacks". As a whole, however, the Milky Way forms one continuous great circle, girdling the entire celestial sphere and dividing it into two equal parts. The plane of this circle is called the "Galactic Plane", and the two points each ninety degrees from it are known as the "Galactic Poles", since they bear the same relation to the Galactic Plane as do the terrestrial poles to the plane of the terrestrial equator. The adjective "Galactic" is of course derived from "Galaxy", the Greek name of the Milky Way. Nebulae, as distinguished from clusters and the Milky Way, are undoubtedly composed of incandescent gaseous matter as yet unformed into definite spherical suns or stars. About 10,000 nebulae are at present known and recorded, the brightest being those in Andromeda and Orion, which are visible to the naked eye. The size of most nebulae must be well-nigh incomprehensible, for whilst the stars, some of which are thousands of times larger than our sun, present no sensible surface as seen from the earth, yet many of the nebulae cover comparatively large areas in our sky.

Dr. Wolf has recently estimated the diameters of certain nebulae at from 900 to 2000 light years (a light year equals 5,869,588,236,000 miles); these bodies being situated from 33,000 to 578,000 light years away. While the stars, both individually [and] in clusters, seem to abound mainly near the Galactic Plane; the nebulae, with the exception of the "planetary" variety, are most numerous around the galactic poles, where the stars are but thinly scattered. Nebulae differ widely in figure and extent. The massive nebula in Andromeda is oval in form, having a sort of nucleus or central condensation, as well as two bright and apparently attendant nebulae beside it. The outer parts suggest the belief that it is of spiral shape. The great nebula in Orion is widespread and diffuse, being wholly without definite outlines. The rather rare "planetary" nebulae, which unlike the others are found in and near the Milky Way, are round and of uniform brilliancy like the discs of the planets. The nebula in Lyra is annular or ring-like in form, whilst one in Sagittarius appears to be split up into three great divisions, the rifts being plainly visible. The spiral nebula in Canes Venatici seems to consist of a central body in the act of throwing off part of its component matter in the form of a second condensation. The "Horseshoe" and "Dumb-bell" nebulae in Sagittarius, and the "Crab" nebula in Taurus, resemble in large telescopes the objects from which they are named. According to the best authorities, the normal type of non-planetary nebula is spiral. The well-known Pleiades cluster possesses a vast nebulous background obviously connected with the component stars themselves, since many of the larger Pleiades have small particles of nebulous matter about them. Although according to the best authorities all nebulae are affected by a slow continuous change, nothing of the kind has as yet been noted, in connection with any of them. That they are actually composed of self-luminous gas, was satisfactorily demonstrated with the spectroscope in 1864 by the late Sir William Huggins.[1] The rotation of nebulae on their axes has long been assumed on theoretical grounds, yet not until 1914 was the assumption verified by observation. In that year Dr. Slipher of the Lowell Observatory found with the spectroscope that a nebula in Virgo performs such a motion. All the nebulae have "proper motions" like stars through space, most of them proceeding with a tremendous velocity. Our notions as to the structure of the great universe whereof we form so infinitesimal a part depend largely upon observations concerning the distribution of the stars and nebulae, and especially their relation to the Milky Way. More than a century ago Sir William Herschel made a most diligent survey of the heavens, and enunciated that theory of the universe which with but few modifications we still accept. From a long and accurate enumeration of the stars in all parts of the sky, Dr. Herschel found that most of them form a great circle, or rather a broad circular band; roughly coinciding with the Galactic Plane, and consisting mainly of the Galaxy itself. The stars outside this belt he saw to be few and scattered. Upon these facts he built his hypothesis, which assumes the visible stellar universe to consist of an immense cluster of stars, the components disposed with moderate uniformity and the whole so shaped that it forms a thin flat disc of incredible magnitude, near whose centre lies our own solar system. When we look along that circle in the sky which corresponds to the plane of the cluster wherein we are situate, we are of course looking through a deep circular layer of stars, whose thickness is equal to the radius of the great cluster itself, and which appears to us as the Milky Way and its stellar neighbours; but when we gaze at the Galactic Poles, the number of stars seen by us is very small, since our vision is then directed at an attenuated layer of stars, whose depth is but half the thickness of the great flat cluster. The spiral nebulae, which abound near the Galactic Poles, may perhaps constitute a gigantic spherical aggregation, with the stellar disc as one of the great circles. That most nebulae belong to our universe seems probable, though it was once believed that they, as well as clusters, are other universes, or external Galaxies, as it were. Whether or not such things as other universes do exist, is a question of the highest interest, involving conceptions of the most awful grandeur. It is very likely that these colossal universes of suns are widely scattered through boundless space, though separated by such terrifying and abysmal distances that their light, sent on its way at the time of their creation, has not yet reached from one to the other. It were useless here to speak of the ultimate confines of space itself. If the monstrous distances dealt with in the ordinary study of astronomy be stupefying in their immensity, what may be said of infinity itself? The idea of a boundary to all space is even more repellent than the terrible conception of the illimitable.

Among the attractive stars and constellations of the month we may mention Vega, high in the sky and almost in transit; Altair, soon to attain the southern meridian; Scorpio, just past transit; Corona Borealis and Boötes in the west; and Perseus, Andromeda, and Cygnus, forming a line from the northeastern horizon to the zenith. By midnight the Pleiades come to view, foretelling in unmistakable terms the sad proximity of chilling autumn.

EDITOR'S NOTE FP: *EN* 51, No. 49 (31 July 1917): 3.

Notes

1. Sir William Huggins (1824–1910), British astronomer, president of the Royal Society (1900–05), and a pioneer in the investigation of nebulae and the use of the spectroscope.

SEPTEMBER SKIES

Venus is now prominent in the early evening heavens, shining brightly in the west as soon as the sun has set, and long before the twilight gathers thickly. Its appearance against the sunset sky much precedes that of any other star-like object, hence it glimmers in solitary splendour until the darkness has become pronounced. On the 1st, it sets at 7:35 p.m., and on the 30th at 7. In a telescope it exhibits a diminishing gibbous phase, though possessing no superficial configurations discernible by the amateur observer. During September Venus moves from the constellation Virgo into Libra, passing close to the bright star Spica on the 9th.

Jupiter, the sole planetary rival of Venus, arrives at quadrature on the 3d; rising on the 1st at 10:09 p.m., and on the 30th at 8:16. To the telescopic observer it presents the spectacle of a large and rather flattened disc, streaked with dark and light horizontal belts, and surrounded by four well visible satellites. The motions of these satellites, their eclipses, occultations, and transits, form a pleasing picture of celestial activity to the diligent astronomer; and are predicted with great accuracy in the National Almanack. Jupiter now lies in the constellation Taurus, in direct motion.

Saturn is now well visible in the morning sky, rising on the 1st at 2:34 a.m., and on the 30th at 12:50. It lies in the constellation Cancer, and is in direct motion. Through a telescope Saturn reveals a disc of substantial size, encircled by the famous system of rings, now fairly well extended to the eye, though gradually narrowing in perspective. The system will be turned edgewise to the earth five years hence, as it was ten years ago, causing it to disappear from all ordinary vision. The satellites of Saturn are less interesting than those of Jupiter, though several of them are visible in small telescopes.

Mars, whose very slow synodic revolution causes it to change but little from month to month, is a pleasing though not conspicuous figure in the morning sky. On the 1st it rises at 1:18 a.m., and on the 30th at 12:50, exactly the same time as Saturn, near which it now lies. The two planets will be in conjunction with each other on the first of next month. During September Mars moves from the constellation Gemini well into Cancer.

Mercury will be in inferior conjunction on the 18th, therefore being virtually invisible throughout the month. The advanced telescopist frequently studies this planet in the daytime, locating it by means of mathematical devices when it cannot be found or seen with the naked eye. This mode of observation is of twofold advantage; eliminating the glare and low altitude encountered during morning or evening twilight visibility and allowing the observer to view it during a much longer period of time than that in which it appears to the unassisted sight. Mercury, however, generally disappoints the novice as a telescopic object.

Uranus, just past opposition, is comparatively well seen in the evening sky, whilst Neptune has now emerged far enough from solar conjunction to be caught by the telescope in the early morning.

The moon goes through five phases during August, as follows:

Full Moon, 1st ....7:36 a.m.

Last Quarter, 8th... 3:05 p.m.

New Moon, 16th ....5:28 a.m.

First Quarter, 24th ....12:41 a.m.

Full Moon, 30th .... 3:31 p.m.

Perigee occurs on the 1st and 29th, Apogee on the 14th. The moon runs high on the 8th, low on the 23d, crossing the equator on the 1st, 15th, and 29th. It will be near Jupiter on the 7th, Mars on the 11th, Saturn on the 13th, and Venus on the 19th. The second full moon this month will be the "Harvest Moon", celebrated alike in science and story. Its particular feature is that it rises at nearly the same time for several nights after the full, permitting the early evening watcher to enjoy its beauties far into its wane.

The Sun enters the Zodiacal sign Libra on the 23d at 10:01 a.m., thereby inaugurating the dreary season of Autumn. The days and the nights are now of equal length, the former decreasing about an hour and 20 minutes during the month. The solar disc is now the seat of considerable activity; 46 spots having been visible last month in a small telescope, several of which could also be discerned with the naked eye. In viewing the sun, the eye must always be protected by means of smoked or heavily tinted glasses, lest the overpowering radiance cause injury to the sight.

The most captivating feature of the September sidereal sky is the return of the Pleiades. For the most part, the heavens are dull, since the gay groups of summer are passing toward the west whilst the dazzling stars of winter have not yet appeared; but just above the northeastern horizon we may glimpse that delightful sight which Tennyson must have appreciated so keenly when he wrote:

> "Many a night I saw the Pleiads,
>   Rising through the mellow shade,
> Glitter like a swarm of fireflies
>   Tangled in a silver braid."[1]

This exquisite cluster, a herald of the brighter pageant soon to be unfolded, scintillates alluringly and prophetically; half reconciling us to the wintry era it portends.

Another beauty of September evenings is the Milky Way, traversing the vault from the northeast to the southwest like a broad and majestic road of ethereal phosphorescence. Best seen in the rural districts and in the absence of the moon, it seems at times of striking vividness; as though we might literally ascend its glowing slope and reach with our own feet those celestial heights which in reality we may know only from an infinite distance.

The Zodiacal constellation on the meridian this month is Capricornus, the Sea-Goat, which formerly marked the sun's position at the winter solstice, and whose traditions are consequently associated with the wintry season. Of this group the Grecian poet Aratus wrote:

> "When Capricorn the radiant sun contains,
> Impetuous winds tumultuate the mains.
> The freezing sailors tremble in the blast,
> And numbly cluster round the ice-deck'd mast."[2]

As viewed casually, Capricornus is a dull group, attracting attention only because of its two brightest stars, Giadi and Dabih, which lie directly below Altair in the Eagle. These stars are of the third magnitude and are bright only by contrast with the surrounding void. Giadi is an apparent double star; that is, is composed of two independent stars which chance to be nearly in the line of sight. This duplicity, which is perceptible to the naked eye, was not remarked by the ancients; since the angular distance between the components was not great enough for notice till comparatively modern times. Dabih is also double, though a binocular is required to reveal this condition. The smaller component is of beautiful blue colour which never fails to impress the observer.

Above Capricornus is Aquila, with the bright Altair, north and east of which lie the three tiny but ancient groups Delphinus, Equuleus and Sagitta. Of these Delphinus, the Dolphin, is best known; since its stars form a delicate but noticeable figure of diamond shape, popularly called "The Coffin".

Above this assemblage and almost in the zenith, is the magnificent Cygnus, or the Swan, which Macpherson[3] has described as "perhaps the most interesting constellation in the entire heavens". Lying immediately east of Lyra, it vastly surpasses that group in magnitude, though it boasts no star equal to Vega in lustre. The general shape of Cygnus is cruciform, giving rise to the common appellation "Northern Cross". At the head of the cross is Deneb, the Alpha of the constellation and a gem of first magnitude. At the centre is Gamma, and at the base is Beta, or Albireo, a striking double star of the third magnitude whose larger component is topaz yellow and whose smaller component is sapphire blue. Albireo is one of the most celebrated and beautiful sights in the heavens, only a good field glass being necessary to exhibit its duplex nature and contrasted colours. The Milky Way completely immerses Cygnus, adding its own splendour to that of the constellation itself. Near the upper part of the cross lies the celebrated "Northern Coal Sack", a starless area whose blackness is doubly emphasised by the brilliancy of the surrounding regions. Cygnus contains the famous 61 Cygni, one of the nearest of all the stars, which lies seven light-years or 459,000 astronomical units away from our system. An astronomical unit is about 93,000,000 miles, being the mean distance of the earth from the sun.

Just west of Cygnus is Lyra, the Lyre, a small but noted asterism whose effulgent star Vega is one of the most splendid objects in the northern sky. Beta, in this constellation, is of changing brilliancy, and has been taken as typical of a well-defined species of variable stars. It shifts betwixt the third and fourth magnitudes in somewhat less than 13 days; probably being composed of two stars, one brighter than the other, revolving round a common centre of gravity and alternately eclipsing each other. Epsilon Lyrae appears double to the keen naked eye, and in the telescope each of the components is shewn to be double as well; making a quadruple system. Lyra, and in particular its star Delta, occupies that part of space toward which our own solar system is believed to be moving at the rate of 11 miles per second, though many thousand years will be required to effect any sensible alteration of present conditions.

The summer constellations, including Sagittarius, Scorpio, Ophiuchus et Serpens, Hercules, Corona Borealis, and Boötes, are all in the western sky; Scorpio indeed having partly set.

In the north we behold Ursa Major preparing to glide beneath the pole, whilst Ursa Minor lies due west of that point. Cassiopeia, preceded by Cepheus, is about to climb above the pole.

In the northeast Auriga is rising, bearing with it the matchless Capella. Just as the advent of Arcturus marks the approach of spring, so does Capella herald the autumn and the harvest. Above Auriga, Perseus reveals his brilliant presence, presenting a multitude of stellar gems set in the richest portion of the Milky Way. Looking still higher we discover Andromeda at an advantageous altitude. Just south of Auriga the Pleiades are appearing, above them lying Aries and Triangula. Due east and south Cetus is rising, while Pisces is entirely above the horizon. High in the east is Pegasus, with the Zodiacal group Aquarius below it. Low in the southeast shines Fomalhaut in lone glory; a bright transient star whose beams are thrice welcome in a generally dismal season.

The 100-inch mirror of the long awaited Mount Wilson reflector has now been successfully transported to its final destination, and the colossal instrument may soon be counted amongst the active heavy artillery of astronomical research. This largest of all telescopes may well be expected to add much to our knowledge of the visible universe, and it is with keen anticipation that the scientific world awaits its completion and dedication.

EDITOR'S NOTE FP: *EN* 51, No. 76 (31 August 1917): 3.

Notes

1. Alfred, Lord Tennyson (1809–1892), "Locksley Hall" (1842), ll. 9–10 (HPL has divided each line into two lines).
2. Aratus, *Phaenomena* 288–93.
3. Hector Macpherson (1888–1956), Scottish writer on astronomy.

OCTOBER SKIES

Mercury this month attains greatest western elongation on the 4th, being visible about that date in the morning twilight just above the sunrise point. The elongation is a reasonably favourable one, since those west of the sun are best displayed in autumn. There is little of interest to recommend Mercury to the casual observer, yet the glimpsing of this elusive planet is not without a certain satisfaction.

Venus dominates the evening sky, shining in the west with intense lustre, setting on the 1st at 6:58 p.m. and on the 31st at 6:45. Its gibbous phase is rapidly shrinking, and by the end of next month the planet will have become a half circle. During October Venus moves from the constellation Libra into Scorpio and Ophiuchus, passing near the flaming red star Antares on the 18th. Needless to say, its superlative radiance quite outshines the humbler yet not inconsiderable lustre of the fixed star.

Venus is the only bright planet technically in the evening sky; but Jupiter, in opposition next month, gorgeously adorns the east in the later evening hours. On the 1st it rises at 8:16 p.m., and on the 31st at 6:10. At the beginning of the month Jupiter's direct motion changes to retrograde, and throughout October the planet will recede amongst the stars of the constellation Taurus. Its enormous brilliancy, though much inferior to that of Venus, will impress the observer after the brighter body has set.

Mars and Saturn are close neighbours in the morning sky, being in conjunction with each other on the 1st of the month. At that time they rise together at 12:49 a.m. Saturn moves but slowly, remaining in the eastern part of the constellation Cancer; but Mars, less sluggish a traveller, journeys well into Leo before the month is over, passing close to the bright star Regulus on the 30th. On the 31st Saturn rises at 1 p.m.; Mars at 12:19 a.m. Saturn will quadrature next month, though Mars will not reach that aspect till December.

Uranus is to be numbered amongst the inconspicuous evening planets; whilst Neptune, in quadrature on the 20th, adorns the morning sky with even feebler beams. Neither is to be discerned without optical assistance.

The moon's phases for October will be as follows:

Last Quarter, 7th.. 5:14 p.m.
New Moon, 15th .... 9:41 p.m.
First Quarter, 23d...9:38 a.m.
Full Moon, 30th ....1:19 a.m.

Apogee falls on the 11th, Perigee on the 27th. The moon runs high on the 5th, low on the 20th; crossing the equator on the 13th and 26th. It will pass near Jupiter on the 5th, Saturn and Mars on the 10th, Venus on the 19th, and Uranus on the 24th. The full moon this month is known as the "Hunter's Moon", since our satellite remains visible in the evening sky for some time after the full phase is past. This is a feeble repetition of the more noted "Harvest Moon" of the preceding month.

The sun enters the Zodiacal sign Scorpio on the 23d, thus proclaiming the near approach of the unwelcome season of frost and chill. That this dismal period is not without its redeeming features, however, is well illustrated by the anonymous verses, which head the page for October, 1800, in our perennial friend and companion, "The Old Farmer's Almanack". Written 118 years ago, they are equally true for the present age:

> "Pomona joyous spreads her copious stores,
>   And with her blessings glads the fertile shores;
>   The sky serene assumes a deep'ning blue,
>   And ev'ry grove puts on a motley hue."

In the evening sky of October we behold the first heralds of winter's magnificent stellar display. Taurus, with its bright Aldebaran and its two attractive clusters, the Pleiades and the Hyades, is fully above the horizon; whilst Auriga, with the gorgeous Capella, now shines at a great altitude. The Zodiacal constellation on the meridian this month is the dull Aquarius, the Water-Bearer, from whose urn flows the chilly stream wherein disports Piscis Australis, the Southern Fish. The brightest star of the latter group, Fomalhaut by name, is nearly in transit low in the south. Fomalhaut, though but ill seen in the Mother Country, appears to considerable advantage in America, lending its brilliant beams to a region otherwise quite desolate. Mr. Garrett P. Serviss has said of this star, that it is "like a distant watch-fire gleaming in the midst of a lonely prairie". It is worth noting that the name of Fomalhaut is not to be pronounced in the French fashion, as many textbooks erroneously direct through false etymology. The word is an Arabic one, and is sounded exactly as spelled.

On the meridian above Aquarius is the expansive constellation of Pegasus, the Winged Horse. The most conspicuous feature of this group is its "Great Square", one of whose stars is held in common by the constellations Pegasus and Andromeda. The Square is not quite in transit at 9 p.m., our chosen hour of observation. Just west of the meridian are Cygnus, Lyra, Delphinus, Equuleus, Sagitta, Aquila, and Capricornus, all well seen; whilst Hercules, Boötes, Corona Borealis, Ophiuchus et Serpens, and Sagittarius are setting or about to set. Grus, the Crane, scrapes the southern horizon below Fomalhaut, though it is not readily noticeable save in the Southern states.

In the North we behold the "Plough" or "Dipper" or Ursa Major below the pole and right side up. Ursa Minor and Draco are west of the pole, Cepheus in upper transit, and Cassiopeia about to assume that position. In the eastern sky are Auriga, Taurus, Perseus, Aries, Pisces, Cetus, and Andromeda; the latter containing one of the most famous nebulae in the entire sky. In our August article we noted that the nebula in Andromeda is of elliptical aspect, having a central condensation and at least two attendant nebulae beside it. We suggested that such an object might afford a key to the evolution of planetary or solar systems from the nebulous condition. Let us now see what astronomers have done toward the development of such a theory.

Whilst the origin of the universe is a problem whose solution has so far defied the efforts of the scientist and the philosopher; we may nevertheless trace the process of creation for a great distance into the past, and be reasonably certain that all the stars, and whatever planets may attend them, are the results of evolution from the nebulous form. In fact, we may picture a remotely ancient age in which our universe contained nothing but nebulae. The celebrated French mathematician and astronomer Pierre Simon, Marquis de la Place, has given us the clearest of all theories concerning the metamorphosis of a nebula into a solar system. His hypothesis is borne out as well by the forms and motions of the sun and planets of our own system, as by the figures of those sidereal bodies still in the nebulous condition. In tracing the evolution of the solar system, Laplace's Nebular Hypothesis assumes the existence at first of an immense mass of highly heated gaseous matter; in other words, a great nebula. This nebula takes a roughly spherical shape from the action of gravitation; and on account of differences in the original motion of its parts, it begins to rotate on its axis at an extremely rapid rate. The centrifugal force generated by this rotation causes the mass to bulge out at the equator, and at length to throw off matter at that place, leaving a ring like that of Saturn. Later, as the original mass cools and contracts, it throws off and leaves behind other rings; all of which breaks up into globular planets which rotate on their axes and revolve around the original mass, and which in turn throw off rings of their own to form satellites. The smaller planets doubtless cool and solidify more swiftly; so that in our own solar system the four inner planets, though they must be more recently formed, have now become quite cold and solid, at least superficially; whilst the outer planets are still hot and molten. The parent mass is of course now represented by the radiant sun itself, whose great size will keep it hot and luminous for thousands of years to come. Although some parts of the hypothesis of Laplace have lately been challenged, the theory rests upon too sound a basis to be lightly shaken; and is still the most probable explanation of the origin of the sun and stars. Since we perceive that all the bodies in the universe appear to be cooling off, we just need inquire how long the present order of things will endure; how long before our sun, as well as the other suns of space, will have lost their fires, and whirl onward; cold, dark, and unnoticed. To this it is impossible to reply. That all the stars are not of equal age, is obvious. When one dies out, it is possible that some object now a nebula will have by that time evolved into a stellar system to take its place; so that no matter how many of the present stars expire, the universe will never want for suns so long as the nebulae hold out. Whether or not new nebulae are being created by some unknown means, it is difficult to say. It is a fundamental principle in the science of physics, that neither matter nor energy may be created or destroyed. Since the stars and nebulae are constantly distributing energy in the form of light and heat, and since they cannot create more to replace that which they are losing, it follows that some day their activity must all be dissipated into infinity as unavailable waves of radiant heat, too feeble to produce any perceptible effects. The resulting scene of desolation will be terrible indeed. A vast sepulchral universe of unbroken midnight gloom and perpetual arctic frigidity, through which will roll dark, cold suns with their hordes of dead, frozen planets, on which will lie the dust of those unhappy mortals who will have perished as their dominant stars faded from their skies. Such is the depressing picture of a future too remote for calculation, yet the understanding shrinks from its conception. Though the strict canons of natural science foretell this result, the philosophical mind cannot accept it without qualification. Infallible as physics may be in ordinary matters, it cannot trace back to its source the energy with which all creation is now pervaded; so why must we accept these attempts to predict its ultimate disposition? Almost inconceivable as is an eternity of the universe of space, a definite beginning and end are still more repugnant to rational reflection.

EDITOR'S NOTE FP: *EN* 51, No. 96 (2 October 1917): 4.

NOVEMBER SKIES

During the present month both Venus and Jupiter, the brightest and next brightest of the planets, reach their most favourable positions for evening observation.

Venus, now high above the western horizon each evening after sunset, arrives at greatest eastern elongation on the 30th; then being at its greatest apparent distance from the sun, and setting about three hours and a quarter after the luminary. To the naked eye it is of intense brilliancy, though not yet at its maximum. In the telescope it displays, at the time of elongation, an exactly semicircular phase; which will shrink to a crescent during the ensuing weeks. The phases of Venus are very easy to discern with even a small instrument, but beyond them the planet is of little interest as a telescopic object. Its high albedo or reflective power gives rise to a trying glare which prevents clear observation except by daylight; and its surface is apparently so densely enshrouded by a cloudy atmosphere, that few or no permanent markings are visible. Not even the most powerful telescopes can furnish conclusive evidences of the topography of Venus; the dubious state of our knowledge being plainly shewn by the fact that observers are divided into two factions regarding the planet's period of rotation, as determined by its surface. Whilst one group of astronomers believe that the day of Venus is much like that of the earth, amounting to about 23 hours and 21 minutes; another and equally numerous group declare with equal positiveness that the rotation period is of the same length as the planet's period of revolution around the sun, a condition analogous to that of the moon in its behaviour toward the earth. If the latter theory be true, then Venus keeps one hemisphere perpetually turned toward the sun and the other perpetually turned away. It is very singular that different observers, studying the same planetary disc, should arrive at conclusions so widely different; but the case at least illustrates the very vague and elusive nature of such markings as may exist. Attempts at solving the rotation problem by other means, mainly spectroscopic, seem to be almost equally indefinite. Venus this month moves eastward amongst the stars of the constellation Sagittarius. On the 1st it sets at 6:53 p.m., and on the 30th at 7:28.

Jupiter, second only to Venus in lustre, gleams gorgeously in the eastern evening sky. On the 29th it will be in opposition to the sun, and therefore nearest the earth, its refulgence then attaining its maximum. The large flattened disc of Jupiter, with its broad horizontal belts of alternate light and dark shading, may be clearly seen in almost any telescope; and the four larger satellites with their various configurations are scarcely less prominent. Jupiter is thought to be radically different from the earth in its physical composition, and probably contains relatively little solid matter. It is a sort of hot, molten, semi-sun, with the exterior at least of a gaseous nature. That the majority of the markings we see are real topographical features, is very likely; since only certain isolated details like the celebrated "Red Spot" shew any permanence. The belts, like the dark stratus clouds of our own sunset sky, are in all probability atmospheric phenomena of some sort. The fluid or semi-fluid consistency of Jupiter is vividly shewn by the planet's unequal rotation, certain parts such as the white spots moving at an appreciably greater speed than other regions. The four larger satellites of Jupiter form an interesting telescopic picture as they move through their various aspects, transiting over the disc of the planet preceded or followed by their shadows, suffering eclipse, or occultation by their primary, and continually altering their relative positions. Jupiter is this month in retrograde motion, its brief course lying through the constellation Taurus, near twinkling Pleiades and Hyades. It rises on the 1st at 6:09 p.m. On the 29th it is opposite the sun, and on the 30th it sets at 6:47 a.m. Generally speaking, it is visible all night throughout the month.

Saturn shines brightly in the morning and late evening sky, rising on the 1st at 10:38 p.m., and on the 30th at 9:04. On the 6th it passes quadrature. Its place amongst the stars changes but little from week to week. It is still in the eastern part of the constellation Cancer, moving directly till the 26th and thereafter retrograding. Its brilliancy is increasing steadily, and shews to advantage against a dull stellar background. In a telescope the rings and larger satellites of Saturn are ever an attractive sight.

Mars, last month in close conjunction with Saturn, now lags somewhat behind its fellow planet in point of rising; appearing above the horizon at 12:19 a.m. on the 1st, and at 11:40 p.m. on the 30th. It is in direct motion through the constellation Leo, being rather near the bright star Regulus at the beginning of the month. The brilliancy of Mars is at present much below that of Saturn.

Mercury, in superior conjunction on the 3d, will be virtually invisible throughout the month. Its next appearance will be in December, in the evening sky.

Uranus, an evening planet, comes to quadrature on the 12th, its position then being in the constellation Capricornus. Neptune is in the morning sky past quadrature, lying in the constellation Cancer. Both of these faint objects require a telescope for observation.

The moon's phases for November will be as follows:

Last Quarter, 6th.. 12:04 p.m.
New Moon, 14th .... 1:28 p.m.
First Quarter, 21st .... 5:29 p.m.
Full Moon, 28th .... 1:41 p.m.

Apogee falls on the 8th, Perigee on the 24th. The moon runs high on the 2nd and 29th, low on the 16th; crossing the equator on the 9th and 23d. It will be near Jupiter on the 1st, Saturn on the 6th, Mars on the 8th, Venus on the 18th, and Jupiter again on the 28th.

The sun enters the Zodiacal sign Sagittarius on the 23d, moving southward 7 degrees and 14 minutes during the month. Between the 1st and the 30th the days lose about one hour in length.

November is generally replete with meteors, or shooting stars, most of which appear in the early morning hours of the 14th, 15th, and 16th, when the earth encounters the Leonid group; or on the evenings of the 23d, 24th, and 25th, when the Andromedes strike our atmosphere. These small celestial objects, impinging forcibly on the upper atmospheric strata, are ignited by friction and generally consumed to dust before they can reach the ground. Those few which are not reduced to ashes, are frequently discovered as meteoric stones.

In the siderial skies of November we behold the advent of the refulgent winter groups. Perseus, Auriga, and Taurus are high in the eastern heavens, whilst Orion is rising due east, with Gemini somewhat north of it. By midnight the two Dogs will have appeared in full splendour. The Zodiacal constellation on the southern meridian at 9 p.m. is the dull and diffuse Pisces, whose uninteresting expanse is chiefly notable for the fact that it contains the so-called "vernal equinox" or point in the sky where the sun crosses the equator on its northward journey. This point marks the prime meridian from which Right Ascension is reckoned eastward. The vernal equinox is often called the "First Point in Aries", since at the time it was defined, the sun's path intersected the equator at the westernmost boundary of that constellation. But a slow circling of the earth's axis called "precession" causes the equator to move through the sky, shifting the vernal equinox backward as the centuries pass, and carrying the arbitrary "signs of the Zodiac" out of the twelve constellations with which they originally coincided, and from which they were named.

Above Pisces, and not far below the zenith itself, is an immense quadrilateral of bright stars which no observer can mistake. This is the "Great Square of Pegasus"; three of whose stars belong to the constellation of that name, the fourth being claimed jointly by Pegasus, and by Andromeda, which adjoins it on the east. Andromeda is a very attractive group, besides having distinction as the possessor of the great nebula described last month.

In the western sky we find the groups of summer and early autumn, many of them about to set. The brilliant Lyra and the scarcely less brilliant Cygnus are still high in the sky, but Aquila is soon to disappear. The small groups Delphinus, Equuleus, and Sagitta are all well seen, while in the southwest Aquarius, Capricornus, and Piscis Australis still shine. Fomalhaut, in the latter group, beams with solitary, almost wistful rays; struggling to glow through the mists above which it may never rise in the latitude of Providence. Farther south are the faint trio of Grus, Sculptor, and Phoenix; the last two on the meridian.

In the north we behold the "Plough" and "Dipper" below the pole, though tilted upward as if preparing for its winter ascent. Draco is slowly gliding beneath the pole, whilst the Lesser Bear is hanging dejectedly downward. Cassiopeia, involved in a splendidly rich region of the Milky Way, is in upper transit. Its characteristic figure, which resembles the letter "W", is nearly upside down. Just ahead of this group, and beginning to shine on the western side of the pole, is the less impressive Cepheus. Looking eastward, along the horizon we find the comparatively modern constellation Lynx coming to view; south of which are the rising brilliants of winter. In the southeast the vaguely defined streams of Fluvius Eridanus are visible, while Cetus, bulky and ponderous, is now at an excellent altitude. Above Cetus is the small but neat figure of Aries.

An asteroid which most astronomers classify as the smallest of all the planets has just been discovered by the celebrated Massachusetts amateur, Rev. Joel H. Metcalf, of Winchester, formerly of Taunton. According to present measurements, this tiny world has a diameter of less than three miles, which places it beneath even the satellites of Mars in magnitude. Much might be said and written by persons of imaginative cast, concerning the features and possible inhabitants of this pygmy sphere.

EDITOR'S NOTE FP: *EN* 51, No. 125 (5 November 1917): 3.

DECEMBER SKIES

Venus, fairest of the planets, is now near the height of its splendour; forming an object of great conspicuousness in the western sky after sunset. So intense is its lustre at this point in its course, that it is frequently mistaken by the ignorant for an artificial light; and it would be not at all improbable if some wily German propagandist were to turn its presence to his advantage by using it as basis for rumours of a conquering air fleet of illuminated super-Zeppelins. In the telescope it exhibits a thick but steadily diminishing crescentic phase, and is increasing markedly in apparent diameter. The conditions are somewhat peculiar, in that the planet's phase shrinks whilst its apparent size grows. As long as the increase of disc outweighs the thinning of the crescent, the net illuminated surface will grow larger, and Venus will continue to grow brighter; but when the visible area becomes so attenuated that the greater size fails to counterbalance the waning phase, the process is reversed, and the planet commences to grow fainter. This turning point will be encountered next month. Since greatest elongation is now past, Venus is approaching the sun; though that circumstance does not at once become apparent in the times of setting. On the 1st the planet sets at 7:30 p.m., about three hours and a quarter after the sun, and on the 31st it will set at 7:53, almost three hours and a half after the sun. During September Venus moves from the constellation Sagittarius into Capricornus, and more than half across the latter group.

Jupiter continues to be the centre of interest in the eastern and southern evening sky. In opposition on November 20th, it still shines refulgently amidst the bright stars of the constellation Taurus. It is now retrograding in the region betwixt the Pleiades and the Hyades. On the 1st Jupiter sets at 6:45 a.m., and on the 31st at 6:30. In lustre it is second only to Venus among the planets.

Mars, a morning planet, arrives at quadrature, or a point 90 degrees from the sun, on the 11th of the month; at that time presenting most noticeably the gibbous aspect which marks its only change of phase. In general it may be said that the superior planets, or those outside the earth's orbit, do not exhibit genuine phases such as those of the inferior planets and the moon; but Mars, and to a vastly less extent Jupiter, plainly suffer a certain [. . .] shading is utterly negligible, and quite difficult to discover; but Mars attains a palpably gibbous appearance, unmistakable even in comparatively small telescopes. None of the more remote superior planets are thus affected, even in the least degree. To the naked eye, Mars is now a prominent object, gleaming with ruddy beams of increasing intensity. At the beginning of the month it is exactly as bright as the star Aldebaran, but by the 31st it will have grown nearly as brilliant as Procyon. During December Mars will be in direct motion, passing from the constellation Leo into Virgo. On the 1st it rises at 11:40 p.m., and on the 31st at 10:40.

Saturn, though not yet in opposition, is virtually an evening planet; rising on the 1st at about 9 a.m., and on the 31st at about 7. It is now retrograding slowly in the constellation Cancer, beaming with much conspicuousness both on account of its intrinsic radiance and on account of its isolation in a region of dull stars. Its brilliancy at the beginning of the month is about the same as that of Procyon, but by the end it will rival that of Rigel.

Mercury arrives at greatest eastern elongation on the 17th, being then visible as a twinkling ruddy spark low in the west just after sunset. The present elongation is not a particularly favourable one. On the 13th Mercury will be only three degrees south of the new moon's extremely attenuated crescent. Whether the conjunction can be well seen is quite doubtful, since the moon will be but little past the change.

Uranus, now past quadrature, is in the evening sky, coming into conjunction with Venus on the last day of the month. Neptune, in opposition next month, is observable in the morning and later evening by the telescope.

The moon's phases for December will be as follows:

Last Quarter, 6th...9:14 a.m.
New Moon, 14th ....4:17 a.m.
First Quarter, 21st..1:07 a.m.
Full Moon, 28th ....4:53 a.m.

Apogee falls on the 6th, Perigee on the 18th. The moon runs low on the 13th, high on the 26th, crossing the equator on the 6th and 20th. It will be near Saturn on the 4th, Mars on the 9th, Mercury on the 15th, Venus on the 17th, Jupiter on the 20th, and Saturn again on the 31st.

Two eclipses will occur this month, an annular eclipse of the sun and a total eclipse of the moon. The solar eclipse, which occurs on the 14th, will be invisible at Providence, but visible in the Antarctic regions and the southern parts of the American and Australian continents. The lunar eclipse falls on the 28th, and will be generally visible here, except for the final emergence of the moon from the earth's penumbra, which will take place after our satellite has set in the morning. The phases are as follows:

Moon enters Penumbra..1:54 a.m.
Moon enters Shadow..3:05 a.m.
Beginning of Totality..4:38 a.m.
Middle of Eclipse ....4:46 a.m.
Ending of Totality...4:55 a.m.
Moon leaves Shadow...6:27 a.m.
Moon leaves Penumbra..7:39 a.m.

The sun enters the Zodiacal sign Capricornus on the 22nd at 4:46 a.m., thereby opening the dismal winter season. However, as we have more than once noted in these articles, this act of attaining the bottom of the Zodiac and turning northward again possesses a certain element of prophetic cheerfulness perceived by the simplest races of primitive antiquity. The aboriginal Mexicans and Peruvians, as well as the prehistoric people of Europe and Asia, held festivals to commemorate the winter solstice as a remote harbinger of Spring and a sign of Nature's immortality. The winter celebrations of the very ancient Italians were called the "Brumalia", and becoming incorporated successively into the classical and Christian religions, formed the parent of our present Christmas merrymakings.

December marks the full advent of the gorgeous winter stars to the evening sky, the eastern heavens now blazing with unparalleled effulgence. This year the lustrous planets Jupiter and Saturn add their radiance to that of the glittering sidereal background. Looking southeast on a clear evening at 9 p.m. about the middle of the month, the learner may commence his study of the constellations with the giant Orion, which is absolutely unique and unmistakable. Shining at a good altitude, it almost forces recognition upon the observer by the brilliant symmetry and majestic magnitude of its parts. Three bright stars in a row form the centre of the group, and represent the "Belt" of the hypothetical giant. Above this Belt burns the bright but slightly variable ruddy star Betelgeux; and as far beneath the Belt as Betelgeux is above it, is Rigel, a paler but generally somewhat brighter star. Immediately below the Belt is a line of attractive but rather faint stars, representing the giant's Sword, around one of which is a slight patch of misty light. This bit of light is the famous Great Nebula of Orion, which is a titanic mass of incandescent vapour thousands of times larger than our whole solar system on earth, sun, and planets. The application of photography to the sky, a modern scientific development which has virtually revolutionised our notions of the universe, reveals the Great Nebula as the centre of a still vaster bulk of luminous matter; involving the entire area of Orion, and having an extent so prodigious that to our finite minds it almost equals infinity itself. The brilliant region above and to the right of Orion is the Zodiacal constellation of Taurus, the Bull; whose brightest star, a reddish orb of the first magnitude, is called Aldebaran. Aldebaran lies at the left hand tip of a celestial letter "V" which constitutes the celebrated Hyades cluster. This cluster represents the head of the Bull, Adebaran being his eye. Prolonging the "V" into space, we find at a moderate distance two stars representing the tips of Taurus' horns. The famous Pleiades lie west of the Hyades, and are more compact and shimmering in aspect. They are, like Orion, involved in nebulous matter. Between the two clusters we now find the planet Jupiter, but in memorising the figure of Taurus we must exclude this refulgent wanderer from our mental map. Low in the southeast we cannot fail to recognise Sirius, the Dog-Star, which surpasses in lustre all the other stars of the heavens. Canis Major, the group in which it lies, will be better visible later in the winter or later in the evening. Much above Sirius, and considerably fainter, we find another star of the first magnitude. This is Procyon, in the Lesser Dog.

Turning our gaze northeast, and keeping Procyon in sight as a guide, we find Gemini, with its two bright stars Castor and Pollux, at a high altitude. The brilliant object below Gemini is not a star, but the planet Saturn. Very high up, above Gemini, is a particular radiant star; the noted Capella in the constellation Auriga. Almost in the zenith above Capella is a curving line of very attractive stars, some of which are entangled in a glistening mesh of light. This is the constellation Perseus, with its well-known cluster. Such are a few of the prominent winter groups which any beginner may identify.

The Zodiacal constellation on the meridian this month is Aries, whose neat figure arrests attention and commands recognition. Below Aries is the gigantic Cetus, southeast of which is the equally immense Fluvius Eridanus. In the west are Andromeda, Pegasus, Pisces, Aquarius, and Cygnus. The bright star about to set in the southeast is Fomalhaut. That about to set in the northwest is Vega. In the north we find Draco and Ursa Minor beneath the pole, Cassiopeia above and to the west of that point, and the Plough below and to the east, headed upward.

A very rich and interesting region of the Milky Way is now coming to view in the southeast, but this will not be seen to best advantage in the early evening until next month.

EDITOR'S NOTE FP: *EN* 51, No. 147 (1 December 1917): 3.

JANUARY SKIES

Venus, arriving at greatest brilliancy on the 5th of the month, is now the supreme planetary object of the evening sky. Unapproached in splendour, it glows refulgently each evening after sunset in the west; where no observer can fail to recognise it, either in the gathering twilight or after the darkness has fully settled over the heavens. The keen vision, indeed, can at this season glimpse the planet in the full glare of daylight if its approximate position be known in advance. On the 1st Venus sets at 7:52 p.m., nearly three and a half hours after the sun, but during the course of the month it approaches the solar orb so closely as to become lost in the latter's overpowering glare. On the 31st it sets about an hour and a half after the sun, being then virtually invisible. Inferior conjunction will ensue before the middle of next month. In the telescope, Venus exhibits a very thin crescent, which is continually becoming more attenuated. By the close of January the phase will be scarce more than a thread of light, though suitable telescopes are able to keep the planet in view till very near the actual time of inferior conjunction. Dr. Thomas Dick remarked many years ago, that he found the planet never hidden at this part of its course for more than two days and 22 hours. The dense atmosphere of Venus produces a singular phenomenon when the planet is a thin crescent, prolonging the cusps so far that they sometimes meet to form a complete circle of light. Such an aspect, of course, is never met with in the case of the moon, since that body lacks the envelope of air whose refractive qualities produce the illusion.

Jupiter is still a conspicuous object in the evening sky, setting on the 1st at 4:27 a.m., and on the 31st at 2:21. It is still in the constellation Taurus, retrograding till the 28th, and thereafter in direct motion. The belts, satellites, and various phenomena of this planet are now observable to best advantage, though opposition occurred some time ago. Jupiter will next month be in quadrature.

Mars, now past its morning quadrature, rises on the 1st at 10:39 p.m., and on the 31st at 9:05. Its lustre is steadily increasing, and it will soon be a very prominent feature of the evening sky. Opposition will occur in March. Mars will be in direct motion throughout January, traversing the constellation Virgo.

Saturn, in opposition on the 31st, is now at its best; gleaming gorgeously in the high eastern heavens. On the 1st it rises at 6:54 p.m.; on the 31st it rises at sunset and sets at 7:10 a.m., thus being visible in full glory throughout the night. The ring system, visible in any small telescope, is narrowing from year to year, and will disappear in 1921. Its last previous period of full expansion was in 1914, and the next will be in

1928. The visibility of the ring system of course depends upon the angle from which Saturn is seen by observers on the earth. A complete set of phases occupies about 30 years, the period of the planet's revolution.

Mercury is in inferior conjunction on the 3d, being then of course invisible. On the 25th, however, it reaches greatest western elongation; then appearing in the eastern heavens just before sunrise, close to the horizon. This appearance is not particularly favourable, but deserves notice by the assiduous astronomer.

Uranus, in conjunction next month, is preparing to quit the evening sky. Neptune comes to opposition on the 26th of the present month, and is visible in the evening with a suitable telescope.

The moon's phases for January will be as follows:

Last Quarter, 5th...6:50 a.m.
New Moon, 13th .... 5:36 p.m.
First Quarter, 19th ....9:38 a.m.
Full Moon, 26th .... 10:14 p.m.

Apogee falls on the 3d and 31st, Perigee on the 18th. The moon runs low on the 10th, high on the 23d, crossing the equator on the 3d, 16th, and 30th. It will be near Mars on the 3d, Venus on the 16th, Jupiter on the 21st, Saturn on the 27th, and Mars again on the 31st.

The sun enters the Zodiacal sign Aquarius on the 21st, but though this event is supposed to signalise the advent of our bitterest weather, it can scarcely bring us a more inclement period than that we have just experienced. The earth will be in perihelion, or nearest the sun, on the 1st at 11 a.m., a circumstance which may or may not be apparent in the tempering of the weather. Theoretically, at least, it mitigates the severity of our northern winter as contrasted with the bleak winters of the southern hemisphere; which occur in June, July, and August, when the sun is most remote from our terraqueous globe. The days this month increase steadily, over three-quarters of an hour being gained between the 1st and the 31st. The sun is now quite replete with spots, visible in a small telescope but not discernible by the unassisted vision. The spectroscope also reveals a corresponding activity in those peculiar eruptions of gaseous flame called the "prominences"; one of these being approximately 36,000 miles in height, as measured by Mr. Seagrave of North Scituate in this state. The sun, being the dominant body of our planetary system and the source of all light, heat, vegetation, and life therein, is worthy of the most careful study. Dazzling though it seem to us, it is itself but a star, of moderate size as compared with other stellar bodies, and seemingly superior only because of its close proximity to us. It is about 866,000 miles in diameter, being 1,300,000 times larger than the earth. Its average distance from the earth is about 93,000,000 miles, light requiring over eight minutes to pass from one to the other. It is not a solid body, but a glowing mass of gaseous or fluid matter, having a density but a fourth of the earth's; yet on account of its enormous size, the force of gravity on its surface is over 27 times greater than that on the surface of the earth; so that if a man were able to reach the centre of the system, he would be crushed and killed by his own weight. Since the sun is not solid, its rotation on its axis is not uniform, the equator travelling more rapidly than the other portions. Twenty-five days represents approximately the average length of one rotation. To the naked eye, the sun has the appearance of a uniformly luminous disc; too bright to admit a direct gaze, and therefore requiring the use of a deeply tinted glass for observation. In the telescope, the surface is seen to be covered with black, irregular, slowly moving spots, surrounded by greyish borders known as "penumbrae". The spots themselves, which are temporary in nature, one seldom lasting more than two or three months, sometimes attain diameters of from 50,000 to 100,000 miles; occasionally verging on visibility to the naked eye. The diameter of some large spots, including their penumbrae, is about 150,000 miles. Solar spots are distributed most thickly in belts extending 30 degrees north and south of the sun's equator, never appearing near the poles. They are especially numerous at intervals of about 31 years, these fluctuations in frequency being connected with certain phenomena of terrestrial magnetism in a way not yet understood. Bright streaks or patches called "faculae" are frequently seen near the spots when the latter are near the edge of the sun's disc. The disc itself is revealed by the telescope to be brightest at the centre, and of a granular or mottled appearance; as though it were composed of white snowflakes or rice grains sprinkled upon a light greyish background. The visible luminous disc of the sun is called the "photosphere". When the sun is eclipsed totally, and its bright rays temporarily intercepted, we see that it possesses a vast amount of matter outside the photosphere, consisting of (1) a bright red atmosphere called the "chromosphere", visible to us mainly as a series of immense fiery jets called "prominences", which form an irregular fringe about the blackened disc, and (2) a far-reaching luminous atmosphere whose exact appearance varies as seen during different eclipses, and which is known as the "corona". The general appearance of the latter is that of a broad halo, with occasional streamers of light. Of the actual constitution of the sun, much has been learned by observation, and by the use of the instrument known as the "spectroscope", which identifies incandescent substances by the character of the light they emit; yet the ultimate facts are still enveloped in the most profound obscurity. That the sun is intensely hot, much more so than may be readily conceived by the human mind, is quite evident; Wilson and Gray estimating its temperature at 7000 degrees Centigrade.[1] Should the earth be placed upon the surface of the sun, it would evaporate like a drop of water, and vanish, dissipated as a trifling cloud of gas. That the sun is, in nature, a mass of fiery incandescent vapour, made up of elements like those composing our own earth, is practically certain. Its heat is probably caused by its contraction in volume, for all contracting bodies radiate energy, and the sun is undoubtedly shrinking, though at so slow a rate, that no change in its apparent size has been observed since its disc was first studied by mankind. The photosphere is in all likelihood composed of solid or liquid particles in the form of clouds, floating in the gas or vapour of which the nucleus or inner part of the sun is constituted. These clouds are probably carbonaceous, giving off light in their incandescence much as do the solid particles of carbon in the flames of hydrocarbons, such as candles. The spots on the sun are considered by most authorities as depressions in the photosphere, caused by titanic eruptions; cooler, therefore darker, than the rest of the disc. This conclusion was reached by observing the changes in their appearance caused by perspective as they are carried across the disc by rotation. However, certain investigators question this theory, some even going so far as to hold that the spots are elevations above the general level of the photosphere. The penumbrae and faculae attendant upon the spots are generally ascribed to the upheaval of the solar surface by the enormous forces displayed in the formation of the spots themselves. The penumbra of a solar spot is ordinarily composed of attenuated filaments converging toward the centre of the spot, and occasionally having a rather spiral contour; thus indicating something of a cyclonic or whirling motion to be possessed by the spots; indeed, the observer Faye[2] advanced the theory that the sun's spots are gigantic cyclones; eddying storms against the incandescent clouds of the photosphere. In actual fact, however, it cannot be said that the spots, penumbrae, and faculae have yet been satisfactorily, or even tolerably well, explained. The sun's chromosphere, as seen during total eclipses in the immense eruptive prominences which fringe the obscured disc, is apparently composed of light gases such as hydrogen and helium. The height to which some of the prominences rise is probably due to forcible ejection from the interior, on a scale that dwarfs all terrestrial standards in comparison. The whole earth itself is tiny beside the most insignificant of these jets of solar fire. The corona, that mysterious crown of pale light which may be seen enveloping the sun during total eclipses, is most inexplicable in its nature. But one thing may be said conclusively of it, namely, that it is composed of self-luminous gas, deriving its light in no manner whatsoever from the inner and more refulgent portions of the sun. Comets traverse its wide expanse without sensible effect, proving that its tenuity must be extreme. Since the sun is the sole source of life upon the earth, it is but natural to inquire into the question of how long its radiant fires will endure for the benefit of remote posterity. Since, as previously stated, the heat of the sun seems to be derived from the slow yet inevitable contraction of its bulk, it is at once apparent that an end to its present condition must some time surely come. According to the late Prof. Simon Newcomb, a date of ten million years hence will mark the end of the existing order of things, after which the sun will become first liquid, then solid, finally ceasing altogether to shine, and rolling on amongst the stars as a dead, cold, unseen mass. However, the discovery of the element radium in its constitution may indicate a longer life; at any rate, the present generation need have no occasion to worry about the immediate future.

The January siderial sky is the most glorious of the entire year, containing all the famed brilliants of the winter season. The groups described last month all shine in unabated splendour, whilst Leo, with its massive sickle-shaped figure and bright star Regulus, has now appeared above the eastern horizon. There is no mistaking this asterism, since its figure is more obvious than that of any other constellation. In the southeast the lower stars of Canis Major are now in view. Themselves of no mean lustre, they are somewhat overshadowed by the superior effulgence of Sirius, the prime brilliant not only of this group, but of the entire sky. Orion and Taurus are now near transit, whilst Canis Minor, Gemini, Auriga, and Perseus add to the bright majesty of the scene.

EDITOR'S NOTE FP: *EN* 52, No. 19 (2 January 1918): 3.

Notes

1. See W[illiam] E[dward] Wilson and P. L. Gray, "Experimental Investigations on the Effective Temperature of the Sun, Made at Daramona, Streete, Co. Westmeath," *Proceedings of the Royal Society* 55 (1894): 250–51.
2. Hervé Faye (1814–1902), French astronomer who was professor of astronomy at the University of Nancy and professor of geodesy at the École Polytechnique. His work concentrated on the sun and on meteorites.

FEBRUARY SKIES

The month of February is marked by the transfer of Venus from the evening to the morning sky. About the 1st it sets an hour and a half after the sun, being just discernible to sharp eyes in the western evening twilight close to the horizon. Shortly afterward it will completely disappear, passing the sun in inferior conjunction on the 9th. Later in the month it may be discerned in the morning just before sunrise, glowing in the east with accustomed radiance, though not rising far before its brilliancy will succumb to the overpowering lustre of the dawn. It will next month be at its brightest again, as it was in January; the waxing crescent then presented to view being of the same thickness as the waning crescent which we observed on that other occasion. By the last of this month, Venus will rise an hour and three quarters before the sun. Its course amongst the stars is now retrograde, taking it from the eastern to the central part of the constellation Capricornus. On March 1st it will turn and commence direct motion.

Mars is now a prominent object of the evening sky, rising on the 1st at 9:04 p.m., and on the 28th at 6:52. Its brilliancy is increasing with great rapidity, so that by the end of the month it will be as bright as the celebrated star Canopus. In March, when opposition occurs, it will almost but not quite rival Sirius. The motion of Mars during February is wholly confined to the western part of the constellation Virgo; direct until the 4th and thereafter retrograde.

Saturn, in opposition on January 31st, is still at the height of its glory; though its brightness is not comparable to that of Mars. It is retrograding in the constellation Cancer, setting on the 1st at 7:10 a.m., and on the 28th at 5:15. During the evening hours it shines high in the south.

Jupiter, in quadrature on the 21st, is still seen to good advantage in the evening sky; creeping in direction motion between the Pleiades and Hyades in the constellation Taurus. On the 1st it sets at 2:31 a.m., and on the 28th at 12:40. At the most convenient hours of observation, it gleams high in the west. Its brilliancy decreases very slowly, and it still outshines anything else in the evening heavens.

Mercury, in greatest western elongation on January 25, may possibly be glimpsed in the early morning during the first few days of February; but it will soon be lost in the sun's rays. Its superior conjunction will fall on the 12th of March.

Uranus, in conjunction on the 13th, will be invisible throughout this month. Neptune, in opposition last month, will present itself favourably for telescopic observers.

The moon's phases for February will be as follows:

Last Quarter, 4th...3:52 a.m.

New Moon, 11th ....5:05 a.m.

First Quarter, 17th .... 7:57 p.m.

Full Moon, 25th .... 4:35 p.m.

Perigee falls on the 12th, Apogee on the 27th. The moon runs low on the 6th, high on the 19th; crossing the equator on the 12th and 26th. It will pass near Jupiter on the 18th, Saturn on the 23rd, and Mars on the 27th.

The sun enters the Zodiacal sign Pisces on the 19th, thus giving a remote prophecy of the eagerly awaited awakening of Nature. The worst of the winter is past, and the Sign of the Fishes, adopted in a slightly warmer clime than this, signifies that the streams are now freed of their icy bondage and open to the net and line of the fisherman. The days are slowly but surely lengthening, an hour and eleven minutes being gained betwixt the 1st and the 28th. The clock and sundial this month are in closest accord, noon coming exactly midway between sunrise and sunset. The fact that we use an artificially regulated system of time, makes the more natural and logical that wise step which every thoughtful citizen wishes and expects to see adopted next summer; the setting ahead of the clock in order to utilise an extra hour of otherwise wasted daylight. This plan will render it necessary to use some calculation in consulting the almanack, but in these articles the revised reckonings will be given during the period of their enforcement. "Daylight Saving", advocated elsewhere even during times of peace, is a war measure so sensible and desirable that its non-adoption would be little short of extravagant.

Encke's comet, which has the shortest period of revolution of any cometary body, reappeared on the 30th of last December, when it was observed by Prof. Schorr of the Bergedorf Observatory.[1] This comet revolves around the sun in about three and a third years, and it is said that this period is growing shorter and shorter, owing to the contraction of the orbit by some unknown resisting medium surrounding the sun. The object was first seen in 1786, but its orbit was not then determined. In 1796 it was observed by Miss Caroline Herschel, sister of the celebrated Sir William Herschel.[2] In 1805 and 1818 it was also noticed, its orbit and period of revolution being determined at this latter appearance by the prominent German astronomer Johann Franz Encke, after whom it was named. Its path is much affected by the attractive force of the immense planet Jupiter, near which it has to pass in certain parts of its course. Jupiter, and other large planets, exercise an important influence in deflecting the orbits of comets. Encke's comet is small, and never visible to the naked eye; its short period of revolution and possible change of orbit being its only qualifications for the astronomical fame it possesses.

Turning to the constellations, we behold the winter groups still in the height of their effulgence. Directly on the southern meridian, and absolutely unmistakable on account of its extreme brilliancy, is Sirius, the Dog-Star, the brightest stellar body in the entire heavens. Sirius is of a white hue, with possibly a tinge of green, but it has been asserted that in ancient times the star was red. Now this is directly opposite to the normal development of a siderial body, for it is generally believed that the stars are at first bluish-white, turning successively yellow, orange, and red as they increase in age through thousands and thousands of years. That is, they tend to emit rays of greater wave length as they grow older. That a star now white should once have been red, is therefore an anomaly quite difficult to explain. Most students believe that the notion of Sirius' ancient redness is due not to fact, but to an error of scholarship on the part of no less a literary celebrity than Cicero; who in translating into Latin the Greek astronomical poem of Aratus, made a misleading rendering of a certain passage alluding to Sirius. Just why a wrongly translated poem should have established its fallacy in opposition to the observation of mankind, is not clear; but Cicero's version of Aratus was probably widely circulated throughout the Roman world until the appearance of Avienus' translation in post-classical times.[3] Those who maintain that Sirius was actually red at the time, quote passages from Seneca and the astronomical writer Claudius Ptolemaseus, who imply, rather than assert, that such was the case in their day.[4] Though of course the most prominent by far, Sirius is by no means the only point of interest in the constellation Canis Major, to which it belongs. Below and somewhat to the left of the Dog-Star are a very attractive array of stars touching the western edge of the Milky Way. There is reason to believe that sixty thousand years ago Canis Major lay on the other side of the Galaxy, and that it has but lately, as time in eternity is reckoned, completed its crossing of the starry stream.

Above and to the left of Sirius, and on the other side of the Milky Way, shines a somewhat fainter, yet really very bright star, which we may identify as Procyon, chief brilliant of the constellation Canis Minor, or the Lesser Dog. The writer Serviss, in describing this body, makes the curious observation that its light impresses him "as lacking the brilliance that one expects from so large a star". This he attributes to its colour, which is a pale yellowish white. The name of Procyon signifies "The Dog Before", and alludes to its appearance in the heavens just before the rising of its more splendid brother Sirius. In setting, however, the reverse is true; for that selfsame northern declaration which makes it rise before, causes it to linger after the Greater Dog-Star. Canis Minor contains one fairly notable star besides Procyon, this being Gomelza, which lies five degrees to the northwest. As to the traditional representation of the group, it is interesting to note that the Lesser Dog is usually considered as a mild watchdog or household pet, as contrasted with Canis Major, the fierce, raging hunting dog. These bits of lore and mythology are of course of no concern to the scientific astronomer, but they lend interest to the studies of the amateur and less pretentious lover of the heavens.

The two bright stars above Procyon, and almost in the zenith, are Castor and Pollux, the Dioscuri or Heavenly Twins which give their names to the constellation Gemini, in which they are situate. In ancient times Castor was the brighter of the two, and received first rating in Bayer's Catalogue as late as the year 1603. During the last three centuries, however, a decided change in brilliancy has occurred; so that Castor is now nearly down to the second magnitude, whilst Pollux holds supremacy with a brightness but little below the first. Castor is white and Pollux orange, colours which appear to have characterised them from the remotest ages. The two have always been fancifully considered as related in some way, probably due to their once equal splendour, and the short distance which separates them. They were therefore named by the Greeks after the famous twin sons of Leda. The still more ancient Egyptians considered them as emblematical of the two gods Horus. In Assyria and Chaldaea they were considered as twins, and even the savage tribes of Africa and the South Sea Islands insist on regarding them as a pair.

West of the meridian we now find the most brilliant groups of earlier winter, among them being the superlatively splendid Orion, still at its best, and the lustrous and extensive Taurus, with the famous Pleiades and Hyades. Capella, in Auriga, is now past transit, whilst Perseus is well down in the west. Eridanus, Cetus, Aries, and Andromeda are all low in the western sky.

In the north we find the Plough east of the pole, Cassiopeia opposite it on the western side, Ursa Minor coming from beneath it, and Cepheus preparing to descend below it. Draco is rearing itself from lower transit, preparatory to its ascent of the sky. In the northeast a few stars of Boötes are appearing as heralds of the ever welcome Arcturus, spring's brightest stellar harbinger. Coma Berenices is also adding its shimmering light to the heavens. Virgo is beginning to rise due east, and Leo is now seen in full majesty.

Cancer, with the faint cluster Praespe, is high in the southeastern heavens. Lower in the southeast Hydra is uncoiling to a considerable extent, the small group Crater, which rests on its back, being now in sight. Soon the typically vernal and easily recognisable Corvus will have appeared. Farther south the Milky Way glows beautifully, its phosphorescent waves bearing upon them the ship Argo, whose best parts are forever hidden from our latitude.

Editor's Note FP: *EN 52*, No. 45 (1 February 1918): 7.

Notes

1. Richard Reinhart Emil Schorr (1867–1951), German astronomer who worked at the Bergedorf Observatory in Hamburg from 1892 to 1941; he was its director from 1902 to 1935.

2. Caroline Lucretia Herschel (1750–1848), German-born British astronomer and sister of William Herschel who assisted her brother in his observations and also discovered three nebulae and eight comets.

3. Cicero's *Aratea* (a translation of Aratus' *Phaenomena*) survives only in fragments. The passage discussing Sirius (= *Phaenomena* 331–37) does not mention its redness. Postumius Rufius Festus Avienus (mid-4th century C.E.) loosely translated and expanded upon Aratus' poem as *Aratea Phaenomena*.

4. See Seneca the Younger (4 B.C.E.?–65 C.E.), *Naturales Questiones* 1.1.7 (which refers to the *rubor* [redness] of the Dog-Star [*Canicula*]). In the *Almagest* (8.1, Constellation 38: Canis Major), Ptolemy refers to Sirius as "reddish."

MARCH SKIES

The prime astronomical phenomenon of March is the opposition of Mars which occurs on the 15th. Though by no means a particularly favourable opposition, such as those of 1907 and 1909, the event is nevertheless one of considerable interest; affording the telescopic observer a good opportunity to study the remarkable red planet, whose physical characteristics and supposed resemblance to the earth have excited such unusual attention both from the scientific and general public during the past quarter-century. Mars is now of extreme brilliancy, rising on the 1st at 6:51 p.m., and on the 10th at 6:00. It sets at 5:02 a.m., on the 31st. The planet is this month in retrograde motion amongst the stars, crossing backward from the constellation Virgo into Leo. During the convenient evening hours of observation it will blaze high in the eastern sky. On the 18th Mars will be actually nearest the earth. Generally speaking, the planet is nearest at the time of opposition, but a few days difference is in practice to be noted. Mars is the fourth planet in order of distance from the sun, and first outside the earth's orbit. It approaches at its most favourable oppositions within 36,000,000 miles of the earth, a closer distance from us than is attained by any other planet save Venus and one or two of the asteroids. At its most unfavourable oppositions, its distance is 61,000,000 miles, the average being about 48,000,000 miles. At conjunction it recedes to a mean distance of 204,000,000 miles. The path of Mars around the sun is very eccentric, the planet's solar distance being at times 26,000,000 miles greater than on other occasions. (Average, 141,000,000 miles.) Gravity on Mars is about three-eights of that upon the earth, whilst its density is about three-fourths. The day of Mars, as determined by the planet's rotation, is but little longer than our own (24h. 37m.), and the similar seasons; although since the year of Mars is nearly twice as long as that of the earth (687 days), these seasons are also double ours in length. The diameter of Mars is roughly half that of the earth, being about 4000 miles. Its synodic or apparent revolution around the earth is by far the longest in the solar system, being 780 days, or about two and one-fifth years as counted between two successive oppositions. To us, Mars shews no variation of phase save a slight gibbous appearance when at or near quadrature. It is best seen, as are all superior planets, when opposite the sun, it then being a conspicuous object for about three months. At other times, the naked eye finds but little of interest in it. The close proximity of Mars to the earth; the fact that it is not, like Venus, invisible when nearest us; and that when visible its surface is not, as is that of Venus, obscured by clouds; all tend to allow terrestrial observers to obtain more positive knowledge concerning it, than may be gathered from any of the other planets. Spots on the surface of Mars were first observed by Huyghens in 1659. Since then, telescopes have greatly improved, and we now see the planet's disc to be divided roughly into two parts; the light or reddish, and the dark or greenish areas. These were formerly regarded as land and water, respectively, and although more recent investigations have quite disproved such an idea, the present nomenclature still refers, like that of the moon, to imaginary oceans and continents. The true nature of these spots is doubtful. It is to the red areas that the general ruddy colour of the planet, as seen with the unassisted vision, is due. Besides the red and green regions, intensely white tracts are seen around each pole, diminishing almost to the point of disappearance on exposure to the direct rays of the sun, as during the summer of Mars in their respective hemispheres, and increases during the winter. These "polar caps", as they are called, are thought to be composed of water in the form of snow, or at least hoar-frost, melting in summer and freezing again in winter. [The] faintest and least clearly defined features of the disc of Mars are the so-called "canals", extremely narrow, dark streaks which cover the planet's surface like a network. They were discovered in 1877 by Schiaparelli, and have since received much attention in connexion with the fantastic idea that they are gigantic ditches, constructed by the hands of intelligent inhabitants of Mars. There is, in truth, [something] worthy of note in the almost mathematical rectitude of these lines, the dark, circular spots called "oases" which mark their intersections, and their probable changes from season to season; but so faint and difficult to see are they, that their very existence was doubted until recently, when some of them were successfully photographed. The true nature of the canals, like that of the spots, is a matter of great dispute. It seems evident that they change from time to time, perhaps with the season of the year of Mars; at times some of them appear double, and a few astronomers believe that a connexion exists between changes in the canals and in the spots. Next month we will note some of the peculiar theories advanced within the last three decades. The atmosphere of Mars must be indefinitely thinner than is that of the earth, for we are able to gain but slight evidence of its existence, and clouds seldom obscure the planet's features. The temperature, owing to the greater distance of Mars from the sun, must be vastly lower than that of our terraqueous globe. Mars has two tiny moons or satellites, discovered in 1877 by the late Prof. Asaph Hall of the U. S. Naval Observatory. Their names are Deimos, or Terror, and Phobos, or Fear, the two mythical attendants of the war-god Mars. Phobos, the inner of the two, revolves round its primary three times during one day of Mars, therefore, as seen from that planet, rising in the west, displaying all its phases whilst above the horizon, and setting in the east after a visibility of only six hours. Deimos revolves in a little more than a day, so rises above Mars' eastern horizon. It remains in sight for 60 hours, and displays two complete sets of phases before setting in the west.

Venus, glowing effulgently near the eastern horizon during the early morning hours, attains greatest brilliancy on the 16th of the present month, when its superlative lustre will excite general attention. On the 1st it rises at 4:36 a.m., an hour and three-quarters before the sun, whilst on the 31st it rises at 3:35, not quite two hours before the great luminary. Turning from retrograde to direct motion amongst the stars on the 1st, the planet will this month advance from the central to the extreme eastern part of the constellation Capricornus. In the telescope Venus shews a steadily thickening crescentic phase; very attractive to view through even a small glass, despite the virtually complete absence of all permanent superficial configurations.

Saturn, not yet in quadrature, is still a prominent object of the evening sky, shining brightly in the constellation Cancer, where it is slowly retrograding. It lies high in the south, almost directly on the meridian, at the usual time of evening observation. On the 1st it sets at 5:14 a.m., and on the 31st at 3:10.

Jupiter is past quadrature, yet not by any means beyond good observation. It is moving directly in the constellation Taurus, shewing no striking change of location from month to month. The planet sets at 12:40 a.m. on the 1st, and at 10:58 p.m. on the 31st, being rather low in the west when most conveniently observed. In brilliancy it is peerless, notwithstanding a considerable decline since opposition.

Mercury, in superior conjunction on the 12th, will be generally invisible throughout March; though it might possibly be spied at the very end of the month, struggling to be seen amidst the evening twilight near the western horizon. Its greatest eastern elongation occurs next month.

Uranus may possibly be visible this month to the telescopic observer, since it is gradually emerging from its conjunctional hibernation into the morning sky. Neptune is well seen in the evening, being not yet in quadrature.

The moon's phases for March will be as follows:

Last Quarter, 5th... 7:44 p.m.
New Moon, 12th .... 2:52 p.m.
First Quarter, 19th ....8:30 a.m.
Full Moon, 27th ....10:33 a.m.

Perigee comes on the 12th, Apogee on the 26th. The moon runs low on the 6th, high on the 18th, crossing the equator on the 12th and 25th. It will pass near Venus on the 10th, Jupiter on the 17th, Saturn on the 22nd, and Mars on the 26th.

The sun enters the Zodiacal sign Aries on the 21st at 5:26 a.m., thus crossing the vernal equinox and sounding the knell of one of the bitterest winters within our remembrance. We do not marvel that this annual blessing was hailed by the primitive ancients with ceremonial rejoicing; nor that such celebrations have persisted in various modified forms throughout the course of time, despite the many and vast changes in man's environment and culture. During March the days increase an hour and 24 minutes, the sun moving northward 11 degrees and 21 minutes. Light and darkness are now evenly balanced.

The stars of March include most of the characteristic winter brilliants, yet are as a whole distinctly vernal. The gorgeous groups which dawned upon us so impressively in the late autumn lost half their subtle magic when beheld declining in the west, through the milder air of early spring. Taurus, Perseus, Gemini, Orion, Canis Major, and Canis Minor are blaze beyond the meridian at various altitudes, though lacking the crisp sparkle of winter. The Zodiacal constellation now in transit is the faint Cancer, for the time being adorned with the transient beams of the planet Saturn. The prime figure of this group is the cluster called Praespe, or the Manger, which appears like a nebula to the naked eye but resolves itself into an assemblage of small stars under even the slightest magnification. East of Cancer are the typical groups of spring; majestic Leo, soaring high with its bright star Regulus, and its Sickle and Triangle; Hydra, rearing its head to the meridian yet stretching down below the southeastern horizon and bearing upon its scaly back the little asterisms Corvus and Crater; and Virgo, almost fully risen, its white gem Spica gleaming cheerfully through the low-hanging mists. In the north we see the Plough high in the heavens, with Draco beneath it, at the right of the pole. Ursa Minor extends east from the pole, while Cepheus and Cassiopeia are descending beneath it. In the northeaster the glittering circlet of Corona Borealis is in sight, above it blazing the characteristic spring star Arcturus, in Boötes. Still higher in the heavens is that cloudy patch of faint light comprising Coma Berenices. The Milky Way stretches from north to south in an arc passing through the western sky, meeting the southern horizon in a sea of glory whereon rides the stately ship Argo.

EDITOR'S NOTE FP: *EN* 52, No. 66 (1 March 1918): 7.

APRIL SKIES

The chief point of astronomical interest at present is undoubtedly the "daylight saving" modification of civil time, which went into effect for six months on the last day of March. According to this system our clocks are turned one hour ahead of the standard time to which we have been adhering, wherefore the civil time of all astronomical phenomena is one hour in advance of what it would have been under the old schedule. Since at Providence, standard time is about fifteen minutes behind local solar time, it follows that the new system will place us but 45 minutes ahead of true astronomical reckoning, such as we employed prior to 1883. The change will have no effect whatever upon our ordinary affairs, since most of us govern our routine by the arbitrary program of mankind, rather than by the actual motions of the earth. When all the nation sets its clocks ahead, we shall perceive no difference save in the additional daylight gained. We shall find that it is not the rising and setting of the sun, but the opening and closing of the business day, which have been guiding our movements. Objectors there will doubtless be, as there were in 1752, when the adoption of the Gregorian year effaced 11 days from our calendar; and in 1883, when standard time reorganised our day; but as in those other cases, a short experience under the new system will suffice to demonstrate the absurdity of objection, and the perfect feasibility of the innovation. Only in consulting the almanack will there be any need to make allowance for the change. In these articles, as in the general affairs of every-day life, the new reckoning will be observed; so that the ensuing columns may be read literally as usual, without calculation or interpretation.

Mars, in opposition last month, still holds principal interest in the evening sky; setting on the 1st at 6:01 a.m., and on the 30th at 3:49. To the naked eye it is a prominent ruddy object, shining brightly in the southern heavens. The planet spends the entire month in the eastern part of the constellation Leo, retrograding until the 26th, and thereafter moving directly. The possessors of large telescopes, notwithstanding the unfavourable nature of this year's opposition, are now watching Mars with great assiduity; since its baffling topographical features, especially the so-called "canals", are always worthy of close scrutiny. To explain these singular markings, whose appearance and variations we noted last month, several theories have been advanced; though none can be said to furnish a very simple or plausible solution to the mystery. The late Prof. Percival Lowell, most diligent of all observers of Mars, constructed an exceedingly elaborate and fairly popular theory on the supposition that the red planet is an inhabited world. He affirmed (1) That the canals all commence at the polar caps, and lead downward toward the centre of the planet in absolutely straight lines, (2) That their many intersections are all marked by small, perfectly round spots or "oases", and

(3) That their breadth increases in the summer, and decreases in the winter of the planet. From these things, Prof. Lowell made the following rather sensational deductions. According to his idea, Mars is an aged body; that is, one which has been in existence much longer than the earth, and whose physical structure is in consequence much more advanced. Its oceans, rivers, and lakes have long been evaporated; leaving it a desert whose only water is that contained in the polar snow caps. These caps, as they melt in summer, give off the needed fluid, which is conveyed to the arid regions by means of the canals; mighty watercourses dug by the highly civilised inhabitants of the planet. Since one cap is always melted whilst the other is frozen, a continual flow of water is secured. The dark "oases" are great cities, placed at the intersection of canals and thus enjoying double allowances of water. The increase in the width of the canals during the summer of Mars is due to the growth of vegetation along their banks, for the ditches themselves could not be seen at so great a distance as ours. In winter, when the vegetation dies from frost and from the withdrawal of water caused by the freezing of the polar cap that feeds the canals, these strange features disappear. The red areas of Mars are desert land; the green, vegetation. Thus the supposed changes in the latter are explained. The difficulty of reconciling the thin air and intense cold of Mars with the sustenance of inhabitants, is overcome by assuming the existence of an atmosphere of different composition from our own; one which though much more attenuated, is yet better adapted to absorb and conserve the solar heat. Such is the more radical and fantastic theory of the canals. Let us now briefly consider the very recent and much more scientific theory advanced by Prof. W. H. Pickering, who has long observed Mars from the clear tropical air of Jamaica. Like Lowell, Prof. Pickering believes the canals to be lines of vegetation nourished by water derived from the polar caps; but here the resemblance ends, for artificial construction has no place in this new "Theory of Aerial Deposition". According to Pickering, the streaks of vegetation forming the canals are due to aqueous precipitation in the form of vapour or moisture, which is deposited along these certain lines as a result of winds or air currents which move in conformity to stated laws of atmospheric circulation. These currents pick up their moisture from hollows at the edges of the polar caps, where water from the melting snow accumulates and evaporates. This state of things is held due to the imperfectly spheroidal shape of Mars. Green's tetrahedral theory of the earth declares that any sphere with a solid surface, slowly contracting, tends to assume a slightly tetrahedral shape; that is, to have four equidistant protuberances and four intermediate flattened surfaces.[1] The inner planets all come under this classification, and Dr. Lau,[2] Prof. Pickering's associate, believes he has accounted for the tetrahedral protuberances and depressions of Mars in a way which explains the collection and distribution of water along the canal lines. The new theory has much to recommend it; and is really the first explanation of the canals ever offered, which may be accorded the dignity of an actual working hypothesis. One point, in particular, seems now settled; namely, that the canals are tracts of vegetation.

Saturn, in quadrature on the 28th, is scarcely comparable to Mars in brilliancy; yet glows with no feeble lustre just west of the meridian during the most convenient evening hours. On the 1st it sets at 4:10 a.m., and on the 30th at 2:13. It lies in the constellation Cancer, retrograding till the 9th, and afterward moving eastward.

Jupiter, though now quite low in the west, is still the brightest planet of the evening sky. At the beginning of the month its stellar magnitude exceeds that of Sirius, but by the end it is slightly fainter than that object. It sets about midnight on the 1st, and at 10:30 p.m. on the 30th. Jupiter is still in the constellation Taurus, moving directly.

Venus, reigning unrivalled in the morning sky, attains greatest western elongation on the 21st, then appearing to best advantage, and shewing in a telescope a phase like that of the half moon. Before this date it will be a crescent, and afterward, gibbous. On the 1st Venus rises at 4:34 a.m., not quite two hours before the sun. At the time of elongation it rises at 4:10, an hour and three-quarters before the sun. On the 30th it rises at about 4:00, 1 hour and 43 minutes before sunrise. During April, Venus moves from the border of the constellation Capricornus entirely across Aquarius and into Pisces. Its lustre is very great, and its beams will prove cheerful in the artificially belated dusk before dawn.

Mercury arrives at greatest eastern elongation on the 7th, then being visible in the west after sunset. The present appearance is rather a favourable one, eastern elongations being most advantageous in spring. On the 12th the planet will be near the very thin crescent of the infant moon. Shortly after this time Mercury will disappear, being in inferior conjunction on the 20th. Mercury can quite readily be found with the naked eye. In the telescope it exhibits a small disc whose phase varies from gibbous to crescentic during the month.

Uranus is in the early morning sky, being in conjunction with Venus on the 2nd, and with the waning moon on the 7th. Neptune, in the evening sky, comes to quadrature on the 24th. It will be near the half moon on the 18th.

The moon's phases for April will be as follows:

Last Quarter, 4th..9:33 a.m.
New Moon, 11th ....12:34 a.m.
First Quarter, 18th ....12:06 a.m.
Full Moon, 26th ....4:05 a.m.

Perigee falls on the 10th, Apogee on the 22nd. The moon runs low on the 2nd and 29th, high on the 7th. [It will pass near] Mercury on the 12th, Jupiter on the 14th, Saturn on the 18th, and Mars on the 22nd.

The sun enters the Zodiacal sign Taurus on the 21st; as Virgil says (in Mr. Dryden's translation),

> "When with his golden horns, in full career,
> The Bull beats down the barriers of the year."[3]

The days gain an hour and 17 minutes in April. On the 1st the sun rises at 6:29 and sets at 7:11. On the 30th it rises at 5:44 and sets at 7:43. In the brilliantly sunlit evenings we may not only obtain our first taste of the boons afforded by "daylight saving", but may form some idea of the usual conditions in more northern latitudes, where the unequal disposition of light and darkness causes the sun to set very late in summer. In England, for instance, the sun does not set till 8:19 on the longest days.

The remarkable display of the Aurora Borealis witnessed early last month, deserves more than a passing mention by astronomical chroniclers. According to many observers, it was the most brilliant phenomenon of its kind seen in New England during this generation. The Aurora is now considered to be an electrical discharge from the sun, consisting of infinitesimally tiny electrons which the solar sphere is always throwing forth. These particles, encountering the earth's atmosphere, are borne by currents to the terrestrial poles, where they furnish the most frequent and splendid displays. At rare intervals, they are carried southward or northward from their respective polar regions, giving the inhabitants of the temperate zones an opportunity to behold their beauties.

The Zodiacal constellation on the meridian this month is Leo, the Lion, one of the most prominent and easily recognisable objects in the sidereal sky. The main figure of the group is that of a sickle or reaping-hook, at the end of whose handle gleams the brilliant Regulus. Some distance to the left of the sickle is the rest of the constellation, a large right triangle, with the fairly bright star Denebola at the intersection of base and hypothenuse. It is in the vicinity of this triangle that the planet Mars is now to be observed. Below Leo is Hydra, with the two small [constellations] Crater and Corvus on its back. Corvus, the more easterly of the pair, is a very attractive trapezium of stars, well-defined in outline, and [a] characteristic feature of the vernal skies. At the right of Leo is Cancer, with its faint cluster Praespe, and with the bright planet Saturn now within its confines.

> "O'er western slopes with feeble beams expire
> The fading embers of Brumalian fire."[4]

Or in plain prose, the bright constellations of winter, robbed of their pristine sparkle, are now sinking low in the western sky, preparing for their annual disappearance. The very bright star in the southwest about 10 p.m. is Sirius, whilst no one can mistake gigantic Orion as he slides down out of sight due west. Taurus is setting in the northwest, carrying with him the refulgent planet Jupiter. Destined for a slightly longer stay with us are Canis Major, high in the west, and Gemini and Auriga, farther north.

Perseus is about to vanish in the far northwest. In the north we behold the Plough above the pole, Ursa Minor and Draco to the right of that point, and Cassiopeia and Cepheus below it. The piercing beams of Vega, newly risen, greet us from the mists of the northeast. The large but somewhat formless and uninteresting Hercules is now partially in sight in the northeast, above it glowing the attractive Corona Borealis and the refulgent Arcturus. Due east we find the first stars of Ophiuchus et Serpens in sight, south of which shines Libra. High in the southeast is Virgo, with the bright star Spica, above which shimmers the misty Coma Berenices.

The winter streams of the Via Lactea are now about to disappear in the west, carrying with them those parts of Argo Navis which we are able to glimpse in this latitude. Next month the glowing ribbon will line the horizon, and in June the quietly beaming summer branches will reward the vision.

EDITOR'S NOTE FP: *EN* 52, No. 92 (1 April 1918): 4.

Notes

1. HPL refers to the British mathematician and natural philosopher George Green (1793–1841), who propounded the theory in a series of papers in the *Transactions of the Cambridge Philosophical Society* (1835–42).

2. Hans Emil Lau (1879–1918), Danish astronomer who, like W. H. Pickering, spent much of his career in the search for trans-Neptunian planets and also did work on the surface features of Mars and Jupiter.

3. Virgil, *Georgics* 1.217–18.

4. The lines are from HPL's poem "April" (*EN*, 24 April 1917), ll. 43–44 (*AT* 278).

MAY SKIES

The month of May is marked by the virtual disappearance of Jupiter from the evening sky. On the 1st the planet sets at 10:30 p.m., about two hours and three-quarters after the sun, but on the 31st it vanishes at 9, only three-quarters of an hour after sunset. Jupiter is in the constellation Taurus, in direct motion, and may be well seen low in the northwest in the early evening during the first half of the month.

Saturn, in quadrature last month, is still seen to excellent advantage in the evening, setting on the 1st at 2:12 a.m., and on the 31st at 12:12. It remains in the constellation Cancer, moving directly throughout May. During the most convenient hours of observation it will be found high in the west. Its ring system, still fairly well expanded, makes it one of the most interesting telescopic objects in the heavens.

Mars is the leading planet of the evening sky, being only two months past opposition. On the 1st it sets at 3:48 a.m., and on the 31st at 1:56. As it draws near quadrature its disc begins to exhibit a slightly uneven or gibbous appearance, due to that slight shadowing of the edge opposite the sun which constitutes the planet's only phase as beheld from the earth. Mars now glows refulgently in the southern and southwestern sky, lying in the extreme eastern part of the constellation Leo, in direct motion.

Venus brilliantly adorns the morning sky, rising on the 1st at 3:58 and on the 31st at 3:20. Having passed greatest western elongation, it is now approaching the sun, shewing in the telescope a slowly expanding gibbous phase. During May the planet moves entirely across the constellation Pisces, from the boundary of Aquarius to the border of Aries. It is visible rather low in the east just before sunrise, vastly outshining all objects in its vicinity.

Mercury reaches greatest western elongation on the 24th, then being visible low in the twilight preceding dawn. The present elongation is not an especially favourable one, but will suffice to reveal the planet to a keen observer. In the telescope Mercury will appear crescentic before elongation, and afterward gibbous.

Uranus, in the morning sky, will come to quadrature on the 19th. It will be near the moon on the 4th. Neptune, in the evening sky, is now past quadrature, being near the moon on the 15th.

The moon's phases for May will be as follows:

Last Quarter, 3d .... 6:26 p.m.
New Moon, 10th ....9:01 a.m.
First Quarter, 17th .... 4:14 p.m.
Full Moon, 25th .... 6:32 p.m.

Perigee falls on the 8th, Apogee on the 20th. The moon runs high on the 12th, low on the 26th, crossing the equator on the 6th and 19th. It will pass near Venus on the 7th, Jupiter on the 12th, Saturn on the 16th, and Mars on the 19th.

The sun enters the Zodiacal sign Gemini on the 21st, travelling steadily northward and very perceptibly lengthening the daylight period. By the 31st there will be 15 hours of sunlight, the sun rising at 5:13 a.m., and setting at 8:13 p.m., according to the new "Summer time" schedule. There will next month be a striking solar eclipse, total in many parts of the United States, and visible as a partial eclipse in Providence. Careful preparations for observation have been made along the path of totality, for the phenomenon is one of no small scientific value. A partial lunar eclipse will also occur in June.

The siderial pageant of May is characteristically vernal; lacking the sparkling effulgence of the winter heavens, yet not without a mild beauty all its own. The Zodiacal constellation on the meridian at 10 p.m. is Virgo, whose bright star Spica is the most noticeable stellar feature of the southern evening sky. Just below Virgo is the neat trapezium of Corvus, a typical spring asterism whose companion group Crater lies just to the west. Both of these rest upon the coils of Hydra, an extensive group reaching far into the western sky. West of Virgo is Leo, still seen to best advantage, and at present containing the bright red planet Mars as an added attraction. Above Virgo on the meridian is the faint shimmering constellation Coma Berenices, which, though appearing like a nebula to the naked eye, may be resolved into its component stars by even the slightest optical assistance.

In the western sky are the last of the winter groups. The vanishing streams of the Milky Way bear with them Canis Minor, whose bright star Procyon shines due west in solitary splendour; Gemini, whose prime brilliants Castor and Pollux gracefully adorn the northwest, and Auriga, whose lustrous gem Capella lends radiance to the extreme northwest. Cancer, now containing the planet Saturn, is still high in the west.

In the north we find the Plough above the pole, tilted downward preparatory to its summer descent of the heavens. Ursa Minor and Draco are not quite at their highest altitudes, whilst Cepheus and Cassiopeia are close to the horizon beneath the pole. Perseus, just west of the north point, has not quite sunk from sight. Cygnus, partly risen in the extreme northeast, balances it. Higher in the northeast is Lyra, with the incomparable Vega. Just south of it Hercules has fully risen, and due east Ophiuchus et Serpens is nearly all in view. Low in the southwest the deep red beams of Antares announce the rising of Scorpio, which is preceded by the somewhat uninteresting Libra. At a good altitude in the east are Boötes, with the bright Arcturus, and Corona Borealis, whose glittering outline is ever pleasing. The Milky Way this month lines the horizon from the southwest through the north to the southeast. To compensate for the departing winter streams, the summer branch is ascending, bringing with it that glowing array of clusters and nebulae which will adorn the south during the months to come.

The appearance in the southeast of the upper parts of Centaurus, whose entire bulk may never be seen from the latitude of Providence, reminds us of a recent discovery concerning our nearest stellar neighbours. Until lately the bright Alpha Centauri, invisible in New England, has been considered as the nearest to our solar system of all the stars. Now, however, another and much fainter star in Centaurus, also invisible here, has been found to possess this distinction. The small object which thus robs Alpha Centauri of its eminence is in some way connected with the latter, sharing its general motion through space. Its parallax, or half its apparent difference of place when viewed from opposite sides of the earth's orbit, is very little less than four-fifths of a second of arc, as contrasted with that of Alpha Centauri, which amounts to only about three-quarters of a second. The nearer a star is, of course, the larger will appear its displacement as observed from opposite points in the earth's annual path. Upon the parallax of the nearer stars depends all our knowledge of their distance. The distances of the farther stars, which present no sensible change of position at opposite seasons of the year, may be estimated only roughly and vaguely, from such unreliable data as brilliancy or actual motion through space. It should be added, that the parallax of even the nearest stars is so slight as to be imperceptible save by means of exceedingly delicate instruments. It is measured with the micrometer, a device consisting of parallel wires which move along a very finely graduated scale. Such an instrument, of course, must be attached to a telescope of adequate power.

As a background against which to detect the apparent motions in question, certain very distinct stars without sensible parallax are employed. Observations for parallax, of course, are made at opposite times of the year, as in May and November, or June and December, when the earth is at diametrically opposite parts of its orbit. When the difference in apparent place has been accurately determined, the distance of the star observed may be calculated with ease, since we know that the observed parallax is simply the apparent angle subtended by the diameter of the earth's orbit at the star's distance. Both the angular and actual space represented by the parallax being known, the distance is readily found, for the ratio of real and apparent size is constant, depending upon distance. An object subtends an apparent angular diameter at one second when situate at a distance 206.265 times greater than its own true diameter, and so on. The quantity technically given as a star's "Annual Parallax" is about half the value as described above, or the arc subtended by the mean radius or semi-diameter of the earth's orbit as seen from the star's distance.

Another recent discovery, or reputed discovery, of interest, is that of an asteroid or minor planet with a satellite. Heretofore these tiny worlds, which revolve in great numbers between the orbits of Mars and Jupiter, have been deemed far too small to possess the attendance of secondary planets. It will be interesting to watch the development of this alleged discovery, and to learn the size both of the new asteroid and of its necessarily microscopic "moon".

EDITOR'S NOTE FP: *EN* 52, No. 119 (2 May 1918): 9.

[SCIENCE VERSUS CHARLATANRY]

SCIENCE VERSUS CHARLATANRY

To the Editor of the Evening News:

It is an unfortunate fact that every man who seeks to disseminate knowledge must contend not only against ignorance itself, but against false instruction as well. No sooner do we deem ourselves free from a particularly gross superstition, than we are confronted by some enemy to learning who would set aside all the intellectual progress of years, and plunge us back into the darkness of mediaeval disbelief.

As a lover of Astronomy, and a writer on that subject, I was the other day very much pained and shocked to see in the Evening News an article on the pseudo-science of Astrology, which has ever been the bane of the seeker after truth. While I entertain no doubt as to the sincerity of the author, a Mr. Hartmann, [it is impossible] for me to comprehend how any person of judgment and education can now give credence to the doctrines of a false and ridiculous system completely exploded over 200 years ago. In this age of enlightenment it ought not the be necessary to shew the utter absurdity of the idea that our daily affairs can be governed by the mere apparent motions of infinitely distant bodies whose seeming arrangements and configurations, on which the calculations of judicial astrology are based, arise only from perspective as seen from our particular place in the universe. It seems very provoking that astronomers and other men of sense should be obliged to waste their time and energy in proving Astrology to be false, when there exists not the slightest reason to believe any part of it true; yet the perverse sophistry of certain misguided individuals still raises up such a body of specious evidence in favour of it, that we must needs attack again what we had thought finally conquered. The fallacies of Astrology are like the many heads of the Lernean Hydra; chop off one, and two grow in its place.

Mr. Hartmann, in his recent article, seems to defend Astrology by assertions that the astronomers and scientists who shew its falsity are unacquainted with its precepts. This statement loses force when we reflect that the whole mass of nonsense which constitutes this study is only a vague distortion and misuse of astronomical principles; indeed, the study of Astronomy absolutely proves the spurious nature of Astrology by elimination, or reductio ad absurdum. It is very amusing to read Mr. Hartmann's hostile allusions to Mr. Garrett P. Serviss and the late Richard A. Proctor.[1] These two popular astronomical writers, similar in many ways, have by means of their double gifts of scientific and literary skill accomplished marvels in dissipating superstition and propagating truth; it is no wonder that they are hated and feared by the leaders of the hosts of ignorance.

Still more amusing is Mr. Hartmann's sober reference to the English astrological almanacks. These wretched pamphlets, though much perused by the vulgar and the ignorant, have been the laughing-stock of the intelligent British public since Queen Anne's time, when Dr. Swift destroyed with such exquisite humour the pretensions of the conceited astrologer and almanack-maker, John Partridge. In 1827 the Society for the Diffusion of Christian Knowledge severely attacked annuals of this sort and later caused most of them either to suspend publication or to discontinue their astrological predictions, so that today only two, Zadkiel's and Raphael's, are in existence. The prophecies of these almanacks are like the utterances of the Delphic Oracle; so vague and ambiguous that they can be made to suit any subsequent events. In many a time of peace have the mystics and seers given forth warnings fully as dire and dreadful as any that have preceded the present war.

The ravings of Raphael about lamentable losses to kings and emperors may be made to fit alike the loss of a handkerchief or of a throne. War in the Balkans, unrest in Russia, and revolutions in Central or South America are among the events most successfully predicted. Mr. Hartmann's mention of the predictions of Pope Pius' death reminds me that this same event was scheduled in 1906 by a learned astrologer of Central Falls, R.I.[2]

I should not take up your time nor seek to occupy your columns with this reply to Mr. Hartmann if I did not consider Astrology a dangerous as well as a silly subject. In the minds of the masses it tends to become confused with Astronomy, and thereby to injure the reputation of that science.

The News has ever been a friend to the improvement and instruction of the public, so that I am confident it will not begrudge me a little space besides that which I regularly occupy on the first of each month, in my humble efforts to diffuse truth and to expose fallacy regarding the heavens.

H. P. LOVECRAFT.

598 Angell Street, Providence, R.I.

EDITOR'S NOTE FP: *EN* 45, No. 95 (9 September 1914): 8. The first of HPL's responses to the astrologer J[oachim] F[riedrich] Hartmann (1848–1930), who had published an article, "Astrology and the European War," in *EN* (4 September 1914), in the very place (the top centre of the last page) where HPL's astronomy articles customarily appeared. For Hartmann's four pieces responding to HPL (and to his pseudonym, Isaac Bickerstaffe, Jr.), see the Appendix (pp. 334–48).

Notes

1. Richard Anthony Proctor (1837–1888), British scientist and author of such works as *Essays on Astronomy* (1872) and *The Moon* (1886).
2. HPL refers to Thomas Hines, Jr., whom he had criticized in his 1906 letter to the *Providence Sunday Journal*, "No Transit of Mars" (p. 16).

THE FALSITY OF ASTROLOGY

To the Editor of the Evening News:
     Since the ordinary modern astrologer is merely a mountebank who seeks to defraud the ignorant by means of crude gibberish which he knows to be untrue, his tribe may very easily be silenced by the proper legal authorities. During the past few years hundreds of these impudent quacks have been disposed of by the United States government through the diligent efforts of the postal inspectors.

     Far more difficult, however, is the task of dealing with that honest minority of star-gazing prophets who actually believe in their own ridiculous teachings, and who can therefore invest their fallacious arguments with the convincing force of genuine though misplaced enthusiasm.

     To the latter class belongs our distinguished local author and astrologer, Mr. J. F. Hartmann, whose long and laboured letter in defence of his belief appears in The Evening News for Oct. 7. Mr. Hartmann is nothing if not sincere. He is very obviously a blindly fanatical devotee of the false science of the heavens; being on that account the more dangerous foe to knowledge, since he appears to deem it his duty to spread the pernicious superstition which he himself so innocently holds.

     In his recent letter Mr. Hartmann says little that he has not said before, and but for the superficial plausibility of some of his attempts at reasoning, I should have taken no notice of it. As it is, I feel impelled to comment a little further on the one oft-repeated foundation of his arguments: the alleged ignorance of astrology on the part of astronomers.

     Mr. Hartmann errs very gravely when he denies that astronomy proves the falsity of astrology. Astronomy investigates every force and influence exerted by the various bodies of space upon one another, measuring with the utmost care and exactitude each slightest manifestation of energy. No considerable influence could possibly escape the attention of the astronomer, for he attacks the subject at every angle, and follows up with the keenest activity every principle for which he can discover any real data whatsoever. The true student, comparing the motions of the heavenly bodies with the varied affairs of mankind, has never found a trace of evidence that there is any connexion between the two, nor has he discovered any reason why there should be. Indeed, astrology is based wholly upon apparent celestial motions, which, as I pointed out in my previous letter, are merely the result of perspective as viewed from this one puny planet which we call Earth. No rational and unprejudiced scholar could for a moment tolerate a "science" thus unsupported. He needs no such "astrological textbooks", as Mr. Hartmann recommends, in order to perceive its absolute unsoundness. Mr. Hartmann himself appears to possess just those intellectual characteristics which he deplores in others. He is certainly bigoted in his astrological belief, and he has evidently studied astronomy no more than the astronomers whom he censures have studied astrology. A simple course in astronomy might do much toward destroying his mediaeval ideas.

Very ridiculous is the statement that any fair-minded astronomer would become a convert to Astrology if he should study the latter subject. It were more correct to say that any astrologer, if unprejudiced and properly instructed, would quickly abandon his superstitious notions. Has Mr. Hartmann forgotten that the great Danish astronomer Tycho Brahe was at first a sincere and enthusiastic believer in Astrology, becoming convinced of its falsity only after he had profoundly studied it for years; or that the eminent French philosopher Gassendi had delved deeply into astrological lore before he cast it aside in disgust?

We need commend but little on the prophecies which Mr. Hartmann in his first article quoted from Raphael's almanack. Though the coincidence concerning the Titanic is very interesting, the general ambiguity of the prediction is self-evident. Prof. George Lyman Kittredge[1] of Harvard University gives similar examples, extracted from Zadkiel's annual, in his interesting book entitled "The Old Farmer and His Almanack".

In replying to one of my arguments, Mr. Hartmann asks: "How do you know that the Delphic Oracles were vague and ambiguous?" My inquisitor would do well to engage in some elementary classical research.

As a supreme test of his pseudo-science, Mr. Hartmann invites me to demand the sort of evidence of its truth which I would deem convincing. I might ask him on what principle the various and complex destinies of men can be connected with the apparent positions of immensely distant bodies, all moving in accordance with regular mechanical laws, and exerting no perceptible influence upon the earth save that of gravitation. I might ask him to state the nature of the powerful, mysterious celestial force which, he declares, moulds our acts and fortunes, and to explain why a few erratic sophists claim the ability to detect and study in detail without instruments a species of energy which no other scientist has yet noticed even with the most elaborate and delicate appliances. But I should pay too much respect to a contemptible system of charlatanry were I to consider these matters seriously.

The baleful effect of Astrology upon the reputation of Astronomy is far too patent for Mr. Hartmann to argue away. I was not long ago asked by a man who had seen my astronomical articles, 'if I did not cast horoscopes or calculate nativities'! It is not pleasant for a serious student of the heavens to be taken for a petty fortune-teller.

I shall not seek to persecute Mr. Hartmann and his false art. Astrology thrives on persecution, as Juvenal knew well when he wrote in his Sixth Satire: "Nemo mathematicus genium indemnatus habebit."[2] My only wish is to warn the reading public against these dead, ancient fallacies which now and then rise like unwelcome spectres from their graves.

Astrology is the legacy of prehistoric ignorance. Since our primitive ancestors saw that the motion of the sun through the Zodiac influenced their affairs by the change of season which it causes, or that the movements and phases of the moon affected their nocturnal pursuits by the alternative presence and absence of moonlight, they must have believed themselves under the direct control of these bodies. Since certain stars appear at certain seasons, apparently announcing such periodic events as the rising of the Nile or the autumn rains, the untutored man of remote antiquity must quite easily have acquired the false belief that events of any sort are predicted by the lanterns of the sky. In time, the ancients came to seek explanations for all the phenomena of earth in the phenomena of the heavens, and arbitrarily to assign a celestial cause for every terrestrial occurrence. Naturally, their religious system became merged into their astrological scheme, and each governing god became identified with some particular "governing" planet; whence comes our present planetary nomenclature.

With such a beginning, it is not difficult to account for the prevalence of astrological beliefs in ancient and mediaeval times, or, on the other hand, to see why such notions cannot hope to survive in this scientific age.

H. P. LOVECRAFT

598 Angell St., Providence, R.I.
    Oct. 8, 1914

EDITOR'S NOTE FP: *EN* 45, No. 122 (10 October 1914): 8. A somewhat intemperate response to Hartmann's letter to the editor of 5 October (see Appendix, p. 338), in which HPL relies largely upon abuse rather than argument to make his points.

Notes

1. George Lyman Kittredge (1860–1941), *The Old Farmer and His Almanack* (1904; *LL* 504). See HPL's discussion of the book (*SL* 2.174).

2. "No astrologer who has not been imprisoned will have any reputation." Juvenal, *Satires* 6.562.

ASTROLOGY AND THE FUTURE

Editor, Evening News:
    Very regrettable is the reluctance lately shewn by the professors of the sublime science of astrology in publishing their predictions. Persecuted as they are by arrogant, intolerant, and materialistic students of less lofty subjects, they seem to confine their glorious art to relatively unimportant matters, as though too proud to exhibit to a cynical, unenlightened, and undeserving world the full majesty of their power.

The most authoritative astrological information now to be obtained is that published each year in Raphael's Ephemeris, as recently quoted by your gifted contributor, Mr. Hartmann; yet this scholarly annual forecasts events only for each following year, neglecting to prepare us for occurrences in the more remote future.

Now since all astrological prophecies are founded on the exact, eternal, and undeviating motions of the heavenly bodies; their houses, exaltations, progressions, aspects, and transits; their oppositions, trines, quartiles, sextiles, and conjunctions; and since by mathematics we can calculate these motions for an infinite distance into the future; why do the astrologers of today content themselves with predictions a mere year in advance, instead of extending their researches through the coming centuries, even to the end of the world itself? It is true that the universal deluge predicted by Stöffler[1] for the year 1524 failed to appear, but we have at the present time far more exact methods of calculation, and are undoubtedly able to determine future events with a much greater degree of accuracy and certainty.

The writer, who was born under the planet Mercury, has spent many years in astrological study, following in general the methods of William Lilly,[2] and giving special attention to remote future. As early as 1897 I predicted the present European conflict, as well as the annexation of Mexico by the United States, which will take place next year, after the anarchy resulting from the displacement of Carranza by Gen. Villa.[3]

In my unpublished book, "The History of the Future", I have recorded many startling things which would not be believed were I to reveal them now. I foresee within the next 2000 years events of the most stupendous nature in the Western hemisphere.

A fortunate ascendant of Mars shews that a man will arise whose fame will outrank Caesar's.

I see changes of a most revolutionary nature about to occur in the very State of Rhode Island. A conjunctional eclipse of Mercury by Saturn indicates that the English language will cease to be spoken in America after the year 2344, at about which time Emperor Theodore IX of the United States will retake California from the Japanese through the remarkable strategy of Field-Marshal Patricio Coeno. The crossed transit of Jupiter and Uranus over the alternately radical sun and moon on March 9, 2448, is certain evidence that the American monarch will be overthrown in that year as a result of a popular uprising led by Gen. Jos, Francisco Artmano and a new republic established; the capital being moved from Mexico City back to Washington.

In Europe every familiar condition will vanish. An opposition of Neptune with the asteroid Ceres tells us that in 1916 the present war will end with a complete victory for the allies, this being followed by the dismemberment of the German and Austrian Empires.

The Tsar will take German and Austrian Poland, as well as the whole of Hungary. France will regain Alsace and Lorraine. England will take over all German colonies, and establish a naval base on the Baltic in Schleswig-Holstein. Holland will enter the war on the side of Germany, and after the defeat will be annexed to Belgium. Italy, having fought bravely with the Allies, will receive a large share of Austrian territory, and will annex all Albanian territory as well. Japan will take but little part in the war, and indeed will engage in no tremendous hostilities until the great Mongolian invasion of 2142. Prussia will retain but little territory outside its own boundaries. Austria, deprived of Hungary, will join with Bavaria, forming a powerful and prosperous Teutonic empire which will conquer Spain in 2010 during the Hapsburg succession to the Spanish throne.

Kaiser Wilhelm and his family will be exiled in Napoleon's old quarters at Longwood on St. Helena, but a supreme ascendant of Mars in Scorpio shews that the crown prince's eldest son will escape in June, 1937, and later reign as king of Prussia. A progressed double quartile of Pallas and Mercury in Taurus and Venus and Juno in Libra indicates the conquest of all Europe by Russia in 1998, and a general invasion of Mongolians in Europe and America in 2142. This invasion will give rise to a frightful struggle between the white and yellow races lasting two and a half centuries, and resulting in the complete defeat of China and Japan, together with the conquest of their lands. A descendant of the circumpolar constellation Ursa Major, accompanied by a corresponding progressive exaltation of the radical Zodiacal sign Leo in 2517, indicates the overthrow of the Russian power in Europe by the English and the subsequent joint rule of earth by America and England.

With Uranus stationary in conjunction with the seventh house of the sextile op-position of Vulcan in Gemini on Aug. 18, 2814, I foresee a terrible plague which will annihilate a quarter of the world's population.

Last and most terrible of all, the collusive quarternary trine of Mars, Mercury, Vulcan, and Saturn, in the 13th progressed house of the sign Cancer on Feb. 26, 4954, stands out as plainly as the handwriting on the wall to shew us the awful day on which this earth will finally and infallibly perish through a sudden and unexpected explosion of volcanic gases in the interior.

Scoffers and unbelievers may smile at my predictions, but these astrological com-putations are founded on a science as old as the human race; a science that has for centuries resisted every attempt of the sceptical and the ignorant to overthrow it.

Were it not a wiser and nobler course for our upstart teachers and scientists to cease their vain cavillings at astrology, to mould their lives and actions in accord with the infinite and the inevitable, and to bow with proper humility before the time-tried precepts of this sacred and venerable species of truth?

ISAAC BICKERSTAFFE, JR.

South Main Street, Providence, R.I.

EDITOR'S NOTE FP: *EN* 45, No. 123 (13 October 1914): 8 (as "Astrlogh and the Future"; as by "Isaac Bickerstaffe, Jr."). The first of HPL's three pseudonymous satires on Hartmann, written before Hartmann had a chance to reply to "The Falsity of Astrology." In this article HPL uses the ploy of making ludicrous astrological predictions of the far future.

Notes

1. Johann Stöffler (1452–1531), German astrologer and student of the astrolabe. HPL's in-formation on him comes from the article "Astrology" (by Jules Andrieu) in the 9th edition of the *Encyclopaedia Britannica.*

2. William Lilly (1602–1681), British astrologer and author of almanacs such as *Merlini Ephemeris* (1644–81).

3. During the Mexican Civil War, revolutionary leader Francisco ("Pancho") Villa (1878–1923) struggled against forces led by Venustiano Carranza (1859–1920). Carranza defeated Villa at the Battle of Celaya in 1915, thereafter ruling Mexico as constitutional president until shortly before his death.

<hr>

DELAVAN'S COMET AND ASTROLOGY

The influence of cometary bodies on the horoscope of mankind is one which most astrologers of the present time have sadly underrated. The uninstructed majority seem to have lost faith in the benefic and malefic potency of these tenuously con-structed celestial wanderers, and to condemn as superstitions what they should investi-gate as scientific phenomena.

Shakespeare knew well the significance of a comet's visitation when he wrote in his immortal tragedy of "Julius Caesar": "When beggars die, there are no comets seen; the heavens themselves blaze forth the death of princes."[1]

Little did I dream when I published my astrological predictions in The Evening News for Oct. 12, what marvellous revelations of interplanetary communications should be made to man through the recent aspect of Delavan's comet, coupled with the retrograde motion of Saturn, the greater in fortune. Prof. Hartmann, the recognised leader of astrological thought in New England, seems even now to have missed these startling disclosures from the sky, though he utters a multitude of profound truths in his masterly essay of Oct. 22.

In brief, I have now been enabled to solve the momentous problem of the future of the human race after the destruction of the earth by the great volcano explosion of February 26, 4954!

It was ever difficult for me to believe that our noble species of mortals could be completely annihilated in an instant; that all the flower of uncounted centuries of evolution could thus be cruelly blasted in the twinkling of an eye; yet what could a true astrologer do but believe it when all the stars, suns, worlds, planets, moons, constellations, and zodiacs in their courses pointed with a grim unrelenting finger to the world's inevitable end?

But the computed alternating back eccentric transit of the future projection of Delavan's comet around the progressed quartile square of the prolonged inclination of the retrograde orbit of Saturn clears up the perplexing situation in a moment, renders the whole matter most simple and obvious, and restores to man that hope without which the heart would sicken and break.

As every schoolboy may perceive, the inequalities in the gravitational direction of the 23d house of Saturn cause a pronounced deflection in the course of the seventh inner circle of that mysterious comet known to astrologers as XY4. Now before the discovery of Delavan's comet it was thought that comet XY4 would not approach that part of space until 4975, or 21 years after the destruction of the world, but the occult separative influence of the new-found body introduces a new factor into our calculations, and our conclusions. From this same cause, most important and hitherto obscure data concerning the ascendant of the 16th benefic of Jupiter over the 11th malefic of Mars in the year 4824 are explained.

From all of which we may easily deduce that on June 29, 4898, or nearly 56 years before the great catastrophe, the comet XY4 will harmlessly encounter our terraqueous globe, safely taking away on its tail the entire human race! The anaesthetic gases of which the comet is composed will preserve in a state of suspended animation the mortals thus whisked off into space, allowing them to be carried toward perihelion and deposited unhurt on the planet Venus, which much resembles the Earth in size, and on which mankind will forevermore dwell in peace and plenty. The processional quadratic equation of Ariel and Callisto in Sagitarrius shews that the present inhabitants of Venus are much superior in intellect to our earthly race, being especially skilled in astrology.

When our remote descendants are set down amidst this enlightened people, they will doubtless lose that stubborn, sceptical devotion to so-called "reason" or "common sense", which now sadly hinders their progress in the higher and more mystical branches of spiritual learning.

It is obvious that all astrological computations beyond the year 4898 must be made not for the Earth but for Venus, where mankind will then reside. I have commenced my labours in this direction, and have succeeded in making certain predictions as far as the year 5025. I find to my extreme regret that several fragments from the terrestrial explosion of 4954 will strike the planet Venus, there creating much damage, and causing grave injuries to Señor Nostradomo Artmano, a lineal descendant of our talented Prof. Hartmann. Señor Artmano, a wise astrologer, will be hit in the cranial region by a large volume of astronomy, blown from the Providence Public Library, and his mind will be so affected by the concussion that he will no longer be able to appreciate the divine precepts of Astrology.

In 5012 an unfortunate event will occur, for the double crossed note of the trine of Neptune and Umbriel on Jan. 3 of that year shews that an evil-minded individual named Serviss will introduce amongst the people a false and pernicious art called "Logic", which will work great havoc with the noble doctrines of astrological truth.

As I delve deeper into the mysteries of the remote future, I shall endeavour to keep the public informed from time to time of my progress; but until then, I must leave the field clear for Prof. Hartmann's expert and brilliant work.

ISAAC BICKERSTAFFE, JR.
Providence, Oct. 24, 1914.

EDITOR'S NOTE FP: *EN* 45, No. 134 (26 October 1914): 8 (as by "Isaac Bickerstaffe, Jr."). Another satire using bogus astrology to predict events of the far future, in this case employing the relatively recent discovery of Delavan's comet (see "May Sky" [p. 113], n. 1) to revise Bickerstaffe's prediction of the extinction of the human race as cited in "Astrology and the Future."

Notes

1. Shakespeare, *Julius Caesar* 2.2.30–31.

THE FALL OF ASTROLOGY

To the Editor of The Evening News:
    In perusing Mr. Hartmann's somewhat belated reply to my letter in The Evening News of October 10, I am impressed with the resentment the astrologer seems to harbour against me for what he deems my abusive treatment of him. It may be that contempt for the puerile fallacies of astrological lore has led me into a rather too caustic procedure with my opponent, yet I would assure him that I respect the sincerity of his opinions, and admire the spirit with which he defends his pseudo-science. In the present letter I shall strive to avoid the use of that denunciation and ridicule against which Mr. Hartmann so strongly protests; but shall instead try the novel experiment of suspending my attack, and of assuming a defensive attitude, endeavouring merely to justify the present universal rejection of astrology by the intelligent public.

Astrology was coeval with astronomy. It was indeed, as I pointed out in a previous article, the natural result of the contemplation of the celestial vault by a young and undeveloped race. In very ancient times it was of real value to science on account of the incentive which it offered to the precise observation and careful study of the heavenly bodies. The astronomical knowledge of the Chaldaeans was in fact wholly due to the zeal of their astrologers. Thus before the advent of modern scientific exactitude, the true and the false studies of the sky were pursued side by side and in perfect harmony. If either might be said to have precedence over the other, astrology was the one so favoured. Throughout the Middle Ages and the early Modern Period astrology enjoyed the condition of a respected branch of learning. Each monarch had his astrologer or astrologers, to whom he referred all projected affairs of state, both in war and in peace. Though at the time of the Renaissance some keener minds penetrated the specious exterior and discovered the fundamental unsoundness of the art, it was none the less very generally cultivated by all classes, foremost among them being the astronomers. Kepler, while discarding many of its more patently absurd notions, stoutly defended the underlying truth of astrology, and made known his views in a pamphlet entitled "De Fundamentis Astrologiae Certioribus" (1602). Lord Bacon and Sir Thomas Browne were likewise believers in the influence of the heavens. As late as Charles the Second's reign the public had scarce begun to doubt the genuineness of astrology, and the notorious William Lilly, though probably a conscious charlatan himself, was credited to a marvellous degree, even being summoned at one time by a committee of the House of Commons to predict the result of a certain piece of legislation.

Thus it may be perceived, that before the discovery of conclusive contrary evidence, astrology encountered no opposition either from the astronomers or from the people in general. So long as any man of science could find any reason to believe it true, it was accepted on a plane of equality with other serious studies. The only bigotry and blind prejudice which astrology ever aroused emanated from the early church; but this hostility did not extend to every department of the subject, and has no connexion with the later overthrow of the art on rational grounds.

The downfall of astrology was the inevitable result of intellectual progress; of new discoveries in science, improved methods of reasoning, more intelligent examination of history, and more discriminating investigation of the prophecies of astrologers. It became apparent that very few definite astrological predictions had ever been fulfilled even approximately, that almost all forecasts were couched in a vague style which might be interpreted in practically any way, that the most successful astrologers were obviously impostors who arrived at their conclusions only through shrewd guesses or profound knowledge of human nature, and that those who most honestly practiced astrology were the most conspicuous in their failures. At the same time, earnest students perfectly familiar with astrology and astrological methods commenced to realise the utter absurdity of the study. They saw that the very fundamental principle of casting horoscopes rests on mere allegory; the analogy of a man's birth to a star's rising. They saw that the various qualities attributed to the several planets and their positions in the Zodiac we derived wholly from the mythical gods and monsters after which the planets and stars were named. Not only was it shewn that astrological predictions were untrue, but also that every method employed to make them is false. Besides, no reason was found why the heavens should in any manner whatsoever influence or indicate the lives and destinies of mankind. What excuse, then, could any man have for adhering to a belief unsupported by the least particle of evidence, and possessing not the slightest shadow of probability? Even had there been no direct evidence against astrology, the complete absence of evidence for it would have been sufficient to justify its abandonment. Astrology died a natural and honourable death; and had the world been content to let it rest in peace, it would never have become an object of contempt and ridicule. But the greed of the charlatan and the vagaries of the eccentric kept it before the eyes of a public who had outgrown belief, and who could not but be intolerant of an art which they knew to be obsolete. The first opponents of astrology were perfectly conversant with its principles, and derived from their knowledge only the more material for use against it. But the study of the pseudo-science naturally disappeared amongst the intelligent as soon as its falsity was well demonstrated. It would of course be ridiculous for men to waste their lives in amassing information which is well known to be false, and which would seriously interfere with their acquisition of real learning. We cannot spend our precious years in repeating all the errors of our remote forefathers; we must rather profit by old blunders, and seek to avoid the false in favour of the true. Wherefore reputable authors, publishers, and institutions of learning have ceased to disseminate the fallacies of astrology, and the present generation have no hesitation in declaring their absolute unfamiliarity with that subject. It has been disproved so many times by those versed in its mysteries, that even were astronomy not enough to brand it false, we should not need to repeat such a redundant performance. Why does not Mr. Hartmann demand that we disprove the old, abandoned Ptolemaic theory of the universe once more?

Let me now consider some of my opponent's statements in greater detail. He declares quite gravely, that "when physicians say the moon's phases influence their patients, the astronomers call it truth". I hardly need answer that no astronomer of the present time would credit such an absurd assertion, nor would any rational physician make it.

Another paragraph of Mr. Hartmann's is truly amazing. He tells us that with but one exception the astronomical books in our public library leave the reader with the impression that planetary orbits are circular. I have read nearly all the volumes in question, and can say with certainty that none of them could possibly convey such an idea to any intelligent person. The elliptical nature of orbits is too well known to be concealed even by the vaguest of books.

Mr. Hartmann inquires of me, in connexion with my denunciation of the "ordinary modern astrologer" as a mountebank, what I would consider an ancient or an extraordinary astrologer. Since the ancient astrologers believed to a greater or less extent their own predictions, I should call them somewhat misguided scientists; while as for the extraordinary modern prophets like Mr. Hartmann himself, I think I gave them sufficient credit for their fanatical sincerity in my previous letter.

Before concluding, I should like to comment on Mr. Hartmann's curious attempt at etymological derivation of the word "superstition". Surely he could not have obtained such a mass of nonsense from the authorities he quotes, for any man of education knows that the word comes directly from the Latin and not from the Greek. "Superstition" is from the Latin "superstare", and in turn derived from "super", over, and "stare", to stand still; the implied meaning being a standing still over anything in dread amazement or reverence. All of this information is obtained from Webster's Unabridged Dictionary, which should invariably be consulted on points of this sort. However, I fail to see how the origin of the word can interest Mr. Hartmann so much more than its present use, which is sufficiently well-known to all.

I have here endeavoured to treat seriously a subject which can scarce be contemplated without a smile. This rather inappropriate method must find its justification in the sober and extremely zealous tone of my opponent's arguments.

H. P. LOVECRAFT

Dec. 15, 1914.

EDITOR'S NOTE FP: *EN* 46, No. 25 (17 December 1914): 8. An attempt at a more sober refutation of Hartmann's astrological claims as presented in "A Defense of Astrology" (p. 344). Hartmann finally gave up the battle and made no further replies either to this article or to HPL's final Bickerstaffe satire.

[ISAAC BICKERSTAFFE'S REPLY]

Editor News:

Seasoned though I am to the heartless attacks of the vulgar scientific public, I was cut to the quick by the recent insinuations concerning me, made by my fellow-astrologer, Prof. J. F. Hartmann. I cannot but infer that it is to my work that he alludes, when he says that "Two recent articles in these columns, by an enemy falsely posing as an astrologer, are real gibberish. Real astrologers never write such ridiculous parodies upon their own sacred science." How can Prof. Hartmann hope to secure belief for his own writings, when he thus basely attacks the humble efforts of a brother? Heretofore only stupid outsiders have cast aspersion and ridicule on our labours. Is the professor about to desert our sublime study, and join the ranks of the mocking unbelievers? In denouncing my work as "gibberish", Prof. Hartmann shews as little genuine spiritual comprehension of the inner truths of astrology as do the pompous pedants who attack us both.

Astrology is indeed like a delicate flower; in its entirety a thing of rare grace and beauty, but utterly ruined when picked to pieces by gross, ungentle hands. Why seek for cold logic in the inspired utterances of a prophet? Obtuse indeed is that intellect which can mistake for parodies the predictions in whose preparation a grave scholar has spent the better part of a long life. Could Prof. Hartmann himself duplicate my achievements in the art of judicial astrology? Does he extend his own timid forecasts to the end of the world and beyond? When he can thus compete with me in my own wider sphere then let him taunt me with his charge of levity and insincerity!

But when the professor pronounces my writings mere "gibberish", he pays me a far greater compliment than he dreams. I perceive by his profound etymological analysis of the word "superstition", wherein he traces it back to the Greek, that he is a thorough master of classical languages; yet his ignorance of the Arabic tongue leads him astray in the use of what he thinks to be an epithet of opprobrium. In employing the word "gibberish", Prof. Hartmann doubtless falls into the error commonly found in the cheap dictionaries, assuming the noun is derived from the Icelandic verb root "gifra", to jabber; but as a student of Arabic, I am able absolutely to controvert this fallacy, and to ascribe the word to its proper root. "Gibberish", or to use the more primitive noun, "al geber isch", arose from the name of Geber, an eminent Arabian astronomer and alchemist, who flourished in the eighth century A.D.[1] The purest signification of "gibberish" is "words of Geber", which later gave rise to the secondary meaning, "astrological wisdom", referring to the Wisdom of Geber's conversation on that subject. Thus do I stand triumphantly vindicated! Prof. Hartmann has indirectly and unwittingly admitted that I am a wise astrologer!

But let me now leave this distasteful controversy and proceed at once to the work which I was preparing before the professor so rudely attacked me. I have the honour herewith to submit my carefully calculated prophecies for the first half of the coming year 1915. I may with all due modesty affirm their complete accuracy, and challenge any of my emulous rivals to produce equal or superior results.

JANUARY.

Conjunction of Mercury and Mars on first indicates prosperous and disastrous year. Earth in perihelion on second, conjoined with greatest brilliancy of Venus, and lunar conjunction of Neptune, predicts cold weather in January and February. Moon on Equator Jan. 19 shews that European war will still be raging. Opposition of Neptune on 20th signifies English or German success about this time.

FEBRUARY.

Greatest elongations of both Venus and Mercury on 6th indicate the following February will have 29 days, that being one extra. Eclipse of Sun on 13th is malefic [so that] several men will die either in Belgium, France, or Prussia.

MARCH.

Entrance of Sun into sign Aries shews that spring will begin on the 21st. Conjunction of Mars and Jupiter on 23d shews disturbances in the Eastern hemisphere.

APRIL.

Moon's double Perigee on 1st and 30th tells one that Kaiser Wilhelm will not yet put into practice his principle of universal peace.

MAY.

Superior conjunction of Mercury in 1st shews that weather will be much warmer than January. Lunar conjunction of Saturn on 17th foretells ill feelings between Austrians and Serbians.

JUNE.

Summer will probably commence this month. Quadrature of Jupiter on the 19th indicates much anxiety felt by Kings and Princes. Conjunction of Saturn on 28th renders it likely that July will arrive no sooner than usual.

The arduous labour necessary for the computation of these prophecies has left me with but little time in which to enlarge my vaster researches into the more remote future, hence I can be sure of very few facts after 5020 A.D.

In concluding, I must again lament the apostasy of my talented colleague, Prof. Hartmann. How can we astrologers hope successfully to promulgate our glorious science, if we have such bitter dissensions amongst ourselves? In exhibiting scepticism of a brother's work and thereby seeking to destroy our faith with the worldly weapons of reason and scorn, the Professor has perpetrated a serious infraction of astrological ethics.

ISAAC BICKERSTAFFE, JR.

EDITOR'S NOTE FP: *EN* 46, No. 28 (21 December 1914): 3 (as by "Isaac Bickerstaffe, Jr."). Here HPL employs the method of making obvious predictions but conveying the impression that they could only have been arrived at by astrological means.

Notes

1. Geber was in fact the pseudonym of a Latin alchemist of the 14th century who wrote four immensely influential astrological works that purported to be Latin translations of the work of an Arabic alchemist, Jabir ibn Hayyan. But the works were in fact original compositions of the 14th century. Geber is cited in *The Case of Charles Dexter Ward* (1927).

MYSTERIES OF THE HEAVENS REVEALED BY ASTRONOMY

T he series beginning with this article is designed for persons having no previous knowledge of astronomy. Only the simplest and most interesting parts of the subject have here been included. It is hoped that this series may help in a small way to diffuse a knowledge of the heavens amongst the readers of The Gazette-News, to destroy in their minds the pernicious and contemptible superstition of judicial astrology, and to lead at least a few of them to a more particular study of astronomical science.

I. THE SKY AND ITS CONTENTS

A stronomy, the oldest of all the sciences, is that branch of knowledge which treats of the heavenly bodies, their size, distances, motions, relations, and physical conditions. The name is derived from the Greek words "astron", a star, and "nomos", a law.

Of the various studies pursued by mankind, none is better adapted to furnish to its followers a rational and intellectual species of enjoyment than is this sublime science, for the grandeur and beauty of its objects, the simplicity and directness of their observation, and the broad conception of the universe obtained from their contemplation, whereby our seemingly boundless earth is relegated to its proper insignificance in the vast system of infinity, all afford to the active and reflective mind an exercise of the most refreshing and pleasurable character.

Astronomy is likewise of great practical use to the human race, for by its aid the size and figure of the earth are measured, the ship guided from port to port, the calendar and clock regulated, and countless other daily affairs facilitated. The book of the heavens is open to all on every clear night of the year, whence there would seem to be little excuse for the great ignorance of celestial science now so lamentably prevalent even in the most highly civilised portions of our globe.

Nature of the Heavenly Bodies

Although the various bodies which shine in our skies appear to us as small flat discs and minute points of light, they are, nevertheless, as everyone has doubtless heard, very different in their actual nature, being for the most part great suns and worlds, the majority of them much, and some vastly larger than the earth on which we reside, whirling around on their axes and rushing with incredible rapidity in their appointed courses; some possibly inhabited by beings not unlike ourselves. This terraqueous globe itself, massive though it seem to us, is in reality a most insignificant object as considered in relation to the rest of the universe. It is, in fact, only one of eight similar globes, called "planets", that revolve in approximately circular paths or "orbits" around the sun, an immense, fiery, central sphere from which they receive all their warmth and illumination. The moon is a small planet revolving around the earth as the earth itself revolves around the sun. Nearly every planet possesses one or more such moons or "satellites" as they are called. The sun, together with its retinue of planets and their satellites, forms what has been designated as "the solar system".

The stars, which should never be confused with the planets, are other suns, similar in many respects to ours, independent of the solar system, and quite likely having attendant planets of their own. The nearest star is 9,000 times more distant from us than is the most remote of the planets; indeed, so far off are the stars that the most powerful telescopes shew them as nothing more than mere points of light. Scattered amongst the stars, however, are the "nebulae", inconceivably great masses of glowing gas, whose prodigious size enables them to present perceptible surfaces to our telescopes.

All the heavenly bodies, stars, nebulae, planets, and satellites alike, are held to their proper places and paths by the laws of motion and the force of universal gravitation. The stars, including the sun, and also the nebulae, shine by their own light, but the moon and the planets of our solar system are made visible only by radiance reflected from the sun.

As will be made evident in the succeeding articles of this series, the domain of astronomy is more unbounded than is that of any other science. In the solar system, distances of millions of miles are relatively short; whilst the stars are so far apart, that the space between them cannot be measured conveniently by terrestrial standards, being marked off by the number of years required by light, at its enormously rapid rate of 186,000 miles per second, to travel from one to the other. Notwithstanding these tremendous gaps, many of the heavenly bodies can be weighed, measured, and analysed by means of modern appliances; while most of the planets, being comparatively near, may be studied and mapped like the earth by the aid of large telescopes. However, the amateur astronomer need not provide himself with any such instruments, as the sky is sufficiently entertaining and instructive as seen by the unaided eye.

The Aspect of the Heavens

The sky seems to us an immense hollow sphere, at whose centre we are situate, and only half of which we are able to see at one time, since the rest is cut off by the earth underfoot. Once in every twenty-four hours this sphere appears to revolve around us from east to west, though we know that this motion is really due to the rotation of our own earth in the opposite direction. By day the dazzling refulgence of the sun prevents us from studying the surface of this celestial sphere, but when the bright orb has sunk from sight, we see that the vault above is bespangled with a vast assemblage of stars, which appear always to keep the same places in relation to one another, and which are arranged by chance into certain well-known permanent figures called "constellations". This seeming lack of motion, however, is only the result of the inconceivable distances at which the stars are situate; actually they are flying in various directions at tremendous rates of speed, though not for thousands of years could we perceive any sensible difference in their apparent places and arrangement. Outlined against this unchanging stellar background, and seeming to move slowly amongst the stars, shine the members of our solar system.

But whilst we cannot observe the real motions of the stars, we are impressed plainly enough by their two apparent motions; their diurnal rising and setting, due to the earth's rotation on its axis, and their annual progress westward, due to the earth's motion around the sun. Since the stars are fixed on the celestial sphere, we may with greater inclusiveness say that these are motions not simply of the stars, but of the celestial sphere itself. The heavens are different at different hours of the same night, because the earth is swiftly turning us to face different parts of the sky; they are different for the same hour at different seasons, because the sun appears to be moving eastward, carrying the day with it, as it were, overtaking the stars, and causing them to rise and set four minutes earlier every day. The morning sky is that which the sun has just left behind; in several months, the sun having travelled around from the eastern part of it to the western part, that same area of sky with all its stars will have become the evening sky. Thus new constellations appear in the east just before sunrise, become visible earlier and earlier at night as time passes, at length rise so early that they are already high in the heavens when darkness falls, shine farther and farther westward as the nights pass, until at last they drift into the western twilight of early evening, and are lost in the sun's rays; later to appear afresh in the morning sky.

The pole or pivot about which the heavens seem to turn is that part of the sky to which is pointed the earth's axis. This spot is roughly marked by a fairly bright star called "Polaris" the "north star", or the "pole star", which is of course exempt from the general motions of the celestial vault, and which is stationed due north, as far above the horizon or skyline of any place, as that place is north of the earth's equator. In our latitude, it lies somewhat less than half way between the horizon and the "zenith", or point overhead, so that there is a very considerable part of the northern sky, having as a radius the distance between Polaris and the horizon, wherein the stars never set, but remain permanently visible, describing circles about the pole, and therefore being called "circumpolar". There is an opposite area of extreme southern sky which can never be seen in this part of the world.

The equator of the heavens is an extension of the plane of the earth's equator, girdling the sky ninety degrees from the celestial pole, and cutting the horizon at the east and west points. Bodies in this region spend equal periods above and below the horizon, whereas others stay longer above or below, according as they are situate north or south of the equator.

The "ecliptic", or apparent annual path of the sun, is in reality an extension of the plane of the earth's orbit into space. Since the earth's equator is inclined 23 and a half degrees to the plane of the orbit, it follows that in the sky the ecliptic and celestial equator must intersect each other at a similar angle. That intersection at which the sun crosses the equator on its northward journey is called the "vernal equinox", and is a most important point on astronomical charts.

In order to determine the position of objects on the celestial sphere, that imaginary globe is supplied with a system of circles like those of latitude and longitude on the earth. "Right ascension" corresponds to longitude, and is distance east of the vernal equinox, whilst "declination" is like latitude, being distance north or south of the equator.

The "meridian" of the sky is a line extending due north and south, and marking the central and highest points in the apparent diurnal courses of the heavenly bodies. A body on the meridian is said to "culminate" or to be in "transit". Circumpolar bodies cross the meridian twice in one revolution; once in culmination, or upper transit, above the pole, and twelve hours later in lower transit, below the pole.

EDITOR'S NOTE FP: *AGN* 20, No. 4 (16 February 1915): 4. The first of a unified series of articles outlining the fundamentals of astronomy, announced in several early columns as being in 14 sections, although only 12 and part of the 13th were apparently published. Several sections were divided into two parts, and these were not always published consecutively. In this edition, the sections are published sequentially, although their division into parts has been retained.

[II.] THE SOLAR SYSTEM

Having obtained a crude idea of the general nature and appearance of the heavens, let us now seek to learn some facts concerning that particular family of celestial bodies to which our own earth belongs. Though of small importance indeed in the vast universe of stars, the solar system is yet to us an object of the greatest concern, since it is the only part of creation whose workings we may study in any degree of detail.

At the centre lies the dominant member, a star of moderate size as stars are reckoned, known to us as the sun. Around this seething ball of fire revolve eight large "major" planets and their satellites, almost a thousand small "minor" planets, or "asteroids", many comets, and countless little rockets known as "meteors". The planets, which are the most important bodies in the system except the sun itself, all resemble one another in the following particulars:

(1)   They are all nearly round bodies, flattened at the ends, or poles.
(2)   They all revolve from west to east around the sun, in nearly the same plane.
(3)   They all rotate, or turn, on their axes, also from west to east.
(4)   Their satellites, with very few exceptions, revolve and rotate in the same manner as themselves.

The time of a planet's revolution round the sun forms its "year", while its axial rotation is its "day". Its seasons are determined by the inclination of its axis to the plane of its orbit, or path around the sun.

The order of the planets from the sun outward is as follows. First come four rather small bodies, nearly alike, called Mercury, Venus, the Earth, and Mars. They are cold and solid in nature, all (save Mercury) probably rotating in a period of about 24 hours, and having few or no satellites. Next is a zone or belt of myriads of tiny worlds, smaller by far than even the smallest of the eight major planets, and called "asteroids" or "minor planets". Beyond the asteroids are four large bodies, Jupiter, Saturn, Uranus, and Neptune. These are in a state of great heat, probably being molten or semi-fluid, perhaps even gaseous; swift of rotation, the average period being about ten hours; and for the most part possessing many satellites.

The times of revolution of the planets are arranged in the same order as their distances from the sun, those nearer to the latter revolving the more swiftly. Planets inside the earth's orbit are called "inferior" planets. They are never visible opposite the sun, being seen only in the east just before sunrise, and in the west just after sunset. In a telescope they shew all the phases of the moon. Those outside the earth's orbit are known as "superior" planets, and are seen in any place along their path save for short periods when they are lost in the solar rays. They are visible when opposite the sun, when at right angles to it, as well as when in its immediate vicinity. Their discs exhibit little or no change of phase. Of course, Mercury and Venus are the inferior planets; Mars, Jupiter, Saturn, Uranus, and Neptune being superior.

The shape of the path or "orbit" of a planet is that of ellipse, or oval, very nearly approaching a circle in form. The point nearest the sun is called "perihelion", whilst that opposite point which is farthest away from the sun is known as "aphelion".

Comets are included in the solar system, since most of them are bodies revolving round the sun in very elongated orbits.

Another class of bodies belonging to the solar system are meteors, the smallest of all celestial objects. These revolve like planets, but move usually in numerous clusters. Some of them are scarcely larger than pebbles, or even grains of dust, yet they obey the same laws that govern Jupiter, a body 1300 times larger than the earth.

While the stars, as we have already learnt, are so far off that they never seem to change their relative position, keeping to the same apparent arrangement into groups or constellations for many centuries, the planets constantly alter their relative apparent places in the sky, moving from week to week amongst the stars. This is due both to their real motion about the sun, and to the earth's motion. The moon's real motion around the earth is that which causes it to change its apparent position with such great speed, while it is scarce necessary to repeat that the apparent annual motion of the sun is the result of the real motion of the earth in its orbit.

Apparent Motions of the Planets

The various typical or important points in the apparent course of a planet are called "aspects". The principal aspects of the inferior planets, or planets within the earth's orbit, are four in number, viz.: inferior and superior conjunctions, and greatest elongations east and west. In order successfully to comprehend the meaning of these terms, let us follow an inferior planet throughout one of its apparent revolutions. We will begin at a time when it is invisible to our eyes, lying on a line between us and the sun, and therefore rising and setting with the latter. It is then nearest to us, and is said to be in "inferior conjunction". "Conjunction" is a word used to express the relation of two celestial bodies which are in a line north and south; in this case the two bodies are the planet and the sun, but when the sun is one of the bodies concerned its name is not generally mentioned, the expression "in conjunction", when applied to one body without the mention of another, meaning, by general custom, that the body is in conjunction with the sun. Usually when an inferior planet is in inferior conjunction, it passes just a little north or south of the sun, but at rare intervals it passes directly across the disc of the great luminary, becoming visible as a black speck on the shining surface. Such a phenomenon is called a "transit", and is far more common with Mercury than with Venus.

Some time after inferior conjunction, the planet emerges from the solar glare, shining low in the eastern sky just before sunrise, and shewing in the telescope a very thin, crescent phase. As time passes, the phase increases, and the planet withdraws more and more from the sun, being visible higher and higher in the early morning sky, until at length it shews a phase like that of the half-moon, and is at its greatest apparent distance west of the sun. It is then said to be in "greatest elongation west". This is the best time to observe an inferior planet in the morning. After this, the planet turns and approaches the sun, its phase meanwhile increasing and becoming gibbous. Finally, having attained an approximately full phase, it is again lost in the solar rays, coming once more in line with the sun and earth, but this time lying beyond the sun, instead of between us and that body. It is now farthest from the earth, and is said to be in "superior conjunction". Were it not rendered impossible by the blinding refulgence of the sun, it would shew a perfectly round disc, like that of the full moon. Having passed beyond the sun, the planet next becomes visible low in the western sky just after sunset, still shewing in the telescope a practically full phase. As it recedes from the sun, mounting higher and higher in the early evening sky, its phase decreases, after a while becoming a semicircle. The planet is then at its greatest distance east of the sun, and is said to be in "greatest elongation east". This is the best time to observe it in the evening sky. Now the planet appears again to approach the sun, and the crescentic phase is a second time assumed. At last it becomes lost in the sun's radiance, and once more arrives at inferior conjunction. The foregoing description applies equally to Mercury and Venus, though Venus, of course, recedes at its elongations nearly twice as far from the sun as does Mercury.

In considering the case of the superior planets, or planets outside the earth's orbit, we are confronted by an entirely different set of aspects and conditions of visibility, for these bodies are not confined to the eastern morning sky, or the western evening sky, but partake to a great degree of the general annual drift of the constellations from east to west. The principal aspects of the superior planets are four in number, viz.: opposition, conjunction, and two quadratures. In tracing the apparent course of a typical superior planet, we had best begin when it is nearest the earth, and opposite the sun, as seen by us. It is then said to be in "opposition", rising at sunset, culminating, or reaching its highest point in the heavens, at midnight, and setting at sunrise. Shewing in the telescope a full, round disc, it is at its best for observation, a condition quite in contrast with that of the inferior planets, which are invisible when nearest the earth. Thus we are enabled to study the superior bodies with a far higher degree of facility and success. After opposition, a superior planet rises earlier and earlier each day, thus appearing higher and higher in the evening sky each night, until, having advanced a quarter of a circle, or 90 degrees of angular measure, it culminates at about six in the evening, being then in "quadrature". When at this point Mars shews a perceptible phase, or departure from the circular form, while Jupiter exhibits a slight shading off on the edge turned away from the sun. The other superior planets, however, are too far distant to be affected in this manner. After quadrature, the planet drifts farther and farther westward, until at length it approaches the sun and is lost in the glare of that body, passing beyond it in "conjunction". It is then farthest from the earth. Soon the planet reappears in the morning sky on the other side of the sun, emerging from invisibility as does an inferior planet after its inferior conjunction. As time passes it rises earlier and earlier, until after a while it comes above the horizon about midnight, and is in "quadrature" again. This is on the other side of the orbit, or 180 degrees from the other quadrature. Mars and Jupiter here repeat their exhibitions of phase. Continuing to rise earlier each night, the planet now enters the evening sky, finally rising at sunset, and reaching another opposition. The foregoing general aspects are shared, of course, by Mars, Jupiter, Saturn, Uranus, and Neptune. In middle northern latitudes planets always culminate in the southern sky, hence the expression "to south" is often used as an equivalent for "culminate" or "transit". The existence and apparent motion of Mercury, Venus, Mars, Jupiter, and Saturn were known to the ancients, but Uranus, Neptune, and the asteroids were later discovered.

Motions of the Planets Amongst the Stars

The real motion of the planets round the sun is, as we have noted before, a motion from west to east in roughly circular paths which lie approximately in the same plane. Now as viewed from the earth, which is itself one of these planets, the others appear to travel amongst the stars, sometimes eastward, or in "direct" motion, and sometimes westward, or in "retrograde" motion. Since their orbits all lie in nearly the same plane, it is obvious that all of them must seem to us to travel over the same parts of the sky, as must also the sun, whose apparent annual path must in reality be the plane of the earth's orbit extended infinitely into space. So closely do the planes of the various orbits coincide, that the apparent motions of all the major planets are confined to within eight degrees on either side of the "ecliptic" or apparent annual path of the sun.

The Zodiac

Thus there extends through the heavens a circular band, sixteen degrees wide, with the ecliptic in the centre, which contains the apparent paths of the sun and planets, as well as that of our own moon, whose orbit lies in the same general plane. This belt is called the "Zodiac", and is marked off into twelve equal parts or "signs", each of which formerly coincided with a constellation of the same name. One sign of the zodiac is equivalent to the apparent motion of the sun along the ecliptic for one month. The signs were named at a very remote and prehistoric period, and are closely associated with the seasons in which the sun occupies them. The following is a list of the twelve signs, together with the months on or around the 21st or 22nd of which they are entered by the sun in its apparent journey around the earth: (1) Aries, the Ram; March. (2) Taurus, the Bull; April. (3) Gemini, the Twins; May. (4) Cancer, the Crab; June. (5) Leo, the Lion; July. (6) Virgo, the Virgin; August. (7) Libra, the Scales; September. (8) Scorpio, the Scorpion; October. (9) Sagittarius, the Archer; November. (10) Capricornus, the Sea-Goat; December. (11) Aquarius, the Water-Bearer; January. (12) Pisces, the Fishes; February. The first point of Aries is of course the vernal equinox, where the sun, on the equator, gives equal day and night. As the sun ascends north to Cancer, the highest sign, the length of the days increases. The first degree of Cancer marks the "summer solstice", where the sun turns and commences its descent of the zodiac, a thing made evident by the decreasing days. The equator is again crossed at the autumnal equinox, or first point in Libra, after which the sun sinks to Capricornus, whose first point is the winter solstice, or most southern part of the zodiac. Here the sun gives the shortest days, but soon begins to climb toward Aries again, once more opening the season of spring on its arrival thither. Of course, this is all the result of the earth's journey about the sun, our northern hemisphere being turned alternately toward and away from the great luminary.

EDITOR'S NOTE FP: AGN 20, No. 8 (20 February 1915): 4.

III. The Sun

To us, and to all who may inhabit any of the planets of the solar system; light, heat, and vegetation, in short, life itself may be considered as emanating from but one tremendous source—the sun.

The sun is the centre of the solar system, and by far the largest body therein. Its attraction holds all the other members to their various courses, while its rays furnish to them all of the light and heat that they receive. It is, however dazzling though it seems to us, itself but a star of moderate size in comparison to the other stars, and seeming superior to the rest only because it is so much nearer to us than any other.

The sun is about 866,000 miles in diameter, being 1,300,000 times larger than the earth. Its average distance from the earth is about 93,000,000 miles, light requiring over eight minutes to pass from one to the other. It is not a solid body, but a glowing mass of gaseous or fluid matter, having a density but a fourth of the earth's; yet on account of its enormous size, the force of gravity on its surface is over 27 times greater than that on the surface of the earth, so that if a man were able to reach the centre of the system, he would be crushed and killed by his own weight.

Since the sun is not solid, its rotation on its axis is not uniform, the equator travelling more rapidly than the other portions. Twenty-five days represents approximately the average length of one rotation.

To the naked eye, the sun has the appearance of a uniformly luminous disc, too bright to admit a direct gaze, and therefore requiring the use of a deeply tinted glass for observation. In the telescope, the surface is seen to be covered with black, irregular, slowly moving spots, surrounded by greyish borders known as "penumbrae". The spots themselves, which are temporary in nature, one seldom lasting more than two or three months, sometimes attain diameters of from 50,000 to 100,000 miles, occasionally verging on visibility to the naked eye. The diameter of some large spots, including their penumbrae, is about 150,000 miles. Solar spots are distributed most thickly in belts extending 30 degrees north and south of the sun's equator, never appearing near the poles. They are especially numerous at intervals of about 11 years, these fluctuations in frequency being connected with certain phenomena of terrestrial magnetism in a way not yet understood. Bright streaks or patches called "faculae" are frequently seen near the spots, when the latter are near the edge of the sun's disc.

The disc itself is revealed by telescopes to be the brightest at the centre, and of a granular or mottled appearance, as though it were composed of white snowflakes, or, as some observers say as a comparison, grains of rice, sprinkled upon a light greyish background. The visible luminous disc of the sun is called the "photosphere".

When the sun is totally eclipsed, and its bright rays temporarily intercepted, we see that it possesses a vast amount of matter outside the photosphere, consisting of (1) a bright red atmosphere called the "chromosphere", visible to us mainly as a series of immense fiery jets called "prominences", which form an irregular fringe about the blackened disc, and (2) a far-reaching luminous atmosphere whose exact appearance varies as seen during different eclipses, and which is known as the "corona". The general appearance of the latter is that of a broad halo, with occasional streamers of light.

In regard to the actual constitution of the sun, much has been learned by observation, and by the use of the instrument known as the "spectroscope", which identifies incandescent substances by the character of the light emitted by them; yet the ultimate facts are still enveloped in the most profound obscurity. That the sun is intensely hot, much more so than may be readily conceived by the human mind, is quite evident; Wilson and Gray estimate its temperature at 7000 degrees centigrade. Should the earth be placed upon the surface of the sun, it would evaporate like a drop of water, and vanish, dissipated as a trifling cloud of gas.

That the sun is, in nature, a mass of fiery incandescent vapour, made up of elements like those composing our own earth, is practically certain. Its heat is probably caused by its contraction in volume, for all contracting bodies radiate energy, and the sun is undoubtedly shrinking, though at so slow a rate, that no change in its apparent size has been observed since its disc was first studied by mankind. The photosphere is in all likelihood composed of solid or liquid particles in the form of clouds, floating in the gas or vapour on which the nucleus or inner part of the sun is constituted. These clouds are probably carbonaceous, giving off light in their incandescence much as do the solid particles of carbon in the flames of hydrocarbons, such as candles.

The spots on the sun are considered by most authorities as depressions in the photosphere, caused by titanic eruptions; cooler, therefore darker, than the rest of the disc. This conclusion was reached by observing the changes in their appearance caused by perspective as they are carried across the disc by rotation. However, certain investigators question this theory, some even going so far as to hold that the spots are elevations above the general level of the photosphere. The penumbrae and faculae attendant on the spots are generally ascribed to the upheaval of the solar surface by the enormous forces displayed in the formation of the spots themselves. The penumbra of a solar spot is ordinarily composed of attenuated filaments converging toward the centre of the spot, and occasionally having a rather spiral contour, thus indicating something of a whirling or cyclonic motion to be possessed by the spots; indeed, the observer Faye advanced the theory that the sun's spots are gigantic cyclones; eddying storms amongst the incandescent clouds of the photosphere. In actual fact, however, it cannot be said that the spots, penumbrae, and faculae have yet been satisfactorily, or even tolerably well, explained.

The sun's chromosphere, as seen during total eclipses in the immense eruptive prominences which fringe the obscured disc, is apparently composed of light gases such as hydrogen (atomic weight, 1) and helium (atomic weight, 4). The height to which some of the prominences rise is probably due to forcible ejection from the interior, on a scale that dwarfs all terrestrial standards in comparison. The whole earth itself is tiny beside the most insignificant of these jets of solar fire.

The corona, that mysterious crown of pale light which may be seen enveloping the sun during total eclipses, is most inexplicable in its nature. But one thing may be said conclusively of it, namely, that it is composed of self-luminous gas, deriving its light in no manner whatsoever from the inner and more refulgent portions of the sun. Comets traverse its wide expanse without sensible effect, proving that its tenuity must be extreme.

Since the sun is the sole source of light and heat, and therefore of life, on all of its attendant planets, including the earth, it is but natural to inquire into the question of how long its radiant fires will endure for the benefit of remote posterity. Since, as previously stated, the heat of the sun seems to be derived from the slow yet inevitable contraction of its bulk, it is at once apparent that an end to its present condition must some time surely come. According to the late Prof. Newcomb, a date 10,000,000 years hence will mark the end of the existing order of things, after which the sun will become first liquid, then solid, finally ceasing altogether to shine, and rolling on amongst the stars as a dead, cold, unseen mass. However, the reputed discovery of the element radium in its constitution may indicate a longer life; at any rate, for countless generations it may be relied upon to continue its existence as a great donor of life-giving energy.

EDITOR'S NOTE FP: *AGN* 20, No. 10 (23 February 1915): 4.

IV. THE INFERIOR PLANETS

Mercury

(Distance from sun, 36,000,000 miles. Diameter, 3,000 miles. Revolution, 88 days. Rotation unknown. Inclination of axis unknown.)

In the early evening, whilst the twilight yet remains, we may often behold near the western horizon, just above the sunset point, a sparkling speck of ruddy or pinkish light, brilliant after a fashion, yet withal elusive to the untrained eye. This scintillating orb is Mercury, the smallest and nearest to the sun of all the planets, and of all the most difficult to observe, since it never recedes more than 28 degrees from the sun, and can therefore never be seen with the naked eye except at or near the times of its greatest elongations; low down in the west soon after sunset, or in the east before the break of day. Its most favourable evening appearances are those which take place in the spring; as a morning star, it is best seen in the autumn.

As seen in the morning sky, this planet was thought by the ancients to be a different body from that seen in the evening, hence was known by them by two names; [Mercury as an evening star] and Apollo as a morning star. The difficulty of glimpsing Mercury is well illustrated by the fact that Copernicus, the great father of modern astronomy, was never in his life able to see it, and that Mr. Hind, an English astronomer, is said to have observed it but once without the aid of a telescope.

The planet is brightest when in a gibbous phase.

Mercury's synodic period, or time of apparent revolution around the earth from one inferior conjunction to another, is 116 days.

The surface of Mercury reflects light but feebly, and has but few definite markings. The older observers believed that they could distinguish high mountains on the planet, but later astronomers have failed to corroborate their conclusions. The time of rotation of Mercury is a matter of warm dispute, since while some declare that it is much like the earth's, others affirm quite as strongly that the planet turns on its axis only once during its revolution about the sun, thus acting as does our own moon toward the earth, and keeping one half always turned to the central body, the other half always turned away. If this condition be true, then Mercury must possess in one hemisphere perpetual sunlight, and in the other, perpetual darkness. The existence of an atmosphere around Mercury is likewise disputed. Of all the members of the solar system Mercury has the greatest density, being, curiously enough, about equal to the metal Mercury in specific gravity. The planet has no satellite. The excessive amount of solar light and heat received by Mercury on account of its proximity to the sun precludes the possibility of the existence upon its surface of inhabitants in any way similar to those of the earth.

Mercury passes in transit between the earth and the sun at intervals of from three to thirteen years, then being visible in the telescope as a black spot crossing the solar surface. Such phenomena always take place either in May or in November. Gassendi, in 1631, was the first to observe a transit of Mercury. Mercury last performed a transit on November 7, 1914, whilst future transits will occur in 1924, 1927, 1937, and 1940. However, not until November 14, 1953, can the inhabitants of this part of the country have the privilege of beholding one.

Venus

(Distance from sun, 66,000,000 miles. Revolution, 225 days. Diameter, 7,816 miles. Rotation, 23 hours, 21 minutes. Inclination of axis unknown.)

The planet Venus has in all ages been an object of admiration on the part of mankind. Like Mercury, it appears on each side of the sun, and it never recedes more than 43 degrees from that luminary. As a morning and evening star it was thought by the ancients to be two distinct bodies; Phosphorus, the light bearer, as a morning star, and Hesperus in the evening. Since this planet departs so much farther from the sun than does Mercury, it can be observed much longer after sunset or before sunrise. Venus is the brightest star-like object in the heavens; so brilliant, indeed, that it cannot only be occasionally glimpsed in full daylight, but can cast a shadow at night. Its extreme brilliancy while in certain parts of its course causes it to be mistaken by the uninformed for an artificial light. The present writer recalls an amusing instance of this fallacy which occurred on Christmas eve, 1909, when many persons were deluded into the belief that the planet was the searchlight of an aëroplane! One cultivated and apparently well-educated gentleman was heard to remark on "the perfect control to which the airship must be subject, in order that the light shine so steadily", whilst another made estimates, varying from half a mile to two miles, of its "distance above the ground".[1]

Venus is the second planet in order of distance from the sun, being just within the orbit of the earth. Since it is an inferior planet, it presents during each apparent revolution of 584 days a complete set of phases, which were discovered in 1610 by Galileo, the founder of telescopic astronomy. Venus approaches at inferior conjunction to a point within about 25,000,000 miles from the earth. It thus comes nearer to us than does any other heavenly body save the moon, the asteroid Eros, occasional comets, and meteors. At conjunction it recedes to a distance of about 160,000,000 miles from the earth. Its extreme proximity to us at inferior conjunction is of course offset by the fact that it is then invisible. The planet is brightest when a large crescent.

Venus has so dense and cloudy an atmosphere, that we probably see its true surface but seldom. This atmosphere is especially evident during the entrance of Venus into a transit over the sun's disc, when it is seen as a thin border of light, arising from the refraction of the solar rays, encircling that part of the planet which is not yet projected against the face of the great luminary. This brilliantly reflective atmosphere, which renders the planet such a striking object to the naked eye, gives rise to a glare that makes its telescopic observation a matter of great difficulty. It is best studied by daylight, when the glare is least offensive. Even then, however, the obscuration of the surface by the atmosphere causes its topographical configurations to be most elusive, and subject to the most violent discussion. Another difficulty in observing Venus is, that in the display of its phases, it becomes invisible when nearest the earth, not exhibiting a disc of any considerable rotundity until it has attained a great distance from us.

As previously intimated, little is definitely known concerning the surface and rotation of Venus. A long line of observers extending from 1666 to the present time, and using various methods, have declared that the planet turns on its axis in about 23 hours and 21 minutes, yet this result has, during the past 25 years, been contradicted very strongly by certain astronomers, particularly the late Prof. G. V. Schiaparelli of Milan, and Prof. Percival Lowell of Flagstaff, Arizona, who maintain that Venus rotates but once in a revolution, thus keeping the same face toward the sun. The shorter period, however, is still the more favoured by those best informed on this subject. Dark, indefinite shadings, with perhaps a few high mountains, are probably the principal features of the disc of Venus, though Lowell insists on the reality of certain spoke-like markings which he says radiate outward from the centre of the surface.

Transits of Venus are much rarer than those of Mercury, occurring in pairs about once a century, eight years intervening betwixt the two transits of a pair. Sometimes much more than a century elapses without a transit; thus the last previous transit occurred in 1882, while the next will not take place until 2004. Transits of Venus occur either in June or in December. These rare phenomena are anxiously awaited by astronomers, who, if necessary, travel half across the earth to points whence they will be best visible, since they afford an excellent means of determining the sun's distance by a method too complicated for description here. The first transit of Venus ever seen by human eye was that of December 4, 1639. Its occurrence was calculated in advance by a young English gentleman named Horrox,[2] who with his friend Crabtree observed it successfully.

Venus is quite like the earth in character and dimensions, gravity, density, and rotation, but is much nearer the sun, thus receiving a far greater amount of light and heat. If the planet possesses inhabitants, as possibly it may, they must seldom see the heavens on account of the cloudy canopy which seems to envelop them. However, when their sky is clear, the earth must appear in their eyes as resplendent as is their abode in ours; in other words, our terraqueous globe must shine in the heavens of Venus as a brilliant planet, having motions like those of Mars as seen by us. The moon, of course, would also be conspicuous, resembling a small star beside its primary. Venus itself is not known to be attended by a satellite, though at times the existence of one has on insufficient grounds been suspected.

EDITOR'S NOTE FP: AGN 20, No. 14 (27 February 1915): 4.

Notes

1. See "Venus and the Public Eye" (p. 99).

2. HPL refers to British astronomer Jeremiah Horrocks (1618–1641) and his friend, the clothier and amateur astronomer William Crabtree. Cf. HPL's discussion of the transit of Venus in 1769 in *The Case of Charles Dexter Ward* (1927).

V. ECLIPSES

First of all astronomical events to be recorded and transmitted in writing to posterity were eclipses, those seemingly miraculous obscurations of the two great natural luminaries, the sun and moon. A total and unexpected blotting out of the light of day must be to anyone a source of awe, whence it is but natural that early nations, following systems of natural theology and attributing all events to the direct action of various benign or malevolent deities, regarded eclipses, particularly total eclipses of the sun, as direful portents, and derived from them the most profound trepidation. The prevailing view was, and still is amongst uncultivated races, that the sun when eclipsed is being devoured by a black and frightful monster, who must be scared away by means of loud clamour and harsh noises, else he will consume the source of all the light of day, and plunge the world into a state of perpetual night. Accordingly, savage tribes raise a terrific din, both with voice and with primitive drums, upon the advent of one of these phenomena.

Eclipses are, as before stated, of two kinds, solar and lunar. Solar eclipses are caused by the intervention of the moon between the sun and the earth, whilst eclipses of the moon are the reverse of these, being interventions of the earth between the sun and the moon, so that the latter is immersed in the shadow of our globe. These phenomena may be further classed as partial, or those in which only a fraction of the disc of the eclipsed body is obscured; and total, those in which the entire disc is hidden. A third sort of eclipse, called "annular", occurs only in connexion with the sun. In this, the central part of the disc is eclipsed, while a narrow ring of light remains uncovered, owing to the fact that when these phenomena occur, the moon is farthest from us, being seen at its least apparent magnitude, and failing to cover the sun completely. The earth's shadow is so much larger than the moon at all distances, that our satellite can never suffer an annular eclipse.

The shadows of the earth and moon, since they are shadows of spheres cast by the sun, a vastly larger sphere, are conical, according to the optical laws governing such cases. Since the length of a shadow depends as well upon the distance between the obscuring body and the source of light as upon their relative magnitudes, it follows that these cones vary in length as the earth and moon vary in their solar distance. As an average, the shadow of the earth is 657,000 miles in length, that of the moon, 232,000 miles.

The greyish fringe of a shadow, or that border from which the source of light is somewhat yet not wholly cut off, is called the "penumbra". (This must not be confused with the same term as applied to the border of a solar spot.) Penumbrae are always divergent, even though the shadow proper, or "umbra", as it is called, be convergent, as in the case of the earth and moon.

It is evident that solar eclipses can occur only at new moon, when our satellite lies between the earth and the sun; and lunar eclipses at full moon, when the earth lies between the moon and the sun. Also, that the moon must be at or very near one of its "nodes", or places where its orbit crosses the ecliptic, or plane of the earth's orbit, so that all three, sun, moon and earth, shall be in a line and on a level. This last named fact gives to the ecliptic its name, the relation between "eclipse" and "ecliptic" being easily traceable. When the time of new moon coincides with the presence of the moon at or very near a node, a solar eclipse occurs; whilst a coincidence of the phase of full moon with our satellite's presence at or very near a node gives rise to a lunar eclipse.

The moon's nodes have a motion from east to west around the eclipse, occupying 18 years and 235 days in a complete revolution back to the place whence they set out. This motion, in connexion with the moon's own motion in its orbit, causes every eclipse, lunar and solar alike, to be repeated under the same conditions for about a thousand years at intervals of 18 years, 11 and one-third days. This latter period is called the "Saros", and was much used by the ancients in the prediction of eclipses.

It is evident that when the moon is exactly at a node during an eclipse, the phenomenon will, since the bodies are exactly level and in a line, be total (or annular), whilst eclipses occurring when the moon is only near a node may be partial in varying degrees.

A moment's thought shews that what is seen by us as a lunar eclipse, is also an eclipse of the sun by the earth as viewed from the surface of the moon, it being total to such parts of our satellite's face as we see darkened by the earth's umbra. The penumbra as well as the umbra crosses the moon's disc in every lunar eclipse, preceding and following the darker shadow, yet seldom being noticed by the casual observer. To those portions which it touches, is presented the spectacle of a partial eclipse of the sun by the earth.

A total eclipse of the sun as seen by us is, as seen from the moon, an eclipse of the earth by the moon's shadow; never, however, appearing even nearly total, since the small size of the lunar umbra is such that even under the most favourable circumstances it produces a mere dot of wholly darkened territory, and sweeps over only that limited region called by us the "path of totality", from which alone we may behold the solar eclipse as total. This is one great difference between the conditions met in observing lunar and solar eclipses, for whilst an eclipse of the moon is a real darkening of that body, and may be watched from any place on the earth above whose horizon our satellite has arisen, one of the sun is only an apparent darkening, and is to be viewed only from points along the path of the moon's shadow. A total solar eclipse can be seen as total only from the narrow zone swept by the moon's umbra, this fact sometimes forcing astronomers to make long expeditions in order to perform their work in connexion with one of these phenomena. Of course, the moon's penumbra touches a much wider area than the umbra itself, producing a belt on each side of the path of totality, from which the eclipse can be seen as partial. Solar eclipses seen only as partial upon the earth are caused by the passage of the moon's penumbra alone over those parts of our globe in which the eclipse is visible. In annular eclipses, the moon is farther distant from the earth than the length of its umbra, which consequently falls just short of us. An annular eclipse is in principle merely a much magnified transit, differing only in proportion from those of Mercury and Venus. A total solar eclipse is a most inspiring sight, the sun's corona and prominences being visible in full splendour.

The moon in its total eclipses never quite disappears, even when in the centre of the earth's umbra, for a faint reddish illumination, due to light refracted by the earth's atmosphere, always pervades the disc.

The greatest possible number of eclipses in a year is seven; five of the sun and two of the moon. The least possible number is two, both of the sun. Usually, a year contains about four or five eclipses. The duration of totality varies in the case of the sun from an almost instantaneous period to nearly eight minutes. Three to five minutes is the most common length. In the case of the moon, the great size of the earth's shadow sometimes allows a totality of almost two hours.

EDITOR'S NOTE FP: AGN 20, No. 16 (2 March 1915): 8.

VI. THE EARTH AND ITS MOON

(Distance from sun, 93,000,000 miles. Revolution, 365 days. Diameter, 7,918 miles. Rotation, 24 hours. Inclination of axis, 23 and a half degrees from upright to plane of orbit.)

At first sight, it appears unnatural that the solid earth underfoot should be included in a survey of the heavens, yet after all, what is this sphere whereon we dwell but a rather small planet, the third in order of distance from the sun, and the fifth in point of size? The earth is the theatre whence we view all the rest of the universe, and as we have seen, its position and motions give our sky most of the familiar features which we behold in the latter.

But the globe itself is best known through the sciences of geography, geology, meteorology, and the like, so that we find our chief astronomical interest directed toward that faithful attendant which ever circles around it; the moon.

The Moon

(Distance from earth, 240,000 miles. Revolution and rotation, 27 and one third days. Apparent revolution, 29 and one half days. Diameter, 2,163 miles. Inclination of axis, one and one half degrees from upright to plane of orbit.)

Most beautiful of all the various heavenly orbs unfolded to the gaze of man, is the moon, whose bright beams invest the nocturnal landscape with a radiance inferior only to the light of day. To us, the moon appears as of about the same size as the sun, for although it is in reality about 400 times smaller in diameter, it is also 400 times nearer, being the nearest to earth of all the celestial bodies. Its apparent diameter is 31 degrees and 24 minutes of angular measure, or about one-360th of the distance across the visible sky from horizon to horizon through the zenith. The moon is larger in proportion to the earth than is any other satellite to its primary. It performs its monthly revolution round the earth in 27 and a third days, during which time the earth itself has changed place, thus causing over two more days to elapse before the moon appears to have completed its circuit, and to have returned to the same place in relation to the sun and earth, from whence it started. This longer apparent or synodic revolution comprises about 29 and a half days. The moon performs its axial rotation in exactly the same time that it revolves around the earth, therefore turning us but one face, and leaving almost an entire hemisphere which may never be seen by human eye. Yet this circumstance is somewhat modified by certain features of the moon's motion called "librations", by which we are afforded certain glimpses of the edges of the hidden side. About six-tenths of the lunar surface may at various times be beheld; four-tenths is always turned to the earth, two-tenths revealed alternately by librations, and four-tenths forever withheld from our vision. That the territory which under no circumstances can be seen by man differs in any way from the visible portions of the moon, there is no reason to believe, yet its inaccessibility to the eye invests it with a species of mysterious interest. Fanciful tales have been written concerning this unknown land,

and at least one theory has been seriously advanced, which holds it to be of a different nature from the rest of our satellite.

The force of gravity on the moon is a seventh of that upon the earth, hence could an object of seven pounds terrestrial weight be transported to the moon, it would there weigh but one pound. The density of the moon is three-fifths of the earth's.

The moon's orbit departs slightly from the circular form, causing its distance from the earth to vary somewhat. When nearest us, the moon is said to be in "Perigee", and when farthest away, in "Apogee".

The most striking phenomena connected with the moon as seen from the earth are the phases, or different aspects caused by the progress of night and day over its surface during its monthly revolution. When our satellite is on a line between the earth and the sun, rising and setting with the latter like an inferior planet at inferior conjunction, it is of course invisible unless it happens to eclipse the solar disc by passing across it like Mercury or Venus in transit. This phase is called "new moon". On the second evening after new moon, our satellite can be seen in the west as a slender crescent, with horns pointing east, setting about two hours after the sun. Each night the crescent is thicker, and the time of setting almost an hour later. About a week after it is new, or five days after its first appearance, the moon shews a semicircle of light, culminating about sunset, and setting about midnight. It is then 90 degrees from the sun, like a superior planet at quadrature, and is said to be in "first quarter". From then on, the eastern edge becomes more and more convex, our satellite exhibiting what are termed "gibbous" phases, until about a week after first quarter (for the various phases all occur about a week apart) we see that entire illuminated circle called the "full moon". It then rises at sunset, souths at midnight, and sets at sunrise, being like a superior planet in opposition, since the earth is between it and the sun. If now it passes on the exact level of the sun and earth, it will enter the shadow of the latter, suffering an eclipse. After full moon, the side of the disc which has hitherto been untouched commences to diminish, and the time of rising grows later and later, carrying our satellite out of the evening sky, until in another week the disc is again a half-circle, the illuminated side being that which was invisible at first quarter. This phase is called "last quarter", and the moon at this time rises about midnight, and culminates about dawn. The western edge now becomes concave, and the disc assumes the shape of a crescent with the horns pointing westward. The moon draws near the sun, and five days after last quarter is barely visible near the eastern horizon before sunrise. The next day it is gone, not to be seen again until it has been once more a new moon, and begun a new set of phases. Ignorance of the moon's phases gives rise to many ridiculous errors in literature and art, such as representations of the full moon in the west in the evening, or the young crescent moon high up in the sky late at night.

When the moon is a slender crescent, we see not only the slight area brightened by sunlight, but the remainder of the disc as well, illuminated by a faint reddish radiance. The latter, often called "the old moon in the new moon's arms", is light reflected from our own earth, which must of course appear from the lunar surface as a great disc thirteen times larger than that which our satellite presents to us, and possessing all the phases of the latter, being new when we see the moon is full, and vice versa. The earthlight on the moon disappears as the lunar disc waxes; since the earth, nearly full when the moon is young, correspondingly wanes.

Harvest and Hunter's Moon

In most seasons of the year the moon, after being full, rises as usual about an hour later every night, thus soon withdrawing its light from the early nocturnal sky. In September, however, as though to guide the actions of the harvester and permit him to continue his labours after the sun has set, our satellite lingers in the evening sky long into its wane, rising but a few moments later each successive night. This fact is caused by the full moon's presence in the zodiacal sign Aries, which makes so small an angle with the eastern horizon, that the moon when passing through it is less depressed in relation to the horizon at consecutive risings than when in any other part of its course, though its rate of motion be in each case the same. This phenomenon is known as the "harvest moon". The following full moon, that of October, partakes in a lesser degree of the same qualities, and is called the "hunter's moon". Of course, the moon occupies the sign Aries at other times than these, but in such instances it is not near full, hence the small difference in the time of its successive risings is not generally remarked.

The apparent altitude at which the moon makes its circuit of the southern sky as seen in our latitude is, of course, like that of the sun, due to the sign of the zodiac wherein it happens to be situated. Therefore, when the moon is in Cancer it runs high, and when in Capricornus runs low. Since the full moon is always opposite the sun, it runs high in winter, when the sun runs low, and low in summer, when the sun runs high.

There is scarce anyone who can have failed to notice the seemingly enormous size of the moon (or sun as well) as it hovers over the horizon just after rising, or just before setting, as contrasted with its apparently lesser magnitude when high in the sky. This false enlargement has at all times been a subject of much discussion. If we view the question scientifically, we shall see that a body should rightly appear smaller instead of larger when on or near the horizon, since it is then more distant from us by half the earth's diameter, or about 4,000 miles, than when it is at or near the zenith. Also, we cannot attribute the phenomenon to any actual magnification due to the great thickness of the air through which we see an object low in the sky, for measurements with delicate instruments have proved the truth of the scientific fact, namely, that the lunar disc is really smaller when so situated. We must therefore seek a psychological rather than an optical or astronomical explanation for this strange state of affairs, and content ourselves with the belief that the seeming immensity of the horizontal moon is due only to the variety of terrestrial objects such as trees, houses, hills, and the like on land, and waves and ripples at sea, which lie between it and the observer, and which by imparting an illusory appearance of great distance, cause our satellite to loom up in greater prominence than when it is high in the heavens, and, for want of intervening objects, seemingly nearer, and proportionately insignificant. Thus a dotted line appears longer than an exactly equal distance which is marked only at its extremities. When the horizontal moon is viewed through a tube which excludes all else from sight, it appears of proper smallness.

The brilliancy of the full moon is 600,000 times less than that of the sun. Were the entire visible sky crowded with full moons, the illumination thus afforded would be but an eighth of full sunlight.

Appearance of the Moon

To the naked eye, the moon appears as a bright disc, more or less spotted by those darker areas which the fancy of primitive man has moulded into such imaginary shapes as "the man in the moon", the "lady in the moon", and many others. These spots were once thought to be seas and oceans, whilst the bright portions were considered as tracts of land, and the moon's principal topographical features were accordingly named. Even now, though it is known that the entire lunar surface is destitute of water, and that the spots are simply regions of darker materials, the old nomenclature still adheres. Since the dark spots are much smoother than the light areas, it has been suggested that the former are the dry beds of old seas and oceans.

When viewed with a telescope, the lunar disc is seen to be covered with mountains, on a scale far greater than that to which we are accustomed on the earth. Although we behold lofty peaks, pinnacles, and ranges of towering mountains which cast shadows of the most profound blackness on account of the total absence of air, by far the most common type of formation is the volcanic crater, the majority of which are incomparably greater than those of earth. Some of these craters are so wide that they are more appropriately called ringed or walled plains, for most of them consist of extensive areas surrounded by lava rims, and having volcanic peaks in their centres. They are extremely numerous throughout the bright portions of the moon's surface, and occur somewhat less frequently in the darker spots. Many of them are overlapping, and some are within the boundaries of larger ones, thereby shewing that all were not formed at the same time. In general, these craters are mute witnesses of extremely violent volcanic forces that once convulsed the moon's now practically changeless surface. Of other species of formations there are many. In various parts of the lunar disc may be seen valleys, circular pits over three miles deep, straight narrow trenches with raised sides, and long streaks of extreme brilliancy radiating from some of the craters.

The moon is generally considered to be a dead world; a body without air, water, life, or volcanic activity. Prof. W. H. Pickering, however, has lately concluded from his observations that slight traces of atmosphere, hoar-frost, and vegetation of a low type, as well as feeble remnants of volcanic force, are to be found upon our satellite.

The conjectures of the earlier astronomers concerning the "inhabitants of the moon" seem now quite amusing. Gruithulsen announced that he had discovered "great artificial works in the moon, erected by the lunarians". Frauenhofer declared he had seen "a lunar edifice, resembling a fortification, together with several lines of road", while Schroeter spoke of "a great city on the east side of the moon, an extensive canal in another place, and fields of vegetation"![1]

Throughout the ages of recorded history various terrestrial phenomena such as changes of weather have been falsely attributed to the influence of the moon. In this twentieth century it is perhaps needless to say that all speculations are absolutely unfounded, and that beyond having a principal part in the ebb and flow of the tides, and a slight effect on certain magnetic forces, our satellite is powerless to govern in any way the state of things upon its primary.

EDITOR'S NOTE FP: *AGN* 20, No. 20 (6 March 1915): 3.

Notes

1. Franz von Paula Gruithuisen (1774–1852), German natural philosopher, author of *Senelog-*

nostische Fragmente (1821?). Joseph von Fraunhofer (1787–1826), German scientist chiefly known for his work in optics. For Schröter see "Is There Life on the Moon?" (p. 26), n. 1.

VII. MARS AND THE ASTEROIDS

Mars

(Distance from sun, 141,000,000 miles. Revolution, 687 days. Rotation, 24 hours, 37 minutes. Diameter, 4000 miles. Inclination of axis, 24 degrees, 50 minutes from upright to plane of orbit.)

When, upon some clear evening as the darkness increases, there is seen ascending above the eastern horizon a remarkably brilliant red orb which pales to insignificance even the brightest of the fixed stars around, it is known that Mars is approaching its opposition, and will for months to come adorn the evening sky.

Mars is the fourth planet in order of distance from the sun, and first outside the earth's orbit. It approaches at its most favourable oppositions within 36,000,000 miles of the earth, a closer distance from us than is attained by any other planet save Venus and one or two of the asteroids. At its most unfavourable oppositions, its distance is 61,000,000 miles, the average being 48,000,000 miles. At conjunction it recedes to a mean distance of 234,000,000 miles. The path of Mars around the sun is very eccentric, the planet's solar distance being at times 26,000,000 miles greater than on other occasions. Gravity on Mars is but three-eighths of that upon the earth, while its density is about three-fourths. The day of Mars, as determined by the planet's rotation, is but little longer than our own, and the similar inclination of its axis to the plane of its orbit gives rise to similar seasons, although since the year of Mars is nearly twice as long as that of the earth, these seasons are also double ours in length. To us, Mars shews no variation of phase save a slight gibbous appearance when at or near quadrature. Its synodic or apparent revolution around the earth is by far the longest in the solar system, being 780 days, or about two and one-fifth years as counted between two successive oppositions. Mars is best seen, as are all superior planets, when opposite the sun, it then being a conspicuous object for about three months. At other times, the naked eye finds but little of interest in it. The close proximity of Mars to the earth, the fact that when it is nearest us it is not, like Venus, invisible, and that when visible its surface is not, as is that of Venus, obscured by clouds, all tend to allow terrestrial observers to obtain more positive knowledge concerning it than may be gathered from any of the other planets.

Spots on the surface of Mars were first observed by Huyghens in 1659. Since then, telescopes have greatly improved, and we now see the planet's disc to be divided roughly into two parts; the light or reddish, and the dark or greenish areas. These were formerly regarded as land and water, respectively, and although more recent investigations have almost disproved such an idea, the present nomenclature still refers, like that of the moon, to imaginary oceans and continents. The true nature of these spots is doubtful. It is to the red areas that the general ruddy colour of the planet, as seen with the unassisted vision, is due. Besides the red and green regions, intensely white tracts are seen around each pole, diminishing almost to the point of disappearance on exposure to the direct rays of the sun, as during the summer of Mars in their respective hemispheres, and increasing during the winter. These "polar caps", as they are called, are thought to be composed of water in the form of snow, or at least hoar-frost, melting in summer and freezing again in winter. The faintest and least clearly defined features of the disc of Mars are the so-called "canals", extremely narrow, dark streaks which cover the planet's surface like a network. They were discovered in 1877 by Schiaparelli, and have since received much attention in connexion with the fantastic idea that they are gigantic ditches, constructed by the hands of intelligent inhabitants of Mars. There is, in truth, something worthy of note in the almost mathematical rectitude of these lines, the dark, circular spots called "oases" which mark their intersections, and their probable changes from season to season; but so faint and difficult to see are they, that their very existence was doubted until recently, when some of them were successfully photographed. The true nature of the canals, like that of the spots, is a matter of great dispute. It seems evident that they change from time to time, perhaps with the seasons of the year of Mars; at times some of them appear double, and a few astronomers believe that a connexion exists between changes in the canals and in the spots.

The atmosphere of Mars must be infinitely thinner than is that of the earth, for we are able to gain but slight evidence of its existence, and clouds seldom obscure the planet's features, (See, however, Prof. W. H. Pickering's monthly reports on Mars for 1914, published in *Popular Astronomy*.) The temperature, owing to the greater distance of Mars from the sun, must be vastly lower than that of our terraqueous globe.

The public press has of late years overflowed with senseless and carelessly written matter concerning the physical condition and habitableness of Mars, the chief and most persistent idea being that the canals are artificial. Most of these speculations may be dismissed as unworthy of serious consideration, but the theories of Prof. Percival Lowell, a private observer whose excellent telescope is situate in the clear air of Flagstaff, Arizona, and who has since 1890 been a leading authority on all matters relating to the planet Mars, deserve some attention. Prof. Lowell affirms: (1) That the canals all commence at the polar caps, and lead down toward the centre of the planet in absolutely straight lines. (2) That their many intersections are all marked by small perfectly round spots or "oases", and (3) That their breadth increases in the summer and decreases in the winter of the planet. From these things, Prof. Lowell has constructed the following wild and grotesque theory. By him, Mars is supposed to be an aged body, that is, a planet which has been in existence much longer than our own earth, and whose physical structure is in consequence more advanced (for slow changes are constantly being undergone by every body in the universe). Its oceans, rivers, and lakes, declares Lowell, are long since evaporated, water existing only in the polar caps, which, as they melt in summer, give off the fluid, which is conveyed to the arid regions of the planet by means of the canals, mighty watercourses constructed by the highly civilised inhabitants. Since one cap is always melted whilst the other is frozen, a continual flow of water is secured. The dark "oases" are held to be great cities, placed at the intersections of the canals and thus enjoying double allowances of water. The increase in the width of the canals during the summer of Mars is ascribed to the growth of vegetation along their banks, for the ditches themselves could not be seen at so great a distance as the earth's. In winter, as the vegetation dies, owing to the frosts as well as to the withdrawal of water caused by the freezing of the polar cap that feeds the canals, these strange features disappear. The red areas are considered as desert land, the green as tracts of vegetation. Thus the supposed changes in the latter may be explained. The difficulty in reconciling the thin air and intense cold of Mars with the sustenance of inhabitants is overcome by assuming the existence of an atmosphere of different composition than our own, one which though much more attenuated, is yet better adapted to absorb and conserve the solar heat. The immense scale, out of all proportion to the known works of mankind, on which are "constructed" the canals, is explained by the lesser gravity on Mars, whereby weight is less, and the activity of the inhabitants is greater, than on the earth.

Now, baseless as most of these speculations may be, it is nevertheless not impossible that living beings of some sort may dwell upon the surface of this planet. It is, however, left to the imagination of the reader, or to that of the ingenious novelist, to portray their appearance, size, intelligence, and habits.

Satellites of Mars

Not until 1877 were the two tiny satellites of Mars discovered. In that year the late Prof. Asaph Hall of the United States Naval Observatory at Washington espied them for the first time. Their names are Deimos, or Terror, and Phobos, or Fear, the two mythical attendants of the war-god Mars. Phobos, the inner of the two, revolves around its primary three times during one day of Mars; therefore, as seen from that planet, rising in the west, displaying all its phases whilst above the horizon, and setting in the east after a visibility of only six hours. Deimos revolves in a little over a day, so rises above Mars' eastern horizon, remains in sight for 60 hours, and displays two complete sets of phases before setting in the west.

The Asteroids

Betwixt the orbits of Mars and Jupiter there lies a region filled with tiny planet-like bodies, some of which are scarce larger than good-sized rocks. Save for the four largest, and possibly a fifth discovered in 1914 by Dr. Metcalf of Winchester, Mass., but few exceed a hundred miles in diameter. Of these peculiar bodies only about a thousand are as yet discovered, but it is likely that thousands more exist unrecorded. So small and numerous are the asteroids, or minor planets, as they are called, that only a few hundred have received names, the rest being designated by numbers and letters. Only one is visible to the naked eye, and that but faintly. Most of the asteroids are now discovered by the art of photography, and each year many are added to the list already so long. The most remarkable of these bodies is that which has received the name of Eros. So eccentric is the orbit of this small world, that it sometimes comes nearer to us than does Mars; nearer, in fact, than any other known heavenly body of regular motions, save our own moon. Its least distance from the earth is only about 13,000,000 miles. Eros is variable in brilliancy, and it has been suggested that it consists of two planetoids, circling about a common centre of gravity. It has also been thought that its shape departs considerably from the spheroidal or approximately spherical form; but so small is its size, that no well-defined disc can be seen even when it is viewed with the most powerful telescopes.

Asteroid No. 588 is worthy of notice on account of the fact that it sometimes recedes beyond the orbit of Jupiter. Pallas, one of the larger asteroids, follows a path more highly inclined to the ecliptic than that of any other planetary body.

Of the real nature and physical constitution of the asteroids nothing definite is known. It was formerly believed that they are the fragments resulting from the explosion of a large planet; indeed, this theory has never been wholly disproved. Four of the asteroids were discovered some time before the rest. Their names, with their diameters in miles, are: Ceres (488), Pallas (304), Vesta (248), and Juno (118). To these must perhaps be added the fifth large asteroid found in 1914.

The discovery of the asteroids was prompted by the belief that according to the regular proportion of planetary distances outward from the sun, some body ought to exist between Mars and Jupiter. Ceres, discovered by Piazzi on January 1, 1801, was the first to be found; Pallas was discovered by Olbers in 1802, Juno in 1804 by Harding, and Vesta in 1807 by Olbers. In 1845 Hencke discovered another, and three more were found in 1847, since which time no year has passed without the discovery of from one to over a hundred.

EDITOR'S NOTE FP: *AGN* 20, No. 22 (9 March 1915): 5.

VIII. THE OUTER PLANETS

Jupiter

(Distance from sun, 483,000,000 miles. Revolution, about twelve years. Rotation, about ten hours. Diameter, 88,000 miles. Synodic period, 299 days. Inclination of axis, three degrees from upright.)

Jupiter, the largest of the planets, called by Proctor the "Giant of the Solar System", is 1,300 times greater in size than the earth on which we dwell. When at its best, shining resplendently in the eastern sky, it rivals even Venus in brilliancy, sometimes casting a perceptible shadow. At opposition Jupiter is but 390,000,000 miles away, whilst at conjunction its distance from the earth is about 580,000,000 miles. The planet stands nearly upright in its orbit, its axis being inclined but three degrees from a perpendicular. The result of this fact is the absence of well-defined seasons, perpetual spring reigning everywhere on its surface. However, we shall soon see that other conditions offset any benefits caused by this seemingly happy state. Gravity on the surface is Jupiter is nine times greater than that upon the earth, so that a man would find difficulty in moving about on the colossal globe. Jupiter, or at least the visible portion, appears to be in a somewhat plastic state; in fact, may be regarded as almost liquid or gaseous. Like the sun, it does not rotate uniformly; the average axial period is only nine hours and 55 minutes. This rapid rotation, together with the pliant structure of the planet, have caused the equatorial parts to bulge out, thus producing a very great polar compression, which at once strikes the eye of the telescopic observer.

Telescopic Appearance of Jupiter

Even through very small instruments the surface of Jupiter is seen to be covered with broad, alternate light and dark belts parallel to the equator. The disc is brightest and most clearly defined at the centre, the belts becoming indistinct toward the edge.

As has been previously stated, Jupiter is not a solid body. It is the first of the group of outer planets, which as we noted in an earlier chapter are large and plastic, as contrasted with the inner planets, which are smaller and solid. The atmosphere of Jupiter is very dense, as shewn by the conduct of the belts, which are palpably atmospheric phenomena of some sort. These belts frequently change shape, move, join each other, or break up, like the stratus clouds of our own sunset skies. Since the planet receives but a 27th of the amount of solar light and heat that is given to the earth, it is evident that in order to account for the rapid formation and motions of its clouds, phenomena requiring a high temperature, the body beneath these clouds must itself possess and radiate great heat. In fact, we may well assume that Jupiter is in a half-molten state; is a kind of semi-sun, as it were, although it gives forth no light. Its density is nearly the same as that of the sun.

Occasionally spots more permanent than the belts are noted upon the surface of the planet. These are probably connected with the great mass beneath the stratum of clouds, thus indicating that although very hot and plastic, this mass is at least in some degree coherent. The famous red spot which appeared in 1878 is even now visible at times, though infinitely fainter than when it was first observed. It is unnecessary to state that no inhabitants could possibly dwell upon Jupiter, or, as may as well be said here, upon any of the four outer planets.

Satellites of Jupiter

Jupiter is attended by nine satellites, four of which are very large, and easily seen in small telescopes. These four were discovered in 1610 by Galileo. They present a most interesting sight in any telescope, being often eclipsed by the shadow of their primary, occulted by that body itself, or preceded or followed by their shadows as their position with respect to the sun determines. Their names, in order of distance outward from Jupiter, are Io, Europa, Ganymede, and Callisto. In powerful telescopes they shew sensible discs, and upon their surfaces spots may be discerned. Prof. W. H. Pickering has discovered that Callisto always faces Jupiter as the moon faces the earth, and Mr. Douglass, an assistant of Prof. Percival Lowell, believes that Ganymede behaves likewise, a fact suspected by Dr. Herschel over 100 years ago. Conclusions respecting the habitability of these orbs would be baseless. If they do possess inhabitants, a thing by no means impossible, their astronomers must be fortunate indeed, for words cannot describe the grandeur with which Jupiter shines in their nocturnal skies.

The other five satellites of Jupiter are very faint indeed. One of these was discovered by Barnard in 1892, two more by Perrine in 1905, another by Melotte in 1908, and the ninth and latest by Nicholson in 1914. The last four are so difficult to observe, that they have never been directly glimpsed by human eye. They were discovered by photography, for the camera is much more sensitive to faint beams of light than is the sight of man, and the exposure can be prolonged to a great extent. The satellite which was discovered in 1892 lies within, and the four more recently found lie outside the orbits of the four larger moons. The satellites discovered by Melotte and Nicholson, respectively, behave in a most extraordinary manner, revolving around Jupiter backwards, thus appearing to break a fundamental law of the system. We shall soon note some instances of this retrograde sort of revolution.

Saturn

(Distance from sun, 886,000,000 miles. Revolution, 29 and one-half years. Rotation, ten hours, 14 minutes. Diameter, 73,000 miles. Synodic period, 378 days. Inclination of axis to upright, 28 degrees.)

We now approach that which is without doubt the most impressive and unique object in the solar system. The naked eye, dwelling upon the bright yet strangely leaden-hued Saturn, is wholly unprepared for the sight revealed by a telescope of moderate power, for through the latter is beheld a golden ball, much like that of Jupiter in appearance, yet entirely surrounded by three immense flat rings of light, which nowhere touch the planet itself. This arrangement is absolutely unparalleled. In all the expanse of heaven no counterpart exists. Saturn itself is inferior only to Jupiter in size amongst the planets, and is believed to have the same constitution; an extremely high temperature, and a plastic or molten nature. Upon its surface may be discerned belts which, though not so readily seen in small telescopes, are nevertheless like those of Jupiter, and which are believed to arise from the same causes. That Saturn is hotter and even less solid than Jupiter may be inferred from its very low specific gravity, for the planet is lighter than water. It is, in fact, the least dense of all the planets. Gravity upon the surface of Saturn is variable. At the equator, it is less than on the earth, but at the poles it is greater. Because of its plastic condition, Saturn, like Jupiter, has an irregular rotation and great polar compression. The polar compression, indeed, is the greatest possessed by any planet in our system. Saturn's distance from us varies from 774,000,000 miles to 1,028,000,000 miles. It was once the most remote of the known planets, of which place it was deprived by the discovery of Uranus in 1781. When viewed with a telescope, Saturn's disc, like that of Jupiter, appears brightest at the centre. The belts, owing to the planet's greater axial inclination, are sometimes seen as curved lines, while Jupiter's always appear horizontal. The brightest belt, that at the equator, is of a faint pink colour. The poles are surrounded by dull areas.

EDITOR'S NOTE FP: AGN 20, No. 26 (13 March 1915): 3.

[THE OUTER PLANETS, PART II]

The Rings of Saturn

The rings of Saturn were discovered by Galileo, who did not, however, understand their real nature. Huyghens, in 1656, first knew them for what they were. With low magnifying powers they appear as one, and such they were first thought to be. Cassini, twenty years after their discovery, found that there are at least two, with a clear black line of demarcation between, and in 1850 Bond discovered the third ring, which is nearer the planet than the others, and so dark and transparent that it has been called the "gauze" or "crepe" ring. The opinion has been recently held by some, that the crepe ring is not separate, but a continuation of the inner bright ring. The plane in which the rings of Saturn lie is that of the planet's equator, which departs 28 degrees from that of the earth's orbit. The result of this is that we see them tipped at various angles, sometimes edgewise, when on account of their extreme tenuity they all but dis-appear, but never behold them as circles with the ball or body of Saturn in the centre. The set of phases resulting from the angles at which the rings are beheld from the earth occupies a complete revolution of Saturn round the sun, that is, about 30 years. Twice during this time, once in 15 years, the rings disappear, being turned edgewise to our planet. The last such disappearance took place in 1907; the next will occur in 1922. The rings of Saturn are not solid bodies, as they seem, but are merely swarms of tiny separate particles like miniature satellites, all revolving together in the same plane, and thus giving an appearance of solidity whilst actually pursuing independent paths. This fact was first suspected as early as 1715, but not proved until after 1850. The stability of the system of rings has often been discussed. It has even been intimated that the rings have contracted, thus approaching the planet, since the beginning of their tele-scopic observation. The rings of Saturn do not exceed 100 miles in thickness. The out-ermost ring is about 170,000 miles in diameter, and 11,000 miles in width. The division discovered by Cassini is 2,000 miles wide. The inner bright ring is 10,000 miles wide, and about 9,000 miles from the surface of Saturn.

Satellites of Saturn

Saturn has ten satellites, more than attend any other planet, five of which are visible in ordinary telescopes. Titan, the largest, was discovered in 1655 by Huyghens. The tenth, a body of incredibly small magnitude for such an object, was discovered by Prof. W. H. Pickering in 1905. It is called Themis. The names of the satellites in order of distance from Saturn are: Iapetus, Hyperion, Themis, Titan, Rhea, Dione, Tethys, Enceladus, Mimas, and Phoebe. The prodigious spectacle presented to their possible inhabitants by the ball and rings of Saturn defies our conception.

Uranus

(Distance from sun, 1,778,000,000 miles. Revolution, 84 years. Rotation unknown. Diameter, 30,000 miles. Synodic period, 370 days. Inclination of axis unknown.)

The large but remote planet Uranus was discovered on the night of March 13, 1781, by Sir William Herschel, who was at that time making a minute survey of the starry heavens. Though at first mistaken for a comet, its true nature was soon realised. It was the first planet to be discovered since prehistoric times, since the brighter mem-bers of the system were known to the ancients. Uranus is barely visible to the naked eye when near opposition. In the telescope it exhibits a very small disc of greenish hue, destitute of all markings save possibly a faint suggestion of belts like those of Jupiter and Saturn. The planet is probably a hot and molten semi-sun. Of the rotation of Ura-nus, nothing definite is known, though some doubtful changes on the disc suggest a day of 11 hours. The atmosphere about Uranus is undoubtedly very dense. Uranus is attended by four satellites, called, in order of distance outward, Ariel, Umbriel, Tita-nia, and Oberon. They revolve in a most peculiar manner, their paths being almost perpendicular to the orbit of their primary, even tending toward a retrograde direction.

Neptune

(Distance from sun, 2,772,000,000 miles. Revolution, 164 and a half years. Rotation unknown. Diameter, 35,000 miles. Synodic period, 366 days. Inclination of axis unknown.)

Neptune, the most distant from the sun of all the planets of our system, was discovered in 1846 through mathematical calculations. Uranus had previously been noticed to shew in its motions certain effects of the gravitation or attraction of some large unknown planet outside its own orbit, so Adams in England and Le Verrier in France simultaneously began to calculate the orbit and position of the attracting body. Dr. Galle, of Berlin, acting on the data of Le Verrier, first saw the new planet on September 23, 1846. The discovery of Neptune was one of the greatest triumphs of the human reason, since the planet's exact place and motions were calculated before it had itself been seen. So great is Neptune's distance from us, that it is invisible to the naked eye at all times, and but ill seen in the best of telescopes. Its surface, like that of Uranus, is of greenish colour, but is not diversified by any visible markings. It is probably hot and of small density, like the other outer planets.

To an observer situate upon the surface of Neptune, the sun would appear as but little more than an intensely brilliant point of light, giving, however, a light equal to that of 700 full moons. Of all the other planets, Saturn and Uranus alone would be visible, both being, of course, "inferior". Neptune possesses a solitary satellite, discovered in 1846 by Lassell. It moves in a retrograde direction, like the eighth and ninth satellites of Jupiter.

Whether or not there are unknown planets beyond Neptune, is a question still unsettled. In all probability such exist, but that we shall ever discover them is not likely, since the small amount of solar light received by them would scarce be enough to make them visible to us.

EDITOR'S NOTE FP: *AGN* 20, No. 38 (27 March 1915): 9.

IX. COMETS AND METEORS

Comets

In ancient times, no portent was regarded as more dreadful than the advent of a great comet, with its fiery head and sweeping tail. Extracts from almost all poetical writings reveal the tendency of untutored man to associate these refulgent celestial wanderers with the severest calamities to nations and princes. But intellectual enlightenment has brought about a change in our attitude toward these as well as other things, and comets are now welcomed with scientific interest, rather than feared with superstitious terror.

So far as we know, comets may be divided into two classes with respect to their relation to the solar system: (1) Periodic Comets, bodies which regularly revolve about the sun in elliptical though highly elongated or eccentric orbits, or (2) Comets which are apparently solitary and independent bodies; bodies that come rushing out of the unknown depths of space, temporarily attracted by the sun, curve around the latter, and vanish again into infinity, never to return.

Periodic Comets, like the planets, have definite times of revolution, and their motions may be quite accurately predicted. It is one of their peculiarities, that in many cases two or more pursue each other around the sun, one after the other, in exactly the same orbit, a condition probably due to successive disintegrations of one original mass; for of all known heavenly bodies, save meteors alone, comets are the most prone to be affected by rapid and sudden changes. Comets vary greatly in size, brilliancy, and constitution; all, however, having the common property of extreme lightness in weight, that is, incredibly small density.

Comets become visible to us only when they are in rather close proximity to the sun. As they draw toward perihelion their brightness increases, until, having undergone a period of invisibility while lost in the solar rays, they gradually fade and soon disappear. The average period during which a comet is visible from the earth is about three months.

The great comets which have in one way or another so often excited the peoples of our globe form but a trifling fraction of the total number of cometary bodies observed and studied by astronomers. It has been estimated that only one out of five is at all visible to the naked eye, and that but about five in the course of an entire century are visible in the full light of day. Roughly speaking, a fairly bright and prominent comet appears about once in every ten years.

Most comets are composed of three principal parts: (1) The Nucleus, a bright, star-like mass, (2) The Coma, a hazy, luminous mist surrounding the nucleus, and (3) The Tail, a thin luminous appendage preceding, following, or surrounding the other parts. The coma is the essential part of a comet; whatever other portions may be absent, the coma must remain. In fact, some small telescopic comets consist of a coma alone. The sun, probably by the mechanical pressure of its intense luminous radiations, always repels the tail of a comet, so that when the latter is approaching the solar orb, the tail follows the nucleus and coma, preceding them, however, as the comet emerges from perihelion. In general, a comet's tail is always pointed away from the sun. While some comets lack tails, many possess two or more. The nucleus and coma of a comet, as distinguished from the tail, are frequently designated by the collective term "head". When there is no nucleus, the coma alone forms the head.

Nature of Comets

There are many conflicting theories regarding the physical constitution of comets. The most recent assumption is that they are composed of collections of extremely small solid meteoric masses, spread far apart, and possessing individual gaseous atmospheres of rare consistency. A comet's light is considered as either derived from sparks of electricity formed by discharges from one tiny mass to another, or as generated by some as yet unknown agency of the sun. In any case, comets are mainly self-luminous, though they may also reflect some light from the sun.

That no extensive solid masses exist in comets seems satisfactorily proved. The comet of 1882, and Halley's Comet in 1910, crossed the sun's disc in transit like Mercury and Venus, yet were not visible as black spots against the solar surface, being entirely lost to sight. Thus we perceive that even the nucleus of a comet is so thin that it is practically transparent. The extremely light weight of comets render them easily liable to deviation from their courses by the attraction of the larger planets, so that many comets have been "captured" by such orbs as Jupiter, and made to move in such a manner that their aphelia, or points of greatest distance from the sun, lie just outside the orbit of the capturing body. It is indeed thought by some astronomers, that all the periodic comets of our system have been acquired from space by the gravitation of the heavier planets. Two groups of cometary aphelia located beyond the orbit of Neptune render it likely that two corresponding planets of great size exist near them, though unseen by us.

It is considered possible for a comet to collide with a planet, such as the earth, though the chances for such a collision are but slight. Even should one occur, the lightness of the comet would prevent any disaster; indeed, it is thought that the earth has sometimes passed through portions of the tails of comets. Such passages are believed to have taken place in 1861 and 1910, yet on neither occasion were any unusual phenomena observed.

The head of the average comet is, according to Young,[1] about 40,000 or 50,000 miles in diameter. Many, however, exceed these figures; indeed, the head of the great comet of 1811 had a diameter of 1,200,000 miles. The nucleus of a comet is usually from 100 to 5000 miles in diameter. The exact size, as well as that of the entire head, varies from time to time. The tail of a comet is usually of great length; in fact, 50,000,000 miles is not considered unusual, while instances are recorded wherein a length of 100,000,000 miles, a far greater distance than that from the earth to the sun, has been attained. So light, however, are these vast objects, that they are acted upon by forces too light to be felt by even the smallest of other bodies.

Periodic Comets

Of all known comets, Encke's has the shortest period of revolution, completing its circuit round the sun in only three and a quarter years. In all, there are about twelve known comets whose revolutions are performed in less than 14 years. The celebrated comet of Halley, which is visible to the naked eye, has a period of about 76 years, the history of its successive advents being traceable back to ancient times. It was last seen in 1910, and will next be visible in 1986. Some of the most brilliant and famous comets ever beheld by man are periodic, but revolve in such prodigiously long periods, some of them comprising thousands of years, that nations and races are born and have perished ere they are observed a second time.

Famous Comets

Some of the principal comets which have appeared in modern times are the comet of 1680, which terrified New England and caused the Rev. Increase Mather[2] of Boston to preach a sermon entitled "Heaven's Alarm to the World"; the comet of 1744, which had five principal tails and many lesser off-shoots, and which was of so strange and splendid an appearance that many doubted its cometary nature; the comet of 1811, whose magnificent tail was 25 degrees long and six degrees wide; the comet of 1843, which had a tail 40 degrees long, and of great lustre; the comet of 1858, which was called "Donati's Comet", and which had a brilliant nucleus and a somewhat curved tail about 60 degrees long; the comet of 1861, whose tail, 80 degrees in length, is said to have brushed the earth; the comet of 1882, which was visible in full daylight, and which had a sweeping bifurcated tail; and the comet of 1910, which far outshone the planet Venus.

EDITOR'S NOTE FP: AGN 20, No. 28 (16 March 1915): 3.

Notes

1. Charles Augustus Young (1834–1908), American astronomer who taught for many years at Dartmouth and Princeton and wrote *Elements of Astronomy* (1890; LL 978), *Lessons in Astronomy* (1893; LL 979–80), and *Manual of Astronomy* (1902).
2. Increase Mather (1639–1723), *Heavens Alarm to the World; or, A Sermon Wherein Is Shewed, That Fearful Sights and Signs in Heaven Are the Presages of Great Calamities at Hand* (1681).

COMETS AND METEORS [PART II]

Meteors

While closely viewing the nocturnal sky, we may occasionally see its seeming repose broken by the swift passage of one or more brilliant streaks of light through the constellations, as though some of the stars themselves were falling to earth. Although these fleet objects are commonly known as "shooting stars", they are in fact more widely different from true stars than are any other bodies in the heavens; for whilst the stars are the largest and most distant things we can behold, these "shooting stars", or "meteors", as they are more properly called, are the smallest and nearest of the celestial orbs, being scarce larger than rocks, pebbles, or grains of dust, and coming into actual contact with our atmosphere, some indeed reaching the surface of the earth itself. Meteors are members of the solar system, revolving around the sun in the same manner as do comets; in fact, it is thought probable that meteors have taken their origin from the disintegration of comets. Their brilliancy is due to their combustion in our air, which latter ignites them with the intense heat caused by its friction upon them as they strike it at extremely high rates of speed. So small are most meteors that they are entirely consumed before reaching the ground, depositing only an ash or dust which has been recognised amongst the arctic and antarctic snows, and upon the beds of the great oceans. Meteors are the only heavenly bodies which forcibly encounter the earth during their passage through space, for while the general laws of motion do not permit of collisions between the various members of the system, these tiny "shooting stars" are so widely diffused, that it would be strange indeed if one did not occasionally strike our planet; either because the latter may happen to lie in its path, or because terrestrial gravity may deflect it toward us. It is thought that meteors become incandescent about 75 miles above the earth's surface.

At regular periodic intervals the earth encounters large clusters of meteors, causing great numbers to be seen during a single night. Such a phenomenon is called a "meteoric shower". Each year at stated dates occur many meteoric showers, some of which are much more conspicuous than others. The meteors in such a shower all seem to come from a single point in the sky, which lies, of course, in the direction from which the cluster strikes the earth. This point is called the "radiant point" of the shower, and all showers are named from the constellations in which their respective radiant points are situate; for instance, the meteors whose radiant point is in Leo are called "Leonids". Two annual meteoric displays are of especial prominence, the Perseid shower of August 10, and the Leonid shower of November 13. Of these, the Leonid shower is the richer in "shooting stars". In November, 1833, when an unusually heavy display took place, 240,000 meteors are estimated to have fallen. This phenomenon occasioned much terror amongst the ignorant, driving into frenzies the simple-minded blacks of the southern states.

While most meteors are so small that they are wholly burnt up before striking the earth, there are a few of greater magnitude that pass through the atmosphere without completely losing their solidity, descending to us as meteoric stones, extremely hot from friction and combustion. Such bodies are known as "meteorites" or "aerolites", and are the only kind of celestial objects that may be touched by earthly hands. Specimens of these objects are carefully preserved in museums, and subjected to chemical analysis, whereby they are found to consist either of rocky matter or of nearly pure metals such as Iron and Nickel. Within their pores are frequently included great volumes of the inert gas Helium. In size they vary from immense masses to fragments scarcely larger than pebbles. At times many aerolites fall at once, as in the showers of stones over the middle western states in 1876 and over Spain in 1896. Besides those stones which are seen to descend from the sky, many great masses bearing indisputable evidences of celestial origin have been found in various parts of the earth. One found in Greenland by Admiral Peary weighs about 100 tons, while others weighing 27, 17, and 15 tons are known.

The Zodiacal Light

Connected perhaps with meteoric phenomena is the "Zodiacal light", a faint diffuse area of luminosity which seems to surround the sun, reaching out beyond the earth's orbit, and lying approximately in the plane of the latter. That portion which is closest to the sun is fairly bright at times, though the rest is discernible only with the greatest effort. In our latitude this light may be seen for a short period twice each year; in spring just after sunset in the west, and in autumn before sunrise in the east. It must be observed in the absence of all artificial lights, then appearing as a large, faintly luminous cone, tapering upwards with its apex at a considerable distance from the horizon. The spring appearances are the most favourable. In the tropics the Zodiacal light may be observed on any clear evening after sunset or any clear morning before sunrise.

Opposite the Zodiacal light in the sky is that faintest of all celestial phenomena, the "Gegenschein" or "Counterglow", an illumination so dim that the light of the Milky Way completely obliterates it from view. In the words of the late Prof. Newcomb, the Gegenschein is "an extremely faint impression of light, to which no exact outline can be assigned."

The Zodiacal light is manifestly composed of some medium surrounding the sun, probably a dense swarm of meteoric bodies. The nature of the Gegenschein is more obscure. Since it is seen only opposite the sun, it may perhaps be formed of those parts of the Zodiacal light which extend beyond the earth's orbit, and which therefore appear in opposition like the superior planets.

EDITOR'S NOTE FP: AGN 20, No. 40 (30 March 1915): 8.

X. THE STARS

Vast and illimitable as seems the sun's domain, to whose contemplation we have hitherto been confined; grand and majestic as appears the solar orb itself, with its massive circumvolent worlds, we have now to consider distances and magnitudes which dwarf to insignificance all that we have previously studied. Nine thousand times farther away from the sun than is Neptune, the most remote of the planets, lies Alpha Centauri, the nearest of the fixed stars. This adjective "fixed" as popularly applied to these bodies is not at all correct, since all of them are moving at rapid rates. The term was formerly used to distinguish them from the planets, for their great distance from us causes them to change but little in apparent place, even through centuries, as opposed to the relatively swift apparent motions of the planets, which appear like them, and which were therefore called by the ancients "wandering stars".

As we have previously learnt, the stars are other suns, in comparison to which our own sun is of but moderate size. In constitution, they all appear to be similar, each shining with its own independent incandescence. The brilliancy of a star as seen from the earth is probably determined by three causes; its distance, its size, and its intrinsic brightness. It is thought probable that many stars exist unseen, even near to us, whose luminous energy has departed, and which now roll on, dark, cold, and desolate. As our own star, the sun, is followed by a large retinue of planets, asteroids, comets, and meteors, forming the solar system, so is it extremely likely that some of the other stars are the centres of similar systems, some of whose planets may or may not be inhabited. Of course, since the nearest of the stars is so far away from us that it exhibits no perceptible disc, even as seen through the greatest of telescopes, it is needless to say that we may never hope to behold these stellar planets, nor could their possible inhabitants ever see our own tiny world or any other of the sun's revolving minions. In short, the planets surrounding one star may not be seen from those attending any other star.

In all the heavens as seen from the earth, there are over 7,000 stars visible to the naked eye, their approximately even distribution leaving about 3,500 in whatever half of the sky is visible at one time from any place. However, only about 2,500 of these are actually to be seen at a given moment, since the fainter stars are obscured when low in the sky by the density of the air around the horizon. The number of stars visible with optical aid is enormous. An opera glass will shew 100,000, whilst the most powerful telescopes reveal over 125,000,000.

The old Alexandrian astronomers, Hipparchus[1] and Ptolemy, divided the visible stars into six classes or "magnitudes" according to their brilliancy. A star of each magnitude is about two and a half times brighter than one of the magnitude next below it. The brightest stars are said to be of the "first magnitude", those second in brilliancy of the "second magnitude", and so on down to the sixth, which comprises the faintest stars visible to the unassisted vision. There are 21 stars of the first magnitude, 65 of the second, 200 of the third, 500 of the fourth, 1,400 of the fifth, and 5,000 of the sixth. After the invention of the telescope the system was continued down to the stars which are seen only by optical aid, thus extending the number of visible magnitudes to about 17. The photographic plate, indeed, will record stars even of the 24th magnitude. Since the brilliancy of most stars does not coincide exactly with any standard magnitude, astronomers are now accustomed to deal with fractional, zero, and negative magnitudes, but the amateur, in his casual survey of the sky, need not depart from the simpler and more ancient system.

Whilst the more important stars are distinguished by individual names bestowed upon them by the astronomers of bygone ages, the scientific system of stellar nomenclature now in general use is that devised by Bayer in 1603, which assigns to the stars the small letters of the Greek alphabet. The brightest star in a constellation receives the letter Alpha, first of the alphabet; the next, Beta, the second letter, and so on, until the Greek alphabet is exhausted, after which our common Roman alphabet is used. This, if inadequate, is followed by numerals, which of course form an endless system. After the letter or number of a star is placed the Latin genitive or possessive case of the name of the constellation, for all the latter have Latin names. This system in no way displaces the individual names of the stars, both being equally correct. Thus Sirius, the brightest star in the constellation Canis Major, is also known as Alpha Canis Majoris.

In considering the distances of the stars, we have to deal with more appalling gaps in space than can be comprehended by the human brain. We may measure the distances only of those stars which are comparatively near our system, yet even these by far surpass in length any readily conceivable standard of linear measure. The nearest star, Alpha Centauri, lies 25,000,000,000,000 miles from our system, whilst 61 Cygni, the next in order of distance from us, is 43,000,000,000,000 miles away. Since these monstrous spaces are as nothing in comparison to most stellar distances, it is evident that some new and enormous standard must be employed in order to measure the latter. Such a standard is the "light year" or the vast linear distance over which the ethereal waves of light, at their incomprehensibly rapid rate of 186,000 miles per second, travel in the course of one entire year. The length of this immensely extended interval is 5,869,588,236,000 miles. According to this system of reckoning, the distance of Alpha Centauri is four and one-third light-years, and of 61 Cygni, seven and one-fifth. Most of the stars visible to the naked eye lie from 200 to 300 light-years away, and their distances from each other are of the same degree of immensity. This being so, how are we to regard those celestial bodies whose distances from us Dr. Wolf has very lately estimated to be about 578,000 light-years?

EDITOR'S NOTE FP: AGN 20, No. 32 (20 March 1915): 10.

Notes

1. Hipparchus of Rhodes (2nd century B.C.E.), prolific writer on astronomy whose works largely perished as a result of the prominence of Ptolemy's *Almagest*. The only complete work that survives is a commentary on Aratus.

[THE STARS, PART II]

Our intellects cannot adequately imagine such a quantity as this. If the light that reaches us from one of these bodies has consumed 578,000 years in its journey, then we must now behold them not as they are at present, but as they were 578,000 years ago; a time possibly previous to the existence of the human race upon the earth! By this time, the bodies whose light we behold may themselves have faded forever. Yet is it not improbable that all the great universe unfolded to our eyes is but an illimitable heaven studded with an infinite number of other and perhaps vastly larger clusters? To what mean and ridiculous proportions is thus reduced our tiny globe, with its vain, pompous inhabitants and arrogant, quarrelsome nations!

As we have noted before, the stars, though seemingly fixed, are actually in extremely rapid and probably rectilinear motion. While it was formerly believed that each one follows a random independent course, the Dutch astronomer Kapteyn demonstrated in 1904 that certain stars are moving in company, bound together by some law yet unknown. These stellar wanderings are called "proper motions" to distinguish them from certain apparent changes in place to which some stars are subject. Delicate instruments are able to record the changes in a star's position during many years, and the spectroscope, whose prismatic image or spectrum of an object moves in one direction when the object is receding and in the other when it is approaching, enables us to learn that many stars apparently at rest are in reality moving in the line of sight, that is, moving exactly toward or away from us. The rates at which the stars are travelling differ greatly. All are very high, yet the distances involved are such that a period of over 3,000 years is necessary for us to perceive any distinct alterations in the figures of the constellations. Certain nebulae are thought to move 621 miles per second, but the rates of the visible stars are considerably less. 1830 Groombridge, the most swiftly moving of all the stars, flies on at the velocity of 200 miles per second, while 61 Cygni, the next in speed, advances about 100 miles per second. About 25 to 50 miles per second is the speed most frequently observed. Our own star or sun is of course in motion like the rest, carrying the whole solar system at the rate of 16 miles per second toward a point in the sky marked out by the constellation Hercules.

The amount of luminous energy which we receive from the stars is very small. The combined light of all the stars in the visible sky is not over one sixtieth of full moonlight, or one thirty-three millionth of sunlight.

In colour the stars are by no means uniform as one might believe from a casual glance at the nocturnal sky; indeed, their chromatic differences are in certain cases quite marked. Of the stars of the first magnitude, Vega and Rigel are bluish white. Sirius and Spica are slightly less white, the former possessing an almost greenish tinge. Capella, Procyon, and Pollux are white, with a slight tendency toward yellow. Arcturus is orange, Betelgeux and Aldebaran are reddish, whilst Antares is of a deep, fiery red. Some of the less brilliant stars have colours even more prominent than these. It is believed that the comparative ages of the stars are revealed by their colours; these bodies being bluish white when new or recently formed, turning successively yellow and orange during their later existence, and assuming deeper and deeper shades of red whilst expiring, after which they become extinct and invisible. Our own sun is considered as belonging to the yellow class, though our proximity to it causes its light to appear almost white to us.

Double and Multiple Stars

Although appearing as single points of light to the unassisted vision, many stars are discovered by the telescope to be double or even multiple. This condition may arise either from the mere effect of perspective, or from a real connexion with the components of the double or multiple system. In the latter case, the components are found to be revolving round a common centre of gravity. Actual systems of two stars revolving about their centre of gravity are known as "binary stars". The shortest known period of revolution of a binary system is five and a half years; the longest, over 1,500 years. The orbits of the components are elliptical, and of about the same size as those of Uranus or Neptune. The relative masses of the stars may be equal or unequal. Obviously, their relations are not like those between a planet and its central sun. Some double stars are coloured, the components presenting to the eye the most attractive contrasts, as in the case of Albireo in Cygnus, which consists of a dark blue and an orange star. Systems of three actually connected stars are called "ternary stars", of which a well-known example is Zeta Cancri. We find there one star revolving around another in a period of over 60 years, whilst a third revolves around both of these in a period of over 500 years. Epsilon Lyrae is quadruple, two binary systems revolving around each other. There are some systems of stars in which one of the members has died out and ceased to give light, being detected only by the motion of its still luminous companion. Procyon in Canis Minor is known to possess such a dark attendant.

Variable Stars

Upon continuous observation, it has been found that many stars do not maintain a uniform brilliancy, but fluctuate during certain intervals. These objects are called "variable stars", and may be divided into several distinct types or classes. Variable stars of the "Algol type", named [from] Algol in Perseus, are usually bright, but suffer temporary diminutions in brilliancy at brief, regular intervals, probably being eclipsed periodically by dark companions. Algol itself is ordinarily a star of the second magnitude, but once in every two and a half days it suffers a temporary obscuration which lasts over eight hours, and which when greatest reduces it to about the fourth magnitude. Another sort of variable star is that represented by Mira in Cetus. Mira is sometimes as bright as the second magnitude, remaining thus for two weeks, when it begins to fade. In about ten weeks it becomes invisible to the naked eye, and finally sinks to the ninth magnitude. Having been invisible for six months, it reappears, and in ten more weeks is again of the second magnitude. For this species of variation we can as yet assign no certain cause, though many conflicting theories have been advanced to explain it.

Besides the ordinary variable stars, we sometimes behold the more impressive spectacle of new, temporary stars, which blaze out unannounced, shine for a while, and finally fade from our vision. In B. C. 134 a new star burst out in the constellation Scorpio, a phenomenon which led the Alexandrian astronomer Hipparchus to compile his famous catalogue of the stars. The new star of 1572 in Cassiopeia was the brightest recorded in history, having surpassed the planet Jupiter in brilliancy. It was observed with great diligence by the celebrated Danish astronomer Tycho Brahe. Tycho's new star was rivalled by that of 1604 in Serpentarius, which was observed by the noted Johann Kepler. In 1866 a star of the second magnitude appeared in Corona Borealis, whilst the new star of 1901 in Perseus attained great brilliancy, and is still remembered by all who beheld it. It is worthy of note, that all temporary stars have appeared in or very near the Via Lactea, or Milky Way.

The origin of temporary stars is still rather uncertain, though it is generally believed that they result from collisions between dark celestial objects, which suddenly liberate vast amounts of light and heat from the concussions.

EDITOR'S NOTE FP: AGN 20, No. 34 (23 March 1915): 4.

XI. CLUSTERS AND NEBULAE

When we view the nocturnal sky with great care, our attention is here and there arrested by a cloudy, luminous patch amongst the constellations. Some of these patches are shewn by the telescope to be dense aggregations of stars, whilst others are continuous gaseous masses called "nebulae". Though most clusters appear as mere specks of misty light to the naked eye, a few, such as the noted Pleiades and Hyades in Taurus, exhibit their true nature without a telescope. Clusters are never the chance results of perspective; there being in all cases a real proximity and relation between the various component stars, as frequently proved by a common motion in the same direction. Two very beautiful clusters are those in Perseus and Hercules. Most clusters and nebulae are designated by numbers, together with the letter "M", the latter signifying Messier's catalogue, in which they are enumerated.

The Milky Way

The Via Lactea, Milky Way, or Galaxy, as it is variously called, is one of the most beautiful objects of the night sky. This faint stream of silvery light, spanning the heavens as it sometimes does in a great arch reaching from horizon to horizon, has in all ages inspired the fancy of poet and philosopher alike. That this apparently continuous glowing ribbon is in reality an aggregation of innumerable stars is now understood by all, and though not actually proven until the time of Galileo and his telescope, was suspected by many, even in ancient times. Pythagoras, Democritus, and Aristotle alike believed in its stellar nature, whilst Manilius, referring to the Milky Way in his "Astronomicon", half inquires 'whether a greater aggregation of stars in a dense ring joins flames and shines with solid light, and the brighter circle glitters in collected splendour?'[1] Since the ancients possessed no telescopes, these surmises as to the starry character of the Galaxy confer much credit upon their powers of imagination. It is not probable that the Via Lactea is merely a fortuitous collection of stars; certain facts soon to be mentioned render it likely that this shining band affords to us a veritable index to our position in space, and possesses a fundamental relation to the structure of the visible universe. It is remarkable that all temporary stars, most of the brighter ordinary stars, and a large proportion of the fainter stars are grouped in or near the Milky Way. The Via Lactea is not a perfectly regular band of light, its contour being diversified by numerous rifts, divisions, and ramifications. Two places along its course are especially destitute of stars, standing out in black contrast to the surrounding fields of light, and receiving the apt name of "Coal Sacks". As a whole, however, the Milky Way forms one continuous great circle, girding the entire celestial sphere and dividing it into two equal parts. The plane of this circle is called the "Galactic Plane", and the two points each ninety degrees from it are known as the "Galactic Poles", since they bear the same relation to the Galactic Plane as do the terrestrial poles to the plane of the terrestrial equator.

Nebulae

Amongst the many bits of misty light scattered about upon the surface of the nocturnal sky are some which even in the most powerful telescopes fail to resolve themselves into clusters of separate stars, but stand out distinct from all other celestial objects as dim, diffuse areas of continuous illumination. These are the "nebulae", and are undoubtedly composed of glowing gaseous matter as yet unformed into definite spherical suns or stars. About 1,000 nebulae are at present known and recorded, the brightest being those in Andromeda and Orion, which are visible to the naked eye. The size of most nebulae must be well-nigh incomprehensible, for whilst the stars, some of which are thousands of times larger than our sun, present no sensible surfaces as seen from the earth, yet many of the nebulae cover comparatively large areas in our sky. Dr. Wolf has recently estimated the diameters of certain nebulae at from 900 to 2,000 light years; these bodies being situate from 33,000 to 58,000 light years away.

While the stars, both individually and in clusters, seem to abound mainly near the Galactic Plane; the nebulae, with the exception of the "planetary" variety, are most numerous around the galactic poles, where the stars are but thinly scattered.

Nebulae differ widely in figure and extent. The massive nebula in Andromeda is oval in form, having a sort of nucleus or central condensation as well as two bright and apparently attendant nebulae beside it. Its outer parts suggest the belief that it is of a spiral shape. The great nebula in Orion is widespread and diffuse, being wholly without definite outlines. The rather rare "planetary nebulae", which, unlike the others, are found in and near the Milky Way, are round and of uniform brilliancy, like the discs of planets. The nebula in Lyra is annular or ring-like in form, whilst one in Sagittarius appears to be split up into three great divisions, the rifts being plainly visible. The spiral nebula in Canes Venatici seems to consist of a central body in the act of throwing off part of its component matter in the form of a second condensation. The "Horseshoe" and "Dumbbell" nebulae in Sagittarius, and the "Crab" nebula in Taurus, resemble in large telescopes the objects from which they are named. According to the best authorities, the normal type of non-planetary nebula is spiral. The well-known Pleiades cluster possesses a vast nebulous background obviously connected with the component stars themselves, since many of the larger Pleiades have small particles of nebulous matter about them.

Although according to the best authorities all nebulae are affected by a slow continuous change, nothing of the kind has as yet been noted in connexion with any of them. That they are actually composed of self-luminous gas was satisfactorily demonstrated with the spectroscope in 1864 by the late Sir William Huggins. The rotation of nebulae on their axes has long been assumed on theoretical grounds, yet not until 1914 was this assumption verified by observation. In that year Dr. Slipher of the Lowell Observatory at Flagstaff, Arizona, found with the spectroscope that a nebula in Virgo performs such a motion. All the nebulae have proper motions through space, most of them proceeding with a tremendous velocity.

The Magellanic Clouds

In that part of the southern sky which is perpetually hidden from dwellers in our latitude lie two remarkable objects called the "nubeculae" or "Magellanic Clouds",[2] the latter name being in honour of Magellan, the Portuguese explorer, who observed them during his celebrated voyage around the globe. These faintly luminous clouds appear to the naked eye like separated and isolated parts of the Galaxy, but investigation shews them to be quite different in nature, and composed of a mixture of nebulae, clusters, and independent stars. The Nubecula Major, or Greater Magellanic Cloud, lies in the constellation Dorado, and covers 40 square degrees in the sky, being about four times larger than the Nubecula Minor, or Lesser Magellanic Cloud, which lies in Hydrus. The lesser cloud, however, is decidedly the brighter of the two. The nubeculae are best observed in the absence of the moon, whose refulgent rays overpower the faint glimmering of these strange objects.

Structure of the Universe

Our notions as to the structure of the great universe whereof we form so infinitesimal a part depend largely upon observation concerning the distribution of the stars and nebulae, and especially their relation to the Milky Way. More than a century ago Sir William Herschel made a most diligent survey of the heavens, and as the result of his researches enunciated that theory of the universe which with but few modifications we still accept. From a long and accurate enumeration of the stars in all parts of the sky, Dr. Herschel found that most of them form a great circle, or rather a broad circular band, roughly coinciding with the galactic plane and consisting mainly of the Galaxy itself. The stars outside this belt of close distribution he saw to be few and scattered. Upon these facts he built his hypothesis, which assumes the visible stellar universe to consist of an immense cluster of stars; the components disposed with moderate uniformity, and the whole so shaped that it forms a thin, flat disc of incredible magnitude, near whose centre lies our own solar system.

EDITOR'S NOTE FP: AGN 20, No. 44 (13 April 1915): 5.

Notes

1. Manilius, *Astronomica* 1.755–57 (HPL's rendering).
2. Cf. HPL's cryptic reference to "the secret behind the Magellanic Clouds and globular nebulae" in "The Whisperer in Darkness" (1930).

[CLUSTERS AND NEBULAE, PART II]

When we look along that circle in the sky which corresponds to the plane of the cluster wherein we are situate, we are of course looking through a deep circular layer of stars, whose thickness is equal to the radius of the great cluster itself, and which appears to us as the galaxy and its stellar neighbours; but when we gaze at the galactic poles, the number of stars seen by us is very small, since our vision is then directed at an attenuated layer of stars, whose depth is but half the thickness of the great flat cluster. According to Prof. Young, the thickness of the disc or cluster is about a tenth of its diameter. The spiral nebulae, which abound near the galactic poles, may perhaps constitute a gigantic spherical aggregation, with the stellar disc as one of its great circles. That most nebulae belong to our universe seems probable, though it was once believed that they, as well as clusters, are other universes, or external galaxies, as it were. Whether or not such things as other universes do exist is a question of the highest interest, involving conceptions of the most awful grandeur. It is very likely that these colossal universes of suns are widely scattered through boundless space, though separated by such terrifying and abysmal distances, that their light, sent on its way at the time of their creation, has not yet reached from one to the other! It were useless here to speak of the ultimate confines of space itself. If the monstrous distances dealt with in the ordinary study of astronomy be stupefying in their immensity, what may be said of infinity itself? The idea of a boundary to all space is even more repellent than the terrible conception of the illimitable.

The Nebular Hypothesis

Whilst the origin of the universe is a problem whose solution has so far defied the efforts of the scientist and the philosopher, we may nevertheless trace the process of creation for a great distance into the past, and be reasonably certain that all the stars, and whatever planets may attend them, are the results of evolution from the nebulous form. In fact, we may picture a remotely ancient age in which our universe contained nothing but nebulae. The celebrated French mathematician and astronomer Pierre Simon, Marquis de Laplace, has given us the clearest of all theories concerning the metamorphosis of a nebula into a solar system. His hypothesis is borne out as well by the forms and motions of the sun and planets of our own system, as by the figures of those sidereal bodies still in the nebulous condition.

In tracing the evolution of a solar system, Laplace's Nebular Hypothesis assumes the existence at first of an immense mass of highly heated gaseous matter; in other words, a great nebula. This nebula takes a roughly spherical shape from the action of gravitation; and on account of differences in the original motion of its parts, it begins to rotate on its axis at an extremely rapid rate. The centrifugal force generated by this rotation causes the mass to bulge out at the equator, and at length to throw off matter at that place, leaving a ring like that of Saturn. Later, as the original mass cools and contracts, it throws off and leaves behind other rings, all of which break up into globular planets which rotate on their axis and revolve around the original mass, and which in turn throw off rings of their own to form satellites. The smaller planets doubtless cool and solidify more swiftly, so that in our solar system the four inner planets, though they must be more recently formed, have now become quite cold and solid, at least superficially; whilst the outer planets are still hot and molten. The parent mass is of course now represented by the radiant sun itself, whose great size will keep it hot and luminous for thousands of years to come.

Although some parts of the hypothesis of Laplace have lately been challenged, the theory rests upon too sound a basis to be lightly shaken, and is still the most probable explanation of the origin of the sun, the stars, and their encircling systems of planets and satellites.

Future of the Universe

Since we perceive that all the bodies in the universe appear to be cooling off, we must needs inquire how long the present order of things will endure; how long before our sun, as well as the other suns of space, will have lost their fires, and whirl onward; cold, dark, and unnoticed. To this it is impossible to reply. That all the stars are not of equal age is obvious. When one dies out, it is probable that some object now a nebula will have by that time evolved into a stellar system to take its place, so that no matter how many of the present stars expire, the universe will never want for suns so long as the nebulae hold out. Whether or not new nebulae are being created by some unknown means, it is difficult to say. It is a fundamental principle in the science of physics, that neither matter nor energy may be created or destroyed. Since the stars and nebulae are constantly distributing energy in the form of light and heat, and since they cannot create more to replace that which they are losing, it follows that some day their activity must all be dissipated into infinity as unavailable waves of radiant heat, too feeble to produce any perceptible effects. The resulting scene of desolation will be terrible indeed. A vast, sepulchral universe of unbroken midnight gloom and perpetual arctic frigidity, through which will roll dark, cold suns with their hordes of dead, frozen planets, on which will lie the dust of those unhappy mortals who will have perished as their dominant stars faded from their skies. Such is the depressing picture of a future too remote for calculation, yet the understanding shrinks from its contemplation. Though the strict canons of natural science foretell this result, the philosophical mind cannot accept it without qualification. Infallible as physics may be in ordinary matters, it cannot trace back to its source the energy with which all creation is now pervaded, so why must we accept these attempts to predict its ultimate disposition? Almost inconceivable as is an eternity of the universes of space, a definite beginning and end is still more repugnant to rational reflection.

EDITOR'S NOTE FP: AGN 20, No. 46 (16 April 1915).

XII. THE CONSTELLATIONS

The exquisite and enduring pleasure engendered by a familiar knowledge of the stars and constellations is beyond the power of mortals to describe. The friendly face of the heavens has smiled down upon the earth in all ages, cheering the people and inspiring the poets of every race since the dawn of human life. In no other manner can we attain an equal degree of sympathetic kinship to the men of other lands and other times, than by establishing an intimacy with these pictured gods and heroes of the sky, the eternal and unchanging companions of all mankind, ancient and modern alike. To him who knows the constellations, each season brings expected and beloved acquaintances. With the spring comes the bright Arcturus above the northeastern hills, whilst Altair as surely leads on the summer. In the autumn majestic Perseus greets us familiarly from the north, and kindly Fomalhaut from the south. The frigid horrors of the northern winter are alleviated by the splendid beams of Taurus, Orion, and the Dogs, besides a whole gorgeous host of starry friends that never fail to comfort us through the months of storm and snow.

In a strictly scientific sense, the study of the constellations is scarce a part of astronomy at all, since these figures are merely apparent arrangements of stars, known by ancient mythological names; yet an accurate knowledge of them is of course as essential to the astronomer as a knowledge of geography is to the terrestrial explorer. It is impossible here to give more than a very meagre account of the various groups with which the fancy of primitive man has adorned the sky, yet the author must needs regret his present limitations, and hope at some later time to say more on this most fascinating of subjects.

While some of the constellations are of modern making, most of them have existed since prehistoric times. They were well known in their present form to the ancients, and are the subject of frequent allusions in classical writings. Ptolemy, in the second century A. D., recorded constellations which were recognised in his day. The number now recognised is 93; 12 in the Zodiac, 35 north of it, and 46 south of it. Some of the latter are wholly or partly invisible in our latitude.

The resemblance of the constellations to the object for which they are named is in most cases very remote, so that we are often inclined to wonder how the ancient nomenclature came to be established.

In learning the features of the sky, a good star-atlas or planisphere, particularly the latter, is much to be desired. Hammett's planisphere, which may be obtained at any bookstall for a dollar, was used by the writer in his early studies, and seems quite unequalled for its purpose.

The Circumpolar Constellations

In learning the constellations we should at first seek to become familiar with groups which are always or almost always visible in our latitude. Of these the well-known "Plough" or "Dipper" in Ursa Major, the Greater Bear, is the most readily recognised, and should serve as to a starting point from which we may proceed to other parts of the sky. The Dipper, which contains seven stars, may always be found with ease. In spring it is in the north above the pole, in an inverted position; in summer it is in the northwest with the bowl downward; in autumn (latitude of Asheville) it partly sets below the horizon under the pole; whilst in winter it is in the northeast with the bowl uppermost. The two stars in front of the bowl are called "the Pointers", since the line which they form points directly to the star Polaris, at the north celestial pole. In our latitude, Polaris is about 35 degrees above the northern horizon, that is, considerably less than half way up to the zenith. Polaris is the principal star of Ursa Minor, the Lesser Bear, which swings round it in a very restricted circle, and possesses the general appearance of a small dipper. Almost exactly opposite Ursa Major, on the other side of the pole, is Cassiopeia, which has the shape of a flattened letter "W". It may be found beneath the pole, partly set, in spring; east of it in summer, above it in autumn, and west of it in winter. Cepheus is a faint group that precedes Cassiopeia in its circuit of the sky. Draco, the Dragon, a dull, extensive constellation, lies beyond Ursa Minor from the pole.

The Spring Groups

The stars of spring, though neither brilliant nor numerous, are none the less attractive to the eye. In spring the great Zodiacal constellation Leo, the Lion, is near the southern meridian and forms the principal feature of the heavens. Leo consists of two divisions: one shaped like a sickle and containing at the base of the handle the star Regulus, a bright gem of the first magnitude; the other a right triangle, lying east of the sickle. East of Leo is Virgo, the Virgin, also a member of the Zodiacal band, whose principal star, called Spica, is of the first magnitude. Below Leo and Virgo extends the enormous length of Hydra, the Water-Snake, on whose back are situate the two small groups Corvus, the Crow, and Crater, the Cup. Corvus, the more easterly of the two, is a very easily recognisable trapezium of stars. West of Leo is the faint Zodiacal constellation Cancer, the Crab, whose leading feature is a cluster of stars called Praespe, visible to the naked eye as a nebulous blur. The head of Hydra lies just beneath Cancer. Northeast of Virgo is Boötes, the Herdsman, with the very bright orange star Arcturus. East of Boötes is the beautiful circle of stars composing Corona Borealis, or the Northern Crown, while west of it we may behold the attractive cluster forming the principal part of Coma Berenices, or Berenice's Hair.

EDITOR'S NOTE FP: AGN 20, No. 64 (27 April 1915): 4.

[THE CONSTELLATIONS, PART II]

The Summer Stars

The constellations of summer have a mild brilliancy appropriate to the genial languor of the season. Lyra, the lyre, with the superbly brilliant bluish-white star Vega, is almost in the zenith, just east of which is Cygnus, the swan, with the somewhat fainter Deneb. South of Cygnus is Aquila, the eagle, with Altair, a star of the first magnitude. West of Aquila is the immense, indefinite group Ophiuchus et Serpens, above which is the equally vague form of Hercules. East of Aquila lies the small diamond-shaped figure commonly called "Job's Coffin", which is the constellation Delphinus, the dolphin. Delphinus is one of three tiny groups in this part of the sky; Sagitta, the arrow, being northwest, and Equuleus, the little horse, southeast of it. On the southern horizon we find Scorpio, the scorpion, a zodiacal group partly in the galaxy, which has the form of a boy's kite, and contains the bright red star Antares. West of Scorpio is the small and inconspicuous Libra, the balances, also of the zodiac, while east of it is the zodiacal constellation Sagittarius, the archer, a rich though not extremely brilliant collection of stars immersed in the Milky Way. In the northern part of Sagittarius is a sub-group of five stars shaped like an inverted ladle, and called the "milk dipper".

The Stars of Autumn

The characteristic constellations of autumn are the dullest of all the year; fit symbols of that gloomy, foreboding period. Just south of the zenith, and adjacent to the circumpolar group Cassiopeia, is Andromeda, west of which is Pegasus, the winged horse. Four rather bright stars at the place where Pegasus and Andromeda join form what is called the "great square of Pegasus". Below these groups are three faint and uninteresting members of the zodiac; Capricornus, the sea goat, Aquarius, the water bearer, and Pisces, the fishes.

Pisces now contains the vernal equinox, or point where the sun crosses the celestial equator on its northward journey. East of Pisces, the small zodiacal group Aries, the ram, presents a pleasing appearance, though it has but three bright stars. Below Pisces is Cetus, the whale, which contains the famous variable star Mira. Low in the south we behold Piscis Australis, the southern fish, whose principal star Fomalhaut is of the first magnitude.

The Winter Constellations

As though designed to compensate us for the inclement conditions of the winter months, the constellations of that season are the most magnificent of all the starry host. Near the southern meridian is Orion, the grandest object in the whole sidereal sky, with its two splendid stars of the first magnitude, Betelgeux and Rigel, its famous "belt" of three bright stars, which lies midway between the two, and its curving "sword" below the belt. In the sword of Orion is the famous nebula. Northwest of Orion is Taurus, the bull, a member of the zodiac, with its bright red star Aldebaran and its two beautiful clusters, the Pleiades and the Hyades. Below Taurus is Eridanus, whose brightest parts are never seen in this latitude, and below Orion is the small group Lepus, the hare. East of Taurus is the zodiacal constellation Gemini, the twins, with its brilliant pair of stars Castor and Pollux. Beneath Gemini is Canis Minor, the lesser dog, with Procyon, a star of the first magnitude. In the zenith is Capella, an intensely brilliant star which is part of Auriga, the waggoner. West of Auriga is the glittering Perseus, which contains a beautiful cluster, besides the celebrated variable star Algol. On the southern horizon, immersed in the Milky Way, are the northern parts of Argo Navis, whose most splendid stars never rise here. Between Argo and Orion is Canis Major, the greater dog, that famous refulgent constellation which contains Sirius, or the dog star, the brightest stellar body in all the heavens.

The elegant amusement afforded by the study of the constellations is immensely enhanced by a knowledge of their mythological history, which can be obtained from any one of the numerous works on this subject.

EDITOR'S NOTE FP: AGN 20, No. 68 (1 May 1915): 4.

XIII. TELESCOPES AND OBSERVATORIES

Foremost among all instruments used by astronomers in their study of the celestial vault stands that greatest invention of the seventeenth century, the telescope. By the aid of this indispensible means of magnification we have gained nearly all our present knowledge of the constitution of the moon and planets, the surface of the sun, and the strange configurations of the misty nebulae.

Telescopes, as everyone well knows, are combinations of lenses or of mirrors and lenses, arranged in such a manner that they produce enlarged images of distant objects. There are two kinds of telescopes; refracting and reflecting. The former, as the name implies, have only lenses to collect and bend the rays of light that reach them, whilst the latter collect and bend the rays on great concave mirrors, more or less supplemented by lenses or combinations of lesser mirrors [. . .] ocular or visual observation, since their size is less than that of reflectors of corresponding power, and since they generally furnish clearer, brighter images. Reflectors, however, are unsurpassed for use in celestial photography, on account of their freedom from certain optical defects which may never be wholly removed from refractors. The principal lens of a refractor is convex, whilst the great mirror of a reflector is concave. Convex lenses and concave mirrors have similar optical properties. All telescopes consist of two principal parts: the great convex lens or concave mirror used to collect and form into an image the rays of light from distant objects; and the eye-piece at the other end of the tube, consisting of two or more small lenses designed to magnify the image. The great lens or mirror, ground and polished with the most exquisite care, is the fundamental and most expensive feature of a telescope; various eye-pieces, each to furnish a different magnifying power, are generally used. The mirrors of reflectors are constructed either of speculum metal or of silvered glass. The great lenses or "object-glasses" of refractors are made in two parts in order to render them "achromatic" or free from false colour. Each consists of a double-convex lens of crown glass and a plano-concave lens [. . .] telescope may for various reasons be made much larger and at vastly less expense than refractors. In a reflector the heavy mirror lies at the bottom of the tube, where it may be supported and balanced with comparative ease, the light being thrown to an eye-piece at the side of the tube. In a refractor, however, the observer must gaze directly at the heavens through the great lens, wherefore the latter must be fixed at the upper end of the instrument, thus creating a rather more difficult engineering problem in mounting the telescope. In making a concave mirror there is but one surface to grind and polish, as opposed to four in the construction of an achromatic object-glass. Furthermore, there is much difficulty in obtaining large glass discs of a quality suitable for grinding into lenses.

The image obtained in an ordinary astronomical telescope is inverted, but since the righting of it would require extra lenses and thus cause more light to be lost, astronomers are content to view the universe upside down, and accordingly publish all their maps and drawings with the south at the top.

Mounting of Telescopes

Telescopes are mounted in various ways in order to be directed with ease to any part of the heavens. Small instruments, such as are used by amateurs, have "altazimuth" stands; light, portable pillars or tripods equipped so that the telescope may be moved both vertically and horizontally by the hand of the observer. Large telescopes are mounted on specially contrived stands called "equatorials", which enable them to follow the apparent diurnal revolutions of the heavenly bodies by one simple motion. They are often driven by clockwork, so that the observer need do nothing himself but observe. These delicately adjusted instruments are fitted with graduated circles of right ascension and declination, by whose aid they may be pointed at will to any desired spot on the visible celestial hemisphere. Thus an object wholly invisible to the naked eye can be found with ease if its right ascension and declination be accurately known. In order to secure absolute steadiness and freedom from the jars caused by the passage of heavy vehicles, the pier or support of a large telescope is made of masonry and sunk far below the surface of the ground, usually extending down farther than the deepest of cellars.

EDITOR'S NOTE FP: AGN 20, No. 76 (11 May 1915): 8.

[Telescopes and Observatories, Part II]

Magnifying Power

The magnifying power of a telescope, that is, the number of diameters by which it enlarges an object seen through it, is determined by the optical relation of object-glass and eye-piece; hence if a proper variety of eye-pieces be provided, the same telescope with its one object-glass may be made to yield different degrees of magnification to suit different purposes and conditions. However, the higher the power applied, the smaller the field of view and the less the amount of light obtained, so that beyond certain limits, high powers cannot be employed without providing large objectives in order to secure more illumination from the objects viewed. It has been found, that in general not much more than 50 diameters of magnification should be used with an object-glass whose diameter or "aperture" is one inch, so that in determining what shall be the highest power for use with a certain telescope, it is well to allow 50 diameters to each inch of aperture. Thus a three-inch telescope can bear a maximum power of 150, and so on. Sometimes better results are obtained with low powers than with higher, for the latter magnify the obscuring mists and disturbances of the atmosphere through which we must always observe the heavens. Powers as high as 2,000 have been employed on the largest instruments, yet 200 is more suitable for ordinary use. Small telescopes are far more efficient for the amateur's purposes than is ordinarily imagined, a three-inch instrument magnifying from 50 to 150 times being an ideal outfit for the beginner in astronomy.

The small field of view afforded by a telescope of high power makes it very difficult for the observer to find celestial objects, and renders necessary the use of a "finder" or small telescope of low power and wide field affixed to the tube of the larger instrument in such a manner that when an object is in the centre of its field, it is also in the field of the principal telescope.

Great Telescopes

The largest telescope in the world is the great reflector of 100 inches clear aperture now being constructed at the Mt. Wilson Observatory in California. Next to this, but no longer in use, is the famous 72-inch reflector made and used by William Parsons, third Earl of Rosse, and long renowned as the greatest of all telescopes. The Rosse mirror was cast in 1842, and the instrument completed in 1845, with a tube 5 feet in length and 7 feet in diameter. The mounting was not equatorial, owing to the excessive weight of the mirror. Instead, the telescope was provided with an universal joint at the base, and supported by chain and pulley, attached to a structure of masonry. Its scope was somewhat restricted, since its arrangement prevented its being directed to all parts of the sky. In 1914 the Rosse telescope was removed from its original site at Birr Castle, Ireland, and placed as a curiosity in the Science Museum at South Kensington, London.

Third in size are the two 60-inch reflectors; one constructed in 1889 by the late Mr. A. A. Common, F.R.S.,[1] of Ealing, England, and now mounted in a peculiar but extremely effective manner at the Harvard Observatory; the other made more recently at Pasadena, California, and used at the Mt. Wilson Observatory. The observatory at Melbourne, Australia, contains a reflector of four feet aperture, made in 1867 by Grubb,[2] and equatorially mounted, whilst another of this size is in use at Paris. The four-foot reflector employed by Sir William Herschel is now dismantled.

With the exception of a huge but ineffective instrument of 47 inches aperture clumsily mounted at Paris, the largest refracting telescope is the 40-inch equatorial of the Yerkes Observatory at Lake Geneva, Wisconsin. The tube supporting the immense lens is almost 70 feet in length. Second only to this is the renowned 36-inch refractor of the Lick Observatory on Mt. Hamilton, California. The National Observatory at Meudon, near Paris, possesses a 32 and one-half inch glass, the Astrophysical Observatory at Potsdam, in Prussia, one of 31 inches, and the observatories at Nice, in France, and Pulkowa, in Russia, each contain a refractor of 30 inches aperture. The Royal Observatory at Greenwich has a telescope of 28 inches aperture, and the Vienna telescope is 27 inches in diameter. The twin telescopes of the United States Naval Observatory at Washington and The University of Virginia are each of 26 inches aperture.

The family of Clark, whose works are at Cambridge, Massachusetts, is generally conceded to excel in the manufacture of great object-glasses.

Observatories

Without a suitable location and sheltering observatory from which to direct it toward the heavens, the most powerful of telescopes or most precise of other instruments would be of small value. An astronomical observatory should be situate if possible upon some elevated or at least level spot, which may command a wide view of the heavens, unobstructed alike by trees, hills, and the various works of man. In selecting a site it is also well to choose a place in which the atmosphere is clear and steady. High mountains, towering above the dense lower strata of clouds, are especially favour-[. . .] brick, or stone, as the occasion directs. It usually contains a large circular tower, surmounted by a revolving dome, in which is kept the large telescope that forms the principal feature. The telescope is pointed at the sky through a large slot in the dome, the latter being turned with the instrument as necessary. The interior of the dome must be of the same temperature as the air outside, in order that troublesome atmospheric currents, arising from the motions of unequally heated air, may not play about the great instrument and thus obscure the objects at which it is directed.

(TO BE CONTINUED.)

EDITOR'S NOTE FP: AGN 20, No. 81 (17 May 1915): 2. It would appear that this article was to have been continued further, since the discussion of observatories is anomalously restricted to a single paragraph. It is likely, therefore, that the indication "(To Be Continued)" refers specifically to Part XIII rather than to the series as a whole, although of course Part XIV also apparently failed to appear in AGN.

Notes

1. Andrew Ainslee Common (1841–1903), British astronomer and instrument maker.
2. Howard Grubb (1844–1931), Irish optical engineer.

EDITOR'S NOTE TO "THE IRISH AND THE FAIRIES"
BY PETER J. MACMANUS

In the following remarkable article we are brought face to face with that is probably the most conspicuous of all genuine survivals from prehistoric Aryan mythology. The Celtic races of the British Isles, both from their simple mode of living and from the native vivacity of their imagination, have preserved with great fidelity the legends of their ancestors, to which they accord a faith almost incredible in this prosaic age. The Irish of today, as startlingly shewn by Mr. MacManus, has as vital and as real a belief in the various Aryan personifications of Nature as had the Greeks of the Homeric period.

Quite naturally, the long existence of the Christian religion in Ireland has somewhat obscured the primal significance of the old pagan deities; but as to a lesser extent in other lands, the ancient gods, goddesses, heroes, nymphs, and fauns yet flourish under slightly altered aspects as "fairies", "banshees", "leprechauns", and the like, and we are confronted with the unique spectacle of a thriving contemporary system of true Indo-European legend. It is this lingering breath of primitive antiquity which doubtless contributes largely to the captivating atmosphere of romance and glamour which has ever enveloped the Green Isle. Perhaps old Erin, in its rural districts at least, is a realisation of that sweet Arcadia of which generations of poets have vainly dreamt; for it is there and there only that we may behold in life that beautiful ancient polytheism which is the real ancestral faith of every Aryan white man from the Ganges to the Shannon. It is curious to note that the Irish seem to assume that the fairy species is peculiar to their country.

In the personal anecdote of Mr. MacManus, we may trace what Fiske classifies as the "cloud-maiden" type of legend;[1] and from the narrator's implicit faith in the reality of his vision, we may gain a striking conception of the vitality with which the ancient lore still pervades Hiberian thought.

EDITOR'S NOTE FP: *Providence Amateur* 1, No. 2 (February 1916): 2–3. A curious preface to an article by Peter J. MacManus, a member of the Providence Amateur Press Club: HPL the rationalist feels obliged to make particular note of the fact that MacManus actually believes in the fairies he discusses. HPL was, along with John T. Dunn, the guiding force behind the press club, which he notes consisted largely of "Micks [Irishmen] who dwelt in the dingy 'North End' of the city" (HPL to Alfred Galpin, 29 August [1918]; *Letters to Alfred Galpin* [New York: Hippocampus Press, 2003], p. 40).

Notes

1. John Fiske (1842–1901), American historian and folklorist. HPL was much influenced by Fiske's popular study, *Myths and Myth-Makers: Old Tales and Superstitions Interpreted by Comparative Mythology* (1872; LL 317), which discusses the "cloud-maiden" legend chiefly in Chapter 3 ("Werewolves and Swan-Maidens").

BRUMALIA

Brumalia commemorates the prehistoric winter festival held by all primitive races to celebrate the northward turning of the sun at the Winter Solstice. On December 21st the days are at their shortest, and the weather is drawing toward its coldest; but the act of the sun in commencing its return to the north is a prophecy of Spring, to be hailed with rejoicing, and typified by evergreen wreaths symbolic of the survival of Nature. The Yule Log, with its blazing glow, is representative of warmth presaged by the return of the sun to its northward track.

This type of festival was amongst the early Latin [races] called "Brumalia", from the word "bruma", which signifies winter, or the winter solstice. In later days, when Rome became the seat of learning and government, Brumalia became the Saturnalia, or festival of Saturn, though it was some time before the primitive significance was really lost. Late in the Imperial age, after the adoption of Christianity, the 25th of December, heretofore the date of the Saturnalia, was selected as the proper time to observe Christmas; a festival previously held on Epiphany, or January 6th, since the day and month of Our Saviour's birth are unknown. Thus the immensely ancient Brumalia may be considered, in a sense, as the primitive pagan ancestor of our Christmas celebration.

EDITOR'S NOTE FP: *Tryout* 3, No. 1 (December 1916): [22]. A brief discussion of a Roman festival, accompanying HPL's poem "Brumalia" (AT 274), published on the first page of this number of the *Tryout*.

THE TRUTH ABOUT MARS

The faintest and least clearly defined features of Mars are the so-called "canals", extremely narrow dark streaks which cover the planet's surface like a network.

They were discovered in 1877 by Schiaparelli of Milan, and have since received attention in connexion with the fantastic notion that they are gigantic ditches, constructed by the hands of intelligent inhabitants of Mars.

There is in truth something worthy of note in the almost mathematical rectitude of these lines, the dark circular spots called "oases" which mark their intersections, and their probable changes from season to season; but so faint and difficult to see are they, that their very existence was doubted until recently, when some of them were successfully photographed.

They change from time to time, perhaps with the seasons of the years of Mars. The immense scale, out of all proportion to the known works of mankind, on which are "constructed" the canals, is explained by the lesser gravity on Mars.

The true nature of the canals is a matter of great dispute, although the late Percival Lowell, a private observer whose excellent telescope was situated in the clear air of Flagstaff, Arizona, developed an elaborate theory, averring that the canals which lead from the polar caps toward the center of the planet in absolutely straight lines were built by the inhabitants.

How baseless as most of these speculations may be, and probably are, it is never-theless not impossible that LIVING BEINGS OF SOME SORT MAY DWELL UPON THE SURFACE OF MARS. It is, however, left to the imagination of the reader or of the ingenious novelist to portray their appearance, size, intelligence, and habits.

In these days, when our planet is so convulsed with the absurd hostilities of its in-significant denizens, it is calming to turn to the vast ethereal blue and behold other worlds, each with its unique and picturesque phenomena, where no echo of terrestrial strife or woe can resound.

EDITOR'S NOTE FP: *Phoenician* 1, No. 3 (Autumn 1917): 8. A nearly verbatim copy of a section of "Mars and the Asteroids" (p. 291), made more sensationalised by all-capitals in reference to the possible habitation of Mars.

THE CANCER OF SUPERSTITION

1. Widespread scope of superstition. Presence in every phase of our daily life. Present is an age of "isms." Men have run mad and are chasing phantoms. Universal ac-ceptance of some phase or other of it among the ignorant. Regions (Kentucky etc.) and classes (sailors, etc.) especially affected. Astonishing instances of super-stition among apparently educated people. Lack of all scientific basis—persists only through mental indolence of those who neglect to assimilate and correlate re-sults of modern science. Harmful effects of superstition—Need of widely diffused, systematic, and authoritative campaign of refutation—This work hitherto ne-glected because competent academic writers think superstition unworthy of no-tice, while those who do take it seriously enough to fight it are generally unscholarly and unconvincing arguers. Attitude should be one of sympathetic in-quiry—psychological and scientific data of highest interest. (Climax—absurdity of superstition in contrast to advanced state of modern knowledge)

2. All superstitious and religious ideas due to primitive man's effort to assign causes for the natural phenomena around him. Ignorant of any cause and effect save his own volition and agency in performing the acts of daily life, he cannot conceive of any cause for natural phenomena save invisible wills or personalities behind the observed appearances. Examples—thunder, earthquake. No act can be conceived without quasi-human *motive*—gods must be *pleased, angry, hungry,* etc. Naturally, these groping efforts are not only to *explain* Nature, but also to secure good for-tune, *influence* Fate, and avoid Evil. Perhaps the most characteristic feature of magic and superstition is its effort to *influence* the powers of Nature.

3. Being too primitive to form a generalised conception, early man attributes special and separate governing personalities to each type of phenomenon he observes; usually fancying that every object in Nature, either organic or inorganic, has a definite personality or soul of its own. This belief is called "animism". Examples—African fetichism. See Frazer.[1]

4. As the mind and observation of early man expand, he learns of certain obvious details in the working of natural phenomena; and is obliged to expand every one of his conceptions of a governing spirit for each class of phenomena into a large body of mythology—in order to account for the visible workings of the various de-

partments of Nature as he now sees them.

5. And at the same time, man's imagination and poetic faculty are expanding. He not only sees new details in the workings of natural phenomena, but invents details and principles which do not exist—based on fancied analogies. Imperfect repetition as the tales are handed down gives rise to omissions, amplifications, distortions, and sometimes parallel versions; this haphazard process usually creating special features (often highly irrational and even contradictory) which eventually become more or less standardised as popular folklore. Example—detailed history of any superstition.

6. The most basic nature-myths are the same among all races and cultures, no matter how widely separated—even if they have never heard of one another's existence. This is because the reactions of the human brain to the general, universal forces of Nature* are always the same. Examples—parallel myths among Aztecs in Mexico and other cultures in Europe and Asia. See Fiske's Myths and Myth-Makers.

7. But it must be remembered that in the case of other than general or universal phenomena, the kind of myth invented will depend greatly upon the character of the race involved, and upon the geographical nature of its habitat—i.e., whether a light-hearted or pensive race—whether backward or intelligent—whether unimaginative or poetic, and whether the country be hot or cold, an earthquake region or a flood region, with heavy rainfall or little rainfall, etc. Examples in Fiske—Myths and Myth-Makers.

8. More than this, as soon as different races come into contact, whether by conquest, trade, proximity, or the reports of travellers, they begin borrowing from one another's mythologies; naturally adapting the tales to their own racial and geographical conditions. Thus a certain tale, originated by one tribe or race, may acquire a great number of variants as it passes by word of mouth from tribe to tribe, modified at each repetition and always distorted to suit the conditions prevailing among whatever tribe adopts it. Examples—the common fairy tales of Germanic folklore—their parallelism with classic myths, and their undoubted tracing back to ancient India. Compare with spread of *language*—all Aryan tongues derived from a common source. Fiske—Myths and M. M. Trench—Study of Words.[2]

9. Still further progress in knowledge of natural phenomena, together with a sharpened faculty of reasoning as developed by evolution and competitive conflict with nature, wild animals, and other tribes of men, gives to a primitive race a gradual comprehension of the real way in which certain natural phenomena work; hence as civilisation appears, the intelligent part of a race begins to cast off its more obvious beliefs in personal agencies behind natural phenomena. The idea gains ground that the forces behind Nature (religious forces—whatever they are—differently conceived by different races) work mainly according to fixed laws and without direct intervention except in the few unusual cases classed as "miracles". At this point *religion* separates from *superstition*;† and the latter, cultivated by a less and less intelligent class of people as time passes, acquires an extravagant and fantastic cast which it would not have had if subjected to the sterner analysis of better minds or the organised discipline of orthodoxy. It tends to become localised, and to break up into several rival and perhaps conflicting versions. At the same time, it receives occasional accretions

---

*sun, moon, tides, wind, thunder—light & darkness, clouds, etc.

†Religion expressing man's actual emotional relationship to the infinite, while superstition continues to explain by false means phenomena whose natural cause has become known

from the dominant religion which runs parallel to it, occasionally adopting religious ideas in a debased or popularised form. (Good Friday beliefs etc) Encyclopaedias—Religion—Magic—Superstition. See Golden Bough.

10. Superstitions have a later growth, among ignorant and irrational people, along the exact lines followed in primitive times; because the elements involved are the same—uninformed and unreasoning minds confronted by natural phenomena which they fear, do not understand, and wish to influence. New discoveries and developments—new customs or modes of daily life—all give birth to new superstitions among the ignorant on exactly the same principle by which the very first superstitions were evolved.

11. Thus every race and culture has its immense body of massed superstition—a combination of (1) primal beliefs common to all mankind, (2) special beliefs in the early history of the culture, (3) borrowings and adaptations, both early and late, from other cultures, (4) adoptions from the prevailing religion, and (5) recent coinages from new phenomena in the experience of the culture. All the parts of this body of myth tend to interact upon one another and produce a sort of rough homogeneity of tone and atmosphere—occasionally causing modifications of certain of the beliefs in question. This array of superstition, always divided into classes, each of which preserves certain characteristrics and very persistent features, is handed down for generations; slightly coloured by additions in the course of repetition, but in the main faithful to certain traditional lines. Impossible to consider all superstitions, but so far as we are concerned, only those of our own European races are of vital significance. While individual European races each have their separate bodies of myth, all are so closely connected culturally that they frequently adopt one another's; so that we may justly assume the existence of such a thing as a collective fund of European superstition—which we may regard as a unit and divide into its various departments according to subject (witchcraft, astrology, spiritualism, etc.) irrespective of national lines. Now prepare for treatment of separate superstitions in any desired order.

12. (Conclusion) Summary. Superstition, whether actually ancient or of later origin, is the result of purely primitive mental processes—the same old attitude of ignorance facing the unknown and seeking explanations, favours, safeguards, and glimpses into the future. Absence of all rational basis—its processes wholly alien and hostile to spirit of modern science and intellectual reflection. Also hostile to all accepted religions—contradicts their principles of the relation of divine powers to mankind, so that the existence of supernaturalism in religion cannot be used as confirmation of superstitious beliefs. Harm and need of refutation already referred to. What refutation better than wide diffusion of facts surrounding its sources and history? Publicity in these matters urged—supplant blind acceptance by alert study and intelligence, and free man of an age-old burden.

EDITOR'S NOTE FP: *The Dark Brotherhood and Other Pieces* (Sauk City, WI: Arkham House, 1966), pp. 246–61. Text derived from the AMS (JHL). HPL's synopsis for a book combating superstition, commissioned by Harry Houdini; the work was halted by Houdini's sudden death on 31 October 1926. His colleague, C. M. Eddy, Jr., then attempted to write out the synopsis.

Notes

1. Sir James George Frazer (1854–1941), British anthropologist and author of *The Golden*

Bough (1890 [2 vols.], 1907–15 [12 vols.]), a landmark in the anthropology of religion.

2. Richard Chevenix Trench (1807–1886), British theologian and author of *On the Study of Words* (1851; *LL* 893).

[SOME BACKGROUNDS OF FAIRYLAND]

The term *fairy* has in modern times been applied to so wide a variety of imaginary entities, that its original meaning is almost lost in favour of a more inclusive significance. The true fairy, as developed by early Celtic folklore, was undoubtedly a female nature-spirit equivalent to the dryads, naiads, and other local nymphs of classical antiquity. Such a spirit is in essence a personification of some aspect of the natural world, and every branch of Aryan Mythology teems with examples. Dawn-maidens, cloud-maidens, fountain-maidens, tree-maidens and the like exist abundantly, under various names, in the legends of all Aryan peoples; and it is not remarkable that the highly imaginative Celts should have evolved one of the most notable of all systems of such beings.

Evidence seems to indicate that the pre-classical Gauls—and, by inference, other Celts—possessed an active belief in beings corresponding to what we recognise as true fairies. After the coming of Roman influences many classical features were undoubtedly woven into this belief, though not so many as to destroy its distinctiveness.

The true Celtic fairy was originally a female of graceful human aspect and average size, dwelling in some specific environment and possessing such supernatural attributes as the power to change form, control the sea and the wind, heal sickness, and divine future events. From these powers the name of *fay, fée,* or fairy was derived in mediaeval times from the Low Latin *fatare,* to enchant; itself derived from the standard Latin *fatum,* fate.

True fairies were generally benignant rather than malignant, though when wronged their revenges were ample and certain. They were frequently loved and married by mortal men, and always exacted heavy penalties when such favoured mortals broke faith with them. Fairies often took it upon themselves to preside at the birth of individuals, over whom they would retain a protective guardianship throughout life. This linkage of the beings with human destiny or *fate* may have been instrumental in the choice of their final name—derived indirectly from *fatum.*

Such are the original fairies commonly met with its pre-Elizabethan tradition and literature. Parallel to them, however, had always existed a wholly separate line of mythological creation whose attributes were eventually to become mixed with those of the fairy world—just as the attributes of both were likewise to become mixed with a third element derived from actual experience. This separate line of myth was also one of natural personification, albeit of a far different and darker cast; having to do with those *night-daemons* or personifications of *darkness* which appear in all Aryan mythologies as thieves or mischief-working entities more or less inimical to man. The element of thievery or mischief-making symbolises the theft of daylight by darkness.

Typical examples of the Aryan night-daemon are the *Panis* of the Hindoos; the characters Cacus, Polyphemus, Cerberus, and Orthos (Geryon's dog) in classical mythology; the Genii and Afrits (to cite a Semitic borrowing) of the Arabians, and the elves, daergar, or trolls of the Teutonic north. As time progresses, and antiquity fades into mediaevalism, we see many of the traits of these night-daemons transferred to the fairy species—causing the latter to become mischievous, predatory, nocturnal, and sometimes hostile to mankind. Discrepancies in fairy nature increase with the years, so that eventually different groups and orders of fairies—good and bad, large and small, male and female—came to be recognised. Finally we reach a point where all sorts of dissimilar beings of air, earth, sea, and nether caves are lumped together in the popular mind under the single and erroneously collective term of "fairies". There are sylphs of the air, gnomes of the earth, undines of the sea, and salamanders of the fire. Each element and region has its especial sort of fairy, till the list includes such things as nixies, leprechauns, kobolds, brownies, goblins, mermaids, banshees, little people, and countless other variants. In many of these beings the attributes of different lines of myth are blended complexly and inextricably, creating extreme types of mongrelism.

So much for the purely mythical side. It is now time to consider an antipodally diverse side of the fairy's ancestry which has no connexion with the primal legends of our Aryan heritage—a side which from the earliest ages had tended to mix itself with the lore of night-daemons, and which consequently became adopted into fairyland along with the contact of Aryan races with some alien stock of darker colouring and diminutive physique encountered during the struggle for the settlement of Europe. That such a contact occurred, can for many reasons scarcely be doubted; and we see reflections of it in all the traditional descriptions of such "fairies" as embody chiefly the attributes of night-daemons.

Such earthy or underground spirits have, in European folklore, a peculiar set of fixed, special qualities in no way to be traced to the general night-daemon myth. They are conspicuously small, conspicuously repulsive, consistently subterranean in habit, generally primitive in their arts and crafts, usually hostile or fearful toward human beings, and given to certain definite practices such as the theft of human infants accompanied by the substitution of their own. They have a profound lore connected with nature, and indulge in secret communal rites varying from the merely grotesque to the unutterably repulsive. Their weapons are generally bows with primitive stone-headed arrows.

Viewing all the evidence, anthropologists have for many generations felt certain that these persistent elfin or fairy characteristics are due to historic memory rather than to mythological imagination. That is, the traditional elf, troll, gnome, kobold, leprechaun, brownie, or imp is not purely an Aryan night-daemon, but a synthesis of the night-daemon with a very genuine dwarf or pigmy race of men whom the Aryans at one time or another displaced and drove into underground hiding, and who afterward kept up a furtive and vindictive course of reprisals against their conquerors.

Driven underground, decimated in numbers, and hunted down whenever seen, the vanquished dwarfs became sly creatures of the night—sallying forth by stealth to waylay lone travellers, steal infants for nameless sacrifices, despoil lonely farm houses, shoot from ambush, and otherwise vent their hatred of their Aryan conquerors. In time it is certain that many Aryan renegades went over to them and joined their number— as men in savage places "go native" today—and that they succeeded in inculcating their repulsive system of fertility-worship amongst a decadent stratum of the Aryans, thus giving rise to the furtive *Witch-Cult* with its sinister organisation and ceremonies, and its obscene and orgiastic Sabbat.

Memories of these waspish, uncouth, and miniature enemies could not but be extremely vivid among the conquerors of Europe; and it is not remarkable that the creatures—so unlike men as the tall, blond Aryans conceived humanity—became blended with the ancient hereditary lore of night-daemons which antedated our ancestors' entrance to the region. Had the Aryans not encountered this squat, dark race, it is probable that their night-daemon myths would have continued to remain in a more or less ambiguous and plastic form. To the conquered little people we undoubtedly owe the existence of elves, duergars, trolls, gnomes, and kobolds as our forefathers conceived them.

It now remains to enquire who those conquered dwarfs really were, where they lived, and when and where our invading forefathers encountered them. Also, whether the whole body of Aryans found such beings in their path, or whether the conflict was limited to a part of the Aryan people and merely reported by hearsay to the rest. We must remember that the presence of a certain legend among a certain people in a certain region by no means proves that the events of the legend really happened to that people in that particular place. The legend may have been borrowed outright from some other people—either of that region or of another region—or it may concern something which happened to the given people in another place—perhaps a very distant place—which the people occupied at some earlier stage of its racial history.

In the opinion of the older mythologies, and of many modern ones, the little people of elfin lore represent none other than the squat Mongoloid stocks of northern Europe—Lapps and Finns—whom the Aryans found upon their entrance to that region. The size, colour, accomplishments, and manners of these stocks in their purest forms lend much plausibility to the hypothesis; and it is highly probable that they covered a much larger area of the European continent than is now the case. Another argument is the fact that most of the legends of small underground beings seem to come primarily from the North—from those Teutons who most directly encountered the squat Mongols in the battle for the continent.

A more modern and much bolder theory identifies our dwarfish foes of prehistoric times with the Neanderthaloid sub-men which shambled over Europe about 30,000 B.C., and which were exterminated by the successive waves of true human beings who swept into the region after that date. This theory, while vastly interesting, has much less standing than the one previously mentioned.

A third theory—taking into account the existence of evil-dwarf legends in regions remote from the Lapp-Finn belt—(for example, the Little People of the British Isles, and the Kalli Kanzari of modern Greece,[1] which are not wholly traceable to nature—spirits of the faun-satyr order) postulates some hitherto unknown race of dwarfs (either Mongoloid or otherwise) which populated wide areas of Europe at a very remote though not palaeolithic period. This theory has considerable vogue at the present time, and is upheld by the existence of certain prehistoric excavations in Southern Austria which seem to have been made by men of less than normal stature. At the same time it would not do to make too much of the idea, since an originally wider diffusion of the Lapp-Finn (or easterly Hunnish) stocks might easily account for dwarf architecture and artifacts in areas remote from their historic habitat. Most conservative anthropologists think it unlikely that—despite the vivid legends of diminutive Picts and elfin brownies in Scotland, tiny fairies and subterrene leprechauns in Ireland, sinister underground "little people" in Wales, and Robin Goodfellow's merry crew in England—any miniature race has ever actually inhabited the British Isles. We derive such tales entirely from the experience of our ancestors at a former stage of migration on the European continent.

A fourth theory—the least probable of all—holds that the small, dark opponents of the Aryans were merely members of those less blond Caucasian stocks which disputed the possession of Europe at the dawn of history—Mediterranean and Iberian races whose stature and pigmentation would naturally seem aberrant to a pure Nordic. This view would of course provide for an actual meeting of Celts and "little people" in the

British Isles. However, it is easy to detect the weakness of such a theory. To begin with, Mediterraneans are not small enough to be called dwarfish—certainly not small enough to inhabit the subterranean *Erdstalle* of Southern Austria. Secondly, they are not enough unlike Nordics to give rise to the tremendous sense of alienage and repulsion evident in most legends. It is ridiculous to imagine normal, regular-featured Iberians as the models for trolls and kobolds. The most that can be said is that possibly some episodes of conflict betwixt Nordics and Mediterraneans may have been confused in Nordic folklore with other tales dealing with encounters with the older dwarf race. Such complexities must always be reckoned with in anthropology—indeed, we cannot swear that two, three, or four wholly different dwarf races, encountered at different times, did not play a part in forming the traditional picture of the elf, kobold, or mischievous fairy. Lapp-Finns of the north, Hunnish stocks of the southeast, unknown stocks of varied habitats, and even dark Iberians of later times may all have figured in the composite legend-building—later encounters being interpreted in terms of earlier ones, and battles on one terrain being twisted into connexion with bygone battles in far different regions. Nor should it be forgotten that the purely mythical element of the night-daemon, with which the early Aryans confused their strange opponents, must always be looked for.

Recent discoveries of large numbers of *Erdstalle* in Austria make it likely that the Danube region was at least a leading seat of the prehistoric dwarf-Aryan conflict. These artificial caverns, plainly constructed by a race not over five feet tall, and holding artifacts indicating a late stone, copper, and early bronze-age date, are occasionally of great elaborateness; some apparently being temples, while others are clearly refuges (like the burrows of small animals) from enemies of larger physique. About 700 of them are known, many of which have been used for centuries as cellars by the inhabitants of the region. The artifacts betray considerable skill—as indeed does the engineering of the caves. Occasional skeletons found nearby reveal a race of about the size of the degenerate Ainos of Japan, the Veddahs of Ceylon (whom Haeckel placed lowest in the human scale),[2] or certain pigmy races of Africa. Ethnologists hesitate to name racial affiliations, but there is nothing to prove that these *Erdstallerbauer* (as the Austrians call them) were not of the same Mongoloid stock as the Lapp-Finn and Hunnish races. Much research remains to be performed in both the archaeological and ethnological field.

Meanwhile, however, there is no dispute concerning the part played by some small, dark race in shaping the hostile, mischievous, diminutive, and subterranean side of the later traditional fairy. Added to the myth of the night-daemon, this element has thoroughly mongrelised the earlier genuine fairy of Celtic nature-myth.

That many other elements, mythical, legendary, and historical, have gone into the making of many types of elf or fairy, it would be absurd to deny. All natural legend-building is infinitely mixed and complex, involving numerous borrowings from every conceivable source; so that we may justly regard the three main fairy origins—nature-spirit, night-daemon, and earthly dwarf—as merely the essential or dominant backgrounds in a field of limitless variety and compositeness.

Fairyland as a whole—the differing superstitions of different nations, and the various streams of myth or memory entering into the weird folk of various regions—is a profound study in itself, and one which has received much attention from scholars such as the Grimms, Keightley, and Lang.[3] The Celt has no monopoly—even of the true fairy which he created. Needless to say, each race and country adds to its traditional elves and fairies an abundance of local and family traits all apart from the more generalised heritage of the elusive creatures. Racial and national temperament, too, plays a large part in any country's selection of a favourite fairy type. Thus some countries may lay emphasis on a mythic being close to the pure-fairy of Celtic antiquity, whilst others may specialise in beings derived mostly from the dwarf and night-daemon elements. Early English fairy-lore includes some examples of the pure type—as in the legend of Thomas of Erceldoune and his seven years in the domain of the fairy queen—though a larger number of legends depict a miniature, good-natured, prankish race of pleasing aspect. Welsh, Scottish, and Irish fairies are less genial on the whole— the complimentary terms "good folk" or "gentry" being euphemisms designed to placate a somewhat feared element. Continental fairies vary widely, those of Germany being perhaps the best-developed. Germanic legend includes magnificent examples both of the pure fairy and of the impish troll and gnome. In the more southerly nations, the importance of the grotesque elf seems to diminish. Many nations assign to the fairies a definite social and political organisation, with King, Queen, and other dignitaries— thus the Mab, Titania, and Oberon of popular legend. Fairy lore in the East, as developed by the Islamic nations, is an extensive separate study; as is the elaborate world of classified elemental spirits described by Paracelsus and the Comte de Gabalis.[4]

Another separate topic for research is the manner in which each nation correlates its fairy lore with its more formal and serious religious beliefs. Thus in rural England a fairy is held to be the wandering spirit of a dead person, too earth-bound for heaven, yet not lost enough for assignment to the realm of Lucifer.

Belief in fairyland is today largely a matter of history in most parts of the world, though in Ireland many surprisingly literate persons still profess to retain faith in the "good folk". To such devout disciples, our present survey will no doubt appear equally blasphemous and unnecessary.

EDITOR'S NOTE FP: *Marginalia* (Sauk City, WI: Arkham House, 1944), pp. 174–83. Presumably an extract of a letter to Wilfred B. Talman, dated 23 September 1932. The ms. of the letter has not been made available for consultation. The title was apparently devised by August Derleth. The item represents HPL's most mature thought regarding the anthropology of religion and superstition.

Notes

1. Cf. the mention of *kallikanzari* in "The Whisperer in Darkness."

2. Ernst Haeckel (1834–1919), German biologist and natural philosopher. HPL was much influenced by his *Die Welträthsel* (1899; tr. as *The Riddle of the Universe*), a materialistic account of the origins of the universe. His discussion of the Veddahs is found in *Anthropogenie* (1874).

3. Jakob Ludwig Karl Grimm (1785–1863) and W. K. Grimm (1786–1859), German philologists and folklorists whose *Fairy Tales* (1812–15; LL 379) was one of HPL's earliest readings. Thomas Keightley (1789–1872), British author of *Fairy Mythology* (1828). Andrew Lang (1844–1912), Scottish editor of a succession of books of fairy tales (1889–1910) and the author of books on folklore and mythology.

4. Paracelsus (Philippus Aureolus Theophrastus Bombastus von Hohenheim, 1493–1541), *Liber de Nymphis, Sylvis, Pygmaeis, et Salamandris, et de Caeteris Spiritibus*, usually translated as *Treatise on Elemental Sprites*. HPL cites the work in "Supernatural Horror in Literature," ch. 6 (CE 2.97). The Comte de Gabalis is not an author but a fictional character created in the Abbe de Villar's *Le Comte de Gabalis* (1670), translated as *The Count of Gabalis: Being a Diverting History of the Rosicrucian Doctrine of Spirits* (1714). HPL derived his information on this work from Lewis Spence's *Encyclopaedia of Occultism* (1920; LL 827).

APPENDIX

DOES "VULCAN" EXIST?

Of late much interest is directed to the question of whether or not an intra-mercurial planet exists. In this article both sides of the question are stated. It began in about 1858, when Leverrier published the result of a calculation of the perturbations of Mercury, and shewed that an unknown planet must cause this. Then Dr. Lescarbault, a physician of Orgeres, France, who had a 2½ inch telescope, announced the discovery of a planet that he said he saw in transit over the sun's disc. Leverrier went to see him, and was soon satisfied that the discovery was genuine, and the new planet was called "Vulcan". Years passed, and nothing was heard of the planet until 1878, when Prof. Watson[1] of Ann Arbor, Mich. said that he had seen *two* such bodies in a total solar eclipse, one of which was probably Vulcan, while the other was undoubtedly new. This discovery was confirmed by Prof. Lewis Swift.[2] This is the evidence in *favour* of its existence. But, on the other hand, it has never been seen since then, and many times have its transits been predicted, but they never have occurred. Probably the body in transit was a peculiar solar spot, and the two bodies seen by Swift & Watson were stars. So, in spite of the favourable evidence, we must still believe that Mercury is nearest to the sun.

EDITOR'S NOTE FP: In August Derleth, *H. P. L.: A Memoir* (New York: Ben Abramson, 1945), pp. 91–92. Derleth claims that this item was published in the *Providence Journal* in 1906, but this does not seem to be the case. It is more likely that this is actually a juvenile ms., similar to others Derleth acquired after HPL's death (see, e.g., "Celestial Objects for All" [p. 89]). The item probably does date to around 1906, as the apparently contemporaneous article "Are There Undiscovered Planets?" (p. 29) comes to approximately the same conclusions in regard to an intra-Mercurial planet as those expressed here.

Notes

1. James C. Watson (1838–1880), American astronomer, professor of astronomy and director of the observatory at the University of Michigan (1858–79), and author of *Theoretical Astronomy* (1868).

2. Lewis Swift (1820–1913), American astronomer and successively director of the Warner Observatory (Rochester, NY) and the Lowe Observatory on Echo Mountain in southern California.

ASTRONOMICAL NOTEBOOK

Astronomical
Observations
Made

———

By
H. P. Lovecraft,
598 Angell St.
Providence,
R. I.
U.S.A.

Years 1909–1910–1911–1912–1913–1914–1915

[Page 1]

ASTRONOMICAL
OBSERVATIONS
1909
Begun Sept. 1, 1909.

[. . .]

Special Observation.
June 3—1909

Moon's eclipse. Clouds interfered but several glimpses were obtained. Total 7.58.

Feb. 1[, 1912]—Observed a lunar halo at about 6.30 p.m. Moon 1 d of full. Halo was of about 46° diameter, with rather noticeable paraselenae on a horizontal line with the moon. The left hand (northern) paraselena was more or less obscur'd by clouds and appeared only at intervals. The right hand mock moon was prominent and attracted much attention. The two paraselenae were seen as diffus'd patches of light. The northern part of the halo was by far the brightest part.

Feb. 26[, 1914]—The moon's crescent very thin. Earthshine visible in strong twilight. The moon was almost at the vernal equinox. Earlier in the day the moon and Mercury had been in conjuction.

Sept. 16[, 1914]—4 a.m. to dawn. Obs. Delavan's Comet and heavens in general. Delavan's Comet lay in R. A. 10h 08m 06s Dec. 49° 14″ in Ursa Major, as shown in diagram. It had about the brightness of a star of the 4th magnitude, appearing to the naked eye as a blurred spot of light; rather faint, yet easily visible. In the opera glasses this blue resolved itself into a star-like nucleus, a bright coma, and a short broad tail. In the prism binocular these details were better seen. Whilst in the 3″ telescope with powers of 50 and 100 the comet was indeed a beautiful sight. A small telescope star could at that time be seen shining through the faint lumination of the tail. The best view was with 3″ tel Ten, Eyepiece 50 diameters. Tail about 1 [   ] in length. Observations made from grounds of residence and somewhat hampered by electric street lights. At this same time moon was a beautiful crescent 3rd before new. Earthshine very powerful. Could see Maria Orisian, Seren Tranq. Rec. Nect. very plainly on dark part of disk. Saturn also fine object.

Winter stars fully in view—Orion, Cosmis Major and Orion's nebula very beautiful in 3″ with pr. 50

Sept. 17—Obs Delavan's comet 4–5 a.m. Also Moon. Earthshine on moon very strong, especially rising above house top and bright thin crescent hidden. Comet appears brighter as Moon wanes.

[Page 99]

Principal Astronomical Work.

1. To keep track of all celestial phenomena month by month, as positions of planets, phases of the moon, Sign of Sun, occultations, Meteor Showers, unusual phenomena (record) also new discoveries.
2. To keep up a working knowledge of the constellations and their seasons.
3. To observe all planets, etc. with a large telescope when they are favorably situated (as 7 h 30″ in winter, abt. 9 h in summer, supplemented by morning observations).
4. To observe opera or field glass objects among the stars with a low power instrument, recording results.
5. To keep a careful record of each night's work.
6. To contribute a monthly astronomical article of about 7 p. Ms. or 4 p. Type to the Providence Evening Journal (begun Jan. 1, 1914).

[Page 100]

Position of Residence
598 Angell St. Prov. R.I.
Latitude 41° 50″ 00″ N.
Longitude 71° 23′ 09″ W.

Fundamental data [. . .]

[Page ___]

Instruments
Dimensions of Telescope.

Clear aperture ---3 inches
Eyepieces, 2. 50 (Ten) and 125 (Ast.) Focus (with Astro) -----------------------44 in.
            ″   (″ Ten) ---------------------------------------52 in.
Manuf. by Bardore.
Altazimuth Stand by R. L. Allen.
Purchased 1906 (Sept. 13)

Accessories
Lunar Map by Wright
Year Book—Farmer's Almanack
Planispheres—Whitaker & Barrett-Serviss.
Atlas by Upton—Library.
Opera glasses—Prism Binoculars
Am. Exh. & Want Almanac.

EDITOR'S NOTE FP: *Lovecraft Collector* No. 3 (October 1949): 1–4 (as part of David H. Keller's article "Lovecraft's Astronomical Notebook"). A notebook detailing HPL's (apparently) sporadic astronomical observations during his period of hermitry. Keller notes that for the years 1911 and 1913 there were no observations at all. Keller goes on to state that on 26 May 1910 there was a "lengthy description" of Halley's Comet, although he inexplicably failed to transcribe it in his article. The complete notebook (formerly part of the Grill-Binkin collection of Lovecraftiana and subsequently sold to an unknown purchaser by the Book Sail, Boston, MA) has not been published or made available for consultation.

[ASTROLOGY ARTICLES BY J. F. HARTMANN]

Astrology and the European War

The vulgar prejudice against the noble science of astrology by otherwise learned men is greatly to be deplored.

Almost every author on astronomy, mythology, anthropology and philosophy; school teachers, professors of universities and the clergy, while willfully ignorant of astrology, yet never tire loading it with slurs and abuse, ridicule and misrepresentation; ever insinuating that astrologers must either be fools or knaves.

Proctor, banking on his knowledge of astronomy, though ignorant of astrology, fills page after page with ridicule of what he disdained to properly investigate.

Garrett P. Serviss, also banking on his astronomical knowledge, parades as an authority on what he don't [sic] know when he says, "Astronomy finds no indication of the existence of any such influences."

It is only those who have never studied this science who in their self-sufficient conceit dare assume authority to condemn it.

They argue that they "cannot understand how the planets can influence human events," as if their ignorance was the limit of truth.

With like reason might all the sciences be argued away by those ignorant of them.

Astrologers themselves are not agreed among themselves about planetary influence. Some say the planets influence our lives; others say they only indicate events, while yet others hold no opinion either way. A good astrologer need not have any opinion about it.

Another argument is that astrology teaches fatalism. But all science is fatalistic. The study of astronomy cannot cause the sun to rise a minute sooner or later than fate decrees it.

Study mathematics a lifetime and you cannot alter the relation of numbers.

Fatalism gives assurance that we can depend upon certain things, such as the multiplication table; without it there could be no dependence upon anything, and there could be no knowledge, no science, and all thinking would be of no use to us.

The other sciences would gain much if pursued in connection with astrology, such as evolution, eugenics, agriculture and statecraft.

Franz Cumont, the Belgian scholar, condemns astrology as a pagan superstition, establishing the divine right of kings to oppress the people.

But a king's horoscope shows only his exaltations over his fellow men, that he will be kind or cruel, wise or foolish, strong or weak, etc. Cumont writes strongly against astrology, but shows how its introduction from Asia into Rome transformed the many religions of Italy into a unison preparatory to Christianity, which was constructed out of these "pagan" religions, thanks to astrology, without which there would have been no Christian religion.

The church has ever fought astrology, which teaches that the immutable laws of nature will not be suspended for a God to answer prayer.

Nor can the Christian doctrine of the freedom of the will stand before the astrological doctrine that we are creatures of conditions, and must ever will and act within the laws of our being; that our bodies and our surroundings force upon us motives which determine what our will shall be.

This conflict between the church and astrology, and the tremendous influence which the church still wields over popular thought, goes far to explain the antagonism of learned men to a science which prejudice prevents them from studying.

The church condemns the prediction of future human events, as if that was a crime, and holds that there is no authentic case of prophecy on record since "Bible times." That God has forbidden it. As if prognostication was astrology's only or most important claim, whereas it constitutes a great philosophy and connects with all the other sciences and philosophies. And the art of practical astrology is well worthy of the best minds.

The English astrologers publish annually ephemerises of the planet's daily places, which have tremendous sales throughout the English-speaking world.

Raphael's reaches nearly a half million copies at 40 cents each, but years ago was sold at a dollar.

A page of pictures, printed in color, depicts events to come. These are printed in the summons previous to the year in which the events are to happen.

The Messina earthquake was thus foretold, the latitude and longitude given. Had the people of that region believed in astrology they could have fled the city in time with their animals and goods.

In these picture predictions, for 1912 published in 1911, there is shown a huge steamship going down in front of a great iceberg and small boats with people in them nearby.

This was literally fulfilled by the Titanic disaster. While the danger was there it could nevertheless have been avoided by the owners of the ship consulting the ship's horoscope, and sailing only when in that way a safe voyage was indicated.

Another picture shows the assassination of a statesman, who is lying on the ground with the assassin nearby trying to sit up. Literally fulfilled by the assassination of Canalejas, where the assassin failed to commit suicide, but only disabling himself so he could not get away.

Another picture shows Turkish soldiers fighting among rough mountains; fulfilled by the Balkan war.

The pictures for 1914 show besides the horrors of war, a royal funeral, and the coffin of the Pope, covered with a purple cloth, and around the base a scarlet cloth, with a crown on top and four large candles at the corners.

While historians publish the pictures of events after they have happened, the astrologer published the pictures before the events come to pass.

But the opponents of astrology call such proofs "mere coincidences that prove nothing." However, everything is "coincidence," without it existence would be inconceivable.

Raphael's ephemeris, published a year ago, makes the following predictions concerning European conditions for 1914:

ENGLAND.

The influences operating in King George's horoscope are very unfavorable. The sun has reached the parallel of Mars, which is evil for health, and denotes the continuation of warlike tendencies. As Mars is in transit over the progressed moon twice during the early months of the year, the danger of war predicted in last year's Messenger will continue. Saturn is also stationary on the radical sun, denoting much depression of trade and commerce and trouble among the people. The autumn is an evil time, for the moon meets the square of Saturn, indicative of bereavement.

A critical period is forming for the fortunes of this country, but as the sun meets the sextile of the radical moon after it leaves the evil direction of Mars, it will be but the darkest hour before the dawn, and a brighter future awaits the empire. Neptune's transit over the progressed sun is indicative of much socialistic aggression, which will cause anxiety and worry.

THE PRINCE OF WALES.

The autumn is very unfavorable, for Saturn falls stationary on the sun's place at birth, which is evil for health and constitution. Some honors are shown in November.

GERMANY.

The Kaiser is under very adverse directions, and danger both to health and person is indicated. The year opens with Mars in square to the radical sun, and with Uranus transiting the sun's place at birth, and Mars passing over the ascendant, the indications for war and disaster are strongly marked. The moon is opposed to Uranus in January, a further indication of trouble. A crisis is apparent in the history of the German Empire; the terribly evil array of influences will leave their mark for many a long day to come.

AUSTRIA.

The sun is closer to an evil direction of Mars, and with that planet near the meridian in the early months of the year, war is threatened. As Saturn is in close parallel with the radical moon, the condition of the health of the emperor will be very precarious, and the end may come at any moment. The stationary position of Saturn on the meridian of the horoscope in the autumn is evil for reputation.

FRANCE.

The president of France was born on Aug. 20, 1860, with the sun conjoined with Saturn in the sign of Leo and the moon in square to Mars. These are not reassuring influences. The sun is now just leaving the square of Mars, and with that planet in transit over the opposition of Mars, and square of the sun, the indications of war are very powerfully shown; still, as the sun leaves the evil direction of Mars it meets the sextile of Jupiter, which should bring about a more favorable time.

RUSSIA.

Adverse influences are shown in the Tsar's horoscope, for the sun meets the conjunction of Uranus at birth, which will cause much trouble in his empire, and great personal danger. Saturn is stationary in opposition to the progressed moon in the autumn and this denotes bereavement and indisposition.

ITALY.

Martial influences are still in operation in the king of Italy's horoscope. The sun is still close to the parallel of Mars, and Mars in stationary opposition to the progressed sun in the early months of the year is ominous of war. Mars has also progressed to the opposition of Uranus, which points to some outrage, or an attempt on his life.

SPAIN.

The King still remains under adverse influences. The sun is still near the square of Mars and both August and December are evil months, and his health and person will be in danger.

JAPAN.

The Mikado is now coming under some severe afflictions which will bring a crisis in his empire. The sun is forming an opposition to Saturn, and is in semi-square to Mercury. The moon has only just left the conjunction of the radical Mars. With Mars stationary on his meridian war is probable, and serious trouble. Disputes with the other powers are shown, and there is grave danger of an Anglo-Japanese difference.

The above illustrates how astrologers publish prognostications year after year— "since Bible times," too.

There are good and evil times for beginning any new undertaking. The emperors of both Austria and Germany chose about the most evil time in the whole year. The sun was going to a close opposition of Uranus, a planet which when evilly aspected brings evil surprises and utterly unlooked for disappointments like lightning out of a clear sky. It breaks up families, partnerships, agreements between nations, etc.

But the wise men of this world don't know everything, and therefore suffer for their ignorance.

J. F. HARTMANN.

EDITOR'S NOTE FP: *EN* (4 September 1914): 8.

[Letter to the Editor]

To the Editor of The Evening News:

It is unfortunate that the advocates of unpopular truth must contend against the prejudice, venom and false teachings of the influential and learned who misuse their reputation for knowledge in their warfare against truth.

My critic, Mr. Lovecraft, "was very much pained and shocked to see in The Evening News an article on the pseudo-science of astrology, which has ever been the bane of the seeker after truth."

If Mr. Lovecraft had studied the textbooks of astrology, and tested their rules he could not have called it a false science; assuming, of course, that he is a seeker of truth, possesses the scientific spirit and is honest with himself.

He queries: "How any person of judgment and education can give credence to the false and ridiculous system completely exploded over 200 years ago."

No one ever heard the explosion; where and when did it occur? We have only heard mere fizzles that have never exploded anything, and these fizzles are still being set off by learned men; weak-minded on this particular subject.

The ancient Greeks, enemies of Astrology, wrote the most plausible arguments against it, plausible to the ignorant. But to astrologers such writings have merely advertised the ignorance of their authors. And no modern critic has gone beyond the ancients.

The moderns, wilfully ignorant of its rules, and mentally too indolent to study and test them, content themselves with making themselves funny over it, indulging in pointless ridicule, cheap denunciation, misrepresentation and downright lying. A course quite unworthy of men parading as scientists.

Mr. Lovecraft complains: "It seems very provoking that astronomers and other men of sense should be obliged to waste their time and energy in proving astrology to be false—that we must needs attack again what we had thought finally conquered."

But no astronomer has ever disproven it, and there is no piece of literature in existence that disproves it.

If they really feel "obliged" to disprove astrology, why don't they try it, and in a manner becoming the scientific method.

Years ago W. H. Chaney contracted with a New York publisher to write a scientific refutation of astrology, seeing that no one had written such a book. After writing all he could think of, he consulted the astrologers for more points to refute, when to his amazement he found it a real science, broke his contract with the publisher, studied it and became a skilful astrologer.

Under the religious persecution of astrologers Boss Tweed locked him up, quite curiously in the same cell which Tweed occupied later on.

He wrote improved books on the science and promulgated it in the West, becoming known as the "Father of Astrology" in the region from the Mississippi to the Pacific.

And so any one who will honestly attempt a sincere and scientific refutation of it will surely become converted to it.

Mr. Lovecraft continues, "Mr. H. seeks to defend astrology by asserting that the astronomers and scientists, who show its falsity, are unacquainted with its precepts."

They certainly are when at the People's Forum we once interrupted a clergyman's rantings against astrology by asking, "What astrological textbooks have you studied?" He replied, "None," and continued his ignorant ranting. And this man is but an example of the enemies of astrology everywhere.

My critic continues: "The whole mass of nonsense, which constitutes this study is only a vague distortion and misuse of astronomical principles; indeed the study of astronomy absolutely proves the spurious nature of astrology."

What astronomical principles, please tell us what you mean. It certainly is not a distortion and misuse of astronomy when we apply it for the promotion of truth and the good of mankind in a more beneficent way than the astronomers are willing for us to use.

The astronomers hurt their own science by narrowing it down to its lesser uses, valuable enough as these are. To set limits to the usefulness of astronomy, when there is already a greater field for it, comes very near being a "misuse of the principles."

There exists not the slightest reason to believe that "the study of astronomy proves the spurious nature of astrology."

There should be just as much sense in saying that the study of anatomy "absolutely proves the spurious nature of medical science." Or that the healing art "is only a vague distortion and misuse of anatomical principles."

Once a learned botanist, ignorant of medicine, meeting a physician, denounced herbal medication as an exploded superstition, and refused to listen to any facts in support of it, because his botanical studies had disproved all medical virtues in herbs. Which well illustrates the astronomer's attitude toward astrology.

Again he says: "The English astrological almanacs. These wretched pamphlets, though much perused by the vulgar and the ignorant, have been the laughing-stock of the intelligent British public since Queen Anne's time." Yes, the laughing-stock of conceited bigots.

And again: "In 1827 the society for the diffusion of Christian Knowledge severely attacked" (severely, that's right) "annuals of this sort and later caused most of them either to suspend publication or to discontinue their astrological predictions, so that today only two, Zadkiel's and Raphael's, are in existence."

There is no such thing as Christian knowledge or Christian science. But there is Christian faith, Christian bigotry and Christian persecution.

The British astrologers were "severely attacked" by Christian policemen, sheriffs, courts and jailors, ruined by Christian persecution, ever the last resort of bigots in the warfare against truth.

In the early Christian centuries astronomy was idolatry, blasphemy, and all that was vile. The astronomers faced the maledictions of the church, its dungeons, hot pinches, the faggot and the ox. If force is a good argument against astrology why was it not against astronomy?

Again he says: "The prophecies of these almanacs are like the utterances of the Delphic Oracles; so vague and ambiguous that they can be made to suit any subsequent events."

How do you know that the Delphic Oracles were "vague and ambiguous"?

I published in *The Evening News* a long list of European predictions from Raphael's Ephemeris published in August, 1913, to come to pass in 1914. There is nothing vague about them, and the daily papers report their fulfillment.

It is hard to comprehend how any person of common sense can stigmatize such proof of correct predictions as "vague and ambiguous."

When the prediction of the Titanic disaster was accompanied by a picture of the great steamer going down in front of an iceberg, how can that be called "vague," "made to fit subsequent events"?

It is hard to argue with men who stubbornly refuse to be shown any facts in support of truth.

Mr. Lovecraft refers to prophets whose predictions went wrong as disproving astrology. But just think of all the astronomers who have made mistakes. Then astronomy must be a superstition. There is no science but its votaries have made mistakes. Then all the sciences must be false.

Think of all the mistakes in calculation made by bookkeepers and bank clerks. Then what a wretched pseudo-science must be arithmetic.

What a poor rule that won't work both ways!

Mr. Lovecraft might make himself interesting if he would demand of us the kind of evidence he would consider proof of the truth of astrology. He might think of something and then challenge us to produce it.

Our enemies never do that for they are determined to listen to no facts.

Mr. Lovecraft considers astrology a dangerous subject which "in the minds of the masses tends to injure the reputation of astronomy." How can that be when astrology gives astronomy a far more respectful and broader meaning. A respect akin to reverence additional to our ordinary conception of it. Mr. Lovecraft has given not a single fact against astrology. Calling names proves nothing.

At another time I hope to illustrate the benefits of astrology, and how that, if universally applied, it would be a most far-reaching means for the progress and uplift of the human race.

J. F. HARTMANN.

77 Aborn Street, Oct. 5, 1914.

EDITOR'S NOTE FP: *EN* (7 October 1914): 12. A response to HPL's "Science versus Charlatanry" (p. 260).

The Science of Astrology

Astrology, built up through observation, reflection, and experience, long ages ago became a science, a philosophy and an art; continually verifiable by whosoever may come to test its rules and aphorisms on himself, his friends or strangers.

It rests upon the relation that is proven to exist between what we are in body and mind, the events of our lives, the evolution of life, and geological disturbance on the one hand and the ever changing mutual aspect between the celestial bodies of our solar system and their places in the zodiac as seen from earth.

We don't know the final explanation more than we know the final secret of gravitation which affects every little particle of matter, or why invisible Neptune billions of miles away affects our earth by perturbation.

The zodiac, from the Greek circle of beasts, is the circle of 12 star groups, or constellations, in the apparent path of the sun, pictured as animals on our star maps from Aries the ram to Pisces the fishes, and as shown in almanacs.

Astrology, however, does not use the constellations, but the 12 signs of the celestial circle measured from the vernal equinox, the sun's place in spring when the days and nights are of equal length.

The signs, or twelfths of a circle, are named like the constellations, but do not coincide with them, for the equinoctial points recede through them 52½ seconds per year.

The "malefics" are those planets which denote evil more often than good.

The "benefics" are those which denote good more than evil.

The evil aspects, as seen from the earth, as square and opposition, denote evil; the trine and sextile denote good.

The hour of the day is also important, the daily horoscope being divided into 12 parts, or "houses," each "house" having its special meaning, as the house of money, of friends, home, health, etc. It makes a difference in reading a horoscope whether a given planet be rising or setting, whether on the midheaven or at the nadir, whether the planets, sun or moon, above or below the earth in the horoscope.

A horoscope is a star map for some particular time at some particular place. Many persons born at the same time but in different parts of the world would not have the same horoscopes, each one's horoscope would be different from that of all the others, but they would be alike only in some particulars.

A "chart" is a written delineation or "reading" of a horoscope.

In mind and body persons are classified by signs and planets, for these denote various characters.

The sign rising at birth, those containing the sun, moon or most planets describe the person. The sign that is stronger than the rest is the chief ruler of the person.

A Taurus person is short and stout with broad shoulders.

A Gemini person is tall and straight, with straight arms.

An Aries person has much mental energy, is a natural leader, organizer and pioneer, headstrong and impulsive.

An Aquarius person is patient, quiet, unobtrusive, fond of art, science, music and literature.

Where one planet is decidedly stronger than the rest the person is known by such a planet. As when a planet is above the earth and the rest under the earth.

A representative Mercury person is tall and thin, with a narrow face, long nose, thin lips and chin, and little beard. A subtle imagination and good memory; philosophical and mathematical; writer, poet, orator, etc.

A Saturn person is of middle stature; small, black, leering eyes, thick nose and lips, large ears, dark hair and of melancholy expression. Tends to engage as a farmer, miner, brick maker, butcher, etc.

Every person, however, is a combination of the 12 signs of the sun, moon and planets.

The planets being in constant motion, each with a different velocity, never twice form the same combination throughout eternity. Hence no two persons can be exactly alike nor have precisely the same fate.

Inasmuch as astrology reveals to each person his strong and weak points, and to what line of efforts he is best adapted it follows that his education and training should accord with it. A child so brought up would learn faster with greater pleasure, and with greater profit to itself and to society than under our present ignorantly conducted school systems.

Hence applied astrology would revolutionize our educational methods.

In our ex-Governor Dr. Garvin's horoscope the medical sign Scorpio is decidedly strong, showing that he would naturally incline to the medical profession.

The planet Uranus is in trine to the sun, denoting that he rises to a high position in government. Which could have been foreseen from his horoscope when he was yet an infant.

In Edison's horoscope is rising a "fixed" sign denoting great persistency of purpose and bodily endurance, and skill in chemistry.

The Sun and Mercury in the scientific and humanitarian signs Aquarius, with the planet Uranus in Aries, denotes great inventive ability.

The symbol for Aquarius is the lightning. It denotes electricity, light, sound, the voice, music, art, etc., and great ability for mental application. Edison's inventions have been well along these lines.

Jupiter alone above the earth is a scientific sign, of itself denotes him a high-minded and noble man of science; and all the other planets below the earth denote that his greatest success and his most brilliant achievements will come in the closing years of his life.

But most persons with such similar horoscopes have no means for engaging in their natural mission. Hence it would pay society to seek them out, particularly the thousands of children with such horoscopes, and put them back to work at the public expense. Financially and for the progress of civilization society could make no investment more profitable.

Natural affinity between two persons is determined by comparing their horoscopes; a matter of supreme importance in sex relations.

Permanent affection is shown where the planets in one horoscope make good aspects to those in the other.

More temporary affection followed by aversion is shown where the mutual aspects are some of them good and some evil, with the evil ones stronger than the good.

When all persons shall know how to compose horoscopes, each will carry his horoscope as he does his watch, and will ally himself only with those whose horoscopes agree with his own.

We live for happiness, in sex relations as in all else. And a happy sex union is a most important factor in begetting improved offspring.

Astrology also shows how so to conduct the marital indulgence by the aspect between Venus and the moon as to regulate the number of offspring within the bounds of reason, for large families are a curse to themselves and to society as the Malthusians have well made clear.

And again, as there are good and evil times to be born, the parents can so time conception that the birth nine months later shall fall under fortunate planetary configurations, thus producing children far superior to those conceived like brutes in man's present ignorance.

Such a course universally practiced would in a few generations create an ideal race having a state of enjoyment not possible to the kind of people that now inhabit the earth.

In the great pyramid of Cheops is an inclined shaft to the south, not for making astronomical discoveries, but for astrological purposes.

On one side of its floor are steps for the astrologers to ascend, and benches to sit upon, while observing the shadows of the sun or moon on the floor of the tube, or the planets' places in the zodiac.

The flattened apex of the pyramid shows a horoscope blank whereon to chalk the planets' places when calculating horoscopes.

It must have well paid the kings to maintain numerous astrologers to decide for them the fortunate times and season for engaging in their projects, to learn what dangers threaten, the intentions of their enemies, what friends to trust, the disposition of their subjects, and a thousand other things.

This pyramid, not built as a tomb for kings, like other pyramids, but for occult purposes, is the largest telescope ever built, a most mighty monument to astrology.

We may well infer that astrology must have been very old and widely known even before this pyramid was built.

Much of the astrological literature has no doubt perished in the wreck that overtook the great writings of ancient times. But some of it has come down to us in most of the 60-odd pamphlets which constitute the Bible, written by astrologers. A book which, without a knowledge of astrology, cannot be properly understood.

In Genesis the zodiac is called "the tree of the fruit of knowledge of good an evil," which by "eating," or appropriating thereof, is calculated to make one wise concerning the good and evil in ourselves and our fate, and of the best "times and seasons" for engaging in the important matters of life.

This "fruit," or knowledge, was forbidden the tillers of the soil and tree keepers of rich men's gardens, lest they become wise "even as one of us" and make an end of their oppressors.

Jacob and his twelve sons is the story of the sun and the twelve signs of the zodiac, each sun, or sign, denoting an astrological character.

The "twelve tribes of Israel" are the twelve classes of persons whose characteristics answer to the twelve signs respectively. Each of us answers to one or more of these "tribes," the tribes of Aries, Taurus, etc.

The astrologers who were to interpret Belshazzar's dream feigned inability, for it was no doubt dangerous to tell the king of impending misfortunes, as dangerous as it would be to tell the Kaiser to his face that he would lose the war.

The Apocalypse calls the zodiac "the tree of life which is the midst of paradise." Paradise, from the Persian, means among the stars, and of course that is where we find the zodiac to be.

It is also called "the book of life," which is to be "eaten" or studied, wherein everyone's life is written, and which only the astrologer knows how to read.

The ancients knew only the seven visible bodies of our solar system, but understood certain influences in their horoscopes which we know to be those of Uranus and Neptune, to be seen through our telescopes.

The ancient Hindu astrologer, however, charted nine bodies, having discovered the two invisible ones from their effects on the horoscopes.

John writes: "The seven stars are the angels of the seven churches; and the seven candlesticks are the seven churches."

Here we are classified by the seven planets instead of by the 12 signs of the zodiac. Each planet is called an angel, as when Jacob, lying on his back at night, watched the "angel" stars rising and settling in their celestial paths, or "ladder."

The "seven candlesticks" are seven star clusters in which the seven "angel" stars exert their most beneficent influence.

The "seven churches" are the seven classes of people that answer to the astrological influence of these celestial candlesticks. The 12 candlesticks being the 12 constellations of the zodiac.

"In the midst of the street of it, (path of the Sun and planets) and on either side of the river, (equinoctial circle) was there the tree of life, (zodiac) which bore 12 manner of fruits, (12 manner of people) and yielded her fruit (births) every month, and the leaves (teachings) of the tree were for the healing of the nations."

When "the nations of them which are saved shall walk in the light of it; and the kinds of the earth do bring their glory and honor into it," "there shall be no more curse."

Disease, poverty, vice and war will disappear and in its place will appear the Christian "millennium."

Then the tears of the world shall be wiped away "from their eyes; and there shall be no more death, (fear of death) neither sorrow, nor crying, neither shall there be any more pain; for the former things are passed away." Rev. xxxi, 4.

J. F. HARTMANN.

77 Aborn Street.

EDITOR'S NOTE FP: *EN* (22 October 1914): 8. A sober, patient outline of astrology, in which Hartmann deliberately takes no notice either of HPL's response to his previous letter to the editor ("The Falsity of Astrology" [p. 262]) or to the first Isaac Bickerstaffe, Jr. article, "Astrology and the Future" (p. 268).

A Defense of Astrology

To the Editor of The Evening News:

Dear Sir—Mr. Lovecraft's abusive treatment of astrology and the astrologers, of Oct. 8, exemplifies the unreasoning attitude of the influential intellectuals, the clergy, college professors, authors and scientists, especially the astronomers, toward a science as thoroughly established in fact and reason as is any science, but whose claims these proud, self-sufficient men will not investigate. Keeping themselves wilfully ignorant of this noble science, they yet imagine themselves fair judges of what they don't understand, and belabor with vilest abuse and slander those learned therein.

Ridicule and bitter denunciation should only be employed when accompanied by facts that justify it, a rule of fairness that is never observed by the enemies of astrology.

Mr. Lovecraft begins this his second tirade:

"Since the ordinary modern astrologer is merely a mountebank" (what about the ancient, or not ordinary one?) "who seeks to defraud the ignorant by means of crude gibberish which he knows to be untrue, his tribe may very easily be silenced by the proper legal authorities."

Here he justifies the revival of the brute force, prison and torture of medieval practices as the proper argument for a scientist to use as a substitute for facts and reason when debating with astrologers. Ever the first and last word of bigotry.

The pulpit, which never defiles itself with science lectures, while it cannot now crush all the sciences as once it had the power to do, allies itself with the scientific bigots in including legislatures to enact laws for the suppression of all such other sciences as remain as yet unpopular in their superstitious, knowledge-fearing circles. Superstitious, because their frightful terror of astrology seems unaccountable to right-thinking people.

Many astrologers, good, honest, useful men, have thus been persecuted, cast into prison, their lives ruined through the machinations of these learned bigots; and the people are by law denied their rightful liberty to consult astrologers, men and women more useful than lawyers. People should have the same right to choose their science that they have to choose their religion, the same right to visit their astrologer that they have to visit their pastor and their prayer meetings.

If everything is to be suppressed whereby the ignorant are defrauded nearly all the religious institutions would be the first to go, and all those astronomers who by misrepresentations defraud the ignorant of the knowledge of astrology.

Honest opponents never attack a thing without first testing it. Before denouncing astrology they would test hundreds or thousands of horoscopes, reading them by the rules in the textbooks, on friends and strangers.

It is a rule of science that to be a science it must be predictive, that like phenomena will recur under like conditions; a rule to which astrology conforms remarkably, placing it among the sciences.

Knowing that under certain celestial phenomena certain mundane phenomena do occur we can predict with assurance that under a recurrence of the celestial the mundane will also recur and to this the astrologer's daily experience continually testifies.

Until our defamers will make and test horoscopes they have no argument that appeals to reason.

Of the many books on astronomy none show how to make a horoscope, one of the first lessons an astronomy student ought to learn, namely a map of the heavens for a given time and place. Innocent as it seems to calculate such a celestial map the professors think it something disgraceful for an astronomer to perform.

As Mr. Lovecraft complains: "The baleful effect of astrology upon the reputation of astronomy is far too patent for Mr. Hartmann to explain away. I was not long ago asked by a man who had seen my astronomical articles, if I did not cast horoscopes or calculate nativities! It is not pleasant for a serious student of the heavens to be taken for a petty fortune-teller."

Rather should astronomers feel shame for not knowing how to calculate such a map. A nativity being a horoscope at birth.

How any astronomer can feel annoyed at being thought capable of making a star map seems beyond comprehension.

That astrologers don't talk "gibberish" any one can see by consulting them, but which our enemies never do, and cannot therefore know how the astrologers talk. But no doubt they call "gibberish" everything that comes from the mouth or pen of an astrologer, however serious.

Two recent articles in these columns, by an enemy falsely posing as an astrologer, are real "gibberish," the kind which our critic does not criticise.

Real astrologers never write such ridiculous parodies upon their own sacred science, which Mr. Lovecraft calls a "base superstition."

But what is superstition? Edward B. Tylor in "Primitive Culture", defines it as derived from two Greek words meaning that which has "stood over" from past times. The implication being that the past can teach us nothing. As if we who now live in the world were the only people who ever knew anything worth knowing.

Under Tylor's definition all literature, history, sciences, and art of past times is superstition.

Andrew D. White, in "Conflict Between Science and Religion", defines it as derived from the Greek "super," the supernatural, and "stitio," to fear—"the fear of God."

But astrology is not "the fear of God." Fear and the supernatural are no more a part of it than of astronomy or any science. Hence astrology is not a superstition, save in the diseased imagination of those learned ignoramuses, who, trembling in mortal fear, beseech governments to help them, and cry "Police! Police!" at the mere sight of an astrologer.

As for astrologers defrauding the ignorant, they enlighten and help them, and frequently serve poor persons with troubled minds free of charge, which they would not do were they "mountebanks." Not only are they studious persons, which their science requires them to be, but they are sympathetic, feeling pity for suffering, which is the foundation of the moral sense.

Astrology goes deep into human nature and deals with the good and evil of existence, which is more evil than good, with the joys and sorrows, hopes and fears of struggling mortals, with whom sorrow and fear outweigh the passing joys of life; and where the astrologer's knowledge becomes of far greater value, a hundred fold, than the person's beliefs and prayers.

Mr. Lovecraft's charge [is] that astrologers are the enemies of knowledge, when their very mission is, in the nature of things, one of enlightenment. Wherever you meet a good astrologer, you almost invariably meet a person of broad views and a well-informed mind: one who wants to see the world wiser and happier, and who never thinks of calling the police to help him settle a question in science.

How any self-respecting astronomer can make such a false charge against astrologers one is at a loss to explain.

It is the astronomer who, by means of base falsehoods, causes disrespect for astrology, and to that extent prevents the spread of knowledge.

Mr. Lovecraft objects to my article: "The one oft repeated foundation of his arguments: the alleged ignorance of astrology on the part of astronomers. He errs very gravely when he denies that astronomy proves the falsity of astrology. Astronomy investigates every force and influence exerted by the various bodies of space upon one another, measuring with the utmost care and exactitude each slightest manifestation of energy."

As if the astronomer's brass and glass tools had now reached their final perfection, further improvements being for all time impossible.

But astrology has means not made of metal incomparably more sensitive than anything the astronomer has yet known, the human brain itself.

When physicians say the moon's phases influence their patients the astronomers call it truth, but when the astrologers say it they call it superstition, and run to the telescope to prove it so.

The astronomer refuses to test astrology by its own methods, which of course would prove it a true science. But if it was a "false science," as Mr. Lovecraft charges, then its own methods would be just the course by which to prove it false.

The astronomer's method is like that of the anatomist who disproved the existence of mental faculties in the head by sawing up skulls and finding none.

My critic continues: "The astronomer attacks the subject at every angle, and follows up with the keenest activity every principle for which he can discover any real data whatsoever."

Just what the astronomer does not do. He rejects the very data and principle that alone will give him results. He stubbornly insists that his ignorant ways which he knows and admits give no results are the only means to be employed.

He never really tests astrology at all, if he thinks so he is deluded, misled by his ignorant professors.

Again he says: "The true student, comparing the motions of the heavenly bodies with the varied affairs of mankind, has never found a trace of evidence that there is any connexion between the two."

He means the false student who doesn't want to find out, for he denounces astrological literature as "miserable pamphlets," unfit for serious study.

The true student of these despised books does find what the untrue-to-truth student can never find. Hence it seems ridiculous to have him conclude: "No rational and unprejudiced scholar could for a moment tolerate a science thus unsupported"—namely, unsupported by himself and all those who keep wilfully ignorant of the facts that do support it, as found in those "miserable pamphlets," in study which he thinks a waste of time and a lowering of his dignity.

The Australian bushman who can't count over three thinks the multiplication table "unsupported." So is the astronomy "unsupported" with those who don't believe in it. And the infallible Bible has often proven astronomy to be of the devil, while early Christian governments made short shrift of the "mountebank" astronomers.

Our critics err when they imagine that the disproving of planetary influence disproves astrology. They don't seem to know that our science does not rest on planetary influence but on the fact that mundane affairs coincide with celestial phenomena and can be read by them.

If your watch keeps good time, what matters it whether you think it makes the time or only indicates it. To prove that it doesn't create time doesn't hurt the watch; just so with astrology.

"Planetary influence" becomes a convenient technical term, because from reading horoscopes they come to seem or appear as if they influenced mundane affairs.

The astronomer also speaks of appearances as if they were real. He speaks of sunrise and sunset, knowing that the sun doesn't rise and set; of retrograde planetary motion, when he knows that planets don't retrograde, and of circular orbits that are only apparent.

About all the books on astronomy in our public library leave the reader with the impression of circular orbits. One author merely adds as a sort of afterthought, "but these are not the real motions."

There is probably but a single explanation of the true planetary motions in all this literature, and that is in the Popular Astronomy magazine. Hence a carping critic could have a better case against astronomy as a "false science" than has the astronomer against astrology.

Mr. Lovecraft having been challenged, in a former reply to his strictures, to test the rules and aphorisms of our textbook, replies: "No rational and unprejudiced scholar needs astrological textbooks in order to perceive its absolute unsoundness." An admission of wilful ignorance of the contents and teachings of astrological books.

What would he think of a "rational and unprejudiced' judge who refused to hear his side, on the ground that he didn't "need" to, and then sentence him with abusive language, insults and billingsgate?

Mr. Lovecraft continues: "Mr. Hartmann himself appears to possess just those very intellectual characteristics which he deplores in others. He is certainly bigoted in his astrological belief, and he has evidently studied astronomy no more than the astronomers whom he censures have studied astrology. A simple course in astronomy might do much toward destroying his mediaeval ideas."

Mediaeval ideas used to imprison astronomers as now the astronomers imprison the astrologers. We are by no means ignorant of astronomy, which we must study in order to become astrologers. It is in astronomy that we find our astrology.

A bigot is one who will not reason, one who persistently condemns a science whose textbooks he will not study, and whose results he will not test. He is a bigot who seeks to refute another's ideas by mere bald denials, abusive language and vulgar personalities, and a bigot is he who in a scientific debate gloats over the tyrannical arrest and imprisonment of those whose views he cannot meet with fact and reasons; one who sets up false reasons and misstatements which he thinks to drive home with a policeman's club and prison bars.

Having been invited to tell what sort of evidence he would consider as proving astrology to be true, my critic evasively refuses the challenge by asking: "on what principle the various and complex destinies of men can be connected with the apparent positions of immensely distant bodies?"

Easily answered by comparing men's lives with their horoscopes.

But as our critic is wilfully ignorant of how to read a horoscope, and has resented it as an annoyance when a man asked him if he could do it, he has no way to test the matter, and can be no judge of it.

Inability to explain all about why observed facts are facts is no argument against their being facts.

Some astronomers don't seem to know that.

What lovely logic: That a thing is not a thing unless we can explain it is a thing.

He asks: "explain why a few erratic sophists claim the ability to detect and study in detail without instruments a species of energy which no other scientist has yet noticed even with the most elaborate and delicate appliances. But I should pay too much respect to a contemptible system of charlatanry were I to consider these matters seriously."

Mr. Lovecraft is mistaken in thinking that astrologers study certain species of planetary energy, which they don't need to study, being no part of astrology, which is a complete science without that sort of study.

He might make himself interesting by telling us what sort of instruments astronomers have used, and how and in what way they have gone about it to decide that there is no astrological relation between earth and sky, and have they gone to any considerable expense of time, money, study and patience in the matter.

Evidently they have done nothing whatever, for in the language of our critic they do not "consider these matters seriously."

Until they tell their story we will doubt their having anything to tell.

So far only false statements, angry contempt, abusive language, and vulgar personalities have come from their lips and pens. Methods so very unbecoming the dignity of scientific gentlemen, the professor's gown, or the sacred cloth.

As for "Tycho Brahe and Gassendi" abandoning astrology for other studies being any argument against it, if it were legitimate, would prove every one of the sciences false. What about the thousands of astrologers who did not abandon their art? And what about their opponents who upon investigation became converted to it? And have not astrologers the same rights as have all men to abandon one profession for another?

While the astronomers have not disproven planetary influence, but only the failure of their instruments to detect any, they have persistently rejected the only instrument suitable for the purpose of proving the astrological relationship between the heavenly bodies—the horoscope. If their failure to discover astrological energy refutes astrology, then, to be consistent, their failure to discover energy in the stars that make them rise and set every night ought to be a sure refutation of astronomy.

J. F. HARTMANN.

77 Aborn Street.

EDITOR'S NOTE FP: EN (14 December 1914): 8. A very belated response to HPL's "The Falsity of Astrology" (p. 262), in which Hartmann reveals his ignorance that HPL was the author of the two "ridiculous parodies" of astrology written by Bickerstaffe.

LOVECRAFT'S JUVENILE SCIENTIFIC MANUSCRIPTS

The following is a list of Lovecraft's surviving juvenile scientific manuscripts, now in the John Hay Library of Brown University. Bibliographical annotations have been added where necessary. As much of Lovecraft's own manner of dating and numbering his works as possible has been retained.

Annals of the Providence Observatory: Vol. I: Observations of a General Character During 1903. 190[4]: Providence: Printed at the Observatory. A.Ms., (v), 11 pp. [Contains cover, signature, frontispiece (drawing of the moon), title page, table of contents, and text. With seven chapters, many illustrations, and an appendix listing "Books in the astronomical library."]

The Art of Fusion Melting Pudling & Casting. A.Ms., 10 pp. [Perhaps Lovecraft's earliest work of scientific juvenilia, and one of his earliest surviving works: perhaps dating to 1899.]

Astronomy.
    Vol. I, No. 1: August 1903. A.Ms., (i), 8 + pp.
    Vol. I, No. 2: September 1903. A.Ms., (i), 12 pp.
    Vol. I, No. 3: October 1903. A.Ms., (i), 4 pp.
    Vol. I, No. 4: November 1903 (combined with *Monthly Almanack*). A.Ms., (i), 10 pp. [Includes *An Annual of Astronomy for the Year 1903: First Edition: Novr. 25, 1903.*]
    Vol. I, No. 5: December 1903. A.Ms., (i), 8 pp.
    The (New) Monthly Almanack for December, 1903. A.Ms., (ii), 6 pp.
    Astronomy: January 1904: Combined with the Monthly Almanack. A.Ms., (iv), pp.
    The Monthly Almanack: Combined with "Astronomy": Feb'y, 1904. A.Ms., (iv), 11 pp.

Chemistry. A.Ms., 12 pp.

Chemistry, Magic & Electricity. A.Ms., 10 pp.

Chemistry III. A.Ms., 31 pp.

Chemistry IV. A.Ms., 21 pp. [In a catalogue of his works dating probably to 1902 (see *CE* 5.260), Lovecraft noted a series of chemistry books in 6 volumes; evidently, therefore, the two final volumes have been lost.]

A Good Anaesthetic. A.Ms., 15 pp.

My Opinion as to the Lunar Canals. A.Ms., 3 pp.

The Planet, Vol. I. No. 1; Saturday August 29, 1903. A.Ms., 2 pp.

Providence Observatory: Forecast for Providence & Vicinity Next 24^h. A.Ms., 1 p. [Forecast for 4–5 April 1904.]

The Railroad Review. December 1901. A.Ms., 3 pp.

The Rhode Island Journal of Astronomy. [All issues copiously illustrated with draw-ings and charts by Lovecraft. Title sometimes varies; different colours of ink sometimes used.]

Vol. I, No. I: Sunday, August. 2, 1903. A.Ms., 4 pp.
Vol. I, No. II: Sunday, August 9, 1903. A.Ms., 2 pp.
Vol. I, No. III: Sunday, August 16, 1903. A.Ms., 2 pp.
Vol. I, No. IV: Sunday, August 23, 1903. A.Ms., 2 pp.
Vol. I, No. V: Sunday, August 30, 1903. A.Ms., 2 pp.
Vol. I, No. VI: Sunday, Septr. 6, 1903. A.Ms., 3 pp.
Vol. I, No. VII: Sunday, Septr. 13, 1903. A.Ms., 3 pp.
Vol. I, No. VIII: Sunday, Septr. 20, 1903. A.Ms., 3 pp.
Vol. I, No. IX: Sunday, Septr. 27, 1903. A.Ms., 2 pp.
Vol. I, No. X: Sunday, Octr. 4, 1903. A.Ms., 2 pp.
Vol. I, No. XI: Sunday, Octr. 11, 1903. A.Ms., 2 pp.
Vol. I, No. XII: Sunday, Octr. 18, 1903. A.Ms., 4 pp.
Vol. I, No. XIII: Sunday, Octr. 25, 1903. A.Ms., 2 pp.
Vol. I, No. XIV: Sunday, Novr. 1, 1903. A.Ms., 2 pp.
Vol. I, No. XV: Sunday, Novr. 8, 1903. A.Ms., 2 pp.
Vol. I, No. XVI: Sunday, Novr. XV, MDCCCIII. A.Ms., 2 pp.
Vol. I, No. XVII: Sunday, Novr. 22, 1903. A.Ms., 2 pp.
Vol. I, No. XVIII: Sunday, November 29, 1903. A.Ms., 2 pp.
Vol. I, No. XIX: Sunday, December 6, 1903. A.Ms., 2 pp.
Vol. I, No. XX: Sunday, December 13, 1903. A.Ms., 2 pp.
Vol. I, No. XXI: Sunday, December 20, 1903. A.Ms., 2 pp.
Vol. I, No. XXII: Sunday, December 27, 1903. A.Ms., 2 pp.
Vol. I, No. XXIII: Sunday, January 3, 1904. A.Ms., 2 pp.
Vol. I, No. XXIV: Sunday, January 10, 1904. A.Ms., 2 pp.
Vol. I, No. XXV: Sunday, January 17, 1904. A.Ms., 2 pp.
Vol. I, No. XXVI: Sunday, January 24, 1904. A.Ms., 2 pp.
Vol. I, No. XXVII: Sunday, January 31, 1904. A.Ms., 2 pp.
Vol. III, [No. I]: Sunday, Apr. 16, 1905. A.Ms., 4 pp.
(Extra): Monday, Apr. 17, 1905. A.Ms., 2 pp.
Vol. III, No. II: Sunday, April 23, 1905. A.Ms., 4 pp.
Vol. III, No. III: Sunday, April 30, 1905. A.Ms., 4 pp.
Vol. III, No. IV: Sunday, May 7, 1905. A.Ms., 4 pp.
Vol. III, No. V: Sunday, May 14, 1905. A.Ms., 4 pp.
Vol. III, No. VI: Sunday, May 21, 1905. A.Ms., 4 pp.
Vol. III, No. 7: Sunday, May 28, 1905. A.Ms., 4 pp.
Vol. III, No. 8: Sunday, June 4, 1905. A.Ms., 4 pp.
Vol. III, No. 9: Sunday, June 11, 1905. A.Ms., 4 pp.
Vol. III, No. 10: Sunday, June 18, 1905. A.Ms., 4 pp.
Vol. III, No. 11: Sunday, June 25, 1905. A.Ms., 4 pp.
Vol. III, No. 12: Sunday, July 2, 1905. A.Ms., 4 pp.
Vol. III, No. 13: Sunday, July 9, 1905. A.Ms., 4 pp.
Vol. III, No. 14: Sunday, July 16, 1905. A.Ms., 4 pp.
Vol. III, No. 15: Sunday, July 23, 1905. A.Ms., 2 pp.
Vol. IV [i.e. III], No. I (new series): Sunday, July 30, 1905. A.Ms., 6 pp.
Vol. III, No. 2: Sunday, August 6, 1905. A.Ms., 4 pp.
Vol. III, No. 3: Sunday, August 13, 1905. A.Ms., 4 pp.

Vol. III, No. 5: Sunday, August 27, 1905. A.Ms., 4 pp.
Vol. III, No. 6: Sunday, September 3, 1905. A.Ms., 4 pp.
Vol. III, No. 7: Sunday, September 10, 1905. A.Ms., 4 pp.
Vol. III, No. 8: Sunday, September 17, 1905. A.Ms., 4 pp.
Vol. III, No. 9: Sunday, October 8, 1905. A.Ms., 4 pp.
Vol. III, No. X: Sunday, October 22, 1905. A.Ms., 6 pp.
Vol. III, No. 11: Sunday, November 12, 1905. A.Ms., 4 pp. [Last page written on 23 November 1905.]
Vol. III, No. 6 [sic]: January 1906. A.Ms., (ii), 12 pp.
Vol. III, No. 7 [sic]: February 1906. A.Ms., (ii), 8(+2) pp.
Vol. 3, No. 8: March 1906. A.Ms., (ii), 8(+2) pp.
Vol. III, No. 9: April 1906. A.Ms., (ii), 9(+l) pp.
Vol. III, No. 10: May '06. A.Ms., (ii), 8(+2) pp.
Vol. 3, No. 11: June 1906. A.Ms., (ii) 8(+2) pp.
Vol. IV, No. I (Special Anniversary Number): August 1906. A.Ms., (ii), 12(+2) pp.
Vol. IV, No. 2: September 1906. A.Ms., (ii), 8(+2) pp.
Vol. IV, No. 3: October 1906. A.Ms., (i), 10 pp.
Vol. IV, No. 4: November 1906. A.Ms., (i), 10 pp.
Vol. 4, No. 5: December 1906. A.Ms., (ii), 9(+1) pp. [With a "Cumulative Index of Illustrations—1906."]
Vol. 4, No. 6: January 1907. A.Ms., (ii), 10 pp.
Vol. 4, No. 9: April 1907. A.Ms., 2 pp.
Vol. VI, No. 6: January 1909. A.Ms., 2 pp.
Vol. VI, No. 7: February 1909. A.Ms., 2 pp. [Never completed.]

Appended is a "Notice" announcing the publishing history of the *Journal* and its termination. As can be seen, much of the series is not preserved; this includes any additional numbers of Volume I (February–April? 1904), the whole of Volume II (April? 1904–April 1905), Vol. III (new series), No. 4 (August 20, 1905), Vol. IV, Nos. 7 and 8 (February and March 1907), any additional numbers of Volume IV (May?–July? 1907), and the whole of Volume V (August? 1907–December 1908). The periodical may have been in abeyance for some of these periods.

The R.I. Journal of Science & Astronomy. Vol. I, No. I: Sunday, Septr. 27, 1903. A.Ms., 2 pp.

The Science Library.
No. 1: Naked Eye Selenography. A.Ms., 8 pp.
No. 2: The Telescope. A.Ms., 8 pp.
No. 5: On Saturn and His Ring (From the Author's "Astronomy"). A.Ms., 8 pp.
[The missing volumes are: No. 3: Life of Galileo; No. 4: Life of Herschel (revised); No. 6: Selections from Author's "Astronomy"; No. 7: The Moon, Part I; No. 8: The Moon, Part II; No. 9: On Optics.]

The Scientific Gazette.
Vol. I, No. I: March 4, 1899. A.Ms., 4 pp.
Vol. CXI, No. III (New Issue Vol. I, No. I): May 12, 1902. A.Ms., 3 pp.
Vol. III, No. I: Sunday, August 16, 1903. A.Ms., 2 pp.
Vol. III, No. II: Sunday, August 23, 1903. A.Ms., 2 pp.
Vol. III, No. III: Sunday, August 30, 1903. A.Ms., 2 pp.

Vol. III, No. IV: Sunday, Septr. 6, 1903. A.Ms., (iv), 3 pp.
Vol. III, No, V: Sunday, Septr. 13, 1903. A.Ms., (ii), 3 pp.
Vol. III, No. VI: Sunday, Septr. 20, 1903. A.Ms., (ii), 3 pp.
Vol. III, odd number I: Tuesday, Sept. 22, 1903. A.Ms., 2 pp.
Vol. III, odd number II: Wednesday, Septr. 23, 1903. A.Ms., 2 pp.
Vol. III, No. X [i.e. VII]: Sunday, Septr. 27, 1903. A.Ms., 2 pp.
Vol. III, No. XI [i.e. VIII]: Sunday, Octr. 4, 1903. A.Ms., 2 pp.
Vol. III, No. XI [i.e. VIII] odd: Thurs. Octr. 8, MDCCCCIII. A.Ms., 2 pp.
Vol. III, No. IX: Sunday, Octr. 11, 1903. A.Ms., 2 pp.
Vol. III, No. X: Sunday, Octr. 18, 1903. A.Ms., 2 pp.
Vol. III, No. IV odd [sic]: Tuesday, Octr. 20, 1903. A.Ms., 2 pp.
Vol. III, No. XI: Sunday, Octr. 25, 1903. A.Ms., 2 pp.
Vol. III, No. XII: Sunday, Novr. 1, 1903. A.Ms., 2 pp.
Vol. III, No. XIII: Sunday, November 8, 1903. A.Ms., 2 pp.
Vol. III, No. XIV: Sunday, November 15, 1903. A.Ms., 2 pp.
Vol. III, No. XV: Sunday, November 22, 1903. A.Ms., 2 pp.
Vol. III, No. XVI: Sunday, November 29, 1903. A.Ms., 2 pp.
Vol. III, No. XVII: Sunday, December 6, 1903. A.Ms., 2 pp.
Vol. III, No. XVIII: Sunday, December 13, 1903. A.Ms., 2 pp.
Vol. III, No. XIX: Sunday, December 20, 1903. A.Ms., 2 pp.
Vol. III, No. XX: Sunday, December 27, 1903. A.Ms., 2 pp.
Vol. III, No. XXI: Sunday, January 3, 1904. A.Ms., 2 pp.
Vol. III, No. XXII: Sunday, January 10, 1904. A.Ms., 2 pp.
Vol. III, No. XXIII: Sunday, January 17, 1904. A.Ms., 2 pp.
Vol. III, No. XXIV: Sunday, January 24, 1904. A.Ms., 2 pp.
Vol. III, No. XXV: Sunday, January 31, 1904. A.Ms., 2 pp.
Vol. X, No. 11: January 1909. A.Ms., 2 pp.

[As with the Rhode Island Journal of Astronomy, some (perhaps much) of the series is missing; this includes any numbers between the original Vol. I, No. 1 (4 March 1899) and the new series (12 May 1902); the whole of Volume I after Vol. I, No. 1 (May–August? 1902), and the whole of Volume II (August? 1902–August 1903). The gap between Vol. III, No. XXV (31 January 1904) and Vol. X, No. 11 (January 1909) is to be noted; in an advertisement in the Rhode Island Journal of Astronomy for September 1906, Lovecraft declares that the Scientific Gazette had been defunct since September 1905, but that his friend Arthur Fredlund had revived it and taken it over. No doubt this run did not last long. The final number of the Scientific Gazette, like the last two numbers of the Rhode Island Journal, seems to represent a nostalgic end to the series.]